Environmental Problems

wcb

WM. C. BROWN COMPANY PUBLISHERS   Dubuque, Iowa

Environmental Problems

Principles,
Readings,
and
Comments

WILLIAM H. MASON
GEORGE W. FOLKERTS

Auburn University

Contents

v

PART IV   MAN AND HIS FELLOW INHABITANTS

Preface

When the shelves of bookstores are sagging under the burden of seemingly myriads of paperback books on environmental problems, the rationale behind adding another to the heap might be questioned. The presently available books vary considerably in length, inclusiveness, purpose, and the level at which they are presented. Some are rather incomplete in their coverage. Others strive hard to reflect all views, leaving the reader better informed but just as lacking in direction as before the book was read. Many make good reading, but are not informative enough for classroom use, while still others present so much data that the average student bogs down and loses interest. Additionally, the viewpoints of all of them differ in some respects from our own. This work reflects our viewpoint, hopefully a viewpoint that will be shared by the reader. This hope was the main stimulus behind the book's preparation.

We intend this to be a book for students. It is not a book of science nor was it compiled for the scientist. We have selected readings which draw their information from factual sources, without distracting and overburdening the reader with formulae, detailed graphs, and intricate empirical reasoning. A number of articles were selected for their readability rather than for the amount of detailed information they contained. As a result, many of the selections were taken from semi-popular and popular periodicals rather than from scientific journals.

In Part I we have attempted to explain in a simplified fashion the basic ecological principles necessary to an intelligent understanding of the readings and their implications. We have made no attempt to appear erudite. Scientists with lofty and sophisticated viewpoints may find our explanations oversimplified, our reasoning mundane, and our examples trite and hackneyed. We hope that the student will find them understandable.

The comments that appear at the end of many of the selections have a number of purposes. In some cases they are explanatory; in others they include additional information. A number are intended to stimulate thought, discussion, or even classroom controversy.

Often, readers or teachers who select text materials make the mistake of looking for a book that reflects all points of view. We make no such claim, and feel that authors and editors that do are deluding themselves and confusing the reader. A banal, middle-of-the-road, point of view is comfortable because it allows one to choose the viewpoint that mirrors the rut of his own opinion. It makes it easy to decide that little action is needed and that the way of least resistance is best. Unfortunately, like the middle of the road on the highway, it is often fatal.

Those who think that compromise is the answer to solving environmental problems, and look for reflections of such an opinion in this book, will be disappointed. One does not compromise with a strangler by asking him to choke a bit less vigorously. One does not meet a manufacturer of inflammable childrens clothing halfway by requesting that in the future only half of the clothing manufactured be made inflammable. The answer to most environmental problems involves the cessation of the activity that has caused the problem. Anything less will only slow the processes which will eventually make this planet uninhabitable.

Many people have contributed to the preparation of this book. We are especially thankful to the authors of the selections for allowing us to reprint their thoughts and information. Mr. Wayne Schotanus at the Wm. C. Brown Company provided stimulus and assistance. Dr. Robert H. Mount read the first section and his comments enabled us to measurably improve it. Mrs. Joan Broom and Mrs. Shirley Burson skillfully typed portions of the manuscript and provided other stenographic assistance. The list of others who have helped us in some way is too long to include, but our sincere thanks go to all of them.

The Gadarene swine mill and grunt at the top of the encarpment, readying themselves unkowningly or uncaringly for the final plunge into the sea. If this book can in some small way contribute to the awakening of man necessary to avert that plunge, then perhaps it will be something more than an additional bit of cellulose to be recycled.

William H. Mason

George W. Folkerts

Part I

Some Basic Ecological Principles

WILLIAM H. MASON and GEORGE W. FOLKERTS

Some Basics About Ecology

Introduction

Ecology is the science which deals with understanding and interpreting the total environment. The word ecology is derived from the Greek *oikos* meaning "place to live." Ecology is the study of organisms and their surroundings. The environment is a system composed of highly-interrelated living and nonliving components. The living components of a given area, the plants and animals, together make up a community. The nonliving components include such things as soil, atmosphere, minerals, water — everything except the plants and animals. Such factors as temperature, humidity, wind, latitude, and altitude influence the living and nonliving parts of the environment of the area and play an important part in determining the types of plants and animals that will live there.

The ecologist is primarily interested in relationships. Three basic types of ecological relationships can be distinguished: (1) those among individual organisms; (2) those among populations of organisms; and (3) those between organisms and the nonliving components of their environment. Ecologists attempt to answer such questions as: What are the effects of climatic changes on natural populations? What effect does an increase in the carbon dioxide content of the air have on plant populations? How does overpopulation of one species affect other species? What are the feeding relationships among individual animals living within a natural area? How do plants and animals acquire and use energy? What would be the effect on native species if a non-native species of plant or animal were introduced? What are the environmental effects of emptying sewage into a lake? What are the effects of removing certain species from a natural area — such as cutting most or all the evergreen trees within a woodland or harvesting most or all the blue whales in the ocean?

The ecologist is clearly an "environmental biologist." We all realize that modern man of today's highly technological culture is modifying the environment to a much greater extent than did his predecessors. Ecologists recognize that changes in the environment which seem to be relatively minor can lead to major changes in the component plant and animal species and produce entirely different patterns of relationships. For example, slightly decrease the rainfall on a natural grassland, and a desert develops; increase the rainfall slightly, and a forest develops. Likewise, increase the amount of organic material in a stream, and drastic changes may take place in the kinds and numbers of plants and animals present. Increased levels of ionizing radiation within a community lead to increased mutation rates in both plants and animals. In general, these mutations are harmful to the individuals in which they occur. The release of man-made chemicals into a natural area can selectively eliminate certain species of plants or animals. The organisms eliminated may have been the main food source for several other species, may have provided a unique type of shelter or nesting site for certain animals of the area, or may have been predators which kept other populations in check. Thus, it is easily seen that changes which may result in the elimination of a native species from a community must be considered carefully before they are made, especially since the initial change may ultimately have a drastic affect upon the entire environmental unit.

There is no way to predict with certainty what modern man's activities will finally lead to in terms of overall environmental change. It is clear that such practices as improper waste disposal, unregulated combustion of fuel, over-exploitation or elimination of our native plants and animals, improper use of pesticides, and poor land management are modifying our environment. Many of these modifications are, or ultimately will be, detrimental to man. Many ecologists fear that the most damaging effects are yet to be realized, much less understood.

Energy in the Environment

Virtually all energy we can use is derived directly or indirectly from sunlight. Green plants are able to use the energy of sunlight directly to unite water and carbon dioxide to form new organic molecules. The process by which this is accomplished is called photosynthesis. Organisms capable of carrying out photosynthesis are referred to as producers. The summary equation for photosynthesis:

$$\text{carbon dioxide} + \text{water} \xrightarrow[\text{chlorophyll}]{\text{sunlight}} \text{sugar} + \text{oxygen}$$

has several implications which should be stressed. Photosynthesis requires carbon dioxide, a gas present in the atmosphere. Atmospheric carbon dioxide is replenished by all living organisms as they chemically break down food molecules to obtain energy, or as any organic matter such as coal, oil, gas, or wood is burned. Water required for photosynthesis in land plants is generally absorbed from the soil and is replenished through rainfall.

Only a relatively small proportion of the total amount of solar energy reaching the earth is used by plants in photosynthesis. The amount of available energy reaching plants is determined by several factors. The angle at which sunlight enters the atmosphere depends on the latitude and the season of year — the greater the angle, the less sunlight delivered. Dust and clouds reflect sunlight which would otherwise reach the ground or water surface below. Through shading, large plants often reduce the light available to smaller ones. Turbidity and water depth greatly affect the amount of sunlight reaching submerged aquatic plants.

The sugar molecules produced by photosynthesis may be used to fuel the metabolic machinery of the plant, or they may be stored. When stored they are often converted to other organic substances. Most of the oxygen produced by photosynthesis is released into the atmosphere. This release of oxygen replenishes that which is constantly being removed from the atmosphere by processes such as respiration (metabolic breakdown of food), combustion, and certain decay processes. Approximately 21 percent of the atmosphere consists of oxygen, all of which has been produced as the result of photosynthesis. Photosynthesis in tiny ocean plants (mostly algae) produces much of the total oxygen being released today. It is obvious that animals depend on plants not only as a direct or indirect source of food. but also for the oxygen they require for respiration.

The world operates on solar energy. Even the energy derived from combustion of fossil fuels (i.e., coal, natural gas, and petroleum) represents solar energy trapped by photosynthesis many millions of years ago. Energy is defined as the capacity to do work. Important aspects of the behavior of energy are described by the *Laws of Thermodynamics.*

The First Law of Thermodynamics states that energy may be converted from one form to another but can never be created or destroyed. The energy conversion principle can be illustrated by the manner in which solar energy is converted into a form which we can use to perform mechanical work. The radiant energy of sunlight is converted to potential energy by photosynthesis. This potential energy is present in the chemical bonds which hold the atoms of organic molecules together. Many organic substances can be burned for fuel. Burning converts much of the potential energy within the molecules to heat energy. The heat can then be used to boil water and create steam which, in turn, can power a turbine. The mechanical energy represented by the turning of the turbine may be converted by a generator to electrical energy. This can then be reconverted to mechanical energy in the form of a rotating power saw blade which will cut wood.

Ecologists are interested in the uses and conversions of energy within plant and animal populations. The organic molecules produced by photosynthesis may be used in several ways. The sugar initially produced by a plant may be broken down by the plant during respiration. During this process, the sugar molecule is converted to water and

carbon dioxide and energy is released which may be used to meet the plant's energy requirements. The summary equation for this process, the respiration of sugar, is the opposite of the photosynthesis equation:

$$\text{sugar} + \text{oxygen} \xrightarrow[\text{enzymes}]{\text{respiratory}} \text{water} + \text{carbon dioxide} + \text{energy}$$

Instead of using its sugar for energy, a plant may convert it to one of several compounds to be stored or used for construction. Stored compounds include the starches and complex sugars in tubers and fruits. Sugars may be converted to cellulose or used in the synthesis of proteins, both of which are important structural materials. Any of these products may be used eventually by other organisms.

The organisms which feed on the bodies of other organisms are called consumers. Most consumers are animals. Consumers that feed mainly on producers (plants) are called primary consumers. Primary consumers obtain usable energy when the organic molecules of plants are digested and used in respiration. The potential energy of the plant's organic molecules may, finally, be reflected in physical motions of the animal's body, synthesis of new molecules, maintenance of electrical charges, and discharge of body heat.

Plant materials which are neither used by the plant nor eaten by an animal must finally decay. (Minor exceptions to this are the seeds and spores which are discharged and successfully germinate, and plant material which is buried, escapes decomposition, and eventually forms coal, peat, or petroleum.) Decay of organic material results largely from the action of bacteria and fungi. These decay-causing organisms are called decomposers. Therefore, regardless of whether a particular organic molecule is used by the plant that produced it, eaten by an animal, or decayed by bacteria or fungi, it is ultimately reduced largely to carbon dioxide and water, and makes its contribution to the energy requirements of the system.

The Second Law of Thermodynamics states that no conversion of energy from one form to another is 100 percent efficient. In other words, some energy is always wasted in energy conversions. All the heat energy used to produce steam cannot be converted into the mechanical energy turning a turbine. Some of the heat is always dissipated into the cooler surroundings. Similarly, when a consumer feeds on the organic molecules of a producer, the transfer of energy from producer to consumer is not 100 percent efficient. The efficiency of most such transfers is around 10 percent. To an ecologist, this means that grasshoppers feeding on plants only obtain one-tenth of the energy required to produce the plant material on which they feed. It also means that an acre of grain contains 10 times as much food energy as the beef which could be produced on that grain. This becomes a

highly significant factor in the plans of a government trying to feed a large population — many more people can be supported on grain than on the beef it can produce.

Energy flow in the environment is diagrammed in a general way in figure 1. The fact that energy moves from one box to the next is an example of *The First Law of Thermodynamics.* Each succeeding box in the energy chain is smaller than the one before it, reflecting the loss of usable energy as it is transferred from one kind of organism to another. The fact that successive boxes are smaller is an example of *The Second Law of Thermodynamics.* Note that the movement of energy is unidirectional — it is noncyclic. This system can remain functional only if energy is continually supplied to it. Later we will see that the other basic transfer patterns in nature are cyclic, at least in those systems which are reasonably well-balanced.

Food Chains and Food Webs

A food chain exists in situations in which an animal feeds on plants and is, in turn, eaten by another animal. Two simple food chains are illustrated in figure 2. You should be able to envision numerous other examples of food chains. Each link in a food chain is called a trophic level. The word trophic refers to type of nourishment. In the food chains represented here, grass and phytoplankton (small aquatic plants) are the producers. They are autotrophic (i.e., self-nourishing) in that they produce their own food by photosynthesis. Consumers in food chains are heterotrophic (i.e., other nourishing). Heterotrophs must obtain nourishment by feeding on other organisms. The cow and the zooplankton (small aquatic animals) in figure 2 represent heterotrophs and are primary consumers since they feed on autotrophs. The other animals in the food chains are secondary (feeding on pri-

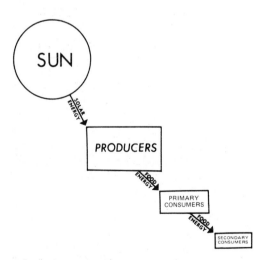

Figure 1. Transfer of Energy in the Environment

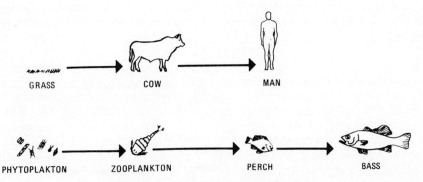

GRASS   COW   MAN

PHYTOPLAKTON   ZOOPLANKTON   PERCH   BASS

Figure 2. Two Simple Food Chains

mary consumers) and tertiary (feeding on secondary consumers) consumers.

The food chain is another way of expressing the *energy chain* illustrated in figure 1. Since usable energy decreases as it moves from one trophic level to another, it is sometimes convenient to express the relationship of usable energy to trophic levels by a diagram which always forms a pyramid (fig. 3). The size of each compartment of the pyramid represents the usable energy present at that particular trophic level. It can be seen that there is a decrease in usable energy as nutrients pass from a lower trophic level to a higher one.

This same energy relationship in the community food chain may also be expressed in terms of numbers of organisms at each trophic level (fig. 3). From one trophic level to another, in an upward direction, the total number of organisms usually decreases markedly; the phytoplankton in a one-acre pond may consist of several billion individuals (producers); the zooplankton may number several million individuals (primary consumers); there may be several thousand bluegills (secondary consumers), while only a few hundred largemouth bass (tertiary consumers) will be present.

Biomass represents the total mass of living and recently-living material within an area. The relationship of biomass to trophic levels is similar to the relationships of energy and numbers to trophic levels (fig. 3). Five acres of pasture may produce several tons of hay in one season. This hay may sustain the growth of a few hundred pounds of cattle which will support still fewer pounds of people. It is obvious that food taken from lower trophic levels is cheaper and more abundant in both availability and energy expended in its production. The three pyramidal relationships discussed are all ways of depicting *The Second Law of Thermodynamics*.

In reality, simple food chains such as those illustrated rarely exist. Even in a seemingly simple system such as a pasture, feeding relationships are much more complex than might be imagined. There is a multitude of plants and small animals present, and their dependency upon one another for food forms a complex food web rather than a simple food chain. The complexity may be more readily evident in a forest than in a pasture (fig. 4).

In general, if all other factors are equal, complex food webs involving large numbers of species are more stable than those with fewer species. Considering that each consumer in a diverse system can rely on more than one species for food decreases

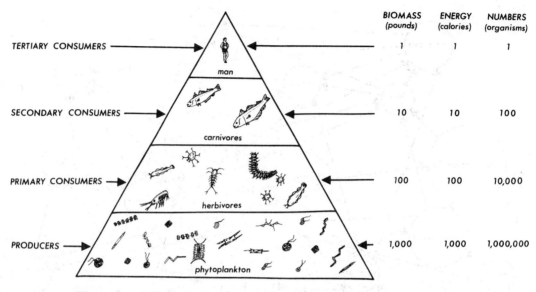

	BIOMASS (pounds)	ENERGY (calories)	NUMBERS (organisms)
TERTIARY CONSUMERS — *man*	1	1	1
SECONDARY CONSUMERS — *carnivores*	10	10	100
PRIMARY CONSUMERS — *herbivores*	100	100	10,000
PRODUCERS — *phytoplankton*	1,000	1,000	1,000,000

Figure 3.   A Hypothetical Pyramid of Energy, Biomass, and Numbers

the likelihood that the elimination of one species will cause severe disruption of the system. This is not the case with simple systems. Ecological systems in arctic regions, where only a few species of plants and animals live, are often simple and involve readily apparent relationships. In some arctic regions, the arctic fox relies almost altogether on the arctic hare for food. If arctic hares were to disappear, the foxes would probably disappear also. In contrast to arctic systems, tropical forest systems contain a high diversity of organisms and have the most complex food webs of any terrestrial situation. A herbivore, or even a carnivore, may often rely on any one of a dozen or more food species. Therefore, the complete elimination of a single food species would probably have little effect on other plants or animals in the system.

Ecological Cycles

The utilization of energy in ecological systems, as we have seen, is noncyclic. The sun must continually replenish the energy used or the systems would disintegrate. On the other hand, the basic elemental components (i.e., carbon, nitrogen, sulfur, etc.) of living things are cycled and reused over and over again. The significance of this is clear — if these raw materials were not recycled, they would soon be expended and life would cease to exist. The carbon cycle is perhaps the best understood of these cycles (fig. 5).

The cyclic movement of carbon in ecological systems involves its uptake as carbon dioxide from the atmosphere by producers, movement from producers to consumers, and ultimately from producers and consumers to decomposers. As decomposers function in the decay process, carbon is returned to the atmosphere in the form of carbon dioxide. Respiration by both producers and consumers also returns considerable amounts of carbon dioxide to the atmosphere. However, respiratory activities of decomposers account for most of the return of this essential gas to the atmospheric reservoir. Small amounts of carbon are

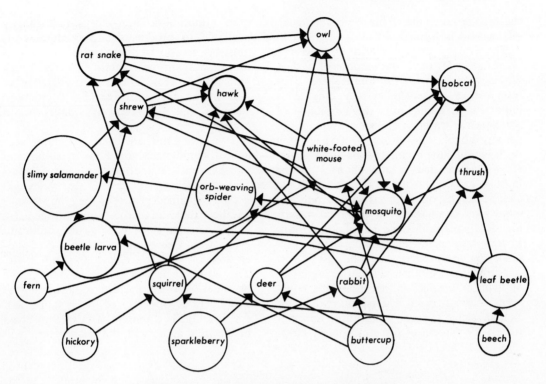

Figure 4. A Hypothetical Forest Food Web

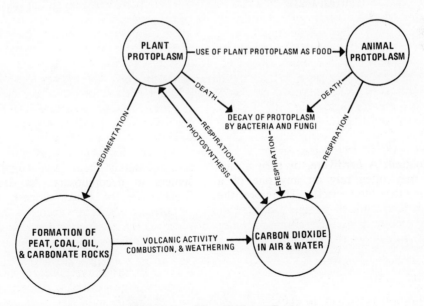

Figure 5. The Carbon Cycle

captured or taken out of the cycle when coal, oil, or peat is formed.

The oceans of the world contain approximately 50 times the amount of carbon dioxide contained in the atmosphere. This reservoir of dissolved carbon dioxide is important in maintaining the constancy of atmospheric carbon dioxide levels, since carbon dioxide may move freely back and forth between the ocean and the atmosphere. It is obvious that drastic changes in the level of carbon dioxide in the oceans could change atmospheric levels of carbon dioxide — a change whose potential results are easily realized since all photosynthesis in terrestrial plants depends upon the availability of atmospheric carbon dioxide.

Nitrogen is another element essential to all living organisms. At first thought, it might seem that nitrogen acquisition would be simple, since nitrogen constitutes approximately 79 percent of the atmosphere. However, atmospheric nitrogen is not directly available to producers and consumers. It must be incorporated into organic molecules by microorganisms (certain bacteria, fungi, and algae) before it can be used by other plants. The nitrogen cycle (fig. 6) is more complex than the relatively simple carbon cycle.

Two other nutrient cycles of major ecological significance are those of sulfur and phosphorous. Neither of these have significant atmospheric phases. These cycles will not be explained here, but their importance parallels those of carbon and nitrogen.

No discussion of ecologically-important cycles would be complete without a consideration of the hydrologic (water) cycle. The water cycle represents an interchange of water between the atmosphere and the earth's surface by way of precipitation and evaporation. The amount of rainfall received by an area, along with the temperature, will

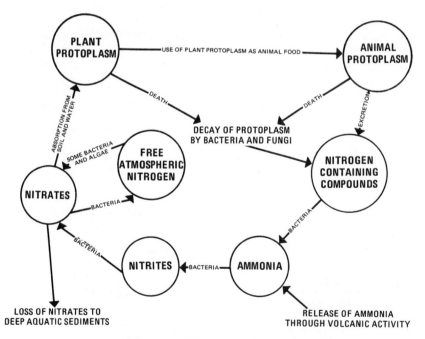

Figure 6. The Nitrogen Cycle

determine in large measure the types of plants which grow there. The nature of the vegetation is, in turn, a major factor in determining the kinds of animals that will be found in the area. A relatively small difference in total rainfall, or in its seasonal distribution, can often mean the difference between a forest, grassland or desert. Seasonal shifts in wind patterns, locations of mountain ranges, and the borders of large land masses affect the hydrologic cycle in general, and an area's annual precipitation pattern in particular.

Niches and Habitats

Simply viewed, an organism's habitat may be thought of as its address, while the niche may be likened to its "life style." The niche, in a sense, is the role of the plant or animal in the ecological system of which it is a part. The complete description of the niche of an organism would include a large, if not infinite, set of physical and biological characteristics. Some of the most obvious information required to determine the niche of a species include the following: its source of nutrients; its predators and parasites; how temperature and humidity fluctuations affect the species; how rainfall patterns affect it; its reproductive habits; how it affects the nutrient cycles in its system. Obviously we can never know everything about the niche of any plant or animal.

Even though the niche is difficult to define precisely, the concept is very important to the ecologist. When an ecologist determines what food two species of fish in a stream eat, he has compared an aspect of their niches. When he compares the behavioral characteristics of crayfish in a mountain stream to those of crayfish in an irrigation ditch, he has compared features of the animals' niches. By obtaining enough information about the niches of the plant and animal species making up a community, an ecologist may make intelligent predic-

tions concerning what would happen if the environment were to undergo certain modifications. Knowing certain things about aquatic animals' niches, for instance, allows the ecologist to predict changes that might occur in aquatic communities if the water were to be warmed by the release of heat from a nuclear power plant, enriched by the release of sewage, or invaded by organisms from another aquatic habitat when canals are constructed. Generally, the more similar the niches of two species, the more intensively they will compete. When two species compete for the same food, shelter, and space, it is likely that one of the species will be eliminated from the area of competition. In natural situations, animals with very similar niches are rarely found living together in the same area.

A non-native species should not be introduced into an area until careful study of its niche indicates that its activities will not interfere with the organisms already there. Introduced organisms may have abundant food while their numbers are low. In the new habitat, the introduced organism may lack major predators or parasites. It may change its feeding and nesting habits. If natural factors fail to control population increase, the exotic species may become a problem rather than an asset. The foregoing considerations are of major importance because of the increasing tendency to introduce non-native species in attempts to control pest populations. Even though the introduced form may be a predator or a parasite of the pest species, it must be firmly established prior to introduction that the exotic species will not itself become a pest. These facts illustrate that knowledge of an organism's niche is necessary before man can make intelligent decisions about manipulating natural populations.

The concept of the habitat is easier to grasp than that of the niche. An organism's habitat can be defined in fairly concrete terms and can be observed in nature.

The habitats of some organisms are very simple or homogeneous. The tundra of the far North is an example. Certain species of beetles live only in decaying logs of certain tree species. Some species of fish live only in streams having a narrow range of water temperatures. Some organisms are capable of living under a wide variety of environmental conditions; the whitetail deer is found in virtually every type of forest and woodland in the eastern United States, ranging from the coniferous forests of northern Michigan to the everglades of Florida.

It should be obvious that changes in a habitat affect the niches of organisms living in that habitat. Destruction or alteration of the habitat destroys some niches and creates new ones. Damming a stream destroys populations of many species restricted to flowing water. The water in the newly-formed lake will be too deep in many areas to support the life characteristic of a stream. Nutrients may accumulate and bring about an increase in numbers of tiny plants. Water temperature may become more stable, and oxygen and carbon dioxide levels may fluctuate more in the newly-formed lake than in the former stream. These and other changes will all affect the niches of the organisms formerly inhabiting the stream and many, if not all, of these organisms will be eliminated and replaced by organisms whose niches are compatible with the newly-formed habitat. Granted, this is an extreme example of habitat modification; however, it should be realized that even the slightest habitat change may affect the niches of virtually all residents of the habitat.

The Ecosystem Concept

As previously stated, the plants and animals of a defined environmental area make up a community. That the plants and animals making up a community are interrelated through a complex system of mutual dependencies should now be evident. However, a consideration of environmental energy flow and of the hydrologic and nutrient cycles reveals that both plants and animals are also highly dependent upon dynamic interrelationships with the abiotic or physical features of the environment. When both the biotic (plants and animals) and abiotic (inanimate matter) features of an environmental area are taken together, the term ecosystem is used to designate the unit.

An excellent example of an ecosystem may be seen in a freshwater pond (fig. 7). In studying such an ecosystem, ecologists attempt to answer many questions: How efficient is the ecosystem in using solar energy to produce biomass? How many pounds of secondary consumers can be harvested yearly from the pond? What relationships can be seen in the food web of this ecosystem? What role do bottom sediments play in recycling nutrients? What would be the effect of introducing a new animal species into the ecosystem? What happens to the relative abundance of the component plant and animal species as the ecosystem ages? What would be the effect on the different plant and animal species if a pesticide were added to the ecosystem in a certain concentration?

Other major types of ecosystems include forests, fields, deserts, streams, and oceans. Even the earth and the atmosphere can be thought of as an ecosystem in the broadest sense of the term. Additionally, the word ecosystem may be used at different levels. A large forest may be properly referred to as an ecosystem; however, there may be several well-defined smaller ecosystems present within it. Ponds may occur in the forest, or clearings in the form of old fields may be present, and even a decaying log with its populations of beetles, millipedes, spiders, ants, bacteria, fungi, and other organisms may be referred to as an ecosystem.

In general, the simpler the ecosystem, the more delicately balanced it is. In a simple ecosystem, complex food webs are

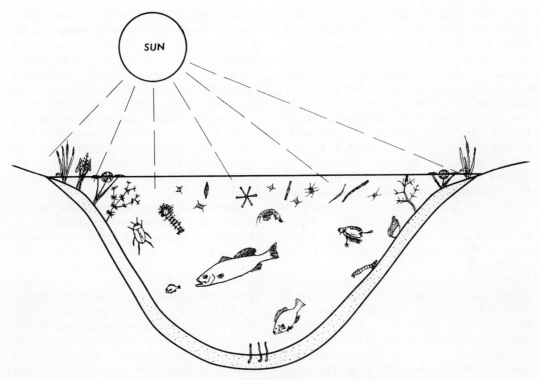

Figure 7. A Fresh-Water Ecosystem

absent. There may be few weather changes during the year, and the water and soil may be relatively homogeneous throughout such a system. The North American tundra is such an ecosystem. An important plant in the tundra is reindeer lichen. Lichens are often called "mosses" but are actually combinations of algae and fungi growing together in a mutually beneficial arrangement. Other less important plants present in the tundra include sedges, dwarf willows, and grasses. The main animals include caribou, arctic foxes, arctic hares, lemmings, wolves, snowy owls, and arctic grouse. The food chains are simple here — the caribou feed on the plants and wolves feed on the caribou. The lemmings, hares, and grouse feed

on the plants, and, in turn, are eaten by the snowy owls and arctic foxes. Any drastic changes in the numbers of one member of a system with such simple food chains will result in drastic changes in the numbers of the other members of the chain. If something were to kill the lichens, the entire ecosystem would be significantly altered because of the lack of a major producer which could live in the harsh environment.

The tropical rain forest represents the other extreme in ecosystem complexity. The plants include many species, and are so numerous that they completely shade the ground's surface. The total standing (living) plant biomass is very large in such an ecosystem. The plant variety present in this ecosystem is paralleled by the animal variety. Thousands of species of invertebrates and vertebrates occupy the animal niches available in a rain forest. The food web is so complex that we can only arrive at a rough approximation of its nature. Species diversity is one strong point of the complex ecosystem — its food web complexity means that one or a few members of the community would hardly be missed by the other community members. Contrary to popular belief, the tropical rain forest has little agricultural potential. High amounts of seasonal rainfall wash the soil nutrients away or leach them deep into the soil. When the forest is cleared for cultivation, it will support crops profitably for only a few years.

Neither the tundra nor the rain forest provide much for man if they are modified. If ecosystems are to be managed, they must be maintained in a state which closely resembles the natural one. We have destroyed many of our natural ecosystems and have modified others to the point that their original state can no longer be determined. Some of these modifications, such as the conversion of many of our natural grasslands to grain fields, have been necessary. Others, such as the conversion of vast areas of our native forestlands to single-species tree farms, are of questionable value in the long-term view. The widespread destruction of natural terrain for building roads and pipelines, and for extracting coal and other minerals is a practice we may later regret. The modification of our aquatic ecosystems by pollution, channelization and canal building may not, in the final analysis, contribute to the quality of life. In too many instances, thorough ecological studies with a view toward the distant future do not precede such modifications.

Ecologists can predict, with some accuracy, the long term effects of continued ecosystem modification. There are defined limits within which ecological systems can function effectively. Man's shortsightedness often results in his failure to appreciate his dependency on natural ecosystems. Small ecosystems can be destroyed and are hardly missed by most of the public. The larger ecosystems represent another story. If man drastically changes the climate through air pollution, he could cause disastrous changes in the worldwide vegetation pattern. If man continues to pollute the oceans, significant reduction in the phytoplankton might ultimately affect the atmospheric oxygen supply.

Ecosystems have only limited healing powers. Slight ecosystem disruption can be repaired by nature, while major modification can leave an ecosystem permanently changed. Connecting two river systems, or other large bodies of water by canals will permit mixing of the plant and animal species of the two systems. The ecological consequences of such an action cannot be accurately determined beforehand — what is known is that undesirable effects of these projects can seldom be reversed. When poor land management causes extensive erosion, the land can lose its ability to support significant plant life for hundreds or thousands of years. Such a modified ecosystem is often beyond repair. Evidence of this can be seen throughout much of Italy. The stark, barren hillsides will never again support the magnificent forests which were removed repeatedly to build ships for the Roman fleet. The Tigris-Euphrates Valley, a very productive area in ancient times, is now hardly distinguishable from the Sahara Desert due to hundreds of years of mistreatment.

Ecological Succession

Ecological succession refers to the series of physical and biological changes which follow the disturbance of an ecosystem. These progressive changes lead toward the reestablishment of ecological maturity. In one sense, ecological succession is a form of "ecological healing." A good example of succession may be seen in the changes which follow when land in an oak-hickory forest in the eastern United States has been cleared, cultivated, and later abandoned. Unless erosion has been extensive, the abandoned land will return slowly to something resembling its former state. At the time of abandonment, the field would harbor few biological residents. During the first year, several species of plants, which most persons would call weeds, would cover the field. Insects and other small invertebrates characteristic of a "weedy field community" would also be present, and, typically, a few rodents and other small vertebrates would move into the area. During this stage of succession there are likely to be large numbers of individual organisms representing relatively few species. A young ecosystem such as this would be very productive in terms of total biomass. Although biomass is accumulating rapidly in the young ecosystem, diversity of life is low, and low diversity in an ecosystem results in poor stability.

During the second year, the species composition in the old field would be noticeably different from that of the first year, particularly with respect to the plants. Weeds would still be present, but much of the field would be covered with broomsedge, and close examination might show that some trees are sprouting — especially pines, whose windblown seeds germinate readily in the absence of leaf cover and shade. The animal life would also change during the second year. Rabbits and other small mammals, generally low in numbers the first year, now find the habitat more suitable. Quail and other birds would be present, and hawks, owls, foxes, and other predators of small mammals would be more abundant. Diversity is increasing in the ecosystem, and it can be predicted that stability is also increasing. Food webs are becoming more complex as the numbers of interrelationships

between the living members of the community increase.

However, succession is only beginning in the old field. The old field vegetation during the next few years will shift slowly from herbs to small shrubs and trees. At first the trees may be mostly pines, since the wind may scatter their seeds over the entire area. As the trees increase in size there will be obvious changes in animal populations. Deer and squirrels will move in and greater numbers of birds will appear. Insects and other invertebrate populations will become more diverse as the vegetation changes.

Even if the area is initially covered with pine, the trees characteristic of the original area will ultimately return. The extreme shade produced by the dense stand of pine will inhibit further germination of pine seeds. However, oak, hickory, sweetgum, and other hardwoods will germinate under such conditions. As the pine trees mature and die, the young hardwoods replace them, and finally pine may be virtually eliminated as the vegetation of the natural area is restored. The time needed for these successional changes to produce the end result may have extended over 200 years or more. The resulting forest type, called the climax ecosystem, would be the most stable and hence the most successful ecosystem capable of developing under the soil and climatic conditions characteristic of the area.

In such a climax ecosystem as the mature oak-hickory forest, we find species diversity and ecosystem stability at its highest since the field was abandoned. Species of trees other than oak and hickory are present; however, the oaks and hickory are particularly numerous, and we refer to them as dominants. There are also numerous smaller species of woody plants, as well as smaller individuals of the larger tree species of the community. Many herbs and mosses cover the ground in shaded areas, and in open areas grasses may be present. Dead trees are standing as well as lying on the forest floor.

Vines of various kinds entangle many of the trees, their stems reaching upward toward the light. The number of niches available for animal life is greater than the number present in the old field or the young forest. Animal life here may not be as conspicuously abundant as in some earlier stages; but of more importance, species diversity is high, and interdependence between all members of the community forms an intricate and stable network of natural relationships not easily disrupted by minor changes which could spell catastrophe to a simpler ecosystem. The climax ecosystem is a well-balanced, self-perpetuating system which only great natural disasters or man can truly disrupt.

In the foregoing example of succession, the early stages of ecosystem development may be referred to as young ecosystems. More photosynthesis than respiration is occurring in the young ecosystem. In other words, living materials are accumulating faster than they are decaying or otherwise being disposed of. Such an ecosystem is very productive. Its productivity (building of molecules) exceeds its respiration (tearing down of molecules). It is obvious that this has to be the case since the old field progresses from barren ground with little accumulated biomass to a complex forest with a great deal of accumulated biomass. As succession proceeds, the productivity-to-respiration ratio declines. At first, productivity was many times higher than respiration; however, the ratio approaches one-to-one in a climax ecosystem. In other words, in a mature climax ecosystem, production equals respiration. This should not be surprising. A balance exists in the climax community in such a way that highly efficient use is being made of what is available. Energy is being incorporated into the system by means of photosynthesis, and the organic molecules thus produced are passing through the system providing energy to all trophic levels. The climax system has

reached its permanent level of complexity, and the capture of energy (production) balances or equals the use of energy (respiration).

Man can harvest relatively little from climax ecosystems — even the earliest men realized this. Efficient agriculture depends on the greater productivity of young ecosystems, with a view toward producing large crop-yields on relatively small acreages. However, crop lands represent low-diversity ecosystems and therefore are easily disturbed. Corn blight can ruin an entire crop over a large area. An important question today concerns the extent to which we can modify our ecosystems to continue to feed, house, and clothe the ever-increasing number of humans without bringing on major ecological catastrophes. Obviously, we must continue to convert climax ecosystems to young, productive, crop ecosystems if the ever-expanding human population is to be provided with even the basic necessities — a practice which must stop sometime.

Regardless of the type of ecosystem involved, successional changes occur after disruption. In general, the principles illustrated by old field succession apply to any young ecosystem as it moves toward maturity. These include: (1) an increase in diversity of plant and animal species; (2) an increase in the complexity of relationships among the living organisms present; (3) an increase in the amount of organic matter (biomass) present; and (4) a movement toward stability in metabolic activity of the community in terms of the ratio of productivity to respiration. Since the above changes are directional, the ecologist is able to predict with some accuracy what the results of ecosystem disruption will lead to in terms of both biological and physical changes. The dumping of sewage into lakes will hasten their conversion to marshes and swamps through natural succession. The results of such a process produce conditions which can be reliably predicted before they take place. When ore or coal is mined directly from the earth's surface, the ecologist can describe with considerable accuracy the succession changes which will take place after mining operations have ceased. Of course, details of the ecologist's predictions are largely dependent on the conditions present when succession begins. For instance, open pits and piles of slag produce different types of successional events than carefully replaced topsoil planted with seedlings.

Population Control

A population is defined as all the members of a given species living within a defined area. Dramatic fluctuations in population size are commonplace in the early stages of succession and in simple ecosystems. This should not be too surprising since the interrelationships within such a system are too few to bring about stability. An insect popu-

lation in an old field may increase at a very rapid rate until food is exhausted or cold weather curbs reproduction. In northern Europe, lemmings reproduce far more rapidly than foxes and owls can eliminate them through predation. Every few years the lemming population literally explodes; individuals become very aggressive, and large numbers undergo mass migrations resulting in death of the vast majority. In both instances of the insects and lemmings described here, population size is drastically reduced by the periodic death of most of the members of the population.

The growth of a population can be illustrated by a growth curve. A growth curve is constructed by plotting the numbers of organisms present on the vertical axis against time on the horizontal axis. A curve depicting a dramatic oscillation in population size is illustrated in figure 8. Note that the total number of individuals increases

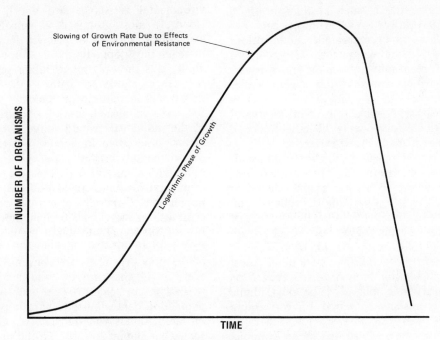

Figure 8. J-Shaped Population Growth Curve

steadily until a dramatic increase in death rate results in a downward plunge in population size. This curve represents the pattern of population growth characteristic of the seasonal insect and lemming populations discussed earlier.

Most natural populations do not undergo the changes illustrated by the J-type curve shown in figure 8. Rather than undergo extreme fluctuations, most natural populations do not fluctuate markedly from year to year. A growth curve for such a population is illustrated in figure 9. Notice that this curve levels off and shows only minor fluctuations after the population reaches its optimum size. A curve such as this is referred to as an S-type curve.

The factors responsible for regulating population size are complex. All the factors which collectively regulate population growth are referred to as environmental resistance. In a climax ecosystem species rarely demonstrate a complete history of population growth, such as that shown in figure 9. However, when large-scale natural disasters or man-made modifications drastically alter ecosystems, the ecologist has the opportunity to trace the entire history of population growth for a species under an observable set of conditions. In instances where this is possible, the identification of the various components of environmental resistance is made much easier.

In young populations, the birth rate usually exceeds the death rate. The slow acceleration of initial population growth shown in figures 8 and 9 is partially dependent upon low breeding efficiency when the number of individuals is small. This slow initial growth is usually followed by a period of accelerated population growth. The period of most rapid population growth is referred to as the logarithmic phase. [The logarithmic phase represents a period of very rapid population growth. Reasons for such rapid expansion can be illustrated by an example. Suppose a pair of small mammals produces litters of 10 offspring every month. Assume that sexual maturity in this species is reached at the age of one month. At the end of the first month of population growth, this pair would have increased to a total of 12 animals, at the end of the second month 72, the third month 432. Logarithmic rates increase rapidly due to the combined effects of both the original and the added components.] Finally, the logarithmic phase is followed by a negatively accelerating phase which eventually results in zero growth and subsequent stability (fig. 9), or a rapid decrease in population size (fig. 8). The negatively accelerating phase is the portion of the curve at which environmental resistance is playing its regulatory role. Zero growth is attained at the point where death rate becomes equal to birth rate. Of course, death rate must equal birth rate in a population which remains stable in size.

Many of the factors contributing to environmental resistance are poorly understood. In most groups of organisms, food availability is rarely of primary importance in regulating population size. If food availability was the only major factor governing the size of stable populations, the population would increase logarithmically until the food was exhausted, and all or virtually all of the individuals would starve. Obviously, factors other than food must contribute to environmental resistance.

Predation may also play a role in environmental resistance regulating prey species populations. Generally, as a prey population enlarges, the individuals become more readily available to predators. The predator numbers tend to increase and greater numbers of the prey organisms are consumed. However, as in the case of food availability, predation can seldom be the sole factor in population control. Arctic hare populations on large islands will fluctuate in a manner somewhat similar to those on the mainland, even though predator species are absent.

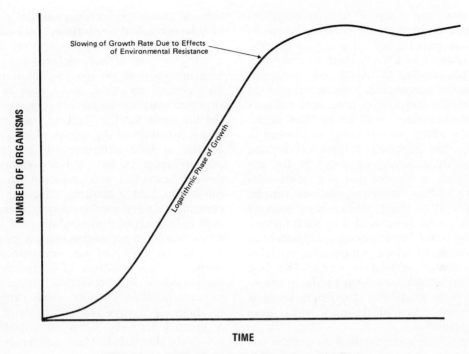

Figure 9. S-Shaped Population Growth Curve

Also, some species lack major predators — grizzly bears and lions obviously have no major natural predators.

Another important factor contributing to environmental resistance is parasitism. A successful parasite rarely kills its host. Host-parasite relationships evolve slowly and, in most natural populations of animals, parasites cause little damage when the population is not crowded. However, parasite infestations become heavier when host density increases beyond a given level. In many cases increased parasite loads eventually results in increased host mortality. In this way, parasitism may contribute to population control. A good example of this may be seen in whitetail deer populations. The occurrence of brain nematode infestations is typically low in moderate-sized deer populations living in climax forest ecosystems.

However, if lack of predation or some other factor causes a dramatic increase in the number of deer, the parasite may spread from individual to individual more readily and thus destroy significant numbers of the population.

Competition between different species for food, space, or cover can become important as population levels increase. There may be little competition while population levels are low; but, as their numbers increase, factors such as the exploitation of new types of foods may result in competition with other species. The effects of population size on competition are generally easier to visualize in plants than in animals. When one species of alga increases to a certain point, the sheer mass of algal cells may limit the reception of light by another species, thus eliminating the second species. A species of tree may "out compete" nearby neighbors for soil moisture and nutrients when its numbers increase beyond a certain density.

You can undoubtedly think of other factors contributing to overall environmental resistance; nevertheless, such factors as food availability, competition, predation, and parasitism sometimes seem to be "last ditch" devices which are effective only when a species has increased its numbers beyond the ability (carrying capacity) of the environment to support that population adequately. Many stable populations can be thought of as being self-regulating systems which are rarely controlled by such factors. Biologists are just beginning to comprehend the extent to which intraspecific relationships control population levels. The best way to explain how intraspecific relationships serve to stabilize population levels is to discuss a few of the ones which have been studied.

The size of some mammalian populations may be regulated to a large extent by endocrine system responses to sociopsychological factors. In many species of small herbivorous mammals, when individuals see more than the usual number of other members of their own species, their adrenal glands tend to enlarge. The increase in adrenal size is thought to be a response caused by increased pituitary activity which was triggered by nerve impulses arising from the visual areas of the brain. As the adrenals enlarge, they produce excessive amounts of adrenal hormones resulting in a reduction of gonad size (reproductive organs). Decrease in gonad size inhibits reproduction. The females in such a population will tend to have fewer offspring, or they may fail to breed at all. This type of physiological response to overcrowding generally occurs prior to the point that a population will be severely limited by food availability, parasitism, and other such factors.

Certain behavioral responses in populations are also important as intraspecific factors affecting population size. The individuals of many species demonstrate a type of behavior called territoriality. Individuals, or small groups of individuals, will select a territory and actively defend it against other members of the species. The territory may contain the food, cover, and nesting sites necessary for successful completion of the life cycle for the "holders" of the territory. Members of the species which do not acquire or hold a territory do not breed and are more subject to being eliminated through starvation and predation than are those who hold a territory. Since an area contains a limited number of territories, and only individuals who successfully hold a territory breed, the population will not increase beyond the ability of the environment to support it. The existence of a nonbreeding component in the population further promotes population stability, since extra individuals are always available to move into a vacated territory when an established holder is eliminated. Many mammals and birds are well known for demonstrating territoriality, and the populations of such species are usually remarkably stable.

The role of behavior in population control may also depend on physiological response to environmental changes. Research in this area has not proceeded as rapidly as it has in many other areas of the zoological sciences. Behavior is known to play a role in population control in many invertebrate populations as well as in the vertebrates. In some of the social insects, removal of the queen stimulates subordinate females to begin egg laying within a matter of hours. Shortly, one of these becomes queen, and the others cease egg laying. The physiological mechanisms involved here are unknown, and many other similar kinds of population regulation through behavior undoubtedly exist.

Migration is a type of behavior which can have a regulatory effect on population size. Not only does migration lead to an increased death rate in the population, but it also prevents overuse of habitat during certain seasons of the year. The singing of a chorus of birds may even contribute to population control. The strength of the chorus is an index of population density and may directly affect the individual members of the species within hearing, especially the males. These individuals are stimulated to heightened display activities such as prolonged singing, strutting, and parading. The increase in these activities may lead to a reduction of breeding efficiency.

An excellent example of the effects of ecosystem modification on population size can be seen by considering a deer management program initiated on the Kaibab Plateau in 1907. The Kaibab Plateau consists of about 727,000 acres on the north side of the Grand Canyon in Arizona. In 1907, a bounty was placed on wolves, cougars, and coyotes. These were all natural predators of deer, and the program was designed to protect the deer population. At about the same time, livestock grazing was restricted in the area and forest fires stimulated an abundant growth of the types of plants eaten by deer. At the initiation of the protection program, it was estimated that the deer herd numbered approximately 4000. In the following 20 years, over 8000 predators were removed. During this time, the deer herd grew rapidly. By 1918, the deer numbered about 50,000. Naturalists now pointed out that habitat damage was occurring, and the herd should probably be thinned, or at least the predator control program discontinued. Neither of these recommendations were followed.

In 1920, the herd numbered about 60,000 and some fawns were noted to be starving. In 1924, the herd may have numbered as high as 100,000 and during the following two winters thousands of deer starved. By this time extensive damage had occurred to the vegetation. Even the bark of trees had been eaten away as starving deer literally ate everything in sight. Feeding pressure applied by the surviving deer prevented full recovery of the vegetation even after

significant numbers of deer had starved to death.

By 1935, the herd was down to approximately 10,000 and has remained at about that level. It is estimated that this natural area could have originally supported about 40,000 deer without undue habitat destruction, but the actual carrying capacity of the environment was ultimately reduced substantially below that level. This seems to be a case in which an ecosystem was not able to fully recover from disaster, even with 40 years of "healing" time.

Adaptation and the Environment

Although space will not permit a detailed discussion of evolutionary principles, a brief review might be appropriate. Evolution is the mechanism by which species change through time. The forces which necessitate, and in fact cause this change, are the environmental factors under which a species exists. The process by which these forces acting together bring about the evolution of organisms is called natural selection. In any population there are differences among the organisms. These differences are mainly due to differences in their genetic make-up. Different individuals have different kinds and different combinations of genetic material. The different kinds of genetic material are the result of mutations which have occurred during the past history of the lineage. Mutations are changes, usually small, in the kind, amount, or position of genetic material present in a cell's chromosomes. Most mutations are detrimental to the individuals possessing them. A few, however, are beneficial. It is the latter that eventually are incorporated into the genetic makeup of the species. Different genetic combinations are created when reproductive processes combine the hereditary material in different ways.

All organisms, by reproductive processes, produce in excess of the number of offspring which can survive. It is reasonable to assume that the ones which are most successful will be those with the most advantageous sets of characteristics. These individuals will, on the average, be more successful reproductively than those with less advantageous sets of characteristics. Thus a greater portion of the next generation will possess the favorable characteristics. Natural selection, therefore, is a process by which the most favorable genetic combinations are perpetuated and enhanced. The forces of natural selection in the environment can be thought of as a sieve, straining out over time those individuals not well-suited to meeting the needs which their mode of life places on them.

The result of natural selection is adaptation. This term may be used in several different ways, but the basic idea is the same. Adaptation can be thought of as a process by which species change in response to natural selection. Adaptation may also refer to any feature of a species which promotes the survival of the species.

Generally, the characteristics of most organisms can be thought of as adaptations. In this sense, adaptations are of three basic types: structural, physiological, and behavioral. The enlarged fur-soled feet of the snowshoe hare are an adaptation enabling the animal to move about freely on snow and ice. The presence of the pigment hemoglobin in the red blood cells of vertebrates is an adaptation which makes it possible for the blood to transport oxygen from the lungs to various parts of the body. The fact that roaches scuttle away into cracks when a light is turned on is a behavioral adaptation, the function of which is escape from predation.

The intricate relationships among organisms and between organisms and the physical environment are the result of adaptation. These adaptations result in success for the organisms possessing them, but they also result in dependency. The laterally flattened bodies of fleas enable them to move swiftly between the hairs of the mammals they parasitize. However, they would be unsuccessful as parasites of any other kind of animal. The barnacle goose is successful, because it is adapted to feed on eelgrass, a plant utilized by few other birds. This also means that its existence depends on the continued abundance of eelgrass. One species of fungus grows only on the wings of living beetles inhabiting caves in southern Europe. This may seem like adaptation carried to the extreme. Presently the fungus is successful in maintaining its population level, but minor alterations in its habitat might destroy it. The process of adaptation is continuous and dynamic, because the environment is constantly changing. Except in localized situations, natural environmental change is a slow process, and the changes it necessitates in organisms are correspondingly slow.

No organism possesses an unlimited ability to adapt, especially over short periods of time. The ability of a species to adapt depends on its genetic variability, its reproductive potential, its lifespan, and a number of other less obvious factors.

Some hopeful individuals discount environmental degradation as a problem by explaining that living things will adapt to the changing conditions. Unfortunately, this is largely wishful thinking. Evolutionary change is, of necessity, rather slow. Even small adaptive modifications may require hundreds or thousands of years. In the hundred or so years that man has been studying evolution, no organism is known to have undergone phenomenal evolutionary change. Several dozen species of insects have changed from light to darker colors in indirect response to the soot-darkened surfaces on which they rest. A number of insects and a few other organisms have developed resistance to chemical insecticides. House sparrows in the United States show slight differences in color and feathering from the European populations from which they originally came. These and other such changes which man has been able to study are very minor from an evolutionary viewpoint. Minor changes, when they accumulate, may ultimately result in major changes, but obviously this does not occur in a short period of time.

If present trends continue, the next few decades will see widespread modifications of the natural world — more drastic and much more rapid than any which have occurred during historical times. Most species will be unable to adapt to these changes. Failure to adapt can only lead to a dead end, e.g., extinction of the species involved. This is easily demonstrated by comparing the rate of extinction in the past several hundred years to the rate of extinction during the previous history of the earth. The changes wrought by man have caused this rate to increase manyfold.

Extinction will compound the problem of environmental degradation, because intricate ecological relationships will be destroyed as important species in food webs become extinct; and prey populations explode when their predators are eliminated. Ecosystems will be irreversibly changed and species adapted to former conditions within the ecosystem will disappear.

It is impossible to predict accurately which species will be the first to succumb. The osprey, brown pelican, and bald eagle have not been successful in adapting to the large quantities of DDT in their diets. Nutrient enrichment of lakes and the subsequent depletion of oxygen results in conditions to which few aquatic organisms can adapt. If the human population continues to increase, urbanization will drastically alter the face of the earth. Few species will adapt to an "ecosystem" composed largely of steel, concrete, and asphalt.

Man's ability to adapt does not compare with that of the insects, rodents, fungi, or bacteria. It is unreasonable to hope that man of the near future will not be harmed by high levels of air pollution. If contamination of the environment by radioactive materials continues, a threshold will be reached beyond which serious damage will be done to man. Evolutionary adaptation to a world whose natural systems have been altered in major ways is an interesting topic on which to speculate, but realistically it holds out little hope to man and other higher animals.

If environmental degradation continues, man may survive for a time, not by evolutionary adaptation, but rather by withdrawal from the dangerous world he has created. Air pollution problems can be met by hiding behind filters and staying indoors. This will also eliminate the trauma caused by the ugliness of smoky skies, monotonous landscapes, and anonymous buildings. Food can be heavily processed to remove contaminants. Water can be chemically and mechanically purified and stringently recycled. Man can increase his dependence on his contrivances until his life differs little from that of another cog or piston. If this is man's goal, he is rapidly approaching it.

Knowledge of the evolutionary process of adaptation leads to a generalization which can be used to guide man's future treatment of the natural earth. The organisms which exist on this planet are adapted to natural conditions and are capable of changing at the relatively slow rate at which nature changes naturally. Speeding the rate of environmental change and creating conditions radically different from those present in nature can lead to only one consequence — failure to adapt and subsequent extinction. It is not a question of "if" but "when."

SOURCES OF ADDITIONAL INFORMATION

BASIC ECOLOGICAL PRINCIPLES

Clarke, G. 1965. *Elements of ecology.* rev. ed. John Wiley and Sons, New York.

Dyson, F. J. 1971. Energy in the universe. *Scientific American* 225(3):50-59.

Gates, D. M. 1971. The flow of energy in the biosphere. *Scientific American* 225(3):88-100.

Kendeigh, S. 1961. *Animal ecology.* Prentice-Hall, Englewood Cliffs, N.J.

Kormondy, E. J. 1969. *Concepts of ecology.* Prentice-Hall, Englewood Cliffs, N.J.

Lowry, W. P. 1969. *Weather and life: an introduction to biometeorology.* Academic Press, New York.

Odum, E. P. 1963. *Ecology.* Holt, Rinehart and Winston, Inc., New York.

Odum E. P. 1971. *Fundamentals of ecology.* 3d ed. W. B. Saunders Co., Philadelphia, Pennsylvania.

Smith, R. L. 1966. *Ecology and field biology.* Harper and Row, New York.

Summers, C. M. 1971 The conversion of energy. *Scientific American* 225(3):148-160.

Wiens, J. A., ed. 1971. *Ecosystem structure and function.* Oregon State University Press, Corvallis, Oregon.

Woodwell, G. M. 1970. Effects of pollution on the structure and physiology of ecosystems. *Science* 168:429-433.

ENVIRONMENTAL PROBLEMS

Anderson, P. 1971. *Omega: murder of the ecosystem and suicide of man.* Wm. C. Brown, Dubuque, Iowa.

Clawson, M. 1972. *America's land and it's uses.* Johns Hopkins University Press, Baltimore, Maryland.

Darnell, R. M. 1970. The new ecology. *BioScience* 20(13):746-748.

Farvar, M. T., et al. 1971. The pollution of Asia. *Environment* 13(8):10-17.

Guthry, D. A. 1971. Primitive man's relationship to nature. *BioScience* 21(13):721-728.

Harrington, C., et al. 1971. *If you want to save your environment . . . start at home.* Hawthorn Books, New York.

Hickel, W. 1971. *Who owns America?* Prentice-Hall, Englewood Cliffs, New Jersey.

Hutchinson, G. E. 1970. The biosphere. *Scientific American* 223(3):44-53.

Jackson, W. ed. 1971. *Man and the environment.* Wm. C. Brown, Dubuque, Ia.

Kendeigh, S. 1965. The ecology of man, the animal. *BioScience* 15(8):521-523.

Killeen, J. ed. 1971. *Ecology at home.* 101 Productions, San Francisco.

Koestner, E., et al. 1972. *The do-it-yourself environmental handbook.* Little, Brown, Boston, Massachusetts.

Lauda, D., and R. Ryan. 1971. *Advancing technology: its impact on society.* Wm. C. Brown, Dubuque, Iowa.

Leisner, R., and J. Kormondy, eds. 1971. *Foundations for today,* vol. 1. *Poplation and food,* vol. 2. *Pollution,* vol. 3. *Ecology.* Wm. C. Brown, Dubuque, Ia.

Littleton, T., ed. 1970. *Approaching the Benign Environment.* University of Alabama Press, University, Alabama.

McHarg, I. 1969. *Design with nature.* Natural History Press, New York.

National Academy of Sciences. 1969. *Resources and man.* W. H. Freeman, San Francisco.

Shepard, P., and D. McKinley, eds. 1969. *The subversive science.* Houghton-Mifflin, Boston.

Wagner, R. H. 1971. *Environment and man.* W. W. Norton and Company, Inc., New York.

Watt, K. E. F. 1968. *Ecology and resource management.* McGraw-Hill, New York.

Watt, K. E. F. 1972. Man's efficient rush towards deadly dullness. *Natural History* 81 (2):74-82.

Part II

Human Population:
Characteristics, Controls,
Policies, and Survival

WALTER E. HOWARD

The Population Crisis Is Here Now

Walter E. Howard is Professor of Wildlife
Biology and a vertebrate ecologist at the
University of California, Davis. He has over
160 publications on the population-environ-
ment crisis and the ecology, behavior, and
control of rodents and other wild vertebrates in
disturbed ecosystems.

Preface

At the present world rate of population
growth of 2% per year, a mere dozen
people a thousand years ago could have
produced the present world population, and
in another thousand years each one of us
could have 300 million living descendants.
Obviously, that cannot be — something must
be done. Either the birth rate must be significantly curtailed or the death rate drastically increased.

The world's overpopulation crisis is of a
magnitude beyond human comprehension,
yet the government and the public remain
seemingly indifferent. Better awareness and
a more forthright leadership are obviously
needed, from biologists and politicians alike.
Will you help? A vastly increased rate of
involuntary premature deaths can be prevented only by an informed public, here and
abroad, following dynamic leadership. No
population can continue to increase indefinitely, no matter how much food there
is. If civilization is to be viable, we must
end the arrogant assumption that there are
unlimited resources and infinite air and
water. People must develop much greater
voluntary restraint in reproduction — or conception itself will have to come under government control.

This earth does not have the resources
necessary to provide even the present world
population with the degree of affluence that
the middle-class citizen enjoys. Even though
the average birth rate in the United States
has declined during the past decade from
about seven children per family to fewer
than three, the population density has been
growing much more rapidly than before.
The reason is the high population base level;
there are now so many more women that
their "small" families add a greater number of new people to the population each
year than did their grandmothers, even with
much larger families.

No population can continue to grow beyond certain limits; eventually, involuntary
self-limitation — in the form of premature

Reprinted by permission from the author and
publisher from *BioScience* 19:779-784. September
1969. Copyright © 1969 by the American Institute
of Biological Sciences.

deaths from starvation, pestilence, and wars — will prevent any further increase in density. Since all finite space is limited, it is an indisputable fact that birth rates and death rates must someday be balanced. Already the rich are devouring the poor — the survival of the fittest.

Introduction

The intent of this article is not to alarm the reader unnecessarily. But how is that possible? Alarm is called for; man should be alarmed. Man must be aware of his dilemma, for if he attempts to feed the world without effective control of the birth rate, he actually is only deferring the starvation of an even greater number of people to a later date.

The world is facing this acute overpopulation situation specifically because of advances in agriculture and health, through science and technology, and a lack of similar progress in the field of sensible birth control. Families are not having more babies, it is just that more now survive.

Passion between the sexes must, of course, remain a basic human right, but it cannot include the having of children at will. While intercourse remains an individual and private matter, procreation must become of public concern. Conception should not be a euphemism for sexual relations. The obvious goal for all societies wishing an abundant life and freedom from want should be a low-birth-rate, low-death-rate culture. Man's responsibility to the next generation includes a primary duty of limiting the size of that generation.

Our problem is uncontrolled human fertility — not underproduction and maldistribution — and corrective action is being dangerously delayed by wishful thinking that some miracle will solve the problem. There is a prodigious need for immediate public awareness of the current critical situation, since overpopulation is intimately involved with political, economic, and sociological problems — in fact, with everyone's peace, security, and general well-being. All of the world's desperate needs — ample food, permanent peace, good health, and high-quality living — are unattainable for all human beings both now and in the foreseeable future for one obvious reason: there are too many people. A soaring population means a shrinking of man's space on this earth.

Not only is population growth the most basic conservation problem of today, but its dominating influence will affect the ultimate survival of mankind. Man can no longer be indifferent to this basic population problem. Its severity behooves all to act now. Hunger and overpopulation will not go away if we do not discuss them, and the bringing of too many babies into this world is not just someone else's problem; it is everyone's concern. The destiny of overpopulation is erosion of civilized life.

The World's Population

To appreciate the recent rapidity with which the world's population has grown — it took from the beginning of man until 1850 to reach a population of one billion people, only 80 years more (1930) to reach two billion, then only 30 years (1960) to reach the three billion mark, and in less than 15 years after 1960 we expect four billion. In the next 25 years after that, the population is expected to increase by another three and one-half billion people. If there have been about 77 billion births since the Stone Age, then about 1 out of every 22 persons born since then is alive today; but in only 30 or 40 years from now, if current rates of increase continue, 1 out of every 10 people ever born will be living at that time. The youth of today might see the United States with a population equal to what India has now.

Only a small proportion of the world's population has made the demographic transition of attaining both a lower fertility and a lower mortality; most have decreased only the premature death rate. The population has continued to increase rapidly because reductions in fertility have not been sufficient to offset the effects of current reductions in mortality produced by technological sanitation, disease control, and pesticide use.

The reproductive potential of the world is grim, for 40 to 45% of the people alive today are under 15 years old. How can this tremendous number of babies soon be fed solid foods? And look how soon those who survive will be breeding.

Even though technology exists that could manufacture enough intrauterine devices for every woman, the problems of distribution and the shortage of doctors make it impossible for the devices to be inserted fast enough to control the world's population growth. Within a few years the number of people dying each year from causes related to poor nutrition will equal what is now the entire population of the United States.

In the United States if the fertility and mortality trends of 1950-60 should be re-established, replacing the 1968 low birth rate, in only 150 years our country alone could exceed the current world population of over 3.3 billion, and in 650 years there would be about one person per square foot. This will not happen, of course, because either the birth rate will decline, or more likely, the death rate will increase.

Rate of Population Increase

The basic factor is the difference between birth and death rates, not what the levels of births and deaths happen to be. Continued doubling of a population soon leads to astronomical numbers. If the world population increase continued at the low rate of only 2%, the weight of human bodies would equal the weight of the earth in about 1500 years.

The world population is reported to be currently growing by 180,000 a day, more than a million a week, or about 65 million a year, and each year it increases in greater amounts. If current trends continue, the population will reach 25 billion in only 100 years.

Prior to Christ, it took about 40,000 years to double the population, but the current growth rate of about 2% would require only 35 years to double the present population. Populations that grow by 3% per year double within a generation and increase eighteen-fold in 100 years.

Population Dynamics

If 90% of a population survives long enough to reproduce, an average of 2.3 children per family will keep the population stable. Only a very slight increase to 2.5 children would produce an increase of 10% per generation, and 3.0 children per family would cause an increase of 31% per generation. If child-bearing families averaged 3.0 children, about one woman in four would need to be childless for the population to remain stable.

A sustained geometric increase in human beings is, of course, impossible; once the population's base level of density is high, as it now is, birth rates cannot continue much above the death rates for long without a truly impossible density being produced. As the base population density rises, even a lower birth rate can still mean that there will be a greater absolute increase in total numbers than was occurring before, when population was less and birth rates were higher.

Obviously, if input (natality) continues to exceed outgo (mortality), any finite space must eventually fill up and overflow. Populations increase geometrically, whereas food and subsistence increase arithmetically. The geometric ratio of population growth is also known as the ever-accelerating growth rate, the logistic curve, the well-known S-shaped or sigmoid growth curve, and compound interest.

When populations of people are exposed to stressing pressures, including those due to overpopulation, they may respond in a strange way of breeding earlier and more prolifically, further aggravating the situation. The principal way in which man differs from other animals is in his intellect, his ability to read and communicate, to learn, to use tools, and his society; and he also differs from other species in that he attempts to protect the unfit and all "surplus" births.

Predisposition to Overpopulate

Nature has seen to it that all organisms are obsessed with a breeding urge and provided with the biological capacity to overproduce, thereby ensuring survival of the species. Since man now exercises considerable control over so many of the natural factors which once controlled his population, he must also learn to control his innate trait to reproduce excessively.

It is not a question of whether this earth has the resources for feeding a much greater population than is now present — of course, it has. The point is that the human population is now growing too fast for food production ever to catch up without stringent birth control.

Carrying Capacity and Self-Limitation

No matter how far science and technology raise the carrying capacity of the earth for people, involuntary self-limiting forces will continue to determine man's upper population density. Surplus populations do not just quietly fade away — quite the contrary. Before surplus individuals die, they consume resources and contribute in general to other population stresses, all of which make the environment less suitable, thus lowering its carrying capacity. Man needs space to live as much as do plants and animals.

The balance of nature is governed primarily by the suitability of the habitat and species-specific self-limitation, where members of each species involuntarily prevent any further increase in their kind. This self-limitation consists of undesirable stresses which cause individual births in a family to be unwanted or cause a compensating increase in death rates. Members of the population become their own worst enemy in the sense that they are responsible for the increased rates of mortality and, perhaps, also some reduction in natality.

Nearly all organisms that are well-adapted to their environment have built-in mechanisms for checking population growth before the necessary food and cover are permanently destroyed. But nature's population control processes are unemotional, impartial, and truly ruthless, a set of conditions that educated men will surely wish to avoid.

Instead of man learning how to conquer nature, he may annihilate it, destroying himself in the process. In current times at least, there is no hope that man as a species will voluntarily limit his birth rate to the low level (zero or even minus replacement) that the overall population must have. Also, unfortunately, when a population level is below carrying capacity the innate desire to have larger families then becomes very strong, making human husbandry difficult to practice.

Nature does not practice good husbandry — all its components are predisposed to overpopulate and, in fact, attempt to do so, thus causing a high rate of premature deaths. If food supply alone were the principal factor limiting the number of people, man would long ago have increased to a density where all of the food would have been consumed and he would have become an extinct species.

When other organisms follow a population growth curve similar to what man is currently experiencing — and they do this only in disturbed (usually man-modified) environments — they can then become so destructive to their habitat that the subsequent carrying capacity may be dramatically reduced if not completely destroyed, thus causing not only mass individual suffering and a high rate of premature deaths but also a permanent destruction of the ecosystem.

Whenever man's population density has been markedly reduced through some catastrophe, or his technology has appreciably increased the carrying capacity of his habitat (environment), the growth rate of his population increases. The population then tends to overcompensate, temporarily growing beyond the upper limits of the carrying capacity of the environment. The excess growth is eventually checked, however, by the interaction of a number of different kinds of self-limiting population stress factors. These include such forces as inadequate food and shelter, social stress factors, competition for space, wars, an increase in pestilence, or any of many other subtle vicissitudes of life that either increase the death rate, reduce successful births, or cause individuals to move elsewhere. Unfortunately, in the developed countries, science and technology are developing at an exponential rate, so the population growth may not again be sufficiently halted by self-limitation until the earth's resources are largely exploited or a world famine or other drastic mortality factors appear.

Athough nature practices survival of the fittest, man believes that all who are born should be given every opportunity to live to an old age. If this is to be our objective, and I am sure it will, then we have only one other alternative, i.e., to restrict the number of births. And to accomplish this, it seems better to reduce conception rather than to rely on abortions. Abortions are a solution, however, when other means of preventing conceptions have broken down. Surprising to most people, abortions induced by a doctor are safer than childbearing.

There is a need too for man to establish a stable relationship with the environment. Man must recognize that he also responds to many, in fact, most of the laws of nature. And his population checks are largely famine, pestilence, and war. Man has transferred himself from being just a member of the ecosystem to a dominant position, where he now mistakenly assumes that the ecosystem is his to control at will. He forgets that he is part of nature. To see his true place in the world he must not attempt to transcend too much over nature, but to discover and assimilate all he can about the truth of nature and his own role in nature.

Only self-limitation can stem the population tide, and the only voice man has in the matter is whether it will be done involuntarily by nature's undesirable stresses, as witnessed by the history of civilization, or will be done consciously by not allowing his kind to exceed an optimum carrying capacity.

Socio-Economic Situations

It is incongruous that student unrest is so great and race problems so much in the front, yet almost everyone seems unaware that the basic cause of most of these socioeconomic stresses is overpopulation, about which almost nothing is said by all of these energetic and sometimes vociferous groups. The daily economic pressures of individuals attempting to provide a decent civilization, especially for themselves, may lead to the ultimate destruction of all ecosystems. Surplus individuals do not quietly fade away.

In spite of man's power of conscious thought, the only species so endowed, he seldom thinks beyond his lifetime or his own family's particular needs. The great desire of most people to provide their children and themselves with all of today's advantages is an important factor in reducing family size. That is not enough, however, for these families are still raising the population level.

At the same time that the world's population is increasing, both the number and the percentage of the "have-nots" increase and, in addition, the gap widens between the "haves" and "have-nots." As tragic as it may sound, when an underdeveloped country's population density is growing rapidly, both health and agricultural aid from the United States may not only be wasted but may severely aggravate the already deplorable social and economic situation in that country.

In industrially developed countries, middle-class couples often have fewer children than they would like (if they only had more money, domestic help, etc.), whereas in underdeveloped countries and ghettos the reverse is too frequently true. High birth rates tend to nullify national efforts to raise average per capita income since there is less money for savings and developmental investments. Neither families nor a nation can escape when life is held close to the margin of subsistence.

Overpopulation inevitably commits too many people to poverty and despair. With perpetual pregnancies the bonds of welfare become inescapable, for unskilled parents cannot feed a large family from the wages they can earn. No matter how you look at it, families of more than two or three children intensify the problem of national development, and this happens whether the parents are poor, middle class, or wealthy.

A complete reorientation of social values and attitudes regarding births is urgently needed now. We need new baby ethics, an awareness of the tragedies associated with too many babies. Bringing births and deaths into balance will demand great social, economic, and political changes.

With reference to our affluence, we cannot turn back — if for no other reason than the fact that there are now too many people to permit going back — to a less materialistic existence without cars, pesticides, diesel exhaust, sewage and garbage disposal, etc.

The stork has passed the plow. Food prices in developing nations are rising faster than the purchasing power.

Economic Interests

Man seems to be governed by economic self-interest. Societies become conditioned to the tenets of the economists — that money can buy anything. Without the basic resources there can be no wealth and affluence; but, unfortunately, the exploitation of resources seems to be considered the very foundations of all "progress."

"Progress" is the magic word. It means to increase property values and returns on one's investment: it is the deity of modern civilization. Yet, do any of us really know what we are progressing toward? Too often, the chamber-of-commerce form of "progress" is the next man's destruction.

Man seems to be more concerned with the quality of his goals than with the quantity of his goods. The more slowly a population increases the more rapid is the growth of both its gross and per capita income.

The harmful consequences of overpopulation are blindly overlooked by those who favor an expanding population for reasons of military strength, economic progress, scientific and agricultural development, and eugenics.

Man's economic dreams, his selfishness, and his materialism interfere with his awareness of the fate of the unborn. He is too busy in the United States in covering two acres per minute with houses, factories, and stores. His highways are now equivalent to paving the entire state of Indiana. Every day, California loses 300 acres of agricultural land.

Unfortunately, little planning has been done on how the socio-economic problems can be handled once the population growth is stopped. If the rush of today's living and industrial development or defense spending just slows down, a painful recession is upon us. We have no government study on how the nation could exist without a growing population.

Resource Management

Insidious economic pressures seem to prevent any effective management of resources in a manner that would provide for their utilization in perpetuity. Concrete and pavement surely are not the epitome of the human species' fulfillment. An ecological appreciation of resource management is needed, and ecological ethics must replace ecological atrocities.

Man is rapidly depleting the nonreplenishable resources. Half of the energy used by man during the past 2000 years was used in the last century. Man is reported to have mined more in the past 100 years than during all previous time. But, every barrel has a bottom; unbridled technology promises to speed us faster toward that bottom. Our planet's resources diminish faster as society's affluence is increased. Our qualitative sense of appreciation of our environment seems to be replaced by mere quantitative values. Why cannot civilization fulfill its obligation of being a competent steward of all resources?

It is inevitable that the limited legacy of natural resources must steadily yield in the face of the current explosion in the world population. As the population swells, open spaces are inundated by a flood of housing, and resources shrink faster. The United States and other developed nations are consuming a disproportionately large share of the world's nonrenewable and other resources at an ever-accelerating rate, perhaps 20 to 30 times as much on a per capita basis as are individuals in undeveloped countries. In 1954, the United States was reported to be using about 50% of the raw-material resources consumed in the world each year, and by 1980 it might be 80%. But we do not have an endless earth of boundless bounty. Any finite resource is subject to eventual exhaustion.

Effect of Science and Technology

The world may have sufficient resources, but it has never provided enough food and other necessities of life for all people at any one time. As technology improved, enabling better utilization of resources, the population similarly increased, so that there have always been many who died prematurely, as Malthus predicted.

No one anticipated the scope and rapidity of the technological changes that have occurred in Western society. About one-third of the people now consume about two-thirds of the world's food production, while the other two-thirds go undernourished. But, unfortunately, these starving people reproduce at a high rate. As individual aspirations rise and per capita resources fall, the widening gap between the haves and the have-nots could well generate some serious social and political pressures.

In recent times spectacular gains have been made in controlling mass killers such as typhus, malaria, yellow fever, small pox, cholera, plague, and influenza; but no corresponding checks have been made on birth rates. It is ironic that the root of our overpopulation problem is technical advances brought about by our increasing intellect (the knowledge explosion of the last hundred years).

Technology can produce almost anything, but only at the usually recognized high price of resource consumption and waste accumulation. As our technology advances, the amount of resources utilized per person also increases, and the supply is not endless.

Technology and science can and do progress at an ever-increasing rate, but can social, political, and religious views change rapidly enough to cope with this "progress"? The fruits of all our scientific and technological advances will be ephemeral if the world's population continues to explode. Our intelligence is so powerful that it may destroy us because we lack the wisdom and insight to recognize and correct what we are doing to ourselves and, especially, to future generations. We are passing on an enormous population problem to the next generation.

Pollution and Waste Disposal

Affluent societies have also been labeled "effluent" societies. That man is a highly adaptable species that can live in polluted environments, in extremely crowded conditions, in situations of acute malnutrition, and in some of the most depressing of environments is well exemplified today. But why should he? And how much lower can he sink and still survive as a "successful" species?

Mushrooming with the population are pollution and litter. We produce 70% of the world's solid wastes but have only 10% of the world's population. There is a need to make the reuse and disposal of rubbish more economical.

Popular Solutions and Misconceptions

Hopeful but inadequate panaceas include synthetic foods (proteins and vitamins), hydroponics, desalinization of seawater, food from the ocean, more agricultural research, fertilizers, irrigation, the vast unused lands, land reforms, government regulation, price support, migrations, redistribution of food and wealth, and private enterprise.

Science and technology may find a way to produce more food and to accommodate more people, but in the end this, of course, will only make matters that much worse if birth control is not effective. It should be obvious that the only solution is a drastically reduced birth rate or a greatly increased death rate. The one inescapable fact about

a country's population — about the world's population — is that the death rate must someday equal the birth rate, regardless of how plentiful food may be.

Unfortunately, a basic American philosophy is the belief that our free-enterprise system can produce anything that is necessary, a false cornucopian faith that our population growth is not a real threat. Our overpopulation-underdevelopment dilemma is not a matter of increasing production to meet the demand for more food; rather the only solution is to limit demand for food so that production may someday catch up to the population's needs.

Role of Family Planning

There is no question that family planning has made great progress. But today's society and religious groups must recognize the urgency for adopting the pill, IUD, other chemical and mechanical devices (both undependable), sterilization, abortion — in fact, any means of limiting childbirth. The promotion of some form of effective means of artificial birth control is the only moral, human, and political approach available to prevent the misery and suffering which will result if people are permitted to have as many "planned" children as they want.

Despite the great benefits of family planning programs, especially the benefits to the families concerned, family planning is not a euphemism for birth control. We need to develop a social and cultural philosophy that even a family of three children is too large and to overcome the fear of some ethic and religious sects that other groups may multiply faster, becoming more dominant. Family planning per se has little relevance to the underdeveloped countries of the world or to poverty groups in the more advanced countries. Therefore anything other than government control of conception may be self-defeating.

Sexual Desire and Love of Children

The basic conflict with the overpopulation problem is that of desires — actually drives — and the fact that most young women are fecund; without either the strong drives or the ability of women to conceive, there would be no problem. As with all organisms, man's potential fecundity and predisposition to overproduce are the basic causes for his excess fertility over deaths. Most babies are the consequence of passion, not love. But children are loved.

Motherhood must become a less significant role for women. We must forego some of our love for children and learn to be content with fewer numbers. What is needed in the way of governmental control of births is not control of an individual's behavior but control of the consequence of such behavior, the prevention of intemperate breeding.

There is no question that children make family ties more intimate, but man has already done too well toward "fathering" the country. Compassionate relations between spouses, not the having of children, must become the primary goal of marriages in the future. There is no need to find drugs that destroy sexual desire; the objective is to control the conception rate, not frequency of intercourse.

Is Having Children a Basic Right?

One price that society must be willing to pay for sustained world peace is a stringent universal birth-control program, which will require revolutionary revisions of modes of thought about our basic human rights with regard to family planning.

The increasing disparity between population density and food supply, by itself, justifies effective birth control regardless of the "morality" associated with depriving parents of the right to have as many planned children as they choose.

Having too many children can no longer be dismissed as an act of God, for it is now truly the consequence of a complacent society that is unwilling to take any of many steps available for preventing surplus births. Our primitive reproductive instincts cannot be condoned in the face of modern survival rates. The two are no longer in balance.

To say that the opportunity to decide the number and spacing of children is a basic human right is to say that man may do whatever he wants with nature without thought of its inevitable consequence to future generations. Our legal and ethical right should be to have only enough children to replace ourselves.

No longer can we consider procreation an individual and private matter. Intercourse, yes, but not unregulated numbers of conceptions since they affect the welfare of all other individuals living at that time plus those to be born in the future.

Religious Complications

It needs to be said over and over again that the bringing of surplus children into this world, whether from personal desire or from religious edicts, destines not only some of these children but many others to a premature death. Overproduction actually lowers the maximum density that can be sustained for normal life spans, thereby increasing the number of souls in need of salvation.

The "morality" of birth control in today's burgeoning human population has taken on an entirely new aspect. God clearly never meant for man to overpopulate this earth to the point where he would destroy many other forms of life and perhaps even himself. The religious doctrines we lean on today were established before science and technology had dramatically raised the carrying capacity for man.

The question of complete abstinence as the only acceptable means of family regulation is as ludicrous as compulsory euthanasia. The mortal sin, if there is one, in God's eyes surely would be associated with those who do *not* practice birth control, for to let babies come "as they naturally do" will prove to be a form of murder — through starvation, pestilence, and wars resulting from excess babies. It must be recognized that the number of children can no longer be left to "the will of God" or to our own desires and family plans, and if population controls are to be successful, they may have to be determined by government regulations.

Religious views that do not condone rigorous birth control must realize that every surplus birth their philosophy promotes will guarantee, on the average, a horrible death some day to more than one individual.

Although the Christian attitude implies that everything on this earth was created for man's use, in reality man is inescapably also part of nature.

Some form of compulsory control of birth rates is essential, although I see no reason why various religious groups cannot be permitted to achieve birth limitations in whatever manner they choose. If a woman or a couple exceeds the limit set by society, however, then they must be dealt with by law compelling them to be sterilized, to have an abortion, or by some other repayment to society.

Birth control is not murder, as some claim, but lack of it in today's overpopulated world most surely will be. For those who strongly oppose the setting of any limit on the number of children a family can have, I ask them to tell the rest of us just how they think the premature death rate should be increased to offset their extra births.

Wealth vs. Number of Children

Civilization can no longer endure a way of life in which people believe they have the right to have as many children as they can afford. This is hypocritical, for those who can "afford" luxurious living are already utilizing many times their share of the limited food and other resources, and also they are contributing much more pollution to the environment than are the have-nots. The affluent population needs to be made aware of the overpopulation problems, for they often desire to have more children per family than those who are in poverty.

Too much of today's religious climate makes birth control a politically sensitive area, thus constraining public officials. But, as citizens, are we not justified in asking why our government officials have not done more to make us aware of the urgency of population control — political sensitivities notwithstanding?

Governments should be guiding the development of a better life and world to live in, but if it does not recognize the need for human husbandry, then it will be fostering the ultimate destruction of the earth rather than the goals it seeks.

Man, in spite of his intellect, is so concerned with the present that he too often turns a deaf ear to alarming sounds of the future. Another difficulty in stabilizing the population is that our standard of living and our economy cannot survive in a static state.

Limiting Size of Families

We can no longer be prophets and philosophers; we must act. The biomagnification of births must be brought to an abrupt halt. Procreation must come under governmental control if no other way can be found. Perhaps what is needed is a system of permits for the privilege of conceiving, or compulsory vasectomies of all men and sterilization of all women who have been responsible for two births.

Since the taboo against birth control is inviolable to some, regardless of the dire consequences of overpopulation, laws must be passed to regulate conceptions and births. Each individual needs to have the right to produce or adopt only a replacement for himself or herself.

The general public must be made to realize that from now on, for a married couple to have more than two children or three at most, is a very socially irresponsible act. We must advocate small families. When business is good and living has quality, marriages will naturally tend to be earlier and births more numerous; therefore, only through the development of new nonfamilial rewards can later marriages be made to appear attractive to people. Taxes now subsidize children, whereas we should be taxed for the privilege of having children.

A rising age at marriage is an effective way of reducing births, and, sociologically and economically, it gives women more time to become better educated, acquire non-family sorts of interests, and develop greater cautions toward pregnancy.

Up to now, only death has been of public concern; procreation has remained an individual and highly cherished private matter. But this privilege cannot continue, and regulation of the number of conceptions, or at least births, must also become a government function.

Population Control or Premature Deaths

Man must decide whether the future growth of populations will be governed by famine, pestilence, and war, or whether he will use his intellect to control birth rates artificially. If the population growth is not controlled by lower birth rates, hundreds of millions of people must soon die prematurely each year.

Man must use his intellect to counteract his excessive fertility, for all species have been endowed by nature to be over-fecund. If he does not, the extra individuals will be eliminated by the natural process of "struggle for existence — survival of the fittest," which causes all surplus individuals

to die prematurely as a result of nature's ruthless laws of involuntary "self-limitation" whenever the carrying capacity has been exceeded. That territoriality and aggression are life-preserving functions of the social order of animals is frightening when man applies these same principles to his own species.

There have always been hungry people in the world, but both the total number of individuals and the percentage of the total population that are destined to go hungry in the future will be dramatically increased if birth rates are not drastically checked. Many like to think that nature will somehow take care of things. They fail to remember how nature has taken care of many species that were no longer adaptable to existence on this earth — they are now preserved as fossils.

Modern public-health methods and medical technology have lessened the chronic hunger, general economic misery, and other vicissitudes that once caused high mortality rates. But, sooner or later, any increase in births over deaths will be balanced by an increase in the rate of premature deaths.

Human Husbandry and Quality Living

Human husbandry implies that we regulate the population density before the natural self-limiting demographic and societal stress factors do it for us. But human motivation will always work against good human husbandry, because to each individual who has quality living, a large family will seem desirable.

The population of the world is so great that what used to be a ripple when it doubled now means catastrophic effects because of the great numbers involved and the lack of this earth's ability to support them. Man is not practicing good husbandry when he lets his population density expand beyond the carrying capacity.

The most important thesis regarding the need for human husbandry is that human beings will not voluntarily restrict their number of children to just two when economic, social, and political conditions appear to be personally favorable. A quality society with quality existence is now unattainable in many parts of the world, and may soon be unattainable any place in the world. The "economic" struggle of overpopulation is the world's greatest threat to quality living, enriched leisure, and even man's ultimate existence.

Conclusion

The ultimate goal must be a zero population growth. To achieve "quality living" instead of nature's "survival of the fittest," as has persisted throughout the history of mankind, the birth rate must not continue to exceed the death rate. If the birth rate of nations and the world are not greatly reduced, an ever-increasing amount of starvation and other types of premature deaths are inevitable. There is a prodigious need for mankind to practice human husbandry (Human Husbandry, a guest editorial in *BioScience,* 18:372-373, 1968, by Walter E. Howard).

A conscientious regulation of fertility is needed, or a calamitous rise in premature mortality rates is inevitable. Without this tremendous voluntary restraint or the development of a strong social stigma against bearing more than two or three children, the rate of conceptions must come under some form of governmental control. It can no longer be a basic human right to have as many children as one wants, especially if such action dooms others to a premature death.

Even though the above picture is bleak, the world is not going to come to an end. In fact, none of the people who read this article are going to starve, but their very existence is going to cause others who are less well off to perish. As overpopulation becomes worse, the percentage of the people who will fall into this nonsurviving unfit category must obviously increase. If babies of the future are to live, there must be fewer of them now.

EDITOR'S COMMENTS

Anyone reading Dr. Howard's article should be frightened by the pictures he presents. He leaves little doubt that the human population is in a logarithmic growth phase (see illustration below). It is clear that man will soon exceed the world's carrying capacity. A point eventually will be reached at which environmental resistance will begin to regulate human population size.

It is an ecological fact that the 3.7 billion people alive today cannot possibly have the kind of life presently pursued by the average American. Food, space, and natural resource availability dictate that fewer than one billion people could live the American way of life. In this respect, the world's carrying capacity has already been exceeded.

If we are frightened by the mass of people already alive (one of every 22 people to ever have lived is alive today), what about the prospects for the future? Most individuals believe that the freedom to make their own decision as to the number of children they will have, is a basic human right. Local, state, and national governments operate in such a way as to encourage human population growth and, indeed, lament the fact that slow growth may sometimes occur. Our entire economy is geared to continued population growth. Slowing of population growth

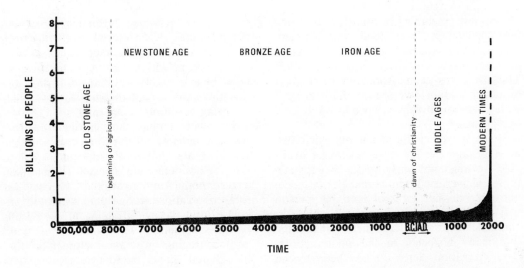

to zero today might cause a recession of catastrophic proportions. It is past time that governments and economists prepare for a static economy based on zero population growth — a climax human ecosystem. Human population growth is a problem that nearly everyone thinks will take care of itself or, at least, will be solved by someone else.

When I teach a course titled "Biology of Human Affairs," I approach the topic of human population cautiously. It has been my experience that a certain amount of self-induced realization as to the magnitude of the problem is worth many words delivered in the classroom. We begin the topic by moving outside and measuring an acre of ground. As it turns out, the acre is represented by a relatively small plot, a square area measuring just over 200 feet per side. A football field encompasses about 1⅓ acres.

The following day I ask the class to arrive at an average amount of land they think would be necessary to sustain the American way of life for one person. It is not unusual to encounter estimates such as 50 acres per person for recreation, 100 acres per person for food, 20 acres per person simply be-

cause everyone should own land, 25 acres per person for building materials and clothing — the class usually requires at least 100 acres per person.

Are the above estimates realistic? Hong Kong has a population of four million persons living on 398 square miles. From here it is simple arithmetic — Hong Kong has .06 acres per person, a space 51 feet square. Japan has .9 acres per person, West Germany 1, India 1½, Philippines 2, Yugoslavia and China 3, U.S. 11, Brazil and Russia 23. If the entire world's land surface were parcelled out (exclusive of Antarctica) each living person would receive 9.2 acres of real estate. Of course, much of this consists of deserts, lakes, mountains, and glaciers — poor places to build houses and raise crops.

It quickly becomes obvious that the world's logarithmic population growth will surely slow, and soon. Already each American has a piece of land only 688 feet square; it is only a matter of a short time until the earth will be unable to support its inhabitants. The American way of life can be supported by a per capita outlay of one and one-half acres for producing food, one acre for producing fibers, two acres for natural use (including recreation, waste disposal, greenbelts, etc.) and one-half acre for artificial systems such as highways, parking lots, factories, and housing sites. This five acres per person *must* be thought of as a minimum—we are rapidly nearing it with no national plans yet produced to slow our growth.

When we reach the point at which five acres of land per person is no longer available we must obviously begin to encroach on the above listed minimums. For instance, one and one-half acres of land per person will not be needed if we are all willing to eliminate meat from our diet — something that many residents of the poorer, overcrowded nations have already been forced to do.

An unbridled population will be controlled, either by its own efforts or by environmental resistance. Environmental resistance most probably will take the form of starvation, disease, or thermonuclear war. Control from within may have to be legislated birth control — humans will probably not make the logical decision to limit their offspring to simple replacement.

It is heartening that during the first seven months of 1972 the birth rate in the United States fell to a level just equal to the replacement rate needed to maintain a zero population growth. Of course, our total population will still continue to increase until the age grouping of Americans becomes stabilized. Even though the trend is encouraging, we must remember that the United States population represents a relatively small proportion of the world's people and that seven months is a relatively small segment of time.

Population Policy: Will Current Programs Succeed?

▶ Grounds for skepticism concerning the demographic effectiveness of family planning are considered.

Kingsley Davis is Ford Professor of Sociology and Comparative Studies, and Director of International Population and Urban Research at the University of California, Berkeley. He is past president of the Population Association of America and formerly the United States representative on the Population Commission of the United Nations. He is the author of *World Urbanization, 1950-1970,* and co-editor of a recent volume, *California's Twenty Million: Research Contributions to Population Policy.*

Throughout history the growth of population has been identified with prosperity and strength. If today an increasing number of nations are seeking to curb rapid population growth by reducing their birth rates, they must be driven to do so by an urgent crisis. My purpose here is not to discuss the crisis itself but rather to assess the present and prospective measures used to meet it. Most observers are surprised by the swiftness with which concern over the population problem has turned from intellectual analysis and debate to policy and action. Such action is a welcome relief from the long opposition, or timidity, which seemed to block forever any governmental attempt to restrain population growth, but relief that "at last something is being done" is no guarantee that what is being done is adequate. On the face of it,

one could hardly expect such a fundamental reorientation to be quickly and successfully implemented. I therefore propose to review the nature and (as I see them) limitations of the present policies and to suggest lines of possible improvement.

The Nature of Current Policies

With more than 30 nations now trying or planning to reduce population growth and with numerous private and international organizations helping, the degree of unanimity as to the kind of measures needed is impressive. The consensus can be summed up in the phrase "family planning." President Johnson declared in 1965 that the United States will "assist family planning programs in nations which request such help." The Prime Minister of India said a year later, "We must press forward with family planning. This is a programme of the highest importance." The Republic of Singapore created in 1966 the Singapore Family Planning and Population Board "to initiate and undertake population control programmes."[1]

Reprinted by permission of the author and publisher from *Science* 158:730-739. November 10, 1967. Copyright © 1967 by the American Association for the Advancement of Science.

As is well known, "family planning" is a euphemism for contraception. The family-planning approach to population limitation, therefore, concentrates on providing new and efficient contraceptives on a national basis through mass programs under public health auspices. The nature of these programs is shown by the following enthusiastic report from the Population Council:[2]

> No single year has seen so many forward steps in population control as 1965. Effective national programs have at last emerged, international organizations have decided to become engaged, a new contraceptive has proved its value in mass application, . . . and surveys have confirmed a popular desire for family limitation . . .
>
> An accounting of notable events must begin with Korea and Taiwan . . . Taiwan's program is not yet two years old, and already it has inserted one IUD [intrauterine device] for every 4-6 target women (those who are not pregnant, lactating, already sterile, already using contraceptives effectively, or desirous of more children). Korea has done almost as well . . . has put 2,200 full-time workers into the field, . . . has reached operational levels for a network of IUD quotas, supply lines, local manufacture of contraceptives, training of hundreds of M.D.'s and nurses, and mass propaganda . . .

Here one can see the implication that "population control" is being achieved through the dissemination of new contraceptives, and the fact that the "target women" exclude those who want more children. One can also note the technological emphasis and the medical orientation.

What is wrong with such programs? The answer is, "Nothing at all, if they work." Whether or not they work depends on what they are expected to do as well as on how they try to do it. Let us discuss the goal first, then the means.

Goals

Curiously, it is hard to find in the population-policy movement any explicit discussion of long-range goals. By implication the policies seem to promise a great deal. This is shown by the use of expressions like *population control* and *population planning* (as in the passages quoted above). It is also shown by the characteristic style of reasoning. Expositions of current policy usually start off by lamenting the speed and the consequences of runaway population growth. This growth, it is then stated, must be curbed — by pursuing a vigorous family-planning program. That family planning can solve the problem of population growth seems to be taken as self-evident.

For instance, the much-heralded statement by 12 heads of state, issued by Secretary-General U Thant on 10 December 1966 (a statement initiated by John D. Rockefeller III, Chairman of the Board of the Population Council), devotes half its space to discussing the harmfulness of population growth and the other half to recommending family planning.[3] A more succinct example of the typical reasoning is given in the Provisional Scheme for a Nationwide Family Planning Programme in Ceylon:[4]

> The population of Ceylon is fast increasing . . . . [The] figures reveal that a serious situation will be created within a few years. In order to cope with it a Family Planning programme on a nationwide scale should be launched by the Government.

The promised goal — to limit population growth so as to solve population problems — is a large order. One would expect it to be carefully analyzed, but it is left imprecise and taken for granted, as is the way in which family planning will achieve it.

When the terms *population control* and *population planning* are used, as they frequently are, as synonyms for current family-planning programs, they are misleading. Technically, they would mean deliberate influence over all attributes of a population, including its age-sex structure, geographical distribution, racial composition, genetic quality, and total size. No government attempts such full control. By tacit understanding, current population policies are concerned with only the *growth* and *size* of populations. These attributes, however, result from the death rate and migration as well as from the birth rate; their control would require deliberate influence over the factors giving rise to all three determinants. Actually, current policies labeled population control do not deal with mortality and migration, but deal only with the birth input. This is why another term, *fertility control,* is frequently used to describe current policies. But, as I show below, family planning (and hence current policy) does not undertake to influence most of the determinants of human reproduction. Thus the programs should not be referred to as population control or planning, because they do not attempt to influence the factors responsible for the attributes of human populations, taken generally; nor should they be called fertility control, because they do not try to affect most of the determinants of reproductive performance.

The ambiguity does not stop here, however. When one speaks of controlling population size, any inquiring person naturally asks, What is "control"? Who is to control whom? Precisely what population size, or what rate of population growth, is to be achieved? Do the policies aim to produce a growth rate that is nil, one that is very slight, or one that is like that of the industrial nations? Unless such questions are dealt with and clarified, it is impossible to evaluate current population policies.

The actual programs seem to be aiming simply to achieve a reduction in the birth rate. Success is therefore interpreted as the accomplishment of such a reduction, on the assumption that the reduction will lessen population growth. In those rare cases where a specific demographic aim is stated, the goal is said to be a short-run decline within a given period. The Pakistan plan adopted in 1966[5](p. 889) aims to reduce the birth rate from 50 to 40 per thousand by 1970; the Indian plan[6] aims to reduce the rate from

40 to 25 "as soon as possible"; and the Korean aim[7] is to cut population growth from 2.9 to 1.2 percent by 1980. A significant feature of such stated aims is the rapid population growth they would permit. Under conditions of modern mortality, a crude birth rate of 25 to 30 per thousand will represent such a multiplication of people as to make use of the term *population control* ironic. A rate of increase of 1.2 percent per year would allow South Korea's already dense population to double in less than 60 years.

One can of course defend the programs by saying that the present goals and measures are merely interim ones. A start must be made somewhere. But we do not find this answer in the population-policy literature. Such a defense, if convincing, would require a presentation of the *next* steps, and these are not considered. One suspects that the entire question of goals is instinctively left vague because thorough limitation of population growth would run counter to national and group aspirations. A consideration of hypothetical goals throws further light on the matter.

INDUSTRIALIZED NATIONS AS THE MODEL

Since current policies are confined to family planning, their maximum demographic effect would be to give the underdeveloped countries the same level of reproductive performance that the industrial nations now have. The latter, long oriented toward family planning, provide a good yardstick for determining what the availability of contraceptives can do to population growth. Indeed, they provide more than a yardstick; they are actually the model which inspired the present population policies.

What does this goal mean in practice? Among the advanced nations there is considerable diversity in the level of fertility.[8] At one extreme are countries such as New Zealand, with an average gross reproduction rate (GRR) of 1.91 during the period 1960-64; at the other extreme are countries such as Hungary, with a rate of 0.91 during the same period. To a considerable extent, however, such divergencies are matters of timing. The birth rates of most industrial nations have shown, since about 1940, wave-like movement, with no secular trend. The average level of reproduction during this long period has been high enough to give these countries, with their low mortality, an extremely rapid population growth. If this level is maintained, their population will double in just over 50 years — a rate higher than that of world population growth at any time prior to 1950, at which time the growth in numbers of human beings was already considered fantastic. The advanced nations are suffering acutely from the effects of rapid population growth in combination with the production of ever more goods per person.[9] A rising share of their supposedly high per capita income, which itself draws increasingly upon the resources of the underdeveloped countries (who fall farther behind in relative economic position), is spent simply to meet the costs, and alleviate the nuisances, of the unrelenting production of more and more goods by more people. Such facts indicate that the industrial nations provide neither a suitable demographic model for the nonindustrial peoples to follow nor the leadership to plan and organize effective population-control policies for them.

ZERO POPULATION GROWTH AS A GOAL

Most discussions of the population crisis lead logically to zero population growth as the ultimate goal, because *any* growth rate, if continued, will eventually use up the earth. Yet hardly ever do arguments for population policy consider such a goal, and current policies do not dream of it. Why not? The answer is evidently that zero population growth is unacceptable to most nations and to most religious and ethnic communities. To argue for this goal would be to alienate possible support for action programs.

GOAL PECULIARITIES INHERENT IN FAMILY PLANNING

Turning to the actual measures taken, we see that the very use of family planning as the means for implementing population policy poses serious but unacknowledged limits on the intended reduction in fertility. The family-planning movement, clearly devoted to the improvement and dissemination of contraceptive devices, states again and again that its purpose is that of enabling couples to have the number of children they want. "The opportunity to decide the number and spacing of children is a basic human right," say the 12 heads of state in the United Nations declaration. The 1965 Turkish Law Concerning Population Planning declares:[10]

> *Article 1.* Population Planning means that individuals can have as many children as they wish, whenever they want to. This can be ensured through preventive measures taken against pregnancy. . . .

Logically, it does not make sense to use *family* planning to provide *national* population control or planning. The "planning" in family planning is that of each separate couple. The only control they exercise is control over the size of *their* family. Obviously, couples do not plan the size of the nation's population, any more than they plan the growth of the national income or the form of the highway network. There is no reason to expect that the millions of decisions about family size made by couples in their own interest will automatically control population for the benefit of society. On the contrary, there are good reasons to think they will not do so. At most, family planning can reduce reproduction to the extent that unwanted births exceed wanted births. In industrial countries the balance is often negative — that is, people have fewer children as a rule than they would like to have. In underdeveloped countries the reverse is normally true, but the elimination of unwanted births would still leave an extremely high rate of multiplication.

Actually, the family-planning movement does not pursue even the limited goals it professes. It does not fully empower couples to have only the number of offspring they want because it either condemns or disregards certain tabooed but nevertheless effective means to this goal. One of its tenets is that "there shall be freedom of choice of method so that individuals can choose in accordance with the dictates of their consciences,"[11] but in practice this amounts to limiting the individual's choice, because the "conscience" dictating the method is usually not his but that of religious and governmental officials. Moreover, not every individual may choose: even the so-called recommended methods are ordinarily not offered to single women, or not all offered to women professing a given religious faith.

Thus, despite its emphasis on technology, current policy does not utilize all available means of contraception, much less all birth-control measures. The Indian government wasted valuable years in the early stages of its population-control program by experimenting exclusively with the "rhythm" method, long after this technique had been demonstrated to be one of the least effective. A greater limitation on means is the exclusive emphasis on contraception itself. Induced abortion, for example, is one of the surest means of controlling reproduction, and one that has been proved capable of reducing birth rates rapidly. It seems peculiarly suited to the threshold stage of a population-control program — the stage when new conditions of life first make large families disadvantageous. It was the principal factor in the halving of the Japanese birth rate, a major factor in the declines in birth rate of East-European satellite countries after legalization of abortion in the early 1950s, and an important factor in the reduction of fertility in industrializing nations from 1870 to the 1930s.[12] Today, according to *Studies in Family Planning,*[13] "abortion is probably the foremost method of birth control throughout Latin America." Yet this method is rejected in nearly all national and international population-control programs. American foreign aid is used to help *stop* abortion.[14] The United Nations excludes abortion from family planning, and in fact justifies the latter by presenting it as a means of combating abortion.[15] Studies of abortion are being made in Latin America under the presumed auspices of population-control groups, not with the intention of legalizing it and thus making it safe, cheap, available, and hence more effective for population control, but with the avowed purpose of reducing it.[16]

Although few would prefer abortion to efficient contraception (other things being equal), the fact is that both permit a woman to control the size of her family. The main drawbacks to abortion arise from its illegality. When performed, as a legal procedure, by a skilled physician, it is safer than childbirth. It does not compete with contraception but serves as a backstop when the latter fails or when contraceptive devices or information are not available. As contraception becomes customary, the incidence of abortion recedes even without its being banned. If, therefore, abortions enable women to have only the number of children they want, and if family planners do not advocate — in fact decry — legalization of abortion, they are to that extent denying the central tenet of their own movement. The irony of antiabortionism in family-planning circles is seen particularly in hair-splitting arguments over whether or not some contraceptive agent (for example, the IUD) is in reality an abortifacient. A Mexican leader in family planning writes:[17]

> One of the chief objectives of our program in Mexico is to prevent abortions. If we could be sure that the mode of action [of the IUD] was not interference with nidation, we could easily use the method in Mexico.

The questions of sterilization and unnatural forms of sexual intercourse usually meet with similar silent treatment or disapproval, although nobody doubts the effectiveness of these measures in avoiding conception. Sterilization has proved popular in Puerto Rico and has had some vogue in India (where the new health minister hopes to make it compulsory for those with a certain number of children), but in both these areas it has been for the most part ignored or condemned by the family-planning movement.

On the side of goals, then, we see that a family-planning orientation limits the aims of current population policy. Despite reference to "population control" and "fertility control," which presumably mean determination of demographic results by and for the nation as a whole, the movement gives control only to couples, and does this only if they use "respectable" contraceptives.

The Neglect of Motivation

By sanctifying the doctrine that each woman should have the number of children she wants, and by assuming that if she has only that number this will automatically curb population growth to the necessary degree, the leaders of current policies escape the necessity of asking why women desire so many children and how this desire can be influenced.[18(p. 41)19] Instead, they claim that satisfactory motivation is shown by the popular desire (shown by opinion surveys in all countries) to have the means of family limitation, and that therefore the problem is one of inventing and distributing the best possible contraceptive devices. Overlooked is the fact that a desire for availability of contraceptives is compatible with *high* fertility.

Given the best of means, there remain the questions of how many children couples want and of whether this is the requisite number from the standpoint of population size. That it is not is indicated by continued rapid population growth in industrial countries, and by the very surveys showing that people want contraception — for these show, too, that people also want numerous children.

The family planners do not ignore motivation. They are forever talking about attitudes" and "needs." But they pose the issue in terms of the "acceptance" of birth control devices. At the most naive level, they assume that lack of acceptance is a function of the contraceptive device itself. This reduces the motive problem to a technological question. The task of population control then becomes simply the invention of a device that *will* be acceptable.[20] The plastic IUD is acclaimed because, once in place, it does not depend on repeated *acceptance* by the woman, and thus it "solves" the problem of motivation.[21]

But suppose a woman does not want to use *any* contraceptive until after she has had four children. This is the type of question that is seldom raised in the family-planning literature. In that literature, wanting a specific number of children is taken as complete motivation, for it implies a wish to control the size of one's family. The problem woman, from the standpoint of family planners, is the one who wants "as many as come," or "as many as God sends." Her attitude is construed as due to ignorance and "cultural values," and the policy deemed necessary to change it is "education." No compulsion can be used, because the movement is committed to free choice, but movie strips, posters, comic books, public lectures, interviews, and discussions are in order. These supply information and supposedly change values by discounting superstitions and showing that unrestrained procreation is harmful to both mother and children. The effort is considered successful when the woman decides she wants only a certain number of children and uses an effective contraceptive.

In viewing negative attitudes toward birth control as due to ignorance, apathy, and outworn tradition, and "mass-communication" as the solution to the motivation problem,[22] family planners tend to ignore the power and complexity of social life. If it were admitted that the creation and care of new human beings is socially motivated, like other forms of behavior, by being a part of the system of rewards and punishments that is built into human relationships, and thus is bound up with the individual's economic and personal interests, it would be apparent that the social structure and economy must be changed before a deliberate reduction in the birth rate can be achieved. As it is, reliance on family planning allows people to feel that "something is being done about the population problem" without the need for painful social changes.

Designation of population control as a medical or public health task leads to a similar evasion. This categorization assures popular support because it puts population policy in the hands of respected medical personnel, but, by the same token, it gives responsibility for leadership to people who think in terms of clinics and patients, of pills and IUD's, and who bring to the handling of economic and social phenomena a self-confident naiveté. The study of social organization is a technical field; an action program based on intuition is no more apt to succeed in the control of human beings than it is in the area of bacterial or viral control. Moreover, to alter a social system, by deliberate policy, so as to regulate births in accord with the demands of the collective welfare would require political power, and this is not likely to inhere in public health officials, nurses, midwives, and social workers. To entrust population policy to them is "to take action," but not dangerous "effective action."

Similarly, the Janus-faced position on birth-control technology represents an escape from the necessity, and onus, of grappling with the social and economic determinants of reproductive behavior. On the one side, the rejection or avoidance of religiously tabooed but otherwise effective means of birth prevention enables the family-planning movement to avoid official condemnation. On the other side, an intense preoccupation with contraceptive technology (apart from the tabooed means) also helps the family planners to avoid censure. By implying that the only need is the invention and distribution of effective contraceptive devices, they allay fears, on the part of religious and governmental officials, that fundamental changes in social organization are contemplated. Changes basic enough to affect motivation for having children would be changes in the structure of the family, in the position of women, and in the sexual mores. Far from proposing such radicalism, spokesmen for family planning frequently state their purpose as "protection" of the family — that is, closer observance of family norms. In addition, by concentrating on *new* and *scientific* contraceptives, the movement escapes taboos attached to old ones (the Pope will hardly authorize the condom, but may sanction the pill) and allows family planning to be regarded as a branch of medicine: over-population becomes a disease, to be treated by a pill or a coil.

We thus see that the inadequacy of current population policies with respect to motivation is inherent in their overwhelmingly family-planning character. Since family planning is by definition private planning, it eschews any societal control over motivation. It merely furnishes the means, and, among possible means, only the most respectable. Its leaders, in avoiding social complexities and seeking official favor, are obviously activated not solely by expediency but also by their own sentiments as members of society and by their background as persons attracted to the family-planning movement. Unacquainted for the most part with technical economics, sociology, and demography, they tend honestly and instinctively to believe that something they vaguely call population control can be achieved by making better contraceptives available.

The Evidence of Ineffectiveness

If this characterization is accurate, we can conclude that current programs will not enable a government to control population size. In countries where couples have numerous offspring that they do not want, such programs may possibly accelerate a birth-rate decline that would occur anyway, but the conditions that cause births to be wanted or unwanted are beyond the control of family planning, hence beyond the control of any nation which relies on family planning alone as its population policy.

This conclusion is confirmed by demographic facts. As I have noted above, the widespread use of family planning in industrial countries has not given their governments control over the birth rate. In backward countries today, taken as a whole, birth rates are rising, not falling; in those with population policies, there is no indication that the government is controlling the rate of reproduction. The main "successes" cited in the well-publicized policy literature are cases where a large number of contraceptives have been distributed or where the program has been accompanied by some decline in the birth rate. Popular enthusiasm for family planning is found mainly in the cities, or in advanced countries such as Japan and Taiwan, where the people would adopt contraception in any case, program or no program. It is difficult to prove that present population policies have ever speeded up a lowering of the birth rate (the least that could have been expected), much less that they have provided national "fertility control."

Let us next briefly review the facts concerning the level and trend of population in underdeveloped nations generally, in order to understand the magnitude of the task of genuine control.

Rising Birth Rates in Underdeveloped Countries

In ten Latin-American countries, between 1940 and 1959,[23] the average birth rates (age-standardized), as estimated by our research office at the University of California, rose as follows: 1940-44, 43.4 annual births per 1000 population; 1945-49, 44.6; 1950-54, 46.4; 1955-59, 47.7.

In another study made in our office, in which estimating methods derived from the theory of quasi-stable populations were used, the recent trend was found to be upward in 27 underdeveloped countries, downward in six, and unchanged in one.[24] Some of the rises have been substantial, and most have occurred where the birth rate was already extremely high. For instance, the gross reproduction rate rose in Jamaica from 1.8 per thousand in 1947 to 2.7 in 1960; among the natives of Fiji, from 2.0 in 1951 to 2.4 in 1964; and in Albania, from 3.0 in the period 1950-54 to 3.4 in 1960.

The general rise in fertility in backward regions is evidently not due to failure of population-control efforts, because most of the countries either have no such effort or have programs too new to show much effect. Instead, the rise is due, ironically, to the very circumstances that brought on the population crisis in the first place — to improved health and lowered mortality. Better health increases the probability that a woman will conceive and retain the fetus to term; lowered mortality raises the proportion of babies who survive to the age of reproduction and reduces the probability of widowhood during that age.[25] The significance of the general rise in fertility, in the context of this discussion, is that it is giving would-be population planners a harder task than many of them realize. Some of the upward pressure on birth rates is independent of what couples do about family planning, for it arises from the fact that, with lowered mortality, there are simply more couples.

Underdeveloped Countries with Population Policies

In discussions of population policy there is often confusion as to which cases are relevant. Japan, for instance, has been widely praised for the effectiveness of its measures, but it is a very advanced industrial nation and, besides, its government policy had little or nothing to do with the decline in the birth rate, except unintentionally. It therefore offers no test of population policy under peasant-agrarian conditions. Another case of questionable relevance is that of Taiwan, because Taiwan is sufficiently developed to be placed in the urban-industrial class of nations. However, since Taiwan is offered as the main showpiece by the sponsors of current policies in underdeveloped areas, and since the data are excellent, it merits examination.

Taiwan is acclaimed as a showpiece because it has responded favorably to a highly organized program for distributing up-to-date contraceptives and has also had a rapidly dropping birth rate. Some observers have carelessly attributed the decline in the birth rate — from 50.0 in 1951 to 32.7 in 1965 — to the family-planning campaign,[26] but the campaign began only in 1963 and could have affected only the end of the trend. Rather, the decline represents a response to modernization similar to that made by all countries that have become industrialized.[27] By 1950 over half of Taiwan's population was urban, and by 1964 nearly two-thirds were urban, with 29 percent of the population living in cities of 100,000 or more. The pace of economic development has been extremely rapid. Between 1951 and 1963, per capita income increased by 4.05 percent per year. Yet the island is closely packed, having 870 persons per square mile (a population density higher than that of Belgium). The combination of fast economic growth and rapid population increase in limited space has put parents of large families at a relative disadvantage and has created a brisk demand for abortions and contraceptives. Thus the favorable response to the current campaign to encourage use of the IUD is not a good example of what birth-control technology can do for a genuinely backward country. In fact, when the program was started, one reason for expecting receptivity was that the island was already on its way to modernization and family planning.[28]

At most, the recent family planning campaign — which reached significant proportions only in 1964, when some 46,000 IUD's were inserted (in 1965 the number was 99,253, and in 1966, 111,242)[29,30(p. 45)] — could have caused the increase observable after 1963 in the rate of decline. Between 1951 and 1963 the average drop in the birth rate per 1000 women (see table 1) was 1.73 percent per year; in the period 1964-66 it was 4.35 percent. But one hesitates to assign all of the acceleration in decline since

TABLE 1. *Decline in Taiwan's fertility rate, 1951 through 1966.*

Year	Registered births per 1000 women aged 15—49	Change in rate (perecnt)*
1951	211	
1952	198	—5.6
1953	194	—2.2
1954	193	—0.5
1955	197	+2.1
1956	196	—0.4
1957	182	—7.1
1958	185	+1.3
1959	184	—0.1
1960	180	—2.5
1961	177	—1.5
1962	174	—1.5
1963	170	—2.6
1964	162	—4.9
1965	152	—6.0
1966	149	—2.1

*The percentages were calculated on unrounded figures. Source of data through 1965, *Taiwan Demographic Fact Book* (1964, 1965); for 1966, *Monthly Bulletin of Population Registration Statistics of Taiwan* (1966, 1967).

1963 to the family-planning campaign. The rapid economic development has been precisely of a type likely to accelerate a drop in reproduction. The rise in manufacturing has been much greater than the rise in either agriculture or construction. The agricultural labor force has thus been squeezed, and migration to the cities has skyrocketed.[31] Since housing has not kept pace, urban families have had to restrict reproduction in order to take advantage of career opportunities and avoid domestic inconvenience. Such conditions have historically tended to accelerate a decline in birth rate. The most rapid decline came late in the United States (1921-33) and in Japan (1947-55). A plot of the Japanese and Taiwanese birth rates (fig. 1) shows marked similarity of the two curves, despite a difference in level. All told, one should not attribute all of the post-1963 acceleration in the decline of Taiwan's birth rate to the family-planning campaign.

The main evidence that *some* of this acceleration is due to the campaign comes from the fact that Taichung, the city in which the family-planning effort was first concentrated, showed subsequently a much faster drop in fertility than other cities.[30(p. 69)32] But the campaign has not reached throughout the island. By the end of 1966, only 260,745 women had been fitted with an IUD under auspices of the campaign, whereas the women of reproductive age on the island numbered 2.86 million. Most of the reduction in fertility has therefore been a matter of individual initiative. To some extent the campaign may be simply substituting sponsored (and cheaper) services for those that would otherwise come through private and commercial channels. An island-wide survey in 1964 showed that over 150,000 women were already using the traditional Ota ring (a metallic intrauterine device popular in Japan); almost as many had been sterilized; about 40,000 were using foam tablets; some 50,000 ad-

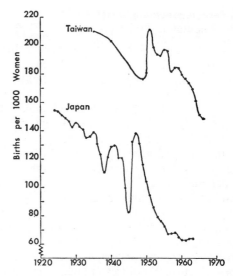

Figure 1.   Births per 1000 women aged 15 through 49 in Japan and Taiwan.

mitted to having had at least one abortion; and many were using other methods of birth control.[30(pp. 18, 31)]

The important question, however, is not whether the present campaign is somewhat hastening the downward trend in the birth rate but whether, even if it is, it will provide population control for the nation. Actually, the campaign is not designed to provide such control and shows no sign of doing so. It takes for granted existing reproductive goals. Its aim is "to integrate, through education and information, the idea of family limitation *within the existing attitudes, values, and goals* of the people"[30(p. 8)] (italics mine). Its target is *married* women who do not want any more children; it ignores girls not yet married, and women married and wanting more children.

With such an approach, what is the maximum impact possible? It is the difference between the number of children women have been having and the number they want to have. A study in 1957 found a median figure of 3.75 for the number of children wanted by women aged 15 to 29 in Taipei, Taiwan's largest city; the corresponding figure for women from a satellite town was 3.93; for women from a fishing village, 4.90; and for women from a farming village, 5.03. Over 60 percent of the women in Taipei and over 90 percent of those in the farming village wanted 4 or more children.[33] In a sample of wives aged 25 to 29 in Taichung, a city of over 300,000, Freedman and his co-workers found the average number of children wanted was 4; only 9 percent wanted less than 3, 20 percent wanted 5 or more.[34] If, therefore, Taiwanese women used contraceptives that were 100-percent effective and had the number of children they desire, they would have about 4.5 each. The goal of the family-planning effort would be achieved. In the past the Taiwanese woman who married and lived through the reproductive period had, on the average, approximately 6.5 children; thus a figure of 4.5 would represent a substantial decline in fertility. Since mortality would continue to decline, the population growth rate would decline somewhat less than individual reproduction would. With 4.5 births per woman and a life expectancy of 70 years, the rate of natural increase would be close to 3 percent per year.[35]

In the future, Taiwanese views concerning reproduction will doubtless change, in response to social change and economic modernization. But how far will they change? A good indication is the number of children desired by couples in an already modernized country long oriented toward family planning. In the United States in 1966, an average of 3.4 children was considered ideal by white women aged 21 or over.[36] This average number of births would give Taiwan, with only a slight decrease in mortality, a long-run rate of natural increase of 1.7 percent per year and a doubling of population in 41 years.

Detailed data confirm the interpretation that Taiwanese women are in the process of shifting from a "peasant-agrarian" to an "industrial" level of reproduction. They are, in typical fashion, cutting off higher-order births at age 30 and beyond.[37] Among young wives, fertility has risen, not fallen. In sum, the widely acclaimed family-planning program in Taiwan may, at most, have somewhat speeded the later phase of fertility decline which would have occurred anyway because of modernization.

Moving down the scale of modernization, to countries most in need of population control, one finds the family-planning approach even more inadequate. In South Korea, second only to Taiwan in the frequency with which it is cited as a model of current policy, a recent birth-rate decline of unknown extent is assumed by leaders to be due overwhelmingly to the government's family-planning program. However, it is just as plausible to say that the net effect of government involvement in population control has been, so far, to delay rather than hasten a decline in reproduction made inevitable by social and economic changes. Although the government is advocating vasectomies and providing IUD's and pills, it refuses to legalize abortions, despite the rapid rise in the rate of illegal abortions and despite the fact that, in a recent survey, 72 percent of the people who stated an opinion favored legalization. Also, the program is presented in the context of maternal and child health; it thus emphasizes motherhood and the family rather than alternative roles for women. Much is made of the fact that opinion surveys show an overwhelming majority of Koreans (89 percent in 1965) favoring contraception,[38(p. 27)] but this means only that Koreans are like other people in wishing to have the means to get what they want. Unfortunately, they want sizable families: "The records indicate that the program appeals mainly to women in the 30-39 year age bracket who have four or more children, including at least two sons. . . ."[38(p. 25)]

In areas less developed than Korea the degree of acceptance of contraception tends to be disappointing, especially among the rural majority. Faced with this discouragement, the leaders of current policy, instead of reexamining their assumptions, tend to redouble their effort to find a contraceptive that will appeal to the most illiterate peasant, forgetting that he wants a good-sized family. In the rural Punjab, for example, "a disturbing feature . . . is that the females start to seek advice and adopt family planning techniques at the fag end of their reproductive period."[39] Among 5196 women coming to rural Punjabi family-planning centers, 38 percent were over 35 years old, 67 percent over 30. These women had married early, nearly a third of them before the age of 15;[40] some 14 percent had eight or more *living* children when they reached the clinic, 51 percent six or more.

A survey in Tunisia showed that 68 percent of the married couples were willing to use birth-control measures, but the average number of children they considered ideal was 4.3.[41] The corresponding averages for a village in eastern Java, a village near New Delhi, and a village in Mysore were 4.3, 4.0, and 4.2, respectively.[42,43] In the cities of these regions women are more ready to accept birth control and they want fewer children than village women do, but the number they consider desirable is still wholly unsatisfactory from the standpoint of population control. In an urban family-planning center in Tunisia, more than 600 of 900 women accepting contraceptives had four living children already.[44] In Bangalore, a city of nearly a million at the time (1952), the number of offspring desired by married women was 3.7 on the average; by married men, 4.1.[43] In the metropolitan area of San Salvador (350,000 inhabitants) a 1964 survey[45] showed the number desired by women of

reproductive age to be 3.9, and in seven other capital cities of Latin America the number ranged from 2.7 to 4.2. If women in the cities of underdeveloped countries used birth-control measures with 100-percent efficiency, they still would have enough babies to expand city populations senselessly, quite apart from the added contribution of rural-urban migration. In many of the cities the difference between actual and ideal number of children is not great; for instance, in the seven Latin-American capitals mentioned above, the ideal was 3.4 whereas the actual births per women in the age range 35 to 39 was 3.7.[46] Bombay City has had birth-control clinics for many years, yet its birth rate (standardized for age, sex, and marital distribution) is still 34 per 1000 inhabitants and is tending to rise rather than fall. Although this rate is about 13 percent lower than that for India generally, it has been about that much lower since at least 1951.[47]

Is Family Planning the "First Step" in Population Control?

To acknowledge that family planning does not achieve population control is not to impugn its value for other purposes. Freeing women from the need to have more children than they want is of great benefit to them and their children and to society at large. My argument is therefore directed not against family-planning programs as such but against the assumption that they are an effective means of controlling population growth.

But what difference does it make? Why not go along for a while with family planning as an initial approach to the problem of population control? The answer is that any policy on which millions of dollars are being spent should be designed to achieve the goal it purports to achieve. If it is only a first step, it should be so labeled, and its connection with the next step (and the nature of that next step) should be carefully examined. In the present case, since no "next step" seems ever to be mentioned, the question arises, is reliance on family planning in fact a basis for dangerous postponement of effective steps? To continue to offer a remedy as a cure long after it has been shown merely to ameliorate the disease is either quackery or wishful thinking, and it thrives most where the need is greatest. Today the desire to solve the population problem is so intense that we are all ready to embrace any "action program" that promises relief. But postponement of effective measures allows the situation to worsen.

Unfortunately, the issue is confused by a matter of semantics. "Family *planning*" and "fertility *control*" suggest that reproduction is being regulated according to some rational plan. And so it is, but only from the standpoint of the individual couple, not from that of the community. What is rational in the light of a couple's situation may be totally irrational from the standpoint of society's welfare.

The need for societal regulation of individual behavior is readily recognized in other spheres — those of explosives, dangerous drugs, public property, natural resources. But in the sphere of reproduction, complete individual initiative is generally favored even by those liberal intellectuals who, in other spheres, most favor economic and social planning. Social reformers who would not hesitate to force all owners of rental property to rent to anyone who can pay, or to force all workers in an industry to join a union, balk at any suggestion that couples be permitted to have only a certain number of offspring. Invariably they interpret societal control of reproduction as meaning direct police supervision of individual behavior. Put the word *compulsory* in front of any term describing a means of limiting births — *compulsory sterilization, compulsory abortion, compulsory contraception* — and you guarantee violent opposition. Fortunately, such direct controls need not be invoked, but conservatives and radicals alike overlook this in their blind opposition to the idea of collective determination of a society's birth rate.

That the exclusive emphasis on family planning in current population policies is not a "first step" but an escape from the real issues is suggested by two facts. (i) No country has taken the "next step." The industrialized countries have had family planning for half a century without acquiring control over either the birth rate or population increase. (ii) Support and encouragement of research on population policy other than family planning is negligible. It is precisely this blocking of alternative thinking and experimentation that makes the emphasis on family planning a major obstacle to population control. The need is not to abandon family-planning programs but to put equal or greater resources into other approaches.

New Directions in Population Policy

In thinking about other approaches, one can start with known facts. In the past, all surviving societies had institutional incentives for marriage, procreation, and child care which were powerful enough to keep the birth rate equal to or in excess of a high death rate. Despite the drop in death rates during the last century and a half, the incentives tended to remain intact because the social structure (especially in regard to the family) changed little. At most, particularly in industrial societies, children became less productive and more expensive.[48] In present-day agrarian societies, where the drop in death rate has been more recent, precipitate, and independent of social change,[49] motivation for having children has changed little. Here, even more than in industrialized nations, the family has kept on producing abundant offspring, even though only a fraction of these children are now needed.

If excessive population growth is to be prevented, the obvious requirement is somehow to impose restraints on the family. However, because family roles are reinforced by society's system of rewards, punishments, sentiments, and norms, any proposal to demote the family is viewed as a threat by conservatives and liberals alike, and certainly by people with enough social responsibility to work for population control. One is charged with trying to "abolish" the family, but what is required is selective restructuring of the family in relation to the rest of society.

The lines of such restructuring are suggested by two existing limitations on fertility. (i) Nearly all societies succeed in drastically discouraging reproduction among unmarried women. (ii) Advanced societies unintentionally reduce reproduction among married women when conditions worsen in such a way as to penalize childbearing more severely than it was penalized before. In both cases the causes are motivational and economic rather than technological.

It follows that population-control policy can de-emphasize the family in two ways: (i) by keeping present controls over illegitimate childbirth yet making the most of factors that lead people to postpone or avoid marriage, and (ii) by instituting conditions that motivate those who do marry to keep their families small.

Postponement of Marriage

Since the female reproductive span is short and generally more fecund in its first than in its second half, postponement of marriage to ages beyond 20 tends biologically to reduce births. Sociologically, it gives women time to get a better education, acquire interests unrelated to the family, and develop a cautious attitude toward pregnancy.[50] Individuals who have not married by the time they are in their late twenties often do not marry at all. For these reasons, for the world as a whole, the average age at marriage for women is negatively associated with the birth rate: a rising age at marriage is a frequent cause of declining fertility during the middle phase of the demographic transition; and, in the late phase, the "baby boom" is usually associated with a return to younger marriages.

Any suggestion that age at marriage be raised as a part of population policy is usually met with the argument that "even if a law were passed, it would not be obeyed." Interestingly, this objection implies that the only way to control the age at marriage is by direct legislation, but other factors govern the actual age. Roman Catholic countries generally follow canon law in stipulating 12 years as the minimum *legal* age at which girls may marry, but the actual average age at marriage in these countries (at least in Europe) is characteristically more like 25 to 28 years. The actual age is determined, not by law, but by social and economic conditions. In agrarian societies, postponement of marriage (when postponement occurs) is apparently caused by difficulties in meeting the economic prerequisites for matrimony, as stipulated by custom and opinion. In industrial societies it is caused by housing shortages, unemployment, the requirement for overseas military service, high costs of education, and inadequacy of consumer services. Since almost no research has been devoted to the subject, it is difficult to assess the relative weight of the factors that govern the age at marriage.

Encouraging Limitation of Births within Marriage

As a means of encouraging the limitation of reproduction within marriage, as well as postponement of marriage, a greater rewarding of nonfamilial than of familial roles would probably help. A simple way of accomplishing this would be to allow economic advantages to accrue to the single as opposed to the married individual, and to the small as opposed to the large family. For instance, the government could pay people to permit themselves to be sterilized;[51] all costs of abortion could be paid by the government; a substantial fee could be charged for a marriage license; a "child-tax"[52] could be levied; and there could be a requirement that illegitimate pregnancies be aborted. Less sensationally, governments could simply reverse some existing policies that encourage childbearing. They could, for example, cease taxing single persons more than married ones; stop giving parents special tax exemptions; abandon income-tax policy that discriminates against couples when the wife works; reduce paid maternity leaves; reduce family allowances;[53] stop awarding public housing on the basis of family size; stop granting fellowships and other educational aids (including special allowances for wives and children) to married students; cease outlawing abortions and sterilizations; and relax rules that allow use of harmless contraceptives only with medical permission. Some of these policy reversals would be beneficial in other than demographic respects and some would be harmful unless special precautions were taken. The aim would be to reduce the number, not the quality, of the next generation.

A closely related method of deemphasizing the family would be modification of the complementarity of the roles of men and women. Men are now able to participate in the wider world yet enjoy the satisfaction of having several children because the housework and childcare fall mainly on their wives. Women are impelled to seek this role by their idealized view of marriage and motherhood and by either the scarcity of alternative roles or the difficulty of combining them with family roles. To change this situation women could be required to work outside the home, or compelled by circumstances to do so. If, at the same time, women were paid as well as men and given equal educational and occupational opportunities, and if social life were organized around the place of work rather than around the home or neighborhood, many women would develop interests that would compete with family interests. Approximately this policy is now followed in several Communist countries, and even the less developed of these currently have extremely low birth rates.[54]

That inclusion of women in the labor force has a negative effect on reproduction is indicated by regional comparisons.[18(p. 1195)][55] But in most countries the wife's employment is subordinate, economically and emotionally, to her family role, and is readily sacrificed for the latter. No society has restructured both the occupational system and the domestic establishment to the point of permanently modifying the old division of labor by sex.

In any deliberate effort to control the birth rate along these lines, a government has two powerful instruments — its command over economic planning and its authority (real or potential) over education. The first determines (as far as policy can) the economic conditions and circumstances affecting the lives of all citizens; the second provides the knowledge and attitudes necessary to implement the plans. The economic system largely determines who shall work, what can be bought, what rearing children will cost, how much individuals can spend. The schools define family roles and develop vocational and recreational interests; they could, if it were desired, redefine the sex roles, develop interests that transcend the home, and transmit realistic (as opposed to moralistic) knowledge concerning marriage, sexual behavior, and population problems. When the problem is viewed in this light, it is clear that the ministries of economics and education, not the ministry of health, should be the source of population policy.

The Dilemma of Population Policy

It should now be apparent why, despite strong anxiety over runaway population growth, the actual programs purporting to control it are limited to family planning and are therefore ineffective. (i) The goal of zero, or even slight, population growth is one that nations and groups find difficult to accept. (ii) The measures that would be required to implement such a goal, though not so revolutionary as a Brave New World or a Communist Utopia, nevertheless tend to offend most people reared in existing societies. As a consequence, the goal of so-called population control is implicit and vague; the method is only family planning. This method, far from de-emphasizing the family, is familistic. One of its stated goals is that of helping sterile couples to *have* children. It stresses parental aspirations and responsibilities. It goes along with most aspects of conventional morality, such as condemnation of abortion, disapproval of premarital intercourse, respect for religious teachings and cultural taboos, and obeisance to medical and clerical authority. It deflects hostility by refusing to recommend any change other than the one it stands for: availability of contraceptives.

The things that make family planning acceptable are the very things that make it ineffective for population control. By stressing the right of parents to have the number of children they want, it evades the basic question of population policy, which is how to give societies the number of children they need. By offering only the means for *couples* to control fertility, it neglects the means for societies to do so.

Because of the predominantly pro-family character of existing societies, individual interest ordinarily leads to the production of enough offspring to constitute rapid population growth under conditions of low mortality. Childless or single-child homes are considered indicative of personal failure, whereas having three to five living children gives a family a sense of continuity and substantiality.[56]

Given the existing desire to have moderate-sized rather than small families, the only countries in which fertility has been reduced to match reduction in mortality are advanced ones temporarily experiencing worsened economic conditions. In Sweden, for instance, the net reproduction rate (NRR) has been below replacement for 34 years (1930-63), if the period is taken as a whole, but this is because of the economic depression. The average replacement rate was below unity (NRR = 0.81) for the period 1930-42, but from 1942 through 1963 it was above unity (NRR = 1.08). Hardships that seem particularly conducive to deliberate lowering of the birth rate are (in managed economies) scarcity of housing and other consumer goods despite full employment, and required high participation of women in the labor force, or (in freer economies) a great deal of unemployment and economic insecurity. When conditions are good, any nation tends to have a growing population.

It follows that, in countries where contraception is used, a realistic proposal for a government policy of lowering the birth rate reads like a catalogue of horrors: squeeze consumers through taxation and inflation; make housing very scarce by limiting construction; force wives and mothers to work outside the home to offset the inadequacy of male wages, yet provide few childcare facilities; encourage migration to the city by paying low wages in the country and providing few rural jobs; increase congestion in cities by starving the transit system; increase personal insecurity by encouraging conditions that produce unemployment and by haphazard political arrests. No government will institute such hardships simply for the purpose of controlling population growth. Clearly, therefore, the task of contemporary population policy is to develop attractive substitutes for family interests, so as to avoid having to turn to hardship as a corrective. The specific measures required for developing such substitutes are not easy to determine in the absence of research on the question.

In short, the world's population problem cannot be solved by pretense and wishful thinking. The unthinking identification of family planning with population control is an ostrich-like approach in that it permits people to hide from themselves the enormity and unconventionality of the task. There is no reason to abandon family-planning programs; contraception is a valuable technological instrument. But such programs must be supplemented with equal or greater investments in research and experimentation to determine the required socioeconomic measures.

References and Notes

1. *Studies in Family Planning, No. 16* (1967).
2. *Ibid., No. 9* (1966), p. 1.
3. The statement is given in *Studies in Family Planning* (1, p. 1), and in *Population Bull.* 23, 6 (1967).
4. The statement is quoted in *Studies in Family Planning* (1, p. 2).
5. *Hearings on S. 1676, U.S. Senate, Subcommittee on Foreign Aid Expenditures, 89th Congress, Second Session, April 7, 8, 11* (1966), pt. 4.
6. B. L. Raina, in *Family Planning and Population Programs,* B. Berelson, R. K. Anderson, O. Harkavy, G. Maier, W. P. Mauldin, S. G. Segal, Eds. (Univ. of Chicago Press, Chicago, 1966).
7. D. Kirk, *Ann. Amer. Acad. Polit. Soc. Sci.* 369, 53 (1967).
8. As used by English-speaking demographers, the word *fertility* designates actual reproductive performance, not a theoretical capacity.
9. K. Davis, *Rotarian* 94, 10 (1959); *Health Educ. Monographs* 9, 2 (1960); L. Day and A. Day, *Too Many Americans* (Houghton Mifflin, Boston. 1964); R. A. Piddington, *Limits of Mankind* (Wright, Bristol, England, 1956).
10. *Official Gazette* (15 Apr. 1965); quoted in *Studies in Family Planning* (1, p. 7).
11. J. W. Gardner. Secretary of Health, Education, and Welfare. "Memorandum to Heads of Operating Agencies" (Jan. 1966), reproduced in *Hearing on S. 1676* (5), p. 783.
12. C. Tietze. *Demography* 1, 119 (1964); *J. Chronic Diseases* 18, 1161 (1964); M. Muramatsu. *Milbank Mem. Fund Quart.* 38, 153 (1960): K. Davis, *Population Index* 29, 345 (1963); R. Armijo and T. Monreal, *J. Sex Res.* 1964, 143 (1964); Proceedings World Population Conference, Belgrade, 1965; Proceedings International Planned Parenthood Federation.
13. *Studies in Family Planning, No. 4* (1964), p. 3.
14. D. Bell (then administrator for Agency for International Development), in *Hearings on S. 1676* (5), p. 862.
15. *Asian Population Conference* (United Nations, New York. 1964), p. 30.
16. R. Armijo and T. Monreal, in *Components of Population Change in Latin America* (Milbank Fund, New York, 1965), p. 272; E. Rice-Wray, *Amer. J. Public Health* 54, 313 (1964).
17. E. Rice-Wray, in "Intra-Uterine Contraceptive Devices," *Excerpta Med. Inter. Congr. Ser. No. 54* (1962), p. 135.
18. J. Blake, in *Public Health and Population Change,* M. C. Sheps and J. C. Ridley, Eds. (Univ. of Pittsburgh Press, Pittsburgh, 1965).
19. J. Blake and K. Davis, *Amer. Behavioral Scientist,* 5, 24 (1963).
20. See "Panel discussion on comparative acceptability of different methods of contraception," in *Research in Family Planning,* C. V. Kiser, Ed. (Princeton Univ. Press, Princeton, 1962), pp. 373-86.
21. "From the point of view of the woman concerned, the whole problem of continuing motivation disappears, . . ."[D. Kirk, in *Population Dynamics,* M. Muramatsu and P. A. Harper, Eds. (Johns Hopkins Press, Baltimore, 1965)].

22. "For influencing family size norms, certainly the examples and statements of public figures are of great significance . . . also . . . use of mass-communication methods which help to legitimize the small-family style, to provoke conversation, and to establish a vocabulary for discussion of family planning." [M. W. Freymann, in *Population Dynamics,* M. Muramatsu and P. A. Harper, Eds. (Johns Hopkins Press, Baltimore, 1965)].

23. O. A. Collver, *Birth Rates in Latin America* (International Population and Urban Research, Berkeley, Calif., 1965), pp. 27-28; the ten countries were Colombia, Costa Rica, El Salvador, Ecuador, Guatemala, Honduras, Mexico, Panama, Peru, and Venezuela.

24. J. R. Rele, *Fertility Analysis through Extension of Stable Population Concepts.* (International Population and Urban Research, Berkeley, Calif., 1967).

25. J. C. Ridley, M. C. Sheps, J. W. Lingner, J. A. Menken, *Milbank Mem. Fund Quart.* 45, 77 (1967); E. Arriaga, unpublished paper.

26. "South Korea and Taiwan appear successfully to have checked population growth by the use of intrauterine contraceptive devices" [U. Borell, *Hearings on S. 1676* (5), p. 556].

27. K. Davis, *Population Index* 29, 345 (1963).

28. R. Freedman, *ibid.* 31, 421 (1965).

29. Before 1964 the Family Planning Association had given advice to fewer than 60,-000 wives in 10 years and a Pre-Pregnancy Health Program had reached some 10,000, and, in the current campaign, 3650 IUD's were inserted in 1965, in a total population of 2½ million women of reproductive age. See *Studies in Family Planning, No. 19* (1967), p. 4, and R. Freedman *et al., Population Studies* 16, 231 (1963).

30. R. W. Gillespie, *Family Planning on Taiwan* (Population Council, Taichung, 1965).

31. During the period 1950-60 the ratio of growth of the city to growth of the noncity population was 5:3; during the period 1960-64 the ratio was 5:2; these ratios are based on data of Shaohsing Chen. *J. Sociol. Taiwan* 1, 74 (1963) and data in the United Nations *Demographic Yearbooks.*

32. R. Freedman, *Population Index* 31, 434 (1965). Taichung's rate of decline in 1963-64 was roughly double the average in four other cities, whereas just prior to the campaign its rate of decline had been much less than theirs.

33. S. H. Chen, *J. Soc. Sci. Taipei* 13, 72 (1963).

34. R. Freedman *et al., Population Studies* 16, 227 (1963); *ibid.,* p. 232.

35. In 1964 the life expectancy at birth was already 66 years in Taiwan, as compared to 70 for the United States.

36. J. Blake, *Eugenics Quart.* 14, 68 (1967).

37. Women accepting IUD's in the family-planning program are typically 30 to 34 years old and have already had four children. [*Studies in Family Planning No. 19* (1967), p. 5].

38. Y. K. Cha, in *Family Planning and Population Programs,* B. Berelson *et al.,* Eds. (Univ. of Chicago Press, Chicago, 1966).

39. H. S. Ayalvi and S. S. Johl, *J. Family Welfare* 12, 60 (1965).

40. Sixty percent of the women had borne their first child before age 19. Early marriage is strongly supported by public opinion. Of couples polled in the Punjab, 48 percent said that girls *should* marry before age 16, and 94 percent said they should marry before age 20 (H. S. Ayalvi and S. S. Johl, *ibid.,* p. 57). A study of 2380 couples in 60 villages of Uttar Pradesh found that the women had consummated their marriage at an average age of 14.6 years [J. R. Rele, *Population Studies* 15, 268 (1962)].

41. J. Morsa, in *Family Planning and Population Programs,* B. Berelson *et al.,* Eds. (Univ. of Chicago Press, Chicago, 1966).

42. H. Gille and R. J. Pardoko, *ibid.,* p. 515; S. N. Agarwala, *Med. Dig. Bombay* 4, 653 (1961).

43. *Mysore Population Study* (United Nations, New York, 1961), p. 140.

44. A. Daly, in *Family Planning and Population Programs,* B. Berelson *et al.,* Eds. (Univ. of Chicago Press, Chicago, 1966).
45. C. J. Goméz, paper presented at the World Population Conference, Belgrade, 1965.
46. C. Miro, in *Family Planning and Population Program,* B. Berelson *et al.,* Eds. (Univ. of Chicago Press, Chicago, 1966).
47. *Demographic Training and Research Centre (India) Newsletter* 20, 4 (Aug. 1966).
48. K. Davis, *Population Index* 29, 345 (1963). For economic and sociological theory of motivation for having children, see J. Blake [Univ. of California (Berkeley)], in preparation.
49. K. Davis, *Amer. Economic Rev.* 46, 305 (1956); *Sci. Amer.* 209, 68 (1963).
50. J. Blake, *World Population Conference* [*Belgrade, 1965*] (United Nations, New York, 1967), vol. 2, pp. 132-36.
51. S. Enke, *Rev. Economics Statistics* 42, 175 (1960); ———, *Econ. Develop. Cult. Change* 8, 339 (1960); ———, *ibid.* 10, 427 (1962); A. O. Krueger and

L. A. Sjaastad, *ibid.,* p. 423.
52. T. J. Samuel, *J. Family Welfare India* 13, 12 (1966).
53. Sixty-two countries, including 27 in Europe, give cash payments to people for having children [U.S. Social Security Administration, *Social Security Programs Throughout the World, 1967* (Government Printing Office, Washington, D. C., 1967), pp. xxvii-xxviii].
54. Average gross reproduction rates in the early 1960's were as follows: Hungary, 0.91; Bulgaria, 1.09; Romania, 1.15; Yugoslavia, 1.32.
55. O. A. Collver and F. Langlois, *Econ. Develop. Cult. Change* 10, 367 (1962); J. Weeks, [Univ. of Califoria (Berkeley)], unpublished paper.
56. Roman Catholic textbooks condemn the "small" family (one with fewer than four children) as being abnormal [J. Blake, *Population Studies* 20, 27 (1966)].
57. Judith Blake's critical readings and discussions have greatly helped in the preparation of this article.

EDITOR'S COMMENTS

There are increasing signs that governments are slowly becoming aware of some of the hazards inherent in continued population growth. On July 18, 1970, President Nixon reported to Congress:

I believe that many of our present social problems may be related to the fact that we have had only 50 years in which to accommodate the second hundred million Americans. In fact, since 1945 alone some 90 million babies have been born in this country. We have thus had to accomplish in a very few decades an adjustment to population growth which was once spread over centuries. It now appears that we will have to provide for a third hundred million Americans in a period of just 30 years.

Yet, nations are doing little more than sanctioning family planning programs.

There are a few countries with zero, or near zero, population growth rates. These are already crowded countries. If the entire world were as heavily populated, the natural ecosystems on which man depends would have long since collapsed. In 1970, Belgium, East Germany, and Luxembourg all reported annual growth rates of 0.1 percent. At this rate, it will take 700 years for these populations to double.

Perhaps the best evidence to support Dr. Davis' contention that present family planning programs will not succeed at the national level is illustrated by what happened in Rumania in 1970. For many years contraceptives have been readily available in this small, crowded country, and abortion has been legal and within the financial reach of virtually everyone. In 1969, the nation's leaders awoke to the startling fact that Rumania's population growth was at an all-time low. The government proceeded to outlaw abortion, and the birth rate doubled in 1970. A nation which had achieved that which is necessary for the survival of mankind abandoned sanity for the sake of artificial economic growth. Current programs most certainly will not succeed in achieving a zero birth rate.

Preventing Pregnancy:
A Review of Contraceptive Methods

William H. Mason is Associate Professor and Coordinator of General Biology at Auburn University, Auburn, Alabama. His research interests include energy flow and food relationships in invertebrate populations, and the development of innovative teaching methods.

Contraception is most satisfactorily achieved by preventing a meeting of egg and sperm or by causing the embryo to be rejected by the uterus, preferably before it has implanted in the uterine wall. Contraception actually has a long history. Egyptian writings of 1850 B.C. described crocodile dung prepared in a paste-like manner for insertion in the vagina where it probably acted somewhat like a sponge to trap sperm. Three hundred years later (1550 B.C.), some Egyptians were using a vaginal preparation containing honey and gum arabic from the acacia shrub. The fermentation of gum arabic produces lactic acid, an effective spermicidal agent used in many modern spermicidal preparations.

One of the earliest effective contraceptives was the condom. Made of animal skins at first, the condom covered the penis and caught the sperm at ejaculation, thus preventing fertilization. Today condoms are made of latex rubber. Used properly they effectively prevent pregnancy.

Withdrawal is another means by which pregnancy can be prevented by the male. As its name implies, withdrawal involves removing the penis from the vagina prior to ejaculation. This is a very undependable contraceptive practice. Sperm can be released prior to ejaculation, and the best of good intentions may be disregarded at the last moment; also of importance, withdrawal is not too satisfying to either party involved.

The most effective means of male contraception is by sterilization. This is a simple operation. It is routinely performed in the physician's office, and the patient may even return to work that day. The procedure is referred to as a vasectomy. It involves making two small incisions in the wall of the scrotum, isolating the small vasa deferentia which convey sperm from the testes to the penis, and cutting them. Sperm are now trapped in the testes where white blood cells regularly destroy them. The man is not affected by this operation in any way other than in his capability to sire children. He still is capable of achieving an erection and produces an ejaculate — there simply are no sperm in the ejaculate.

A vasectomy is safe and is a foolproof contraceptive method. Its only drawback is that it is sometimes permanent. Restoration of the broken ends of the sperm ducts is possible roughly one-half of the time. It is thought that severing of the sperm ducts may be replaced soon by the insertion of plugs. Such plugs could be removed easily if the person wished to produce children again.

About six million American women practice contraception by taking the pill. The pill contains two chemical substances, an estrogen and a progestin. These substances are closely related to the naturally-occurring estrogens and progesterone and, biologically, they exert effects similar to the action of the naturally-occurring hormones.

A certain amount of basic knowledge relating to the human female's menstrual cycle is required for an understanding of the pill's mode of action. The pituitary gland secretes follicle-stimulating hormone (FSH) early in the menstrual cycle. FSH stimulates egg production in the ovary. After about two weeks, the pituitary begins to release sufficient amounts of luteinizing hormone (LH) to cause a release of the maturing egg from the ovary. The egg now moves down a Fallopian tube and may be fertilized during about a 48-hour period.

FSH and LH also cause the ovary to release estrogens and progesterone. Both of these hormones affect the uterine lining in such a way as to prepare it for reception of the tiny embryo in case the egg is fertilized in the Fallopian tube. Estrogens and progesterone also act to depress the continued pituitary secretion of FSH and LH.

The reduction of FSH and LH causes the ovaries to reduce their secretion of estrogens and progesterone, and at about 28-day intervals the uterine lining sloughs away, thus ending the cycle. At this time the pituitary again begins to secrete FSH and LH, and the cycle begins again. If fertilization and implantation occurs, the cycle is not terminated, estrogen and progesterone secretion continues, and a normal pregnancy is usually maintained.

Taken 20 consecutive days a month, the pill is virtually 100 percent effective in preventing pregnancy. Its mode of action is simple; the estrogen and progestin interfere with the normal pituitary release of FSH and LH. This depression of pituitary activity prevents the development of eggs within the ovary. No eggs — no pregnancy.

There are drawbacks to use of the pill. Some women suffer from nausea, some gain weight; also, increases in circulatory problems associated with pill use have been reported. However, the possible complications involved in unwanted pregnancy are far greater than the possible side effects of the pill. The pill causes no damage to the pituitary or the ovaries. A woman can become pregnant the month after she discontinues use of the pill.

Rhythm, as a contraceptive technique, relies on refraining from sexual intercourse during the time an egg is present in the Fallopian tube and can be fertilized. This period is about 48 hours in duration each menstrual cycle. The problem with this method involves identification of the 48-hour period. By abstaining from intercourse during the middle 10 days of each period, the chances of pregnancy are significantly reduced. A further aid in determining the "danger period" is the fact that most women run a slight temperature at the time the egg is released from the ovary. However, women are variable in regard to the time the egg may be released each month; therefore, this method of contraception is not regarded as being generally effective.

Well over two million American women now employ the intrauterine device (IUD) as a contraceptive. The IUD is a small, flexible object inserted into the uterus by a physician. Most IUD's are made of plastic or stainless steel. The mode of action of the IUD is not fully understood. It is believed to speed the embryo through the uterus thus preventing implantation. It seems clear that the IUD does not prevent fertilization; it prevents implantation. Newer IUD's contain small amounts of copper. For an unknown reason, copper increases the IUD's effectiveness.

The IUD has few side effects. It may cause initial bleeding and discomfort, and may be expelled spontaneously. In most women it is not expelled and all discomfort soon disappears. It is not thought to produce cancer and certainly does not affect the body's hormone levels. The IUD is from 95 to 99 percent effective. If abortion-on-demand were available for the small number of women it fails in each year, the IUD could quite possibly be considered the "best choice" of present contraceptives.

The diaphragm has been used by women for many years as a contraceptive device. Diaphragms are made of latex rubber and are shaped in such a way as to cover the cervix (a neck-like portion of the uterus containing its opening into the vagina). This prevents the entrance of sperm into the uterus and therefore prevents fertilization, since the sperm cannot enter the Fallopian tubes. There are no side effects associated with use of the diaphragm — none except the high incidence of pregnancy in women relying on this method. The diaphragm may be improperly placed or may be dislodged during intercourse. Its use requires prior planning — all too often that prior planning is not done, and it's just too much trouble to take time out for diaphragm placement — after all, "nothing will happen this one time."

A variety of chemicals which destroy sperm can be inserted into the vagina; however, these are not dependable, and a woman using them should count on becoming pregnant. Douching, the rinsing out of the vagina after intercourse, certainly is not effective; two of five women depending on this will become pregnant in a year's time.

Tubal ligation (tying off the Fallopian tubes) is the surest means of contraception in women. For many years, tubal ligation was accomplsihed by opening the abdominal wall — an operation requiring about 15 minutes and possessing many of the dangers always inherent in abdominal surgery. A new method of tubal ligation is called laproscopic sterilization. This method relies on the insertion of a tiny tube through the abdominal wall. With this instrument the Fallopian tubes are found and sealed off. Laproscopic sterilization is inexpensive, leaves no scars, and is safe. Tubal ligation is presently considered to be a permanent procedure.

Abstention is another absolutely safe contraceptive method, especially when both members of the mating pair agree to it. As a method, it leaves something to be desired when only one member agrees to it.

TABLE 1. *Effectiveness of Different Contraceptive Procedures in Women of Childbearing Age.*

Method	Probability of Becoming Pregnant During a Given Year
No contraceptive	.80
Douche	.38
Foam tablets	.22
Jelly alone	.20
Withdrawal	.16
Condom	.15
Safe period	.14
Diaphragm	.12
Intrauterine device	.05
Oral contraceptives	.002

The future certainly holds many promises of newer, safer, and more effective contraceptives. One drug has already been discovered which renders males temporarily sterile but does not cause impotence. However, if a man on this drug drinks alcoholic beverages, his blood pressure reacts sharply, and the eyes become very red. It is possible that a drug similar to this, but lacking side effects, will soon be available. Such a drug may be taken orally or may be implanted just beneath the skin in such a way as to release its active ingredients slowly over a period of months or years. Such an implant could be removed as easily as it is inserted.

A new pill for women is being developed which does not contain estrogens — the probable cause of side effects associated with today's pill. This new so-called mini-pill contains only a low dose of progestin. The mini-pill is taken daily and contains only a fraction of the hormone-like substances found in previous preparations. After two years of testing in England, it is thought that this method may be free of possible circulatory complications.

Development of the low progestin implant is thought to have several advantages over the pill. The implant, placed under skin, would release progestin slowly over long periods of time. With this method there is no pill to remember to take each day.

The morning-after pill would be taken after intercourse. The present-day morning-after pill consists of a series of oral doses of estrogen. This prevents implantation; however, the high doses of estrogen can make a woman quite ill. This method is best used sparingly, for example, after rape if pregnancy is suspected.

A better and more efficient morning-after pill may soon be available. It will contain substances called prostaglandins. Prostaglandins are natural substances found in the body in low quantities. They cause contraction of certain muscles and large doses can be used to cause uterine contraction, thereby effecting a spontaneous abortion. It is very probable that these substances will soon be available for once-a-month use if the bleeding phase of the menstrual cycle fails to occur, indicating pregnancy.

Someday it may be possible to immunize a woman against her husband's sperm. New IUD's are being developed and new spermacidal chemicals are being experimentally tried. Men may soon be able to take pills which keep sperm from maturing, and pills may even be available which increase the chances of having either a boy or a girl.

It has recently been found that each sperm is surrounded by a fluid which must be removed if the sperm is to fertilize an egg. An enzyme which removes this fluid is present in the uterus. An effective means of contraception could be developed if it were discovered how to turn off a woman's production of this enzyme. Recent discovery of the hormone which controls the release of FSH and LH from the pituitary may even herald a new type of pill. Many investigators feel that this substance may produce none of the side effects of today's pill. This pill may also be used to prematurely stimulate egg release in the middle of the month — an obvious benefit for Roman Catholics.

It is clear that pregnancy can be prevented. It should also be clear that many millions of pregnancies must soon be prevented each year. At present, the world's plans for using these methods seem to be inadequate.

V. C. WYNNE-EDWARDS

Self-Regulating Systems in Populations of Animals

► A new hypothesis illuminates aspects of animal behavior that have hitherto seemed unexplainable.

V. C. Wynne-Edwards is Regius Professor of Natural History at the University of Aberdeen, Aberdeen, Scotland. He is well known throughout the world as an authority on mechanisms of population control in animals and is the author of numerous books and technical publications on the subject.

I am going to try to explain a hypothesis which could provide a bridge between two biological realms.[1] On one side is that part of the "Balance of Nature" concerned with regulating the numbers of animals, and on the other is the broad field of social behavior. The hypothesis may, I believe, throw a bright and perhaps important sidelight on human behavior and population problems. I must emphasize, however, that it is still a hypothesis. It appears to be generally consistent with the facts, and it provides entirely new insight into many aspects of animal behavior that have hitherto been unexplainable; but because it involves long-term evolutionary processes it cannot be put to an immediate and comprehensive test by short-term experiments.

Human populations are of course increasing at compound interest practically all over the world. At the overall 2 percent annual rate of the last decade, they can be expected to double with each generation. In

the perspective of evolutionary time such a situation must be extremely short-lived, and I am sure we are going to grow more and more anxious about the future of man until we are able to satisfy ourselves that the human population explosion is controllable, and can be contained.

Populations of animals, especially when they are living under primeval undisturbed conditions, characteristically show an altogether different state of affairs; and this was equally true of man in the former cultural periods of the stone age. These natural populations tend to preserve a continuing state of balance, usually fluctuating to some extent but essentially stable and regulated. The nature of the regulatory process has been the main focus of study and speculation by animal ecologists during the whole of my working life, and in fact considerably longer.

Charles Darwin[2] was the first to point out that though all animals have the capacity to increase their numbers, in fact they do not continuously do so. The "checks to increase" appeared to him to be of four kinds — namely, the amount of food available, which must give the extreme limit to which any species can increase; the effects of predation by other animals; the effects of physical factors such as climate; and finally, the inroads of disease. "In looking at Nature," he tells us in the *Origin of Species,* "it is most necessary . . . never to forget that every single organic being may be said to be striving to the utmost to increase in numbers." This intuitive assumption of a universal resurgent pressure from within held down by hostile forces from without has dominated the thinking of biologists on matters of population regulation, and on the nature of the struggle for existence, right down to the present day.

Setting all preconceptions aside, however, and returning to a detached assessment of the facts revealed by modern observation and experiment, it becomes almost immediately evident that a very large part of the regulation of numbers depends not on Darwin's hostile forces but on the initiative taken by the animals themselves; that is to say, to an important extent it is an intrinsic phenomenon.

Forty years ago Jespersen[3] showed, for example, that there is a close numerical agreement between the standing crop of planktonic organisms at the surface of the North Atlantic Ocean and the distribution density of the various deep-sea birds that depend on these organisms for food. Over the whole of this vast area the oceanic birds are dispersed in almost constant proportion to the local biomass of plankton, although the biomass itself varies from region to region by a factor of about 100; the actual crude correlation coefficient is 85 percent. This pro rata dispersion of the birds must in fact depend solely on their own intrinsic efforts and behavior. Even though the dispersion directly reflects the availability of food, the movements of the birds over the ocean are essentially voluntary and not imposed against their will by hostile or other outside forces.

Turning to the results of repeatable experiments with laboratory animals, it is a generally established principle that a population started up, perhaps from one parental pair, in some confined universe such as an aquarium or a cage, can be expected to grow to a predictable size, and thereafter to maintain itself at that ceiling for months or years as long as the experimenter keeps the conditions unchanged. This can readily be demonstrated with most common laboratory animals, including the insects *Drosophila* and *Tribolium,* the water-flea *Daphnia,* the guppy *Lebistes,* and also mice and rats. The ceiling population density stays constant in these experiments in the complete absence of predators or disease and equally without recourse to regulation by starvation, simply by the matching of recruitment and loss. For example, a set of particularly illuminating experiments by Silliman and Gutsell,[4] lasting over 3 years, showed that when stable populations of guppies, kept in tanks, were cropped by removal of a proportion of the fish at regular intervals, the remainder responded by producing more young that survived, with the consequence that the losses were compensated. In the controls, on the other hand, where the stocks were left untouched, the guppies went on breeding all the time, but by cannibalism they consistently removed at birth the whole of the surplus produced. The regulating methods are different in different species; under appropriate circumstances in mice, to take another example, ovulation and reproduction can decline and even cease, as long as the ceiling density is maintained.

Here again, therefore, we are confronted by intrinsic mechanisms, in which none of Darwin's checks play any part, competent in themselves to regulate the population size within a given habitat.

The same principle shows up just as clearly in the familiar concept that a habitat has a certain carrying capacity, and that it is no good turning out more partridges or planting more trout than the available habitat can hold.

Population growth is essentially a density-dependent process; this means that it tends to proceed fastest when population densities are far below the ceiling level, to fall to zero as this level is approached, and to become negative, leading to an actual drop in numbers, if ever the ceiling is exceeded. The current hypothesis is that the adjustment of numbers in animals is a homeostatic process — that there is, in fact, an automatic self-righting balance between population density and resources.

I must turn briefly aside here to remind you that there are some environments which are so unstable or transitory that there is not time enough for colonizing animals to reach a ceiling density, and invoke their regulatory machinery, before the habitat becomes untenable again or is destroyed. Populations in these conditions are always in the pioneering stage, increasing freely just as long as conditions allow. Instability of this kind tends to appear around the fringes of the geographical range of all free-living organisms, and especially in desert and polar regions. It is also very common in agricultural land, because of the incessant disturbance of ploughing, seeding, spraying, harvesting, and rotating of crops. In these conditions the ecologist will often look in vain for evidences of homeostasis, among the violently fluctuating and completely uncontrollable populations typical of the animal pests of farms and plantations. Homeostasis can hardly be expected to cope unerringly with the ecological turmoil of cultivated land.

I return later to the actual machinery of homeostasis. For the present it can be accepted that more or less effective methods of regualting their own numbers have been evolved by most types of animals. If this is so, it seems logical to ask as the next question: What is it that decides the ceiling level?

Food Supply as a Limiting Factor

Darwin was undoubtedly right in concluding that food is the factor that normally puts an extreme limit on population density, and the dispersion of oceanic birds over the North Atlantic, which so closely reflects the dispersion of their food supply, is certain to prove a typical and representative case. Just the same, the link between food productivity and population density is very far from being self-evident. The relationship between them does not typically involve any signs of undernourishment; and starvation, when we observe it, tends to be a sporadic or accidental cause of mortality rather than a regular one.

Extremely important light is shed on this relationship between population density and food by our human experience of exploiting resources of the same kind. Fish, fur-bearing animals, and game are all notoriously subject to overexploitation at the hands of man, and present-day management of these renewable natural resources is based on the knowledge that there is a limit to the intensity of cropping that each stock can withstand. If we exceed this critical level, the stock will decline and the future annual crops will diminish. Exactly parallel principles apply to the exploitation of natural prairie pastures by domestic livestock; if overgrazing is permitted, fertility and future yields just as fatally decline.

In all these situations there is a tendency to overstep the safety margin while exploitation of the resource is still economically profitable. We have seen since World War II, for example, the decimation of stock of the blue and the humpback whale in the southern oceans, under the impetus of an intense profit motive, which persisted long after it had become apparent to everyone in the industry that the cropping rate was unsupportably high. The only way to protect these economically valuable recurrent resources from destruction is to impose, by agreement or law, a man-made code of rules, defining closed seasons, catch limits, permitted types of gear, and so on, which restrict the exploitation rate sufficiently to prevent the catch from exceeding the critical level.

In its essentials, this is the same crucial situation that faces populations of animals in exploiting their resources of food. Indeed, without going any further one could predict that if the food supplies of animals were openly exposed to an unruly scramble, there could be no safeguard against their overexploitation either.

Conventional Behavior in Relation to Food

When I first saw the force of this deduction 10 years ago, I felt that the scales had fallen from my eyes. At once the vast edifice of conventional behavior among animals in relation to food began to take on a new meaning. A whole series of unconnected natural phenomena seemed to click smoothly into place.

First among these are the territorial systems of various birds (paralleled in many other organisms), where the claim to an individual piece of ground can evoke competition of an intensity unequaled on any other occasion in the life of the species concerned. It results, in the simplest cases, in a parceling out of the habitat into a mosaic of breeding and feeding lots. A territory has to be of a certain size, and individuals that are unsuccessful in obtaining one are often excluded completely from the habitat, and always prevented from breeding in it. Here is a system that might have been evolved for the exact purpose of imposing a ceiling density on the habitat, and for efficiently disposing of any surplus individuals that fail to establish themselves. Provided

the territory size is adequate, it is obvious that the rate of exploitation of the food resources the habitat contains will automatically be prevented from exceeding the critical threshold.

There are other behavioral devices that appear, in the light of the food-resource hypothesis we are examining, equally purposive in leading to the same result — namely, that of limiting the permitted quota of participants in an artificial kind of way, and of off-loading all that are for the time being surplus to the carrying capacity of the ground. Many birds nest in colonies — especially, for example, the oceanic and aerial birds which cannot, in the nature of things, divide up the element in which they feed into static individual territories. In the colony the pairs compete just as long and keenly for one of the acceptable nest sites, which are in some instances closely packed together. By powerful tradition some of these species return year after year to old-established resorts, where the perimeter of the colony is closely drawn like an imaginary fence around the occupied sites. Once again there is not always room to accommodate all the contestants, and unsuccessful ones have to be relegated to a nonbreeding surplus or reserve, inhibited from sexual maturation because they have failed to obtain a site within the traditional zone and all other sites are taboo.

A third situation, exemplifying another, parallel device, is the pecking order or social hierarchy so typical of the higher animals that live in companies in which the individual members become mutually known. Animal behaviorists have studied the hierarchy in its various manifestations for more than 40 years, most commonly in relation to food. In general, the individuals of higher rank have a prior right to help themselves, and, in situations where there is not enough to go round, the ones at the bottom of the scale must stand aside and do without. In times of food shortage — for example, with big game animals — the result is that the dominant individuals come through in good shape while the subordinates actually die of starvation. The hierarchy therefore produces the same kind of result as a territorial system in that it admits a limited quota of individuals to share the food resources and excludes the extras. Like the other devices I have described, it can operate in exactly the same way with respect to reproduction. In fact, not only can the hierarchical system exclude individuals from breeding, it can equally inhibit their sexual development.

It must be quite clear already that the kind of competition we are considering, involving as it does the right to take food and the right to breed, is a matter of the highest importance to the individuals that engage in it. At its keenest level it becomes a matter of life and death. Yet, as is well known, the actual contest between individuals for real property or personal status is almost always strictly conventionalized. Fighting and bloodshed are superseded by mere threats of violence, and threats in their turn are sublimated into displays of magnificence and virtuosity. This is the world of bluff and status symbols. What takes place, in other words, is a contest for conventional prizes conducted under conventional rules. But the contest itself is no fantasy, for the losers can forfeit the chance of posterity and the right to survive.

Conventionalized Rivalry and Society

It is at this point that the hypothesis provides its most unexpected and striking insight, by showing that the conventionalization of rivalry and the foundation of society are one and the same thing. Hitherto it has never been possible to give a scientific definition of the terms *social* and *society,* still less a functional explanation. The emphasis has always been on the rather vague element of companionship and brotherhood. Animals have in the main been regarded as

social whenever they were gregarious. Now we can view the social phenomenon in a new light. According to the hypothesis the society is no more and no less than the organization necessary for the staging of conventional competition. At once it assumes a crisp definition: a society is an organization of individuals that is capable of providing conventional competition among its members.

Such a novel interpretation of something that involves us all so intimately is almost certain to be viewed at first sight a bit skeptically; but in fact one needs no prompting in our competitive world to see that human society is impregnated with rivalry. The sentiments of brotherhood are warm and reassuring, and in identifying society primarily with these we appear to have been unconsciously shutting our eyes to the inseparable rough-and-tumble of status seeking and social discrimination that are never very far to seek below the surface, bringing enviable rewards to the successful and pitiful distress to those who lose. If this interpretation is right, conventional competition is an inseparable part of the substance of human society, at the parochial, national, and international level. To direct it into sophisticated and acceptable channels is no doubt one of the great motives of civilized behavior; but it would be idle to imagine that we could eliminate it.

A corollary of the hypothesis that deserves mention is the extension of sociality that implies, to animals of almost every kind whether they associate in flocks or seek instead a more solitary way of life. There is no particular difficulty of course in seeing, for example, cats and dogs as social mammals individually recognizing the local and personal rights of acquaintances and strangers and inspired by obviously conventional codes of rivalry when they meet. In a different setting, the territory-holding birds that join in the chorus of the spring dawn are acting together in social concert, expressing their mutual rivalry by a conventional display of exalted sophistication and beauty. Even at the other extreme, when animals flock into compact and obviously social herds and schools, each individual can sometimes be seen to maintain a strict individual distance from its companions.

Social Organization and Feedback

We can conveniently return now to the subject of homeostasis, in order to see how it works in population control. Homeostatic systems come within the general purview of cybernetics; in fact, they have long been recognized in the physiology of living organisms. A simple model can be found in any thermostatic system, in which there must of course be units capable of supplying or withdrawing heat whenever the system departs from its standard temperature and readjustment is necessary. But one also needs an indicator device to detect how far the system has deviated and in which direction. It is the feedback of this information that activates the heating or cooling units.

Feedback is an indispensable element of homeostatic systems. There seems no reason to doubt that, in the control of population density, it can be effectively provided simply by the intensity of conventional competition. Social rivalry is inherently density-dependent: the more competitors there are seeking a limited number of rewards, the keener will be the contest. The impact of stress on the individuals concerned, arising from conventional competition and acting through the pituitary-adrenal system, is already fully established, and it can profoundly influence their responses, both physiological and behavioral.

One could predict on theoretical grounds that feedback would be specially important whenever a major change in population density has to take place, upsetting the existing balance between demand and resources. This must occur particularly in the breeding season and at times of seasonal migrations. Keeping this in mind, we can obtain what we need in the way of background information by examining the relatively long-lived vertebrates, including most kinds of birds and mammals, whose individual members live long enough to constitute a standing population all the year round. The hypothesis of course implies that reproduction, as one of the principal parameters of population, will be subject to control — adjusted in magnitude, in fact, to meet whatever addition is currently required to build up the population and make good the losses of the preceding year. *Recruitment* is a term best used only to mean intake of new breeding adults into the population, and in that sense, of course, the raw birth rate may not be the sole and immediate factor that determines it. The newborn young have got to survive adolescence before they can become recruits to the breeding stock; and even after they attain puberty, social pressures may exclude them from reproducing until they attain a sufficiently high rank in the hierarchy. Indeed, there is evidence in a few species that, under sufficient stress, adults which have bred in previous years can be forced to stand aside.

There are, in fact, two largely distinct methods of regulating reproductive output, both of which have been widely adopted in the animal kingdom. One is to limit the number of adults that are permitted to breed, and this is of course a conspicuous result of adopting a territorial system, or any other system in which the number of permissible breeding sites is restricted. The other is to influence the number of young that each breeding pair is conditioned to produce. The two methods can easily be combined.

What we are dealing with here is a part of the machinery for adjusting population density. What we are trying to get at, however, is the social feedback mechanism behind it, by which the appropriate responses are elicited from potential breeders.

Birds generally provide us with the best examples, because their size, abundance, and diurnal habits render them the most observable and familiar of the higher animals. It is particularly easy to see in birds that social competition is keenest just before and during the breeding season, regardless of the type of breeding dispersion any given species happens to adopt. Individuals may compete for and defend territories or nest sites, or in rarer cases they may engage in tournaments in an arena or on a strutting ground; and they may join in a vocal chorus especially concentrated about the conventional hours of dawn and dusk, make mass visits to colony sites, join in massed flights, and share in other forms of communal displays. Some of these activities are more obviously competitive than others, but all appear to be alike in their capacity to reveal to each individual the concentration or density level of the population within its own immediate area.

Communal Male Displays

Some of these activities, like territorial defense, singing, and the arena displays, tend to be the exclusive concern of the males. It has never been possible hitherto to give a satisfactory functional explanation of the kind of communal male displays typified by the arena dances of some of the South American hummingbirds and manakins, and by the dawn strutting of prairie chickens and sharp-tailed grouse. The sites they use are generally traditional, each serving as a communal center and drawing the competitors from a more or less wide surrounding terrain. On many days during the long season of activity the same assembly of males may engage in vigorous interplay and mutual hostility, holding tense dramatic

postures for an hour or more at a stretch without a moment's relaxation, although there is no female anywhere in sight at the time. The local females do of course come at least once to be fertilized; but the performance makes such demands on the time and energy of the males that it seems perfectly reasonable to assume that this is the reason why they play no part in nesting and raising a family. The duty they perform is presumably important, but it is simply not credible to attribute it primarily to courting the females. To anyone looking for a population feedback device, on the other hand, interpretation would present no difficulty; he would presume that the males are being conditioned or stressed by their ritual exertions. In some of the arena species some of the males are known to be totally excluded from sexual intercourse; but it would seem that the feedback mechanism could produce its full effect only if it succeeded in limiting the number of females fertilized to an appropriate quota, after which the males refused service to any still remaining unfertilized. I hope research may at a not-too-distant date show us whether or not such refusal really takes place.

The conclusion that much of the social display associated with the breeding season consists of males competing with males makes necessary a reappraisal of Darwinian sexual selection. Whether the special organs developed for display are confined to the males, as in the examples we have just considered, or are found in both sexes, as for instance in most of the colony-nesting birds, there is a strong indication that they are first and foremost status symbols, used in conventional competition, and that the selective process by which they have been evolved is social rather than sexual. This would account for the hitherto puzzling fact that, although in the mature bullfrog and cicada the loud sound is produced by the males, in both cases it is the males that are provided with extra-large eardrums. There does not seem much room for doubt about who is displaying to whom.

Communal displays are familiar also in the context of bird migration, especially in the massing and maneuvering of flocks before the exodus begins. A comparable build-up of social excitement precedes the migratory flight of locusts. Indeed, what I have elsewhere defined as *epideictic* phenomena — displays, or special occasions, which allow all the individuals taking part to sense or become conditioned by population pressure — appear to be very common and widespread in the animal kingdom. They occur especially at the times predicted, when feedback is required in anticipation of a change in population density. The singing of birds, the trilling of katydids, crickets, and frogs, the underwater sounds of fish, and the flashing of fireflies all appear to perform this epideictic function. In cases where, as we have just seen, epideictic behavior is confined in the breeding season to the male sex, the presumption is that the whole process of controlling the breeding density and the reproductive quota is relegated to the males. Outside the breeding season, when the individuals are no longer united in pairs and are all effectively neuter in sex, all participate alike in epideictic display — in flighting at sundown, like ducks; in demonstrating at huge communal roosts at dusk, like starlings, grackles, and crows; or in forming premigratory swarms, like swallows. The assumption which the hypothesis suggests, that the largest sector of all social behavior must have this fundamentally epideictic or feedback function, gives a key to understanding a vast agglomeration of observed animal behavior that has hitherto been dubiously interpreted or has seemed altogether meaningless.

Maintaining Population Balance

Having outlined the way in which social organization appears to serve in supplying feedback, I propose to look again at the machinery for making adjustments to the population balance. In territorial birds, variations in the average size of territories from place to place and year to year can be shown to alter the breeding density and probably also the proportion of adults actually participating in reproduction. In various mammals the proportion of the females made pregnant, the number and size of litters, the survival of the young and the age at which they mature may all be influenced by social stress. Wherever parental care of the young has been evolved in the animal kingdom, the possibility exists that maternal behavior and solicitude can be affected in the same way; and the commonly observed variations in survival rates of the newborn could, in that case, have a substantial functional component and play a significant part in regulating the reproductive output. This would, among other things, explain away the enigma of cannibalism of the young, which we noticed earlier in the guppies and which occurs sporadically all through the higher animals. Infanticide played a conspicuous part in reducing the effective birth rate of many of the primitive human peoples that survived into modern times. Not infrequently it took the form of abandoning the child for what appeared to be commendable reasons, without involving an act of violence.

Reproduction is of course only one of the parameters involved in keeping the balance between income and loss in populations. The homeostatic machinery can go to work on the other side of the balance also, by influencing survival. Already, in considering the recruitment of adults, we have taken note of the way this can be affected by juvenile mortality, some of which is intrinsic in origin and capable of being promoted by social pressures. Conventional competition often leads to the exclusion of surplus individuals from any further right to share the resources of the habitat, and this in turn compels them to emigrate. Research conducted by Aberdeen in the last years has shown how important a factor forced expulsion is in regulating the numbers of the Scottish red grouse. Every breeding season so far has produced a population surplus, and it is the aggressive behavior of the dominant males which succeeds in driving the supernumeraries away. In this case the outcasts do not go far; they get picked up by predators or they mope and die because they are cut off from their proper food. Deaths from predation and disease can in fact be substantially "assisted" under social stress.

On the income side, therefore, both reproductive input and the acquisition of recruits by immigration appear to be subject to social regulation; and on the loss side, emigration and what can be described as socially induced mortality can be similarly affected. Once more it appears that it is only the inroads of Darwin's "checks to increase," the agents once held to be totally responsible for population regulation, which are in fact uncontrollable and have to be balanced out by manipulation of the other four components.

Attention must be drawn to the intimate way in which physiology and behavior are entwined in providing the regulatory machinery. It seems certain that the feedback of social stimulation acts on the individual through his endocrine system, and in the case of the vertebrates, as I have said, this particularly involves the pituitary and adrenal cortex or its equivalent. Sometimes the individual's response is primarily a physiological one — for example, the inhibition of spermatogenesis or the acceleration of growth: sometimes it is purely behavioral, as in the urge to return to the breeding site, the development of aggressiveness, or the demand for territory of a given size. But often there is a combination of the two — that is to say, a psychosomatic response, as when, for instance, the assumption of

breeding colors is coupled with the urge to display.

Sources of Controversy

There is no need for me to emphasize that the hypothesis is controversial. But almost all of it is based on well-established fact, so that the controversy can relate solely to matters of interpretation. Examples have been given here which show the ability of the hypothesis to offer new and satisfying interpretations of matters of fact where none could be suggested before. Some of these matters are of wide importance, like the basic function of social behavior; some are matters of everyday experience, like why birds sing at dawn. Very seldom indeed does the hypothesis contradict well-founded accepted principles. What, then, are the sources of controversy?

These are really three in number, all of them important. The first is that the concept is very wide-ranging and comprehensive; this means that it cannot be simply proved or disproved by performing a decisive experiment. There are of course dubious points where critical tests can be made, and research is proceeding, at Aberdeen among many other places, toward this end. Relevant results are constantly emerging, and at many points the hypothesis has been solidified and strengthened since it was first formulated. On the other hand, there has been no cause yet to retract anything.

The second source of controversy is that the hypothesis invokes a type of natural selection which is unfamiliar to zoologists generally. Social grouping is essentially a localizing phenomenon, and an animal species is normally made up of countless local populations all perpetuating themselves on their native soil, exactly as happens in underdeveloped and primitive communities of man. Social customs and adaptations vary from one local group to another, and the hypothesis requires that natural selection should take place between these groups, promoting those with more effective social organizations while the less effective ones go under. It is necessary, in other words, to postulate that social organizations are capable of progressive evolution and perfection as entities in their own right. The detailed arguments[5] are too complex to be presented here, but I can point out that intergroup selection is far from being a new concept: It has been widely accepted for more than 20 years by geneticists. It is almost impossible to demonstrate it experimentally because we have to deal with something closely corresponding to the rise and fall of nations in history, rather than with success or failure of single genes over a few generations; it is therefore the time scale that prevents direct experiment. Even the comparatively rapid process of natural selection acting among individuals has been notoriously difficult to demonstrate in nature.

The third objection is, I think, by far the most interesting. It is simply that the hypothesis does not apply to ourselves. No built-in mechanisms appear to curb our own population growth, or adjust our numbers to our resources. If they did so, everything I have said would be evident to every educated child, and I should not be surveying it here. How is this paradox to be explained?

The answer, it seems clear, is that these mechanisms did exist in primitive man and have been lost, almost within historic times. Man in the paleolithic stage, living as a hunter and gatherer, remained in balance with his natural resources just as other animals do under natural conditions. Generation after generation, his numbers underwent little or no change. Population increase was prevented not by physiological control mechanisms of the kind found in many other mammals but only by behavioral ones, taking the form of traditional customs and taboos. All the stone age tribes that survived into modern times diminished their effective birth rate by at least one of three ritual practices — infanticide, abortion, and abstention from intercourse. In a few cases fertility was apparently impaired by surgery during the initiation ceremonies. In many cases, marriage was long deferred. Mortality of those of more advanced age was often raised through cannibalism, tribal fighting, and human sacrifice.

Gradually, with the spread of the agricultural revolution, which tended to concentrate the population at high densities on fertile soils and led by degrees to the rise of the town, the craftsman, and the merchant, the old customs and taboos must have been forsaken. The means of population control would have been inherited originally from man's subhuman ancestors, and among stone age peoples their real function was probably not even dimly discerned except perhaps by a few individuals of exceptional brilliance and insight. The continually expanding horizons and skills of modern man rendered intrinsic limitations of numbers unnecessary, and for 5,000 or 10,000 years the advanced peoples of the Western world and Asia have increased without appearing to harm the world about them or endanger its productivity. But the underlying principles are the same as they have always been. It becomes obvious at last that we are getting very near the global carrying capacity of our habitat, and that we ought swiftly to impose some new, effective, homeostatic regime before we overwhelm it, and the ax of group selection falls.

References

1. V. C. Wynne-Edwards, *Animal Dispersion in Relation to Social Behaviour* (Hafner, New York. 1962).
2. C. Darwin, *The Origin of Species* (Murray, London, 1859) (quoted from 6th edition, 1872).
3. P. Jespersen, "The frequency of birds over the high Atlantic Ocean," *Nature* 114, 281 (1924).

4. R. P. Silliman and J. S. Gutsell, "Experimental exploitation of fish populations." *U.S. Fish Wildlife Serv. Fishery Bull.* 58, 214 (1958).

5. V. C. Wynne-Edwards, "Intergroup selection in the evolution of social systems," *Nature* 200, 623 (1963).

EDITOR'S COMMENTS

Dr. Wynne-Edwards makes a point of immense importance — modern day human populations are not controlled by the intrinsic factors regulating many natural animal populations. It is interesting to suppose that primitive peoples were controlled by intrinsic mechanisms; however, the hope for tomorrow lies only in man's will to force himself to have fewer children than he desires. Dr. Wynne-Edwards' "ax of group selection" is a familiar story — it is starvation, disease, or thermonuclear warfare.

WILLIAM C. PADDOCK

How Green Is the Green Revolution?

William C. Paddock is a Consultant in Tropical Agricultural Development. After living for ten years in Central America where he was a corn breeder for Iowa State University and the Director of the Panamerican School of Agriculture (in Honduras), he is now based in Washington, D.C. but still spends half his time in the American Tropics. He is co-author of *Hungry Nations* and *Famine-1975* and has a third book in press.

Three years ago, any agricultural specialist worth his salt was warning of impending famine in the underdeveloped nations of Asia, Africa, and Latin America. The less developed world, it was said, was losing the capacity to feed itself. Disaster lay as close as the year 1975.[1]

Today the warnings are of a wholly different sort. The world has an overabundance of grain. Wheat stocks have reached the level of 60 million tons. If anything, the danger immediately ahead would seem to be oversupply and glut.

In three short years, a startling turnaround has apparently taken place in the agricultural output of several parts of the developing world. The Philippines report achieving self-sufficiency in rice for the first time in history this year. Malaysia and South Vietnam are predicting the same for 1971 and Indonesia for 1973. Pakistan says it will shortly be self-sufficient in all cereals, and India expressed a similar hope. Optimism, clearly, rides tall in the saddle this year.

The increases are laid to a "Green Revolution" which is based on the introduction and the rapidly spreading use of so-called "miracle grains" in the rice paddies and wheat stands of South Asia. These are new, high-yielding varieties of wheat researched in Mexico by the Rockefeller Foundation and rice developed at the International Rice Research Institute in the Philippines, cosponsored by the Rockefeller and Ford Foundations.

Among many agriculturalists, there is euphoria about man's potential for feeding himself for years and even centuries ahead of a kind that has not been seen since the introduction of the potato into Ireland. Reams of prose are being written and conferences held on the potential of the new seeds. The general theme is that now, at last, the chance exists to eradicate hunger from our planet.

[1]Adapted from address given at the symposium, "Man: His Environment, His Future," at North Carolina State University at Raleigh. 25 February 1970.

At the risk of offending some good friends who are writing so hopefully, I say . . . no. The revolution is green only because it is being viewed through green-colored glasses. (Remember the Emerald City in the Wizard of Oz? It could be seen only when you put on a pair of green glasses.) Take off the glasses, and the revolution proves to be an illusion — but devastating in the damage it can do to mankind's tardy efforts to limit the world's horrendous population growth. For optimism about man's ability to feed himself as today's rate of population growth continues is precisely what we do not need and cannot afford in the race with the population bomb.

The Green Revolution, in short, could do us all in — if it worked. The cruel joke is that it does not work.

To many, the Green Revolution is a turning point in man's long war against the biological limitations of the earth. On examination, however, "skirmish" seems a more accurate description. Because, win or lose this round, the final outcome of the war will not be altered.

Here is the "official" U.S. AID story of the Agricultural Revolution in South Asia:

> What has happened in less than three years is revealed in a few statistics . . . overall food production has risen 14 percent in the period 1967-69. And, in South Asia alone — the crucial countries of India and Pakistan — the increase has been 27 percent. AID worked with foundations, universities and others in developing new farming methods, including the most efficient use of "miracle" wheat and rice seeds that have brought about the Green Revolution? (Tollefson 1970)

The statement is misleading for it places all the emphasis on new technology. Consider the following items.

WEATHER

1965 and 1966 were poor weather years for the farmer of South Asia, and the succeeding years have been good. A drought followed by rain will cause a spurt in production with or without new technology! In the last 3 years, India, for instance, has increased her production of barley, chickpeas, tea, jute, cotton, and tobacco by 20 to 30% and did so with no new high-yielding varieties.

Throughout Asia, agricultural yields on virtually all crops are up. Thus, rubber production in West Malaysia was 12% higher last year than the year before. Pakistan's peanut crop is double that of 4 years earlier. Even Red China, which has only recently been reported to have the new high-yielding grains, has been able to perform agriculturally as well as India and the rest of Asia. This has been possible although fertilizer shipments to China have been interrupted (because of the closed Suez Canal and the civil disturbances of the Cultural Revolution).

Far and away the most important factor for increased production is the improvement in weather. But weather seldom gets the credit it deserves. When crops are *poor,* governments blame it on the weather. When crops are *good,* governments take the credit for the foresight and wisdom of providing fertilizer and loans to the farmer and for the clairvoyance of having conducted the research needed to develop improved crop varieties.

Thus, AID, when asking Congress for this year's money, said, "India's current successes in agriculture are largely due to a reappraisal of its agricultural strategy . . . with the help of the United States, the World Bank and other interested agencies and countries, India developed a new strategy which placed top priority on investment in agriculture. . . ."[2]

HIGH-YIELDING VARIETIES

Since the early 1950s, most of the developing world has been increasing its total

[2]Agency for International Development Congressional Presentation, p. H-3, 29 May 1969.

agricultural production and yields per acre. This has been possible through greater use of fertilizer and irrigation, improved varieties, and the opening up of new agricultural land. The concern of most who study the problem is whether or not this increase can continue to keep pace with the growth in population.

Thus, India from 1951 to 1961 was able to increase agricultural production by 46%. This was done partially with new technology but primarily by putting new land into production. As new land became scarce, the increase tapered off. To simply maintain current per capita consumption levels, India must now increase cereal production by three million tons each year (Shertz 1970). If the Green Revolution is to be a reality, production must now grow faster than it has in the past. Bernard Nossiter, whose book on India will be published this fall, has looked at India's grain production figures from 1965 to 1970 and says that the increase "is something less than 2.5 percent. In other words, the 'revolution' has not yet increased food supply at the same rate as the growth in population" (Nossiter 1970).

This does not mean that the new high-yielding wheats in India and Pakistan have not increased production spectacularly. Where irrigated and fertilized, crops have flourished. The same has been true in southeast Asia with rice. But while there is a promise of other crops on which to base a Green Revolution, to date there are only the two: wheat and rice.

The development of the new wheat and rice varieties having high fertilizer response without lodging resulted from imaginative research justifiably meriting recognition. However, the press agent's "miracle" and "wonder" appellation given these cereals distorted out of proportion their impact on the world.

In India, where one-third of Asia's population lives, *only* the new wheats have made an impact. This is unfortunate since in India wheat is a far less important crop than is rice (the production of which is three times that of wheat). Actually, according to a recent study by economic forecaster Louis Bean, the trend in increased rice yields which began in the early 1960s as a result of new technology has leveled off and stagnated at the 1964-65 level. Thus, the "miracle" rice has produced no miracle in India or in East Pakistan, the traditional rice-growing area of that country, although it has done extremely well in West Pakistan, an area not normally recognized as a major rice producer.

In discussing the new rice varieties for India, a recent U.S. Department of Agriculture report ended by saying: "For the immediate future, modest increases in yield from local (i.e., *not* the "miracle" rice) varieties through improved fertilizer use offer the most promise" (Haviland, 1969).

Bean calls it the "Brown and Green Revolution" to underscore its sporadic influence. In India, for instance, a third of the wheat land has been affected, but only 3% of the rice production has been touched, with the rest of the crops escaping its influence.

Irrigation

Irrigation is the life blood of the new cereals. For those who are accustomed to seeing wheat grown only in the United States, where no wheat is irrigated, this point needs to be understood. Virtually all the new wheats in Mexico, India, Pakistan, and Turkey — the areas where they have made an impact — are grown under artificial irrigation. They are grown, then, on the very best land in the nation, the most expensive land, the land which receives the largest capital investment, and the land with the best farmers. In the United States, we consider wheat too low in value to put on irrigated land.

The new rice varieties also require carefully controlled irrigation. In the Philippines, where the new rice is grown under irrigation, harvests are reported as two to three times that of the traditional local varieties. However, on nonirrigated land, the new varieties do no better than the standard ones.

This is important to understand. Ford Foundation's Lowell S. Hardin says that if one looks at a map "the land where this new technology, this Green Revolution, applies is a postage stamp on the face of the earth" (Hardin 1969). The major reason is that, unfortunately, there is very little irrigated land in this world. To expand the current Green Revolution, therefore, will require expanding the amount of irrigated land, an extremely expensive operation. Even with capital, the potential land for irrigation is limited by its location, slope, and availability of water.

The hungry nations have been and are hungry because they have a poor piece of real estate. The soils are too dry, too wet, too rocky, too thin, or too mountainous to fulfill adequately the agricultural needs of the country. A Green Revolution may minimize these disadvantages, but it can never do away with them.

SUBSIDIES

Green Revolution advocates ignore the cost at which wheat and rice production has been achieved in some countries. To understand the role of subsidies, the Department of Agriculture's Director of Economics Don Paarlberg says:

> This is the inescapable fact that a price artificially held above the competitive level will stimulate production, retard consumption and create a surplus. This will be true even if the commodity was originally in deficit supply. Thus a surplus is the result of deliberate intervention in the market. It is the product of human institutions, not simply a consequence of rapid, technological advance. It may or may not be accompanied by a scientific revolution. We could create a surplus of diamonds or ura-

nium or of avocadoes or rutabagas simply by setting the price above where the market would have it and foregoing cost production control. A surplus is not so much a result of technology as it is a result of intervention in the market.[3]

The much-heralded Philippine rice self-sufficiency is a classic example of how Paarlberg's statement applies to the developing world. In 1966, the Philippine Rice and Corn Administration initiated a self-sufficiency program. Within a year, it increased the price support paid for rice by 50%. The support price of corn was also raised but to a lesser degree than rice. Rice production went up. Corn became cheaper to eat than rice, thus more people ate corn — result: a "surplus" of rice in the Philippines. With much fanfare, it was publicized that the Philippines were now able to export rice. Yet this was done at a *loss* because the world market price for rice was less than the government paid the Philippine farmer. In the words of James Keefer of the U.S. Department of Agriculture, the Philippines have "administered self-sufficiency" because they have artificially defined the level of consumption in the country. The nation's people could consume more rice, but the people cannot buy more at the price at which the government pays for it.

While many of the Green Revolution countries not only subsidize in part the price of fertilizer, pesticides, and irrigation water, *all* subsidize the production of the new cereals. Thus, Mexico supports her wheat at $1.99 a bushel or 33% above the world's market price for quality grain; Turkey, at 63%; India and Pakistan, at 100%. But since the quality of the grain from the new miracle cereals is low and they are sold at a discount, the subsidies are, in real terms, significantly higher.

[3]Don Paarlberg. Address before the 12th Annual Meeting of the Agricultural Research Institute, National Academy of Sciences, Washington, D.C., 18 October 1963.

Currently, there is fear of a glut in world cereal markets, but the fear "is largely attributable to expansion of production in the developed world" (Shertz 1970) rather than to any Green Revolution in the hungry nations. The current glut is related to the support policies which all grain-producing nations follow (wheat supports range from $1.40 a bushel in the United States to $4.29 a bushel in Switzerland), policies which are often used as justification for similar subsidies in Asia, Africa, and Latin America. It should be obvious, however, that what a developed nation may do with ease an undeveloped nation might find nearly impossible to do.

The United States will subsidize her farmers with a sum approaching $4 billion this year, but this is in a nation where agriculture generates only 3% of the gross national product. India's agriculture accounts for 49% of her GNP; Pakistan's, for 47%; and the Philippines', for 33%. In these countries, there are not enough other sources of income to generate for long the money needed to subsidize the large agriculture segment of the economy.

It was interesting that the *very* day the House Foreign Affairs Subcommittee was holding its recent symposium on the Green Revolution and repeatedly pointing out to all the attendees the self-sufficiency achieved in rice production by the Philippines, the Philippine Government asked the United States for an advance of $100 million on its 1970 payments (due it for our use of military bases) in order to "stave off the emergency" arising from threatened bankruptcy.

Unfortunately, most of the developing world totters on the brink of bankruptcy with little hope of improving its situation. Within the next few years, the debt service of countries such as Indonesia, India, and Pakistan will equal nearly 50% of their export earnings.

Yet, the new varieties require irrigation water, fertilizer, and additional labor. All are expensive. For the farmer, this means financial risks. For him, risk is justified because of the support price. But, take that crutch away and fewer would take the risk.

With these high support prices, one of two things becomes obvious. Either the farmers are getting rich on the government subsidies or else the new technology is much more costly to use. There are reports of land prices skyrocketing in the area of the Green Revolution, of incipient social revolution with formerly absent landlords returning to farm their land and evicting their tenants. All of this may be true, but to what extent?

My guess is that the best farmers on the best land are profiting substantially from the Green Revolution. But the report that "hundreds of millions of rural people" (Borlaug et al. 1969) are benefiting is open to question.

In 1969, during the wheat harvest, this writer visited Sonora, Mexico, to see the experiment station where the new wheats were developed.

While there, a delegation of wheat farmers from the area left for Mexico City to ask the government to raise still higher their wheat subsidy. This may have been simply a ploy to keep pressure on the government and prevent it from lowering the subsidy. Yet the U.S. Department of Agriculture's Vernon Harness has studied the incomes of these farmers and concluded that the "man with average yields is not making much of a profit." In Sonora, the average wheat farmer made $12.00 an acre while in adjacent Sinaloa, he *lost* $12.00 (Harness 1969).

The U.S. Department of Agriculture's Dana Dalrymple cites two surveys of farmers in the Philippines who decided to stop growing improved rice varieties. Over 50% gave as their reason the "low price or added expenses" while another 10 to 15% said the new rice involved too much additional labor. He also cites a Burmese village which reduced its acreage because of the poor consumer demand for the miracle rice on both the free and black markets. The Burmese wanted to raise the rice if the government would buy the production but not otherwise. Dalrymple says, "It has been widely assumed that the increased returns from growing the new variety have exceeded the cost. Incomes have probably generally been increased in the short run. Yet there is little solid evidence on this point" (Dalrymple 1969).

The Green Revolution and the 1970s

In his book, *Seeds of Change,* Lester Brown has projected a highly hopeful agricultural future because of the Green Revolution. He reflects the opinions of many who feel that "thanks to the breakthrough in the cereal production, the problems of the seventies will be much more political and less technological than were those of the sixties. Their solutions lie more in the hands of politicians, less in the hands of scientists and farmers" (Brown 1970).

Such a view would be correct if the new varieties were as good as the press often suggests. But to overcome the biological limitations imposed by the land on agricultural production will require greater technological breakthroughs in the 1970s than anything we have ever seen. "What we have accomplished so far in the Green Revolution is the easiest part," says Will Meyers, Vice-President of the Rockefeller Foundation (Horne 1969).

The new wheat varieties are essentially a transfer of temperate zone technology to temperate zone areas in Mexico, India, Pakistan, and Turkey. Tropical rice has so far had only limited success. Corn is going to be a more difficult crop with which to work because of its inability to be moved from latitude to latitude.

The "wonder" wheats and "miracle" rice varieties have been quickly accepted in Asia partly because governments encouraged their acceptance. Farmers who grew them were the ones who found loans for fertilizer and pesticides available to them. Governments were encouraged to do this partially out of fright stemming from the crop failures of 1965 and 1966 and partially from the pressure and salesmanship of foreign scientists and aid givers. Already many fear the consequences of this action.

The U.N.'s Food and Agriculture Organization recently held a round-table discussion on the "genetic dangers in the Green Revolution" and concluded that progress in one direction "represents a calamitous loss in the other." Plant breeders unanimously agree that it is dangerous to produce over large areas varieties with similar disease-resistant characteristics. By eliminating the great number of genetically different types of wheat and rice and replacing them with substantially the same variety, there is a loss of variability from which to select resistance to new and still unknown diseases. Speaking of this, Dr. Jack R. Harlan, professor of Plant Genetics at the University of Illinois, says, "The food supply for the human race is seriously threatened by any loss of variability" (Anonymous 1969).

The danger of a disastrous attack by either insect or disease is greatly enhanced when a region is planted to genetically similar varieties. The consequences of this are surely to be seen in the 1970s.

"All across southern Asia (not just India) there has been a rush toward one dominant family of wheats prized for its yielding ability. . . . All of this wheat carries the same kind of rust resistance, which means that if a new race of rust to which it would be especially susceptible were suddenly to appear, much of the wheat crop of that whole vast stretch of the world could be devastated almost overnight."[4]

This is not theory without precedent. In 1946, 30 million acres of U.S. land were

[4]Streeter, Carroll P. 1969. A partnership to improve food production in India. A report from the Rockefeller Foundation.

planted to a new group of oats (two-thirds of the oat crop), all having what was called "Victoria type" resistance to rust. Within 2 years, these oats had virtually disappeared from the country's oat fields. The reason was the emergence of a new disease which had been unknown only 4 years earlier.

In 1950, there was probably no single phase of the plant sciences more highly developed than that related to the control of a disease on wheat known as "stem rust." A strain of that rust (called 15B) had been known and watched in the United States for 10 years. Nevertheless, 15B was able to build up to epidemic levels and, in 1953 and 1954, cause the almost total destruction of our durum-wheat crop. If this were to happen in India today, the results would be disastrous.

Yet a country like India is particularly vulnerable. She has too few technicians to keep track of what is going on in her wheat and rice fields as well as too few scientists to develop new disease-resistant varieties and have them ready when needed. Furthermore, her seed industry cannot quickly multiply a new variety and get it into the hands of the farmer if a crisis arises.

The recent epiphytotics of the developed world involved highly selected crop varieties derived from a narrow genetic base. The hungry world has had a degree of protection against this because of the multiplicity of types found within its unselected crops. However, the sudden introduction and widespread use of the new Mexican wheats and Philippine rice into South Asia shows how quickly this can change.

If the 1970s is to see an agricultural revolution, another problem must be solved: the efficient use of fertilizer and water. Fertilizer is expensive; most countries lack the natural resources to produce it. What the subsidies now do is make it economically possible for the farmer to use the high-cost fertilizer and water required by the new cereals.

Where the Green Revolution is said to exist, it would die tomorrow without any one of its three legs: subsidies, irrigation, and fertilizer. The economics of the developing world make all three legs fragile supports.

Finally, for the Green Revolution to produce a revolution in this coming decade, some way must be found to bring it to the tropics where a majority of the free world's hungry live. Little technological progress has been made with the basic food crops of the tropics, and virtually no aspect of the Green Revolution has reached Africa south of the Sahara or Latin America south of Mexico.

The Danger in the Green Revolution Optimism

Many believe that the Green Revolution has bought time to solve the world's population problem.

To me this hope is premature at best and disastrous at worst.

The potential of the current Green Revolution is too limited to expect it to provide anywhere near adequate time in which to find a solution to the population problem. Bert Tollefson, Assistant Administrator of the Agency for International Development, recently told a campus group that "AID hopes to see a breakthrough similar to the Green Revolution in individual country efforts to control population growth" (Tollefson 1970). Like a litany, our AID officials tell of Taiwan, Hong Kong, Singapore, and South Korea lowering their birth rate without adding that even these prize examples will double, on the average, their population size within 27 years — one year longer than the rest of the developing world!

The 1969 study of India's population by Emerson Foote puts the hungry world's population growth in true perspective. When India began her population control program 17 years ago, her population was growing at the rate of 6 million a year; to-day, it grows at an annual rate of 15 million. If things continue this way, Foote says, the population of India would be one billion in 2000. He continues: "Long before the one billion figure would be reached, the break point would occur . . . it is entirely possible that in India and in other parts of the world for the next three years, five years or even a bit longer, the 'Green Revolution' will increase food production faster than population grows. But if this is the case, it will be a very temporary and misleading solace — only postponing the day of reckoning. . . . (The) growth will be slowed either by rational means or by indescribable catastrophe" (Foot 1969).

Premature hope stemming from the Green Revolution contains two dangers. They are (1) the governments of the hungry nations will once again turn their thoughts away from the No. 1 problem of solving the agricultural and rural problems of their countries and resume their emphasis on pacifying the cities and worshipping the idol of industrialization; (2) of greater danger, however is the likelihood of lessening concern over the exploding world population.

In 1968, at the Second International Conference on the War on Hunger, the Philippine "success" with the Green Revolution (although it was yet to be called the Green Revolution) was a major topic. In fact, the Philippine Undersecretary for Agriculture, Dr. Dioscoro Lopez Umali, came to Washington and brought with him a Philippine farmer who had markedly increased his production through the use of the new "miracle" rice. Before a distinguished audience, Umali translated the farmer's story as he spoke. The farmer had 10 children and said that because of the new high-yielding variety, he and his neighbors would now have enough food for all, and all could enjoy seeing their women in the condition in which they were most beautiful — pregnant. This sudden switch from concern about food shortages to praise for pregnancy was a frightening specter to some of the audience. The Philippino farmer cannot be criticized for waxing poetic over the beauties of his pregnant wife. But some felt that the Undersecretary for Agriculture, with a Cornell University Ph.D., might have suggested the danger such beauties held for his country. The Philippines, which among the world's 15 largest nations has the fastest population growth rate, will double the number of her citizens in 20 years.

Some time earlier, the Rockefeller Foundation's Norman Borlaug, while discussing the impact of the high-yielding varieties said, "It seems likely that through a combination of improvements in conventional and non-conventional food production methods, man can feed the world's mushrooming human population for the next 100-200 years" (Borlaug 1965). More recently, however, he shortened the time to "two or three decades" (Borlaug et al. 1969).

Green Revolution Not Enough

Virtually all authorities accept the fact that if the developing world is to be fed, the purchasing power of its people must be raised. Yield per acre is only part of the equation. *Cost* of production is of equal importance. Even with its highly efficient agricultural productivity, the United States has 5 million citizens who are malnourished because they cannot afford to buy the food they need.

Jean Mayer, President Nixon's Advisor on Food and Nutrition, says that it would take $3.5 billion more than is now being spent to solve the U.S. hunger problem. Much more than just food for the hungry is involved in Dr. Mayer's $3.5 billion figure because food cannot be separated from other problems of poverty. Nevertheless, if such a figure is accurate, think what the cost will be to solve the food needs of the developing world.

In 1967, the President's Science Advisory Committee's report on the "World Food Problem" said that it is meaningless to consider a nation's demand for, and supply of, foodstuffs independently from overall economic growth. That report put a price tag for achieving the goal at approximately $12 billion more a year in external investment than was then going into the hungry nations.

The report of the Commission on International Development to the World Bank (commonly known as the Pearson Report) stated in September, 1969 (when the Green Revolution was already a household phrase among development people) that in order to achieve the goals to which the Commission had addressed itself, foreign assistance must be increased by $10 billion annually during the next 7 years.

The FAO's enormous new Indicative World Plan, which was 6 years in the making and was presented to the Second World Food Conference at The Hague in June, "indicates" what the hungry nations must do. By 1985, the plan says, food demand in developing countries will be nearly two and a half times the level of 1962 (two-thirds of the extra demand will be a consequence of population growth). The FAO plan to meet this food requirement calls for an expenditure of $112 billion ($37 billion alone is required for expanding irrigation!). In the understatement of the decade, the plan says that the need for foreign aid will continue and "is likely to increase."

So, taking your pick among the authorities, you still need from $7 to $12 billion more a year for the developing world to feed its expanding population. Because that part of the world can barely handle its current $3 billion annual debt servicing charges, this extra demand placed on the area's agriculture must come from the developed nations. But such aid to the developing countries is now at a low ebb with no upswing in sight. Without outside financing, the Green Revolution will never get out from behind the barricades.

The conclusion is clear. Current optimism that the world food problem is being solved is premature.

Production Versus Reproduction

Whether the Green Revolution is a fact or a myth, the consequences of an agricultural breakthrough without an accompaning breakthrough in population control are ominous.

To feed today's world population requires the use of agricultural chemicals, the pollutants of which will have a deleterious effect on our children and on their children. But we have seen nothing yet! By 1985, the demand for food in the hungry world will more than double. If the hungry world is to then feed itself, it must increase its use of fertilizers by 100% and pesticides by 600% (President's Science Advisory Committee 1967). Such an inrease in the use of chemicals to feed the projected populations could wreck our environment.

Man has, through the use of his land, turned far more into desert than he has reclaimed through irrigation. Lord Richie Calder says that in the Indus Valley in West Pakistan the population grows at the rate of 10 more mouths to be fed every 5 minutes. In that same 5 minutes in that same place, an acre of land is being lost through water-logging and salinity.

Paul Ehrlich says, "Those clowns who are talking of feeding a big population in the year 2000 from make-believe 'green revolutions' . . . should learn some elementary biology, meteorology, agricultural economics and anthropology."

Today's accelerating rate of population growth is due primarily to the consequences of modern medicine which has lowered the world's death rate without an accompanying lowering of the birth rate.

Rereading the 1936 best seller, *An American Doctor's Odyssey,* is today a disturbing experience. The author, Victor Heiser, tells of activities when he headed the Asian section of the Rockefeller Foundation's International Health Division. In a chapter entitled, "Dividends from Philanthropy" he tells not only of the successful attack on hookworm and other diseases but on the "great progress" achieved by 1934 in upgrading the "backward public health situation of 1914 for which I rejoice to feel the Foundation is largely responsible (this progress) fairly staggers the imagination."

In retrospect, the highly motivated, well-intentioned staff of the Rockefeller Foundation and other similar good Samaritans might well have been advised to slow down the dissemination of modern medicine until Asia's resources could be developed, until educational facilities and agricultural technology could be expanded, *and* some way found to motivate man to limit his population. Herman Kahn, reflecting on the good and bad effects of prematurely bringing modern medicine to a nation says, perhaps only half facetiously, the United States was fortunate to develop her resources before the Rockefeller Foundation began its good works.

Agriculturalists (and this writer is one) too glibly damn modern medicine while striving to do exactly the same thing through improved agricultural technology. More food will certainly mean that more people will live. This will accelerate the population explosion still more. Obviously, without effective population control, an agricultural breakthrough resulting in increased yields might be as detrimental to some countries as was the use of DDT on the malaria-bearing anopheles mosquito.

Perhaps no one, with a clear conscience, can deny a hungry nation the technology for an agricultural revolution. Even if he wanted to, he could not. Today's transistor radio and the jet provide the means for the knowledge and the theft of the new seeds.

However, simultaneously with the release of improved food crop varieties to a hungry nation, an effort must be made to limit that nation's population growth. Not to do so is to ignore history, and he who ignores history, the axiom says, is condemned to relive it. In this case, to relive history is to endure still another spurt in population growth.

Should we then be disappointed that the Green Revolution is neither very green nor very revolutionary? Indeed, is the world ready for a Green Revolution?

Malthus' dismal theorem said, essentially, that if the only check on the growth of population is starvation and misery, then no matter how favorable the environment or how advanced the technology, the population will grow until it is miserable and starves. Kenneth Boulding has, however, what he calls the "Utterly Dismal Theorem." This is the proposition "that if the only check on growth of population is starvation and misery, then any technological improvement will have the ultimate effect of increasing the sum of human misery as it permits a larger proportion to live in precisely the same state of misery and starvation as before the change" (Boulding 1956).

Boulding uses Ireland as an example of this "Utterly Dismal Theorem." In the 17th century, the population of Ireland had come into balance with the carrying capacity of her land. Two million Irish lived there destitute.

Then came the 18th Century truly Green Revolution. The Irish potato was introduced to the Emerald Isle from the Western Hemisphere. Agricultural production shot up. The carrying capacity of the land increased. The Irish multiplied accordingly. By 1835, eight million Irish lived where only two million had lived in the previous century.

Then arrived a totally new plant disease caused by the previously unknown fungus *Phytophthora infestans* and the potato crop was destroyed. In the resulting Irish famines of the 1840s, two million Irish starved to death, two million Irish emigrated, and four million Irish were left on the land in abject poverty.

When there is such a thing as a Green Revolution, its name will be disaster if it arrives ahead of a Population Control Revolution.

EDITOR'S COMMENTS

An important ecological principle discussed in Part I of the text should now be considered in relation to the problem of feeding the present and future people of the world. I am referring to the relationship of ecological complexity to ecological stability. Dr. Paddock explains the significance of this relationship to modern agricultural practices when he refers to the increased chances of sustaining a significant loss to crop diseases when a single variety of plants is used to cover a broad area of agricultural land.

The successful farmer, the one who harvests the largest yield from his crop, strives to maintain a true monoculture (i.e., a crop consisting of a single variety of organism). To attain the highest degree of success he must virtually eliminate all other plants, soil invertebrates, insects, birds, and any other animals or microorganisms which could possibly harm his crop. Such a scheme is, of course, ecologically unsound — it represents the ultimate in ecosystem simplicity. An extensive monoculture is a disaster waiting to happen. Such an ecosystem can be destroyed by a single flaw — such as susceptibility to viruses, insects, floods, or droughts.

Monocultures are unstable for two reasons. The lack of diverse life forms creates a situation which does not respond satisfactorily to change. Relationships are simple in such an ecosystem and is, therefore, unstable. The second reason monocultures are unstable has to do with the crop organisms themselves. High yielding varieties of rice, corn, and wheat are bred in such a way

as to capitalize on the genes responsible for producing large quantities of fruit. This gives us vast expanses of plants having very low genetic diversity. Such plants are all virtually identical twins. This low genetic diversity means that there may not be enough different traits present in the population to successfully combat a new disease organism, a new predator, a flood, or a drought. This is rarely a problem in mature ecosystems. When a new pest or disease appears, individuals are usually present that are resistant or immune — these resistant or immune forms are available because of the genetic variability always present in a natural population. As discussed in Part I, this variability is the stuff from which adaptation or evolution is made.

The dilemma here is somewhat comparable to a man standing on the 50th story ledge of a burning building — if he jumps he will be killed, if he doesn't jump, he will be burned to death. As the human population continues to grow, if we do not practice more and more monoculture surely many people will starve. On the other hand, the practice of more and more monoculture may produce more of an environmental disaster and more starvation than if monocultures had been regulated.

Many optimistic persons point to the oceans thinking that they represent a virtually untapped source of human food. There is certainly a great deal of photosynthesis occurring in marine waters. However, in most of the oceans of the world, the amount of productivity going on will not support the large schools of fish which must be present if man is able to harvest them in adequate numbers. In about 90 percent of the oceans, there is less than than 50 grams (554 grams = one pound) of carbon fixed by primary producers per year per square meter of ocean surface. In shallow coastal waters (depths of less than 500 to 600 feet), the value may go to 100 grams of carbon per square meter per year. This area represents about 7.5 percent of the total ocean surface. About 2.5 percent of the deep areas of the ocean have a productivity comparable to the shallow coastal waters. Productivity in these areas is increased since a number of factors work to bring small amounts of nutrient-rich subsurface water to the surface. In about 1/10 of one percent of the ocean surface, we find that prevailing winds and ocean currents work together to divert surface waters and cause a massive upwelling of deep, nutrient-rich waters. In these areas there may be as much as 11 grams of carbon fixed per day per square meter of water surface. These areas are well-known since they represent the most heavily fished and most productive parts of the ocean. They are found off the coasts of Peru, parts of Africa, California, Somalia, Arabia, and Antarctica. These areas of upwelling average approximately 300 grams of carbon fixed per square meter per year.

If man could somehow harvest and use the primary producers of the sea, we certainly could significantly increase the food available for our tables. Most marine producers (algae) are very small. In much of the ocean, we find that five or six trophic levels are involved in the food chains leading from marine primary producers to man. Referring to our earlier consideration of energy and trophic levels, we see this means that the energy man derives from eating marine fish can represent only .01 to .001 of one percent of the energy initially fixed by the primary producers. This certainly is not a very efficient means of utilizing marine food. Of course, it may be that we will ultimately harvest food from a lower trophic level than that represented by large fish. In regions of upwelling there are as few as two trophic levels from producer to man.

Regions of upwelling represent a total area about the size of California. About one-half of the marine fish harvested today come from these areas comprising about 1/10 of 1 percent of the total ocean surface. The other ½ of the fish harvested comes from shallow coastal waters. It is estimated that the ocean produces 200 to 240 million tons of edible fish per year. Much of this fish is eaten by natural predators (i.e., seals, birds, squid, other fish, etc.). Man can probably harvest about 100 million tons a year and still leave enough fish to guarantee continued maximum breeding success. In 1967 man harvested 60 million tons of fish from the ocean! Man's harvest will probably be over 80 million tons in 1973. Obviously, marine fish cannot and will not solve any of our long-range, future food needs. As a matter of fact, without planning and regulations, the productivity of the oceans could be seriously impaired in the near future by over-fishing — sort of a Kaibab deer story in reverse.

The obvious solution to the world food problem is less mouths to feed. At our present rate of population growth, natural ecosystems are rapidly disappearing as we strive to produce enough food, consumer goods, and living space — something must soon give, since neither food, consumer goods, nor space are infinite.

SOURCES OF ADDITIONAL INFORMATION

HUMAN POPULATION

Bajama, C. J. 1971. The genetic implications of population control. *BioScience* 21(2):71-75.

Baker, J. J. W. 1970. Science, birth control, and the Roman Catholic church. *BioScience* 20(3):143-150.

Barnett, L. D. 1971. Zero population growth, Inc. *BioScience* 21(14):759-765.

Blake, J. 1971. Reproductive motivation and population policy. *BioScience* 21(5):215-220.

Chandrasekhar, S. 1971. India: two must do. *Ecology Today* 1(7):6-8.

Ehrlich, P. R., and A. H. Ehrlich. 1972. *Population, resources, environment.* 2d ed. W. H. Freeman and Co., San Francisco.

Ehrlich, P. R., and J. P. Holdren. 1969. Population and panaceas: a technological perspective. *BioScience* 19(12):1065-1071.

Eisenhower, M., and J. D. Tydings. 1972. A national population policy. *Ecology Today* 1(11):18-20.

Hardin, G. 1968. The tragedy of the commons. *Science* 162:1243-1248.

Hardin, G., ed. 1969. *Population, evolution, and birth control.* 2d ed. W. H. Freeman, San Francisco.

Hulett, H. R. 1970. Optimum world population. *BioScience* 20(3):160-161.

Keyfitz, N., and W. Flieger. 1968. *World population: an analysis of vital data.* University of Chicago Press, Chicago.

Lamson, R. W. 1970. Federal action for population policy — what more can we do now? *BioScience* 20(15):854-857.

McElroy, M. D. 1969. Biomedical aspects of population control. *BioScience* 19(1):19-23.

Odum, E. P. 1971. The optimum population for Georgia. *The Ecologist* 1(9):14-15.

Russell, W. S. 1971. Population and inflation. *The Ecologist* 1(8):4-8.

Taeuber, C. 1972. Population trends of the 1960's. *Science* 176(4036):773-777.

Taylor, C. E. 1970. Population trends in an Indian village. *Scientific American* 223(1):106-114.

Tienhoven, A. van, et al. 1970. Education and the population explosion. *BioScience* 21(1):16-19.

Williamson, F. S. L. 1969. Population pollution. *BioScience* 19(11):979-983.

Wrigley, E. A. 1969. *Population and history.* McGraw-Hill, New York.

Zimmerman, A. 1961. *Catholic viewpoint on overpopulation.* Hanover House, Garden City, New York.

HUMAN FOOD RESOURCES

Aldrich, S. R. 1972. Some effects of crop-production technology on environmental quality. *BioScience* 22(2):90-95.

Boerma, A. H. 1970. A world agricultural plan. *Scientific American* 223(2):54-69.

Borgstrom, G. 1967. *The hungry planet.* rev. ed. Collier Books, New York.

Boyko, H. 1967. Salt-water agriculture. *Scientific American* 216(3):89-96.

Brown, L. R. 1970. Human food production as a process in the biosphere. *Scientific American* 223(3):160-170.

Carlson, C. W., and J. D. Menzies. 1971. Utilization of urban wastes in crop production. *BioScience* 21(12):561-564.

Champagnat, A. 1965. Protein from petroleum. *Scientific American* 213(4):13-17.

Chase, H. P., and H. P. Martin. 1970. Undernutrition and child development. *New England Journal of Medicine* 228(17):933-939.

Dasmann, R. F. 1964. *African game ranching.* Pergamon-Macmillan, New York.

Harpstead, D. D. 1971. High-lysine corn. *Scientific American* 225(2):34-42.

Harris, M. 1972. How green the revolution. *Natural History* 81(6):28-30.

Holt, S. J. 1969. The food resources of the ocean. *Scientific American* 221(3):178-194.

Paddock, W., and P. Paddock. 1967. *Famine 1975.* Little, Brown and Co., Boston.

Pinchaot, G. B. 1970. Marine farming. *Scientific American* 223(6):14-21.

Pirie, N. W. 1967. Orthodox and unorthodox methods of meeting world food needs. *Scientific American* 216(2):27-35.

Pratt, C. J. 1965. Chemical fertilizers. *Scientific American* 212(6):62-72.

Robinson, H. F. 1969. Dimensions of the world food crisis. *Bio-Science* 19(1):24-28.

Ryther, J. H. 1959. Potential productivity of the sea. *Science* 130:602-608.

Ryther, J. H. 1969. Photosynthesis and food production in the sea. *Science* 166:72-76.

Ryther, J. H., et al. 1972. Controlled eutrophication — increase in food production from the sea by recycling human wastes. *BioScience* 22(3):144-152.

Vogl, R. J. 1971. Monotonous monocultures. *Ecology Today* 1(7):43-45.

Wharton, C. 1969. The green revolution: cornucopia or Pandora's box? *Foreign Affairs* 47(3):464-476.

Effects of Urbanization

Calhoun, J. B. 1962. Population density and social pathology. *Scientific American* 206 (2):139.

Davis, K. 1965. The urbanization of the human population. *Scientific American* 213 (3):40-53.

Hammilton, W. F., II., and D. K. Nance. 1969. Systems analysis of urban transportation. *Scientific American* 221(1):19-27.

Herber, L. 1968. *Crisis in our cities.* Prentice-Hall, Inc., Englewood Cliffs, N. J.

Isenberg, I., ed. 1968. *The City in Crisis.* H. W. Wilson, New York.

Lynch, K. 1965. The city as environment. *Scientific American* 213(3):209-219.

Mayer, J., and T. G. Harris. 1970. Affluence: the fifth horseman of the Apocalypse. *Psychology Today* 3(8):43-58.

Means, R. L. 1970. *The ethical imperative: the crisis in American values.* Anchor Books, Garden City, New York.

Milgram, S. 1970. The experience of living in cities. *Science* 167:1461-1468.

Mumford, L. 1961. *The city in history: its origins, its transformations and its prospects.* Harcourt, Brace and World, Inc., New York.

Peck, E. 1971. *The baby trap.* Bernard Geis Associates, New York.

Pirages, D., ed. 1971. *Seeing beyond: personal, social and political alternatives.* Addison-Wesley Publishing Co., Reading, Massachusetts.

Sidenbladh, G. 1965. Stockholm: a planned city. *Scientific American* 213(3):106-118.

Simpson, D. 1968. The dimensions of world poverty. *Scientific American* 219(5):27-35.

Sjober, G. 1965. The origin and evolution of cities. *Scientific American* 213(3):54-63.

Skinner, B. F. 1971. *Beyond freedom and dignity.* Knopf, New York.

Spilhaus, A. 1969. Technology, living cities, and human environment. *American Scientist* 57:24-36.

Srole, L., et al. 1962. *Mental health in the metropolis, the midtown Manhatten study.* Vol. 1. McGraw-Hill, New York.

Tunnard, C., and B. Pushkarev. 1963. *Manmade America: chaos or control?* Yale University Press, New Haven, Connecticut.

Birth Control

Calderone, M. S. 1970. *Manual of family planning and contraceptive practice.* Williams and Wilkins Co., Baltimore.

Culliton, B. J. 1970. Improving mechanical birth control methods. *Science News* 97 (6):121-123.

Guttmacher, A. F. 1966. *The complete book of birth control.* Ballantine Books, New York.

Hall, R. E., ed. 1970. *Abortion in a changing world.* Vol. 1. Columbia University Press, New York.

Holden, C. 1972. Sperm banks multiply as vasectomies gain popularity. *Science* 176 (4030):32.

Kistner, R. W. 1969. *The pill, facts and fallacies about today's oral contraceptives.* Delacorte Press, New York.

Peel, J., and M. Potts. 1969. *Textbook of contraceptive practice.* Cambridge Univ. Press.

Pike, E. 1971. Prostaglandins. *Scientific American* 225(5):84-92.

Tietize, C., and S. Lewit. 1969. Abortion. *Scientific American* 220(1):21-27.

Westoff, L. A., and C. F. Westoff. 1971. *From now to zero: fertility, contraception and abortion in America.* Little, Brown and Co., Boston.

Wood, H. C., Jr. 1967. *Sex without babies.* Whitmore Publishing Co., Philadelphia.

Man of the Future

Augenstein, L. 1968. *Come, let us play god.* Harper and Row, New York.

Dobzhansky, T. 1962. *Mankind evolving.* Yale University Press, New Haven, Connecticut.

Dubos, R. 1965. *Man adapting.* Yale University Press, New Haven, Connecticut.

Dubos, R. 1968. *So human an animal.* Scribner's, New York.

Editors of Time Magazine. 1971. Man into superman: the promise and peril of the new genetics. *Time* Apr. 19, 1971.

Fleming, D. 1969. On living in a biological revolution. *Atlantic Monthly* 223(2):64-70.

Leaf, A. 1970. Social consequences of new developments in medicine. *Bulletin of the Atomic Scientists* 26(1):21-22.

Lerner, I. 1968. *Heredity, evolution, and society.* W. H. Freeman, San Francisco.

Newman, M. Biological adaptation of man to his environment: heat, cold, altitude, and nutrition. *Ann. N. Y. Acad. Sci.,* 91:617-633.

Penrose, L. 1950. Propagation of the unfit. *Lancet* 259:425-427.

Ramsey, P. 1970. *Fabricated man: the ethics of genetic control.* Yale Univ. Press, New Haven, Connecticut.

Sinsheimer, R. L. 1969. The prospect for designed genetic change. *American Scientist* 57:134-142.

Sonneborn, T. M., ed. 1965. *The control of human heredity and evolution.* Macmillan, New York.

Part III

Air and Water:
The Not-So-Infinite
Resources

Air Conservation and the Kinds of Air Pollutants

The Chairman of the Air Conservation Commission is Dr. James P. Dixon, President of Antioch College.

Introduction

The initial evolution of man took place in an environment that, whatever its other hazards, was characterized by the virtually unlimited availability of what we now refer to as "pure air." That is, man's respiratory apparatus was evolved to breathe a mixture of nitrogen, oxygen, water vapor, and small traces of carbon dioxide, the rare gases, and a few other simple substances. Although there were natural outbreaks of pollution from volcanoes and the like, the usual response was migration; there was not enough preference for one area over another to hold a tribe in an uncomfortable location. Then mankind began to build or seek shelter for itself, and discovered the use of fire — the deliberate release of stored energy to modify the local environment.

The discovery of how to control fire also marked the start of air pollution. As tribes settled in villages, and villages grew into cities, the levels of concentration of the combustion products, and of the other by-products of human living, increased. This early urbanization was accompanied by the first evidences of industrialization, which further added to the general pool of atmospheric substances to which man was not genetically accustomed. However, since the average human life span was only a few decades, the slow chronic workings of airborne toxicants probably did not have time to seriously affect the human system before death claimed it.

The past century has seen a radical change in man's existence. Improvements in nutrition, agriculture, communication, hygiene, and medicine have extended the human life span tremendously. During this same period, improvements in heating methods and standards of sanitation were so great that the level of insult to the organism probably decreased substantially. As industry continued to introduce new substances into the air, it also put into effect improved industrial hygiene practices, which further decreased the exposure of the individual to high concentrations of many toxic materials.

This environmental improvement, however, much as it may have ameliorated con-

Reprinted with the permission of the chairman and the AAAS from the summary of the commission's report, pages 23-36 in *Air Conservation*. AAAS Publication No. 80. Washington, D. C. Copyright © 1965 by the American Association for the Advancement of Science.

ditions inside homes and factories, was accomplished in most cases by removing the objectionable substances to the outside air. This process, accompanied by rapid industrial development and concentration, began producing, in the outdoor air of the cities, the phenomena that had previously occurred indoors. There were even a few catastrophic, acute pollution episodes, such as the one at Donora, Pennsylvania.

Meanwhile, increasing population and increasing longevity, together with a high standard of living, generated pressure from all population groups for cleaner air. The youngest, the oldest, and those whom medicine had spared without fully curing make up groups who are especially sensitive to pollutants. The younger adults, with long lives ahead, object to any threat to longevity. All ages and conditions have become intolerant of discomfort and annoyance.

Finally, the enormous increase in world population now taking place, an increase apparently destined to continue, raises an entirely new kind of problem. The oxygen in our atmosphere is not a permanent feature, but is rather the result of a delicate balance between its formation in the photosynthetic process and its removal by animals, by combustion, and principally by the slow oxidation of minerals on the earth's surface. This balance completely renews the oxygen supply in the atmosphere in the course of a very small number of millenia. A change of a few percent in the rate of either production or removal could well result in an enoromus change in the steady oxygen level.

Although it is unlikely that man or his machines could "breathe" enough oxygen to seriously contribute to upsetting this balance, he could, either through nuclear war or through sheer numbers, destroy enough green plants to seriously decrease the renewal rate of atmospheric oxygen. At present there are no data on which to base a quantitative statement; however, the possibility seems very real. It has also been

postulated that the amount of carbon dioxide that human activities are injecting into the atmosphere may be sufficient to upset the global balance.

These considerations suggest that the time has come for man to stop regarding the atmosphere as unlimited and to undertake its conservation.

It may be worthwhile at the outset to restate the fundamental nature of atmospheric pollution. All creatures live by a process of converting one form of energy into another. Man has raised himself above the animal level to the extent that he deliberately converts this energy by processes outside the limitations of his body. All extensions of the human senses, of the human frame, and of the human muscle, which is to say, our tools and the trappings of civilization, use this energy. Energy conversion has certain material by-products. When they become airborne, in sufficient concentrations to be troublesome to man, we call the resulting airborne material "air pollution." At a very high stage of technology, pollution may also occur from by-products of processes other than the liberation of energy, but they are seldom as widespread as the energy by-products.

Some material by-products from this process of energy conversion are inevitable. The only choices are the relative proportions of the various by-products and the way in which they will be removed. Nothing is gained by removing them from the air if we thereby pollute the waters of nearby streams and make them unusable, or contaminate the soil to the extent that it will not support vegetation. In some respects, the problem resembles the old one of attempting to bury a pile of dirt.

In order to obtain an optimum balance of benefit and risk for ourselves and for our posterity, the problem of air conservation is to select the appropriate means for either disposing of or using these by-products and to employ appropriate forms of energy. The definition of such an optimum — the risks we are prepared to take for the benefits we enjoy — is not a matter of scientific judgment, but rather one of moral and ethical judgment; hence, it will not be discussed here. Mankind will probably face enough moral decisions during the next decade to keep occupied; probably the precise setting of an optimum balance will not receive a great deal of attention. However, mankind must ultimately make such a decision; it must decide what the balance of risk and benefit will be. We cannot abandon our technology without relapsing into savagery. But we cannot continue our present course of technological development without the risk of making the earth unfit for human habitation.

The Pollutants

The sources, then, of air pollutants are anywhere that energy is converted under human direction. From the smallest hearth fire to the latest factory, all contribute their share. The pollutants are even greater in number than the sources. However, a small number of groups of substances comprise the vast bulk of human emissions to the atmosphere and they have been singled out for special attention in this report.

The greatest single product of the energy conversion processes is of least concern here — water. Only in very rare instances can it qualify as a pollutant. Occasionally, the vapor from the stack of a large factory may reduce visibility on a nearby highway. But normally, water vapor does not represent an air pollution problem.

GASES

Carbon dioxide. Carbon dioxide is next in quantity of the waste products produced by our use of organic fuels. It is naturally abundant in the atmosphere, and mankind is well adapted to living with widely varying levels of it. However, while water vapor precipitates out of the atmosphere to join the oceans, carbon dioxide normally remains in a gaseous state for a long time. The liberation of this gas has been so great that we have already increased the global concentration by a substantial figure. This increase has had no effect on any known living organism. However, carbon dioxide is intimately involved in the mechanism that maintains the overall temperature of the earth. Although so many factors are involved in this overall atmospheric heat balance that it is impossible to evaluate the effect of any given increase in atmospheric carbon dioxide, a continued increase over a long period could possibly change the global climate. And, if such a change were to involve an increase of the earth's temperature, thereby causing a large portion of the global ice caps to melt and the oceans to rise, available land area would be reduced at precisely the time when more land is needed for an increasing population. In the light of this possibility, the use of fossil fuels as the principal source of our energy should be continually evaluated.

Carbon monoxide. The complete combustion of carbonaceous fuels produces carbon dioxide; the incomplete combustion, characteristic of many processes involving the conversion of energy, yields carbon monoxide. In American cities, the primary source of this gas is the automobile. Carbon monoxide begins to be hazardous to most human beings at concentrations of about 100 parts per million (ppm) if experienced over a period of several hours. Particularly susceptible individuals may be affected at lower levels. Although the toxic level seems very high when compared with other pollutant gases, this level has actually been reached occasionally in areas where traffic is heavy; more frequent occurrences may be expected unless automotive emissions can be effectively controlled.

Sulfur dioxide. In addition to substances emitted in massive amounts, there are a variety of materials that normally occur in much lower concentrations. However, these materials are much more toxic. Sulfur dioxide and the sulfuric acid that forms when the gas comes in contact with air and water seldom reach levels above a few parts per million. However, the present consensus is that these two substances have been principal factors in all the air pollution disasters of recent history, including the London smog of 1952 in which some 4000 persons died. (There are many scientists who believe that factors as yet undiscovered contributed materially to these deaths, but most of them would identify sulfur dioxide and sulfuric acid as the major causative agents, perhaps combined with soot or other particles.) Sulfur dioxide results primarily from the combustion of coal or oil, both of which contain substantial percentages of sulfur in various chemical forms. To some extent in the combustion itself, and to a greater extent in the external atmosphere, sulfur dioxide is converted by the action of atmospheric oxygen and water to sulfuric acid. Sulfur dioxide by itself is extremely irritating to the upper respiratory tract in concentrations of a few parts per million. Sufuric acid appears as a fine mist that can be carried deep into the lungs to attack sensitive tissues. In addition, droplets of sulfuric acid carry absorbed sulfur dioxide far deeper into the system than the free gas alone could penetrate, thus spreading the effect of this irritant over the entire respiratory tract. On the other hand, because of the ease with which sulfur dioxide is converted into sulfuric acid and sulfates, its lifetime in the atmosphere is seldom more than a few days. Consequently, it would not be expected to accumulate in the atmosphere.

Hydrogen sulfide. Hydrogen sulfide can result from a variety of industrial and other processes, but it usually enters the atmosphere as a result of the accumulation of industrial wastes in stagnant waters. Here bacterial action reduces the sulfur-containing compounds to hydrogen sulfide, which is relatively insoluble in water. It has the well-known odor of rotten eggs and it is highly objectionable. In high concentrations, it is also rapidly lethal. However, there are only a few cases in which concentrations of hydrogen sulfide in the open atmosphere exceeded the level of mere nuisance. (In one such case, a score of deaths resulted from an accidental release from a refinery in Poza Rica, Mexico.) The bacterial processes described constantly occur in nature, and by far the bulk of the total sulfur found in the atmosphere comes from natural causes. However, concentrations at any one place are usually not sufficient to be detected by the senses, or, in fact, by any but the most delicate measuring devices.

Nitrogen oxides. There are six known oxides of nitrogen, and there is presumptive evidence for a seventh. However, only two are normally considered as pollutants: nitric oxide and nitrogen dioxide. These are what might be called "status symbol" pollutants. Only a highly mechanized and motorized community, is likely to suffer serious pollution from them. Nitric oxide, the primary product, is formed when combustion takes place at a sufficiently high temperature to cause reaction between the nitrogen and oxygen of the air. Such temperatures are reached only in highly efficient combustion processes or when combustion takes place at high pressure. A great deal of nitrogen is fixed in the latter way in automobile cylinders. Electrical power plants and other very large energy-conversion processes will also fix nitrogen in this fashion. However, in most cities, automobiles are the largest single source.

Nitric oxide is generally emitted as such into the atmosphere. However, a complex of processes, some of them photochemical in nature, may convert a substantial portion of the nitric oxide to nitrogen dioxide, a considerably more toxic gas and the only important and widespread pollutant gas that is colored. As a result, nitrogen dioxide can significantly affect visibility. Nitrogen oxides are also liberated from a variety of chemical processes, such as in the manufacture of guncotton and nitric acid. In large-scale pollution, these sources are usually less significant than the broad area source represented by vehicular traffic.

Ozone. There is little or no ozone emitted as such into the atmosphere. However, this gas, which is extremely toxic, is formed in the atmosphere on sunny days as a result of the interaction of nitrogen oxides with certain organic compounds.

Hydrogen fluoride. In addition to the inorganic gases just mentioned, nearly any other objectionable inorganic gaseous material that is used in industry can become a pollutant if it escapes into the atmosphere. However, these are not the general emissions of what might be called the metabolic processes of civilization and they are likely to be restricted to a few locations. Consequently, only one of them, hydrogen fluoride, deserves separate attention. Because of its extreme toxicity for some living organisms, it is likely to be an acute problem wherever materials containing fluorides are processed. Hydrogen fluoride is apparently taken up from the air by nearly all plants, and certain species are damaged by concentrations as low as 1 part per billion. Furthermore, since vegetation tends to concentrate the fluoride that it receives, continuing low atmospheric levels of fluoride can produce toxic levels in forage and probably in some leafy vegetables as well. The manufacture of phosphate fertilizer, the smelting of certain iron ores, and the manufacture of aluminum are all sources of hydrogen fluoride gas as well as of some particulate fluoride.

Organic gases. The organic gases are very numerous. The chemical process industries inevitably release into the atmosphere some of almost everything they manufacture. However, only a few general classes need separate consideration since a number of the organic materials that can be identified in the atmosphere appear to have no adverse effects.

Probably the simplest organic substance significant to air pollution is ethylene. Aside from its participation in the "smog" reaction, it is a potent phytotoxicant (plant damaging agent) in its own right. Concentrations of a few parts per billion, for example, are extremely damaging to orchids, and only slightly higher concentrations adversely affect the growth of tomatoes. Ethylene, like the bulk of other simple hydrocarbons, emanates in part from industrial sources, but it is primarily a product of automotive exhaust.

The higher members of the series to which ethylene belongs, the olefins, appear to have no direct effect upon vegetation or animal life. However, when they (together with several other classes of organics) are exposed to sunlight in the presence of nitrogen dioxide or nitric oxide, an extremely complex reaction sequence ensues. The end products appear to be ozone, aldehydes, and a variety of organic compounds that contain nitrogen. In adequate concentrations, this mixture injures plants and irritates the eyes and mucous membranes in human beings. There is some indication that animals are also affected. This reaction was first noticed in Los Angeles, and is therefore popularly referred to as the "Los Angeles smog reaction." The substances needed for this reaction can be produced by the right combinations of industries, but they are present in almost ideal concentrations in automotive exhaust. Consequently, the presence of this type of pollution is characteristic of areas having a high density of automobile traffic.

Some of the aldehydes characteristic of the Los Angeles smog can also arise from other sources. Formaldehyde and acrolein, which are particularly irritating to the eyes and nose, are found in the smoke of poorly operating incinerators and also in stockyards and a number of other sources.

Mercaptans, which are organic substances related to hydrogen sulfide, are among the most odorous materials known. Aside from chemical processes that directly employ or produce these compounds, they are undesired by-products of Kraft paper mills and of some petroleum refineries.

Finally, there is a large class of organic vapors generally referred to as "solvents." They escape from such processes as dry cleaning and painting. They are very diverse chemically, and some of them can probably participate in the smog reaction. Others have objectionable odors. Most of them are toxic to some degree, although it would be difficult to produce toxic concentrations over any period of time in the open air.

PARTICULATE MATTER

Aside from these gases and vapors, large quantities of more or less finely divided particulate matter are put into the air or are formed there as a result of human activities. The largest single particle in nearly all urban atmosphere is dust. This word is used here to denote soil from areas denuded of vegetation, whipped up by natural wind, by the passage of vehicular traffic, or by agricultural activities. For the most part it is without physiological effect, but it is a very substantial nuisance. The particle sizes are usually large, so that, under most circumstances, such dust will not travel great distances. Obvious exceptions occur during times of high winds, as was demonstrated during the dust storms of the middle 1930s.

In many cities, the next most prevalent substance among the airborne particles is soot. Soot is very finely divided carbon clumped together into long chains and networks. Because the individual particles are so fine, they present an enormous surface per unit weight. This surface is extremely active, and it can absorb a large variety of substances from its environment. Soot generally carries with it a substantial load of heavy hydrocarbons that are formed si-

multaneously with it in smoky flames. These hydrocarbons include organics that are either known or are suspected causes of environmental cancer on sufficiently prolonged contact. Soot can also act under some circumstances in the same manner as sulfuric acid mist; that is, it can absorb vapors that would normally be removed in the upper respiratory tract and carry them deep into the lungs. In addition to all known or suspected physiological effects, soot is a nuisance because it obscures visibility and soils buildings and clothing. The fall of combined soot, dust, and other particulate materials on a single square foot of horizontal surface in a city may easily exceed a pound per year.

Another variety of fine particles is one of the end results of the photochemical smog reaction. The nature of the particulate matter formed is not understood, but it is oily, not easily wetted, and of a size that is highly effective in obscuring visibility.

The typical urban atmosphere also contains particles caused by practically every process carried on within the city. There are lead salts from the combustion of leaded gasoline and particles of airborne ash from all the solid and liquid fuels burned in the area. The metallurgical industries, the manufacture of fertilizer, the storing of grain, and the milling of flour all add particles that are characteristic of their own processes.

Finally, there is a quantity of material generally referred to as "resuspended matter," refuse dropped into the streets or onto the ground, there to be slowly pulverized and blown into the air. Bits of newspaper, residue of plant matter, particles of glass and tire rubber, all go to make up the complex found suspended in the atmosphere of a typical city.

There are two additional classes of particulate matter which, while not of peculiarly urban origin, have had a substantial impact on human well-being and have received a great deal of attention recently. The first of these are the economic poisons. They include insecticides, herbicides, and other chemicals used by man. A number of them are normally disseminated through the air, and some portion may well find its way substantial distances from the intended site of application. While many of them are toxic to man, they can also harm other forms of life not intended as their targets.

The second category is radioactive material. There are three major sources of radioactive gases and particles. The first is research, which is generally not an important source of contamination except in the case of a major accident. The second is nuclear power plants, which almost continuously give off some gaseous materials. There is no evidence to date that their accumulation in the atmosphere is a major hazard. The nuclear power industry is said to be one of the most carefully controlled of all industries on the face of the earth. However, an accidental discharge can distribute highly toxic concentrations over a rather large area. The final source is, of course, nuclear weapons. They belong in a special category, not because of any chemical or physiological difference in the compounds involved or in their effects, but because the political and economic considerations that govern their use are so special.

Transport of Pollutants

Once a pollutant, or a group of pollutants from a given source, has been ejected into the air, its movement with the air will depend upon a number of factors.

Particles larger than approximately 1 micron are significantly affected by gravity. They tend to settle out from the air and are eventually deposited, the distance from the source usually depending on the size of the particle. In addition to gravity, the movement of pollutants is affected by turbulent diffusion. The wind contains many eddies, ranging in size from millimeters to miles, and these eddies tend to disperse the cloud of pollutants.

Less important over short distances, but of crucial importance on a large scale, are the effects of aggregation and growth. Particles in a pollution cloud tend to increase in size, sometimes by collisions that form larger aggregates, and sometimes by the condensation of vapors on them, with or without chemical reaction. This process may occur in and under water clouds, where the water droplets may form on the particles, thereby increasing their size, or falling raindrops may collide with the particles, thereby carrying them to the ground.

At substantial wind speeds, pollutants are rapidly removed from the point of origin and turbulent diffusion usually dilutes them below the level of significant effect within a short distance. However, under some conditions, turbulence can bring the plume from a stack to the ground in great loops at a point quite close to the source and before extensive dilution has occurred, resulting in brief exposure to extremely high concentrations. Thus, a period of strong winds is likely to be characterized by low mean values of pollutants, with occasional high peaks of short duration near the point of origin. When the air is still, both horizontally and vertically, all pollutants tend to stay near their source and to blend in slowly with other sources in the same area. Generally the result is a very high average level of pollution with a few abrupt short-term variations.

While the horizontal travel of pollutants is largely controlled by wind velocity, the primary factor that regulates the vertical dispersal of pollution is the vertical profile of temperature. The rate of temperature change with height is referred to as the "lapse rate." In the lower atmosphere the temperature usually decreases with increasing height.

A substantial amount of misinformation has been disseminated concerning the effect of lapse rate on pollution. The facts are rather simple. According to well-established physical law, if a parcel of air is carried from a low altitude to a high one, it will expand with the decreasing pressure and its temperature will decrease, provided there is no exchange of heat with its surroundings. By the same token, if the parcel of air is taken to a lower altitude without gaining or losing heat, its temperature will increase. For a given change of altitude, the corresponding temperature change is constant and determinable. This rate of change is referred to as the "adiabatic lapse rate."

If the actual lapse rate is greater than this theoretical rate, a parcel of surface air that begins to rise will continue to do so. This situation is called "unstable." If, on the other hand, the change in temperature with height is less than the adiabatic rate, surface air that begins to rise will tend to sink back to the surface; this is called a "stable" lapse rate. If there is no change in temperature with altitude, or an increase, the atmosphere will be particularly stable. The difference between this and the unstable situation is one of degree, not of kind. An increase in temperature with altitude, a so-called inversion, is not a unique phenomenon.

During unstable conditions, there is a great deal of vertical mixing, in addition to whatever horizontal dispersion the wind may induce, and so the dilution of pollutants takes place in three dimensions. On the other hand, under conditions of high stability, vertical dispersion will be greatly inhibited; if this is accompanied by low winds, a layer of highly polluted air may build up over a large area, such as an entire city or an entire basin.

Shifts from stable to unstable conditions and back are set in motion by three major forces. Since winds tend to have vertical eddies, and since rapid vertical air motions tend to be adiabatic, the wind helps to establish a precisely adiabatic lapse rate. The sun, by heating the surface more than the air, tends to steepen the lapse rate and thus acts as a force for instability. Conversely, at night the ground loses more heat by radiation than the air does, which tends to make the surface colder than the layer overlying it. This cooling of the ground is a force working for stability. Under most circumstances, there is a continuous diurnal cycle from stability to instability and back. When, for a variety of reasons, this cycle is broken, a serious accumulation of pollutants is possible.

The Fate of Pollutants

For virtually every known pollutant, there are natural processes that tend to remove it from the atmosphere, thus preventing man from smothering in his own by-products.

Reference was made earlier to the tendency of particulate pollutants to coagulate, to increase in size, and to fall. Rain and snow carry large amounts of both particulate and gaseous pollutants out of the atmosphere and into the soil and the water of the earth. Trees and grasses act like the fibers of an enormous filter mat to collect particles and some gases.

The oxygen of the air combines with many pollutants, either directly or indirectly, gradually changing them into forms that are more readily removed. In many cases, sunlight plays a role in this reaction, and frequently particulate matter is formed from gases. These particles can then enter the cycle of filtration, aggregation, and washout, and can thus be removed from the atmosphere. It is worth noting that the droplets of sulfuric acid that have been implicated by many as contributing to the death toll in London, and the photochemical smog that is characteristic of the West Coast, are actually steps in the atmosphere's own process of self-purification. The misfortune is that these intermediate products are physiologically active and that they frequently form in heavily inhabited areas.

A few miscellaneous substances do not participate rapidly enough in the reactions of photochemical oxidation to be removed by that process. The outstanding examples are methane and a few of its relatives and carbon monoxide. They are ultimately destroyed by oxidation, entirely in the gas phase, and become carbon dioxide, although the rate of destruction is not known. Carbon dioxide appears to be removed effectively by direct solution in the ocean, the disposal point for most of the soluble inorganic substances. The capacity of the ocean to ultimately consume such materials by dilution is enormous. However, our rapid production of carbon dioxide seems to be outstripping the ocean's ability to remove it from the atmosphere. It appears that roughly one-third of the carbon dioxide put into the air by combustion remains there and, as noted earlier, it may have an effect on the world's weather.

Thus, the atmosphere has tremendous powers to dilute, disperse, and destroy a large variety of substances that man, for one reason or another, elects to discharge into it. Pollution occurs when these processes cannot keep up with the rate of discharge, and when this happens, only one more factor is needed to constitute pollution — a susceptible receptor, such as man.

Man removes some of the pollutants from the air, for if he did not, the pollutants would not affect him. (The only exception is when pollution is manifested by loss of visibility. This can have economic repercussions in delaying aircraft schedules, in increasing automobile accidents, and by making a location less favorable to paying tourists, or its effect may be purely aesthetic.)

Pollutants collect on, and may affect, buildings, plants, and animals, including man. They enter the lungs of creatures that breathe the air. With the pollution density of the atmosphere increasing rapidly, the possibility of any pollutant leaving the atmosphere without contacting man, his property, plants, or animals is becoming increasingly small. Although it is certainly necessary to use the atmosphere as one of the places to dispose of our wastes, it is going to become more and more difficult to find a parcel of air that can be used for waste disposal and that can adequately detoxify its load of pollutants before it is needed again.

EDITOR'S COMMENTS

Air pollution existed prior to man. Since the beginning of geological time, various natural phenomena resulted in the production of vast quantities of airborne materials. Even now the release of volcanic ash and dust may affect the earth's atmosphere in such a way as to change the earth's climate. However, only since man learned to burn fuels has he directly contributed to air pollution. In the beginning, man's use of fuels primarily produced local effects. As man's numbers increased, and as his fuel-based technology grew, local air pollution spread to become worldwide.

Today the problem of air pollution demands, and is receiving, legislative attention in many countries. In the United States certain laws intended to "clean up the air" have been enacted. By 1975, new cars are to emit 90 percent less hydrocarbons than in 1970, and 90 percent less nitrogen oxides than in 1971. Similar laws must soon govern the emission of harmful airborne substances from all sources.

At this time there are serious questions as to whether the presently proposed air quality standards can actually result in an improvement of air quality. For example: Will the air pollution devices on new cars operate efficiently over a long period of time? Will they be properly serviced? Will a continued increasing demand for energy cause an increase in total air pollution even with enforced emission standards? Demand for electricity in the United States doubles each 8 to 10 years. It is estimated that sulfur dioxide emissions from the power industry (with today's emission standards in effect) will increase two to three times by the year 2000! As our technology and our numbers continue to grow, we will have to continue to run twice as fast just to stay in the same place.

It is impossible to accurately predict where we are headed in terms of controlling air pollution and in terms of what the final effects of air pollution will be. It is clear that air pollution affects ecosystems. Until now the observed primary effects have been the poisoning of certain plants. (The city of Los Angeles recently began to replace air pollution-killed trees and ornamentals along streets with artificial plants.) Animals are certainly affected by many components of industrially polluted air; however, these ecosystem effects are not well-understood at this time. The effects of air pollution on human health are beginning to be accurately documented and will be summarized later. Air pollution may also affect the world's climate. A brief description of these effects follows in the next few paragraphs.

The heat received by the earth's surface must be dissipated or the surface would grow hotter and hotter. Heat is absorbed only by that portion of the earth's surface which is exposed to sunlight; however, the entire earth's surface radiates heat into space. Several factors could affect this relationship of heat absorbed to heat lost. We can assume that the intensity of solar radiation will remain virtually unchanged — there is little we could do if it were to change. If man's technological activities were to increase the earth's ability to absorb solar radiation, or decrease its ability to lose heat by radiation, the earth will grow warmer. On the other hand, if man causes the earth to absorb less of the sun's heat, or if heat

radiation is accelerated, the earth will become cooler. It seems now that air pollution might ultimately cause either one of these — a cooler or a warmer earth.

Most of the sun's heat is absorbed at, or near, the ground since clean air is nearly transparent to wavelengths of solar energy. As this energy is absorbed, much of it is converted to heat. The heat thus formed is represented by infrared radiation. The presence of water vapor, clouds, and carbon dioxide in the air prevents the outward radiation of most of this heat — causes the air to be quite opaque to infrared radiation. If it were not for this opaqueness of our air to infrared radiation, temperatures on the earth's surface would be much lower than those now experienced. This tendency to "trap" heat at, or near, the earth's surface is referred to as the "greenhouse effect."

It is a well-known fact that the earth's mean annual temperature has undergone minor changes during the past 100 years. Some researchers link these fluctuations to sunspot activity and theorize that such activity results in changes in the intensity of solar radiation. An increase of 1 percent in solar intensity would raise the earth's mean temperature by about 1½ degrees. However, other factors could also play roles in the observed temperature changes: dust in the air, amout of cloud cover, extensiveness of snow and ice coverage, and type of vegetation can all affect the absorption or radiation of solar energy. An increase in snow, ice, clouds, or dust makes the earth a brighter planet. An increase in brightness means an increase in the amount of sunlight being reflected. This sunlight is never absorbed, and thus the earth will become cooler. An increase of 1 percent in the reflectivity of the earth would lower its mean temperature about 3 degrees.

We can now begin to see why air pollution may change the earth's mean temperature in either direction. Increases in carbon dioxide and water vapor increase the atmosphere's opaqueness to infrared radiation and will cause warming of the earth's surface. On the other hand, dust, other particulates, smoke, and clouds increase the atmosphere's reflectivity which results in the cooling of the earth's surface.

From 1880 to 1940, the mean temperature of the earth rose nearly 1 degree. The question of whether this change represents a change in solar intensity or a change in absorbative and reflective characteristics of the earth's surface and/or atmosphere is not known. These factors cannot yet be measured this precisely.

Since 1940, the earth seems to have cooled by a quarter of a degree. However, sunspot activity and carbon dioxide content of the air have continued to rise during this time. It seems that air pollution has had a "double" effect on the earth's temperature. Prior to 1940, the net effect of air pollution may have been to decrease the rate at which surface heat escaped, thus causing a warming trend. Perhaps at about 1940, the balance swung in the other direction. In other words, at about this time air pollution may have added sufficient quantities of particulate matter to the air to negate the "greenhouse effect" produced by the build up of carbon dioxide. Thus the beginning of a cooling trend would result as more and more solar radiation was reflected from the atmosphere before it could reach the earth's surface and be converted to heat.

Within the past 100 years, the mean temperature changes experienced by the earth have had little effect on man or on his life-support systems. It is easy to see, however, that we can withstand only minor changes in the mean annual temperature. An increase of only a few degrees would melt the polar ice caps and inundate the world's largest cities and most valuable farm lands. A decrease of only a few degrees would herald the beginning of a new ice age.

The following few figures will help emphasize the magnitude of air pollution in the United States. In 1970, approximately 210 million tons of air pollutants were released. An estimated 91 million tons were from cars, trucks, buses, trains, etc. Of this 91 million tons, 64.5 million tons consisted of carbon monoxide; 17.6 million tons were hydrocarbons, and 7.6 million tons were nitrogen oxides. Transportation was the largest single source of these three pollutants. The largest single source of particulates and sulfur oxides was from the combustion of fuel by stationary sources (9.2 and 22.9 million tons, respectively). Even forest fires contributed an estimated 17.3 million tons to the total.

The control and the ultimate reduction of air pollution must be accomplished within the next few decades. This may be achieved in one of two ways: decrease the total need for energy, or render pollutants harmless at their source by either "trapping" them or by chemical treatment which would convert them to harmless substances. It is improbable that our demand for energy will decrease in the foreseeable future. It is obvious that it will have to level off eventually; however, as long as population increases and as long as living standards are based on a continued increase in the consumption of consumer products, the demand for energy will rise. This means that during the time required for governments to realize that infinite increase in population, energy, and gross national product is an absurd dream, we will have to depend on the relatively new technology directed toward air pollution control at the source. Once population and economy have stabilized, we can hope that this technology will allow us to actually reduce air pollution.

JOHN MACINKO

The Automobile and the Environment

John Macinko is an enginer on the staff of
the University of Colorado. Previously he had
been employed as a Project Engineer in
Cryogenics, and has a number of publications
in that field. His major interest in the environmental field is with automotive developments
and he is a member of the Board of Directors
of several environmental organizations.

Introduction

Although transportation accounts for only
20 percent of total U.S. energy use, it results
in 60 percent of all air pollution nationwide, and as much as 90 percent in urban
areas where air pollution controls on stationary sources are enforced. But even the 60
percent figure is conservative, since it only
includes pollutants emitting directly from the
transportation vehicles themselves. Transportation also has indirect contributions
from the wastes resulting from extraction
and processing of fuel and iron ore, the
manufacture of automobile parts and accessories, the automobile assembly plants,
and the disposal of scrap automobiles. When
these indirect contributions to air pollution
are included, transportation's share would
more likely be 80 percent of the total.

Analysis by individual pollutants shows
the internal combustion engine to be the
major source of carbon monoxide, the hydrocarbons, and the oxides of nitrogen. In
recent years there has been mounting evidence that lead from the high compression
engines and asbestos from brake drums are
reaching dangerous levels in the air we
breathe.

But the environmental effects of the
automobile do not stop with air pollution.
The automobile is also the vector by which
man has brought about urban deterioration
in the form of freeways, parking lots, sign
advertising, and noise. Natural systems have
been permanently disrupted by high-speed
highways, bridges and suburban sprawl. Discarded automobile bodies litter the countryside and tax the abilities of solid waste
disposal systems. And last, but perhaps most
significant, there is the problem of the
rapid rate of depletion of exhaustible resources, primarily iron and petroleum — a
problem which neither industry, government,
nor the public has been willing to face.

Proposed solutions to the automobile
problem should take advantage of present
environmental concern and offer a total
system which would not only reduce air

Reprinted by permission of the author. An article
based on a lecture given in an interdisciplinary
seminar titled "Environment and Public Policy"
and adapted especially for this text.

pollution but reduce resource depletion rates, eliminate the problem of discarded automobile hulks, and halt the urban deterioration directly attributable to automobile use. This means that the automobile as we now use it and the automobile as we now know it must change.

Causes

Since the automobile has been around for more than a half century, one may ask why it is that the automobile has become such a serious environmental threat during the past two decades. There are numerous causes and the most significant should be mentioned: First is the increasing population, the common denominator of most environmental problems. Second is the increase in affluence which has increased the number of automobiles per capita as well as increased the use of the automobile in the conduct of our daily activities. Third is the migration to the urban areas causing increased automobile densities and traffic congestion. Idling and deceleration, common to city driving, greatly increase the rate of pollution.

And fourth, we have automobile design dictated by the wrong people for the wrong purpose. This has resulted in a misdirected technology in which automobile design has been determined not by the best technology available or even the transportation needs of society, but by the stylists, Madison Avenue, and the profit system.

In fact, technology is so misdirected that the April, 1963 issue of *American Engineer,* the journal of the National Society of Professional Engineers, opened a critical analysis of the automobile with these words: "It would be hard to imagine anything on such a large scale that seems quite as badly engineered as the American automobile. It is . . . a classic example of what engineering should *not* be."

Trends in Engine Design

Until 1940, all automobiles other than racing cars had low-speed, low-compression engines. Following World War II, the availability of high-octane gas from expanded war-time facilities prompted a move toward higher compression engines, and in a few years the horsepower race was on. From 1940 to 1954, engine size changed very little, but there were noticeable increases in compression ratios and engine speeds. From 1954 to 1959, the average brake horsepower almost doubled. In the early 1960s, there was a trend toward economy-size automobiles which temporarily slowed down the horsepower race. Since then, horsepower output has continued to increase to the point where today's automobile engines are the most powerful ever built. This increased horsepower was brought about by increased engine size, increased compression ratios, and higher engine speeds. Increased engine displacement is accompanied by a corresponding increase in the volume of exhaust gases. Increased compression ratios result in higher peak temperatures which bring about an increase in the production of oxides of nitrogen. The increased compression ratios also increase detonation, which in turn has required the addition of lead-based compounds to gasoline, resulting in lead compounds in the exhaust gases.

Attempts to extend the increased engine torque over an increased range of engine speeds required the engine designers to compromise in operating efficiency in several ways. The problem of uniform distribution of fuel mixtures to all cylinders at high speeds required the addition of multi-barrelled carburetors and compromises in the air-fuel mixture ratios. To obtain greater power from a given sized engine, carburetion was set to provide a richer mixture. Although the stoichiometric mixture for gasoline is approximately 15 to 1, and best fuel economy is obtained when air-fuel mixtures are near this ratio, best power is obtained when running at mixtures of 11 or 12 to 1.

Valve timing was compromised since low and high-speed engine operations require different degrees of lead, lag, and overlap. Engine ignition was compromised resulting in less than ideal spark advance for high-speed operation in order to reduce detonation tendencies of the high-compression engine. The increased engine speed also required high-speed additives to gasoline.

Thus we see that these design changes, though resulting in increased horsepower, also increased the volumetric rate at which the automobile pollutes in addition to adding new pollutants. But horsepower ratings sell automobiles even though the purchaser seldom realizes what he is buying.

The horsepower gains between 1940 and 1970 are impressive, but a closer look at performance characteristics indicates today's motorists may not be getting all they bargained for. To obtain satisfactory performance from the low-compression, low-speed engine, the 1940 design called for a long piston stroke and small cylinder bore, developing maxium torque (pulling power) at car speeds of 30-40 mph in high gear, and maximum horsepower at 65-75 mph. This principle is still applied in the design of commercial vehicles such as trucks and buses, where economy of operation is important.

TABLE 1. *Horsepower Comparison, 1940 vs. 1969.*

Make & Model	1940 hp	1969 hp	Model
Buick Roadmaster	147	360	GS 455
Cadillac (All V8)	135	375	Eldorado
Chevrolet (All)	85	435	Corvette
Chrysler Imperial	137	375	Imperial
Dodge (All)	87	425	V8
Ford V8	90	375	Torino
Lincoln V-12	120	365	V8
Oldsmobile 8	110	400	455
Pontiac 8	100	390	V8
1970 Greyhound Bus (26,000 lbs.)..........285 hp			

portant. The 1970 Greyhound bus, for example, develops maximum torque at 39 mph in high gear, and maximum hp at 70 mph.

TABLE 2. *Speed Comparison, 1940 vs. 1969*

	*Mph at Max Torque		*Mph at Max HP	
	1940	1969	1940	1969
Buick	40	56	72	92
Cadillac	34	60	68	88
Chevrolet	18	76	64	109
Chrysler	24	64	72	92
Dodge	24	80	72	100
Ford	44	64	76	112
Lincoln	40	56	70	92
Oldsmobile	40	64	72	96
Plymouth	24	80	72	100
Pontiac	32	64	74	104
1970 Greyhound Bus		39		70

*Speeds are based on a ratio of 1000 rpm/20 mph except where literature gave exact mph.

But the current practice of putting high-compression, high-speed engines with racing car speed-torque characteristics in the passenger automobile has little to do with meeting transportation needs. Maximum torque is often generated at road speeds as high as 60-80 mph, and maximum horsepower at speeds often in excess of 100 mph. This may be great for drag racing or road racing, but it has little merit in normal city driving, or even mountain or open highway driving. In fact, some of the modern high-powered cars do not perform as well in high gear on mountain roads as do older cars with ½ the hp rating.

The long-stroke, low-compression engine is limited in maximum speed due to higher inertia forces and design limitations on piston speeds. But the longer stroke and slower speed promote more complete combustion and higher exhaust temperatures. The higher exhaust temperature promotes oxidation of hydrocarbons, resulting in substantial reductions in exhaust hydrocarbon concentration. Despite the lower efficiency of low compression engines and increased gasoline consumption, the net effect is a reduction in both concentration and total volume of exhaust hydrocarbons. For example, a reduction in compression ratio from 8:1 to 6:1 in an experimental engine resulted in hydrocarbon emission reductions up to 43 percent. The major argument against low compression engines is that the motorist will not accept a compromise in vehicle performance. Given a choice between smog and performance, that premise is debatable.

Fuel Composition

Practically all petroleum hydrocarbons found in gasoline are members of four major groups: parafins, olefins, naphthenes, and aromatics. The ratio of these groups in petroleum vary according to the geographic source of the petroleum and the refining process used. The gasolines are then blended to obtain the desired characteristics. But the process does not stop there. Due to the complex nature of the combustion process, engine design, and modes of operation, numerous additives are used to give gasoline the widest range of operating characteristics. The anti-knock compounds, and high-speed additives have already been mentioned.

Scavengers are added to remove lead oxide deposits from valves and spark plugs.

Deposit modifiers are used to alter the chemical character of combustion chamber deposits.

Anti-oxidants are used in nearly all gasolines to prevent deterioration during the normal life of the fuel.

Metal deactivators are used to destroy the catalytic activity of trace amounts of copper, which even in minute quantities promotes oxidation.

Anti-rust agents are incorporated into gasoline to overcome rust and corrosion in storage tanks, pipe lines, tankards, and engine fuel systems.

Anti-icing agents are used to inhibit the formation of ice in fuel lines or carburetors.

Detergent additives are used to prevent the build-up of deposits in carburetors.

Lubricants are added to gasoline to improve the lubrication of cylinders and to prevent valve and ring sticking.

Each of these additives makes it more difficult for the engine — which was not designed in the first place to reduce emissions — to burn the fuel completely. The additives themselves undergo chemical changes during combustion and then are emitted as pollutants into the air.

Some produce exhaust products dangerous to plant and animal life, yet no legislation exists to control gasoline additives, regardless of how dangerous they may be. If you want to give the country a dose of metal poisoning, put the metal in gasoline. It's legal. In fact, the law does not even require that you indicate you have made the addition.

Exhaust Emission Control

Many methods for control of the exhaust emissions from the automobile have been investigated. Three general approaches have been given most attention in recent years: (1) devices to modify the engine operating conditions, (2) devices that treat the exhaust gases, and (3) modification of the fuel to produce exhaust emissions that are less reactive in the atmosphere.

Major emphasis to date has been on treatment of exhaust gases, and a number of control devices have been proposed. These include afterburners, catalytic converters, absorbers, adsorbers, filters, and condensers. Of these, only two presently show promise and are being developed actively: the afterburner and the catalytic converter.

In the first, the afterburner, air is admitted to the exhaust manifold and a direct flame provides some combustion of unburned gases. This device reduces both hydrocarbon and carbon monoxide content of the exhaust gases, but does not reduce, and may increase, the nitrogen oxides.

In the second type, a catalyst is used to convert the hydrocarbons and carbon monoxide to water and carbon dioxide by burning. Catalysts can also reduce the nitrogen oxide content. An important disadvantage of the catalytic converter is its gradual decrease of effectiveness with use. The loss of efficiency is due to fouling by the lead compounds, by sintering or deactivation by high temperatures, and by attrition through abrasive action. Thus we have the dilemma in which the high compression engine, which produces the greatest amount of nitrogen oxide, also requires leaded gasoline which reduces the efficiency of the catalytic converter.

Devices to modify engine operating conditions have considerable promise if cost can be kept down, reliability kept high, and performance not too adversely affected.

Fuel modification should be a relatively easy approach, but engine design must change concurrently.

The Steam Engine

The external combustion engine, better known as the steam engine, is much in the news these days as a possible replacement for the internal combustion engine. The advantage of the steam engine is that combustion takes place at atmospheric pressure with ideal fuel/air ratios, providing more complete combustion than is attainable with the internal combustion engine. The heat of combustion vaporizes the working fluid which becomes the power source for the engine. The vapor is conducted to the engine where it drives the pistons or turbines which turn the shaft and drive the wheels of the vehicle. Due to the difference in combustion processes, there is a phenomenal difference in exhaust products between the steam engine and the internal combustion engine.

	STEAM	I.C.E.
Hydrocarbons	20.0 ppm	900.0 ppm
Carbon Monoxide	0.05	3.5
Nitrogen Oxides (no lead)	40.0	1500.0
Lead	none	unmeasured

In addition, there is virtually no deterioration of emission characteristics with age. The steam engine will operate on lower grade fuels than the internal combustion engine, and give more miles per gallon of fuel than its equivalent counterpart in internal combustion engines.

It is difficult to arrive at any cost comparisons since there is currently no volume production of steam engines. The Battelle Institute estimates that volume production would bring the cost down to a comparable size V-8 internal combustion engine with automatic transmission, a realistic comparison since the steam engine requires no transmission.

Despite these advantages, the steam engine is not about to replace the internal combustion engine overnight for several reasons. First, very little money has been spent on its development and there are still some technical problems to be ironed out. Second, it must be established that cost of installation and service can be competitive with the ICE. And third, the automotive industry has considerable interest and investment in the ICE and will offer resistance to switching over. GM says it's too heavy and costly, Chrysler says it's too hot to hold any known anti-freeze, and Ford says it's inefficient.

At this point in time, there are significant hurdles to be cleared, and research and development is on the rise. The prospects are good that steam will eventually be the alternative propulsion system for automobiles, but there is good reason to believe it is at least a decade away.

Diesel Engines

The motor vehicle exhaust emission standards originally adopted by the California Board of Health on Dec. 4, 1959, contained standards for hydrocarbons and carbon monoxide. Under those standards, the diesel engine qualified without afterburners or other control devices. This was given much publicity, and many believed the solution to transportation pollution was already a reality. But the answer was not so simple.

Aside from the problems of engine weight and limitations on engine speed, there are other emissions which must be considered. There is odor and eye irritation caused by diesel exhaust. Under certain operating conditions, nitrogen oxide emissions can be higher with diesels than with gasoline engines, and present concern over nitrogen oxide levels may require exhaust controls on diesels as well as gasoline engines. The exhaust also contains 3, 4-benzo(a)pyrene, which is suspected of being a contributor to the high incidence of lung cancer.

Electric Vehicles

Current battery technology makes electric vehicles possible and practical for trips of limited length. Their power-to-weight ratio, and therefore their performance, is largely a question of the action radius such vehicles are designed for. If intermittent recharging is made possible by charging stations at points at which the travel can be interrupted for sufficiently long periods, electric vehicles could be quite practical, although their first cost would remain high.

Other Power Systems

Fuel cells, thermoelectric generators, thermionic generators, solar cells, hot-air engines, closed-cycle gas turbines, and others have been proposed or reproposed as future vehicle power plants, in some cases with utter disregard to fundamental and practical limitations. Most of these solutions will not be ready in the near future for anything except very specialized applications. It is extremely doubtful that any will ever become practical for road vehicle propulsion.

Conclusions

Exhaust emission control devices and alternative propulsion systems can solve only part of the problem, since they do nothing for the problems of resource depletion, urban deterioration, and solid waste disposal. With the possible exception of the steam engine, there are no satisfactory alternative propulsion systems in sight.

However, with changes in the use and design of the automobile, the problems mentioned can be solved, at least for quite a few decades. Whether these solutions would be acceptable — or the degree to which they would be acceptable — to industry, government, and the public is the real topic of debate.

EDITOR'S COMMENTS

It is readily apparent that the American car is incompatible with clean air and the conservation of fossil fuel. In Part I of this text, we attempted to characterize most ecosystems in terms of their complexity — a complexity which defies human comprehension. An understanding of the automobile-atmosphere problem also involves complexity — a complexity of mental attitudes and physical situations developed primarily by our shift toward technology, increased leisure time, and an economy heavily dependent on the mobile, internal combustion engine.

There is no simple solution to automobile pollution. Many things can be done to alleviate the problem — many things must be done — however, the most effective actions would be the most distasteful and will be the last to be put into effect. Just as family planning is no solution to overpopulation, the present emission standards for future automobiles are not a solution to automotive air pollution. However, it is hoped that these standards will serve to focus public attention on the problem and will serve as a stimulus for the development of more effective and more permanent solutions.

As with most human problems involving degradation of the environment, a point of permanent stability must finally be reached in regard to automobile-induced pollution. This will probably be represented by a zero growth population level coupled with the development of an automotive power supply which will not be dependent on finite fossil fuel reserves. Neither of these situations can even be envisioned by most persons today. While researching and implementing the programs necessary to achieve these obvious goals, there are interim projects which could prevent further deterioration of air quality.

Urban mass transit systems must be improved and rules regarding their use must be formulated and enforced. This could greatly reduce automobile traffic and, consequently, air pollution levels in and near large population centers. Mass transit systems will be used when automobile parking becomes unavailable and tolls for bridges, tunnels, and expressways become prohibitive. The tax on gasoline (especially high-octane gasoline) could be increased significantly — especially after a consumer had used an annual quota. Such taxes could be used to conduct research directed toward producing cleaner engines and alternative power supplies.

Plans must be adopted for inspecting automobiles for effectiveness of their air pollution control devices. The emission standards applicable to new cars must apply for the life of the car. Significant fines or other suitable punishment must accompany violations detected at such inspections. It is a foregone conclusion that an automobile's pollution devices will require periodic maintenance. An enforcement system will be necessary to ensure that this periodic maintenance is performed.

Pedestrian and bicycle traffic should be encouraged by the construction of special traffic lanes. Certain city streets could even be put "off limits" to powered vehicles. Vast improvements could be made in our railroad passenger service. It is even questionable whether a second family car is needed.

The above suggestions would require little or no new technology; however, they certainly represent no permanent solution. They would have to be followed by more lasting innovations. Obviously the automobile's size must be restricted. The present United States car is not only too large (heavy) but has too great a horsepower and piston displacement and develops too great a maximum speed. These factors must be controlled through legal restrictions. Engine compression ratios should be reduced, removing the need for lead and other anti-knock compounds presently found in gasolines. Limitations should also be placed on other gasoline additives, and no additive should be used prior to careful study as to the effects it would have on exhaust emissions.

The concept of planned obsolescense should be immediately discarded and permanent or semi-permanent body styles should be developed. If the substances present in an automobile were recycled, we could view planned obsolescense as a tolerable evil, not resulting in severe degradation of nature or wastage of natural materials. However, recycling of automobiles does not occur on a wide-spread level. It is obvious why this kind of talk is balleyhooed in Detroit — indeed, in many places other than Detroit. Not only will a degree of permanence in automobiles require a new technology, it will require a new economics. The importance of this cannot be overstated. We must learn to live with and survive the "powering-down" of certain of our present-day economically important industrial giants. Many people must be retrained, and a major shift in economic philosophy will be necessary in determining what is good or bad for the ecological health of the world.

Cleaner burning fuels must be developed while we are finding an alternative to the internal combustion engine. Standards in regard to gasoline composition must be put into effect and enforced. The development and use of small, short-range electrical vehicles should be encouraged. Setting limits on city size and new zoning techniques could "scatter" present pollution in heavily polluted areas. This type of control is certainly hazardous in that it tends to minimize present pollution problems; it is only an interim method of dealing with the problem.

All the changes suggested here, and you can undoubtedly add many other suggestions, could be implemented in the near future. These changes are probably dependent on intelligent legislation and enforcement. They call for little new technology, and they could easily reduce vehicular emissions by 50 percent or more if the total number of operating automobiles were to be stabilized. If the number of automobiles continues to increase, it is obvious that these changes might be necessary just to hold our own.

Finally, permanent solutions must be found if powered transportation remains a way of human life. The numbers of humans and the numbers of powered vehicles must stabilize, and the source of energy to power these vehicles must be renewable, cyclical, or inexhaustible. Many researchers feel that the former (population stabilization) must be achieved soon if man is to survive at all. For the latter (renewable, cyclical, or inexhaustible energy sources), the only present-day practical power source is stored electricity. Our only hope for a continuous and inexhaustible source of electricity may be in either the development of environmentally clean nuclear fusion processes or in the direct utilization of solar energy. Much more time, money, research, and human manpower is needed if these problems are to be solved in a reasonable length of time.

CROSWELL BOWEN

Donora, Pennsylvania

Croswell Bowen is a free-lance writer.

Donora, Pennsylvania, is a steel mill town of 12,300 people, twenty-eight miles south of Pittsburgh. During the last five days of October, 1948, a heavy mixture of fog and smoke settled over the countryside, and by 11:30 Saturday night, October 30, seventeen persons were dead. The first died that morning. Four more, who became seriously ill at the time, died during the next two months. A government report later revealed that a total of 5910 persons, 42.7 percent of the population, were made ill by the smog. Of those, 1440, or 10.4 percent, were "severely affected."

Front-page stories drew a comparison between the Donora incident and what had taken place in the Meuse Valley in Belgium in 1930, when sixty persons died from a concentration of fog and smoke. Both places were located in heavily industrialized areas. News accounts suggested that the Donora disaster, like the Belgium one, was the result of a freak weather condition — what weather authorities called a "temperature inversion." A layer of warm air descended over Donora, which is located at the bottom of a river valley. This sealed in smoke from locomotives and factories, automobile exhausts, and floating solid particles, probably fly ash. There was no wind to blow away this smog.

Two U.S. Steel installations were located in Donora — a zinc manufacturing plant and an enormous factory for forging iron from ore and making various steel products. The great open hearth furnaces used to burn night and day; they were back in full operation the week after the deaths.

Since the Smog

For a year after the disaster, U.S. Public Health officials conducted a study and issued a report on "The Unusual Smog Episode of October, 1948," as they termed it. But the incident at Donora was more or less forgotten until the late 1960s, when the country became aroused over the issue of pollution. Students of the air pollution problem began to see Donora as the Hiroshima of their particular area of concern.

Today, the visitor driving south to Donora from Pittsburgh on Route 88 travels through lush valleys of prosperous towns: Castle Shannon, Library, Finleyville. One passes farms where the farmer himself can do a little strip mining of soft coal on his

Reprinted by permission of the editors from *The Atlantic* 226(5):27-34. November 1970. Copyright © 1970 by The Atlantic Monthly Company, Boston, Mass.

own land to heat his house. Entering Donora, the bus driver points to the site of the U.S. Steel zinc mill, now known to be the chief offender in the 1948 smog. Dismantled in 1956, it was located at the northern end of the town which is spread out on the steep west bank of the Monongahela River. Across the river from the old zinc plant site, the east bank is partly devoid of vegetation, exposing bright tan clay. "It used to be all barren, nothing would grow there," a passenger remarks, "but it began to get green after the zinc plant went down." A Hercules Powder plant (which makes nitric acid) has replaced the zinc plant. Black smoke pours out of its chimney. Some of the stores are boarded up.

There used to be a sign on the road, as you entered Donora, which said: NEXT TO YOURS THE BEST TOWN IN THE U.S.A. Since the smog, the sign has been allowed to disintegrate. They now call their town HOME OF CHAMPIONS because Stan Musial, Arnold Galiffa, Bimbo Cecconi, and other great athletes came from here.

High on the windblown rim of the hill overlooking the bowl-shaped river valley are the town's cemeteries. Each religious denomination has its own. Up here all is peaceful. The family burial plots, planted with dated headstones, tell the story of the generations who lived and died in the town below. In St. Dominic's Catholic Cemetery, near the winding road inside the gates, the visitor can see a headstone marking the grave of Ivan Ceh: May 6, 1879-October 30, 1948. Only the date of his death hints that he figured in the Donora smog tragedy. There is no record in the town, even in the obituaries of the local newspaper, the Donora *Herald American*, that any of the twenty-two dead suffocated to death from smog that weekend. There was no combined memorial service at the time nor since. There is no mass grave, no monument.

U.S. Public Health Bulletin No. 306, titled: "Air Pollution in Donora, Pa., Epidemiology of the Unusual Smog Episode of October, 1948," recorded the sudden passing of the five women and seventeen men meticulously. Ivan Ceh was stricken at four o'clock in the morning of Thursday, October 28, and died forty-six hours later at two o'clock in the morning of Saturday, October 30. Nine more died in the next eight hours. The last of the twenty-one dead, George Weisdak, sixty-five, a retired zinc plant worker, died on Christmas Eve, 1948. As Ivan Ceh's obituary reveals, he was a fairly typical Donora citizen. He was born in Rilka, Yugoslavia, in 1879, arrived in the United States in 1901, settled in Donora in 1902, and worked in the steel mill. He was seventy and retired at the time of his death.

The Monongahela River, once brimming with fish and delightful to swim in, winds into a horseshoe curve that almost makes an island of Donora. Today it is thoroughly polluted, mostly by acid from abandoned coal mines. The three hundred forty-two acres which make up the center of the town were once a farm bought by Nicholas Crist in 1769. In 1899, the plot was purchased by three businessmen: James McKean, for whom Donora's main street is named; Henry Clay Frick, the steel baron; and Andrew W. Mellon, who amassed one of America's largest fortunes.

William Donner built the first industrial plant along part of the three miles of riverfront. Steam locomotives and river barges powered by the soft coal in which the region abounds made the site ideal at the time, because they afforded easy transportation of fuel, raw materials, and steel and iron products. The town derived its name from combining the Don of Donner and Nora, the name of Andrew Mellon's wife. By 1908, the steel town of Donora was an important center in the U.S. Steel empire put together by J. P. Morgan.

From the beginning of the century, people of more than half a dozen nationalities lived and worked together in towns like Donora in the Monongahela Valley. Their children didn't have to leave to find work. They went straight from school into the mills. They married each other and set up new families. The pay was good and got better as the unions upped the wages. Donora grew and prospered. It was a friendly town. Everybody knew everybody else. They cared about each other: "We're a League of Nations town. We say to a guy, you dumb Russian or you Polack or you Guinea. Nobody minds. I'm Polish and my daughter married an Italian."

Living with heavy dense smoke and fog was part of their way of life. They equated factory chimneys, sending forth smoke to the skies, with prosperity: "That smoke coming out of those stacks is bread and butter on our tables."

Steel men in Donora, like most steel men, were a proud lot, proud of their special skills. Wages in various job categories could go to $40 a day. There were three shifts to keep the plants going twenty-four hours a day. Men strolled with their lunchpails down the hillside from their homes and loitered at the factory gates an hour or so before starting time. "When I walked through those doors to go to work I just felt good. I loved my work. I knew my job. And I liked the guys."

"Your Footprints"

The 1948 smog lasted over a long weekend. On Tuesday morning, October 27, smoke from the locomotives stacks spilled down toward the ground. You could hardly see ahead to walk or drive. There was a sweetish smell in the air. (It was sulfur dioxide.) The smog left a layer of dust on porches, on the sidewalks and pavement: "You could see your footprints if you looked back. Tires left the marks of their treads in the streets." The town's eleven doctors were soon getting telephone calls; patients were having trouble breathing or felt as if they were coughing their lungs out. "Everything was black with gas and soot; you could even taste it." Dr. William Rongaus recalls, "The odd thing was that two days later some of the people whom I had treated while they were gasping for breath denied they had been ill."

John Turner, the tall, gaunt driver of the Donora Fire Department truck, can still hear the wailing sirens of ambulances taking people to hospitals in the neighboring towns. "I hauled oxygen tanks around the clock. We'd knock on doors to see if people were all right. You'd put a sheet over the head of somebody who couldn't breathe and then turn on the oxygen. Automobiles kept stalling. I thought something was wrong with the timing. Then we realized it was the lack of oxygen."

Most Donora citizens recall the Halloween parade on Friday evening. It was an eerie sight: marchers striding forward holding white handkerchiefs to their faces, bands playing all barely visible in the smoky haze and the autumn twilight. Donora High School won the $25 prize as the best of the Monongahela Valley bands.

Then, a dead cat was discovered along the parade line, apparently run over by a car. An examination indicated that in fact it had suffocated Halloween night, a black cat mysteriously dead; it seemed to Donora people a terrible omen of the disaster about to engulf the town. The next day, Saturday, word spread that people were sick and dying. Albert Delsandro (who is now Donora's mayor) recalls carrying the ill and the dead out of their homes into ambulances. By ten in the morning Rudolph Schwerha, the town's leading undertaker, had nine bodies spread out in his funeral home.

"No Change in the Process"

"I can't conceive how our plant has anything to do with the condition. There has been no change in the process we use since

1915."—Superintendent, American Steel and Wire Company, October, 1948.

News writers, photographers, air pollution authorities began arriving in Donora as word of the disaster spread in print and on the air. Dr. Clarence Mills, an air pollution expert from the University of Cincinnati, arrived to study the Donora smog. He said chronic damage had been done for years to the lungs of the people in the valley.

Sunday, October 31, rain and winds cleared away the smog. On Tuesday, most of the dead were buried. It was, the citizens recall, one of the most beautiful fall days they had ever seen. The zinc and steel mills resumed their operations. Now Donora people began to resent the cries of alarm. It was disloyal to Donora and, besides, the talk could drive away the mills. But Dr. Rongaus, who had been through a grueling experience ministering to the sick and dying, described the deaths as "murder . . . those who died could have been saved. Those who failed to get a second dose of adrenalin died. The smoke was a silent killer. Something murdered them. One more night and the death toll would have been one thousand and twenty instead of twenty."

Several men across the river in the town of Webster tried to get a valley lawyer to sue U.S. Steel on behalf of the smog victims and the families of the dead. But local lawyers hesitated to take the case, probably, as Al Kline of Webster thinks, because they were afraid of offending U.S. Steel. Finally a Pittsburgh lawyer, Charles J. Margiotti, was engaged. He took the case with a $500 retainer and the proviso that he would get one third of any settlement. If the smog was "an act of God," he announced, there would be no suit, "but if it was the result of smoke from the mills, we'll sue." Doctors Rongaus and Mills felt sure that gases in the smoke fumes were responsible. Margiotti launched a $4 million lawsuit against U.S. Steel. Families of some of the dead did sue in the end, as did some of those made ill.

The Webster citizens were signed up easily, but most Donora people were reluctant to press the suit. The group in Webster insisted on trying to make people aware that smoke from the mills was at fault. The leaders were Al Kline, the sports editor of the *Valley Republican,* and Abe Celapino, owner of a restaurant and a stone quarry. Earl Klein, a lawyer who later became a judge, helped and did legal work without a fee. They organized and incorporated The Society For Better Living, sent out some forty press releases, and enlisted the help of air pollution authorities around the country.

When the U.S. Public Health people came to the valley to do a study, they were wined and dined by Al Kline, Abe Celapino, and others from Webster. "We tried to make them understand what had happened." Kline said recently, "but it didn't do any good. We still got a wishy-washy report. I think they were afraid of making U.S. Steel liable for damages."

The published report was not very enlightening or specific. It did say that weather had something to do with the smog, and that October was the "optimum" month for smog at Donora because of the frequency of "stagnant deep anti-cyclones." Illness from the smog was "essentially an irritation of the respiratory tract and other exposed mucous membranes, and varied in degree from mild to severe." The report discussed the exsitence in the air of fluoride, chloride, sulfur dioxide, hydrogen sulfide, sulfur trioxide, and other gases. But it did not "appear probable . . . that any one of these substances *by itself* [italics added] was capable of producing the syndrome [irritation of the respiratory tract]."

U.S. Steel, despite a virtual clearance by the Public Health Service report, decided to settle the Webster lawsuits out of court as a package deal for about $250,000. Four million dollars had been asked. The lawyers got a third, about $83,000. Families of the dead who sued got $5,000 per fatality. Those made ill got $1,000 apiece.

The Webster group met with Clifford Wood, president of American Steel and Wire, the U.S. Steel subsidiary. As Al Kline recalls, "He was extremely cordial, said he sympathized with us and would feel the same way if he lived in the Donora area. He was very impressive. Said they agreed smoke from the mills killed vegetation."

Forgetting

The crusade against smoke died out, and Donora entered the 1950s with increasing anxiety that all this talk about the smog would result in the mills leaving town. In 1957 U.S. Steel closed the zinc plant for good. People believed the company was angry because of the lawsuits and had concluded Donora was in danger of another smog. Many people viewed the tragedy as, literally, "an act of God." They argued: "Weren't the people who got sick or died all old people?" (Their ages ranged from fifty-two to eighty-four, and the mean age was sixty-five, according to the U.S. Public Health Service report.) "Wasn't the 'temperature inversion' a freak of nature?"

The companies denied rumors that the rest of the mills would leave town. But in 1960, the company discontinued making iron and steel in Donora and shut down two blast furnaces, thirteen open hearth furnaces and five steel product mills. Seventeen hundred out of forty-four hundred workers were laid off. Now the town felt itself thoroughly doomed. The smog seemed to have cast a curse on the valley. Merchants were forced out of business, and many families left town. U.S. Steel did employ some of the Donora steel workers at its new Fairless Hills plant near Philadelphia three hundred miles away.

As it happened, U.S. Steel had tentative plans to phase out its Donora mills long be-

fore the 1948 smog. Already obsolete in the 1940s, they had been kept open owing to the demands of war production. The great coke-burning open hearth furnaces were obsolete. Oxygen and electric furnaces were the new things. Besides, Donora's steep hillside roads made truck access difficult, especially in winter. Rather than modernize an old plant, it was more economic to build new factories in new open space locations with planned housing conditions. Early in February, 1966, U.S. Steel officially announced the end of all its operations in Donora.

Although there was growing national concern about air pollution, the citizens of Donora immediately set about trying to persuade companies to build factories in their town. One of the objectives was to create jobs for young people. The Chamber of Commerce set up what it called Operation Native Son. There was a Society for a Green Donora. Trees, purchased from the state, were planted. Hercules Powder was one of the first plants to move in. A dozen or so followed. Smoke from factory chimneys again rose from the valley.

Donora refuses to pass ordinances designed to control smoke. It is argued that cars, buses, home and commercial heating systems, engines from locomotives and riverboats all are part of the air pollution problem. This view found support in the U.S. Public Health Service report. Reforms suggested in the report were adopted elsewhere in the valley, but not in Donora. The Weather Bureau instituted a system to warn of an impending temperature inversion or bad smog condition. Companies began installing air pollution devices. Wheeling-Pittsburgh Steel, in nearby Monessen, invested $4.8 million in such devices as an electrostatic precipitator and a graphite collection system. The company claimed a 70 percent reduction in dust fall. When a smog warning goes out, companies are told to cut back on production.

But people in Donora take a more traditional view. "Except for the lesson to be learned by other communties," a Donora *Herald American* editor wrote a few years ago, "this small Pennsylvania town could wish for nothing better than to have the world forget 'the Donora episode.'"

EDITOR'S COMMENTS

The fact that incidents similar to the one described for Donora, Pennsylvania have occurred supports the idea that air pollution is a serious threat to human health. Air pollution medical research has actually just begun. Scientists generally realize that most effects of air pollution on human health are the result of several pollutants reacting together. Specific cause and effect relationships are further obscured by a wide variation in individual and population sensitivity to air pollution.

However, certain air pollutants have already been correlated with specific human health disorders. Carbon monoxide undoubtedly lowers the oxygen carrying capacity of the blood and affects heart function. Continued burdens of carbon monoxide may contribute to heart disease in general. Sulfur dioxide and particulates have definitely been linked with pulmonary and respiratory diseases. Several air pollutants may be capable of causing cancer.

Nitrogen oxides are thought to increase general sensitivity to infection and may cause structural changes in cells lining the respiratory passages. Small quantities of asbestos seem to cause damaging respiratory conditions, including cancer and asbestosis. Lead, fluoride, and beryllium poisoning can cause ailments ranging from mental retardation, to liver and kidney damage, and to death.

It is unfortunate that human suffering is necessary to point out the impending perils of continued air contamination. Many scientists think that the relationships between air pollution and disease are not linear. In other words, if air pollution were doubled, the rate of pollutant-caused diseases might be increased by a factor of 5 or 10 or 20 — the answer is simply a guess at this time. It seems obvious that our attempts to reduce air pollution have come none too soon, and hopefully, continued public pressure can lead to permanent control methods compatible with what we have come to consider a modern life style.

GENE BYLINSKY

The Limited War on Water Pollution

Gene Bylinsky is associate editor of FOR-
TUNE magazine. He specializes in writing on
science, medicine, and pollution control efforts.
He is a graduate of Louisiana State University
and a member of the National Association
of Science Writers. He has received a number
of awards for his articles, including the Albert
D. Lasker Award for medical journalism.

To judge by the pronouncements from
Washington, we can now start looking forward to cleaner rather than ever-dirtier
rivers. The Administration has declared a
"war" on pollution, and Secretary of the
Interior Walter J. Hickel says, "We do not
intend to lose." Adds Murry Stein, enforcement chief of the Federal Water Pollution
Control Administration: "I think we are on
the verge of a tremendous cleanup."

The nationwide campaign to clean up ravaged rivers and lakes does seem to be moving a bit. For the first time since the federal
government got into financing construction
of municipal sewage plants in 1956, Congress has come close to providing the kind
of funding it had promised. There are other
signs that the war is intensifying. Under the
provisions of the Water Quality Act of 1965
and the Clean Water Restoration Act of
1966, federal and state officials are establishing water-quality standards and plans for

their implementation, to be carried out eventually through coordinated federal-state action. Timetables for new municipal and
industrial treatment facilities are being set,
surveillance programs are being planned, and
tougher federal enforcement authority is being formulated. Without waiting for these
plans to materialize, Interior is talking tough
to some municipal and industrial polluters,
with the possibility of court action in the
background.

Even with all this, however, the water-
pollution outlook is far from reassuring. Although the nation has invested about $15
billion since 1952 in the construction of
7,500 municipal sewage-treatment plants, industrial treatment plants, sewers, and related
facilities, a surprising 1,400 communities in
the U.S., including good-sized cities like
Memphis, and hundreds of industrial plants
still dump untreated wastes into the waterways. Other cities process their sewage only
superficially, and no fewer than 300,000 industrial plants discharge their used water
into municipal sewage plants that are not
equipped to process many of the complex
new pollutants.

Since the volume of pollutants keeps expanding while water supply stays basically the same, more and more intervention will be required just to keep things from getting worse. Within the next fifty years, according to some forecasts, the country's population will double, and the demand for water by cities, industries, and agriculture has tended to grow even faster than the population. These water uses now add up to something like 350 billion gallons a day (BGD), but by 1980, by some estimates, they will amount to 600 BGD. By the year 2000, demand for water is expected to reach 1,000 BGD, considerably exceeding the essentially unchanging supply of dependable fresh water, which is estimated at 650 BGD. More and more, water will have to be reused, and it will cost more and more to retrieve clean water from progressively dirtier waterways.

Just how bad water pollution can get was dramatically illustrated in the summer of 1969 when the oily, chocolate-brown Cuyahoga River in Cleveland burst into flames, nearly destroying two railroad bridges. The Cuyahoga is so laden with industrial and municipal wastes that not even the leeches and sludge worms that thrive in many badly polluted rivers are to be found in its lower reaches. Many other U.S. rivers are becoming more and more like that flammable sewer.

Even without human activity to pollute it, a stream is never absolutely pure, because natural pollution is at work in the form of soil erosion, deposition of leaves and animal wastes, solution of minerals, and so forth. Over a long stretch of time, a lake can die a natural death because of such pollution. The natural process of eutrophication, or enrichment with nutrients, encourages the growth of algae and other plants, slowly turning a lake into a bog. Man's activities enormously speed up the process.

But both lakes and rivers have an impressive ability to purify themselves. Sunlight bleaches out some pollutants. Others settle to the bottom and stay there. Still others are consumed by beneficial bacteria. These bacteria need oxygen, which is therefore vital to self-purification. The oxygen that sustains bacteria as well as fish and other organisms is replenished by natural aeration from the atmosphere and from life processes of aquatic plants.

Trouble starts when demand for dissolved oxygen exceeds the available supply. Large quantities of organic pollutants such as sewage alter the balance. Bacteria feeding upon the pollutants multiply and consume the oxygen. Organic debris accumulates. Anaerobic areas develop, where microorganisms that can live and grow without free oxygen decompose the settled solids. This putrefaction produces foul odors. Species of fish sensitive to oxygen deficiency can no longer survive. Chemical, physical, and biological characteristics of a stream are altered, and its water becomes unusable for many purposes without extensive treatment.

Pollution today is very complex in its composition, and getting more so all the time. In polluted streams and lakes hundreds of different contaminants can be found: bacteria and viruses; pesticides and weed killers; phosphorus from fertilizers, detergents, and municipal sewage; trace amounts of metals; acid from mine drainage; organic and inorganic chemicals, many of which are so new that we do not know their long-term effects on human health; and even traces of drugs. (Steroid drugs such as the Pill, however, are neutralized by bacteria.)

A distinction is often made betwen industrial and municipal wastes, but it is difficult to sort them out because many industrial plants discharge their wastes into municipal sewer systems. As a result, what is referred to as municipal waste is also to a large extent industrial waste. By one estimate, as much as 40 percent of all waste water treated by municipal sewage plants comes from industry. Industry's contribution to water pollution is sometimes measured in terms of "population equivalent." Pollution from organic industrial wastes analogous to sewage is now said by some specialists to be about equivalent to a population of 210 million.

The quality of waste water is often measured in terms of its biochemical oxygen demand (BOD), or the amount of dissolved oxygen that is needed by bacteria in decomposing the wastes. Waste water with much higher BOD content than sewage is produced by such operations as leather tanning, beet-sugar refining, and meatpacking. But industry also contributes a vast amount of non-degradable, long-lasting pollutants, such as inorganic and synthetic organic chemicals that impair the quality of water. All together, manufacturing activities, transportation, and agriculture probably account for about two-thirds of all water degradation

Industry also produces an increasingly important pollutant of an entirely different kind — heat. Power generation and some manufacturing processes use great quantities of water for cooling, and it goes back into streams warmer than it came out. Power plants disgorging great masses of hot water can raise the stream temperature by ten or twenty degrees in the immediate vicinity of the plant. Warmer water absorbs less oxygen and this slows down decomposition of organic matter. Fish, being cold-blooded, cannot regulate their body temperatures, and the additional heat upsets their life cycles; for example, fish eggs may hatch too soon. Some scientists have estimated that by 1980 the U.S. will be producing enough waste water and heat to consume, in dry weather, all the oxygen in all twenty-two river basins in the U.S.

How clean do we want our waterways to be? In answering that question we have to recognize that many of our rivers and lakes serve two conflicting purposes — they are used both as sewers and as sources of drinking water for about 100 million Americans. That's why the new water-quality standards for interstate streams now being set in var-

ious states generally rely on criteria established by the Public Health Service for sources of public water supplies. In all, the PHS lists no fewer than fifty-one contaminants or characteristics of water supplies that should be controlled. Many other substances in the drinking water are not on the list, because they haven't yet been measured or even identified. "The poor water-treatment plant operator really doesn't know what's in the stream — what he is treating," says James H. McDermott, director of the Bureau of Water Hygiene in the PHS. With more than 500 new or modified chemicals coming on the market every year, it isn't easy for the understaffed PHS bureaus to keep track of new pollutants. Identification and detailed analysis of pollutants is just beginning as a systematic task. Only recently has the PHS established its first official committee to evaluate the effects of insecticides on health.

Many water-treatment plants are hopelessly outmoded. They were designed for a simpler, less crowded world. About three-fourths of them do not go beyond disinfecting water with chlorine. That kills bacteria but does practically nothing to remove pesticides, herbicides, or other organic and inorganic chemicals from the water we drink.

A survey by the PHS shows that most waterworks operators lack formal training in treatment processes, disinfection, microbiology, and chemistry. The men are often badly paid. Some of them, in smaller communities, have other full-time jobs and moonlight as water-supply operators. The survey, encompassing eight metropolitan areas from New York City to Riverside, California, plus the State of Vermont, has revealed that in seven areas about 9 percent of the water samples indicated bacterial contamination. Pesticides were found in small concentrations in many samples. In some trace metals exceeded PHS limits. The level of nitrates, which can be fatal to babies, was too high in some samples. Earlier the PHS found that nearly sixty communities around the country, including some large cities, could be given only "provisional approval" for the quality of their water supply systems. Charles C. Johnson Jr., administrator of the Consumer Protection and Environmental Health Service in the PHS, concluded that the U.S. is "rapidly approaching a crisis stage with regard to drinking water" and is courting "serious health hazards."

Clearly, there will have to be enormous improvement in either the treatment of water we drink or the treatment of water we discard (if not both). The second approach would have the great advantage of making our waterways better for swimming and fishing and more aesthetically enjoyable. And it is more rational anyway not to put poisons in the water in the first place. The most sensible way to keep our drinking water safe is to have industry, agriculture, and municipalities stop polluting water with known and potentially hazardous substances. Some of this could be accomplished by changing manufacturing processes and recycling waste water inside plants. The wastes can sometimes be retrieved at a profit.

A great deal of industrial and municipal waste water now undergoes some form of treatment (fig. 15.1). So-called primary treatment is merely mechanical. Large floating objects such as sticks are removed by a screen. The sewage then passes through settling chambers where filth settles to become raw sludge. Primary treatment removes about one-third of gross pollutants. About 30 percent of Americans served by sewers live in communities that provide only this much treatment.

Another 62 percent live in communities that carry treatment a step beyond, subjecting the effluent from primary processing to secondary processing. In this age of exact science, secondary treatment looks very old-fashioned. The effluent flows, or is pumped, onto a "trickling filter," a bed of rocks three

to ten feet deep. Bacteria normally occurring in sewage cover the rocks, multiply, and consume most of the organic matter in the waste water. A somewhat more modern version is the activated sludge process, in which sewage from primary settling tanks is pumped to an aeration tank. Here, in a speeded-up imitation of what a stream does naturally, the sewage is mixed with air and sludge saturated with bacteria. It is allowed to remain for a few hours while decomposition takes place. Properly executed secondary treatment will reduce degradable organic waste by 90 percent. Afterward, chlorine is sometimes added to the water to kill up to 99 percent of disease germs.

Secondary treatment in 90 percent of U.S. municipalities within the next five years and its equivalent in most industrial plants is a principal objective of the current war on pollution. The cost will be high: an estimated $10 billion in public funds for municipal treatment plants and sewers and about $3.3 billion of industry's own funds for facilities to treat wastes at industrial plants.

But today that kind of treatment isn't good enough. Widespread use of secondary treatment will cut the amount of gross sewage in the waterways, but will do little to reduce the subtler, more complex pollutants. The effluents will still contain dissolved organic and inorganic contaminants. Among the substances that pass largely unaffected through bacterial treatment are salts, certain dyes, acids, persistent insecticides and herbicides, and many other harmful pollutants.

Technical "tunnel vision," or lack of thinking about all the possible consequences of a process, has often been the curse of twentieth-century science and technology. Today's sewage plants generally do not remove phosphorus and nitrogen from waste water, but turn the organic forms of these nutrients into mineral forms that are *more* usable by algae and other plants. As one scientist has noted, overgrowths of algae and other aquatic plants then rot to "recreate the

PRIMARY TREATMENT   SECONDARY

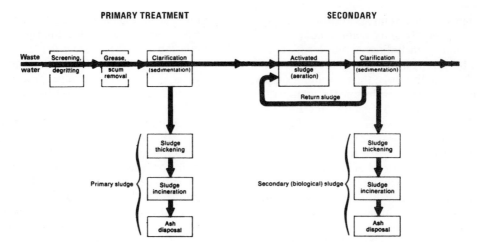

Figure 15.1.   How to take out of water some of what people put in. Advanced techniques that remove more subtle pollutants are in use in only a few places in the U.S., and most such plants are still experimental. The operation of one advanced facility, a 7,500,000-gallon-a-day plant at Lake Tahoe in California, is schematically shown above. The waste water passes through three stages, the first two of which generally correspond to the forms of treatment commonly used in the U.S. Metal screens stop large objects such as sticks and rags from entering the plant. The sewage then passes into a grit chamber where sand and small stones settle to the bottom. Next stop is the sedimentation tank, where speed of flow is reduced and suspended particles sink to the bottom, forming sludge. By itself, this primary treatment removes only about 30 percent of oxygen-

same problem of oxygen-consuming organic matter that the sewage plant was designed to control in the first place." The multibillion-dollar program to treat waste water in the same old way, he says, is "sheer insanity."

Yet the U.S. has little choice. Most of the advanced treatment techniques are either still experimental or too costly to be introduced widely. To wait for those promising new methods while doing nothing in the meantime could result in a major pollution calamity.

The pollutants that secondary treatment fails to cope with will increase in volume as industry and population grow. Phosphates, for instance, come in large amounts from detergents and fertilizers, and from human

wastes. Phosphorus has emerged as a major pollutant only in recent years. Nitrogen, the other key nutrient for algal growth, is very difficult to control because certain blue-green algae can fix nitrogen directly from the air. Since phosphorus is more controllable, its removal from effluents is critically important to limiting the growth of algae.

A few years ago, when it looked as if America's streams and lakes were to become highways of white detergent foam, the manufacturers converted the detergent base from alkyl benzene sulphonate to a much more biologically degradable substance, linear alkylate sulphonate. That effectively reduced the amount of foam but did almost nothing to reduce the amount of phosphates in detergents. The mountains of foam have shrunk,

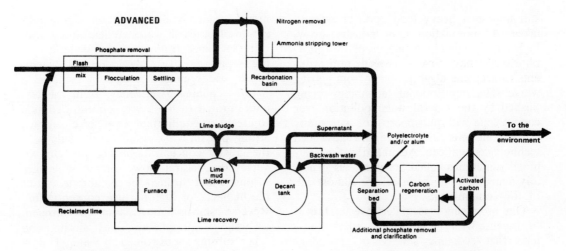

consuming organic matter in sewage. In secondary treatment, most of the remaining organic matter is consumed by bacteria. Aeration speeds up, or "activates," the process. Advanced treatment at Lake Tahoe removes both phosphate and nitrogen, undesirable nutrients that cause proliferation of algae. Phosphate is removed with the help of lime ("flash mix" refers to the rapidity of mixing). Nitrogen, which occurs in sewage mostly as ammonia, is more difficult to eliminate. At Tahoe, the effluent is passed through a stripping tower where ammonia is extracted in a process that involves blowing large amounts of air through the sewage. The effluent then undergoes additional cleansing in passing through separation beds (where chemicals remove more phosphate) and finally through activated carbon. The result is water that's almost good enough to drink.

but green mats of algae keep on growing. The developers of detergents failed to consider the possible side effects; such lack of systematic thinking and foresight is precisely what has led to today's environmental abuses. It might be possible to substitute nonphosphorus bases in detergent manufacture—and work is in progress along those lines.

There is little prospect of substituting something else for the phosphate in fertilizer. It's hard to visualize a fertilizer that is a nutrient when applied to land and not a nutrient when it enters the water. One way to reduce water pollution from farmlands would be to reduce the amounts of chemical fertilizers farmers apply to their fields — it is the excess fertilizer, not ab-

sorbed by plants, that washes into streams or percolates into groundwater. Through some complex of social and economic arrangements, farmers might be persuaded to use less fertilizers and more humus. By improving the texture of soils, as well as providing slowly released nutrients, humus can reduce the need for commercial fertilizer to keep up crop yields. The U.S. produces enormous quantities of organic wastes that could be converted to humus. Such a remedy for fertilizer pollution, of course, might seem highly undesirable to the fertilizer industry, already burdened with excess capacity.

Even if phosphorus pollution from fertilizers and detergents were entirely eliminated — an unlikely prospect — phosphates from domestic and industrial wastes would still impose a heavy load upon rivers and lakes. As population and industry grow, higher and higher percentages of the phosphorus will have to be removed from effluents to keep the algae problem from getting worse. The conventional technology being pushed by the federal water-pollution war cannot cope with phosphorus, or with many other pollutants. But there are advanced technologies that can. Advanced water treatment, sometimes called "teritary," is generally aimed at removal of all, or almost all, of the contaminants.

One promising idea under investigation is to dispense with the not always reliable bacteria that consume sewage in secondary treatment. Toxic industrial wastes have on occasion thrown municipal treatment plants out of kilter for weeks by killing the bacteria. "We've found that we can accomplish the same kind of treatment with a purely physical-chemical process," says a scientist at the Robert A. Taft Water Research Center in Cincinnati.

In this new approach, the raw sewage is clarified with chemicals to remove most suspended organic material, including much of the phosphate. Then comes carbon adsorption. The effluent passes through filter beds of granular activated carbon, similar to that used in charcoal filters for cigarettes. Between clarification and adsorption, 90 percent or more of the phosphate is removed. The carbon can be regenerated in furnaces and reused. Captured organic matter is burned. Carbon adsorption has the great additional advantage of removing from the water organic industrial chemicals that pass unhindered through biological secondary treatment. The chemicals adhere to the carbon as they swirl through its complex structure with millions of pathways and byways.

Other treatment techniques are under study that make water even cleaner, and might possibly be used to turn sewage into potable water. One of these is reverse os-

mosis, originally developed for demineralization of brackish water. When liquids with different concentrations of, say, mineral salts are separated by a semipermeable membrane, water molecules pass by osmosis, a natural equalizing tendency, from the less concentrated to the more concentrated side to create an equilibrium. In reverse osmosis, strong pressure is exerted on the side with the greater concentration. The pressure reverses the natural flow, forcing molecules of pure water through the membrane, out of the high-salt or high-particle concentration. Reverse osmosis removes ammonia nitrogen, as well as phosphates, most nitrate, and other substances dissolved in water. Unfortunately, the process is not yet applicable to sewage treatment on a large scale because the membranes become fouled with sewage solids. Engineers are hard at work trying to design better membranes.

New techniques are gradually transforming sewage treatment, technically backward and sometimes poorly controlled, into something akin to a modern chemical process. "We are talking about a wedding of sanitary and chemical engineering," says David G. Stephan, who directs research and development at the Federal Water Pollution Control Administration, "using the techniques of the chemical process industry to turn out a product — reusable water — rather than an effluent to throw away." Adds James McDermott of the Public Health Service: "We're going to get to the point where, on the one hand, it's going to cost us an awful lot of money to treat wastes and dump them into the stream. And an awful lot of money to take those wastes when they are going down the stream and make drinking water out of them. We are eventually going to create treatment plants where we take sewage and, instead of dumping it back into the stream, treat it with a view of recycling it immediately — direct reuse. That is the only way we're going to satisfy our water needs, and second, it's going to be cheaper."

Windhoek, the capital of arid South-West Africa, has gained the distinction of becoming the first city in the world to recycle its waste water directly into drinking water. Waste water is taken out of sewers, processed conventionally, oxidized in ponds for about a month, then run through filters and activated-carbon columns, chlorinated, and put back into the water mains. Windhoek's distinction may prove to be dubious, because the full effects of recycled water on health are unknown. There is a potential hazard of viruses (hepatitis, polio, etc.) being concentrated in recycling. For this reason, many health experts feel that renovated sewage should not be accepted as drinking water in the U.S. until its safety can be more reliably demonstrated.

Costs naturally go up as treatment gets more complex. While primary-secondary treatment costs about 12 cents a thousand gallons of waste water, the advanced techniques in use at Lake Tahoe, for instance, bring the cost up to 30 cents. About 7½ cents of the increase is for phosphorus removal. Reverse osmosis at this stage would raise the cost to at least 35 cents a thousand gallons, higher than the average cost of drinking water to metered households in the U.S. Whatever new techniques are accepted, rising costs of pollution control will be a fact of life.

Ironically, these new treatment techniques, such as removal of phosphorus with chemicals, will intensify one of the most pressing operational problems in waste-water treatment — sludge disposal. Sludge, the solid matter removed from domestic or industrial waste matter, is a nuisance, highly contaminated unless it's disinfected. The handling and disposal of sludge can eat up to one-half of a treatment plant's operating budget. Some communities incinerate their sludge, contributing to air pollution. "Now in cleaning the water further we are adding chemicals to take out phosphorus and more solids," says Francis M. Middleton, director of the Taft Center. "While we end up with cleaner water, we also end up with even greater quantities of sludge."

Chicago's struggle with its sludge illustrates some of the difficulties and perhaps an effective way of coping with them. With 1,000 tons of sludge a day to dispose of, the metropolitan sanitary district has been stuffing about half of it into deep holes near treatment plants, at a cost of about $60 a ton. The other half is dried and shipped to Florida and elsewhere where it is sold for $12 a ton to citrus growers and companies producing fertilizers — a nonprofit operation. Vinton W. Bacon, general superintendent of the sanitary district, says this state of affairs can't continue. "We're running out of land. Not only that, but the land we're using for disposal is valuable. And even it will be filled within two years."

Bacon is convinced he has an answer that will not only cut costs but also solve disposal problems indefinitely while helping to make marginal lands bloom. Bacon's scheme, tested in pilot projects in Chicago and elsewhere, is to pump liquid sludge through a pipeline to strip mines and marginal farmland about sixty miles southwest of Chicago. "We put the sludge water through tanks where it's digested," Bacon says. "Then it can be used directly without any odor or health dangers. It's the perfect marriage. That land needs our sludge as much as we need the land. Most astounding, even acquiring the required land at current market prices, taking in the cost of a twenty-four-inch, sixty-mile-long pipeline, the pumps, reservoirs, irrigation equipment, and manpower, the cost would still come to only $20 a ton. We could build a pipeline 200 miles long and still not run higher costs than with our present system."

An aspect of water pollution that seems harder to cope with is the overflow of combined sewers during storms. A combined system that unites storm and sanitary sewers into a single network usually has interceptor sewers, with direct outlets to a stream, to protect the treatment plant from flooding during heavy rains. But in diverting excess water from treatment plants, interceptor sewers dump raw sewage into the waterways. Obviously, this partly defeats the purpose of having treatment plants.

So bad are the consequences of sewer overflow that some specialists would prefer to see part of the federal money being channeled into secondary treatment go into correction of the combined-sewer problem instead. But more than 1,300 U.S. communities have combined sewers, and the cost of separating the systems would be huge. The American Public Works Association estimated the cost of total separation at $48 *billion*. The job could be done in an alternative fashion for a still shocking $15 billion, by building holding tanks for the overflow storm water. Still another possibility would be to build separate systems for sewage and to use existing sewers for storm water. The federal war on water pollution discourages construction of combined sewers but strangely includes no money (except for $28 million already awarded for research and development) to remedy the problem of existing combined-sewer systems.

The General Accounting Office recently surveyed federal activities in water-pollution control and found some glaring deficiencies. The G.A.O. prepared its report for Congress and therefore failed to point out that in some of the deficiencies the real culprit was Congress itself. Still largely rural-oriented, Congress originally limited federal grants for construction of waste-treatment facilities to $250,000 per municipality. The dollar ceiling was eventually raised, but was not removed until fiscal 1968. In the preceding twelve years about half of the waste-treatment facilities were built in hamlets with populations of less than 2,500, and 92 percent in towns with populations under 50,000.

In drafting the legislation that provides for new water-quality standards, Congress again

showed limited vision, leaving it up to the states to decide many important questions. Each state is free to make its own decisions on pollution-control goals in terms of determining the uses to which a particular stream or lake will be put. Each state is to decide on the stream characteristics that would allow such uses — dissolved oxygen, temperature, etc. Finally, each state is to set up a schedule for corrective measures that would ensure the stream quality decided upon, and prepare plans for legal enforcement of the standards.

It would have been logical to set standards for entire river basins since rivers don't always stay within state boundaries. What's more, there were already several regional river-basin compacts in existence that could have taken on the job. But with the single exception of the Delaware River Basin Commission, of which the federal government is a member, the government bypassed the regional bodies and insisted that each state set its own standards. Predictably, the result has been confusion. The states submitted standards by June 30, 1967, but by the end of 1969 Interior had given full approval to only twenty-five states and territories. It has now become the prickly task of the Secretary of the Interior to reconcile the conflicting sets of standards that states have established for portions of the same rivers.

Some states facing each other across a river have set different standards for water characteristics, as if dividing the river flow in the middle with a bureaucratic fence. Kentucky and Indiana, across the Ohio from each other, submitted two different temperature standards for that river: Kentucky came up with a maximum of 93° Fahrenheit, while Indiana wants 90°. Similarly, Ohio sets its limit at 93°, while West Virginia, across the same river, chose 86°. One reason for such differences about river temperature is that biologists don't always agree among themselves about safe temperatures for aquatic life. At one recent meeting in Cincinnati, where federal and state officials were attempting to reconcile the different figures for the Ohio, the disagreement among biologists was so great that one exasperated engineer suggested, "Maybe we should start putting ice cubes at different points in the river."

The biggest deficiency in the federal approach is its lack of imagination. Congress chose the subsidy route as being the easiest, but the task could have been undertaken much more thoughtfully. A regional or river-valley approach would have required more careful working out than a program of state-by-state standards and subsidies, but it would have made more sense economically, and would have assured continuing management of water quality.

A promising river-valley program is evolving along the Great Miami River in Ohio. The Great Miami runs through a heavily industrialized valley. There are, for instance, eighteen paper mills in the valley. Dayton, the principal city on the river, houses four divisions of General Motors and is the home of National Cash Register. To finance a three-year exploratory program for river management, the Miami Conservatory District, a regional flood-control agency, has imposed temporary charges, based on volume of effluent, on sixty plants, businesses, and municipalities along the river. These charges amount to a total of $350,000 a year, ranging from $500 that might be paid by a motel to $23,000 being paid by a single power-generating station.

With this money, plus a $500,000 grant from the Federal Water Pollution Control Administration, the district has been looking into river-wide measures that will be needed to control pollution even *after* every municipality along the river has a secondary treatment plant. (Dayton already has one.) The district's staff of sanitary engineers, ecologists, and systems analysts has come up with suggested measures to augment the low flood of the river as an additional method of pollution control. The Great Miami's mean annual flow at Dayton is 2,500 cubic feet a second, but every ten years or so it falls to a mere 170 cubic feet a second. To assure a more even flow, the Miami District will build either reservoirs or facilities to pump groundwater, at a cost of several million dollars. The cost will be shared by river users. District engineers are also exploring in-stream aeration, or artificial injection of air into the river, to provide additional dissolved oxygen. The state has set an ambitious goal for the Great Miami — to make the river usable "for all purposes, at all places, all the time."

To meet this goal, the district will introduce waste-discharge fees, which will probably be based on the amount of oxygen-demanding wastes or hot water discharged. Will these amount to a charge for polluting the river? "No," says Max L. Mitchell, the district's chief engineer. "Charges will be high enough to make industry reduce water use."

Federal money would do a lot more good if it were divided up along river-basin lines instead of municipality by municipality or state by state, with little regard for differences in pollution at different points in a basin. To distribute federal funds more effectively, Congress would have to overcome its parochial orientation. Also, Congress should be channeling more funds into new waste-treatment technologies and ways of putting them to use. Unless pollution abatement is undertaken in an imaginative and systematic manner, the "war" against dirty rivers may be a long, losing campaign.

EDITOR'S COMMENTS

People and factories actually consume nothing but energy. In this process they merely use and transform things. The absolute mass of materials entering a person, city, or factory must either remain there on be transported out as waste. This is an antinature act. In nature, materials are cycled — they are used over and over again. The development of salvage methods which could be economically profitable when applied to waste water represents one of the most challenging problems ever confronted by engineers. Making people, cities, and industries aware of this problem may be just as challenging.

JOEL W. HEDGPETH

The Oceans: World Sump

Joel Hedgpeth is Professor of Biological Oceanography at the Marine Science Center, Newport, Oregon. He has been concerned with man's impact on seashores, is the author of a guide to seashore life, and editor of Treatise on Marine Ecology. He is the author of numerous polemics on the environment, and founder (1944) of the Society for the Prevention of Progress.

We have become much concerned about the potential resources of the oceans of the world. At all levels of the public press, from scholarly books to official reports of presidential and gubernatorial commissions and the ephemeral mimeographed effluvia of ad hoc meetings, there are discussions of the potential yield of all sorts of things from the sea. More fish for our tables, diamonds off Africa, oysters from thermally controlled raceways of power plants, and even the very water itself are being counted upon to make a better life for all by the year 2000, if not shortly after. Presidents and Chairmen of the Board predict at after-dinner speeches that the ocean is the place to go for business and industry, that the development of all these resources will be the glamour business of the 1970s. At the same time, we are beginning to suspect that although the ocean may cover most of the globe, it may

not be an eternally self-renewing cesspool to take care of everything we want to dispose of. Furthermore, our capacity to produce undesirable materials or to create irreducible crud that must somehow be shoved under a rug or washed out of sight is increasing exponentially. Years ago, when I began writing articles about the impending doom of our environment, my old English professor remarked that he could depend on me to take a dim view of things. But the exponential rate of deterioration has caught up with him and it seems almost a personal vindication to have him write a book on the problems of garbage disposal.[1]

It was not very long ago that no one thought much about using the ocean as a dumping ground, and as late as 1966 one of the officials associated with the development of the colossal sewer outfalls of Los Angeles could make the following statements at the First International Conference on Waste Disposal in the Sea:

> The great economy inherent in the discharge of urban sewage and industrial wastes into

Reprinted by permission of the author and publisher from *Environment* 12: 40-46. April 1970. Copyright © 1970, by the Committee for Environmental Information.

1. George R. Stewart, *Not So Rich as You Think* (Boston: Houghton Mifflin, 1968).

nearshore waters for final disposal is apparent to all who will investigate. It is doubly apparent to those charged with the responsibility of disposing of such wastes without excessive cost to the public or menace to public health. If the ocean, or one of its arms, can be reached with a sewer outfall, within the bounds of economy, the grim spectre of an expensive complete treatment plant grows dimmer and dimmer until it fades entirely and, to the great satisfaction of those who have to gather funds for the public budget, as well as they (you and I) who have to pay the bill, the good old ocean does the job free.

And small wonder that we look to the sea for this assist. Its vast area and volume, its oxygen-laden waters, its lack of potability or usefulness for domestic and most industrial purposes, present an unlimited and most attractive reservoir for waste assimilation.[2]

One would almost hope that the gentleman was trying to be a bit humorous except that his statement suggests the same lack of concern for other life on the planet that has governed, for example, our disposal of radioactive wastes.

It does seem that, in an era when many thoughtful scientists recognize that the resources of the sea are finite and can never replace those of land for the supply of food, the concept of the inexhaustible sea is still alive among sanitary engineers.

We have just recently realized that heating up water as a by-product of cooling industrial and power-generating processes is a form of pollution, "thermal enrichment" to the contrary notwithstanding. Removing a part of the environment may be considered pollution as much as adding something that was not naturally there before, and it may not be long before we find ourselves talking of interference with the maintenance of sand on a beach as "pollution." Nor must we be complacent about this matter of inert, solid waste that we dump into the ocean daily in carload lots from every large coastal city.

All seems well if twenty tons of suspended solid disappear every day from a large effluent pipe in the bottom of Puget Sound, as was cheerfully announced by one engineer to his colleagues, but it must not be forgotten that this stuff is going somewhere. What is happening to it today may become a rude shock to some other industry or fishery a few years hence. It is true that rats and seagulls may thrive on city dumps, but we cannot assume that desirable species of marine animals may thrive beneath a steady rain of debris from our city streets and industrial activities.

We forget too easily that "out of sight, out of mind" is our way of least resistance when confronted with unpleasant problems. At least 46 years ago it was recognized that "the exhaust gas of automobiles is extremely poisonous."[3] The authors of this statement went on to suggest some suitable practical measures, specifically that automobiles, garages, and shops should have vertical exhaust pipes to carry the fumes away overhead (the inversion layer was an unrecognized phenomenon at that time). In some unhappy ways this paper sounds all too up-to-date:

. . . it is essential that now, before worse conditions develop, steps should be taken to ameliorate the hazards to health and life arising from the inhalation of automobile exhaust gas. The enactment of certain requirements either in state law or in city ordinances, and also provisions for supervision of automobile fuels and engine construction, are necessary to this end. The matter cannot be left to the voluntary action

2. A. M. Rawn, "Fixed and Changing Values in Ocean Disposal of Sewage and Wastes," *First International Conference on Waste Disposal in the Sea* (New York: Pergamon Press, 1966), pp. 6-11.

3. Yandell Henderson and Howard W. Haggard, "Health Hazard from Automobile Exhaust Gas in City Streets, Garages, and Repair Shops," *Journal of the American Medical Association* 81 (August 4, 1923):385-391.

of the automobile industry. . . . as the secretary of one of the largest automobile manufacturers recently remarked to one of us, "We are in the business to make and sell cars. We will conform to any requirements regarding health hazards only when the public demands it and the laws enforce it."

Now, 46 years later, it is difficult to pick up the morning paper and not find some article about air pollution, or an editorial demanding that something be done about it.

Ours is an exponential age: we are increasing our numbers exponentially, and our capacity to pollute the world with substances potentially if not immediately harmful to our environment and to ourselves is increasing even faster than our own numbers. Unfortunately there does not seem to have been a comparable knowledge explosion, at least among those who must deal with the pollution explosion. It is disturbing to find, as late as 1968, serious proposals for disposal of wastes in the sea based on oceanographic information assembled from a motley collection of data from different years, as if the engineers involved thought that data from one season thirty-five years before could be compared with that of another season in 1966 to provide a model for what might happen in the real ocean.[4] This approach to the problem, especially when supported by large amounts of public money, is dangerous as well as pathetic. For the immediate future at least we are dealing with that part of the ocean about which we know the least — the region inshore, mostly within the three or five-mile limit. We have much to learn of currents, mixing processes, and natural temperature regimes of this part of the ocean into which we are dumping sewage, pesticides, radionuclides, and just plain junk.

This is especially true in the case of the proposed outfalls which would carry off wastewater from central California, perhaps by tunnel under the mountains and across the San Andreas fault, directly to the Pacific Ocean. This project would add a permanent feature to the environment, yet is being recommended on the basis of admittedly short-term, incomplete studies, despite clear, published warning:

> There is abundant evidence, however, that longterm climatic and oceanographic changes of regime take place. Several of these are well documented for the region of the California current and elsewhere. These are accompanied by great fluctuation in the locations of stocks of commercial fish and other organisms. Thus in the circumstances of disposal where the dominant circulation is other than tidal, no long-term confidence can be maintained in the veracity of conclusions drawn from short-term surveys. Even where tidal currents dominate, findings of the composition of the fauna may not be reliable.[5]

The aspect of atmospheric circulation and the contribution of fallout to nearshore concentrations have been clearly overlooked in many considerations of how much pollution we can add to waters of the ocean. Estimates of the permissible amount of materials that might be released into a body of water are meaningless if they do not also take into consideration the potential additions from the atmosphere. Recent advances in our knowledge of how pesticides are distributed in the air indicate very strongly that the concept of acceptable dilution of wastewaters in a bay or the ocean is obsolete, and the most dramatic demonstration of this obsolescence is the reproductive failure of

4. Engineering-Science, Inc., Kaiser Engineers report on San Francisco Bay-Delta Water Quality Program, Raymond Walsh, Project Director. Final Report. Task VII-1a, Special Oceonographic Studies (see VII-13, for example). June 15, 1968.

5. R. T. P. Whipple, "Considerations on the Siting of Outfalls for the Sea Disposal of Radioactive Effluent in Tidal Waters," *Advances in Water Pollution*, edited by Pearson (New York: Macmillan) 3(1964):1-18.

pelicans and other marine birds. The ocean is obviously not an infinite sink into which everything may be dumped; certainly not the upper layers, contaminated at the surface by fallout of man's many antiecological activities and at shallow depths by sewer outfalls. It is a lively, interacting system; indeed, as Wesley Marx called it, "the frail ocean."[6]

As we become aware of new hazards to the survival of life on this planet, we may want to forget the old standbys because it seems that we have blundered into the Grand Guignol by mistake. But we cannot do so; we must sit through the increasing horrors of the melodrama. The immediately noticeable effects of careless use of pesticides should not cause us to forget that radioactivity is still with us, and that certain radioactive wastes are still being discharged into the sea. Since 1952, low-level wastes have been released into the Irish Sea at Windscale, and into the Columbia River at Hanford, 250 miles from the Pacific Ocean. The release at Windscale has been carefully monitored to see that the permissible levels established on the basis of concentration in an edible seaweed are not exceeded.[7] No permissible levels have been established for the Columbia release on the basis of the maximum possible amounts of radioactivity that might be accumulated by a consumer of seafood, but the levels are stated to be well below the maximum permissible concentrations established for man by various authorities.

We know little about the effect of these low levels of radioactivity upon organisms, and even less about the possible effects of introducing artificial radionuclides that have not been part of the natural environment of the sea. Most of our information is based on subjecting organisms to levels of radioactivity they may never encounter in nature and which would doubtless be harmful to us as well as other forms of life. Furthermore, we have used as experimental animals for such studies organisms that have long been used in laboratory studies from carefully selected stocks. Some of these animals are almost indestructible, and others are not appropriate for comparison of experimental results with conditions in the sea. On the basis of experiments with the pelagic eggs of Black Sea anchovies, Soviet investigators find perceptible effects from levels of activity of strontium-90 that are close to permissible levels, whereas American workers experimenting with eggs and young of salmon eggs found no such damage.[8] It would seem obvious that one cannot compare results based on eggs of a fish living near the surface of the Black Sea in a comparatively constant salinity with those based on eggs of a fish adapted to withstanding the full range of salinity. The Russian results suggest caution, and in the opinion of G. G. Polikarpov, we have already reached the maximum permissible limits, and "further radioactive contamination of the seas and oceans is inadmissable."[9]

As Pieter Korringa says, it is not the occasional spectacular local disaster that is significant so much as "the general trends, the stealthy deterioration of environmental conditions in sections of the sea of vital importance for its living resources."[10] Some-

6. Wesley, Marx, *The Frail Ocean* (New York: Coward McCann, 1967).

7. J. Mauchline and W. L. Templeton, "Artificial and Natural Radioisotopes in the Marine Environment," *Oceanography and Marine Biology,* Annual Review, 2(1964): 229-279. W. L. Templeton, "Ecological Aspects of the Disposal of Radioactive Wastes to the Sea," *Ecology and the Industrial Society Fifth Symposium,* British Ecological Society. (1965):65-67.

8. F. L. Parker, "Disposal of Low-level Radioactive Wastes into the Ocean," *Nuclear Safety* 8(4)(1967):376-382.

9. G. G. Polikarpov, *Radioecology of Aquatic Organisms* (New York: Reinhold Book Division, 1966).

10. Pieter Korriga, "Biological Consequences of Marine Pollution with Special Reference to the North Sea Fisheries, *Helgolander wiss. Meeresunters* 17(April 1968):126-140.

thing of this nature may be occurring along the central California coast at this time, where levels of pesticides in eggs of market crabs (*Cancer magister*) and halibut near the Golden Gate are as high as .430 parts per million and .591 parts per million respectively. Reproductive success of crabs in this region has been poor in recent years, and may be related to the discharge of pesticides into San Francisco Bay:

> We do not know what constitutes a lethal level of pesticide residues in eggs of our marine species, but it is entirely possible that pesticide residues are already having deleterious effects on our marine species.[11]

On these grounds, the authors of this report urge that chlorinated hydrocarbons should not be discharged into the marine environment and express the opinion that it may be necessary to achieve this aim by prohibition of use.

Our experiences with destruction of birds and other wildlife by pesticides should be warning enough that they may endanger fisheries' stocks or, indeed, the very productivity of the ocean. Several ecologists have suggested that we might upset the balance of plant life in the oceans with pesticides carried on the wind and deposited with the fall of dust particles.

> Considering the powerful forces for ecological change which are at man's disposal, admitting the impossibility of complete foreknowledge of the consequences of many activities, and granting that a highly technical over-populated world must continue to take risks with natural resources, an "early warning system" for unwanted consequences is extremely important. We do not have such a system at present.[12]

What kind of an early-warning system is needed then? A die-off of ten percent of a species? Are we to say that Polikarpov's warning that we have already reached the maximum permissible level of radioactive contamination of the sea is simply politics or inadequate application of statistics to his experimental results and therefore is not a warning? What about the DDT in penguins? Granted such a warning system, perhaps some sort of red light that turns on when the first plant or animal dies from a new pollutant, will we heed it? We have had ample warning, 20 to 40 years ahead, that the California sardine fishery was in danger from overfishing and that we would exterminate the blue whales, but our reaction was simply to continue until the predictions were verified. We were warned in 1923 that automobile exhaust would kill people, and it has taken 46 years for most of us to admit it. It should be obvious even to a Congressman that we should never have learned to make some chemicals in the first place and that certainly we should not be releasing them into the environment, even in the perpetual "sink" of the ocean and certainly not near the shore: "Pesticides and other very dangerous products should never be admitted in the shallow sea areas, so important as nursery grounds for the fishery resources."[13]

There are real limits to our potential exploitation of the sea, set by difficulties in hunting, processing, and marketing, as well as by the fisheries' stocks themselves. We may be able to increase our total annual harvest as much as fourfold, but in doing so we will be creating circumstances that may

11. Melvyn Odemar, Paul W. Wild, and Kenneth C. Wilson, The final report of the California Department of Fish and Game to the San Francisco Bay-Delta Water Quality Program pursuant to task order VII-1a (DFG). MRO Reference No. 68-12, July 1968.

12. Report of the Subcommittee on Science, Research, and Development to the Committee on Science and Astronautics, U. S. House of Representatives, 89th Congress, 2d session, "Environmental Pollution, a Challenge to Science and Technology," (Committee Print, Serial S.) Washington, 1966, revised August 1968.

13. Pieter Korriga, "Biological Consequences of Marine Pollution with Special Reference to the North Sea Fisheries, *Helgolander wiss. Meeresunters* 17(April 1968):126-140.

render the stock on which we depend more vulnerable to environmental fluctuations that a mass species not under fishing pressure might easily survive. Something of this sort may have contributed to the decline of the sardine stocks of the Pacific Coast

of North America.[14] As we increase our pressure on populations of the sea, we can expect that such added complications as pollutants will have even more effect than predictable on the basis of laboratory survival under artificial stress.

There is some implicit realization of this in a summary statement of the House Subcommittee Report on Environmental Pollution:

> The ocean currents present a partciular problem to storage or dumping in the sea. Although the ocean is big, recirculation and local effects of pollution may mean that the portion available for waste disposal is actually rather small. Further, there is life throughout the ocean. Marine ecology indicates that this life is affected by pollutants and even by temperature changes. . . . It would be tragic if the food producing potential of the sea were decreased by inappropriate waste disposal. . . . It seems that standards and criteria for the ocean, as a receiving body, should be as carefully worked out as for those for inland lakes and rivers. The sea was the original home of life and its ecology still interacts in many ways with man's present domain.[15]

One would wish that this statement had not used the word ecology in this somewhat unsophisticated way. There is danger that the glib pseudolanguage of some ecologists, with its talk of energy input and output and circuit analogies, when combined with the limited biological knowledge of sanitary engineers, may produce dazzling oversimplifications to justify disastrous policies and

---

The tendency of engineers to manipulate language is shown in a recent report from Kaiser Engineers concerning waste disposal in the San Francisco Bay area. The following statement from Chapter X was evidently intended to be reassuring:

Ocean disposal of wastewaters presents opportunities which are unique in the area of wastewater treatment and disposal. Unlike most situations the availability of the ocean makes it possible not only to consider various alternative combinations of treatment and outfall location but also, and most importantly, to consider outfall location with respect to minimizing disturbances to the ecosystem and the associated beneficial uses. That is, based on economics, where applicable, and technological and scientific evaluations, it is possible to locate an outfall along a coast line where the negative benefits are minimized while still accomplishing wastewater disposal. Although such an approach is most desirable in any wastewater management system, ocean disposal is one of the few instances where it can be realized.

In this statement there is a concession to the "ecosystem," but it is to be noted that possible adverse effects are referred to as "negative benefits," a sort of language which, if carried to its logical extreme, will replace "dead" by some such expression as "negatively alive." J.H.

---

14. Garth I. Murphy, "Population Biology of the Pacific Sardine (Sardinops caerulea)." *Proceedings of the California Academy of Science, Fourth Series,* 34(1)(July 26, 1966):1-84.

15. Report of the Subcommittee on Science, Research, and Development to the Committee on Science and Astronautics, U.S. House of Representatives, 89th Congress, 2d session, "Environmental Pollution, a Challenge to Science and Technology," (Committee Print. Serial S.) Washington, 1966, revised August 1968.

decisions for waste disposal. The problems of pollution in the sea are too serious to be obscured by such verbiage.

The magnitude of the problem can be realized when it is remembered that by that magic year 2000 more than 50 percent of the population of the United States will probably be living within 100 miles of the shore of the sea or of the Great Lakes:

> By the end of the century, some 150 to 200 million people may be struggling for places on the beaches and in the narrow coastal waters. Even if the country's entire coastal strip were converted into public beaches, this would mean about two people per foot. Actually only a fraction of the shoreline is available for public recreation. Long stretches are too polluted to be safe for swimming or water sports, and much of it is owned by either industry, shipping, and military interests, or private individuals.[16]

Obviously one of our major efforts in pollution control must be directed towards keeping our beaches hygenically clean as well as aesthetically attractive. In the words of Carl Sauer, in his espousal of the hypothesis that man's first culture may have begun on the seashore:

> We still like to go beachcombing, returning for the moment to primitive act and mood. When all the lands will be filled with people and machines, perhaps the last need and observance of man will be, as it was in the beginning, to come down to experience the sea.[17]

The *Torrey Canyon* and Santa Barbara disasters brought to the attention of the big industrialists just how seriously this matter of beach aesthetics and the preservation of sea life can be. On British shores, the cure (if such it may be called) by detergents may have been worse than the disease.[18] An oil spill is more than a threat to birds and fisheries, it is a threat to man's idea of the sea as an inviolable environmental resource for contemplation and recreation.

Our concern with conservation is more than saving scenery or the lavendar dream of prettying up power plants with flower beds, where the deer and the antelope may play between tepid lily ponds teeming with goldfish; it is with the quality of environment, not only for aesthetics, but for human survival itself. To be "people oriented" is to remember all that people need for living beyond mere survival.[19] Those ecologists and engineers who seem to think that we can solve all our problems by manipulating our natural system to support an ever-increasing population are simply borrowing time that does not exist. Of course, if we want to live like ants under plastic domes to protect us from air pollution, while eating some sort of sludge from artificially eutrophic ponds sustained by our own effluvia, we may last a bit longer as a species, at least as a species of ant. Our most certain knowledge of how to control nature to our own advantage rests not in our ability to tamper with the system, but to reduce our impact upon our environment. Unless and until we do this, everything else is beside the point.

16. Roger Revelle, "Outdoor Recreation in a Hyperproductive Society," *Proceedings of the American Academy of Arts and Sciences* 96(4)(Fall 1967):1171-1191.

17. Carl O. Sauer, "Seashore — Primitive Home of Man?" *Proceedings of the American Philo. Society* 106(1962): 41-47. (Reprinted in Land Life, a selection from the writings of Carl Ortwin Sauer, Berkeley: University of California Press, 1967).

18. J. D. Mercer, ed., "Conservation and the Torrey Canyon," *Journal of the Devon Trust for Nature Conservation, Ltd.,* Supplement, July 1967. See also: E. D. S. Corner, A. J. Southward, and E. C. Southward. "Toxicity of Oil-spill Removers ('detergents') to Marine Life: An Assessment Using the Intertidal Barnacle *Elminius modestus,*" *Journal of the Marine Biological Association* 48(1968):29-47.

19. Ian Burton, "The Quality of the Environment: A Review," *Geographical Review,* 58(3)(1968): 472-481. Joel W. Hedgpeth, "A Fit Home for Earth's Noblest Inhabitant," *Science* 164(May 9, 1969):666-669.

EDITOR'S COMMENTS

Dr. Hedgpeth clearly outlines the dangers inherent in continued misuse of the oceans. I have previously discussed the fallacy held by many that ocean fish will be an ever-increasing source of human food. It may be that many minerals can be recovered from the sea once the easily-accessible ores have been mined from the earth's crust. However, a little known and equally important function of the ocean is the production of atmospheric oxygen. More than one-half of the oxygen being produced by photosynthesis today comes from marine phytoplankton. We know very little as to the long-term effects that continued chemical and radioactive contamination of the seas will have on these plant populations. Of course, marine phytoplankton also represent the basic trophic level supporting virtually all ocean life. If the producers of the ocean were to be de-stroyed, or even if their population densities were to be drastically changed, ocean life as we know it now would change, and within a few hundred years, a noticeable decrease in oxygen content of the atmosphere might be noted.

It is clear that man in general does not respect the ocean. Many European industries place highly toxic chemical wastes in drums which are loaded on outgoing freighters for dumping at sea. These drums are supposed to be pushed overboard when water is reached having a depth of over 6000 feet. The drums are now being recovered in shallow fishing waters along the coast of northern Europe and are even washed ashore sometimes. Eventually these drums corrode and their contents mix with the sea — the ecological effects this will produce are totally unknown — out of sight, out of mind.

MAX BLUMER, HOWARD L. SANDERS,
J. FRED GRASSLE and GEORGE R. HAMPSON

A Small Oil Spill

Max Blumer and Howard L. Sanders are
Senior Scientists at the Woods Hole Oceano-
graphic Institution. J. Fred Grassle is Assistant
Scientist and George R. Hampson is Research
Associate at Woods Hole.

During the last few years the public has
become increasingly aware of the presence
of oil on the sea. We read about the recur-
ring accidents in oil transport and production, such as the disaster of the *Torrey
Canyon* tanker, the oil well blowout at
Santa Barbara, and the oil well fires in the
Gulf of Mexico. To those visiting our shores
the presence of oil on rocks and sand has
become an everyday experience; however,
few of us realize that these spectacular accidents contribute only a small fraction of
the total oil that enters the ocean. In the
Torrey Canyon episode of 1967 about 100,-
000 tons of crude oil were lost. By comparison, routine discharges from tankers and
other commercial vessels contribute an estimated three and one-half million tons of
petroleum to the ocean every year. In addition, pollution from accidents in port and
on the high seas, in exploration and production, in storage, in pipeline breaks, from
spent lubricants, from incompletely burned
fuels, and from untreated industrial and
domestic sewage contribute an equal or

larger amount of oil. Thus, it has been
estimated that the total oil influx into the
ocean is between five and ten million tons
per year.[1]

What are the effects of oil on marine
organisms and on food that we recover from
the sea? Some scientists have said that the
oceans in their fullness should be capable
of assimilating the entire oil input. This,
however, assumes that the oil is evenly distributed through the entire water profile, or
water column, of the ocean. Unfortunately
this assumption is not correct. Oil production, transportation, and use are heavily
concentrated in the coastal regions, and
pollution therefore predominately affects the
surface waters on the continental margins.
J. H. Ryther has stated that the open sea
is virtually a biological desert.[2] Although
the deeper ocean provides some fishing for
tuna, bonito, skipjack, and billfish, the

Reprinted by permission of the authors and publisher from *Environment* 13(2): 2-12. March
1971. Copyright © 1971 by the Committee for
Environmental Information.
1. M. Blumer, "Scientific Aspects of the Oil Spill
Problem," paper presented at the Oil Spills Conference, Committee on Challenges of Modern
Society, NATO, Brussels, Nov. 1970.
2. J. H. Ryther, "Photosynthesis and Fish Production in the Sea." *Science* 166(1969):72-76.

coastal waters produce almost the entire shellfish crop and nearly half of the total fish crop. The bulk of the remainder of the fish crop comes from regions of upwelling water, near the continental margins, that occupy only one-tenth of one percent of the total surface area of the seas. These productive waters receive the heaviest influx of oil. They also are most affected by other activities of man, such as dredging, waste disposal, and unintentional dispersal of chemical poisons like insecticides.

Some environmentalists have expressed the belief that major oil spills such as those from the *Torrey Canyon* and the blowout at Santa Barbara have brought about little biological damage in the ocean.[3] These statements are largely based on statistical measurements of the catch of adult fish. We believe that such statistics are a very insensitive measure of the ecologic damage to wide oceanic regions. Often the migratory history of the fish species studied is unknown. The fish may not have been exposed to the spill itself, or may not have suffered from a depletion of food organisms if their growth occurred in areas remote from the spill. Statistical and observational data on adult fishes will not reveal damage to the often much more sensitive juvenile forms or to intermediate members in the marine food chain. The only other studies on effects of oil on marine organisms have concentrated on relatively tolerant organisms which live between the tides at the margins of affected areas. The main impact, however, would be expected in subtidal areas, and that has never been measured quantitatively.

A relatively small oil spill that occurred almost at the doorstep of the Woods Hole Oceanographic Institution at Woods Hole, Massachusetts, gave us the opportunity to study immediate and long-term ecological damage in a region for which we had extensive previous knowledge about the biol-ogy and chemistry of native marine organisms.[4] On September 16, 1969, an oil barge on the way to a power plant on the Cape Cod Canal came ashore off Fassets Point, West Falmouth, in Buzzards Bay. Between 650 and 700 tons of #2 fuel oil were released into the coastal waters. The oil-contaminated region in Buzzards Bay expanded steadily with time after the accident as the complex interaction of wind, waves, and bottom sediment movement spread oil from polluted to unpolluted areas. Eight months after the grounding, polluted sea bottom, marshes, and tidal rivers comprised an area many times larger than that first affected by the accident. The dispersion was much greater than expected on the basis of conventional studies of oil pollution. The situation even forced changes in our research efforts. As we shall explain later, a control point for marine surveys was established beyond the anticipated limit of the spread of oil. Within three weeks, the contamination had spread to the station. Another was established twice as far away. Three months after the accident, that too was polluted. Bottom sediment was contaminated 42 feet beneath the surface, the greatest water depth in that part of Buzzards Bay.

Ecological effects of the spreading blanket of oil beneath the surface were severe. The oil decimated offshore marine life in the immediate area of the spill during the first few days. As the oil spread out across the bottom of the bay in the following months, it retained its toxicity.

3. Julian McCaull, "The Black Tide," *Environment* 11(9)(1969):10.

4. M. Blumer, G. Souza, J. Sass, "Hydrocarbon Pollution of Edible Shellfish by an Oil Spill," *Marine Biology,* 5(3)(March 1970):195-202. M. Blumer, J. Sass, G. Souza, H. L. Sanders, J. F. Grassle, G. R. Hampson, "The West Falmouth Oil Spill," Reference No. 70-44, unpublished manuscript available from senior author, Woods Hole Oceanographic Institution, Woods Hole, Massachusetts, September 1970.

Even by May 1970, eight months after the spill, bacterial degradation (breakdown into simpler substances) of oil was not far advanced in the most polluted regions. More rapid oil deterioration in outlying, less affected areas had been reversed by a new influx of less degraded oil from the more contaminated regions.

The tidal Wild Harbor River still contained an estimated four tons of fuel oil. The contamination had ruled out commercial shellfishing for at least two years. The severe biological damage and the slow rate of bio-degradation of the oil suggests that shellfish productivity will be affected for an even longer period. Furthermore, destruction of bottom plants and animals reduced the stability of marshlands and sea bottom. Resulting erosion may have promoted spread of the oil along the sea floor. Inshore, the oil penetrated to a depth of at least one to two feet in marsh sediment.

Nevertheless, compared in magnitude to other catastrophes, this was a relatively small spill; the amount of oil lost in the *Torrey Canyon* accident was 150 times larger. The interim results of our survey, coupled with research findings of other studies in this laboratory, indicate that crude oil and other petroleum products are a far more dangerous and persistent threat to the marine environment and to human food resources than we would have anticipated. Pollution from a large oil spill is very obvious and visible. It has often been thought that the eventual disappearance of this visible evidence coincides with the disappearance of any biological damage. This, however, is not true. Sensitive analytical techniques can still detect oil in marine organisms and in sediments after the visual evidence has disappeared, and biological studies reveal that this residual oil is still toxic to the marine organisms. Here we shall discuss first the general results of our study, then go more deeply into the description of the laboratory work involving biology, biochemistry, and chemistry. Our most important findings are these.[5]

Crude oil and petroleum products contain many substances that are poisonous to marine life. Some of these cause immediate death; others have a slower effect. Crude oils and oil products differ in their relative composition; therefore the specific toxic effect may vary. Crude oil, in general, is less immediately toxic than some distilled products, but even crude oil that has been weathered (altered by exposure to the weather) at sea for some time still contains many of the acutely toxic hydrocarbons.[6] The more persistent, slowly acting poisons (for example, the carcinogens) are more abundant in crude oil than in some of the lower boiling distillates. These poisons are quite resistant to the environmental weathering of oil.

In spite of low density, oil may mix with water, especially in a turbulent sea during storm conditions. Hydrocarbons may be dispersed through the water column in solution in the form of droplets, and the compounds may reach the sea bottom, particularly if weighted down by mineral particles. On the sea floor oil persists for long periods and can continue to damage bottom plants and animals. Thus, a single accident may result in long-term, continual pollution of the sea. This is a very important finding since biologists have long agreed that chronic pollution generally has more far-reaching effects than an accident of short duration. Hydrocarbons can be taken up by fish and shellfish. When the oil enters the fat and flesh of the animals, it is isolated from natural degradation processes. It remains essentially constant in amount and chemically intact even after the animals are trans-

5. Ibid.

6. M. Blumer, G. Souza, J. Sass, "Hydrocarbon Pollution," *op. cit.*, p. 198.

planted into clean water for decontamination. Thus, chemicals from oil that may be poisonous to marine organisms and other animals, including man, may persist in the sea and in biological systems for many months after the spill.

By killing the bottom organisms, oil reduces cohesion of the bottom sediments and thereby accelerates transport of the sediments. Sediment movements along the sea bottom thus are a common occurrence after an oil spill. In this way contaminated sediments may be spread over great distances under the influence of tide and wave action, and the oil may be carried to areas not immediately polluted by the spill.

None of the presently available countermeasures can completely eliminate the biological damage of oil spills. The rapid removal of oil by mechanical recovery or by burning appears most promising. The use of sinking agents or detergents, on the other hand, causes the toxic and undegraded oil to spread in the ocean; the biological damage is then greater than if the spill had been left untreated. Reclamation of contaminated organisms, marshes, and offshore sediments is virtually impossible, and natural ecological recovery is slow.

With these conclusions in mind we can now turn to our experience with the West Falmouth oil spill. The effect of this relatively small spill was still acute in January 1971, almost a year and one-half after the accident. Officials in the town of Falmouth have estimated that the damage to local shellfish resources, during the first year after the accident, amounted to $118,000. This does not include the damage to other marine species and the expected damage in coming years. In addition to the loss of the oil and the barge and the cleanup expense (estimated to be $65,000), the owner of the oil paid compensations for the losses of marine and fishery resources to the town of Falmouth ($100,000) and to the Commonwealth of Massachusetts ($200,000). The actual ecological damage may far exceed this apparent cost of almost half a million dollars.

Biological and Chemical Analysis

For our analysis (which is still continuing) bottom samples were carefully taken from the marshes and from the offshore areas. Samples for biological analysis were washed and sieved to recover living or dead organisms. These were preserved, identified, and counted. Results of counts from the affected area were compared with those from control areas that were not polluted by the spill. Some animals can be used as indicators for the presence of pollution, either because of their great sensitivity or because of their great resistance. Thus, small shrimp-like animals, the amphipods of the family Ampeliscidae, are particularly vulnerable to oil pollution. Whenever the chemical analysis showed the presence of oil, these sensitive crustaceans were dying. On the other hand, the annelid worm, *Capitella capitata,* is highly resistant to oil pollution. Normally, this worm does not occur in large numbers in our area. However, after the accident it was able to benefit from the absence of other organisms which normally prey upon it and reached very high population densities. In the areas of the highest degree of pollution, however, even this worm was killed. *Capitella capitata* is well known, all over the world, as characteristic of areas heavily polluted by a variety of sources.

For chemical analysis, the sediments collected at our biological stations were extracted with a solvent that removed the hydrocarbons. The hydrocarbons were separated from other materials contained in the extracts. They were then analyzed by gas-liquid chromatography. This technique separates hydrocarbon mixtures into individual compounds, according to the boiling point and structural type. To do this, a sample is flash-evaporated in a heated tube. The vapor is swept by a constantly flowing stream of carrier gas into a long tube that is packed with a substance (substrate) that is responsible for the resolution of the mixture into its individual components. Ideally, each vaporized compound emerges from the end of the tube at a definite time and well separated from all other components. A sensitive detector and an amplifier then transmit a signal to a recorder which traces on a moving strip of chart paper a series of peaks (the chromatograms) that correspond to the individual components of the mixture. From the pattern of peaks in the gas chromatogram the chemist can learn much about the composition of the mixture. Each oil may have a characteristic fingerprint pattern by which it can be recognized in the environment for weeks, or even months, after the initial spill. Past and continuing work on the composition of those hydrocarbons that are naturally present in all marine organisms (see box, "What is Petroleum?") enabled us to distinguish easily between the natural hydrocarbons and those contained in the fuel oil. These analyses facilitated our study of the movement of the fuel oil from the West Falmouth oil spill into the bottom sediments and through the marine food chain.

Immediate Kill

Massive, immediate destruction of marine life occurred offshore during the first few days after the accident. Affected were a wide range of fish, shellfish, worms, crabs, other crustaceans, and invertebrates. Bottom-living fish and lobsters were killed and washed up on the shores. Trawls made in ten feet of water soon after the spill showed that 95 percent of the animals recovered were dead and others were dying. The bottom sediments contained many dead snails, clams, and crustaceans. Similarly severe destruction occurred in the tidal rivers and marshes into which the oil had moved under the combined influence of tide and wind. Here again fish, crabs, shellfish, and other invertebrates were killed; in the most heavily polluted regions of the tidal marshes almost no animals survived.

The fuel oil spilled at West Falmouth was a light, transparent oil, very different from the black viscous oil associated with the *Torrey Canyon* and Santa Barbara episodes. Within days most of the dead animals had decayed and the visual evidence of the oil had almost disappeared. Casual observers were led to report to the press that the area looked as beautiful as ever. Had we discontinued our study after the visual evidence of the oil had disappeared, we might have been led to similar interpretations. From that point on, only continued, careful biological and chemical analysis revealed the extent of continuing damage.

Persistence of Pollution

Quite recently a leading British expert on treatment of oil spills remarked that "white products, petrol, kerosene, light diesel fuel, and so forth, can be expected to be self-cleaning. In other words, given sufficient time they will evaporate and leave little or no objectionable residue."[7] Our experience shows how dangerously misleading such statements are. Chemical analyses of the oil recovered from the sediments and from the bodies of the surviving animals showed the chromatographic fingerprint of the diesel fuel, in monotonous repetition, for many months after the accident.

7. J. Wardly Smith, "Dealing with Oil Pollution Both on the Sea and on the Shores," paper presented to the Ocean Oil Spills Conference, Conference on Challenges of Modern Society, NATO, Brussels, November 1970.

Bacteria normally present in the sea will attack and slowly degrade spilled oil. On the basis of visual observations it has been said that the oil spilled by the *Torrey Canyon* disappeared rapidly from the sediments. This was interpreted to mean that the action of the bacteria was "swift and complete." Our analyses, which were carried out by objective chemical, rather than by subjective observational techniques, showed the steady persistence of fuel oil that should, in principle, be even more rapidly degraded than a whole crude oil. Thus, in May 1970, eight months after the spill, oil essentially unaltered in chemical characteristics could still be recovered from the sediments of the most heavily polluted areas. By the end of the first year after the accident, bacterial degradation of the oil was noted at all locations, as evidenced by changes in the fingerprint pattern of the oil. Yet only partial detoxification of the sediments had occurred, since the bacteria attacked the least toxic hydrocarbons first. The more toxic aromatic hydrocarbons remained in the sediments.

Spread of Pollution

For our chemical and biological work we established an unpolluted control station, outside of the area that was polluted, immediately after the accident. For a short period after the accident the sediments at this station were still clean and the organisms alive in their normal abundance and distribution. However, within three weeks, oil was found at this station and a significant number of organisms had been killed. Another control station was established twice as far from shore. Within three months fuel oil from the spill was evident at this station, and again there was a concomitant kill of bottom-living animals. This situation was repeated several times in sequence, and by spring 1970 the pollution had spread considerably from the area affected initially. At that time, the polluted area offshore was ten times larger than immediately after the accident and covered 5,000 acres (20 square kilometers) offshore and 500 acres (2 square kilometers) in the tidal river and marshes.

Another significant observation was made in the spring of 1970: Between December 1969 and April 1970, the oil content of the most heavily contaminated marine station two and one-half miles north of the original spill increased tenfold. Similar but smaller increases were observed at about the same time at other stations more distant from shore. The oil still showed the typical chromatographic fingerprint of the diesel fuel involved in the September 1969 oil spill. This and the lack of any further accident in this area suggested that oil was spreading from the most heavily contaminated inshore regions to the offshore sediments. We believe that the increase in the pollution level and the spread of oil to outlying areas are related to a transportation mechanism that we do not yet fully understand. However, the drastic kill of the animals that occurred with the arrival of oil pollution at the offshore stations showed that mortality continued for many months after the initial spill, even though no visible evidence of oil remained on the shores.

We believe these observations demonstrate that chronic oil pollution can result from a single spill, that the decimation of marine life can extend to new regions long after the initial spill, and that, once poisoned, the sea bottom may remain toxic to animals for long time periods.

Destruction of Shellfish Resources

Our analyses showed that oysters, soft-shell clams, quahaugs (another variety of clam), and scallops took up the fuel oil. Because of the pollution, the contaminated regions had to be closed to the harvesting of shellfish. Continuing analyses revealed that the contaminataion of the 1970 shellfish crop was as severe as that of the 1969 crop. Blue mussels that were juveniles in the polluted area at the time of the spill generally were sexually sterile the next season — they developed almost no eggs or sperm. Furthermore, in 1970 distant areas contained shellfish contaminated by fuel oil. Therefore, harvesting prohibitions had to be maintained in 1970 and had to be extended to polluted shellfish grounds that had not been closed to the public immediately after the accident.

It has long been common to transfer shellfish polluted by human sewage into clean water to make the animals marketable again. It has been thought that a similar flushing process would remove the oil from animals exposed to oil. Indeed, taste tests showed that the objectionable oily taste disappeared from animals maintained for some period in clean water. However, we removed oysters from the contaminated areas and kept them in clean running sea water up to six months. Fuel oil was still found in the animals by chemical analysis at essentially the same concentration and in the same composition as at the beginning of the flushing period.

Thus, we discovered that hydrocarbons taken up into the fat and flesh of fish and shellfish are not removed by natural flushing or by internal metabolic processes. The substances remain in the animals for long periods of time, possibly for their entire lives. The presence or absence of an oily taste or flavor in fish products is not a measure of contamination. The reason is that only a relatively small fraction of the total petroleum product has a pronounced taste or odor. Subjective observations cannot detect the presence of the toxic but tasteless and odorless pollutants. Only objective chemical analysis measures the presence of these chemical poisons. It is important to note in this regard that state and federal laboratories in the public health sector are not generally equipped to carry out these important chemical measurements. Such tests are vital, however, for the protection of the consumer.

Thus, our investigation demonstrated that the spill produced immediate mortality, chronic pollution, persistence of oil in the sediments and in the organisms, spread of pollution with the moving sediments, destruction of fishery resources, and continued harm to fisheries for a long period after the accident. Our continuing study will assess the persistence and toxicity of the oil and the eventual ecological recovery of the area. At the present time, one and one-half years after the spill, only the pollution-resistant organisms have been able to reestablish themselves in the more heavily contaminated regions. The original animal populations there have not become reestablished. Many animals that are able to move, early in their life cycles, as free-swimming larvae reach the polluted area and are killed when they settle on the sea bottom or in the marshes at West Falmouth.

In addition, revitalization of bottom areas probably will be hampered by oxygen depletion caused by oxygen-requiring bacteria that degrade oil.[8]

The Significance of West Falmouth

Some scientists are convinced that the effects at West Falmouth are a special case and have little applicability to spills of whole, unrefined crude oils. They contend that #2 fuel oil is more toxic than petroleum and that therefore it has effects that would not be comparable to those of whole petroleum. We cannot agree with this view.

Fuel oil is a typical oil-refining product. It is frequently shipped by sea, especially along coastal routes, and it is spilled in

8. T. A. Murphy, "Environmental Effects of Oil Pollution," presented at American Society of Civil Engineers, Boston; available from author at Edison Water Quality Laboratory, Edison, New Jersey (July 13, 1970), p. 14-15.

accidents like those which occurred at West Falmouth and off Baja California following the grounding of the *Tampico Maru* in 1957.[9]

More importantly, fuel oil is a part of petroleum, and as such it is contained within the whole petroleum. Surely, hydrocarbons that are toxic when they are in fuel oil must also be toxic when they are contained in petroleum. Therefore, the effects observed in West Falmouth are typical both for that fuel oil and the whole crude oil. In terms of chemical composition, crude oils span a range of molecular weights and structures. Many light crude oils have a composition not too dissimilar from that of fuel oil, and their toxicity and effects on the environment are very similar. Other heavier crude oils, while still containing the fuel oil components, contain higher proportions of the long-lasting poisons that are much more persistent and that include, for instance, some compounds that are potent carcinogens (cancer-producing agents) in experimental animals. Such heavy crude oils can be expected to be more persistent than a fuel oil, and they will have longer lasting long-term effects. Even weathered crude oils may still contain these long-term poisons, and in many cases some of the moderately low-boiling, immediately toxic compounds. In our view, these findings differ from those of other investigators principally for two reasons: Our study is based on objective measurement and is not primarily concerned with the mobile, adult marine species — the fish whose migratory history is largely unknown — or the highly resistant intertidal forms of life. We are studying quantitatively the effects of the spill on the sessile (bottom) animals that cannot escape the spill or the polluted sediment and that are thus exposed to chronic pollution. Since all classes of bottom animals are severely affected by the oil, we believe that the effects on free-swimming animals should be just as drastic. The difficulty of measuring the total

impact of oil on the marine life has led many to doubt the ecological seriousness of oil pollution. Our findings, extending far beyond the period when the visual evidence of the oil had disappeared, are based on objective chemical analyses and quantitative biological measurements, rather than on subjective visual observations. They indict oil as a pollutant with severe biological effects.

It is unfortunate that oil pollution research has been dominated so strongly by subjective, visual observations. Clearly, oil is a *chemical* that has severe *biological* effects, and therefore oil pollution research, to be fully meaningful, must combine chemical with biological studies. Those few investigators who are using objective chemical techniques find patterns in the environmental damage by oil that are similar to those demonstrated by the West Falmouth spill. Thus, R. A. Kolpack reported that oil from the blowout at Santa Barbara was carried to the sea bottom by clay minerals and that within four months after the accident the entire bottom of the Santa Barbara basin was covered with oil from the spill.[10] Clearly, this is one of the most significant observations in the aftermath of that accident. A concurrent and complimentary biological study would have appreciably enhanced our understanding of the ecological damage caused by the Santa Barbara oil spill.

G. S. Sidhu and co-workers, applying analytic methods similar to those used by us, showed that the mullet, an edible finfish,

9. Laurence G. Jones, Charles T. Mitchell, Einar K. Anderson, and Wheeler J. North, "A Preliminary Evaluation of Ecological Effects of an Oil Spill in the Santa Barbara Channel," W. M. Keck Engineering Laboratories, California Institute of Technology.

10. R. A. Kolpack, "Oil Spill at Santa Barbara, California, Physical and Chemical Effects," paper presented to the FAO Technical Conference on Marine Pollution, Rome, Dec. 1970.

takes up petroleum hydrocarbons from waters containing low levels of oil pollution from refinery outflows. In their chemical structures the hydrocarbons isolated by the investigators are similar to those found in the polluted shellfish of West Falmouth. The compounds differ markedly from those hydrocarbons present as natural components in all living organisms, yet closely approximate the hydrocarbons in fossil fuels.[11]

Numerous results of crude-oil toxicity tests, alone or in the presence of dispersants, have been published in the literature. However, in almost all cases such tests were performed on relatively hardy and resistant species that can be kept in the laboratory and on adult animals for short time periods under unnatural conditions or in the absence of food. At best, such tests may establish only the relative degree of the toxicity of various oils. We are convinced that the exposure of more sensitive animals, especially young ones, to oil pollution over many months would demonstrate a much greater susceptibility to the damaging effects of the oil. Such effects have been demonstrated in the studies of the West Falmouth oil spill. These studies represent a meaningful field test in open waters.

Thus, we believe that the general toxic potential and the persistence of the West Falmouth oil are typical of most oils and oil products both at the sea bottom and in the water column.

Conclusions

Our analysis of the aftermath of the West Falmouth oil spill suggests that oil is much more persistent and destructive to marine organisms and to man's marine food resources than scientists had thought. With the advent of objective chemical techniques, oil pollution research has entered a new stage. Earlier interpretations of the environmental effect of oil spills that were based on subjective observation, often over a short time span, have questionable validity. Crude oil and oil products are persistent poisons, resembling in their longevity DDT, PCB and other synthetic materials [which have been discussed in these pages]. Like other long-lasting poisons that, in some properties, resemble the natural fats of the organisms, hydrocarbons from oil spills enter the marine food chain and are concentrated in the fatty parts of the organisms. They can then be passed from prey to predator where they may become a hazard to marine life and even to man himself.

Natural mechanisms for the degradation of oil at sea exist — the most important of which is bacterial decomposition. Unfortunately, this is least effective for the most poisonous compounds in oil. Also, oil degrades slowly only in marine sediments, and it may be completely stable once it is taken up by organisms. It has been thought that many of the immediately toxic low-boiling aromatic hydrocarbons are volatile and evaporate rapidly from the oil spilled at sea. This has not been the case at West Falmouth, where the low-boiling hydrocarbons found their way into the sediments and organisms. We believe that the importance of evaporation has been overestimated.

Oil-laden sediments can move with bottom currents and can contaminate unpolluted areas long after the initial accident. For this reason a *single* and relatively small spill may lead to *chronic,* destructive pollution of a large area.

We have not yet discussed the low-level effects of oil pollution. However, a growing body of evidence indicates that oil as well as other pollutants may have seriously damaging biological effects at extremely low concentrations, previously considered harmless. Some of this information was presented

11. G. S. Sidhu, G. L. Vale, J. Shipton and K. E. Murray, "Nature and Effects of a Kerosene-like Taint in Mullet," paper presented to FAO Technical Conference on Marine Pollution, Rome, Dec. 1970.

in Rome at the December 1970 Food and Agriculture Organization's Conference on the Effects of Marine Pollution on Living Resources and Fishing. Greatly diluted pollutants affect not only the physiology but also the behavior of many animals. Many behavioral patterns which are important for the survival of marine organisms are mediated by extremely low concentrations of chemical messengers that are excreted by marine creatures. Chemical attraction and repulsion by such compounds play a key role in food finding, escape from predators, homing, finding of habitats, and sexual attraction. Possibly, oil could interfere with such processes by blocking the taste receptors of marine animals or by mimicking natural stimuli and thus eliciting false responses. Our general ignorance of such low-level effects of pollution is no excuse for neglecting research in these areas nor for complacency if such effects are not immediately obvious in gross observations of polluted areas.

Recent reports suggest an additional environmental threat from oil pollution. Oil may concentrate other fat-soluble poisons, such as many insecticides and chemical intermediates.[12] Dissolved in an oil film, these poisons may reach a concentration many times higher than that which occurs in the water column. In this way other pollutants may become available to organisms that would not normally be exposed to the substances and at concentrations that could not be reached in the absence of oil.

The overall implications of oil pollution, coupled with the effects of other pollutants, are distressing. The discharge of oil, chemicals, domestic sewage, and municipal wastes, combined with overfishing, dredging, and the filling of wetlands may lead to a deterioration of the coastal ecology. The present influx of pollutants to the coastal regions of the oceans is as damaging as that which has had such a detrimental effect on many of our lakes and freshwater fishery resources. Continued and progressive damage to the coastal ecology may lead to a catastrophic deterioration of an important part of marine resources. Such a deterioration might not be reversed for many generations and could have a deep and lasting impact on the future of mankind.

Since present oil-spill countermeasures cannot completely eliminate the biological damage, it is paramount to prevent oil spills. The recent commitment by the United States to take all steps to end the intentional discharge of oil from its tankers and non-tanker vessels by the mid 1970s is important. As a result of this step and of the resolution of the NATO Ocean Oil Spills Conference of the Committee on Challenges of Modern Society in Brussels, December 1970, other countries hopefully also will adopt necessary measures to halt oil pollution from ships. This would eliminate the largest single source of oceanic oil pollution. At the same time steps also must be taken to reduce oil pollution from many other, less readily obvious sources, such as petrochemical operations on shore, disposal of automotive and industrial lubricants, and release of unburned hydrocarbons from the internal combustion engine.

Acknowledgments: The authors acknowledge the continued support of their basic and applied research efforts by the National Science Foundation, The Office of Naval Research, and the Federal Water Quality Administration.

12. R. Hartung and G. W. Klinger, "Concentration of DDT by Sedimented Polluting Oils," *Environmental Science and Technology,* 4(1970):407.
13. W. A. Gruse and D. R. Stevens, *The Chemical Technology of Petroleum,* Mellon Institute of Industrial Research, 2d ed. (New York: McGraw-Hill Book Company, Inc., 1942) p. 2.
14. For example, see: R. C. Clark and M. Blumer, "Distribution of N-paraffins in Marine Organisms and Sediments," *Limnology and Oceanography* 12(1967):79-87.

What Is Petroleum?

Organic materials, deposited at the bottom of the sea millions of years ago have been covered by sediments and deeply buried. Under the influence of elevated temperature over very long periods of time, an immensely complex mixture of hydrocarbons has been formed. Some of these have accumulated in reservoirs from which crude oil can be procured.

Crude oil is one of the most complicated natural mixtures on earth. Compounds made up of only carbon and hydrogen predominate, but small amounts of sulfur, oxygen, and nitrogen-containing substances also occur. [13]

The way in which the individual carbon and hydrogen atoms combine into hydrocarbon molecules helps scientists to classify them. They distinguish four principal types of hydrocarbons.:

The first type, **the aliphatic compounds,** includes straight and branched chain compounds in which each carbon atom is directly linked to four other atoms (saturated). Aliphatic compounds frequently account for a large fraction of crude oil and are common in gasoline and many other fuels.

The second general type is **the alicyclic compounds** (naphthenes). These compounds are also saturated, but the carbon atoms of at least part of the molecules are joined in rings.

The third major type, also cyclic, consists of **the aromatic compounds.** These contain at least one benzene ring. This type includes a large number of one-ring, two-ring, and multi-ring compounds, among them several materials that have been implicated as potent carcinogens (cancer-producing agents) in laboratory animals.

The fourth type, **the olefinic compounds** are unsaturated. Here, double or triple chemical bonds between carbon atoms exist, but not of the regular arrangements found in the benzene ring. Olefins do not occur in crude oil, but are formed in some refining processes and are common in many oil products.

The boiling point is an important physical property of the hydrocarbons. Differences in boiling point between different crude-oil hydrocarbons are useful in separating the oil into fractions with individual characteristics suited to specific fuels or lubricants. Crude oil contains components boiling over a range from below room temperature to well above 500 degrees C. The lowest boiling fractions of crude oil are relatively rich in the simpler chain- and ring-type saturated hydrocarbons. Intermediate fractions have a higher content of the immediately poisonous aromatic hydrocarbons. Conversely, the higher boiling hydrocarbon fractions contain relatively more of the complex polycyclic aromatic compounds, including the carcinogens.

Hydrocarbons are formed by all living organisms. The hydrocarbons in crude oil are very different from those normally found in healthy unpolluted organisms, however. The crude oil mixture is far more complex, the compounds cover a much wider range in structure and boiling point, and many hydrocarbons are present that are toxic to organisms. As a rule, only very few individual natural hydrocarbon compounds are found in unpolluted plants and animals. They are mostly saturated or olefinic, and with a few exceptions they are nontoxic. [14]

M.B.

EDITOR'S COMMENTS

It seems obvious that ocean oil spillage must soon be controlled. It is also obvious that many of the small oil spills simply represent the absence of responsibility by shipping and petroleum industry personnel. However, the spectre of even a greater potential source of marine oil pollution is seen in offshore drilling activities. Many coastal waters of the world lie over extensive petroleum deposits. Offshore wells have already released huge amounts of oil when "blow-outs" occurred. Undoubtedly, this source of petroleum must ultimately be used; but it is also of great importance that a technology be developed which will prevent oil spillage disasters. Surely we can wait for this fuel until such a technology has been developed.

ED CHANEY

Catastrophe Brewing in Quiet Waters

▶ "We just cannot continue to muck up the environment simply
because we can prove no harm at the moment."

Ed Chaney is information director of the
Environmental Defense Fund and a former
Information Director of the National Wildlife
Federation. He has written scores of essays
and magazine articles on various environmental
issues. He is particularly interested in
cracking government's resistance to citizen
participation in the environmental decision-
making process and in the social and cultural
implications of the struggle for environmental
quality.

In the spring of 1970, the American Em-
bassy at Ottawa, Canada telegraphed the
U.S. Secretary of State that a Swedish chemist doing graduate work at the University of
Ottawa had discovered dangerous mercury
concentrations in fish from border waters.

By the end of the year, the American public had experienced an unprecedented flurry
of government activity. The Federal Water
Quality Administration discovered high mercury concentrations in lakes and streams
throughout the United States; the Justice
Department filed cease and desist lawsuits
against some of the nation's largest corporations; and the Food and Drug Administration seized several million cans of contaminated tuna and tons of fresh swordfish.

Federal officials, the news media and the
general public breathed a collective sigh of
relief as the quick action ostensibly averted
what could have become a disaster. But if
you really believe the mercury disaster was
nothing more than a close call; that everything is under control; that there's no cause
for alarm, you're very wrong.

The mercury disaster wasn't averted. It
has us surrounded. And we don't even
know the full extent of the problem yet —
let alone what we are going to do about it.
From what we do know, much of the environmental mercury contamination may be
as irreversible as the effects of mercury
poisoning on the human brain.

Mercury pollution is a bona fide national
disaster. FDA seizures of 3.6 percent (about
six million pounds) of tuna and a stag-
gering 89 percent of the swordfish marketed
in this country constitute the largest case of
pollution contaminated foodstuffs in U.S.
history.

Dangerous concentrations of mercury in
freshwater fish throughout the United States
have thrust thousands of once self-reliant
commercial fishermen and their families into
the vicious welfare cycle. Wholesale fish

dealers, sport charter boat operators, motel owners and the myriad small businessmen dependent upon recreational and commercial fisheries have suffered enormous losses.

The toll of dead and contaminated wildlife is inestimable. Even preliminary sampling has revealed mercury in pheasants and other upland game birds in Montana, Idaho, California and Canada. In ducks of North Dakota and Michigan. Doves in North Carolina. Whales in Hudson Bay and seals in Alaska. Bald eagles, hawks, owls and virtually every variety of creature that lives in or from the aquatic environment.

We know almost nothing about what effect the historic consumption of mercury contaminated fish and wildlife has had on millions of Americans. But the possibilities give you a funny feeling in the pit of your stomach.

Scratch a nit-picker preoccupied with defining mercury in its hundreds of compound forms, and you'll uncover a mercury polluter or his apologist. But with all due respect to the real and masquerading academicians, the average human being really can understand mercury pollution and its consequences.

Mercury is one of the most versatile, useful natural elements. Its use in a wide variety of industrial and agricultural activities has redistributed it in great quantities throughout the environment.

Sources Incredibly Varied

At present, its major known sources in the environment are: (1) natural geologic formations, (2) industrial discharges, (3) pesticides, (4) residues from use in gold and silver mining, (5) miscellaneous garbage, including thermometers, fluorescent lights, mercury lamps, batteries and many other products, (6) and barely understood, the burning of fossil fuels (which may account

for mercury contaminated waters far from any known industrial discharge or natural source).

Mercury does come in an incredible variety of compound forms. Methylmercury is the most highly toxic and is dangerous even in extremely minute quantities. But it is now established that when introduced into the aquatic environment, *all* forms of mercury, even that contained in thermometers, are transformed into deadly methylmercury which moves freely up the natural food chain.

In animals, methylmercury causes irreversible damage to the brain and central nervous system. In high concentrations, the symptoms are convulsions, blindness, coma and death. Methylmercury passes freely through a mother's placenta and damages or kills unborn young. It passes through the oviduct into eggs with similar consequences.

Victor Lambeau of the Federal Environmental Protection Agency's Water Quality Office calls it "a blueprint for the perfect environmentaly hazardous compound. . . ." Methylmercury is cumulative and extreme sublethal effects could be considered worse than lethal effects.

Food Chain Reaches Man

In the 1950s and '60s, scores of Japanese men, women, children and unborn fetuses were killed or mentally and physically crippled after eating fish highly contaminated by mercury. Hundreds of deaths have occured in other countries from accidental consumption of grain seed coated with methylmercury fungicides. In 1969, several members of the Huckelby family in New Mexico suffered severe brain damage after eating pork from a hog mistakenly fed mercury-treated seed.

It is believed that methylmercury has a half-life of about 70 to 90 days in the human body. That is, within 70 to 90 days after consumption, half of the intake would be naturally excreted from the body. Within another 70 to 90 days, half of the remaining half would be excreted and so on, until it was all gone.

But anyone who thinks that man's ability to excrete mercury offers a health loophole is fooling himself. There is plenty of time for the mercury to reach the brain and do its dirty work.

Early signs of low-level methylmercury poisoning are fatigue, lethargy, irritability, etc. But we really don't know just what happens when a human ingests minute levels of mercury over long periods of time. The possibility of insidious brain and genetic damage is genuine.

Though no one's talking about it in public, an unknown but substantial number of Americans have been eating mercury contaminated fish and wildlife for years, some with concentrations well above the FDA's recently established, temporary safety level of 0.5 parts per million (which is ten times higher than the level set by the World Health Organization).

The University of Toronto has even found minute mercury concentrations in toothbrush bristles, poultry, wheat flour, bread, long grain rice, skim milk powder, cheese, tea, beef liver and cosmetics.

No one really knows what all this means in terms of human health. Our ignorance is certainly no cause for panic, but is even less a cause for complacency.

A special Federal task force concluded early this year that "it seems unlikely that we will find overt mercury poisoning from the consumption of fish or other food products, as normally marketed, in this country. This is not to say that there may not be a few individuals, who because of high consumption of contaminated fish, may have signs of mercury poisoning or suffer possible subclinical effects, including delayed neurological or intellectual damage. Also, possibly infants or children may have impaired development. . . . "

The task force of government scientists said the mercury situation in America is "potentially grave." It recommended prohibition of all methylmercury fungicides and severe restrictions on all other mercury pesticides, pending development of safe substitutes. It further advocated reducing industrial discharges to natural background levels and close control of waste disposal and combustion of fossil fuels.

And then came the kicker: ". . . it appears probable that, even with the complete elimination of new discharges of mercury, existing deposits in sediments of waterways will continue to yield the highly toxic methylmercury for decades to come. Interruption of this methylation or decontamination of existing deposits is thus of the utmost urgency."

When government scientists depart from the standard, infinitely qualified bureaucratese and use words like "grave" and "utmost urgency," you better believe we've got a serious problem.

Just how serious can be determined from the task force's conclusion that there are at least three theoretically practical methods for removing the millions of pounds of mercury that have accumulated in our waterways: (1) cover the bottoms of contaminated waterways with absorptive materials like ground quartz or silicates; (2) literally bury the bottoms under something like rocks; and (3) remove the contaminated bottoms by dredging or pumping.

Picture the ecological havoc resulting from covering the bottom of 180 miles of the Savanah River in Georgia with rocks or ground quartz. What would one do with the bottom of 294,400 acres of Lake St. Clair? Have the Corps of Engineers pile it up to create Mount St. Clair and sell lakeview lots to pay for the dredging? What about Lake Erie? Now there's a dredging project for you.

Until someone comes up with better answers, it appears we've committed a devastating, possibly irreversible environmental blunder that may quarantine many of our nation's waterways for years. And in so doing have definitely set off a chain reaction of highly undesirable social consequences.

How did a nation with one foot in the "Environmental Decade" ever get itself into such a mess? Although man's contribution to mercury contamination of ocean fish is not yet understood, with few exceptions, the dangerous contamination of wildlife and fish in inland waters can be laid directly to the use of mercury-based pesticides and various industrial mercury discharges.

No Forethought Shown

Methylmercury fungicides came into vogue in the 1920s. Their toxicity was well known, and someone should have thought about what might happen when song and game birds ate the treated grain seeds. And when predators, including man, ate the birds that ate the seed.

After certain bird populations dropped catastrophically in the 1950s, the Swedish government did start thinking about it, and by 1966 banned the use of all methylmercury fungicides. It wasn't until the Huckelby family tragedy in 1969 that our chemical-dominated, agricultural bureaucracy stirred into action.

The aquatic transformation of all mercury compounds into the deadly methylmercury wasn't fully documented until 1967. After that, ignorance was no excuse. Prior to that time, however, mercury was freely dumped into lakes and streams — without malicious intent — just because it was economically convenient.

No one could then prove it was hurting anything, and that brand of ignorance has always been interpreted as a license to dump anything and everything into the air and water. That attitude is *The Problem,* of which the mercury disaster is really only a symptom.

Conservationists have been harping about The Problem for years. Implicit in their warnings is the fact that a small number of people and institutions are taking some totally unnecessary, long-range gambles with the public's health in a most undemocratic fashion.

For a brief period, it appeared that the mercury disaster would finally shock the public into reasserting control over its air and water. But that didn't happen. What may prove to be the greatest single environmental disaster in our history is now generally perceived as nothing more than a "close call" by those not personally affected. We have now literally settled back to await the next crisis.

After being constantly bludgeoned with bad environmental news, the public was understandably anxious to accept the U.S. Justice Department's grand pronouncement. "We have averted the disaster," after it was forced by then Interior Secretary Hickel to sue ten major mercury polluters.

There was also a ripe audience awaiting U.S. Food and Drug Administration assurances that its interim tolerance level for mercury "offers a broad margin of safety and is adequate to protect consumers." That the confiscated tuna was actually "absolutely" safe to eat. That although 89 percent of the fresh swordfish marketed in the United States was being seized, "there is no cause for alarm."

Self-appointed pollyannas poured out of the woodwork and conjured up a batch of Rube Goldberg formulas to assure us that on the "average" everything was "probably" OK. That "most" public waters were mercury-safe.

Tragically, even many governmental fish and game agencies and fishing industry representatives capitulated to the immediate economic threat of mercury pollution, instead of parlaying it into an attack on The Problem, which is inexorably putting them out of business.

All the official and unofficial assurances were run through the news media whose understandable fear of public panic and unforgivable ignorance of the implications combined to turn out an ersatz message devoid of constructive insight into the mercury disaster.

And with hints of what it desperately wanted to hear roaring in its ears, the public could conveniently tune out the less publicized, flat-out official contradictions, ifs and maybes, the scientists who insist on reminding us that we are virtually ignorant about the subtle effects of mercury poisoning; the fact that albeit sincere, the official assurances are largely assumptions based upon something called the "Average American."

Bill Baab, outdoor editor of the Augusta, Georgia *Chronicle-Herald*, wryly observed, "While 90 percent of the waters in the United states may be free of mercury contamination, 180 miles of Savannah River . . . are still among the 10 percent that aren't safe."

The Governor of Alabama asked the President to declare his state a national disaster area due to industrial mercury pollution — largely due to the heroic efforts of the state's fish and game department — but the Office of Emergency Preparedness couldn't find pollution on its list of approved disasters.

While bureaucrats quibbled, almost no one heeded the cries that the emperor has no clothes. And although many people in and out of government are valiantly trying to grapple with The Problem, their chances of success dwindle daily as public apathy increases.

There is an ominous lack of public outrage over losing the freedom to eat a wild pheasant, walleye or bass when, where and as often as one wants. Or being put out of business because someone upstream didn't think his mercury discharge pipe was loaded.

And yet, as another serious symptom of The Problem, mercury pollution has made some extremely serious inroads into our freedoms. It has contributed substantially to the slow, insidious cancer that is more likely to destroy environmental quality than a cataclysmic stroke.

Sources of mercury pollution

26.56%

Electrolytic preparation of chlorine and caustic soda in chemical industry

23.91%

Electrical apparatus (switches, thermostats, batteries, etc.)

12.74%

Miscellaneous

12.47%

Paint (antifouling and mildew proofing)

8.94%

Industrial and control instruments

3.91%

Dental preparations

3.79%

Catalysts for manufacturing

3.44%

Agriculture (includes fungicides and bactericides for industrial purposes)

2.61%

General commercial laboratory use

.92%

Pharmaceuticals

.71%

Paper and pulp manufacture

It is a living, painful lesson that we cannot continue to muck up the environment simply because we can prove no harm at the moment of mucking. But it is also painfully obvious we have yet to accept the truth that in this closed system called Earth, we can throw nothing away, for there is no away.

EDITOR'S COMMENTS

Mr. Chaney makes it obvious why mercury pollution is so hazardous — mercury is highly poisonous and is concentrated by living organisms. This latter feature of mercury means that higher trophic level organisms will absorb progressively higher body burdens. Such a concentration of many environmental contaminants occurs in food chains. The basic reason for this was explained thoroughly in Part I of the text. Animals from higher trophic levels consume large volumes of organisms from lower trophic levels, and thus expose themselves to ever-increasing levels of the contaminant. Unfortunately, man sits atop the trophic pyramid!

Little can be done about mercury which has already been released in nature. We can hope that present levels of the contaminant will prove to have no generally detrimental effects on human health, and we can only hope that present mercury levels in natural waters will not increase as the present sediments become active.

Continued mercury pollution simply cannot be tolerated. Recently adopted restrictions on mercury release should be made stronger and should be rigidly enforced. Meanwhile, we can hope that mercury represents the most potentially dangerous of our environmental pollutants. It is certainly possible that many other chemical pollutants presently being released will actually represent more of a human health hazard than does mercury.

ARTHUR D. HASLER AND BRUCE INGERSOLL

Dwindling Lakes

▶ Blue-green algae cause the natural aging and disappearance
of lakes. Man hastens the process.

Arthur D. Hasler is Professor of Zoology
and director of the Laboratory of Limnology
at the University of Wisconsin and president
of the International Association for Ecology.
His research career has been devoted to the
ecology of aquatic systems. His students hold
leading positions in limnology and marine
biology. Bruce Ingersoll has been a lumberjack,
a fishing guide, and a reporter for the *Chicago
Tribune*.

Algae, minute and one-celled, ride the
summer waves of every waterway in America. They colonize stagnant sloughs of rivers
and gather in backwaters behind dams.
Under a microscope, these tiny and rather
attractive plants appear innocent enough,
yet they can quickly cover a bay with
scum, form hairy filaments to enslime a
rocky shoreline, or clog an entire lake. With
life-spans of only a few days, algae can make
any lake grow old thousands of years before its time.

To realize their immense potential for
harm, however, algae depend on man. It
takes man to speed up natural eutrophication, the normal process of enrichment and
aging undergone by bodies of fresh water.
By fertilizing the nation's waters with the
nutrients vital to algae growth and reproduction, primarily nitrogen and phosphor-

ous, we turn eutrophication into an accelerated, cultural process—cultural in that we
are perverting nature with municipal sewage, industrial wastes, agricultural drainage,
and other odious by-products of our civilization. Cultural eutrophication, therefore, is
an aberration: a natural process running
amok.

In enriching the water with the nutrients
in sewage, groundwater, and urban and rural
runoff, we promote the exponential reproduction of algae: the seemingly harmless
alga becomes 2 algae, then 4, 8, 16, — mul-
tiplying until there are billions. And during
such a population explosion, lakes become
murky and fetid under the August sun, while
wave-tossed weeds, bloated fish, and dead
algae rot in shoreline windrows.

More than one-third of America's 100,-
000 lakes are showing signs of cultural
eutrophication. The danger of accelerated
eutrophication continues to grow as our
population makes greater demands on national water resources, and lakes continue
to take on the eutrophication syndrome. Besides showing the symptoms of excess nutrients and algae bloom, they are character-

ized by the depletion of dissolved oxygen in deeper waters, a change from cold-water game fish to "rough" bottom feeders, and the encroachment of rooted vegetation from shore.

The appearance of these symptoms follows a definite sequence. First, the algae population skyrockets in a man-fertilized lake. Water fleas (miniature freshwater shrimp), the staple in the diet of fry and minnows, cannot eat enough algae to keep these plants in check. As a result, billions of algae live their languid lives, reproduce, and then die. As they drift toward the bottom, their decomposing bodies exhaust the deep-water oxygen supply. Trout, whitefish, and other fish species suffocate in the oxygen-thin depths.

The lake's ecology, initially upset by excess nutrients, then becomes totally upended, since bacteria can convert only some of the dead algae into plant and animal food. Therefore, generation after generation of algae settle on the bottom, adding layer after layer to the muck. The rate of sedimentation is most rapid in a northern lake where bacteria grow only during the summer while nutrients are added throughout the year. As erosion and sedimentation fill in the lake, shoreline vegetation impinges on the open water. In time, the lake becomes so shallow and overgrown that it becomes a marsh or bog. The accelerated process of aging has taken its toll: the lake's life is ended.

Cultural eutrophication is not new, nor is it solely an American problem. Recent core samples of an Italian lake indicate that ancient Roman road builders caused eutrophication by exposing nearby nutrient-rich limestone strata to erosion.

By the latter part of the nineteenth century, a few scientists in Europe and the United States, alarmed about cultural eutrophication, issued warnings that went unheeded. In 1896, on Switzerland's Lake Zürich, the problem finally received notice, and during the 1920s and 30s worldwide scientific interest began to focus on the problem. But research without implementation is impotent, and by the 1940s eutrophication was no longer confined primarily to farm belts and urban areas. It had followed urban man in his quest for recreation into the wilds.

It took the visual (and olfactory) impact of a huge body of water, Lake Erie, suffocating as a sump for industrial waste, sewage, and urban and rural runoff to bring the problem of water pollution dramatically to the public eye. Some now pronounce Lake Erie "dead." We, however, extend hope for recovery. For if communities and industries in Lake Erie's drainage basin cease polluting and fertilizing its waters, and if a cleansing flow from Lake Huron is permitted to reach and "flush out" the lake via the Detroit River, Erie might show signs of recovery within a decade. True, our hope is contingent upon many "ifs." However, it cannot be too strongly emphasized that these situations are reversible — that bodies of water will respond when the right steps are taken.

There is reason to fear for the other Great Lakes, together the greatest reservoir of clean fresh water in the world. Although Lake Superior and Lake Huron bear only a few signs of eutrophication so far, alarming amounts of DDT and other persistent toxic pesticides have been detected in the highly prized flesh of lake trout caught in their waters.

Lake Michigan is also deteriorating rapidly from increasing effluents and may soon go the way of Erie. The stench of algae and weeds decaying on beaches, compounded by the wave-borne plague of dead alewives, makes eutrophication impossible to ignore in this once pure lake. Such cities as Muskegon, Gary, Chicago, Milwaukee, and Green Bay realize that the fate of Lake Michigan

STAGES OF NATURAL LAKE SUCCESSION

Figures (A-C) portray the natural aging and disappearance of a lake in the Northern Hemisphere. A newly formed lake contains few algae or eroded materials. Later, shoreline runoff brings eroded soil (1) and plant nutrients into the lake; aquatic vegetation (2) (including algae) flourish and die, adding to debris on lake bottom; marsh plants and water-tolerant conifers (3) grow at lakeside. Eventually, the entire lake is filled and covered with forest vegtation (4).

— to which they once owed their existence — is now uncertain.

Stewart L. Udall said a year ago that there is still time to save Lake Michigan, but warned that further delay in action would prove fatal. His statement is admittedly, and of necessity, vague, but it is correct.

The long-range outlook here is not encouraging because the mitten-shaped lake isn't in the mainstream of Great Lakes water circulation, and thus receives very little cleansing flow. Its tributaries carry heavy nutrient loads to its shallows, and consequently, along Michigan's southern rim scientists have found 44 times more phosphorus (in the form of sewage effluent and industrial waste) than the lake can handle.

Lake Michigan's fate would have been decided long ago had Chicago's engineers and city fathers lacked the foresight and imagination to reverse the lakeward flow of the Chicago River and channel it into the Illinois River, a tributary of the Mississippi. The metropolis now draws water from the lake, and discharges sewage effluent into the altered river system. As is sometimes the case in such diversion operations, they have alleviated their own problem but have contributed to the water problems of St. Louis and other cities located farther down the Mississippi.

While concern for the future of the Great Lakes intensifies, distress is being voiced over eutrophication on many smaller bodies of water. Fishermen complain that dense mats of algae and rooted weeds make trolling for pike impossible, and that the few fish they do manage to catch are too tainted to eat. A summer cottager realizes that he will be landlocked if his bay becomes any shallower, and a concerned parent forbids her youngsters to wade in the green slurry of algae.

To stop cultural eutrophication, the sources of nutrients for algae growth and reproduction must be pinpointed. A 1967

survey, representative of the Midwest, indicates that 6 percent of the nitrogen and 2 percent of the phosphorus reaching Wisconsin waters come from septic tank seepage. Twenty-five percent of the nitrogen and 56 percent of the phosphorus come from municipal sewage treatment plants. Runoff from manured fields accounts for 10 and 22 percent of these elements, while urban runoff supplies 6 and 10 percent. Groundwater and direct rainfall on Wisconsin bodies of water contribute, respectively, 42 percent and 9 percent of the nitrogen, but together less than 4 percent of the phosphorus. Industrial wastes which bypass municipal treatment are a source of trace amounts of each of these chemical substances.

The nitrogen contribution of groundwater and rainfall will continue to be significant as long as automobile exhaust and industrial smokestacks keep spewing nitrogen into the atmosphere. Rain, in cleansing the air, picks up this nitrogen and deposits it directly into lakes and streams or indirectly in groundwater. Nitrogen-laden rain falling on land also percolates down to the subterranean water table, the level of groundwater.

It must be remembered that the natural rate of eutrophication is the base rate for cultural eutrophication. Moreover, the natural rate depends on whether the soil in a lake's drainage basin is rich or poor in nutrients. For this reason, the thousands of lakes in a nutrient-poor belt stretching from northern Minnesota and Ontario to Maine and Quebec have changed very little since the last glacier retreated 10,000 years ago. Found in sandy or granitic terrain and unspoiled by man, these deep lakes have kept their gin-clear purity and their youth — they are oligotrophic. However, should we disturb their basins and fertilize their waters, they would immediately undergo cultural eutrophication.

Seepage from the septic tanks of just a few summer cabins and resorts, for example,

CONDITION OF TWELVE U.S. LAKES

LAKE	LOCATION	EXCELLENT	GOOD	FAIR	POOR	ENDANGERED	IMPROVING
Crater	Oregon	■				■	
Superior	Great Lakes	■				■	
Tahoe	Calif.—Nev.	■				■	
George	New York		■			■	
Cayuga	New York		■				
Washington	Washington		■				■
Okoboji	Iowa			■			
Mendota	Wisconsin			■			
Erie	Great Lakes				■	■	
Douglas	Michigan		■				
Apopka	Florida				■	■	
Okeechobee	Florida			■			

is rich enough in nutrients to speed up the aging process. Cochran Lake, once a pure gem set in the northern Wisconsin wilds has deteriorated so rapidly since the first of seven cottages was built on its shores ten years ago that it now looks like a 300-acre caldron of pea soup.

Lakes with large drainage basins in limestone terrain, which is usually high in phosphorus, are far more likely to show their age than lakes in granitic or sandy basins. Because of their high nutrient content, they become shallow and die under encroaching cattails, reeds, and marsh grasses. But even though such lakes are already highly fertilized through natural means, whenever man is present his actions become the determining factor in the rate at which lakes fill in. Unless septic tank seepage is stanched, Cochran Lake — and thousands of other lakes in the resort areas of northern United States, Canada, Scandinavia, and the Alps — will be ruined.

While faulty septic tanks are a major source of nutrients in rural regions, their over-all contribution does not approach that of municipal sewage treatment plants. It has been estimated that 260 million pounds of phosphorus and 511 million pounds of nitrogen reach the nation's surface waters in the form of municipal sewage each year. Substantial amounts of these plant nutrients are discharged in effluent even after sewage is treated. As much as 75 percent of the phosphorus in sewage comes from detergents. In addition to phosphorus and nitrogen, vitamins, amino acids, and growth hormones have been found in effluent — substances which contribute to the growth of algae and weeds. These growth stimulants are synthesized inadvently in the biological processes of sewage treatment.

Since cities and villages across the country are rather impartial in dumping their sewage, rivers too are receiving their share of nutrients for eutrophication. This is most obvious wherever rivers have been dammed and currents slowed enough to give algae a chance to multiply. Because most of the nation's rivers have been systematically converted into series of impoundments since the 1930s, cultural eutrophication in these manmade lakes is now a common problem.

Algae blooms foul many of the man-made lakes in the TVA system, as well as the backwaters of hydroelectric dams on the Missouri and Snake rivers. The Mississippi — "father of waters" — carries partially treated sewage from Minneapolis and St. Paul forty miles downstream to Lake Pepin where algae thrive on sewage nutrients. As algae die and settle to the bottom with other sediments, the sluggish lake becomes shallower, increasing the possibility of spring flooding at Winona, Minn., and other down-river towns.

Formidable as it is, cultural eutroprication isn't inevitable. For example, five years ago officials from 70-plus local government bodies became alarmed about algal slime at sewage outlets on Lake Tahoe on the California-Nevada border, touted as one of the clearest lakes of North America. With the entire Tahoe basin's livelihood — tourism and gambling — at stake, they banded together and consulted sanitary engineers and limnologists. The prescribed cure: sewage treatment and diversion.

The South Tahoe Public Utility District, spurred by action committees of panicked businessmen, obtained a $10 million grant from Washington, raised another $9 million, and this year built a plant to treat sewage and a pipeline to carry effluent over a mountain pass to an irrigation reservoir. In diverting the effluent from the lake basin, the South Tahoe district provided California desert farms with nutrient-rich water. Meanwhile, the 42 voters of Round Hill, Nev., (most being gaming-house owners) floated a $5.8 million bond for their own sewage treatment-diversion project, fearing that

smelly scum would hurt business at their lakeshore casinos and hotels. And if other Tahoe communities act right now, eutrophication should never smirch the lake's reputation for clarity — at least not for several thousands of years.

Diversion is currently the most effective measure we have to combat eutrophication, since it immediately deprives nuisance vegetation of nitrogen, phosphorus, and other nutrients. Morever, until some technological breakthrough occurs in sewage treatment — now far from a completely effective process — diversion will continue to be the logical approach.

Sanitary engineers haven't yet found a process, chemical or biochemical, that offers an economical alternative to diverting effluent around lakes. Nevertheless, research is being pressed throughout the country. A pilot plant, for example, has been built to test a chemical process at Ely, Minn., the launching point for canoe trips into the Superior National Forest. Research teams have investigated the feasibility of using algae to remove nutrients from effluent. The plan is to grow algae in effluent-filled ponds until they have consumed all the nutrients. Then the algae would be harvested and the nutrient-poor effluent discharged directly into a lake, obviating the need for diversion. The researchers, in practice, have been stymied by several technical problems: for one, how can algae be put to use? Unfortunately, there is no demand for algae as a fertilizer or as an animal food.

While the logic of diverting effluent is obvious, particularly in light of the shortcomings of sewage treatment, it often hasn't been accepted. Opponents of diversion in Madison, Wis., for instance, argued that runoff from manured farmland — not municipal sewage — was the chief cause of eutrophication in Lake Monona, one of four lakes linked by the sluggish Yahara River. Nevertheless, soon after Madison began diverting all of its effluent around Lake Monona in 1936, the amount of copper sulfate needed to kill algae dropped from carloads to a few handfuls by 1956.

As Madison learned in the late 1930s, diversion requires a sense of responsibility and a regard for downstream communities. That city, in sparing Lake Monona, poured its effluent into Lake Waubesa and indirectly into Lake Kegonsa. This half-measure promptly fertilized their waters. Residents, enraged by the proliferating algae that threatened to ruin their lakes, sued the city. In 1941 legislators passed an antipollution bill aimed at Madison. Gov. Julius Heil, however, vetoed it on the ground that there was no consensus on the main cause of eutrophication. Although the bill was later enacted, it was not until 1959 that Madison's effluent was diverted completely from Waubesa and Kegonsa.

Foes of diverting sewage plant effluent around Seattle's Lake Washington to Puget Sound claimed that farm runoff was responsible for cultural eutrophication — just as had been claimed in Madison — even though the 24-mile long lake was absorbing the effluent of ten treatment plants by 1950. In this case, it took the lavender bloom of *Oscillatoria rubescens,* the same alga that discolored Lake Zürich, to awaken the public. Mass apathy dissolved, but a welter of conflicting opinions took its place and for a time threatened to defeat the attempts to divert sewage around Lake Washington. Eventually, 5,000 women, backed by the Municipal League and the League of Women Voters, went from door to door, mustering support for a bond issue to be used for diversion. Recently, voters reversed the stand they took in 1956 and approved the bond issue and a charter for a new metropolitan governmental body that would cope with the sewage problem. Although the diversion project hasn't been completed, the picturesque lake is nearly as clear as it

was eighteen years ago. Its clarity should continue to improve as its effluent is diverted to the tide-washed sound.

Diversion projects are sometimes condemned as costly boondoggles, since rainfall inevitably contributes so much nitrogen to lakes, whether or not diversion is practiced. Critics, however, fail to consider, or choose to ignore, the fact that municipal sewage — not rainfall — is the major source of phosphorous, the other stimulant of cultural eutrophication.

There is no standard remedy for ailing lakes. Diversion is no cure-all. It has disadvantages in addition to its expense and capacity for creating or aggravating water problems elsewhere. Diversion can negate itself, particularly in water-scarce regions where sources of clean water that might have flushed lakes clean have been channeled instead into diversion systems to carry away sewage effluent. Thus, the advantage of diverting effluent is sometimes offset by the disadvantage of diverting potentially cleansing inflows. Engineers, aware of this drawback, are exploring the possibility of using "infertile" water from the Columbia River to rinse Moses Lake in central Washington.

Harvesting weeds and fish to remove nutrients from fertilized lakes promises to supplement diversion projects very effectively. Seining crews, for example, hauled 40 pounds of carp per acre from Madison's Lake Mendota. Since the nitrogen and phosphorus content of fish flesh is 2.5 and 0.2 percent, respectively, 500 pounds of carp harvested removed 12.5 pounds of nitrogen and a pound of phosphorus from the lakes. The 1966 carp catch yielded 16,000 pounds of nitrogen and 800 pounds of phosphorus. The nutrient "yield" of this method could be easily expanded in most eutrophic lakes with more intensive harvesting of carp and other rough fish.

A program to perfect weed-harvesting

techniques and to evaluate their effectiveness was begun last summer on Lake Sallie, a densely populated lake in the vacation area of Detroit Lakes, Minn. By "cropping" one-third of the lake three times to a depth of five feet below the surface, the researchers expect to remove substantially more nutrients in one summer than enter the lake in a year. The outlook for harvesting algae on a large scale, however, isn't nearly as bright. No economical equipment has been developed to skim algae off lakes and impoundments.

While inventors are working on a variety of devices that "suck up algae like vacuum cleaners" or "strain algal scum from lakes," members of the National Eutrophication Research Program are hunting for a herbivore, perhaps some water flea or fish, with a huge appetite for algae. The search may be extended abroad if no algae-craving counterparts can be found to the weed-eating snails used in the southeastern United States. Precautions, however, must be taken to screen out "exotic" species that could become nuisances. Also, of two viruses known to cause diseases among blue-green algae, one is being tested, and more virulent species are being sought.

The best that can be said for spraying chemical poisons on lakes in the grip of algae and weeds is that it is usually a futile undertaking. Treating a lake with copper sulfate or other toxic chemicals is no more effective than taking aspirin for a brain tumor. It offers only temporary relief, masking the symptoms of cultural eutrophication. In the long run it makes a lake sicker. Poisoning algae and weeds simply accelerates the natural process of growth, death, and decay, thereby freeing nutrients for another cycle of plant production. This has been borne out by studies of blue-green algae in Oregon's Upper Klamath Lake, which first showed signs of eutrophication eighty years ago. In the peak growth month of August, Klamath algae contain within their cells three times as much nitrogen as is dissolved in the lake. Killing an alga therefore would release this nitrogen for further growth.

Chemical poisons should be used only as a last resort, for once dumped into a body of water, they cannot be confined to one locality. They dissolve and spread far beyond the area treated. Dispersed eventually by wave action throughout a lake, they adversely alter the fragile fabric of aquatic communities of many species. Too little is known about the sublethal effects of such poisons to risk their use.

We can take several steps — all more effective than chemical poisoning — to bolster the two-pronged attack of diverting effluent and removing nutrients. By separating sewer systems for storm runoff and sewage, communities can forestall the lake fertilization that occurs when nutrient-rich combined sewers overflow after heavy rains. Damaging septic tank seepage can be curbed by passing legislation that would require that tanks be installed at a "safe" distance from bodies of water. Wisconsin legislators, for instance, recently decided that lakes and rivers would be safe from fertilization only if septic tanks are set back as far as 1,000 feet and 300 feet, respectively. They also set more stringent specifications for septic tanks themselves. The specifications vary with the porosity of the soil.

Livestock growers could also fight cultural eutrophication by adopting the European practice of fluidizing and storing manure in vats, from winter freeze-up until the spring thaw, and then spraying it on their fields when the soil can better absorb it. The bulk of the manure now spread on frozen cropland runs off with spring meltwater to fertilize lakes and streams. This is significant considering the fact that the amount of manure, produced each year in the Midwest alone, is equivalent to human sewage of a population of 350 million. The chief drawback of the European method is its expense. Federal funds for water and soil conservation, however, could possibly be used to help farmers pay for costly storage tanks and spraying equipment.

We still have much to learn about the complexities of the eutrophication process. There is an urgent need for more research on such factors as a lake's depth, size, and configuration, its drainage basin and sources of nutrients, and its aquatic communities. But such research is complicated because biological and ecological factors vary with every lake, pond, and reservoir. Systems analysis with computers promises to be the research tool that will enable us to supply precise data on the potentialities of eutrophication.

Improved research, however, is only part of the solution to this dilemma. Unfortunately there isn't time to raise an enlightened generation to cope with eutrophication. Although we don't have all the answers, we must heed the warnings given by the waterways around us that have fallen into an advanced state of decay. If we delay, the price may be too dear to pay.

EDITOR'S COMMENTS

There is obviously only one desirable way of stopping cultural eutrophication; namely, to stop allowing excesses of nitrogen, phosphorous and other nutrients to enter natural waters. It has become rather ridiculous to use expense as an excuse not to do this. The cost of water must be increased to bear the financial weight of tertiary sewage treatment. The cost of meat must be increased to pay for effective manure disposal. The cost of consumer goods in general must be increased to defray the cost of industrial water treatment. Pollution is people-caused. Too many people demanding too much of natural ecosystems will surely spell the end of these ecosystems if a new environmental technology is long in coming.

JOHN R. CLARK

Heat Pollution

John Clark is an environmental consultant
specializing in aquatic ecology and an author
of books on aquatic life. He is Board chairman
of the American Littoral Society. He worked
for 21 years in fishery research for the Department of Interior at Woods Hole, Massachusetts
and Sandy Hook, New Jersey.

Scientists consider heat as the primary
environmental control of life on earth; yet
when this great power is misused, it assumes the role of pollutant. Heat in the
form of hot water discharges has much in
common with pollutants more widely known
to the public: it is produced in vast amounts
by basic industry; it is dumped like sewage
into public bodies of water; and, once
dumped, it can generate massive ecological
disturbance.

Thermal discharge and power plants go
hand in hand. Electrical energy is generated
in one of two basic ways; by steam or by
falling water. A generator is driven by a
turbine in either method. In a waterpower
plant the potential energy of river or reservoir water is realized by allowing it to
plunge down a sharp drop and over the
blades of the turbine. In a steam plant the
energy of burning fossil fuels — coal, oil, or
gas — or nuclear fuel is used to produce
steam at high pressure. The steam turns the

turbine, which powers the generator. However, once it has gone through the turbine,
the spent steam must be recondensed into
water, which is done by cooling it in a
condenser with water taken from a lake,
river, estuary, bay, or ocean.

A nuclear power plant represents no great
conceptual departure from the more familiar
coal-fired plant. Both are thermal plants, but
heat is obtained in the so-called "nuke"
plant by fission reaction in an atomic pile.
Nuclear plants obviate need for transport-
ing huge quantities of fossil fuels, thus
widening the choice of plant location. Moreover, they do not pollute the air with smoke.
The price of these advantages is the threat
of radiation hazards (both short and long
term) from such plants, the full extent of
which is unknown; and the additional thermal pollution they create.

Ideally all heat produced should be turned
into electricity. In practice much is wasted;
the amount of waste is the index of plant
efficiency. Nuclear plants waste 50 to 60

Reprinted by permission of the author and publisher from *National Parks and Conservation
Magazine* 43(267): 4-8. December 1969. Copyright © 1969 by the National Parks and Conservation Association which assumes no responsibility
for its distribution other than through the magazine.

percent more heat than fossil fuel plants, and this heat is discharged as additional thermal refuse in the outflow from the condensers.

Of the 60,000 billion gallons of water per year now used by American industry for cooling, about three-quarters is used in power plant steam condensers. As of now, thermal pollution has erupted as a problem only in some limited areas. However, power development apparently is not going to wait for technology to provide easy answers to pollution problems. Relatively few nuclear plants are in operation at the moment, most of them government-subsidized installations designed to develop techniques for economical nuclear power generation. But a new generation of fully commercial plants is under construction, and many more are being planned. It is estimated that within the next decade there will be nearly three-quarters as much electrical energy generated in such plants as in all other thermal plants combined. Because of ever-increasing demands of an exploding population, by the end of the century the power industry will be generating an estimated 2 million megawatts of electricity, by far the largest portion of it in nuclear power plants. This level of energy production will yield, every day, enough waste heat to warm *107 cubic miles* of water by 20°F., a level of thermal addition that could produce catastrophic effects if inflicted on many of our waters. An amount equal to one-third of the daily freshwater runoff of the United States would be needed for plant condensers. Already it has been estimated that half again as much water as occurs in the summertime daily freshwater runoff passes through the cooling systems of thermal electric power plants along certain of the heavily industrialized and populated watercourses of the northeastern United States, which obviously requires the reuse of at least part of the available flow (Summer is generally the low-flow period.) Moreover, much of this water occurs where it is inaccessible to the plants so it is ap-

parent that accessible water is used many times over, often being recycled before it has had a chance to cool down to normal temperature again. (Cooling systems of thermal plants commonly raise the temperature of water used by 10° to 30°F.)

To some people it may seem strange that a temperature rise of "only" 10° or 20°F. in the vicinity of a power plant could be ecologically devastating. That it can indeed be devastating is testimony to the delicacy and complexity of the communities of aquatic life, especially where heat is involved.

A characteristic of most natural bodies of water is that temperatures change slowly; in addition, the fluctuation usually is confined between about 28°F. and perhaps 100°F. Because of this thermal stability, aquatic animals are cold blooded and therefore at the mercy of ambient temperatures. The heat of their surroundings determines their internal temperature and thus the biochemical pace of their lives. Generally speaking, in cold water fish slow down; as the temperature rises, they become more active. Heartbeat and respiration rates go up, and all the fishes' biochemical reactions are accelerated. This acceleration is desirable as it occurs naturally in the spring, when winter torpor gives way to full activity again, but beyond a certain level it can cause trouble.

The difficulty stems from the fact that there is a limit to how much an organism's metabolism can be wound up by rising temperature. The biochemical processes run faster and faster until the delicate mechanisms that keep all running smoothly together are overtaxed and begin to operate abnormally; then the animal ceases to reproduce properly and suffers internal disorders that lead to ill health or even death.

Such consequences may result from a rise of only a few degrees when temperatures are naturally high. The limits of tolerance are sharply defined for each species. Normally the fishes in a particular body of water adapt to extremes in temperature of that water so far as possible by natural selection; those unable to adapt die or seek other waters. However, when a river whose summertime temperature in a particular stretch almost never exceeded 90°F. suddenly has an average summer temperature of 93°F., the apparently small rise over the previous limit can be disruptive to much of the river life of the area. In a river, excessive temperatures can form a "thermal block" preventing migrating adult fish from going upstream to spawn and young fish from returning to estuary or ocean. In many organisms, spawning and migration are triggered by temperature, usually as an automatic reaction. Rising spring temperatures induce development of gonads and the deposition of eggs by the female; in estuarine shellfish, spawning takes place only hours after the critical temperature is reached. Forcing spawning to occur with artificial heat at a time of year when conditions are not right for survival of the young will reduce a population of animals as surely as killing them directly. Lake trout can tolerate water temperatures of up to 77°F. However, satisfactory growth of their young cannot take place in waters over 68°F., and spawning will not occur at temperatures above 48°F. A population of lake trout that can never reach water below 50°F. will die out like the shellfish, from reproductive failure.

Even if adult organisms can manage to lay eggs, thermal pollution still may bring death to their offspring. Higher temperatures result in faster development and hatching of eggs; but beyond a certain point, as with adults, the biochemistry goes awry and the eggs develop abnormally or not at all. The Oregon Fish Commission says that if the temperature of the Columbia River is increased by only 5.4°F., hatchability of Chinook salmon eggs will decline disastrously. Carp eggs exposed to temperatures between 68° and 75°F. will not undergo cell division.

Thermal pollution can have other directly deleterious effects on aquatic life that deeply concern biologists as proposals are advanced for the proliferation of nuclear and other thermal power generating plants. But biologists are not worrying most about direct effects of heat at the present time. More important than the absolute limit of tolerance of a given organism, or even the ability of a population of one species to survive, is the ability of the ecosystem to work smoothly.

Shallow lakes, rivers, and estuaries are among the tighter and more heat-sensitive ecosystems. They do not contain a huge amount of water to dilute heated effluents; furthermore, in many lakes and estuaries water currents are sluggish and inefficient at mixing hot water with cool. And these bodies of water, particularly the estuaries, are the ocean's nurseries. They are placid compared to the churning sea, and many forms of marine life depend on their protected waters as sanctuaries for their young. Their marshes, lagoons, bayous, creeks, and sloughs provide shelter from predators for the tiny larvae and vulnerable fry; and the water is a rich source of minerals and microscopic animals, plants, and bits of organic detritus that comprise the larvae's food.

We have seen how the temperature range in which a creature can spawn, and in which its young will thrive, is much narrower than the range in which it can maintain a toehold on life. Furthermore, ecological relationships of microscopic life such as algae and larvae are extremely complex and subtle. This level of life is even more dependent than adult fish on a stable environment; minute physical changes can reverberate powerfully through such a tightly interdependent level of the ecosystem.

The advent of thermal pollution in some of the most valuable estuarine nurseries could be disastrous. The effect of heat on spawning and egg development already has been mentioned. As another example, three groups of algae commonly found in water form the diet of many small animals and larvae — diatoms, green algae, and blue-green algae. According to one study, although all three forms may be found where temperatures range between 68° and 104°F., the relative abundance of the species of each varies with temperature. At 68° diatoms comprise by far the largest portion of the total number of species of the three forms. At about 83° green algae species have increased and diatoms have declined until both are in equal abundance, and blue-green species have begun to become more numerous. At 95° greens have peaked and are declining, blue-greens have increased to a population two-thirds that of the greens, and diatoms are insignificant. Beyond this temperature blue-green species take over.

Now, many of the tiny organisms naturally present in an estuary depend on diatoms rather than green algae for food, because diatoms normally are more abundant. A change in the abundance of the kinds of algae decreases organisms that depend on diatoms and increases organisms that can best utilize green algae. At the upper end, the blue-green algae are indigestible to many organisms that graze on algae, and consequently the total number of grazing organisms in the estuary drops. This decrease results in the loss of larger animals that had been feeding on the smaller animals, then the loss of even larger predatory animals, and so on up the food chain, inevitably all the way to the producer of the thermal pollution — man.

Of course, any adverse shift in algal populations would reduce the proper food for the larval form of many open-ocean fish species, spoiling the otherwise suitable nursery for those species. If as is often the case, nowadays, a widespread and important oceanic species has relatively few unpolluted nurseries left, the loss of only one could have serious consequences for the species. Again, man, attempting to harvest the

species, will suffer the boomerang effect of his own actions.

Finally, ecological imbalance often results in a population explosion of undesirable algae. At night algae, like all plants, use oxygen instead of producing it. If the algal population reaches a high enough level, there will not be enough oxygen in the water to sustain the plants through the night and many will die. The oxygen-consuming bacterial decay of these algae will further reduce oxygen levels, and more algae will die, even in the daytime. This process is the familiar phenomenon of algal bloom followed by die-off that produces a malodorous slime and water that may be unlivable for all but anaerobic bacteria. Needless to say, higher organisms lose out early in the competition with bacteria for oxygen. This phenomenon is especially likely to occur if water is thermally polluted that already contains overloads of sewage effluents and agricultural fertilizer runoff. Both of the latter contain nutrients for algae that hasten their growth.

Thermal discharges do not have to heat an entire body of water in order to cause concern. Some ecologists are worried about the invaluable Chesapeake Bay ecosystem because of nuclear power plants such as that being constructed at Calvert Cliffs in Maryland by the Baltimore Gas and Electric Company. The company has commissioned baseline studies of the bay in the vicinity of the plant site. Armed with results of such a study, scientists will be able to determine what effect the plant's operation will have on the bay ecosystem. The company says that it will avoid serious consequences for the bay at any cost but claims that inasmuch as it is warming only 35 acres of surface water by 3° F., on the average, no harm will be done. Some scientists studying the bay are not so sure. Their concern is not just that 35 acres of the 2.1-million-acre bay might be ruined. Rather, they fear that the 35-acre thermal "plume" might be spread across the 6-mile-wide waist of the bay near the site, forming a thermal barrier to the passage of surface organisms to spawning grounds in the upper bay. Others fear that even a small rise of 3°F. in mean temperature can have consequences as yet unknown.

What can be done about the thermal pollution threat? Until population is stabilized, demand will continue to increase. Meanwhile, to avoid damage to aquatic life, plans for thermal plants should hinge on thorough ecological studies that map existing conditions and predict areas of special vulnerability. Even if more expensive, other heat disposal methods should be sought.

Many schemes have been advanced for using the waste heat of thermal plants to some advantage, but unfortunately most so far have proven impractical. One of the most promising of these ideas would use the waste heat to aid in evaporating seawater in desalination plants; another would use excess heat to make sewage treatment processes more efficient. Paradoxically, in view of the danger to natural aquatic life of waste heat, sea farming may eventually be a profitable consumer of the thermal energy that now is allowed to escape. In controlled use, such heat could extend the growing season by promoting more rapid growth of marine life during spring and fall because of its speeding up of body processes. Tests now under way in Scotland have shown that two saltwater fish species, plaice and Dover sole, may be grown to market size faster in nuclear plant seawater effluent than in the ocean.

At the moment, however, and for many years to come, most of the waste heat must be released into the environment. Anywhere it is released it will affect the ecosystem to some extent. In view of the impact on the aquatic environment, it would seem that water — even the water at the edge of the ocean — should be the last place chosen for heat disposal. However, if it must be dumped into water, several alternatives are available, choice of which should depend on the ecological nature of the receiving body of water. A discharge method producing least harm in one body of water might produce most harm in another.

The only alternative to water as a waste heat dump is the air. Three possibilities exist.

First, a large, fairly shallow impoundment may be constructed, into the shallowest end of which the heated effluent is pumped. The heat is dissipated from the reservoir into the air; and, once cooled, the water is withdrawn from the deepest end for use again in condensers.

Second, a cooling tower can be used. The heated water is sprayed into a cooling countercurrent of air in the tower. Cooling is partly evaporative. The disadvantage both of this type of tower and of cooling reservoirs is that much of the cooling water is lost by evaporation. More seriously, in cool climates wet towers can produce a large amount of fog and in winter could ice over a considerable area; the towers needed for a 1,000-megawatt plant would emit some 20,000 to 25,000 gallons of water per minute as vapor, the equivalent of an inch of rain a day on an area of 2 square miles.

The third method of dissipation is both most desirable from the environmental point of view and most expensive. (At that, the extra cost might be only about $1 a month for the "average" homeowner.) This is the so-called dry tower. In this kind of tower condenser water is pumped through coils of tubing across which air is drawn. The heat is dissipated as from the radiator of a car. Because the system is closed, there are no evaporation problems.

Power companies, in business for a profit, like to keep costs down. Therefore, they prefer to discharge heat into natural waters first, cooling reservoirs second, wet towers third, and dry towers fourth. The ecologist prefers the reverse order, with perhaps a few exceptions. Before long many natural waters will reach the limit of their heat-absorbing capacity. Then it may pass that energy consumers — homeowners and industries alike — will have to pay the full cost of the product they buy instead of letting the environment pay part of the bill — a bill that, added to all her other bills, may impoverish Mother Earth.

EDITOR'S COMMENTS

The satisfactory answer to the thermal pollution of natural water is so simple that one would wonder at the furor created during the past several years. Dr. Clark explains the solution in his next-to-last paragraph — release of heat from a dry tower. All processes which release heat into natural fresh water systems should be converted to this type of heat dissipating device, and all future heat releasing projects should be designed so as not to release heat into fresh water sources.

It is questionable as to whether the present heat burden being applied to fresh water systems is causing extensive ecological damage. However, much of this heat is released from electrical generating plants, and our demand for electricity doubles every 8 to 10 years. It is obvious that the continued practice of heat disposal in our natural rivers and lakes cannot be continued indefinitely. Consumers must ultimately bear the cost of proper heat disposal through slightly increased utility and consumer goods prices.

Heat released from dry towers enters the atmosphere where it contributes in a minor way to an overall rise in atmospheric temperature. This heat can also cause local climatic modifications such as fogging and icing. However, heat released into the air undoubtedly produces fewer problems than heat released into rivers, streams, and lakes.

SOURCES OF ADDITIONAL INFORMATION

AIR POLLUTION (GENERAL)

Brodine, V. 1970. A special burden. *Environment* 13(2):22.

Brodine, V. 1972. Running in place. *Environment* 14(1):2-11.

Brodine, V. 1972. Point of damage. *Environment* 14(4):2-15.

Bryson, R. A. 1968. All other factors being constant . . . ; a reconciliation of several theories of climatic change. *Weatherwise* 21:56-61, 94.

Craig, P. P., and E. Berlin. 1971. The air of poverty. *Environment* 13(5):2-9.

Craig, R. 1971. Cloud on the desert. *Environment* 13(6):20-35.

Flohn, H. 1969. *Climate and weather.* McGraw-Hill, New York.

Hexter, A. C., and J. R. Goldsmith. 1971. Carbon monoxide association of community air pollution with mortality. *Science* 172:265-266.

Kotin, P., and H. Falk. 1963. Atmospheric factors in pathogenesis of lung cancer. *Advances in Cancer Research* 7:504.

Lave, L. B., and E. P. Seskin. 1970. Air pollution and human health. *Science* 169(3947): 723-733.

Lewis, H. R. 1965. *With every breath you take.* Crown, New York.

Likens, G. E., et al. 1972. Acid rain. *Environment* 14(2):33-40.

McCaull, J. 1971. Building a shorter life. *Environment* 13(7):2-15.

Pack, D. H. 1964. Meterology of air pollution. *Science* 146:1119-1128.

Peterson, E. K. 1970. The atmosphere: a clouded horizon. *Environment* 12(3):32-39.

Schaefer, V. 1969. Some effects of air pollution on our environment. *BioScience* 19 (10):896-897.

Schroeder, H. A. 1971. Metals in the air. *Environment* 13(8):18-32.

Stern, A. C., ed. 1968. *Air pollution.* 2d ed. 3 vols. Academic Press, New York.

Stocks, P. 1960. On the relations between atmospheric pollutions in urban and rural localities and mortality from cancer, bronchitis, and pneumonia. *British Journal of Cancer* 14:397-418.

Stokinger, H. E., and D. L. Coffin. 1968. Biologic effects of air pollutants. *Air Pollution* 1:460-465.

Sultz, H. A., et al. 1970. An effect of continued exposure to air pollution on the incidence of chronic childhood allergic disease. *American Journal of Public Health* 60:890.

Summer, W. 1971. *Odor pollution of air.* Chemical Rubber Co. Press, Cleveland, Ohio.

Waggoner, P. E. 1971. Plants and polluted air. *BioScience* 21(10):455-459.

Winkelstein, W., Jr., and S. Kantor. 1969. Stomach cancer: positive association with suspended particulate air pollution. *Archives of Environmental Health* 18:544-547.

Winn, I. J. 1971. Greetings from Los Angeles. *Natural History* 80(8):12-20.

Wise, W. 1968. *Killer smog: the world's worst air pollution disaster.* Rand McNally, Chicago.

Wolman, A. 1965. The metabolism of cities. *Scientific American* 213(3):178-190.

WATER POLLUTION (GENERAL)

Carr, D. E. 1966. *Death of the sweet waters.* W. W. Norton, New York.

Chesters, G., and J. G. Konrad. 1971. Effects of pesticide usage on water quality. *BioScience* 21(12):565-569.

Commoner, B. 1970. Soil and fresh water: damaged global fabric. *Environment* 12(3): 4-11.

Fonselius, S. H. 1970. Stagnant sea. *Environment* 12(6):2-11.

Hasler, A. D. 1969. Cultural eutrophication is reversible. *BioScience* 19(5):425-431.

Hennigan, R. D. 1969. Water pollution. *BioScience* 19(11):976-978.

Hoult, D., ed. 1969. *Oil on the sea.* Plenum Press, New York.

McCaull, J. 1970. Who owns the water? *Environment* 12(8):30-39.

McClane, A. J. 1968. The ultimate open sewer. *Field and Stream* 73(1):12.

National Academy of Sciences. 1969. *Eutrophication: causes, consequences, correctives.* National Research Council, Washington, D.C.

Rutzler, K., and W. Sterrer. 1970. Oil pollution: damage observed in tropical communities along the Atlantic seaboard of Panama. *BioScience* 20(4):222-224.

Shea, K. P. 1970. Dead stream. *Environment* 12(6):12-15.

Vietes, F. G., Jr. 1971. Water quality in relation to farm use of fertilizer. *BioScience* 21(10):460-467.

Warren, C. E. *Biology and water pollution control.* W. B. Saunders, Philadelphia, Pennsylvania.

Wilbur, C. G. 1969. *The biological aspects of water pollution.* Charles C. Thomas, Springfield, Illinois.

THERMAL POLLUTION

Clark, J. R. 1969. Thermal pollution and aquatic life. *Scientific American* 220(3):18-27.

Cole, L. C. 1969. Thermal pollution. *BioScience* 19(11):989-992.

Krenkel, P., and F. Parker. 1969. *Biological aspects of thermal pollution.* Vanderbilt University Press, Nashville, Tennessee.

Merriman, D. 1970. The calefaction of a river. *Scientific American* 222(5):42-52.

U.S. Senate, Ninetieth Congress, 2d Session, February 1968. Thermal pollution. *Hearing before the subcommittee on air and water pollution of the committee on public works.* U.S. Govt. Printing Office, Washington, D.C.

Woodson, R. D. 1971. Cooling towers. *Scientific American* 224:70-78.

HEAVY METAL POLLUTION

Chisolm, J. 1971. Lead poisoning. *Scientific American* 224(2):15-23.

Friberg, L., et al. 1971. *Cadmium in the environment.* Chemical Rubber Co. Press, Cleveland, Ohio.

Friberg, L., and J. Vostal. 1972. *Mercury in the environment.* Chemical Rubber Co. Press, Cleveland, Ohio.

Goldwater, L. J. 1971. Mercury in the environment. *Scientific American* 224(5):15-21.

Grant, N. 1971. Mercury in man. *Environment* 13(4):2-15.

Hyman, M. 1971. Time table for lead. *Environment* 13(5):14-23.

Miller, M., and G. Berg, eds. 1969. *Chemical fallout.* Charles C. Thomas. Springfield, Illinois.

Peakal, D., and R. Lovett. 1972. Mercury: it's occurrence and effects in the eco-system. *BioScience* 22(1):20-25.

Siccama, T., and E. Porter. 1972. Lead in a Connecticut salt marsh. *BioScience* 22(4):232-234.

Wood, J. 1972. A progress report on mercury. *Environment* 14(1):33-39.

Part IV

Man and His Fellow
Inhabitants

WILLIAM A. NIERING

The Effects of Pesticides

William A. Niering is Professor of Botany at
Connecticut College. His research has involved vegetation management with herbicides.
He is currently editor of the BULLETIN
of the Ecologcial Society of America.

The dramatic appearance of Rachel Carson's *Silent Spring* (1962) awakened a
nation to the deleterious effects of pesticides. Our technology had surged ahead of
us. We had lost our perspective on just how
ruthlessly man can treat his environment and
still survive. He was killing pesty insects by
the trillions, but he was also poisoning natural ecosystems all around him. It was Miss
Carson's mission to arrest this detrimental
use of our technological achievements. As
one might have expected, she was criticized
by special vested industrial interests and, to
some degree, by certain agricultural specialists concerned with only one aspect of our
total environment. However, there was no
criticism, only praise, from the nation's
ecosystematically oriented biologists. For
those who found *Silent Spring* too dramatic
an approach to the problem, the gap was
filled two years later by *Pesticides and the
Living Landscape* (1964) in which Rudd
further documented Miss Carson's thesis but
in more academic style.

The aim of this chapter is to summarize
some of the effects of two pesticides — insecticides and herbicides — on our total
environment, and to point up research and
other educational opportunities for students
of environmental science. The insecticide
review will be based on representative
studies from the literature, whereas the herbicide review will represent primarily the
results of the author's research and experience in the Connecticut Arboretum at Connecticut College. Although some consider
this subject controversial, there is really no
controversy in the mind of the author —
the issue merely involves the sound ecological use of pesticides only where necessary
and without drastically contaminating or upsetting the dynamic equilibrium of our natural ecosystems. I shall not consider the
specific physiological effects of pesticides,
but rather their effects on the total environment — plants, animals, soil, climate, man
— the biotic and abiotic aspects.

Environmental science or ecosystemic
thinking should attempt to coordinate and
integrate all aspects of the environment. Although ecosystems may be managed, they
must also remain in a relative balance or
dynamic equilibrium, analogous to a spider's

web, where each strand is intimately inter-related and interdependent upon every other strand.

The Impact of Insecticides

Ecologists have long been aware that simplifying the environment to only a few species can precipitate a catastrophe. Our highly mechanized agricultural operations, dominated by extensive acreages of one crop, encourage large numbers of insect pests. As insurance against insect damage, vast quantities of insecticides are applied with little regard for what happens to the chemical once it is on the land. Prior to World War II, most of our insecticides were nonpersistent organics found in the natural environment. For example, the pyrethrins were derived from dried chrysanthemum flowers, nicotine sulphate from tobacco, and rotenone from the tropical derris plants. However, research during World War II and thereafter resulted in a number of potent persistent chlorinated hydrocarbons (DDT, dieldrin, endrin, lindane, chlordane, heptachor and others) to fight the ever-increasing hordes of insects, now some 3000 species plaguing man in North America.

In 1964, industries in the United States produced 783 million lb. of pesticides, half insecticides and the other half herbicides, fungicides, and rodenticides. The application of these chemicals on the nation's land-scapes[1] has now reached the point where one of out of every ten acres is being sprayed with an average of 4 lb. per acre (Anonymous 1966).

Positive Effects of Target Organisms

That market yields and quality are increased by agricultural spraying appears to have been well documented. Data from the National Agricultural Chemical Association show net increased yields resulting in from $5.00 to $100.00 net gains per acre on such crops as barley, tomatoes, sugar beets, pea seed, and cotton seed. However, Rudd (1964) questions the validity of these figures, since there is no explanation just how they were derived. His personal observations on the rice crop affected by the rice leaf miner outbreak in California are especially pertinent. The insect damage was reported as ruining 10% to 20% of the crop. He found this to be correct for some fields, but most of the fields were not damaged at all. In this situation, the facts were incorrect concerning the pest damage. It appears that not infrequently repeated spraying applications are merely insurance sprays and in many cases actually unnecessary. Unfortunately, the farmer is being forced to this procedure in part by those demanding from agriculture completely insect-free produce. This has now reached ridiculous proportions. Influenced by advertising, the housewife now demands perfect specimens with no thought of a regard for how much environmental contamination has resulted to attain such perfection. If we could relax our standards to a moderate degree, pesticide contamination could be greatly reduced. Although it may be difficult to question that spraying increases yields and quality of the marketable products, there are few valid data available on how much spraying is actually necessary, how much it is adding to consumer costs, what further pests are aggravated by spraying, and what degree of resistance eventually develops.

Negative Effects on Nontarget Organisms

Although yields may be increased with greater margins of profit, according to available data, one must recognize that these chemicals may adversely affect a whole spectrum of nontarget organisms not only where applied but possibly thousands of miles from

1. Dr. George Woodwell estimates that there are 1 billion lbs. of DDT now circulating in the biosphere.

the site of application. To the ecologist concerned with the total environment, these persistent pesticides pose some serious threats to our many natural ecosystems. Certain of these are pertinent to review.

1. KILLING OF NONTARGET ORGANISMS

In practically every spray operation, thousands of nontarget insects are killed, many of which may be predators on the very organisms one is attempting to control. But such losses extend far beyond the beneficial insects. In Florida, an estimated 1,117,-000 fishes of at least 30 species (20 to 30 tons), were killed with dieldrin, when sand flies were really the target organism. Crustaceans were virtually exterminated — the fiddler crabs survived only in areas missed by the treatment (Harrington and Bidlingmayer, 1958).

In 1963, there was a "silent spring" in Hanover, New Hampshire. Seventy percent of the robin population — 350 to 400 robins — was eliminated in spraying for Dutch elm disease with 1.9 lb per acre DDT (Wurster et al. 1965). Wallace (1960) and Hickey and Hunt (1960) have reported similar instances on the Michigan State University and University of Wisconsin campuses. Last summer, at Wesleyan University, my students observed dead and trembling birds following summer applications of DDT on the elms. At the University of Wisconsin campus (61 acres), the substitution of methoxychlor has resulted in a decreased bird mortality. The robin population has jumped from three to twenty-nine pairs following the change from DDT to methoxychlor. Chemical control of this disease is often overemphasized, with too little attention directed against the sources of elm bark beetle. Sanitation is really the most important measure in any sound Dutch elm disease control program (Matthysse 1959).

One of the classic examples involving the widespread destruction of nontarget organisms was the fire ant eradication program in our southern states. In 1957, dieldrin and heptochlor were aerially spread over two and one-half million acres. Wide elimination of vertebrate populations resulted; and recovery of some populations is still uncertain (Rudd 1964). In the interest of science, the Georgia Academy of Science appointed an ad hoc committee to evaluate this control-eradication program (Bellinger et al. 1965). It found that reported damage to crops, wildlife, fish, and humans had not been verified, and concluded, furthermore, that the ant is not really a significant economic pest but a mere nuisance. Here was an example where the facts did not justify the federal expenditure of $2.4 million in indiscriminate sprays. Fortunately, this approach has been abandoned, and local treatments are now employed with Mirex, a compound with fewer side effects. Had only a small percentage of this spray expenditure been directed toward basic research, we might be far ahead today in control of the fire ant.

2. ACCUMULATION IN THE FOOD CHAIN

The persistent nature of certain of these insecticides permits the chemical to be carried from one organism to another in the food chain. As this occurs, there is a gradual increase in the biocide at each higher trophic level. Many such examples have been reported in the literature. One of the most striking comes from Clear Lake, California, where a 46,000-acre warm lake, north of San Francisco, was sprayed for pesty gnats in 1949, 1954, and 1957, with DDD, a chemical presumably less toxic than DDT. Analyses of the plankton revealed 250 times more of the chemical than originally applied, the frog 2000 times more, sunfish 12,000, and the grebes up to an 80,000-fold increase (Cottam 1965; Rudd 1964). In 1954 death among the grebes was widespread. Prior to the spraying, a thousand of these birds nested on the lake. Then for 10 years no grebes hatched. Finally, in 1962, one nestling was observed, and the following year three. Clear Lake is popular for sports fishing, and the flesh of edible fish now caught reaches 7 ppm. which is above the maximum tolerance level set by the Food and Drug Administration.

In an estuarine ecosystem, a similar trend has been reported on the Long Island tidal marshes, where mosquito control spraying with DDT has been practiced for some 20 years (Woodwell et al. 1967). Here the food chain accumulation shows plankton 0.04 ppm, shrimp 0.16 ppm, minnows 1 to 2 ppm, and ring-billed gull 75.5 ppm. In general, the DDT concentrations in carnivorous birds were 10 to 100 times those in the fish they fed upon. Birds near the top of the food chain have DDT residues about a million times greater than concentration in the water. Pesticide levels are now so high that certain populations are being subtly eliminated by food chain accumulations reaching toxic levels.

3. LOWERED REPRODUCTIVE POTENTIAL

Considerable evidence is available to suggest a lowered reproductive potential, especially among birds, where the pesticide occurs in the eggs in sufficient quantities either to prevent hatching or to decrease vigor among the young birds hatched. Birds of prey, such as the bald eagle, osprey, hawks, and others, are in serious danger. Along the northeast Atlantic coast, ospreys normally average about 2.5 young per year. However, in Maryland and Connecticut, reproduction is far below this level. In Maryland, ospreys produce 1.1 young per year and their eggs contain 3 ppm DDT, while in Connecticut, 0.5 young ospreys hatch and their eggs contain up to 5.1 ppm DDT. These data indicate a direct correlation between the amount of DDT and the hatchability of eggs — the more DDT present in the eggs, the fewer young hatched (Ames, 1966). In Wisconsin, Keith (1964) reports 38% hatching failure in herring gulls. Early in the incu-

bation period, gull eggs collected contained over 200 ppm DDT and its cogeners. Pheasant eggs from DDT-treated rice fields compared to those from unsprayed lands result in fewer healthy month-old chicks from eggs taken near sprayed fields. Although more conclusive data may still be needed to prove that pesticides such as DDT are the key factor, use of such compounds should be curtailed until it is proved that they are not the causal agents responsible for lowering reproductive potential.

4. RESISTANCE TO SPRAYS

Insects have a remarkable ability to develop a resistance to insecticides. The third spray at Clear Lake was the least effective on the gnats, and here increased resistance was believed to be a factor involved. As early as 1951, resistance among agricultural insects appeared. Some of these include the codling moth on apples, and certain cotton, cabbage, and potato insects. Over 100 important insect pests now show a definite resistance to chemicals (Carson 1962).

5. SYNERGISTIC EFFECTS

The interaction of two compounds may result in a third much more toxic than either one alone. For example, Malathion is relatively "safe" because detoxifying enzymes in the liver greatly reduce its toxic properties. However, if some compound destroys or interrupts this enzyme system, as certain organic phosphates may do, the toxicity of the new combination may be increased greatly. Pesticides represent one of many pollutants we are presently adding to our environment. These subtle synergistic effects have opened a whole new field of investigation. Here students of environmental science will find many challenging problems for future research.

6. CHEMICAL MIGRATION

After two decades of intensive use, pesticides are now found throughout the world, even in places far from any actual spraying. Penguins and crab-eating seals in the Antarctic are contaminated, and fish far off the coasts of four continents now contain insecticides ranging from 1 to 300 ppm in their fatty tissues (Anonymous 1966).

The major rivers of our nation are contaminated by DDT, endrin, and dieldrin, mostly in the parts per trillion range. Surveys since 1957 reveal that dieldrin has been the main pesticide present since 1958. Endrin reached its maximum, especially in the lower Mississippi River, in the fall of 1963 when an extensive fish kill occurred and has since that time decreased. DDT and its cogeners, consistently present since 1958, have been increasing slightly (Breidenbach et al. 1967).

7. ACCUMULATION IN THE ECOSYSTEM

Since chlorinated hydrocarbons like DDT are not readily broken down by biological agents such as bacteria, they may not only be present but also accumulate within a given ecosystem. On Long Island, up to 32 lb. of DDT have been reported in the marsh mud, with an average of 13 lb. presumed to be correlated with the 20 years of mosquito control spraying (Woodwell et al. 1967). Present in these quantities, burrowing marine organisms and the detritis feeders can keep the residues in continuous circulation in the ecosystem. Many marine forms are extremely sensitive to minute amounts of insecticides. Fifty percent of a shrimp population was killed with endrin 0.6 parts per billion (ppb). Even 1 ppb will kill blue crabs within a week. Oysters, typical filter feeders, have been reported to accumulate up to 70,000 ppb. (Loosanoff 1965). In Green Bay along Lake Michigan, Hickey and Keith (1964) report up to 0.005 ppm wet weight of DDT, DDE, and DDD in the lake sediments. Here the accumulation has presumably been from leaching or run-off from surrounding agricultural lands in Door County, where it is reported that 70,000

pounds of DDT are used annually. Biological concentration in Green Bay is also occurring in food chain organisms, as reported at Clear Lake, California. Accumulation of biocides, especially in the food chain, and their availability for recycling pose a most serious ecological problem.

8. DELAYED RESPONSE

Because of the persistent nature and tendency of certain insecticides to accumulate at toxic levels in the food chain, there is often a delayed response in certain ecosystems subjected either directly or indirectly to pesticide treatment. This was the case at Clear Lake, where the mortality of non-target organisms occurred several years after the last application. This is a particularly disturbing aspect, since man is often the consumer organism accumulating pesticide residues. In the general population, human tissues contain about 12 ppm DDT-derived materials. Those with meatless diets, and the Eskimos, store less; however, agricultural applicators and formulators of pesticides may store up to 600 ppm DDT or 1000 ppm DDT-derived components. Recent studies indicate that dieldrin and lindane are also stored in humans without occupational exposure (Durham 1965). The possibility of synergistic effects involving DDT, dieldrin, lindane, and other pollutants to which man is being exposed may result in unpredictable hazards. In fact, it is now believed that pesticides may pose a genetic hazard. At the recent conference of the New York Academy of Science, Dr. Onsy G. Fahmy warned that certain chlorinated hydrocarbons, organophosphates and carbamates were capable of disrupting the DNA molecule. It was further noted that such mutations may not appear until as many as 40 generations later. Another scientist, Dr. M. Jacqueline Verrett, pointed out that certain fungicides (folpet and captan) thought to be nontoxic have chemical structures similar to thalidomide.

We are obviously dealing with many biological unknowns in our widespread use of presumably "safe" insecticides. We have no assurance that 12 ppm DDT in our human tissue, now above the permissible in marketable products for consumption, may not be resulting in deleterious effects in future generations. As Rudd warns (1964):

> . . . It would be somewhat more than embarrassing for our "experts" to learn that significant effects do occur in the long term. One hundred and eight million human guinea pigs would have paid a high price for their trust.

Of unpredicted delayed responses, we have an example in radiation contamination. In the Bravo tests on Bikini in 1954, the natives on Rongelap Atoll were exposed to radiation assumed to be safe. Now more than a decade later, tumors of the thyroid gland have been discovered in the children exposed to these presumably safe doses (Woodwell et al. 1966). Pesticides per se or synergisms resulting from their interaction could well plague man in now unforeseen or unpredictable ways in the future.

The Sound Use of Herbicides

In contrast to insecticides, herbicides are chemical weed-killers used to control or kill unwanted plants. Following World War II, the chlorinated herbicide 2, 4-D began to be used widely on broadleaf weeds. Later, 2, 4, 5-T was added, which proved especially effective on woody species. Today, over 40 weed-killers are available. Although used extensively in agriculture, considerable quantities are used also in aquatic weed control and in forestry, wildlife, and right-of-way vegetation management. Currently, large quantities are being used as defoliators in Vietnam.

Although herbicides in general are much safer than insecticides in regard to killing nontarget organisms and in their residual effects, considerable caution must be exercised in their proper use. One of the greatest dangers in right-of-way vegetation management is their indiscriminate use, which results in habitat destruction. Drift of spray particles and volatility may also cause adverse effects on nontarget organisms, especially following indiscriminate applications. In the Conneticut Arboretum, shade trees have been seriously affected as a result of indiscriminate roadside sprays (Niering 1959). During the spring of 1957, the town sprayed the marginal trees and shrubs along a roadside running through the Arboretum with 2, 4-D and 2, 4, 5-T (1 part chemical: 100 parts water). White oaks overarching the road up to 2 feet in diameter were most seriously affected. Most of the leaves turned brown. Foliage of scarlet and black oaks of similar size exhibited pronounced leaf curling. Trees were affected up to 300 feet back from the point of application within the natural area of the Arboretum. White oak twigs near the sprayed belt also developed a striking weeping habit as twig elongation occurred — a growth abnormality still conspicuous after 10 years.

The effectiveness of the spray operation in controlling undesirable woody growth indicated a high survival of unwanted tree sprouts. Black birch and certain desirable shrubs were particularly sensitive. Shrubs affected were highly ornamental forms often planted in roadside beautification programs. The resulting ineffectiveness of the spray operation was indicated by the need for cutting undesirable growth along the roadside the following year.

In the agricultural use of herbicides, drift effects have been reported over much greater distances. In California, drift from aerial sprays has been reported up to 30 miles from the point of application (Freed 1965).

Although toxicity of herbicides to nontarget organisms is not generally a problem, it has been reported in aquatic environments. For example, the dimethylamine salt of 2, 4-D is relatively safe for bluegill at 150 ppm, but the butyl, ethyl, and isopropyl esters are toxic to fish at around 1 ppm (R. E. Johnson, personal communication). Studies of 16 aquatic herbicides on *Daphnia magna,* a microcrustacean, revealed that 2, 4-D (specific derivation not given) seemed completely innocuous but that several others (Dichlone, a quinone; Molinate, a thiolcarbamate; Propanil, an anilide; sodium arsenite and Dichlopenil, a nitrile) could present a real hazard to this lower food organism (Crosby and Tucker 1966).

EFFECTS OF RIGHTS-OF-WAY

The rights-of-way across our nation comprise an estimated 70,000,000 acres of land, much of which is now subjected to herbicide treatment (Niering 1967). During the past few decades, indiscriminate foliar applications have been widespread in the control of undesirable vegetation, erroneously referred to as brush (Goodwin and Niering 1962). Indiscriminate applications often fail to root-kill undesirable species, therefore necessitating repeated retreatment, which results in the destruction of many desirable forms. Indiscriminate sprays are also used for the control of certain broadleaf weeds along roadsides. In New Jersey, 19 treatments were applied during a period of 6 years in an attempt to control ragweed. This, of course, was ecologically unsound, when one considers that ragweed is an annual plant typical of bare soil and that repeated sprayings also eliminate the competing broadleaved perennial species that, under natural successional conditions, could tend to occupy the site and naturally eliminate the ragweed. Broadcast or indiscriminate spraying can also result in destruction of valuable wildlife habitat in addition to the needless destruction of our native flora — wildflowers and shrubs of high landscape value.

Nonselective spraying, especially along roadsides, also tends to produce a monotonous grassy cover free of colorful wildflowers and interesting shrubs. It is economically and aesthetically unsound to remove these valuable species naturally occurring on such sites. Where they do not occur, highway beautification programs plant many of these same shrubs and low-growing trees.

Recognizing this nation-wide problem in the improper use of herbicides, the Connecticut Arboretum established, over a decade ago, several right-of-way demonstration areas to serve as models in the sound use of herbicides (Niering 1955; 1957; 1961). Along two utility rights-of-way and a roadside crossing the Arboretum, the vegetation has been managed following sound ecological principles, (Egler 1954; Goodwin and Niering 1959; Niering 1958). Basic techniques include basal and stump treatments. The former involves soaking the base of the stem for 12 inches; the stump technique involves soaking the stump immediately after cutting. Effective formulations include 2, 4, 5-T in a fuel oil carrier (1 part chemical: 20 parts oil). Locally, stem-foliage sprays may be necessary, but the previous two techniques form the basic approach in the selective use of weed-killers. They result in good root-kill and simultaneously preserve valuable wildlife habitat and aesthetically attractive native species, all at a minimum of cost to the agency involved when figured on a long-range basis. In addition to these gains, the presence of good shrub cover tends to impede tree invasion and to reduce future maintenance costs (Pound and Egler 1953; Niering and Egler 1955).

Another intriguing use of herbicides is in naturalistic landscaping. Dr. Frank Egler conceived this concept of creating picturesque natural settings in shrubby fields by selectively eliminating the less attractive species and accentuating the ornamental forms (Kenfield 1966). At the Connecticut Arboretum we have landscaped several such areas (Niering and Goodwin 1963). This approach has unlimited application in arresting vegetation development and preserving landscapes that might disappear under normal successional or vegetational development processes.

Future Outlook

Innumerable critical moves have recently occurred that may alter the continued deterioration of our environment. Secretary Udall has banned the use of DDT, chlordane, dieldrin, and endrin on Department of the Interior lands. The use of DDT has been banned on state lands in New Hampshire and lake trout watersheds in New York State; in Connecticut, commercial applications are limited to dormant sprays. On Long Island, a temporary court injunction has been granted against the Suffolk County Mosquito Control Board's use of DDT in spraying tidal marshes. The Forest Service has terminated the use of DDT, and in the spring of 1966 the United States Department of Agriculture banned the use of endrin and dieldrin. Currently, the Forest Service has engaged a top-level research team in the Pacific Southwest to find chemicals highly selective to individual forest insect pests and that will break down quickly into harmless components. The Ribicoff hearing, which has placed Congressional focus on the problem of environmental pollution and Gaylord Nelson's bill to ban the sale of DDT in the United States are all enlightened endeavors at the national level.

The United States Forest Service has a selective program for herbicides in the National Forests. The Wisconsin Natural Resources Committee has instituted a selective roadside right-of-way maintenance program for the State. In Connecticut, a selective approach is in practice in most roadside and utility spraying.

Although we have considerable knowledge of the effects of biocides on the total environment, we must continue the emphasis on the holistic approach in studying the problem and interpreting the data. Continued observation of those occupationally exposed and of residents living near pesticide areas should reveal invaluable toxicological data. The study of migrant workers, of whom hundreds have been reported killed by pesticides, needs exacting investigation.

The development of more biological controls as well as chemical formulations that are specific to the target organism with a minimum of side effects needs continuous financial support by state and federal agencies and industry. Graduate opportunities are unlimited in this field.

As we look to the future, one of our major problems is the communication of sound ecological knowledge already available rather than pseudoscientific knowledge to increase the assets of special interest groups (Egler 1964, 1965, 1966). The fire ant fiasco may be cited as a case in point. And as Egler (1966) has pointed out in his fourth most recent review of the pesticide problem: ". . . 95% of the problem is not in scientific knowledge of pesticides but in scientific knowledge of human behavior. . . . There are power plays . . . the eminent experts who deal with parts not ecological wholes."

One might ask, is it really good business to reduce the use of pesticides? Will biological control make as much money? Here the problem integrates political science, economics, sociology, and psychology. Anyone seriously interested in promoting the sound use of biocides must be fully cognizant of these counter forces in our society. They need serious study, analysis, and forthright reporting in the public interest. With all we know about the deleterious effects of biocides on our environments, the problem really challenging man is to get this scientific knowledge translated into action through the sociopolitical pathways available to us in a free society. If we fail to communicate a rational approach, we may find that technology has become an invisible monster as Egler has succinctly stated (1966).

Pesticides are the greatest single tool for simplifying the habitat ever conceived by the simple mind of man, who may not yet prove too simple to grasp the fact that he is but a blind strand of an ecosystem web, dependent not upon himself, but upon the total web, which nevertheless he has the power to destroy.

Here environmental science can involve the social scientist in communcating sound science to society and involve the political scientist in seeing that sound scientific knowledge is translated into reality. Our survival on this planet may well depend on how well we can make this translation.

EDITOR'S COMMENTS

Since Dr. Niering's article was written, the correlation of DDT with reduced reproduction in certain birds has been verified. Eggshell formation in birds is controlled by the hormone estrogen. The presence of DDT in the body of the female bird induces the formation of enzymes which in turn destroy estrogen and thus interfere with shell formation. Lowered reproduction results.

Concerning herbicides, current information indicates that they may not be as safe as previously thought. Recent studies on animals have linked birth defects to the weed killer 2, 4, 5-T, and have resulted in limited government restrictions on it's use. Several variants of 2, 4-D have also been shown to cause birth defects and may affect the liver. Additionally, dioxin, a contaminant contained in both of these herbicides, causes abnormal growth. Some authorities think that continued use of these substances is a dangerous experiment, especially in the face of the scientific evidence that has already accumulated.

CHARLES F. WURSTER

DDT in Mother's Milk

Charles F. Wurster is Associate Professor of Environmental Sciences at the State University of New York at Stony Brook. He is also a member of the board of trustees and chairman of the Scientists Advisory Committee of the Environmental Defense Fund. His research has involved studies on the effects of DDT on non-target organisms.

Twenty-five years ago several scientists reported that DDT fed to dogs soon appeared in their milk. It was hardly surprising then, when another report in 1951 told how DDT, present in the diet of humans since World War II, had also appeared in human milk. The finding has been confirmed many times since then.

Although this contamination has long been "known" to the scientific literature, it was not known to the general public until 1969, when a Swedish scientist, Dr. Göran Lohfroth, testified at the DDT meetings in Madison, Wisconsin, where the petitioner's case was presented by the Environmental Defense Fund. Lohfroth pointed out that human milk now contains .1 to .2 parts per million (ppm) of DDT residues, which is two to four times higher than the 0.05-ppm tolerance limit permitted by the Food and Drug Administration in cow's milk shipped in interstate commerce. This information

was the basis for my own remark, in a newspaper interview made soon afterward in May 1969, that, if mother's milk were in any other container, it would be banned from crossing state lines. The comment found its way into some newspapers, and I was deluged with letters, many from nursing mothers — not all of them were friendly. Some suggested that I was irresponsible and had done harm to nursing women and their babies. The subject is sensitive and controversial, and it deserves a closer look.

DDT residues have become universal pollutants of our biosphere; they contaminate virtually all animal tissues, and they become more concentrated with each step in the food chain. Cattle accumulate DDT from their diet, store some in their tissues, and pass some into their milk. We do likewise. Since we are higher in the food chain than are cattle (we eat cattle and other meat), we store more DDT in our tissues than they do. (In fact, human meat contains more DDT than the FDA permits in meat for human consumption — it's a good thing we're not cannibals!) Human milk is therefore more contaminated than cow's milk,

Reprinted by permission of the author and publisher from *Saturday Review*. May 2, 1970. Copyright © 1970 by *Saturday Review, Inc.*

a difference that is further increased because women secrete a higher proportion of the DDT into their milk than do cows.

The biological significance of the DDT residues we ingest is difficult to interpret. We know that DDT does not kill people outright, even at far higher dosages than we, or nursing babies, take in. Nor are there obvious, overt symptoms of DDT poisoning. Recent studies by a team of scientists supported by the National Cancer Institute, however, have confirmed earlier evidence that DDT is a cancer-causing agent. The experiments were done with mice, and earlier work with rats and trout gave similar results. The tendency of a chemical to cause cancer in test animals indicates a high probability (but not a certainty) that that chemical is also cancer-causing in humans, but we cannot run a controlled experiment on humans to confirm this probability. Two other studies have shown that human cancer victims carry much more DDT in their fat than the rest of the general population, a finding that could be interpreted as being consistent with the animal experiments. In other words, the contamination of human tissues with residues of DDT may well be inducing a low level of cancer in the general population, but this possibility cannot be verified.

Our knowldege of the damage being caused by DDT to other organisms is much more extensive. We know that residues of DDT have caused extreme declines in the populations of many wild species, especially among the larger birds and fish. These effects are caused primarily by reduced reproduction, rather than direct mortality, and in some cases even the physiological and biochemical mechanisms are understood. Some species face extinction because of DDT.

What, then, is the worried nursing mother to do? Certainly she should continue to nurse her infant; the advantages of breast-feeding are well known. Switching to another diet is hardly a solution, because other foods also contain DDT. Nursing infants are little worse off than the rest of us; we are all in the same boat. Babies are born with DDT in their bodies. Fetuses in the womb contain it because DDT passes the placental barrier; it was probably present in the original cell at conception. Mothers can minimize their DDT burden, and thereby the amount in their milk, by avoiding household sprays containing DDT (or other chlorinated hydrocarbons), and by minimizing their intake of eggs, fatty meats, and fish.

I would suggest that any irresponsibility lies not with those scientists who tell the truth about DDT, but with those who continue to advocate its use in spite of acceptable alternatives. It is they who have contaminated our Earth. Reassuring headlines from Washington have told us that DDT would be "phased out" to "essential uses" during the next two years, but our government has been "phasing out" DDT for a decade already, and most current uses (the greatest is on cotton) are apparently considered "essential" by DDT advocates. There has been far more talk than action on the DDT problem, and its use goes on as before.

Federal laws that are intended to protect us from such chemical assaults often have not been enforced by those federal agencies charged with doing so. The Delaney Amendment prohibits the presence in human foods of agents that cause cancer in "man or animal," yet the Department of Health, Education and Welfare has chosen to ignore it. The Environmental Defense Fund (EDF), an organization that goes to court with environmental problems, has asked the Court of Appeals in Washington to compel HEW to enforce this law.

Primary responsibility for regulating pesticides lies with the Department of Agriculture, but getting action from USDA is like moving a barge loaded with sand through thick molasses. The federal law applying to insecticides provides for the protection of man, other vertebrates, and "useful invertebrate animals," but USDA has administered this law more for the benefit of insecticide manufacturers than for the protection of non-target organisms. On a recent TV program, Dr. Theodore C. Byerly, assistant director of science and education for USDA, virtually admitted this by stating that environmental factors had not been considered by USDA in formulating pesticide policies prior to October 1969 — in spite of the fact that this federal law has existed since 1947. Since USDA apparently ignored protection of the environment, is it surprising that we have serious environmental problems with certain insecticides?

Last November USDA announced cancellation of the registration of DDT for uses on tobacco, shade trees, in the household, and in aquatic areas, leaving all other DDT registrations intact. Although the announcement received wide publicity, cancellation is not as meaningful as it may sound, for it takes effect only when manufacturers fail to appeal the move. The law provides a lengthy appeal procedure for manufacturers and users — which may take years — and during the appeal period use of the material continues as before. When the major manufacturers of DDT appealed USDA's cancellation notices in January, they effectively blocked restrictions on DDT usage, thus allowing the continued input of DDT into the environment.

If USDA had seriously intended to stop the use of DDT, it would have canceled *and suspended* the registrations. Only suspension, a procedure also provided in the law, swiftly reduces use of an insecticide. Cancellation without suspension has proved futile when manufacturers oppose the move. EDF has also taken the USDA case into federal court, requesting that the court compel USDA to enforce the law it is supposed to administer by canceling and suspending all registrations of DDT. These two cases are still pending in federal court.

The presence of DDT in human milk is not just a problem for nursing mothers. With a profound impact on the biota of our planet, DDT contamination has become a threat to us all. If all environmental problems require a quarter-century of scientific research, controversy, and legal battle before effective action reduces the continuing biological damage — as has been the case with DDT — it may be too late for mankind. Let us therefore take action not only on a local level, but internationally as well, through such a body as the United Nations, to guarantee the survival of the global ecosystem.

EDITOR'S COMMENTS

In June 1972, the administrator of the U.S. Environmental Protection Agency announced that the use of DDT will be prohibited for general purposes as of December 31, 1972. Although unquestionably a step forward, there is some doubt as to how long the ban will stick. The sole U.S. manufacturer of DDT has filed with the U.S. Court of Appeals to have the ban set aside. Other manufacturers which use DDT in their products have filed similar appeals.

Although typically these suits would have been filed in Washington, D.C., the headquarters of the Environmental Protection Agency, in this case they have been filed in New Orleans, apparently because a cotton-belt judicial body might be more sympathetic.

The ban is not a total one. DDT will still be available for use in public health emergencies. It will also be available under certain conditions for use on a few vegetables.

The ban does not prevent the U.S. manufacturer from continuing to export large amounts of DDT.

The presumed substitute for DDT will be methyl parathion, a pesticide of the organophosphorus class. This compound although extremely toxic and quite indiscriminate in what it kills, has in the past been considered nonpersistent in the environment. However, a June, 1972, release by the American Chemical Society states that parathion "does not degrade rapidly in soil, and spillage areas can retain dangerous levels for more than five years."

Clearly some progress has been made with this ban, if it lasts. But the results of increasing the use of parathion are completely unknown. Unfortunately, throughout much of the debate and discussion, there has been an obvious flaw in the reasoning — an acceptance of the idea that we can no longer grow crops without massive use of chemical sprays. It seems odd that those groups and interests who most frequently accuse environmentalists of hysteria and emotionalism are quite willing to scream "we'll all starve," when the use of one of their multitude of chemicals is limited.

ANTHONY WOLFF

Big Schemes for Little Ants

Anthony Wolff is an associate editor of
Newsweek and a former conservation editor
at *American Heritage* magazine.

Solenopsis saevissima, popularly known
as the Imported Fire Ant, is an unpopular
creature with few natural friends outside
the worldwide circle of its sisters and its
cousins and its aunts, in which company
ants outnumber everything else on Earth.
While ants evoke in otherwise imperturable
men a disproportionate, deep-seated squeam-
ishness, most common species are condemned simply as picnic pests so long as
they stay outdoors where they belong.

The fire ant obviously provokes a more
violent reaction. It is the Vietcong ant, the
object of a technologically sophisticated,
government-sponsored campaign of annihilation that may eventually last 12 years, cost
$200 million, and baptize much of the South
with a chlorinated hydrocarbon insecticide.
A less well-armed but equally vehement
counterattack by scientists and conservation
organizations is intended to defend not the
friendless fire ant, but rather the environment.

Unquestionably, the imported fire ant is
an eminently undesirable alien. Since arriving about 1918 *sans* passport — presumably
traveling steerage-class in the hold of a cargo
ship bound from South America for Mobile,
Alabama (illegal immigrants are hard to
trace) — the fire ant has extended its range
to infest nine Southeastern states as far north
as the Carolinas and west as far as Texas.
It builds elephantine anthills, sometimes
three feet or more in both diameter and
height, preferably in untilled fields but also
along roadsides and fencerows, on levees, in
parks, playgrounds, and orchards, or wherever the proper soil and moisture conditions
exist undisturbed. From 25,000 to 50,000
ants may set up housekeeping in a single
mound, and upwards of 40 such colonies
may crowd into an especially auspicious
acre.

More to the point, a fire ant mound is
an armed camp, equipped to counterattack
even the slightest, most inadvertent violation of its conical stronghold. Though only
a quarter of an inch long or less, the ants
are single-mindedly belligerent and given
to attacking in overwhelming numbers. The
sting is instantly and persistently painful, and
is often followed by a sore or pustule. Secondary effects may be more generalized in
some victims, including headaches, nausea,

and difficult breathing, along with the severe emotional reaction often associated with such an experience. Hyperallergic reactions to the fire ant venom may in rare cases include coma and even death. But out of a total of 460 deaths from venomous animals reported in the United States from 1950 to 1959, only four were attributed to ants of any kind.

Indeed, *Solenopsis saevissima* impinges so little on the dominant species, *Homo americanus,* that as recently as 1958, when the ant was already being touted as a major problem, a government survey unearthed only two states that bothered to include it among their twenty most undesirable pests, and then near the bottom of the list.

It should also be noted that the fire ant mound is usually easily avoided, and colonies can be wiped out by simple control methods when necessary. However, in the last twenty years, as the fire ant has gained in range and population, its reputation has grown out of all proportion to its numbers or its impact. While this exaggeration has been due in some part to the ant's own talent for mischief, it is also the contrived result of effective press agentry by industries and agencies with an interest in waging war on the immigrant invader.

Thus, in the 1950s, Southerners were subjected to a steady barrage of horror stories in government and industry publications as well as the popular press. The fire ant, they read, "is a destroyer of plant, animal, and bird life." "A formidable army of South American fire ants has invaded the United States. . . . Already the destructive insects have captured much of the South's best farmland." The enemy attacked the economy as well as the population: "Fire ants may attack and kill newborn pigs, calves, sheep, and other animals; newly hatched chicks; and the young of ground-nesting birds." "This ant damages vegetable crops by sucking juices from the stems of plants and by gnawing holes in roots, stalks,

buds, ears, and pods. It injures pasture grasses, cereal and forage crops, nursery stock, and fruit trees."

While the citizens were getting a nightmareful of this kind of misinformation, the chemical industry, according to a major trade journal, anticipated "a sales bonanza in the increasing numbers of broad-scale pest elimination programs." The bonanza has not abated. Last year alone, pesticide producers rang up one billion in wholesale business.

Meanwhile, less hysterical advice that showed the fire ant problem to be less than a life-or-death matter was drowned out. The ant, in fact, abjures vegetation and feeds almost exclusively on other insects, including such bona fide marauders as the boll weevil, and is therefore treated with respectful neglect in its native Argentina. Like other ants this one aerates and conditions the soil. Human susceptibility to fire ants is lower than to wasps, hornets, honeybees, bumblebees, and yellow jackets, while reports of animal mortality from fire ant attacks are most kindly described as highly exaggerated. And so on.

But in 1957 the first fire ant war began. In response to public and Congressional demand which it had helped to generate, USDA's Plant Pest Control Division requested Congress to authorize an eradication campaign against the ant. Until then, control had been achieved where necessary by limited, state-sponsored programs, using mostly chlordane in relatively small-scale applications. But under the Federal Plant Pest Act of 1957, a nine-state coordinated program was launched that fall with $2.4 million in federal matching funds. The technique involved dosing each acre with 2 pounds of dieldrin or heptachlor, diluted 1:10. More than 125,000 acres were treated in this way in the first six months. It was discovered, however, that this represented a considerable overdose, and in 1958 the treatment was revised to between 1 and 1.25

pounds of insecticide per acre. Soon afterward, it was decided that even this was too generous, and a more efficient program was adopted using one-eighth the original dose — .25 pounds per acre — in two applications three or four months apart.

Although the rapid and repeated decreases in the dosage indicate USDA's haphazard approach to pesticides — the program was based on $115,000 of outdated federal research — there was some awareness of the dangers that dieldrin and heptachlor posed to domestic animals and people. The Georgia Department of Entomology issued a list of precautions in treated areas, including: "Cover all open wells, springs and other open water sources; turn over or cover all feed and watering troughs, goldfish ponds, cricket boxes, warm beds, rabbit pens; cover or remove bee hives; remove all clothing drying out of doors; close all windows and doors; cover leafy vegetables in gardens." After treatment, the advice was to keep livestock off treated areas for a minimum of 30 days in the case of milk cows (though where they were to be kept for 30 days was not specified); wash vegetables thoroughly before eating; and sprinkle down lawns and other play areas before letting children use them.

No official measures were taken to insure that all affected citizens received the advice, much less that they understood and followed it. Those who did not get the warnings, or who failed for whatever reason to obey them — including, of course, the wildlife — suffered the consequences, and for the wildlife the consequences were dire. As early as May 1958, the Fish and Wildlife Service of the U.S. Department of the Interior found it necessary to respond to "inquires from many sources for interim information on the impact of the fire ant eradication program upon wildlife." Even with incomplete data, the Interior Department reported indications of an extensive die-off of wildlife due to the fire ant spraying. In Wilcox Coun-

ty, Alabama, 14 of 16 coveys of quail on the treated areas disappeared, presumed dead, while quail on an untreated control area were unharmed.

There was heavy mortality of ground-dwelling species, and newly killed animals were still being found seven weeks after treatment. Heavy losses of aquatic life included fish in a pond almost half a mile from the treated area. Heptachlor and heptachlor epoxide were found in all examined specimens. "Bird numbers in the two most extensively studied areas were reduced 75 to 85 percent," the report continued. "In Hardin County, Texas, dead specimens recovered amounted to 33 percent of the estimated pretreatment population. Quail and rabbit populations were decimated or completely wiped out." In addition, there were many reports of fatalities among livestock, poultry, and household pets. And in all cases, delayed reactions to sublethal doses, including possible reproductive failures affecting the populations of future generations, could not be estimated.

Describing this first fire ant eradication program in *Silent Spring,* Rachel Carson called it "an outstanding example of an ill-conceived, badly executed, and thoroughly detrimental experiment in the mass control of insects . . . expensive in dollars, in destruction of animal life, and in loss of public confidence in the Agriculture Department . . ." Eventually, the heptachlor-dieldrin program was stopped, but neither because the USDA admitted its mistake nor because of *Silent Spring.*

As early as 1959, the Food and Drug Administration effectively banned any residues of heptachlor on food. In the same year, the Alabama Legislature failed to appropriate matching funds for the program, followed the next year by Florida. In Louisiana, as farmers began to identify the outbreak of another and far more serious pest as a side effect of the fire ant program, State University entomologist Dr. L. D. Newsom added an ironic epilogue: "The imported fire ant 'eradication' program . . . is thus far a failure. There are more infested acres in Louisiana now than when the program began."

In January 1965, Congress got the same message from the Comptroller General of the United States: "Although since inception of the program in the fall of 1957 through June 30, 1963, over five million acres in nine states had received treatments with insecticides to eradicate the imported fire ant, and the total cost of the eradication program had been about $24.7 million . . . there had not been a net reduction in the number of acres infested with the ant. On the contrary, *there had been a net increase of about eleven million acres in the land reported to be infested with the ant."* [Emphasis added.]

Not until two years later did the Department of Agriculture receive confirmation of what was by then the common wisdom, from a National Research Council study. The council's Committee on the Imported Fire Ant concluded that "an eradication of the Imported Fire Ant is not now biologically and technically feasible." Further, in view of its conclusions that the fire ant was in no respect a major problem, the committee had very grave doubts whether an attempt to eradicate it would be justified, even if it were shown to be feasible at a later date.

At the same time, the committee recommended continued research into the biology, ecology, and behavior of the ant, about which precious little was known, and into developing and refining methods of *control.* This question of eradication versus control often comes into the argument. "Eradicate" seems to occur most often in the press agentry of those tooling up for and funding an ambitious program. When the cry of 'overkill' is raised, the ambition of the ant-hunters is revised to "control."

Whichever it is, eradication or control, it would have been reasonable back in 1961 to

1963 to expect that any large-scale program against the fire ant would be indefinitely postponed. But in a decade which began with clear evidence of the danger of DDT, and which ended with only the beginnings of an adequate limitation on its use, such reasonable expectations seem unreasonable.

Even more to the point, such a noble expectation would underestimate America's infatuation with big ideas, of which massive insect-control programs are one of the most tempting. Like all big schemes, this one has its political-economic, as well as its tactical aspects, and political support for the fire ant program is imbedded in the government from the grass roots to the top of the federal family tree. The individual farmer or landowner is connected by his local Extension Agent to the state department of agriculture, which thrives on USDA's federal programs. (The cutback in the fire ant program deprived the Georgia Agriculture Department, for one, of its biggest budget item, thus much of its power.) State agriculture departments are represented in turn on the Southern Plant Board, which speaks for them to the regional office of the Plant Pest Control Division of the U.S. Department of Agriculture, which reports to the Congress, the Cabinet, and the President.

In addition, there are the less well-charted channels of influences worn by the flow of money and power over the years. Long and mutually profitable association between farmers and pest-control agencies has cemented alliances that have sympathizers on important Congressional committees. In the other direction, money appropriated from the anonymous federal treasury percolates down to the county level with the names of its legislative expediters clearly marked. In Congress, the House subcommittee responsible for passing on appropriations for agricultural programs is chaired by Representative Jamie L. Whitten of Mississippi. Whitten is the author of a book praising the chemical pesticide industry and its products, and is an ardent supporter of the fire ant program.

With such support, it is perhaps not so surprising that the fire ant program did not die of shame as the body count from the original experiments mounted. Rather, after the briefest of pauses the program began anew, substantially unchanged but armed with a different poison. Since 1962, more than 30 million acres have been treated; and now, satisfied with the results, the Plant Protection Division of USDA is ready to reescalate the war against the fire ant.

The impetus for the new assault may originate in the highest levels of government. President Nixon's commitment to the persecution of the fire ant seems to be an element in his strategy to Republicanize, or at least to Nixonize, the South. During the 1968 campaign, Mr. Nixon was asked about his fire ant program during a Georgia telecast of his carefully structured but unrehearsed traveling talk show. When he failed to ad lib the proper enthusiasm for exterminating the fire ant, one of his top aides made a special request of the local press to include in their coverage Mr. Nixon's earlier campaign promise to support fire ant control, and the *Atlanta Journal* responded with the headline, "Nixon Puts His Foot Down on Fire Ant." After the election, the President appointed Georgia's agriculture commissioner, J. Phil Campbell — described in the state press as a "fire ant fanatic" — as Undersecretary of Agriculture.

In the new production of The Great Fire Ant War, the *deus ex machina* is a complex chemical character dubbed *Dodecachlorooctahydro-1,3,4-metheno-2H-cyclobuta [cd] pentalene,* mirex for short, that will be dumped from a fleet of converted World War II bombers equipped with special Decca electronic guidance systems. Each acre slated for treatment will be lightly salted up to three times with 1.25 pounds of a formulation called Mirex Granulated Bait 4X, an Allied Chemical Company concoction of (by

weight) 84.7 percent corncob grits coated with 15 percent soybean oil to attract the ants and 0.3 percent mirex to kill them. Approximately 750,000 of these tiny granules will be dropped per acre per dose.

Until a few weeks ago, the U.S. Department of Agriculture had plotted a 12-year, $200 million war of eradication against the fire ant, with 450 million pounds of mirex bait to be dropped into the ecosystems of 120 million acres of Southland. Then, on January 15th and under mounting pressure from other government agencies as well as scientists and conservationists, USDA substituted a seemingly more modest proposal in a draft statement of environmental impact.

"Eradication is not now a program objective," USDA hedges, prudently adopting the less alarming notion of a continuing "control-oriented program." This is further camouflaged by subdivision into annual installments. Thus, USDA appears to be asking to treat only 6 million acres for one year.

The sham is obvious: the same report claims that 126 million acres are infested with fire ants, 20 million of them within the last three years. A 6-million-acre program, by USDA's own figures, won't even keep up with the problem, much less lick it. The "more than 30 million acres" treated with mirex since 1962 has not effectively hindered the spread of the ants' range. Also, as the report points out, "the continual application of mirex, as would take place in a continuing control program, would increase substantially the chance of resistance" — the "emergence of resistant populations." And, ominously, the report mentions under "Alternatives to the Proposed Action" that "eradication appears to be technically feasible. . . . It is estimated that the fire ant could be eradicated over a 12-year period with 1.8 million pounds of mirex applied to about 175 million acres. . . ." The USDA is ever loathe to forgo a crusade.

This time, however, the government seems to be going to some pains to snow the people about mirex before snowing them *with* mirex. Last October the Plant Protection Division issued a comforting soft sell: "The amount of mirex applied to the average acre of land to control the fire ant is no more toxic than 4 to 5 common aspirin." (Which, if true, suggests a simple solution to the problem.)

Indeed, the promotional techniques employed in this second fire ant crusade recall the days of proprietary potions and patent medicine shows. For instance, a request to Louisiana Agriculture Commissioner Dave Pearce for information about the program brings a selection of stomach-turning photographs of spectacularly allergic fire ant victims, along with a reprint from the American Medical Association Archives in Dermatology, dated April 1957. The article repeats some of the learned misconceptions of its day about the fire ant's destructiveness to crops and wildlife, citing a discredited 1940 reference for the accusation that ". . . during the hatching period . . . the ants enter the pipped shells and consume the chicks before they escape from the egg shells."

The article also includes testimonials to the ant's homicidal capabilities. "Yes, doctor," reads one, "Sonny came in and asked for the fly spray to spray the ants with . . . He laid the spray down in front of the door and kept saying, 'Ants, Mommy, ants' . . . I couldn't find but three bites on his left foot . . . but, doctor, by the time I got to the front room he was in a complete coma . . . We carried him to the hospital after the doctor saw he was not going to regain consciousness, and he lived 29 hours after he was bitten. . . ."

Even discounting such obviously misleading propaganda — as of 1967 there were only two deaths on record resulting from fire ant stings, far fewer than from the stings of other insects — the Plant Protection Division's own statements have been generous both in ascribing damage to the fire ant and safety to mirex. "Mirex is actually

one of the safest insecticides presently on the market," claims an October 1970 report. "It would be impossible for a person to obtain a lethal dose by either breathing fumes from it or from contact with their skin . . . it is comparatively safe even if small amounts were accidentally eaten. . . . Mirex is almost totally insoluble. The amounts that could dissolve in water are exceedingly small (parts per billion or less) . . . only when the dosages are raised by the hundreds, thousands, or even ten thousand times above those used in the field does some mortality or adverse effects on reproduction occur. . . . Examination of over 6,000 shellfish samples from over the U.S. has failed to turn up mirex except for a few samples from estuaries draining areas in the Southern States in which mirex bait was used. . . . Since mirex bait is a typical chlorinated hydrocarbon insecticide, it is presumed that even if it were picked up by an oyster or shellfish it would behave in the normal manner of most of these pesticides and would be rapidly flushed from the mollusk's body. . . . Catfish, like all fish, are very resistant to mirex, and it would be expected that no mortality . . . would ever result from the bait application. While very minute residues have been found in wild catfish, analysis of samples from five catfish farms in Mississippi areas which were treated with mirex failed to show any residues."

Aside from grammatical lapses, this official statement seems beyond repair; some of its assertions are blindly self-incriminating, others are contrary to the commonly available evidence advanced by those opposed to the mirex program, evidence often drawn from other government agencies. Thus, a research progress report from Interior's Bureau of Commercial Fisheries states that "Experiments show that mirex has delayed toxic effects on crabs and shrimp. . . . Juvenile blue crabs and pink shrimp showed no symptoms of poisoning during a 96-hour exposure to 0.1 ppm technical [undiluted] mirex in flowing sea water. All of these crustaceans, however, became irritated and paralyzed, and then died within 18 days after being placed in clean water.

"Mirex bait also causes delayed toxicity to crabs . . . 76 percent (19 of 25) of the crabs were dead or paralyzed two weeks after receiving the mirex bait. No mortality or paralysis occurred in 25 control crabs. The availability of fire ant bait to feeding crabs should be considered in evaluating the effect on field applications of this material on estuarine organisms."

The same report notes that "mirex is not easily metabolized." Far from it, in fact: the livers of shrimp in the experimental situation were found to accumulate mirex to 24,000 times its ambient concentration. Further evidence for the persistence of mirex in both the environment and organic tissues is cited in an Interior Department "Evaluation of Water Quality Effects of the Program to Control the Imported Fire Ant with Mirex," which concludes that "The evidence supports a strong stand by the Federal Water Quality Administration in opposition to the large-scale use of mirex to control the fire ant."

Among the evidence cited is a study made in Oktibbeha County, Mississippi, approximately one year after the second treatment with 1.25 pounds of mirex bait per acre. Concentrations of mirex in birds ranged as high as 104.39 ppm in the extreme case, and from 5.98 to 11.25 ppm in catfish. Noting also that a 1969 study found that mirex was the fourth most abundant pesticide residue in 5,000 samples of oysters and shellfish from estuaries on the Atlantic, Gulf and Pacific coasts over a three-year period (exceeded only by DDT, endrin and toxaphene) the report warns ". . . the greatest potential for damage would result from the accumulation of residues in aquatic organisms which could render them unfit for use as human food."

The report also affirms that "Mirex is extremely stable and resistant to degradation in the water environment. When placed in ponds at the recommended rate . . . residues in such water and vegetation were relatively constant over three hundred days." In addition, "Any large-scale use of this chemical probably would result in water contamination through run-offs. The proposed application would most assuredly result in water contamination and a hazard to aquatic life, as well as the consumers of this life."

Other findings relevant to long-term exposure to low-level mirex indicate that it *may,* like DDT, inhibit reproduction and increase infant mortality. A letter from the director of the Pesticide Registration Division to the director of the Pesticide Regulation Division dated January 19, 1970, warns that ". . . data show that mirex in rodents passes through the placental barrier; is excreted in the milk of nursing parents; leads to a high incidence of cataracts in suckling pups; has an adverse effect on the viability of suckling pups; and produces a reduction in the number of offspring."

Even more ominous was the Department of Health, Education, and Welfare's Mrak Commission report on "Pesticides and their Relationship to Environmental Health," which put mirex — along with DDT, dieldrin, heptachlor, and other old favorites — on its "B" list of "Compounds judged 'positive' for tumor induction." The report recommends that "the exposure of human beings to pesticides in this category "B" be minimized and that use of these pesticides be restricted to those purposes for which there are judged to be advantages to human health which outweigh the potential hazards of carcinogenicity." This was the decisive factor behind a 1970 resolution of the American Medical Association's House of Delegates opposing the mirex program.

But even if there were such "advantages

to human health" — and there almost certainly are not in this case — there is considerable doubt that any eradication or strict control program such as the one now proposed can succeed. For one thing, the Department of the Interior has "restricted" mirex to local mound-by-mound application on lands under its control, pending results of an *in vivo* study of mirex's effects on ecosystems and "a conclusive demonstration of ecological safety." The Interior Department controls six million acres in the states due for treatment. In addition, water quality standards may well preclude the poisoning of aquatic and estuarine areas, and the South is veined with river systems.

The USDA's own fire ant fact sheet suggests the scenario for almost inevitable reinfestation of treated areas: "Fire ants usually spread 5 to 6 miles per year. . . . The fire ant 'hitchhikes' long distances via human transportation. One female fire ant can represent an entire future colony of mounds. . . ." Harvard entomologist Edward Wilson, a specialist on fire ants, reports that "One colony of fire ants can reproduce and repopulate several square miles in less than three years. If one colony is missed, the entire ant population would spring back in a couple of years."

The probability of reinfestation, coupled with the corollary need for repeated mirex applications, more than compounds the dangers of employing chemical poisons in the first place. It also raises the possibility of a mutant strain exhibiting an increased tolerance for mirex. This was precisely the experience with DDT, as predicted by Rachel Carson and others; it now takes 1,800 times as much poison to kill resistant strains of the housefly as it did when DDT was new.

All in all, the evidence suggests overwhelmingly, as the Water Quality Administration's report says, that in the case of mirex and similar poisons "The burden of proof that an environmental hazard will not occur beyond reasonable doubt certainly rests with the applicator." It seems equally obvious that in view of the highly suggestive evidence against mirex, that burden of proof can never be discharged convincingly enough to outweigh the irrepressible suspicion that this is a self-sustaining crusade against a pest for which adequate, less expensive, far less hazardous alternative controls already are available.

Spearheading the public opposition to the mirex program has been a small group of scientists at Mississippi State University, under the acronym CLEAN (Committee for Leaving the Environment of America Natural). CLEAN and the Environmental Defense Fund (joined later by the National Wildlife Federation) filed suit in federal court last August to stop the program on the grounds it is dangerous and unnecessary.

Elsewhere, a formidable array of diverse groups — Gulf of Mexico shrimp fishermen, Tulane University medical students, the Junior League, Friends of the Earth, to name a few — have rallied to support the Louisiana-based Citizens for the Responsible Use of Pesticides, sponsored by the National Audubon Society, its Orleans chapter, and the Ecology Center of Louisiana, in their fight to halt the fire ant campaign.

If USDA is not thwarted by lack of state participation (Florida withdrew from the program in January), the matter may be finally decided on the federal level. There, jurisdiction is divided among the U.S. District Court, the President's Council on Environmental Quality, the new Environmental Protection Agency (which reportedly has a number of pesticides, including mirex, under review), and the White House, where the southern strategy seems now to be diminished to lower case and subject to revision.

In the last two tribunals, if the first should fail, the public voice is presumed still to be audible.

EDITOR'S COMMENTS

Opposing any program initiated by the United States Department of Agriculture is difficult. This agency throws its weight around effectively in Washington and it's pork barrel schemes have enabled it to place many legislators in the position of being obligated to help the U.S.D.A. whenever help is requested. Couple this with the lobbying power of the massive pesticide chemical industry and one comes up with a combination that can successfully promote almost any program, regardless of its true worth.

JULIAN McCAULL

Know Your Enemy

Julian McCaull is Managing Editor of
Environment magazine. His numerous articles
in the magazine have dealt with problems
ranging from oil spills at sea to legislative
measures against pollution.

There is a crisis in agriculture more widespread than that caused by outbreaks of
corn ear blight or drought in the South.
Insecticide-resistant insects, or insects that
have become pests because insecticides have
killed off their natural enemies, have devastated cotton crops in areas of Peru, Central
America, Mexico, Egypt, and Texas,[1] and
now threaten food crops in local areas of
the United States. The situation stems from
ignorance, as well as disregard, of the resil-
ient capacity of pest insects to surmount all-
out chemical warfare. Yet man stubbornly
responds with increasingly powerful poisons
in ever larger amounts. This strategy has
gained temporary victories, but the war is
being lost as the powerful chemicals do immense environmental damage on the one
hand, and promote the evolutionary development of insect pests resistant to the most
advanced poisons on the other.[1]

Serious U.S. crop losses are closer today
than at the time of *Environment's* last report
in 1969.[1] Consider, for example, the advance of "superpest" strains of the tobacco

budworm (*Heliothis virescens*), a tobacco
pest that has also become a threat to cotton
as insecticides have killed off its insect
enemies. The budworm in 1967 forced
abandonment of cotton farming in 700,000
acres of land in the Matamoros-Rio Bravo-
Reynosa area of Mexico, despite heavy use
of powerful insecticides. The cotton-growing
operation was moved to a half-million acre
region of the Valles-Tampico area of Mexico, but farmers again had to move on in
1970 as the insecticide-resistant budworm
decimated all but 20,000 acres of cotton.[2]
No respecter of national boundaries, the
tobacco budworm also ruined 75,000 acres
of cotton in Texas in 1970 despite many
repeated applications of powerful organic
phosphorus and carbamate insecticides.[3] Resistant populations of the insect have now
been found in Louisiana, and it appears to
be moving east toward the tobacco fields
of the Southeast. A close relative, the cotton
bollworm (*Heliothis zea*), also is thriving

Reprinted by permission of the author and publisher from *Environment* 13(5):30-39. June 1971.
Copyright © 1971 by the Committee for Environmental Information.

1. *Environment,* Vol. 11, Nos. 6, 7, 1969.
2. M. J. Lukefahr, personal communication.
3. L. D. Newsom, personal communication.

on the modern insecticide diet. Dr. L. D. Newsom, Department of Entomology, Louisiana State University, reports a population of cotton bollworms in the Bradley River Bottom of southwest Arkansas that experienced farmers cannot control with any registered chemical poisons. In a more localized, but nonetheless representative situation, cabbage growers in the St. Louis, Missouri area were unable to control the cabbage looper (*Trichoplusia ni*) in 1969, despite insecticide applications made every other day. Crops harvested in late spring and early fall were so infested that large numbers of larvae crawled out of the crates during shipment to market.

"The plain truth of the matter is that many important insect pests in limited areas can no longer be controlled with *any* insecticide, and one or two pests have reached this level of resistance over very large areas," declares Francis Lawson, retiring director of the U.S. Department of Agriculture (USDA) Biological Control of Insects Research Laboratory in Columbia, Missouri. A 40-year veteran of the war against insect pests, Lawson asserts that "on a worldwide basis, a concentrated research effort on the five crops — wheat, corn, rice, barley, and oats — that supply 80 percent of the world's calories and protein might result in noninsecticidal controls for most of the major pests, which number only twelve or so, in five to ten years. But the cotton growers of Nicaragua, Guatemala, Mexico, and Texas, and the growers of cabbage, collards, and other cole crops don't have five or ten years. They already have suffered disaster or now are facing it."

The "noninsecticidal controls" of which Lawson speaks are based on a strategy called biological control, by which man has utilized aspects of natural defenses against insects to protect his crops for at least 200 years (see accompanying article by Kevin Shea). This strategy has been augmented by farming methods called "cultural con-

trol" that decrease plant food for insects or increase the number of helpful natural enemies that prey on the pests. This approach has been refined by research such as Lawson's in recent years and in its most comprehensive form is now called "integrated control." Lawson's own definition of integrated control is the use of biological and cultural control whenever possible — with insecticides used locally and in small amounts, but only when necessary to prevent economic loss to the farmer.[4]

If man has an arsenal of weapons against insect pests, why does he so resolutely limit himself to chemical poisons, despite their decreased effectiveness? In Lawson's words, after many years of experience: "The reason is that one can get a quick, easy answer. You don't have to go to a lot of trouble educating the farmer to do something better. The barrier to change now is not fundamentally biological or technical. It is a social, economic, and political problem."

When Lawson arrived in Columbia in 1964, there was no laboratory. The USDA's Entomological Research Division under Director E. F. Knipling had determined that agricultural research in natural control of insects was seriously underdeveloped, in view of insecticide resistance. Public indignation about environmental damage from pesticides, which followed publication of Rachel Carson's book *Silent Spring* in 1962, was an additional spur. Initially Lawson had only ten acres of undeveloped land in Columbia on which to conduct his research, but over the next six years he guided development of a $1 million complex of research and insect-rearing facilities that is the only one of its type within the USDA and one of the few in the world devoted exclusively to research in the biological control of

4. F. R. Lawson, "The Relation of Insect Control to Increased Food Production," Proceedings of the Tall Timbers Conference on Ecological Animal Control by Habitat Management," February 27-28, 1969, pp. 145-173.

insects. At the time of Lawson's retirement this March, the scientific staff consisted of eight research entomologists, four research assistants, and six research technicians. Their research is aimed at improving ways to control insect pests by parasites, predators, or pathogens.

Life History of Insects

The career experiences of Lawson before becoming director of the Columbia laboratory support his assertions about the barriers to change. His work with the USDA began in 1929 after he obtained an A.B. degree in zoology and entomology at the University of Illinois. His first major project was with a team of other entomologists, including R. L. Piemeisel and J. C. Chamberlin, during 1930-38 in the San Joaquin Valley of California. The assignment was to map out the life habits, or life history, of a small insect pest called the sugar beet leafhopper [*Circulifer tenellus* (Baker)]. Despite its small size (3.0 to 3.5 millimeters long), the brown-green insect causes monumental crop damage. It feeds on juices in sugar beets, tomatoes, and beans, and can induce a disease known as "curly top," named for destructive curling of the leaves. The disease produced millions of dollars worth of damage to sugar beet plants in the western United States in the late 1920s.[5]

"It was not uncommon for the insect to cause statewide destruction of sugar beets, tomatoes, and beans in the early '30s," Lawson recalls. "About the only weapon we had was prediction on the basis of what we knew about the insect's life history. We could tell the farmer: 'All right, infestations are going to be so bad that you're going to get wiped out unless you plant something else.' So he would have to plow, then plant something else. That's all we could do for him."

The field work in California, however, produced new insights into the relationship between the beet leafhopper, the plants it lives on, and the environment.[6] The entomologists then devised a control program based on improved agricultural and conservation practices. The research also was an early demonstration of Lawson's ability to discover one or two key vulnerable stages in a pest insect's life on which to concentrate a safe, economical attack.

"We determined that the leafhopper passes the winter in the foothills on the west side of the San Joaquin Valley. It moves into the valley in the spring. The vegetation of the valley was mapped, and we found that the insect spends the summer principally on three species of weeds. I determined that, instead of a dozen or so host weeds, the only really significant one was Russian thistle."[6]

The strategy then became to reduce the availability of Russian thistle, a prickly herb introduced from abroad that has become a serious pest plant in its own right in North America. Farmers could routinely

5. E. O. Essig, *Insects of Western North America,* The MacMillan Company, New York City, 1926, p. 211.

6. R. L. Piemeisel, and F. R. Lawson, "Types of Vegetation in the San Joaquin Valley of California and their Relation to the Beet Leafhopper," *USDA Technical Bulletin* 447(1937):1-28. J. C. Chamberlin, and F. R. Lawson, "A Mechanical Trap for the Sampling of Aerial Insect Populations," USDA ET-163, 1940. F. R. Lawson, D. W. Fox, and G. T. York, "Three New Devices for Measuring Insect Populations," USDA ET-183, 1941. F. R. Lawson, W. C. Cook, and G. T. York, "Russian-thistle as a Summer Host Plant of the Beet Leafhopper in the San Joaquin Valley, California and Methods of Reducing Its Acreage," USDA E-573, 1942. F. R. Lawson, and R. L. Piemeisel, "The Ecology of the Principal Summer Weed Hosts of the Beet Leafhopper in the San Joaquin Valley, California," USDA Technical Bulletin 848(1943): 1-38. F. R. Lawson, J. C. Chamberlin, and G. T. York, "Dissemination of the Beet Leafhopper in California," USDA Technical Bulletin 1030(1951): 1-59. R. L. Piemeisel, F. R. Lawson, and E. Carsner, "Weeds, Insects, Plant Diseases, and Dust Storms," *Scientific Monthly,* 73(2)(1951): 124-128.

destroy the Russian thistle on cropland. At the same time, ranches could eliminate the weed on grazing land, where it frequently was near the insect's spring breeding grounds, by halting overgrazing by cattle. Stopping the overgrazing would promote regrowth of forage grasses that could crowd out the Russian thistle. This regrowth would, in turn, improve grazing conditions and foster soil conservation by reducing water and wind erosion.

As reasonable as this plan of action seemed, it lost out to another one featuring insecticides. "About the time we had the control program for the beet leafhopper worked out in California, one of the sugar company men devised an insecticide spray system using pyrethrum (a natural insecticide available long before synthetic chemical pesticides). He knew that the hopper bred in the northern part of the valley in relatively restricted areas. His idea was to go in there and spray with pyrethrum to cut down the population. We all objected, but our control system was never really put into operation because of the pyrethrum spray plan." The spraying program brought only temporary control, and the defeat foreshadowed many more to come for Lawson and others who favored biological control.

Tobacco Growers' Dilemma

In 1948, the USDA assigned Lawson to the first of several studies he was to do on insect pests of tobacco in southeastern United States.[7] By this time, organic pesticides such as DDT and TDE were widely used, and many entomologists and most administrators within the USDA viewed the emerging spectrum of chemical poisons as the panacea for pest infestations. "We've known for forty years that for some insects there are better, more efficient answers than insecticides, but very few administrators had a very high opinion of biological control. They didn't think it was necessary. The

reason that I went to work on tobacco was that the research problem there required a biologist."

Nevertheless, Lawson's field investigations showed that the insecticides, which were being applied in progressively larger doses, were being needlessly overused. He first studied the green peach aphid (*Myzus persicae*), which had become a serious tobacco pest. Lawson discovered that serious infestations of the aphid could be prevented in most cases by eliminating small stands of wild or cultivated mustard plants and sorrel which grew near tobacco plant beds. The mustard plants provided winter food for the aphids. Destroying this food source — or, at the most, applying insecticide in the plant beds before transplanting the seedlings to the fields — usually would control the aphid. Field applications of insecticides were necessary only on a local basis near fields of wild mustard. But generalized field applications of insecticides continued, despite Lawson's findings.

The story was much the same in the next major research project, a study of the life history and population dynamics of the larvae, or caterpillar, of the tobacco hornworm. (*Manduca sexta*),[8] a serious tobacco pest in the Southeast. Lawson and fellow scientists were again able to pinpoint the

7. F. R. Lawson, G. B. Lucas, and N. S. Hall, "Translocation of Radioactive Phosphorus Injected by the Green Peach Aphid into Tobacco Plants," *Journal of Economic Entomology*, 47(1954): 749-52. F. R. Lawson, and F. S. Chamberlin, "Aphids on Tobacco: How to Control Them," USDA Leaflet No. 405, 1960.

8. R. L. Rabb, and F. R. Lawson, "Some Factors Influencing the Predation of *Polistes* Wasps on the Tobacco Hornworm," *Journal of Economic Entomology*, 50(1957): 778-84. F. E. Guthrie, R. L. Rabb, T. G. Bowery, F. R. Lawson, and R. L. Baron, "Control of Hornworms and Budworms on Tobacco with Reduced Insecticide Dosage, *Tobacco Science*, 3(1959): 65-68. F. R. Lawson, "The Natural Enemies of the Hornworms on Tobacco," *Annnals of the Entomology Society of America*, 52(6)(1959): 741-55. F. R. Lawson, R.

natural weaknesses of the pest. First of all, their studies dramatically showed the degree to which insects are kept in check by natural enemies. About 30 percent of the eggs of the tobacco hornworm were destroyed by an insect called the stilt bug (*Jalysus spinosus*); 60 percent were killed by the larvae of *Polistes* wasps; a variable portion of the remainder were killed by two other parasites. Most of the tobacco damage was done by larvae that managed to survive these and other attacks and reach a certain stage of physical development (the fifth instar, or moult). The number of hornworms reaching that stage was determined primarily by losses to natural enemies rather than by the number of eggs.

An integrated pest control program was designed on the basis of this pattern of insect development. One step in the program was to erect wooden boxes around the tobacco field to serve as nesting shelters for the *Polistes* wasps, which then attacked the hornworm larvae in greater numbers and depressed the number of larvae. Insecticide treatment was necessary only when larvae escaped the assault of natural enemies and reached a predetermined population level. Whether or not they had reached that level could be discovered by counting the number of caterpillars per 50 plants, a system based on Lawson's ecological studies.

Lawson discovered that when insecticide applications were necessary, customary dosages could be reduced by 75 percent. Tobacco growers generally sprayed the entire

L. Rabb, F. E. Guthrie, and T. G. Bowery, "Studies of an Integrated Control System for Hornworms on Tobacco," *Journal of Economic Entomology*, 54(1961): 93-7. Hoffman, J. D. and F. R. Lawson, "Preliminary Studies on Mass Rearing of the Tobacco Hornworm," *Journal of Economic Entomology*, 57(1963):354-55. F. R. Lawson, and R. L. Rabb, "Factors Controlling Hornworm Damage to Tobacco and Methods of Predicting Outbreaks," *Tobacco*, 159(27)(1964): 28-32 and *Tobacco Science*, 8(1964):145-49.

plant with pesticides, but the hornworm eggs were only on the top quarter of the plant and the larvae fed in that area during their early development. Lawson's experiments showed conclusively that one-fourth the recommended dosage of insecticides applied to the top of the plant provided as much control as the full dose applied to the entire plant.

So here was a fairly straightforward, comprehensive system of insect control, based on proven scientific principles, that would reduce the cost to the farmer, improve tobacco yields, and decrease environmental damage from pesticides. But, to Lawson's frustration, "nobody ever used the program. Control recommendations were based largely on how quickly insecticides killed. Entomologists were convinced that farmers wanted to see insects dropping off plants behind them as they sprayed. The entomologists tried to give the farmer what he wanted."

Twice as Much Is Better

This attitude still prevailed during 1962-64 when Lawson became investigations leader in charge of three USDA laboratories in the Southeast (in Florida, South Carolina, and North Carolina). "One of my responsibilities — a job I didn't like much — was to review federal recommendations for application of insecticides on tobacco. The typical attitude of government entomologists and tobacco workers was 'Let's keep the costs down, but let's not take the chance of someone losing part of his crop. If the research data looks like one-fourth-pound treatments will do the job, maybe we better recommend one-half-pound treatments to be on the safe side.' "

This attitude clashed hard with Lawson's entire professional experience. Furthermore, he and other investigators were able to show at the time that populations of tobacco hornworms could be reduced 50 to 70 percent by a method that was even simpler than the previous integrated control program for hornworms. The tobacco farmer merely set up three mechanical light traps per square mile in a tobacco planting area no less than 100 square miles in size.[9] Since the hornworm was a primary pest, controlling it meant that generalized insecticide spraying could be halted. Spraying continued in most of the Southeast, however, with predictable results: "During this period, C. Corley, M. S. Schechter, and I showed that insecticide residues in cured tobacco in nearly all brands of cigarettes, cigars, and snuff were several times the quantity permitted in food by the Food and Drug Administration."[10] (Residues on tobacco were permissible at the time, but since then use of DDT and TDE on tobacco has been banned by most tobacco-growing states, not because of concern about health hazards to smokers, but because European countries that *were* worried about the health hazards and that imported 40 percent of the U.S. tobacco crop, set low tolerances for chlorinated hydrocarbons.)

DDT Addiction

Frutsrated by the relatively low killing power of insecticides such as arsenicals and pyrethrum, agricultural entomologists thought they had found the answer to pest control when DDT became available in the 1940s. They knew that widescale use of DDT would kill enemies of the pest as well as the pest itself, but Lawson remembers the attitude as: "Well sure, there are natural enemies. But they aren't doing the job. So if we knock them off, what difference does it make?"

"The thing that we didn't know that got us into real trouble was the true role of natural enemies of insects. We knew, of course, that this parasite or predator attacked that host. But I don't know that we understood two key facts until after DDT

began to cause trouble. First of all, we didn't have much idea of the extent to which major insect pests like the cotton boll weevil, tobacco hornworm, tobacco budworm, corn ear worm, and coddling moth are held in check by natural enemies. Second, we did not understand how many other *potential* pests on the same plants also are held in check by natural enemies."

To illustrate, Lawson points out that investigators estimate that at least 1,000 species of insects can be found feeding on or living in alfalfa plants. Even the plants which are most unappealing to insects will have at least 250 species, of which 100 will be plant feeders. Some of the other species that do not feed directly on the plant eat dead organic matter, fungi, or other organic material not essential to the life of the plant. A larger proportion of insects not feeding directly on the plant, however, are parasites or predators that attack the plant-eating (phytophagous) insects and are responsible for destroying a large percentage of their populations. A given species of insect thus is usually kept from predominating

9. J. D. Hoffman, F. R. Lawson, and B. Peace, "Attraction of Blacklight Traps Baited with Virgin Female Tobacco Hornworm Moths," *Journal of Economic Entomology,* 59(4)(1966): 809-11. F. R. Lawson, C. R. Gentry, and J. M. Stanley, "Effect of Light Traps on Hornworm Populations in Large Areas," USDA ARS 33-91(1963):1-18. J. M. Stanley, F. R. Lawson, and C. R. Gentry, "Area Control of Tobacco Insects with Blacklight Radiation," *Transactions of the American Society of Agricultural Engineering,* 7(2)(1964):125-27. F. R. Lawson, and C. R. Gentry, "Experiments on the Control of Insect Populations with Light Traps," AAAS Symposium, ARS 33-110, 1966. C. R. Gentry, F. R. Lawson, C. M. Knott, J. M. Stanley, and J. J. Lam, Jr., "Control of Hornworms by Trapping With Blacklight and Stalk Cutting in North Carolina," *Journal of Economic Entomology,* 60(5)(1967):1437-1442.

10. F. R. Lawson, C. Corley, and M. S. Schechter, "Insecticide Residues on Tobacco During 1962," *Tobacco,* 159(12):28-30 and *Tobacco Science,* 8(1964):110-12.

because of the pressure from competitors and natural enemies.

The quick-kill pesticide answer so dominated agricultural entomology, however, that entomologists simply recommended more powerful chemicals as insects became resistant to DDT or as new pests emerged. When environmental damage became apparent from the long-lasting effect of the chlorinated hydrocarbon pesticides such as DDT,[11] they recommended shorter acting, still more powerful chemicals. The objective remained to kill insects indiscriminately, quickly, and in large numbers. "We have always gone from a less toxic to a more toxic compound," Lawson observes. "We went to DDT, to Toxaphene, to Dieldrin, to Aldrin [all chlorinated hydrocarbons], to parathion [an organic phosphorus compound], and now Temik [a carbamate compound]."

One measure of heightened toxicity is lower LD_{50} values, which are estimates of the dosage necessary to kill 50 percent of a large population of test animals. The lower the LD_{50}, the more deadly the substance.

An oral dose of DDT in male white rats has an LD_{50} of 113 (milligrams per kilogram of body weight); applied to the skin of female rats, the LD_{50} is much higher, 2,510. By comparison, Parathion, a chemical with a different and more potent type of physiological action, has an oral LD_{50} of 3.6 in female white rats and a dermal (applied to the skin) LD_{50} of 6.8 in female rats.[12] Manufacturer's data on Temik state an oral LD_{50} of 6.2 in male rats, a dermal LD_{50} of 3,200.[13]

The danger to human beings has increased with intensified chemical warfare. For example, 15 to 20 pesticide poisoning cases a year occurred during 1960 through 1963 in the cotton-growing region of the lower Rio Grande Valley of Texas. These were caused by the chlorinated hydrocarbons. Insects became resistant to these pesticides, and in 1964 growers turned to methyl para-

thion. The number of poisonings promptly jumped to about 70 a year until 1967, when there was a rapid decline due to improved safety precautions. In 1968, insects were resistant to methyl parathion, so growers countered with ethyl parathion, which is more toxic to human beings if it contacts the skin. The number of poisonings (all nonfatal) shot up to 118 that year. (Although tabulated from more extensive surveys than in previous years, the number was indicative of the sharp increase since 1967.) Twenty-three of the victims were cotton-field workers; most of the other were ground-support personnel for aerial spraying companies.[14]

In addition to producing a tragic increase in the occupational hazard to agricultural workers, the unrelenting step-up in indiscriminate killing power of insecticides has had an unfavorable effect on the complex, interdependent relationships between insect pests and their enemies, as can be anticipated from Lawson's observations. To summarize, three serious situations have occurred. First, pest insects have migrated into treated areas from untreated fields and become more numerous than ever since the pesticides have killed off their parasites and predators. A related, but more subtle, side effect is that reduction of the insect pests has denied food to their predators, which then have starved or migrated from the area, leaving the field to resurging pests. Second, previously minor pest insects have become major ones as their plant-eating

11. F. R. Lawson, "History and Development of the Insecticide Syndrome," unpublished.

12. *Clinical Handbook on Economic Poisons,* Public Health Service Publication No. 476, U.S. Government Printing Office, Washington, D.C., 1963.

13. *Technical Information on Temik*[12] 10 *G, Aldicarb Pesticide,* Union Carbide Corporation.

14. R. L. Hatcher and J. S. Wiseman, "Epidemiology of Pesticide Poisoning in the Lower Rio Grande Valley in 1968," *Texas Medicine,* 65(8) (August 1969):40-43.

competitors and natural enemies have been destroyed by insecticides. Third, intensified applications of broad spectrum insecticides have hastened development of resistant strains of insect pests.

These difficulties are compounded by another phenomenon, according to Lawson: "Both the carbamates and the phosphates exert physiological effects on plants that greatly increase the fecundity of many insects, particularly aphids and spider mites.[15] The result of all this is that the pest is breeding faster, and it has fewer enemies."

A Matter of Economics

In view of this dismal outlook — the futility of all-out chemical warfare against insects, the danger that the toxic chemicals pose to field workers, and the serious environmental damage — why don't we do the sensible thing, reduce pesticide use to a minimum and immediately develop biological and other alternative methods of nonpesticide control?

Lawson greets that solution with a grim smile, and returns to underlying economic and social considerations that make timely change unlikely. First of all, chemical companies make a great deal of money from broad-spectrum insecticides. In 1968, the most recent year for which complete USDA data have been published,[16] insecticide sales by manufacturers totaled $304 million in the United States.

This massive output of chemical poisons has a tacit stamp of approval from most agricultural entomologists in the United States. "For example," Lawson elaborates, "the entomologists recommend the dosages and leave the rest to the salesmen. So the average farmer or home gardener gets most of his information from the people who sell the pesticides. A recent study in North Carolina showed that about 80 percent of farmers got their information from the salesmen. By-and-large, agricultural extension

service people have aided and abetted in this. Suppose someone comes to me and says 'I've got a problem with insects. What am I going to do about it?' The quick and easy answer — the answer the farmers get from salesmen and extension agents — is to use insecticides. The biological control answers are not quick and not easy."

The pesticide solution also has captivated the administrative mind of USDA. As a recent example, Lawson cites the statement of J. Phil Campbell, undersecretary of agriculture, before the House Committee on Agriculture, February 23, 1971, during hearings on the proposed Federal Environmental Pesticide Control Act of 1971:[17] "When we consider the beneficial effect, the pertinent fact is that pesticides are essential to the abundance and quality of agricultural production in this country. The balance of nature in our monocultural system of agriculture would be heavily weighted on the side of pests if we did not have pesticides."

Mr. Campbell qualified this: "The acute need — while very real — does not mean that we can ignore the hazard that pesticides represent to man and the environment. . . ."

This qualification was modified, however, in Campbell's closing comments, in which he urged that criteria for enforcement of pesticide control legislation be the benefit — or hazard — to human health and the economic benefit to farmers. In regard to the latter, Campbell said: "It would be untenable to consider human health as the

15. F. Chaboussou, "Nouveaux Aspects de la Phytiatrie et de la Phytopharmacie. Le Phenomene de la Trophobiose," Proceedings of the FAO Symposium of Integrated Pest Control, Rome, (1) (1965): 33-61.

16. "The Pesticide Review, 1969," United States Department of Agriculture, Agriculture Stabilization and Conservation Service, Washington, D.C.

17. "Statement of J. Phil Campbell, Under Secretary of Agriculture before the House Committee on Agriculture on February 23, 1971," available from U.S. Department of Agriculture, Washington, D.C.

only criterion of importance in human welfare aspects of pesticide use. . . . We strongly believe that the impact of pesticide decisions on the opportunity for agricultural producers to make a livelihood must be an important criterion in such decisions when criteria other than public health are being considered. . . . To do otherwise — to put the deleterious effects of pesticides on a few species of esthetically desirable birds ahead of the needs of people would be a perversion of human values."

A hallmark of Lawson's research has been control programs to make farming more profitable, while reducing ecological damage from pesticides. The integrated control programs he has devised — to counteract the tobacco hornworm, for example — have been aimed at preventing increasingly expensive pesticide applications that eventually backfire anyway, as in Mexico, leaving farmers in economic ruin. Against this background, Lawson has this assessment of the implications of USDA official policy as advocated by Campbell: "He's saying it's too bad about the bald eagle and the hawks, but if we *have* to sacrifice these animals in order to feed the population, then they have to be sacrificed. In my opinion, this is a complete misunderstanding of what the situation really is. The man simply does not understand that what's happening to the bald eagle and the peregrine falcon, and to other animals, is a symptom of an extremely serious illness of the whole ecosystem. And furthermore, he does not understand that it is not necessary and that it never was necessary. These urgent problems are due to misuse and overuse of insecticides."

Priorities of Research Support

Official emphasis on the insecticide solution has produced a number of other related problems, Lawson believes. For one thing, research money for other than pesticide control has been limited. "All of that time when I was working out an integrated control program for the tobacco hornworm and other tobacco insects, my USDA allotment for working funds was only $500 a year. The people who got the money were people who were working with insecticides and getting quick answers."

Then, the commitment to rather utilitarian pesticide research may have a questionable effect in some departments of entomology at U.S. universities. Chemical companies furnish funds for a number of research assistantships, as well as working funds for research projects on the effects of given insecticides. "I think it's high time the universities quit taking money from the insecticide companies. The people in the universities who are getting the grants are the people who are working with insecticides. They also are the ones who help write state insect control recommendations for farmers, recommendations that are prepared by extension services in every state."

Deceptive Appearance

Faith in chemical control also has promoted unrealistically high standards regarding insect damage. "There are federal standards as to allowable insect parts in fruits and vegetables that are set not because the parts are a health hazard, but simply because the customer doesn't like them. People won't eat anything that might have an insect in it. What people don't know is they eat insects in food everyday even though they may not see them. For example, ground figs, ketchup, and jams generally are made out of U.S. Grade #2 fruits and vegetables. One of the reasons that they are #2 grade is that they have insect parts in them, but we go right ahead and eat ketchup and jams. State standards sometimes are designed to provide a better market for their own products. For example, by demanding a certain percentage of U.S. #1 grade fruit from its growers a state can improve the appearance of its own product and thus compete better with produce from other states. Other standards are strictly cosmetic. The rust on oranges that you get from Florida is caused by the rust mite. A great deal of insecticide is applied against the rust mite, even though the rust does not affect the quality of the orange in any way. It just spoils the nice orange color, that's all. Another example is that U.S. #1 grade cabbage can have only a minimum number of insect holes in the outer wrapper leaves. But the grocer generally pulls off the [outer] leaves before putting the heads of cabbage out in the market anyway."

Competitive pressures force the grower to strive for the highest grades of fruits and vegetables by using excessive amounts of insecticides. "For any control measure," Lawson calculates, "effectiveness decreases exponentially with the intensity of the dosage. If you apply 'x' amount of an insecticide to get 50 percent control, you have to apply twice that to get 75 percent control. In other words, you have to double the dose to kill half of the 50 percent of insects remaining. The disparity becomes much larger as you approach 95 percent control. Perhaps with the new ecological concern, people would be willing to eat some blemished apples or oranges or green vegetables with a few holes in the leaves, if they knew that doing so would mean lower doses of insecticides released into the environment."

Finally, even if scientists and federal administrators give their full support to integrated control and de-emphasize insecticides, the system will not be easy to apply. Lawson explains: "Integrated control is technically a beautiful system. But it's a sophisticated system that is going to require field supervisors. There already are some supervisors working in California, but if you ask what percentage of cotton in the San Joaquin Valley is under supervised control, the answer is less than five percent. The first problem is to find trained supervisors.

The second is to get farmers to listen to them. I don't think they'll listen or change the present system as long as they have any alternatives."

Lawson considers integrated control a long-term goal. In the meantime, he asserts that crops can be saved and insecticide usage reduced by at least one-half if registration procedures for pesticides are strengthened, entomological advisory services to farmers expanded, grading standards revised to eliminate the need for insecticide treatments aimed at maintaining cosmetic appearance rather than quality of fruits and vegetables, and biological control measures introduced against all plant pests instead of only those most recently introduced from abroad.

For his own part, Lawson intends to influence the trend even though he is retiring from the USDA. In some respects, he feels his chances will be even greater since the department seems so slow to perceive the urgency of the agricultural crisis. Lawson and his brother-in-law have formed a company to rear parasites and predators and to develop pathogens in order to promote the sale and use of biological control methods. They will travel to Gainesville, Florida, to be near entomologists at the University of Florida who are interested in devising biological control techniques. Lawson's brother-in-law, formerly an engineer in the U.S. Department of Defense, will be business manager and will help design some of the equipment necessary. Lawson also intends to give his views public exposure, a luxury which he restrained while in the Department of Agriculture.

Of Friend and Foe

The research which Lawson has done over the past forty years has brought us closer to an understanding of the sensitive, interdependent relationships among insect pests and their enemies. He has shown new ways in which the relationships can be used against the pests, to man's benefit, without poisoning the environment or promoting insecticide resistance.[18]

It has been convenient so far to speak of the pests as enemies of man. And so they seem, with 700,000 species compared to our one, a number of which have the capacity to devour food supplies which must be doubled or tripled in the next few decades if we are to support our rate of reproduction.[19] Yet scientifically, it is more accurate to speak of the plant-eating insects as competitors for our food. They, after all, are no more our direct enemies than are other animals which share the air we breathe. It's just that air is abundant, and food is not.

There appear to be reasons for changing this attitude that are more forceful than a desire for scientific accuracy, however. In our power-conscious age, we are prone to conditioned response against those we categorize as enemies. The response, often enough, is to go to war. This, in fact, is precisely what we have done. We have waged all-out chemical warfare against insects, and now we find the object of our attack stronger than ever. So our response is to hit harder, even though the interwoven dynamics of nature are more powerful than our biggest chemical bomb. Our intelligence tells us that we must learn to live with these forces, but until our will is bent to that task, our insect competitors will enjoy new opportunities.

18. F. R. Lawson, "Theory of Control of Insect Populations by Sexually Sterile Males," *Annals of the Entomological Society of America*, 60(4) (1967):713-722. F. R. Lawson, "Some Features of the Relation of Insects to their Ecosystems," *Ecology*, 39(3)(1958):515-21. F. R. Lawson, "The Relation of Insect Control to Increased Food Production," Proceedings of the Tall Timbers Conference on Ecological Animal Control by Habitat Management, February 1969. F. R. Lawson, "Integrating Control of Pest Populations in Large Areas," Proceedings of the FAO Symposium on Integrated Pest Control, 1965, Food and Agriculture Organization of the United Nations, #3 (Invited speaker for the symposium, which resulted in this publication).

19. Daniel G. Aldrich, Jr., "World Food and Population Crisis," *Science*, 162(3859)(1968):1309-10.

EDITOR'S COMMENTS

In many cases, the amount of knowledge that can be applied to solving man's problems exists in direct relationship to the amount of research effort brought to bear on a particular possible solution Funds used by professional research entomologists in studying the effectiveness of chemical pesticides far outweigh those used in research on methods of biological control. One might wonder if the concentration of biocides in the environment would be as heavy as it is today if two decades ago, government agencies and insecticide companies had pushed research on biological control methods with the same amount of zeal used to push pesticide use.

JEAN CARPER

Danger of Cancer in Food

▶ A controversy is brewing in Washington over chemicals added to what we eat; the report below tells the disconcerting facts.

Jean Carper is a free-lance writer specializing in consumer and health subjects. She is the author of numerous magazine articles and is co-author with Senator Warren G. Magnuson of the Book "The Dark Side of the Marketplace."

The purpose of this report is to alert the American people to the fact that they are in danger of losing the only effective legal protection they have against the addition to their food of chemicals capable of causing cancer.

Congress wrote the now threatened safeguard into the U.S. Food, Drug and Cosmetic Act in 1958. Called "the Delaney clause," after its sponsor, New York Congressman James J. Delaney, this unique bulwark of the law says "no additive [to food] shall be deemed to be safe if it is found to induce cancer when ingested by man or animal or if it is found, after tests which are appropriate for the evaluation of the safety of food additives, to induce cancer in man or animal." Delaney drafted the clause in keeping with a recommendation adopted by the International Union Against Cancer at Rome in 1956.

The first public suggestion that attempts were being made to weaken or abolish the Delaney clause came last October, when most people were just becoming aware of the controversy over cyclamate, the artificial sweetener that had been put into soft drinks and foods in growing amounts for a half dozen years prior. Trouble had arisen because scientists under contract with Abbott Laboratories, a major maker of cyclamate, had conducted tests showing that when the sweetener was fed to rats the animals developed bladder cancers. With disclosure of this information, banning of cyclamate from food and drink became automatic under the Delaney clause.

This was a disastrous blow to West Coast food canners, who had just completed another season of cyclamate use. If the Delaney clause were to operate strictly, the entire year's crop would have to be withheld from the market.

The plight of the canners went unmentioned until later, when Food and Drug Administration officials were called upon by Congressional investigation to explain their behavior. Robert Finch, then President Nixon's Secretary of Health, Education and Welfare, did not refer to it when he pointed-

Reprinted by permission of the author and publisher from *Saturday Review*. September 5, 1970. Copyright © 1970 by Saturday Review, Inc.

ly hedged his announcement that cyclamate would be banned from soft drinks and general purpose foods. In an appearance on the National Educational Network, he said he favored changing the Delaney clause to allow "safe levels" of cancer-producing additives in foods. The Delaney clause does not recognize any level of carcinogenic additive as safe.

Dr. Roger Egeberg, Assistant HEW Secretary for Scientific and Health Affairs, fell into line behind Finch. Egeberg declared his intention to continue to use cyclamate to keep his own weight down because he saw no danger in small amounts of the chemical. Subsequently he appointed an ad hoc "medical advisory committee" to determine whether cyclamate was beneficial in treatment of diabetes and obesity, and the committee recommended that cyclamate in certain dietetic foods be allowed on the market as a drug. The Food and Drug Administration (FDA), an agency of HEW, thereupon approved cyclamate's sale as a nonprescription drug after September 1, 1970.

So far as the outside world could see, the whole of FDA — the whole of HEW, for that matter — opposed strict enforcement of the Delaney clause in the case of cyclamate. However, insiders knew this to be untrue. The FDA staff had split on the question. At least as late as last December 5, the argument still proceeded through written memos. On that date, Alan T. Spiher, Jr., now assistant to the director of FDA's Office of Compliance, addressed Dr. Albert C. Kolbye, Jr., now deputy director of FDA's Bureau of Foods and Pesticides, on the subject of "modification of the anticancer proviso." The communication began:

> A proposed amendment to the Federal Food, Drug, and Cosmetic Act has been drafted. This modifies the so-called Delaney Clause to remove the mandate that no additive shall be deemed to be safe if it is found to induce cancer, and to replace it with a statement that no tolerance shall be established for an additive that induces cancer or any other serious effects on organ systems, unless the Secretary after consultation with experts by scientific training and experience, particularly with respect to the observed adverse effect, determines that the finding raises no substantial question of safety under the proposed conditions of use.

Philosophy of the Delaney Clause

I am opposed to any attempt to water down the Delaney Clause at this time, and particularly in the manner suggested by the draft bill.

That a significant attempt is being made to change the anticancer provision would appear to represent a serious misunderstanding of the intent of the law and the need for conservatism in protecting the public health. This law has been on the books for eleven years. Two years after its inception, Congress carefully studied the implication of the Delaney Clause. In studying this matter, the Congressional Committee considered seriously and at length each of the questions that are now being advanced as reason why the Delaney Clause should be changed. In studying this matter, the Committee consulted a distinguished group of about eleven cancer experts provided by the NRC [The National Research Council, research arm of the National Academy of Sciences]. They were asked to respond individually to the specific question: "Do we think the Food and Drug Administration should set tolerances for carcinogens?" All were not in agreement, but the majority responded in the negative. The major reason for this was clearly that no expert was willing to say that a "no effect" level could be established for a carinogen. The minority supported leaving the decision to FDA scientists clearly with the expectation that only in very rare and exceptional "borderline" cases might FDA consider a finite tolerance.

The legislative change is being proposed without a study comparable to the previous one by Congress which resulted in the retention of the anticancer provision. No scientific breakthroughs have occurred in understanding cancer or learning whether there is in fact a finite level for a carcinogen below which no effect can be expected. No formally appointed group of cancer experts has been consulted.

On the contrary, increasing knowledge of our polluted environment and the stresses to which man is subject on all sides, along with our beginning to understand that cancer may be the body response to the total insult from all stresses, raise the serious question whether we should provide the opportunity for additional potent insults, albeit small in amount.

Because of the internal struggle, Finch had to fudge his department's intentions when he addressed the Pharmaceutical Manufacturers Association last April 10. "We are going to introduce legislation . . . to strengthen and update the Delaney clause," he said. "I repeat and stress the point." Which way would the legislation go? "We could propose that the Delaney clause be extended to apply to irreversible effects in addition to carcinogenesis — to liver, brain, and heart damage, for example, and to mutagenesis (mutations in offspring) and teratogenesis (defects in embryos). And as a suboption we could propose that HEW might be permitted to set tolerance levels for all these substances where there is a compelling reason to do so."

Two months later, on June 10, an AP news dispatch interpreted Finch's ambivalence. AP quoted a confidential memo from Creek Black, Assistant HEW Secretary for Legislation, who attributed the legislative tactics to Surgeon General Dr. Jesse Steinfeld. The memo revealed that proposed extensions of tolerances not only for cancer but for other diseases were "designed to anticipate and counteract criticism that the Department is merely trying to weaken existing safeguards against harmful substances in foods."

In that same month of June, Congressman L. H. Fountain of North Carolina, chairman of the intergovernmental subcommittee of the House, conducted hearings to investigate the FDA. During the hearings he uncovered details of the cyclamate affair. He challenged FDA to show that cyclamate was either effective or safe as a drug. FDA could show neither. On the witness stand, its officials confirmed that they had acted on orders from higher-ups in HEW, partly to avoid imposing calamitous losses on fruit canners. The requirements of the drug law had been avoided by neglecting to ask the industry for evidence it was known not to possess.

At the end of the hearings, Fountain wrote to Finch's successor in the HEW secretaryship, Elliot L. Richardson:

I believe these orders (declaring cyclamate a drug) are not only ill-advised but illegal. The cyclamates were prohibited for public use under the Delaney amendment because they are a potential health hazard to the American people. The subcommittee's hearing record discloses that no benefits with regard to weight reduction have been scientifically demonstrated for the cylamates. On the other hand, the scientific literature indicates that the ingestion of cyclamates may increase the risk of birth defects, genetic damage, and cancer. Further, it has been shown that cyclamates interfere with the desired effects of some drugs taken for treatment of medical conditions, including the oral drug tolbutamide used by diabetics.

Fountain urged Richardson to "rescind the unlawful orders for cyclamates" and reminded him that "Congress never intended the act to be disregarded at certain times on the basis of executive whim."

Fountain was still awaiting reassurances from Richardson when consumer champion Ralph Nader's Center for the Study of Responsive Law filed a petition with FDA asking that cyclamate be totally banned as the law required. Three days later, FDA announced that foods containing cyclamate could not be marketed after September 1, 1970.

A side effect of the Fountain hearings in June was a focusing of general attention on the Delaney clause, which bars carcinogenic additives not only from human food but also from animal feeds unless the feeds do not "adversely affect the animals for which such feed is intended" and if "no residue of the additive will be found in any edible portion of such animal after slaughter or in any food yielded by or derived from the living animals."

Many months before the Fountain hearings began, Wisconsin Senator William Proxmire had received allegations from a former U.S. Department of Agriculture employee in California, Dr. John N. S. White, that some other evasions of the Delaney clause were even more flagrant than the cyclamate case had been. Specifically, White told Proxmire that a synthetic growth hormone, diethylstilbestrol (DES), known to be carcinogenic, was showing up in animal flesh intended for the human diet.

A year before Congress added the Delaney clause to the Food and Drug Act, it had been discovered that DES caused cancer in mice. At that time, DES pellets were being implanted in the necks of chickens to make the fowl grow faster and bigger. After residues of DES were found in the edible portions of chickens, use of DES in poultry was prohibited ten years ago. Dr. Roy Herz, who then was chief of the branch of endocrinology of the National Cancer Institute, made the following statement:

> Stilbestrol is known to produce a variety of tumors in several species after prolonged exposure . . . In rare cases cancers have developed in (human) patients after prolonged use of stilbestrol. . . . It is therefore desirable to eliminate the hazard, no matter how small the dosage, of continued consumption of this material in one's diet. . . .

In spite of this unequivocal warning from an acknowledged cancer specialist, beef cat-

tle growers were allowed to continue feeding DES to steers. Today, three-quarters of the nation's beef supply comes from DES-stimulated animals. The reason for the practice is that the hormone causes a 10 to 16 percent greater weight gain per volume of feed consumed by the cattle. The justification for the risk to the consumer is that if DES is withdrawn from cattle feed forty-eight hours prior to slaughter of the animals, no residue of the hormone will remain in the meat by the time it reaches the human consumer.

What Dr. John White told Senator Proxmire was that USDA meat inspectors had been finding residues of DES in meat intended for human consumption for half a decade. The Fountain hearings gave Proxmire's staff a timely opportunity to call White's complaints to the attention of AP reporter John Lang, who published quotations from a letter USDA had written to Proxmire in response to a query from the Senator. According to Lang's published account of the matter, USDA gave Proxmire the following percentage of cases in which DES residues had been found in beef livers:

1965—2.7 percent
1966—1.1 percent
1967—2.6 percent
1968—0.7 percent

When I asked Dr. Harold Trabosh, a USDA staff officer assigned to the DES inspection program, to confirm or deny the AP story, Trabosh replied that the AP figures were not entirely accurate. For one thing, he said, no data on DES residues were available until 1966. The record thereafter, he said, showed these incidences of hormone residue, all in beef livers:

1966—none out of 207 samples taken
1967—13 out of 469, or 2.7 percent
1968—4 out of 539, or 0.7 percent
1969—3 out of 505, or 0.6 percent

Whatever inaccuracies there may have been in the AP data were not substantial.

Whether AP was correct in reporting that the use of DES had been outlawed in cattle as well as in poultry in Switzerland, France, and the Netherlands, I could not confirm. But I did discover that the tolerances allowed by the USDA sampling system are riskier than the low percentages might indicate.

Under the DES surveillance program, samples of meat are sent to a laboratory for analysis. If DES residue is found, the meat must be condemned. But it takes a month, sometimes more, before the laboratory reports come back and any condemnations can be made. Meanwhile, the cattle from which the sample was taken have been slaughtered and marketed. Dr. James Stewart, another USDA staff officer with the DES project, explained that in practice enforcement consists of tracing a residue back to the grower of the cattle from which it came. The next time he markets cattle, they cannot be approved for marketing until after the sample has been analyzed. Dr. Stewart conceded that thousands of cattle containing DES may be marketed and eaten under this system.

Couldn't all animals be sampled before slaughter? Dr. Stewart replied: "It would cost more than the Vietnam War."

It is not the USDA but the FDA that has responsibility for invoking the Delaney clause. FDA can act only on advice from USDA inspectors. Dr. C. D. Van Houweling, director of FDA's Bureau of Veterinary Medicine, told me USDA does not always find cattle growers who are selling animals with DES residues because records are not that complete. Dr. Van Houweling said that most DES residues are due to failure of cattle growers to observe the forty-eight hour withdrawal period before slaughter. His official position, as he stated it to me, is that small amounts of DES are not harmful to humans. "There are some real advantages to using it, and I don't think at these very low levels there is any danger," he insisted. Referring to a letter from a man in California who claimed he got cancer of the colon from eating meat contaminated with DES, Van Houweling commented: "I don't think there is any more chance he has cancer from eating DES than I can jump from here to the moon."

In the three years since he learned of the DES residue in beef, Dr. Van Houweling said, he has begun an intensified "educational program" to get the cattle industry to control the use of DES. If illegal residues continue to show up, he said, the FDA may have no recourse but to ban DES. But he is not willing to set a timetable for that action. In any event, he believes, "we can never prevent all residues of DES from occurring." He believes further that people would rather eat a little of a carcinogenic chemical than pay the extra 20 percent cost of beef which he estimates would be incurred if DES were totally banned.

Apparently, Dr. Van Houweling's view is the FDA view. For, under a strict reading of the Delaney clause, residues of DES, a known carcinogen, are clearly illegal. But Ray Geremia, press officer for FDA Commissioner Charles C. Edwards, has told me that he was authorized to state that FDA has no plans for prohibiting use of the hormone.

The obvious purpose of the Delaney clause is to take away all discretion from FDA concerning food additives capable of causing cancer. The appearance of *any* cancer-causing substance is sufficient cause for the clause to be invoked. An often heard argument against the clause is that sufficiently high dosages of nearly any chemical will prove carcinogenic. A November 3, 1969, editorial in *Chemical and Engineering News* phrased the argument well: "Raise dosages high enough and make test conditions severe enough and a vast number of chemicals will likely prove to be cancer inducers, even though they are perfectly safe in anything like normal use." A new scientific study, published just last June by Bionetics Research Laboratories of Litton

Industries under contract with the National Institutes of Health, contradicts this widely held point of view. When 120 chemical compounds were fed to mice at the highest doses the animals could tolerate and yet survive, 75 percent of the chemicals did not cause any significant rise in tumors.

Because it seems to preclude decisions based on scientific opinions and judgments, the Delaney clause has been assailed as unscientific. Such criticism was voiced at last year's White House Conference on Nutrition and Health by a number of conference participants, including many from the food industry. But Dr. Umberto Saffiotti, associate scientific director for carinogenesis at the National Cancer Institute, vigorously disagrees. He contends that the Delaney clause allows much room for the exercise of scientific judgment. He points out that cancer experts must determine whether the additive in question did in their judgment induce the cancer. To make that determination, he notes, cancer authorities must consider the validity of the tests.

Dr. Saffiotti was one of the cancer experts who reviewed the Abbott Laboratories' data on cyclamate and subsequently recommended that cyclamate be banned as a carcinogen of unknown potency. After HEW, in announcing the ban, stressed that there was absolutely no evidence to demonstrate in any way that the use of cyclamate has caused cancer in man," Dr. Saffiotti observed that the absence of evidence of human harm is irrelevant and can be misleading: "We would not expect to have any evidence. Cyclamate has been in widespread use only since 1963, and it takes at least 15 to 20 years for cancer to develop. If cyclamate had been such a potent carcinogen that it would have already caused a detectable rise in cancer in the last six years, we would find ourselves in an epidemic of incredible proportions."

According to him, the weight of scientific opinion throughout the world still opposes establishing any "safe" doses for carcinogens, because no one knows how little of a carcinogen it takes to trigger cancer at the cellular level, and the effects of the small levels of carcinogens we are exposed to daily through air pollution, pesticides, radiation, smoking may be cumulative.

"We have produced no evidence there is a safe dose of a carcinogen," he declares. "Exposure to cancer-producing agents . . . shows that the tissue which is exposed acquires *new* susceptibility. The tissue stores the danger, so to speak, so that even with low levels of a carcinogen, if the cells are exposed to additional insults, the damage can add up so you reach a level where a tumor develops. All of this gives us a situation in which we cannot assume that low-level exposure to carcinogens may be insignificant."

Dr. Joshua Lederberg, Nobel Prize-winning geneticist, not only supports the Delaney clause but argues that it should be broadened. His position is that any food additive found to cause mutations or defects in human or animal embryos should be automatically banned. Eventually, he says, "as we develop better theories of and experimental models for other chronic diseases like hypertension and atherosclerosis, these, too, would be covered." Wisconsin Senator Gaylord Nelson has introduced legislation that would extend the effect of the Delaney clause in that general direction. In *The Chemical Feast,* the book James Turner wrote for the Nader's Raiders group that studied FDA, a similar advocacy appears.

Perhaps the most persuasive argument against repeal of the Delaney clause was made in the Alan Spiher memo quoted earlier in this report. The words Spiher used were these:

There seems to be some confusion in assessment of the relative risk from carcinogens and from ordinary chemical toxicants in our food supply and in the environment.

A no effect level can be developed in animals for a chemical toxicant, and the relative risk of translating this information to man can be assessed. If an error occurs and the allowable dietary level produces toxicity in man, the offending agent can be removed and the deleterious effect is reversible and complete recovery is expected.

In the case of carcinogens, mutagens, and teratogens, we have a drastic difference in the result of any miscalculations. If cancer, terata, or mutagenic changes are induced, these are irreversible—no recovery is possible even if the offending agent is removed from the diet, the damage is done. Malignant cancer will develop, a malformed infant will be born, or a gene defect will be transmitted to the next generation.

Under what conditions will it be possible to say that there is an additive which is so needed in our food supply that *any* risk of one of these effects is acceptable? My children would have to be in more than highly theoretical danger of starving before I would want *any* risk.

EDITOR'S COMMENTS

Just as a person suffering from lung cancer cannot prove that his ailment was directly caused by a specific air pollutant emitted from a certain source, so one can never prove that a specific cancer was caused by a certain food additive. Few consumers would argue for a weakening of FDA standards for food additive use when confronted by the facts. The truth is that the forces brought to bear on the politicians who can reduce these standards represent manufacturers and producers who are fighting for continued or elevated profits. They neither care nor think about the possible human ailments which might be caused, but are never traced to their true source. In the world of finance, man may be somewhat less than highly civilized!

JACK SHEPHERD

The Nuclear Threat Inside America

Jack Shepherd was formerly a Senior Editor of *Look* magazine. He is presently associated with *Newsweek* magazine.

For 24 years the Atomic Energy Commission has grown up fat, powerful, unquestioned. Its vast, loyal band of scientists, functionaries, businessmen and politicians talk about "nuclear enhancement," "nuclear events," and "nuclear landscaping," license and run atomic-power generators and weapons factories that dump "rad-waste," which will bubble for thousands of years—lasting longer than governments, records, perhaps man himself. AEC has spent $49 billion. It's got friends.

Now AEC is under attack. More than 112 nuclear power plants are promised by 1980. Private citizens have blocked six in 1970. University of Nevada researchers checking the buildup of iodine-131 in cattle thyroids across the West conclude: "The principal known source of I-131 is exhaust gases from nuclear reactors and associated fuel-processing plants."

Scientists argue that our underground blasts for research — more than 23 so far this year versus two in Russia — are expensive, repetitive and careless. Radioactive plutonium now covers 250 square miles of the Nevada Test Site. AEC admits the desert is contaminated. "It's going to be contaminated a long, long time," says a spokesman. "That's why we're testing here. That's the kind of thing we have to do."

Many AEC officials are working hard to overcome their reputation. Others are skating fastest where the ice is thinnest. Critics bristle at a nuclear policy run by insiders impatient with environmental questions and want a voice in safety and radiation standards used by the AEC. They argue against AEC's dual role of promoter and regulator of atomic energy. "That," says a critic, "is like letting the fox guard the hen house."

AEC sees its mission as a crusade. Howard B. Brown, Jr., assistant general manager, says: "We have circumnavigated the globe many times over, spreading the gospel about the peaceful atom." Opponents are heretics.

Two of them, Drs. John Gofman and Arthur Tamplin of AEC's Lawrence Radiation Laboratory (Livermore, Calif.), argue that AEC's "safe radiation dose" is unsafe. If everyone got AEC's safe dose, they claim, there would be 16,000 to 24,000 more cancer and leukemia deaths a year

Reprinted by permission of the author and publisher from *Look* 34:21-27. December 15, 1970. Copyright © 1970 by Cowles Communications, Inc.

215

in the U.S. They demand an immediate reduction to a tenth of the AEC level.

AEC fumes. "Gofman, Tamplin and their allies are . . . trying their case in the press and other public forums," said James T. Ramey, an AEC commissioner. "We used to call such characters 'Opera Stars.'"

Dr. Gofman has rebutted: "There is no morality . . . not a shred of honesty in any one of them — none. I can assure you, from every bit of dealing I've had . . . there is absolute duplicity, guaranteed duplicity, lies at every turn, falsehood in every way, about you personally and about your motives."

Any exposure to radiation may be cumulative, the damage is irreversible. There are five dangers: cancer, leukemia, genetic defects, fetal and neonatal deaths. They may take generations to show up.

Radioactivity tends to accumulate in specific tissues and organs. Iodine-131 seeks the thyroid; strontium-90 builds into bones and teeth, Cesium-137, muscle. Krypton-85 is already concentrating in our fatty tissues, and this accumulation could exhaust two-thirds of AEC's "radiation budget" for man for the coming century.

Critics charge that the present standards don't consider concentration, or accumulation, that all radiation damages cells, that there is no safe limit or threshold. AEC standards come from two groups of scientists and the Federal Radiation Council, which also balances risk versus benefits.

Dr. Gofman believes: "Citizens . . . will be puzzled by benefit versus risk calculations, where the benefits are expressed in corporate profits and the risks expressed in cancer, leukemia and genetic diseases to themselves and their children."

On Sunday, May 11, 1969, the most expensive fire in American industrial history burned through building 776-777 at the AEC's Rocky Flats plant near Denver. That $45 million fire tells much, good and bad, about the AEC.

The fire alarm that rang at 2:27 p.m. had a familiar sound: Over 200 fires have occurred at Rocky Flats since 1953. The plant, run under contract by Dow Chemical Company, makes plutonium triggers for hydrogen bombs and missiles. An AEC press release brags: "Rocky Flats ranks first in AEC facilities for safety and holds the fourth best all-time mark in American industry. . . ."

Plutonium discs — 3″ x 1″ — burned in uncovered cans in Glovebox 134-24 and spread to cellulose laminate storage cabinets. The fire went uncontrolled for more than four hours. Some $20 million of plutonium burned, enough to build 77 Nagasaki-size atom bombs. AEC assured Coloradans: "No appreciable amount of plutonium escaped from the building and no off-site contamination resulted from the fire."

That was a lie.

Dr. Edward A. Martell is a West Point graduate, a former program director for the Armed Forces Special Weapons Project, and now a biophysicist at the National Center for Atmospheric Research in Boulder. Martell asked Dow for soil samples to check if plutonium had carried beyond the plant. Dow and AEC did nothing. Martell and an aide circled the plant and took 20 soil and seven water samples.

They found: Two to four miles east of the plant, plutonium "of Dow Rocky Flats origin"; that was "five to 300 times" normal readings of plutonium fallout from all nuclear testing. "The estimated total plutonium deposited in off-site areas which we have examined so far is in the range from curies to tens of curies. Depending on the amounts deposited nearer the plant and in other areas, the total could be much greater. Stack effluent data furnished by Dow Rocky Flats indicate that the total stack release during the past year . . . was less than one millicurie. The actual off-site accumulation of plutonium is at least one thousand times greater."

An AEC commissioner has called plutonium a "fiendishly toxic" substance. Its radiation destroys lung tissue and may cause cancer.

Winds at Rocky Flats sometimes reach 120 mph and kick up dust clouds. Almost half of Colorado's population lives within 25 miles of the plant. Denver is 16 miles downwind. So are the suburbs of Westminster, Broomfield Heights and Arvada. Broomfield draws its water from the Great Western Reservoir. Martell found the highest plutonium concentrations at the reservoir.

A 1965 fire exposed 400 Rocky Flats workers to high concentrations of plutonium in the air; 25 workers got up to 17 times the permissible level. In one 18-month period, there were 24 fires, explosions, plutonium spills and contamination incidents. Some 325 workers have been contaminated by the radiation since 1953. Fifty-six workers got cancer; 14 have died. Still, says Lloyd Joshel, general manager of Rocky Flats, "Radiation may very well be good for you."

Martell discovered one other plutonium source. Since 1958, Dow had stored machine cutting oil with high plutonium concentrations outside in 1,400 55-gallon drums. Some were buried. The drums corroded, the oil contaminated the soil and the winds blew plutonium dust toward Denver. In March, 1967, air-filter samples in Denver showed ten times more plutonium than anywhere else in the U.S. Last year, Dow covered the contaminated two-acre area with a four-inch slab of asphalt. Coloradans want Dow to dig it all up and truck it to an AEC burial site. Last spring, Dow began digging up some barrels. Not all the pits have been located. Company records are vague about the locations.

Such short-term disposal doesn't work with plutonium. It takes 24,360 years for only half of plutonium's radioactivity to decay.

In discussions last April 10, at the Joint Committee on Atomic Energy offices in Washington, Rep. Chet Holifield, chairman, met with members of the Rocky Flats union, AEC and others. Holifield complained about "these professors who have been scratching around in the sand trying to find something wrong within the radius of 50 miles" of Rocky Flats. He was worried about the drums of "hot waste": ". . . You know the problems this sort of thing can create from a public-relations standpoint. It can be magnified many times by these sensationalists." Capt. Edward Bauser of the Committee spoke up: "Mr. Chairman, I don't think we know right now whether it was an authorized burial or not. It was a very poorly supervised thing."

Holifield then replied: ". . . This would be a very serious thing if Dow was taking upon itself the burial of plutonium waste without going through established procedures. I would assume if this is low-level waste that there would be probably a prohibition against this convenient burial and that it should have been put in some permanent high level waste burial ground like we have at Hanford."

Capt. Bauser: "I don't know, but I doubt if that site is an authorized burial site for any level waste." Someone thought barrels had been buried outside the plant's fence. Holifield: "Then they had better build a new fence. . . ."

The AEC can't fence its mistakes in western Colorado. Vast uranium deposits were discovered by the early 1950s, and, by 1960, there were 1,000 uranium mines across the West. AEC published its first price schedule in 1948. But it wasn't until July, 1967 that any safety standard was enforced for uranium miners. Then it was too late.

By the end of 1966, 98 uranium miners had lung cancer. A report projects 1,150 cases by 1985.

About 90 million tons of waste ore, or tailings, piled up outside 35 uranium mills from Texas to Oregon. The tailings emit gamma radiation. Excessive exposure can result in leukemia. Radium from tailings decays into radon gas and its daughter products, which cause lung cancer.

Of 26 mills still operating in 1963, ten discharged liquid effluent into streams. In 1958-59, the Animas River below uranium mills in Durango, Colo., contained almost "300 percent" of the maximum daily intake for radium. Crops raised on farms irrigated by the Animas River had twice as much radium-226 as crops irrigated with clean water.

By 1960, the radium downstream was still 20 times higher. It didn't reach acceptable limits for 60 miles. Radium from tributaries of the Colorado mixed with sediment and moved downstream to Lake Mead. Studies of Lake Mead — with its tributaries, a major drinking- and irrigation-water source for seven states — showed radium concentrations in bottom sediments three times the normal level.

By 1966, the U.S. Public Health Service was checking tailings piles. El Paso Natural Gas Company's uranium tailings in Tuba City, Ariz., on Navajo land, showed radium radiation levels up to 1,000 times the average background. Gamma radiation was 12 times the level. El Paso came in and covered the pile. Tailings at the empty A-Z Minerals Corporation mill in Mexican Hat, Utah, in May 1968, also Navajo land, had radon-gas concentrations around the pile up to five times the maximum level.

Things were worse in Grand Junction, Colo. For 15 years, builders removed 300,-000 tons of tailings from the American Metal Climax mill's pile. The gray sand-like material was used to level ground for concrete slabs, as back fill around basements, and underneath the Main Street mall and in children's sandboxes.

The Colorado Health Department first warned residents in 1966 against radon-gas seepage. Some basement walls glowed. G.

A. Franz III, the state-health physicist in Grand Junction, started sampling the air in the homes. This fall, ten teams are checking all 6,500 buildings in town. So far, of 534 buildings checked, 95 have excessive gamma radiation or radon gas. One has 180 times the acceptable level.

Colorado and other states are doing an excellent job stabilizing the tailings piles by leveling and covering. AEC says of the mill tailings: "We aren't responsible for them."

Elsewhere, AEC's Nevada Test Site is riddled with fractures wide enough for a man to stand in. An internal AEC study recommended in 1968 that underground nuclear blasts above one megaton not be made at the Nevada site because of the chance of radioactive leakage through the fissures. A 1969 report by the U.S. Geological Survey said that all large tests in Nevada had been followed by earthquakes. One shot caused earthquakes out to 387 miles for 18 hours. Another created 10,000 earthquakes for nearly four months.

Operation Plowshare is AEC's idea of peaceful development of nuclear energy. There have been 14 ventings of radioactivity from underground tests since the 1963 Nuclear Test Ban Treaty. These ventings have blown 200 to one million curies into the air per explosion — equal to a Hiroshima bomb. These shots violate the National Environmental Policy Act. Project Schooner was a 1968 chain explosion of nuclear devices in an excavation test. It violated the Nuclear Test Ban Treaty. Radioactivity from Schooner was measured in Mexico and Canada.

In fact, Plowshare has found the treaty a bit of a damper. In 1969, Reps. Craig Hosmer and Chet Holifield sponsored an amendment to the Atomic Energy Act, to excuse Plowshare from Test Ban Treaty restrictions. The "Plowshare Amendment" still sits in the Joint Committee.

Project Rulison was a 40-kiloton Plowshare shot September 10, 1969, 8,431 feet below Grand Valley, Colo. It combined private enterprise with the AEC. Austral Oil Co., Inc. footed 90 percent of the bill. CER Geonuclear Corp. advised. Rulison was a test to see how much gas can be freed from the Mesa Verde rock. If Rulison succeeds, it may lead to a series of 100 kiloton shots, two a year, for perhaps ten years. Rulison was based on the argument that we are short on natural gas. Yet we export 50,000 million cubic feet of it a year to Japan alone.

Coloradans brought four lawsuits against AEC over Rulison; AEC was forced to make public daily radioactivity readings from the flaring (burning off of gas). Dr. John Emerson of the Colorado State Health Department says, "We may have picked up radioactivity two-three times the background for tritium at the site. . . . We don't expect to find any increases elsewhere. But, of course, we haven't reached the high level of flaring yet." That level comes this winter.

Strontium-90, iodine-131, krypton-85 and tritium might enter water and plants. David Evans, a geologist at Colorado School of Mines worries about radioactivity getting into the groundwater, flowing into the Colorado River and the Southwest.

Ruth Kiesler, mayor of Grand Valley, is also uneasy: "I've always felt pretty secure by what the AEC said about safeguards. . . . Now, I'm not sure. They seemed more concerned about the dollars and cents than people."

Dollars play a big role in nuclear reactors. AEC licenses nuclear reactors. (Interestingly, there are no physicians, biologists or geneticists on AEC's Safety and Licensing Boards.)

Nuclear power plants provide only 1.2 percent of the country's total electric power. But the demand for electricity is doubling every ten years. AEC estimates that nuclear power plants will furnish 25 percent in ten years, almost 60 percent by 2000.

To meet this demand, AEC has spent $2.3 billion to make nuclear power plants safe, profitable and competitive. In fact, nuclear reactors discharge low-level radioactive gas and liquids into the air and water. Highly radioactive wastes must be shipped for reprocessing or permanent burial. David E. Lilienthal, former AEC chairman, says ". . . You cannot have an atomic power plant unless you produce large quantities of radiation."

A 1957 AEC study, WASH-740, shows what would happen to a hypothetical reactor of 100-200 megawatts, near a large body of water and about 30 miles from a major city of about 1,000,000 if it became super-critical and all safety devices failed.

WASH-740 predicted an explosion that would kill 3,400 people up to 15 miles away, injure 43,000 up to 45 miles, contaminate up to 150,000 square miles — about the size of California — and damage property to $7 billion. Such a catastrophe, says AEC, is unlikely.

But plants of 1,000 megawatts — five times the WASH-740 plant — are planned for Illinois, Michigan, California, Alabama, New Jersey and Pennsylvania. By 1990, most nuclear power plants will be 1,000-4,000 megawatts, a few up to 10,000.

How safe will these plants be?

In 1966, there were 42 accidents at nuclear plants around the world, 37 in the U.S. Six U.S. plants had more than one accident. These included fuel-rod leaks, control-rod failures, explosions in beam tubes, fission gas release, fuel meltdown and plugged cores.

On October 10, 1957, the Number One Pile (reactor) at the Windscale Works in England malfunctioned, spewing radioactivity and contaminating milk and vegetables over a 400-square-mile area. *All* the reactor's safety features failed.

In 1961, an accident at the SL-1 reactor in Idaho killed three workers.

In 1966, the Enrico Fermi plant, within 20 miles of Detroit, nearly had a WASH-740 runaway. A piece of metal blocked the liquid-sodium coolant, causing fuel to heat up dangerously. Fermi was broken down for four years.

Sloppiness, error and surprises abound. At the Big Rock Point Nuclear Plant, a reactor near Charlevoix, Mich., control rods stuck in position, studs failed or cracked, screws jostled out of place and into machinery, a valve malfunctioned, foreign material lodged in critical moving parts, welds cracked at 16 points. At Humboldt Bay in California, fuel tubes cracked because cheaper stainless steel had been used instead of a more reliable alloy. Workers repaired the cracks, and the plant broke down again. AEC files show error elsewhere: 3,844 pounds of uranium hexafluoride lost owing to a mistake in opening a cylinder; a $220,000 fire in a reactor because of accidental tripping of valves by electricians.

In Illinois, the Advanced TRIGA Reactor was humming along at 1.5 million watts last spring. Someone flushed a toilet, which dropped the main water pressure, which stopped a pump that stopped another pump, which triggered a safety device, which shut down the reactor.

"Once a bright hope, shared by all mankind, including myself," Lilienthal said, "the vast proliferation of atomic power plants has become one of the ugliest clouds overhanging America."

Nuclear reactors require enormous amounts of cooling water. A 1,000 megawatt nuclear plant needs 850,000 gallons of cool water a minute. In one day, 1.2 billion gallons will be sucked in and spewed out 10-30 degrees hotter. By 2000, power plants will cool themselves with about one-third of the daily U.S. freshwater runoff. In low-water periods it will be 100 percent. The hot water, called "thermal enrichment" by AEC friends, decreases dissolved oxygen, increases the toxicity of pollutants, cuts off sunlight to water plants, spurs the growth of noxious blue-green algae, changes the metabolic rates, behavior, reproductive cycles, defense mechanisms and eating habits of fish and other organisms.

Sixteen nuclear plants are operating or ordered for the shores of the Great Lakes. Lake Michigan gets ten. This fall, the Federal Water Quality Administration made a decisive attack on thermal pollution: It wants "no significant discharge" into Lake Michigan. The study of Lake Michigan said heat addition was cumulative and would lead to the death of all fish and plant life within 30 years.

There are choices. Power plants could use cooling towers, ponds or canals instead of lakes and rivers.

Nuclear plants may run out of fuel. Dr. Dean E. Abrahamson, in a pamphlet *The Environmental Cost of Electric Power,* says: "Because the reserves of natural uranium in commercially recoverable deposits are extremely limited, today's reactors cannot operate for more than a very few decades without exhausting the total world reserves of uranium-235. . . ." Uranium demands will be about one million tons in 2000. Counting all uranium reserves and AEC estimates of undiscovered resources, there will be just 1,020,000 tons available that year. Then it's gone.

AEC, which has grabbed 84 percent of the Federal energy-research dollar for the past 20 years, is spending more than $2 billion on fast-breeder reactors that could extend the nuclear supply. Little research is being done on solar power, tidal energy, geothermal power, magneto-hydrodynamics (MHD), fuel-cell generation, gas turbines, even garbage incineration for power. The areas of most promise, fuel cells, solar power, MHD, will get just $300,000 for research this year.

All nuclear plants and nuclear-weapons making produce waste. Fuel assemblies must be removed from reactors and shipped to reprocessing plants where contaminants are separated from the salvageable fuel. Liquid residue is highly radioactive, and must be stored until safe.

Some low-level waste is diluted and discharged into the environment. This waste, says an AEC pamphlet, can "have no more than about 1,000 times the concentrations considered safe for direct release." Some 650,000 cubic feet of low-level junk was buried at AEC-licensed plants in 1969. There will be one million cubic feet this year, three by 1980.

High-level waste contains hundreds to thousands of curies per gallon from the chemical processing of nuclear fuels. This waste, says AEC, poses "the most severe potential hazard. . . ." AEC stored 100,000 gallons this year. By 1980, commercial nuclear reactors will produce some 3.5 million gallons of high-level waste a year. AEC already has 80 million gallons of high-level waste stored in 194 underground tanks. It may boil for ten centuries.

By 1963, AEC had reported 47 accidents in waste shipments by public transport: 18 spills; 15 "severe impact accidents." Eleven storage tanks at the Hanford Atomic Products Operation have leaked "some liquid into the dry soil under the tanks." Only 180 feet separates the tanks from underground water. Hanford also dumps diluted waste into the Columbia River, where river plankton now average 2,000 times the radioactivity in the water; fish, 15,000; ducks feeding in the river, 40,000 times; young swallows fed on river insects, 500,000 times. Four ducks recovered by AEC at Hanford had radioactive phosphorus-32.

A report by the National Academy of Sciences, which AEC requested and sat on for four years, advises against dumping high-level wastes at its Savannah River Plant (SRP). Still, AEC has gone ahead with $1.3 million for a 2,000 foot shaft into the bedrock below the plant.

The NAS report warned AEC about escape of radioactivity from the bedrock and recommended that the bedrock studies be stopped. "At the same time," it said, "the entire Committee urges against any thought of permanent storage or disposal of high-level wastes above or in any of the fresh-water aquifers at the SRP site. . . . Apparently the only safe disposal for high-level wastes should be an off-site disposal, presumably involving solidification, before transportation."

Also: "None of the major sites at which radioactive wastes are being stored or disposed of is geologically suited for safe disposal of any manner of radioactive wastes other than . . . very low-level liquids. . . ."

AEC is trying to get permission to bury these wastes in a Lyons, Kan., salt mine. The Kansas Geological Survey has refused to endorse the AEC plans until completing a two-year study on the area's geological safety.

And the NAS committee? "AEC's concerns over the report were not resolved before the decision to dissolve the committee and replace it with one having a broader spectrum of scientific discipline." Like obedience.

If the AEC is lax in handling radioactive wastes, what will be the record of commercial firms?

Nuclear Fuel Services, Inc., of West Valley, N.Y., is the only private company now reprocessing irradiated nuclear-reactor fuel. It's on a 3,000-acre, state-owned site 30 miles from Buffalo. Most nuclear reactors in the Northeast ship to NFS. Every 404 days, for example, the Yankee Atomic Power Reactor in Rowe, Mass., puts 8,000 to 10,000 highly radioactive 12-foot fuel rods on a special flatcar with its own cooling system. The Boston & Maine Railroad hauls it to NFS. But B & M has its difficulties. In April, 1969, there were three accidents in a week on the line.

NFS dissolves the reactor rods in a solution and processes this nuclear soup — to reclaim the fuel — through chemicals. There's waste. "The cheapest thing to do," says the AEC, "is pour it down the nearest stream." That's Buttermilk Creek.

In 1968, scientists from Cornell went, AEC reports, "under the fence." They got samples from the holding ponds and Buttermilk Creek with 36,000 to 100,000 times the maximum permissible radioactivity.

AEC warned NFS in a letter May 31, 1968: ". . . release from the NFS plant should be significantly reduced. . . ." NFS, on July 9, 1969, applied to AEC for permission to drill a 6,000-foot well for discharge of radioactive wastes. On May 27, 1970, AEC responded by urging that NFS put in more chemical cleaning processes. NFS still has its proposals to make.

The New York State Bureau of Nuclear Engineering, formerly the Radiological Bureau, has checked NFS: "Our surveillance program has detected a reconcentration of radionuclides, such as strontium-90 and cesium-137 . . . in fish and wildlife around the facility."

There are 389 dairy herds within ten miles of NFS. About 240 square miles of the nearby land is used as a source of public-water supply. One public system is within five miles, six more within ten. The New York State Public Health Department's *Radioactivity Bulletin* lists water radiation levels near NFS at ten times the AEC limit.

How serious are all these wastes? Dr. L. P. Hatch of the Brookhaven National Laboratory says: "If we were to go on for fifty years in the atomic power industry, and find that we had reached an impasse, that we had been doing the wrong thing with wastes and we would like to reconsider the disposal methods, it would be entirely too late, because the problem would exist and nothing could be done to change that fact for the next six hundred or a thousand years."

Now we must all ask: Should ecologists be added to safety and licensing boards? Should underground weapons testing continue? Should any further blasts for gas be made? Is the state of the art advanced enough so that under highest possible safety standards, utilities can go ahead with nuclear power?

EDITOR'S COMMENTS

The harmful effects of radiation represent one of the most well-worked areas of biological research. Most researchers in this field are convinced that there is no such thing as a safe dose of radiation. It is a foregone conclusion that increasing doses of radiation are responsible for increased rates of birth defects and cancer in persons exposed to sources of ionizing radiation. During the past 70 years, the maximum allowable dose of radiation for persons working in close proximity to a radiation source has been reduced by 99.5 percent. Some investigators feel that it should still be reduced by another 90 percent.

A great deal of radioactive wastes has been released into the environment since 1945. Most of these materials have originated with the explosion of nuclear weapons. These materials have increased the radiation exposure of every living person. Many thousands of deaths have occurred as a result of cancer triggered by this exposure; however, just as with many other environmental poisons, it is impossible to actually link a specific case of cancer with a source of radiation.

Hopefully, man is nearing completion of nuclear weapon testing. Unless nuclear war occurs, the future of most environmental radiation will be primarily from industrial sources. Of these sources, nuclear power generating plants now represent a possible source of much environmental radiation. The use of nuclear power does not stop with industry — at least one nuclear powered warship has already been lost at sea. The reactors in sunken ships will ultimately corrode and the radioactive materials contained therein will be released.

There is little doubt that radiation is hazardous; however, it should be respected rather than feared. In both medical therapy and diagnosis it is an indispensable tool. Radiation treatment can arrest the growth of some forms of cancer and X-rays have long been a source of valuable diagnostic data. However, even in medicine radiation may be used indiscriminately. There are many instances where X-rays are taken when there may be no actual reasons for this service. This is especially true in the dental profession where whole-mouth X-rays may be routinely performed in searching for cavities. This is a highly undesirable practice. Pregnant women certainly should avoid abdominal X-rays and would usually be well advised to consult with another doctor when such a procedure is recommended.

Radioactive materials released into the environment do not necessarily become randomly distributed throughout the air, water, and soil. Particles in the air ultimately move into the soil and water where many radioactive isotopes become concentrated in food chains. Animals in higher trophic levels may concentrate these materials to the point of continuously receiving quite high doses of ionizing radiation. Oysters have been shown to concentrate an isotope of zinc to the extent that the isotope is 250,000 times as abundant in the oyster's tissues as in the surrounding water. The same type of situation exists for many aquatic and terrestrial life forms — including man.

Radioactive materials undergo progressive conversion to nonradioactive substances. Different isotopes require various amounts of time for this conversion to be accomplished. One isotope of iodine is characterized by requiring only eight days (half-life) for one-half of a given quantity of the isotope to be converted to a stable, harmless form.

Still another isotope of iodine requires 17,000,000 years for such a transformation. It is obvious that the environmental consequences associated with release of these two isotopes are quite different; in the case of the former, most of the radiation is gone in a matter of weeks or months; in the case of the latter, most of the radiation will probably outlive the civilization of man.

Different isotopes also emit different types of radiation. Some forms of radiation can be shielded by a sheet of paper. Some forms can penetrate concrete, steel, or lead. Some isotopes are not concentrated in living organisms. The half-life, type of radiation emitted, and the affinity for biological tissues are all characteristics which deserve careful consideration when dealing with processes which might release radioactive substances into the environment.

If nuclear power plants did not routinely release radioactive isotopes into the air and water, if they were absolutely safe in terms of accidents which could release these materials, if they did not produce large quantities of useless radioactive wastes, and if they did not produce large amounts of heat, then the nuclear power plant could be viewed as a very real boon to our power-hungry technological society. However, all these characteristics are not presently realized by the nuclear power industry. A much better technology is needed to prevent the routine release of radioactive materials. The dry tower method of releasing heat (discussed in a previous selection) can satisfactorily dispose of the waste heat generated by such a facility. A new type of breeder-reactor may reduce the total volume of nuclear wastes produced by such a power plant. However, it may be that safety mechanisms which could prevent all forms of nuclear mishap at such a facility are far in the future.

The complex Emergency Core Cooling System developed under the supervision of the Atomic Energy Commission, will supposedly prevent a major accident in the event that the normal coolant for the reactor is accidentally lost. Recent feasibility studies and tests indicate that this emergency system will not be as reliable as it was once envisioned to be. A great many people today think that nuclear power plants are hazardous and, indeed, it is obvious that such fears are well founded. It is unfortunate that our demand for electrical power is such that our society must push for such rapid development in a technologically complex and potentially hazardous area. The best we can hope for today is a continuously successful attempt to develop fail-safe nuclear power systems. Such attempts would be less than full scale if it were not for the pressures being applied by citizens and environmental organizations.

There are also other less well-known disadvantages of present nuclear power plants. (1) Those plants in operation today actually convert less than one percent of the potential energy in uranium to electricity. This energy conversion system is very inefficient and our known rich reserves of uranium will be gone in 10 to 20 years. (2) Taxpayers must subsidize nuclear energy facilities. A very real form of this subsidization is seen in the limits of liability payable to individuals for nuclear accidents. Taxpayers must be self-insured for most of the amount. Private insurance companies refuse to write anything like the necessary amount of liability insurance on such facilities. (3) The amount of cooling water required by some nuclear power plants is disconcerting. (4) The possible ecological consequences of emptying this heated water into natural lakes and streams has already been discussed. (5) Nuclear

power plants could be easily sabotaged by enemy action, resulting in major releases of radioactive materials.

The most pressing problem associated with nuclear power plants is undoubtedly the disposal of wastes. Mr. Shepherd thoroughly discussed the hazards associated with the transport and storage of such materials. It is mind-boggling to consider the enormity of this problem when one takes into account the long life of many of these waste substances. The Atomic Energy Commission recently planned to bury much of these waste materials in abandoned salt mines in Kansas. The wastes would be pumped into vaults surrounded by salt and would presumably be safely stored against environmental release and possible human exposure. The Governor, Attorney General, and the State Geological Survey of Kansas do not agree with the Atomic Energy Commission. It has become obvious that Kansans do not want this facility — indeed, it would be surprising to find a community of informed citizens anywhere who would consent to establishing such a facility nearby. The only satisfactory method of radioactive waste disposal would involve shipping wastes to the sun, something we are not equipped to do at this time.

A possible way out of the present nuclear power dilemma lies in the development of electric power generating plants which operate on thermonuclear fusion — a process similar to the release of energy going on in stars. Nuclear fusion would release less radioactive substances and would produce little radioactive waste. Nuclear fusion very possibly will save the day for electrical power.

JOHN M. MECKLIN

It's Time to Turn Down All That Noise

The late John M. Mecklin was an Associate Editor of *Fortune* magazine.

In the Bronx borough of New York City one evening last spring, four boys were at play, shouting and racing in and out of an apartment building. Suddenly, from a second-floor window, came the crack of a pistol. One of the boys sprawled dead on the pavement. The victim happened to be Roy Innis Jr., thirteen, son of a prominent Negro leader, but there was no political implication in the tragedy. The killer, also a Negro, confessed to police that he was a nightworker who had lost control of himself because the noise from the boys prevented him from sleeping.

The incident was an extreme but valid example of a grim, and worsening, human problem. In communities all over the world, the daily harassment of needless noise provokes unknown millions to the verge of violence or emotional breakdown. There is growing evidence that it contributes to such physical ailments as heart trouble. Noise has become a scourge of our land, a form of environmental pollution no less dangerous and degrading than the poisons we dump into our air and water; it is one of the main causes of the exodus from our cities.

In many ways, noise is the most difficult form of pollution to combat. It has been recognized only recently as a major evil. It works so subtly on the human mind that it has gained a form of acceptance. Shouting over the din of an air compressor in New York recently, a newsman asked a construction foreman what he thought about the noise problem. "What are you," the foreman shouted back, "some kind of a Communist?"

Noise pollution is hardly a new evil. The word itself derives from the same Latin root as nausea. Noise bothered Julius Caesar so much that he banned chariot driving at night. In 1851, Arthur Schopenhauer wrote about the "disgraceful . . . truly infernal" cracking of whips in German streets. In a study published in October, 1955, *Fortune* reported "a rising tide of noise [in] U.S. streets, factories, homes, and skies" and asserted that Americans "have decided that noise should be abated." The optimism was unwarranted. Today the level of everyday noise to which the average urban American is exposed is more than *twice* what it was in 1955; and the cacophony continues to mount: the crash of jackhammers, whirring

Reprinted by permission of the publisher from *Fortune*. October 1969:130-133, 188, 190, 195. Copyright © 1969 by *Fortune*.

air conditioners, snarling lawn mowers, family arguments penetrating the paper-thin walls of homes and apartment houses, and the blast of traffic on freeways. Everyday noise is assaulting American ears at an intensity approaching the level of permanent hearing damage, if indeed the danger point has not already been passed.

A Zone of "Unacceptable Annoyance"

As often happens with a slowly encroaching evil, it has taken a major outrage to stir up public concern. This is being provided spectacularly by the jet aircraft now bombarding some 20 million Americans every few minutes with a thunderous roar around our major airports. In the area of New York's John F. Kennedy airport alone about one million people (including the students in about ninety schools) live within a zone of "unacceptable annoyance," as an official of the Federal Aviation Administration describes it. At Shea Stadium baseball games, the racket regularly drowns out not only the national anthem but also the players calling for fly balls. In Washington, jet noise so disrupted a ceremony attended by President Johnson at the Lincoln Memorial in 1967 that he ordered an aide to call the airport and stop it. In Los Angeles, concerts at the Hollywood Bowl have become virtually inaudible, and residents of nearby Inglewood have filed lawsuits that could total as much as $3 billion against the city.

The federal government is beginning belatedly to recognize that it has a problem — an awakening that may be partly due to the fact that approach paths to Washington National Airport pass directly over the homes of numerous top government officials. Congress last year voted to give the Federal Aviation Administration authority for the first time to fix aircraft noise limits, and the agency's initial order is expected momentarily. Though the effort may result in higher fares for air travelers, there is reason to

hope that jet noise may be rolled back almost to the level of propeller planes within a few years.

But the same cannot be said for noise pollution in general. With a few exceptions, the steps taken so far have been palliatives. Memphis, for example, has enforced a ban on automobile horn blowing (instigated by an angry newspaper editor) since the 1930s. In New York in 1948 a landmark court decision upheld for the first time an award of compensation to an industrial worker who had suffered gradual hearing loss without losing work time. This type of claim is now recognized in some thirty states. Studies indicate, however, that only a small percentage of workers with legitimate claims have gone to court.

In Washington, at least a dozen federal agencies have become involved in the noise problem, and there has been one action of significance. This was the promulgation of a series of new regulations last spring under the Walsh-Healey Public Contracts Act of 1938, which limit industrial noise levels in most plants doing business with the government. The new regulations were initiated by the Johnson Administration, however, and were watered down by the Nixon Administration. Elsewhere a handful of unofficial organizations are agitating for noise abatement, notably in New York City.

Multitudes of special interests are arrayed against anti-noise measures whenever they are contemplated. When a state law was proposed to ban playing transistor radios in public vehicles, Buffalo radio-TV station WGR editorialized against such "inanities." Of about 125 industry representatives who testified last winter at Labor Department hearings leading to the new industrial noise standards, more than 90 percent were opposed to regulation. Sample argument: "It is unrealistic and literally impossible to comply with." The cause of noise abatement wasn't helped any when the *Journal of the American Medical Association* argued in an editorial earlier this year that "some noise must be tolerated as an unavoidable concomitant of the blessings of civilization."

Quiet Doesn't Cost Much

To permit this kind of thinking to prevail is the true inanity. Virtually all man-made noise, whatever its source, can be suppressed. While some major problems, such as thin apartment walls and the roar of New York City's subway, would cost large sums of money to correct, many of the most irritating noises could be reduced at negligible cost. The screech of truck tires on pavement, for example, can be reduced at no extra cost or efficiency loss by redesigning the tread, and a quiet home lawn mower costs only about $15 more than the usual ear-jarring model. Some other examples of added costs: a garbage truck $2,400 (on top of an original cost of $15,600), a small air compressor $500 ($5,300), and on most machinery an additional 5 percent atop the original cost. In some cases there is also a relatively small cost in reduced efficiency. Mass production of silenced equipment would lower costs still more. The expense becomes even less formidable when measured against the savings from noise suppression. The World Health Organization estimates that industrial noise alone costs the U.S. today more than $4 billion annually — in accidents, absenteeism, inefficiency, and compensation claims. The human costs in sleepless nights, family squabbles, and mental illness are beyond measure, but they surely must be enormous.

In the cases of air and water pollution, one of the main obstacles to corrective action is the large governmental outlay required — e.g., for nonpolluting municipal incinerators and sewage-treatment plants. But society's noise-makers are predominantly privately owned machines, many of which wear out and must be replaced within a few years anyway. Moreover, noise is not a uniquely big-city problem of little interest to suburban or rural taxpayers who are not exposed to it. Modern technology, its root cause, is everywhere, from grinding dishwashing machines in farm kitchens to outlying airports and thundering throughways that can be heard for miles.

The first and perhaps the most important course of action is to generate all possible public pressure on governments. It is no coincidence that one of the world's most effective anti-noise programs emerged in West Germany after the leading political parties there began including it in their election platforms. Once it becomes clear to Americans that noise is not an inescapable fact of life, that something *can* be done about it, and at manageable cost, the support for real action could be overwhelming. Says Judge Theodore Kupferman, a former Congressman from Manhattan and long-time anti-noise crusader: "In addition to the merits of the anti-noise cause, I don't see why more politicians don't take up the cudgel. Who's going to be in favor of noise?"

The most effective approach to governmental action probably lies in *federal* regulation. The legal authority already exists in the laws providing federal regulation of interstate commerce, health protection, and such specific functions as federal guarantees of housing loans, and there is a precedent for federal regulation of noise in the 1965 legislation empowering the Department of Health, Education, and Welfare to set limits on air pollutants emitted by motor vehicles. At the same time, state and local governmental action against noise, as well as support from enlightened businessmen, could go a long way toward reducing the problem, and perhaps in setting a trend — as a few localities have already demonstrated.

No Lids to Close

Noise — commonly defined as "unwanted sound" — works on humans in two ways.

One, of course, is to cause deafness through deterioration of the microscopic hair cells that transmit sound from the ear to the brain. A single very loud blast, as from a cannon, can destroy the cells by the thousands and they never recover. (The Veterans Administration is spending about $8 million a year on the claims of some 5,000 servicemen whose hearing has been damaged by gunfire in training or combat.) Constant exposure to noises commonplace in our society can cause slower deterioration as the hair cells gradually rupture. There is a glimpse of the remarkable "redundancy" of the human body — in this case in spare hair cells — in the fact that all of us in modern communities have lost a substantial portion of our hearing mechanism without ever missing it. An experiment conducted by Dr. Samuel Rosen, a leading Manhattan otologist, has shown that aborigines living in the stillness of isolated African villages can easily hear each other talking in low conversational tones at distances as great as 100 yards, and that their hearing acuity diminishes little with age.

The second effect of noise upon humans is psychological and intensely personal. It relates not only to a lifetime of experience, but also to mood. Thus the scream of a siren at night may bring fright and anger to a thousand neighbors, but it means hope to a desperate accident victim. The human ear, unlike the eye, has no lids and cannot be turned off, not even in sleep. Nature's initial purpose in providing animals with hearing presumably was to alert them to enemies, with its function in communication coming at a later stage. Thus the instinctive human reaction to noise, especially unexpected noise, is fear and an impulse to flee. Children play games with this "startle effect," as psychologists call it. But to older people, just home from a hard day's work, for example, a sudden noise like the slam of a door or an automobile backfire or even the bell of an ice-cream vendor often can tip

the balance of self-control and lead to an emotional eruption. Studies of sleep patterns have shown that people never "get used" to noise; on the contrary, the annoyance, and loss of sleep, worsen as the interruptions persist. This is the main reason why there is, rightly, such strong opposition to the use, over populated areas, of supersonic airliners whose sonic booms would cause psychic havoc among millions.

Hypertension and Hallucinations

Clinical evidence has established conclusively that excessive exposure to noise constricts the arteries, increases the heartbeat, and dilates the pupils of the eye. Sigmund Freud wrote that noise could create an anxiety neurosis "undoubtedly explicable on the basis of the close inborn connection between auditory impressions and fright." One recent French study goes so far as to suggest that noise is the cause of 70 percent of the neurosis in the Paris area, compared with only 50 percent four years ago, and it blames noise for three recent premeditated murders. John M. Handley, a New York authority on industrial acoustics, recently wrote that "symptoms of hypertension, vertigo, hallucination, paranoia and, on occasion, suicidal and homicidal impulses, have been blamed on excessive noise . . . 'Noise pollution' may be one of the reasons why the incidence of heart disease and mental illness is so high in the United States." Other authorities have suggested that noise may be related to stomach ulcers, allergies, enuresis (involuntary urination), spinal meningitis, excessive cholesterol in the arteries, indigestion, loss of equilibrium, and impaired vision.

Tests of the effects of noise upon animals have produced dramatic results. Prolonged exposure has made rats lose their fertility, turn homosexual, and eat their young. If the noise is continued still longer, it eventually kills them through heart failure. There is clearly a limit to the amount of noise that any animal, including humans, can tolerate. But at what point does the noise in our daily lives begin to be dangerous? Dr. Vern O. Knudsen, former chancellor of the University of California at Los Angeles and a leading authority on noise pollution, believes we have already reached it. "Noise, like smog," he says, "is a slow agent of death."

Death by Decibels

There is no single universally accepted criterion of what constitutes excessive noise. The most common noise yardstick is the decibel (db) scale, which is an expression of the sound pressure that moves the ear. The scale begins at zero db, which is the weakest sound that can be picked up by the healthy ear. Thereafter, because of physical laws, the scale increases as the square of the change. Thus so soft a sound as human breathing is about ten times greater than zero db, while an artillery blast is one thousand trillion (1,000,000,000,000,000) times greater. To simplify things, the scale is in logarithmic form so that ten times the minimum is 1 db and one thousand trillion times the minimum is 150 db. The db scale does not, however, take account of the tones in the sound being registered — i.e., the frequencies of the sound waves being propagated. Scientists' attempts over the years to work out techniques to weight such factors for accurate registration of the ways that noise sounds to humans have led to a plethora of measuring scales.

There is agreement that high-pitched tones are more annoying and thus should be given more weight than low tones, but there the agreement ends. The most common weighting system is the "A" scale, written dbA, which gives less weight to low tones and thus more nearly matches the effect of sound on people. Beyond that the variations are myriad. For example: dbC ("C" scale), PNdb ("perceived noise"), EPNdb ("effective perceived noise"), SIL ("speech interference level"), and the "sone" and "phon" scales.

Some sample noise readings in the dbA scale at distances at which people are commonly exposed:

Rustling leaves	20 dbA
Window air conditioner	55
Conversational speech	60
(Beginning of hearing damage	
if prolonged	85)
Heavy city traffic	90
Home lawn mower	98
150-cubic-foot air compressor	100
Jet airliner (500 feet overhead)	115
(Human pain threshold	120)

In the case of the laboratory rats mentioned earlier, death occurred after prolonged exposure at 150 dbA, or the equivalent of continuous artillery fire at close range. The take-off blast of the Saturn V moon rocket, measured at the launching pad, is about 180 dbA.

Very roughly, the noise level in busy sections of American communities is doubling every ten years. It has reached the point today where it is often greater than industrial noise levels. The main cause of the trend is the constant growth of the use of power. To cite one of the main new offenders, air conditioners are now in use in some 32 million homes. The giant machines on the top of large buildings often spew out more than 100 dbA and bother people for blocks around. No fewer than 89 million cars (up to 70 dbA) and about 18 million trucks and buses (up to 95 dbA) are cluttering our roads and streets. Millions of them are operating with defective mufflers, which always wear out faster than the vehicle. The beauty of our winters has been defiled by the din of some 700,000 snowmobiles, and our buses, trains, parks, and streets by millions of transistor radios. The racket in a modern American kitchen rises as high as 90 dbA midst an ever expanding profusion of dishwashers, mixers, grinders, exhaust fans, disposers, and the like. The National Institute of Mental Health is considering a proposal to wire up a typical housewife with telemetry like a spacecraft to try to study the effects of the pandemonium on her nervous system.

On top of all that, architects, engineers, and contractors in the $90-billion U.S. construction industry behave, says one acoustical expert, "as though they were born without ears." Thousands of new apartment buildings and homes are being thrown together like cardboard dollhouses, creating multi-million-dollar "noise slums," as one occupant puts it. Privacy, so badly needed by city dwellers, vanishes among the sounds of flushing toilets, electric razors, and family intimacies penetrating the walls, inhibiting conversation, and worsening tensions. Air-conditioning, heating, and ventilation ducts are made smaller and smaller to save space and weight, with the result that machinery must be faster, and therefore noisier, to move the same amount of air. Outside, meanwhile, some three million construction workers all over the U.S. create daily bedlam with jackhammers, air compressors, earthmoving equipment, riveters, and similar mechanical monsters.

Americans often seem to react to noise as if it were a narcotic, as though nature were compelling us to accept it, even savor it, rather than engage in a hopeless struggle. Researchers have found, for example, that workers in noisy jobs often refuse to wear ear plugs because they are proud of their ability to "take it." In truth, this kind of tough-guy syndrome seems to be a subconscious device for sublimating discomfort. Psychologists think a similiar narcotic effect may help explain why teen-agers sit for hours in rock joints, overwhelmed by "music" (as high as 130 dbA) that blots out all else in the world and, like marijuana, enables them to escape temporarily from reality.

Muffling the Jumbo Jets

The first real test of the nation's capability to roll back the engulfing tide of noise will be the FAA regulations on aircraft. At this writing, the FAA is about to announce its plans. The agency reportedly will begin by fixing noise limits on the new generation of planes soon to go into service—such as the huge 325-passenger Boeing 747 due to begin operating early next year. The ruling probably will stipulate that such planes must generate the equivalent of no more than about 95 dbA at a point about four miles beyond the start of the take-off roll; today's big planes register as much as 105 dbA. An improvement of that magnitude is already being built into the 747's by Boeing engineers.

To supplement the new regulations, the National Aeronautics and Space Administration has launched a $50-million program to subsidize development of still another generation of even quieter engines through design and engineering innovations to slow engine fan-blade tips below supersonic speeds and thereby lessen the noise-making air turbulence. The agency hopes this will permit it a few years hence to begin further reducing the limit for new planes, perhaps to the equivalent of heavy city-traffic noise.

A third move, tentatively expected early in 1970, will apply noise limits to the 2,000 airliners now in service on the nation's airways. The problem is much tougher in this case and no decisions have yet been reached. There is a good chance, however, that there will be a dramatic program, to cost about $2 billion, to "retrofit" the whole airline fleet with engine silencers. How such a program would be financed remains to be worked out, but it seems likely that the government would require passengers to share in the added costs; a general fare increase of 5 percent has been suggested. A "retrofit" program might be accompanied by a change in flying procedures. Instead of a gradual three-degree approach to airports, aircraft would make a two-segment approach, first at six degrees, then at three degrees for the final segment. That would permit them to stay longer at higher, and thus quieter, altitudes than is possible today. Such changes in procedure would also involve design changes in the aircraft.

A Nixon Compromise

In the area of general noise pollution other than aircraft, the one step that Washington has taken — new regulations under the Walsh-Healey Act — has been a disappointment to anti-noise advocates. The regulations benefit some 27 million workers in about 70,000 plants, but exclude millions of others in plants with fewer than twenty workers and less than $10,000 in government contracts, thus omitting small businesses where abuses are no less deplorable. The Johnson Administration, which initiated the action, originally proposed to fix a noise limit of 85 dbA, with higher levels permitted for short periods. The proposal was so hotly opposed, however, especially by high-noise industries like textiles, that the Nixon Administration compromised on a maximum of 90 dbA — or 5 dbA more than the experts regard as safe. Even at 90 dbA, however, the new regulations will have a notable, indeed historic, impact if they are enforced. At least half of American industry today permits noise levels above 90 dbA. The American Petroleum Institute estimates the cost of compliance to the oil industry alone at $40 million to $50 million to modify its existing equipment.

Meanwhile, the federal government is acquiring a great deal of valuable expertise in studies ranging from apartment-house noise insulation to a computerized analysis of transportation noise. By far the most significant of the studies is an exhaustive document called "Noise — Sound Without Value," published last fall by a special ten-agency committee. The report asserted:

"Increasing severity of the noise problem in our environment has reached a level of national importance and public concern." With notable political courage, it added that the solution "frequently will require actions that transcend political boundaries within the nation," i.e., it should not be left to the states. Not long afterward, the Johnson Administration, which had promoted the study, went out of business.

Which points directly to a central unknown today: what will the Nixon Administration do about noise? The top authority is the newly created Environmental Quality Council, headed by Nixon himself, which to date has made no decisions on noise. There is fear among anti-noise advocates that Nixon's strong feelings about state responsibilities may lead him to stay out of noise control except perhaps for voluntary — and therefore ineffective — guidelines. Such concern is one reason why the Senate recently passed a bill proposed by Washington's Democratic Senator Henry Jackson to create a prestigious, independent council to recommend policy on all forms of environmental control, including noise. A similar bill is pending in the House.

If the Administration should leave non-aircraft noise pollution to the states, the outlook could be gloomy; few states have taken actions of any consequence. California has a law limiting the vehicle noise on freeways to 88 dbA, and a noise abatement commission will soon begin hearings aimed at producing recommendations by 1971. The law is so loosely enforced, however, that a Los Angeles police official confessed he did not know it existed. In New York State, indignant citizens along the roaring New England Thruway, where some 10,000 trucks create a steady din around the clock, persuaded the state legislature to fix a limit of 88 dbA on each vehicle. There have been only sixty-three arrests since 1965 — and the maximum fine is only $10 anyway. Connecticut also plans to introduce a noise-abatement program soon.

In the long-suffering core cities, where noise works its greatest evil, the record is spotty. Several cities have anti-noise ordinances, e.g., Dayton, Dallas, Chicago, and Minneapolis. In San Francisco the Bay Area Rapid Transit System now under construction is spending $1,250,000 (only one tenth of 1 percent of the total cost) on noise suppression; it is expected to be the quietest subway in the country — 85 dbA on the platforms versus New York's numbing average of 102 dbA. Milwaukee attempted to reduce truck noise by a city ordinance, only to have it overturned by the courts on grounds that it invaded state jurisdiction; the effort was laughed into obscurity anyway when a newsman discovered that the city's own vehicles were violating the ordinance.

The Man Who Moved a City

Despite its multitudes of other problems, New York City probably has tried harder than any other big community to mount a really effective anti-noise campaign. Much of the initiative came from a group of volunteers called Citizens for a Quieter City, Inc., headed by Robert Alex Baron, forty-nine, who was so incensed by the din of a construction project outside his Manhattan apartment that he quit his career as a Broadway play manager in 1966 to do something about it. His efforts helped coax Mayor John V. Lindsay to appoint, in 1967, a special anti-noise task force of technical experts and public-spirited citizens. These and other pressures combined to persuade the city council last year to pass the first building code of any major U.S. city with an anti-noise provision. It requires that new residential buildings must be constructed to cut noise penetration by about 45 dbA, which is appreciably less strict than the codes of several European countries but nevertheless a major stride forward.

To prove that Americans do not have to live with noise, Baron arranged for a public demonstration of silenced machinery in New York's Lincoln Center one day in 1967.

Among other items, he displayed a quiet air compressor imported from Britain. Within a few months, at least one major American manufacturer, Ingersoll-Rand, began actively promoting a similar machine. The city is running a test of the feasibility of using paper bags for garbage instead of cans, and it has contracted with General Motors to develop quiet garbage trucks to replace the present fleet of "mechanized cockroaches," as Baron calls them.

In a report to be published this month, the New York task force has also recommended an extraordinarily ambitious program for further steps, ranging from new zoning rules to creation of a corps of noise inspectors, with the objective of reducing the noise level in busy areas to 85 dbA and the residential level to 40 dbA in daytime and 30 dbA at night. The New York initiative is attracting considerable local attention. On N.B.C.'s Johnny Carson TV show recently, Baron appealed for people annoyed by noise to write him; the result was some 2,500 letters, most of them venting long-pent-up anger and frustration.

But the effort has a very long way to go. The anti-noise forces to date have failed even to persuade the New York Police Department to try to enforce the ordinance against needless horn blowing. The problem is compounded by the fact that the city has no direct authority to act against noisy vehicle engines (which are the state's responsibility), or noisy aircraft (the FAA's), or even the New York subway system (the Transit Authority's).

Even the French Don't Blow Their Horns

There is no mystery about how to control noise. At least sixteen European countries have building codes with anti-noise provisions, many of them tougher than anything even contemplated in the U.S. The Soviet Union, which began a "struggle against noise" in 1960, says it has banned factory noise above 85 dbA and limited the level in residential areas to 30 dbA. The West Germans, among other actions, have set up no fewer than eight categories of noise limits; they offer tax concessions and easy credit to manufacturers willing to silence machinery acquired before the limits were established; and they stamp the maximum noise permitted each vehicle on the owner's driver's license. In France, needless horn blowing has been successfully outlawed — much to the surprise of the French themselves — and other noise regulations are so well enforced that a peasant recently was fined $50 for a noisy cowbell.

Unlike other forms of pollution, noise comes from an infinite number of sources and cannot be cut off simply by cleaning up a few big operations such as garbage dumps. The answer, however, does not lie in brave new proclamations. Ways must be found to get at the problem through appeals to the self-interest of business and community leaders and through governmental regulations that are realistic and easily policed.

Two further federal moves are needed now to provide a legal framework for minimum national standards. One is to broaden the recent anti-noise regulations to protect workers in all factories engaged in interstate commerce. The second is to invoke the interstate commerce principle to permit the fixing of limitations on the noise created by the machines that industry produces. The objective of such a move would be to oblige manufacturers to design noise suppression right into their goods, and its national application would guarantee that no company would be hurt competitively. Says Leo L. Beranek of Cambridge, Massachusetts, chief scientist for the nation's largest acoustical consulting firm: "We have got to have noise regulation at the federal level. Controls in only a few scattered cities won't work; quiet products must have a national market."

A proposal for federal action on such a broad scale obviously invites innumerable problems. For one thing, it would require congressional action. It would compound the infighting already under way among the several federal agencies competing for anti-noise responsibility. Whatever the bureaucratic machinery, however, the approach probably should be to seek a broad mandate from Congress, and then to begin application of specific controls on a progressive basis, beginning with the most urgent problems — e.g., highway vehicle noise and outrageously noisy machines like air compressors.

The Diverse Opportunities

Federal laws, of course, are no panacea. At best they can be expected only to provide minimum standards that could then be reinforced through state and local action. In some cases such action can be carried out most easily through local regulation — e.g., anti-noise insulation of residential buildings, which can be enforced with relative ease through existing building inspectors. The mere existence of federal anti-noise laws would create strong psychological pressures on local governments and industry to act.

Apart from legislation, there are innumerable other opportunities for action. The federal government buys something like 35,000 vehicles annually. To require such vehicles, especially trucks, to be fitted with good mufflers, quiet tire treads, and other noise-suppressing equipment would go a long way toward encouraging manufacturers to make such items standard equipment. State and local governments could easily do the same. Procurement policy can be similarly useful across a broad spectrum of other items that are purchased by both consumers and government agencies — e.g., garbage cans, which can be quieted for about $1.50 apiece. The Federal Housing Authority and other national and local agencies have the power now to make compliance with noise standards a condition for publicly backed loans. The National Park Service has the same kind of authority now to bar noisy vehicles, transistors, and the like from our national parks. It should also be feasible for the federal and local governments to grant tax concessions to encourage industry to suppress noise. By relatively simple fiddling with electronic circuits, buses and trains could be fitted with jamming devices to discourage transistor addicts. And automobiles could be equipped with two horns, one for highways and a quieter beeper for city streets, as is widely done in Europe. The Federal Highway Safety Bureau recently revealed that it is already considering a requirement of this sort.

Contrary to the view among some industrialists that noise control is an expensive luxury, it is in fact good business; the lack of effective noise control at the source, moreover, is bad for business. In the case of aircraft, anti-noise flight procedures — e.g., disuse of some runways — are further reducing the capacity of our congested airports, while popular reaction against aircraft noise is making it increasingly difficult to find sites for new airports. Cities like New York are losing tens of millions of dollars in traffic diverted elsewhere.

For industry in general, the mounting cost of hearing-loss compensation claims could easily become astronomic if workers began going to the courts in large numbers. In view of the growing evidence that noise is a significant health hazard, it would make eminent sense for insurance companies and labor unions to add their considerable weight to the battle. With a few exceptions, businessmen have been surprisingly slow to recognize that noise prevention can be marketed; for example, in advertising for quiet apartments or noiseless kitchen equipment. There is also a major public-relations consideration in the growing feeling among environmentalists that corporations have no more right to dump noise on communities than air and water pollutants.

"Let avoidable noise be avoided," said the late Pope Pius XII in a 1956 appeal from the Vatican. "Silence is beneficial not only to sanity, nervous equilibrium, and intellectual labor, but also helps man live a life that reaches to the depths and to the heights. . . . It is in silence that God's mysterious voice is best heard."

EDITOR'S COMMENTS

As one reads more and more about environmental problems, their causes and their solutions, it is easy to become rather disgusted with the self-centered nearsightedness which is obviously so characteristic of the human species. Approximately 20 million Americans suffer hearing losses, more than all other disabilities combined. Yet, in the face of this ever mounting and increasingly hazardous nuisance, politicians and industrialists cry that the cost of environmental correction is prohibitive. At the risk of resembling a broken record, people problems must be solved by people money; ultimately taxpayers and consumers must pay for a quieter world. And, as is so often the case, people must bring pressures to bear, or noise will just represent another one of those things that emotional "pseudoecologists" go around making more noise about. It would be interesting to know where we would be today if these persons had not awakened literally millions of Americans to the realities of environmental misuse.

FRANK GRAHAM, Jr.

The Mississippi Fish Kill

Frank Graham, Jr. is a Field Editor of *Audubon* magazine and lives with his wife, Ada, in Milbridge, Maine. In addition to *Disaster by Default*, he is the author of several other books on the environment and the conservation movement, including *Since Silent Spring* and *Man's Dominion: The Story of Conservation in America*.

On November 18, 1963, Robert LaFleur of Louisiana's Division of Water Pollution Control called the Public Health Service in Washington to report a massive fish kill in the lower Mississippi River and its tributary, the Atchafalaya. An estimated five million dead fish were floating, belly up, in the great muddy river which drains a third of the United States, provides drinking water for over a million southerners, and supports a vast segment of this country's fishing industry. LaFleur's telephone call, made reluctantly as are most pleas for help by state officials to the federal government, set in motion more than a routine investigation. Before many months had passed, roving teams of water "detectives" had touched off an uproar which was fueled by the fires from many of the basic moral, political, and business controversies of our time.

It was not the first such kill on the Mississippi in recent years. In the summer of 1958, fish, snakes, eels, and turtles died in enormous numbers in streams throughout the sugar-cane areas of southern Louisiana. State chemists could not detect toxic materials in either the water or the fish, but the carnage went on. In 1959 a state report noted that during that year's growing season "these kills reached alarming proportions with complaints being received by the Division of Water Pollution Control on an almost daily basis."

At least 30 major kills were reported during the summer of 1960. Kenneth Biglane, who was then chief of the Louisiana Water Pollution Division, recalls his department's frustration. "The sports public, indignant citizens, harassed elected officials and the press were all demanding that something be done. Dead fish were observed to be clogging the intake of the Franklin, Louisiana, power plant and were dying in Bayou Teche, a stream used as a source of drinking water for the town of Franklin."

In the fall of 1960, nearly four million fish died mysteriously in the Mississippi and the Atchafalaya. The dead fish included threadfin shad, freshwater drum, and buffalo, but by far the greatest number of vic-

Reprinted by permission of the author and publisher from *Disaster by Default*. Chapter 5, pp. 107-135. Copyright © 1966 by Frank Graham, Jr. Published by M. Evans and Co., Inc., New York.

235

tims were catfish (95 percent), the principal source of food for many of the poorer people in the river towns and bayou settlements. Although continued observation did not give scientists any clues to the cause of their death, all the dead and dying fish exhibited strikingly similar symptoms.

"Most of the catfish were bleeding about the mouth," Robert LaFleur recalls, "and many were bleeding about the fins. In every instance examination revealed that this was due to distention of the swim bladder and the digestive tract. The latter was devoid of food material and contained only gas and a small amount of bile-like frothy material. Analysis of the bottom organisms revealed that an abundant food supply was available. Dying fish were swimming at the surface, often inverted, in a very lethargic manner, and were easily captured by hand."

According to the state investigators, this was "the most spectacular fish mortality ever noted in Louisiana," but their only conclusion was that it might be attributed to "abdominal dropsy." When smaller but widespread kills occurred again in 1961 and 1962, the details were not reported to the United States Public Health Service because, according to Biglane, "We did not think pollution was responsible for the mortalities."

By 1963, however, Biglane had joined the Public Health Service in Washington, and he was among the federal pollution experts who were alarmed by the report of the massive fish kill reported that November. Louisiana officials, until then reluctant to call in the federal government on a problem which they considered rightfully belonged to the state, had thrown up their hands in despair. LaFleur's call to Washington was a plea for immediate help.

Teams of federal investigators descended on the lower Mississippi. They talked to local scientists, read reports on previous fish kills, and toured the stricken areas in small boats. There was no scarcity of evidence, and no scarcity of local people waiting to tell their stories. Harry McHugh, who lives along the Atchafalaya, told his in the Franklin *Banner-Tribune*.

"I can look out my front door," he wrote in January, 1964, "and see at least a few fish swimming crazily on the surface of the water — mostly shad and mullet. These will swim in such a fashion for a while, eventually losing their ability to swim, and then either drift on down with the tide toward the Gulf of Mexico or are washed up on the banks where they die."

A reporter for *The New Republic* learned that the streams and bayous were clogged with dead ducks, mostly fish-eating species like scaup and mergansers. "The bodies of turtles floated on the waters," *The New Republic* said. "Tough 150-pound garfish and catfish weighing 70 pounds surfaced, too weak to move. Crabs lay along the banks. Thousands of cranes and robins lay dead. The pencil-size white eels fishermen used for bait were scooped up dead by the net full. Alligators, once plentiful, have disappeared. Otter died or left the swamps."

Though many human beings lived on the product of those waters, there were no reports yet of illness and death among them. Economically, the story was different. The men who had fished the Cajun areas of Louisiana for years were hard hit. The wives of many were forced to go to work in the canneries, while the fishermen themselves took work in nearby towns or in the offshore oil industry. "More fishermen have gone on jobs this year than ever before," one of them told a reporter from the *New York Times*.

"This time the poison hit all types of fish," another fisherman said. "So many died this winter that it got so I couldn't make $10 a week."

A wholesaler reported that he could buy only a small percentage of the fish usually available to him. "You can stand here on the dock any day of the fall and winter and see thousands of dead fish float by with the current," he said. "They would shoot up out of the water and just flop over. Many others died in the nets before the fishermen could bring them in."

These tales were confirmed by the experience of government scientists. Dr. Donald Mount, a young biolgist with the Public Health Service, told of touring the Mississippi in an open powerboat near Baton Rouge.

"Thousands of catfish, drum, buffalo and shad were seen at the surface, unable to maintain an upright position and often having convulsions. Literally acres of minnow schools were also in a state of hyperactivity and convulsions."

Dr. Mount also visited the delta areas where menhaden, a salt-water fish which enters estuaries to cast its eggs in late winter and early spring, were reported dying by the millions. Menhaden, in fact, made up by far the greatest proportion of the fish killed in the estuaries during the winter of 1963-64. Touring the harbor at Venice, 235 miles below Baton Rouge, Dr. Mount observed thousands of convulsing blue catfish, mullet, and menhaden. "On several occasions," he said, "we went into a dead-end canal, and as the boat approached the end, schools of menhaden were trapped and hundreds of these fish began convulsing, jumping onto the boat, the banks and against an oil drilling rig."

Scientists from various government agencies collected dead and dying fish, froze them, and shipped them to laboratories for study. Analysis by the U.S. Fish and Wildlife Service (Department of the Interior) proved that the fish were not killed by parasitic or bacterial disease. Botulism was ruled out, as were organic phosphorous insecticides and toxic concentrations of metals.

But government scientists were for the first time armed with recently developed techniques and machines which brought them within reach of a solution. At the Taft Sanitary Engineering Center in Cincinnati, investigators worked for weeks to find a clue to the mysterious fish kills. Tissues of dying catfish were fed to healthy catfish, but no viral or bacterial diseases were transmitted to them. A major breakthrough resulted, however, when scientists turned to the mud which had been dredged from affected areas of the river. Extracts of the tissues taken from dying fish were then dissolved in water where healthy fish swam. The healthy fish convulsed and died — symptoms exactly similar to those of the stricken fish in the Mississippi and Atchafalaya!

Teams of investigators (one from a private research laboratory) independently analyzed both the mud and the dead fish. Endrin, a chlorinated hydrocarbon insecticide, was found in every extract.

This deadly poison was not new to government scientists. For some years the Bureau of Commercial Fisheries (Department of the Interior) had been studying Endrin and similar poisons, Dieldrin and Aldrin, because of their effect on key commercial fish like shrimp and menhaden. These insecticides, marketed because of their extreme toxicity to arthropods (the phylum to which insect pests belong), were naturally found to be especially harmful to shrimp, which are marine arthropods. Dr. C. M. Tarzwell, chief of the Public Health Service's Aquatic Biology Section, reports that, of all the substances he ever tested, Endrin is the most toxic to fish.

Endrin, indeed, was more than a laboratory goblin. It was known to Louisiana biologists as far back as 1958, the year of the first mysterious fish kill there. They noticed then a cause-and-effect relationship between the spraying of sugar-cane fields with Endrin (to control an insect called the sugar-cane borer) and the subsequent drainage of those fields after heavy rains. Thousands of fish immediately died. When the spraying stopped, the killing stopped. Kenneth Biglane, chief of the state's Division of Water Pollution Control at the time, clearly remembers that sequence of events.

"I have witnessed aerial applications of Endrin on sugar-cane fields around Houma, Thibodaux, and Donaldsonville, Louisiana," he says. "After subsequent rains, I have returned to such streams as Bayou Pierre Part near Donaldsonville, Bayou Black near Houma, and Bayou Chevrieul near Thibodaux, and I have seen thousands of fish and snakes, turtles, eels, dead and dying."

Yet all attempts to pin down Endrin as the cause of the fish kills during those years proved futile. The advanced techniques of fish autopsy and the sensitive instruments capable of detecting minute traces of foreign substances in water and mud (as low as a few parts per billion) were not then available to investigators. The now-familiar pattern of delay began to appear. The federal government was reluctant to move in because, as one Public Health Service scientist said, "it would destroy state relations and dry up future research." State officials, jealous of their sovereignty, refused to allow federal investigators to come in and perhaps put restrictions locally on the sale of suspected pesticides. The state, of course, could have taken strong measures of its own in 1959. Louisiana limited itself to a public education program, pointing out the dangers of the careless use of Endrin.

"Regulations for the supervision of aerial application," Biglane says, "the marking of cane fields, the plugging of drainage ditches leading away from fields, and the halting of applications immediately before a rain was forecast were recommended to the Louisiana Stream Control Commission by our division in August, 1959. No action was taken on these recommendations."

But now, early in 1964, modern science enabled the government teams to isolate the killing substance. Dr. Donald Mount, the Ohio State graduate who had toured the lower Mississippi observing the effects of the kill and picking up dead fish, is de-

scribed as one of the heroes of the investigation. Working on a new method of "fish autopsy," he was able to uncover vital evidence in the fatty tissues of his specimens. Other PHS scientists in Cincinnati, using a gas chromatograph equipped with an electron capture detector, were able to assay extracts and blood from 100 poisoned fish between December 20, 1963, and April 1, 1964. Every sample contained Endrin. When infinitesimal quantities of Endrin, corresponding to the quantities discovered by sensitive instruments in extracts of the stricken Mississippi fish, were injected in healthy fish, the later passed through identical symptoms and died. The next problem was to discover how Endrin got into the streams and rivers.

"Endrin is not found naturally in the Mississippi River," Murray Stein has said. "The fish don't go out to a supermarket or drug store or a package store and buy it. The fish must get Endrin from their total environment."

There was one clue. Although some scientists have said for a long time that insecticides were being washed off fields into streams and rivers, Louisiana officials believed that the big fish kill of November, 1963, was not caused by field drainage. For one thing, the fields are sprayed in the spring, not in the fall. For another, most of the Louisiana sugar-cane fields are cut off from the Mississippi and Atchafalaya by levees, thereby ruling out direct drainage into them; there were no big kills in the smaller streams near the cane fields. State Sanitary Engineer John E. Trygg summed up the state's position in his report of Endrin in the river: "Although the concentrations seem to increase in reaches of the Mississippi River in Louisiana there is really no drainage to the river from Louisiana soils and there are no Louisiana industries discharging insecticide wastes into the river."

Louisiana officials concluded that the great percentage of Endrin must be entering Louisiana from another state. It was on this basis (the pollution of interstate waters) that Louisiana had requested the assistance of the federal government.

Because the Mississippi River is the United States' major inland waterway, it is also its major sewer. Countless industries adhering to the old and once-valid adage that "dilution solves all pollution," have settled on its banks primarily to have access to a natural and therefore inexpensive sewer. Though there is not a major city along the Mississippi below Minneapolis and St. Paul which has an adequate sewage-treatment plant, no one had any qualms about dumping his most noxious wastes into the great but overburdened river. In 1964 St. Louis, Memphis, Vicksburg, Natchez, and New Orleans were still pouring their raw sewage into the Mississippi. New Orleans, as well as 100 other "jurisdictions" within Louisiana, with a total population of 1,094,000, takes its *drinking* water from this cloudy sewer.

"Stream scientists working for Louisiana's Division of Water Pollution Control," Kenneth Biglane says, "soon become educated to the different types of water pollution that are found in their state from time to time. Wastes from sugar factories, sweet potato canneries, pulp and paper mills, oil field brines, naval stores plants, chemical plants, municipal sewages, and slaughterhouses all have two things in common. They can degrade water and they can kill aquatic life. Their point in time, their point source, and their physical and chemical alteration of the aquatic environment, however, offer clues to their dissimilarities."

Today there are about 10,000 industries in 18 states along the Mississippi and its tributaries. Of these, 118 plants manufacture pesticides. Before the development of new techniques and instruments by PHS scientists in the last few years, it would have been nearly impossible to trace a specific poison to a specific source. Now PHS investigators set out to find the source of Endrin in the Mississippi. After talking to agricultural people who had handled Endrin,

and to scientists who had observed earlier fish kills in which Endrin had been suspected, they discovered an interesting fact. The effect on fish trapped in Endrin-infested streams near sugar-cane areas immediately after spraying and heavy rains had been "acute": the fish had died immediately. The effect on most of the fish during the recent kill had been "chronic": the fish had died more slowly or in many cases, had gone through convulsions, righted themselves, and survived. Perhaps, the scientists thought, the more recent infestation of the river was of a different nature. Perhaps the poison had been diluted, after a long passage downstream, by mingling with the enormous flow of the lower Mississippi. At Memphis, Tennessee, some 500 miles up the river, there was a plant which manufactured Endrin. PHS investigators decided to take a close look at it.

The Memphis plant was owned by the Velsicol Chemical Corporation of Chicago. Endrin itself had been developed in Velsicol's Chicago laboratories. In discussing Endrin's widespread use in the South one agronomist put it this way: "I can say without the slightest fear of being contradicted that Endrin is the most effective insecticide ever used on the Louisiana cane crop." It is effective and popular, of course, simply because it is extremely deadly, it does the job.

In April, 1964, a team of Public Health Service investigators visited the Velsicol plant at Memphis. Leading the investigators was Dr. Alfred R. Grzenda, a pesticides expert from the PHS office in Atlanta. The story of what Grzenda and his associates found in Memphis might be enlightening to those who believe industrial pollution can be cleared up merely by "education and friendly persuasion."

Grzenda's job was to gather information on the manufacture of Endrin (including its by-products) and take samples of the water and mud in the vicinity of the plant. William Anthony, Velsicol's plant manager, was apparently reluctant to give Grzenda information about the various processes involved in Endrin's manufacture. "When we asked specific questions about starting and intermediate products," Grzenda said, "Mr. Anthony referred us to the patents for the manufacture of these compounds."

According to later newspaper reports, the PHS officials were barred from the plant, but Grzenda denied this. "We were treated well," Grzenda said, "but the Velsicol Company more or less selected the sites which we sampled. In other words, it was a guided tour through the plant."

Anthony showed Grzenda the plant's waste-treatment facility, a 50-ton lime bed used to produce a lime slurry which is added to a 40,000-gallon agitated retention tank. Anthony said that virtually no waste solids entered the tank. "However," Grzenda said, "sludge was dredged from the sides and middle of the tank and it contained a black, sticky, smelly residue. In the course of sampling, I splashed sludge on my face. It was extremely irritating to my eyes and skin."

Grzenda learned that the treatment plant was comparatively new, having been installed less than a year before (Velsicol had been manufacturing Endrin there since 1954, and discharging its wastes into nearby Cypress Creek until 1963). Asking for information on sewers in the area, Grzenda received contradictory reports from Velsicol people and city engineers about which pipes carried off trade wastes and which were city sanitary sewers. An attempt to enter one sewer was thwarted by noxious fumes, another attempt came to nothing when Grzenda discovered that smoke bombs planted in them by city officials ("to check for leaks") had made the sewers impenetrable. In all of them, including the "sanitary" sewers Grzenda and his assistants detected strong chemical odors similar to that in the Velsicol treatment facility.

But the investigators did not have to rely on odors alone. Unexpectedly, they came across a by-pass line discharging Velsicol's trade wastes into a pipe which flowed into Wolf River, a small tributary of the Mississippi. They also discovered that wastes, solid or semi-liquid, were being hauled daily from the Velsicol plant to a place called the Hollywood Dump. These wastes were carted there in caustic drums and in large containers known commercially as "Dempster Dumpsters." Shortly before the PHS men arrived, one of the workmen carting the drums to the dump had become ill when he was splashed with the wastes.

This material is buried, or left exposed on a portion of the dump located on the flood plain of the Wolf River," Grzenda said. "All of the sites are subject to flooding. Mr. Anthony denied that any solids from the Endrin plant were being hauled to the Hollywood Dump, but we noted drums labeled 'isodrin scraps' at the dump on April 15. Isodrin is one of the compounds used in the manufacture of Endrin. However, Mr. Anthony said that such material is not normally taken to the Hollywood Dump for disposal."

Grzenda and his associates took samples of water and mud from the various sewers and dumps in the vicinity of the Velsicol plant, as well as from such small waterways as Wolf River and Cypress Creek (which he described as a "biological desert"). He found enormous quantities of Endrin and Dieldrin present. Calculating the amounts of Endrin which flowed from this area through streams and city sewers into the Mississippi, he was able to determine that about 7.2 pounds would enter the main stream in a single day, or 2,000 pounds a year. Although Endrin is marketed in a formula amounting to two percent, Grzenda made his calculations against "technical," or 100 percent, Endrin, which is 50 times stronger than the substance used on crops.

"I played with some figures that Dr. Mount gave me relative to blood volume and toxic concentration in the blood of catfish,"

Grzenda said, "and just playing around with a pencil, I figured if only one-*thousandth* of this amount of Endrin — that is if only two pounds a year found its way into the blood of fish, it would have the potential of killing 45 million one-pound catfish."

Grzenda, having completed his investigation, concluded that the concentration of Endrin in the water and underlying mud around Memphis exceeded by far all previous reports of concentrations of chlorinated hydrocarbon insecticides. Most of the contaminated areas were noted at sites "known to be downstream from points used or previously used by the Velsicol Chemical Corporation for waste discharge or disposal."

Soon afterward the Public Health Service made known its findings to the public. The presence of Endrin in the Mississippi had already been disclosed. This report was specific about its sources.

"Endrin discharged in the Memphis, Tennessee, area," the PHS report read, "other sources of Endrin not yet identified, and possibly other pesticides and discharges of sewage and industrial wastes of many kinds, pollute the waters of the lower Mississippi and Atchafalaya Rivers, and thereby, endanger health and welfare of persons in a State or States other than those in which such discharges originate. Such discharges are subject to abatement under the provisions of the Federal Water Pollution Control Act."

The Mississippi River, draining a vast area in the middle of our country, carries with it over 400 million tons of sediment a year. Reaching the sea it drops most of this sediment. Gradually the sediment, or silt, forms a delta. The 12,000-square-mile delta at the mouth of the Mississippi today has been built up over the centuries and is advancing into the Gulf of Mexico at the rate of 300 feet a year. Much of the south-central part of the United States is composed of land carried from the north and laid down by the Mississippi and its tributaries, so that the great river now flows through the land it helped to create. The river, then, is naturally discolored, but this has not always been a menace to the life it supports. On his voyage down the Mississippi, Huck Finn overheard a raftsman tell his colleagues that there was "nutritiousness in the mud, and a man that drunk the Mississippi water could grow corn in his stomach if he wanted to."

Whether there is nutritiousness in the river today is open to question, but there are a great many other things in it. The Mississippi, like every other major river in the country, has been blighted for years by raw sewage. The absence of treatment facilities in most of the cities and nearly all of the river towns is a disgrace with which the people have come to live. Raw sewage is the country's leading killer of fish. It also causes various serious diseases among human beings: hepatitis, poliomyelitis, cholera. The situation, until the recent mild spasm of treatment-plant construction, had grown steadily worse on the Mississippi. The process goes on from year to year, each town taking the river water, perhaps treating it and perhaps not, then using it and turning it back to the river, which carries it just a little bit more contaminated along to the next fellow downstream. The introduction of insecticides to the river in recent years has added another, and potentially more deadly, dimension to the problem. There is a morbid little joke currently circulating among pollution experts on the Mississippi. "Pesticides can't do anything to our fish this year," it goes. "Our sewage has killed them all."

It was not a laughing matter in New Orleans when the Public Health Service released its report on Endrin in the river. Traces of Endrin were found in the drinking water of that big river city, as well as in the water of Vicksburg. (Purification systems for drinking water cannot remove Endrin.)

New Orleans citizens who could afford it took in supplies of bottled water. Only a few hours after the PHS announcement, one New Orleans bottled-water dealer announced that he was placing customers on a five-month waiting list for his product. The uproar continued throughout April. James M. Quigley, Assistant Secretary of Health, Education and Welfare, said that after looking over the evidence he would not care to eat a Gulf shrimp cocktail. Dr. James M. Hundley, Assistant Surgeon General, on the other hand, said that he didn't feel there was any present danger involved in drinking Mississippi water or eating Gulf shrimp, but he added that he did not think it healthy to try to subsist exclusively on a diet of Mississippi catfish. The Food and Drug Administration discovered an interstate shipment of canned oysters containing traces of Endrin, but did not seize it on the grounds that it was not considered "an imminent danger to health." The government decided to survey the entire season's harvest before deciding what to do with Endrin-contaminated samples. Secretary of the Interior Stewart Udall called for an immediate ban from agricultural use on long-lasting pesticides (and ordered such a ban throughout the 550 million acres of public land administered by his department). The *New York Times,* in an editorial, supported Udall's position.

"These pesticides do not break down in nature," the *Times* editorial said. "They retain their potency long after their initial use. Once put into the environment by farmers and others, these chemicals tend ultimately to enter the food chain of living creatures. There is evidence suggesting that the degree of their concentration in organisms increases as contaminated fish, for example, are eaten by birds. Since human beings complete such food chains, there is some ground for suspicion that such increasing concentration can endanger human health.

"Here is a situation," the *Times* continued, "in which the case is strong for imposition of at least some controls quickly while research goes on to accumulate more information and also to find substitute pesticides which do not pose so formidable a threat. Certainly the nation's overcapacity for food production is so great that any potential diminution of crops resulting from such pesticide restrictions would be a lesser risk than that arising from the haphazard use of the chemicals themselves."

Velsicol, under fire, shot back. Bernard Lorant, the company's vice-president in charge of research, issued strong denials. In a statement to the press, he said that Endrin had nothing to do with the Mississippi fish kill, that the symptoms of the dying fish were not those of Endrin poisoning, and that Velsicol's tests proved that the fish had died of dropsy. He went on to question the Public Health Service's accuracy in analyzing fish samples, claiming that, since Dieldrin is not a by-product of Endrin's manufacture, Dieldrin traces could not have been found at Memphis.

The row shifted from the pages of the daily newspapers to the hearing rooms of various committees investigating the fish kill. Hearings were called by both Senator Abraham Ribicoff's Sub-committee on Government Operations and the United States Department of Agriculture. Velsicol continued to question almost every aspect of the Public Health Service's case. Lorant pointed out that the amounts of Endrin in question often amounted to only a few parts per billion. He said that, of the 5,175,000 fish reported killed, five million were menhaden ("which is 96.6 percent," Lorant said, "or in the vernacular of Public Health, 966 million parts per billion"); these menhaden died in the mouth of the river, he went on, and were not collected or sampled by PHS; as there were only 175,000 others, mostly catfish, Endrin could be blamed at most in the death of 3.4 percent. He asked how Endrin could drift 500 miles down the river without causing a fish kill on the way, asked why no fish kills had been reported during 1961 and 1962, although Endrin was being manufactured and applied just as regularly, and said that it would have been impossible for Endrin to contribute to pollution in the lower Mississippi by running off the Louisiana sugar-cane fields, because the fields were cut off from the river by levees.

Velsicol was supported in its arguments by the Shell Chemical Corporation, the only other manufacturer of Endrin. According to a Shell executive, Endrin is readily absorbed into mud. "It is reassuring to realize," this official said, "that the large silt load carried by the Mississippi River acts as its own 'clean-up' agent for chlorinated or other highly absorbable pesticides."

But the Public Health Service stood its ground. One witness pointed out that the so-called infinitesimal quantities of Endrin found in certain areas (measured in parts per billion) are not quite so negligible when one considers the tremendous flow of the Mississippi. Others remarked that there was no major fish kill near Memphis because the fish in Endrin-infested waters had probably been killed off long ago ("Sometimes a sure sign of pollution abatement is a fish kill," one government investigator said. "At least it proves that there are still fish in the vicinity"). Endrin's report that the fish kill could be attributed to dropsy, and that there had been no reports of a kill in 1961 and 1962, were countered with the reminder that older methods of analysis had not been able to detect Endrin, and that earlier fish kills were not reported since they were considered due to natural causes.

In reply to Velsicol's statement that Endrin could not have reached the Mississippi from Louisiana cane fields, one PHS scientist suggested that the Endrin might come from factories where the cane was washed

and treated; some of these plants border the Mississippi.

Witness after witness reflected the alarm that had invaded many sections of our government. It was noted that British authorities had already placed restrictions on these pesticides which have poisoned fish and shrimp in the United States. Dr. Clarence Cottam, a noted biologist, warned, "We're going to find human beings dying of this thing, unless we act with intelligence now." Assistant Secretary of HEW James Quigley testified, "The presence of any of these materials in any food or liquid consumed by human beings is a cause for concern, even though the levels may be far below those which might be considered an imminent health hazard."

When asked what amount of Endrin might be lethal to human beings, Assistant Surgeon General Hundley confessed to Senator Ribicoff's subcommittee that he did not know. "I don't know that an answer is available," he said.

After hearing the evidence that Endrin was present in shipments of shrimps and oysters, Senator Ribicoff commented, "There must be an awful lot of fish going into interstate commerce that should be condemned and removed from the market."

But the reply of George P. Larrick, Commissioner of the Food and Drug Administration, was guarded, "That remains to be seen," he said. "I don't want to just destroy the market for those products. . . . I would prefer to wait until we have run a lot of samples. I hope we won't find massive contamination, and I don't think we will."

Ribicoff, after hearing all the testimony, came to some strong conclusions. He told the Velsicol people that they had disposed of their chemical wastes "in a primitive and dangerous manner. . . . The record is overwhelmingly against your position."

Officials in the Department of Health, Education and Welfare came to similar conclusions. Until that time they had not wanted to restrict the use of dangerous pesticides, but the findings in the Mississippi River had changed their minds. "We cannot proceed in the same way in the future as in the past," Assistant Secretary Quigley testified before Ribicoff's subcommittee. He said that HEW now believed that as a "matter of prudence every possible effort should be made to control the use of the persistent pesticides in our environment."

The Department of Agriculture had also found disturbing evidence of misuse or careless handling of insecticides. Its representatives had accompanied PHS investigators to the Velsicol plant at Memphis. A USDA report confirmed that Velsicol's disposal of its wastes "is contributing substantially to the contamination of the river. It is our understanding, however that the waste disposal system employed by this plant is in compliance with local sanitation codes."

A dispatch printed in the *New York Times* on January 17, 1965, reviewed some of the other curious circumstances in Velsicol's recent history at Memphis. "On June 3, 1963," the *Times* story said, "the Memphis Health Department reported complaints from 20 persons living near Cypress Creek, an open stream flowing through the north side of the city. Nausea, vomiting and watering eyes were the symptoms produced by gas rising from the stream. An official of the Velsicol Chemical Corporation denied responsibility. 'Endrin could not have caused the symptoms,' said Wilson Keyes, director of manufacturing."

"On June 7, 1963, 26 workmen in plants near Velsicol were taken to five hospitals after becoming ill from chlorine gas fumes. Within a year lawsuits totaling over $5 million had been filed by more than 40 persons claiming injury."

"Velsicol reacted in the first weeks of the trouble with a dinner for 150 political, civic and business leaders. 'It came as quite a shock to us to discover that there was some question about whether we were welcome in the city of Memphis', said John Kirk, executive vice-president, down from Chicago for the event. Then Mayor Henry Loeb responded that 'this plant is very much wanted by Memphis.' His successor, William B. Ingram, Jr. took much the same position a year later."

Elsewhere along the Mississippi, Department of Agriculture investigations into pesticide plants proved to be "quite revealing." The USDA report said that "conditions were observed which appear to constitute a definite hazard. For example, it was found that a cooperage company removed material from used drums by heating and then washing them with caustic soda. Periodically, this solution is flushed into the city sanitary system. It was also found that several plants dispose of wastes at city dumps and that as a rule these dumps are located on the river side of the levee."

But the USDA, with the farmer's welfare uppermost in its reasoning, refused to take restrictive action. It confirmed the Public Health Service report that large quantities of Endrin and Dieldrin had been found in the Memphis area, but said that the river contamination had nothing to do with the agricultural use of these insecticides. It called, as usual, for further study. A Public Health Service scientist noted that the USDA, which is charged with the growth and welfare of American farming, continues to move into health research as well. "It's like getting a jewel thief to guard the jewels," he said.

The full-dress parade of all the combatants was reserved for the conference which was held on May 5-6, 1964, at New Orleans. It was called by Anthony J. Celebrezze, Secretary of Health, Education and Welfare, as a direct result of Louisiana's plea for help and the subsequent investigation by various government agencies. Present at the conference were members of these agencies, representatives of Arkansas, Tennessee, Mississippi, and Louisiana, and a number of other interested parties. Murray Stein, as usual, served as chairman. If the conference was not a complete success, at least it dramatized the obstacles to enforcing an effective program against water pollution in this country.

The Public Health Service, occasionally calling on representatives of the Department of the Interior and the Department of Agriculture, presented its lengthy case and its conclusions. Its investigators told the conferees what they had found in Memphis, and its scientists painstakingly reviewed their methods of analysis, and the results of their tests. Velsicol made its defense, and was rebutted by PHS.

Then the states and other industries took their turn before the conferees. Going over the transcript of the conference, one is impressed finally by the doggedness with which each speaker strove not so much for a final solution of this complex problem, but with defending his own position and interests. Those whose concern was with fish or other wildlife pleaded for immediate action. A representative of the Tennessee Fish and Game Commission, after describing the carnage inflicted by insecticides on the state's fish and birds, recommended that "the manufacture, distribution, and use of Endrin, Aldrin, Dieldrin, and other related chlorinated hydrocarbon pesticides be banned until the full effects of these poisons can be determined and evaluated." On the other hand, a representative of the sugar-cane growers asked the PHS to take no action, or, in a euphemistic phrase, to "undertake an extensive survey and study program to determine all the facts in this matter before a decision is made that could possibly do an injustice to agriculture in general and weaken our nation."

The tail end of that phrase struck a chord that seemed to be popular at the time with those under fire from the Public Health Service. "The great fight in the world today is between Godless Communism on the one hand and Christian Democracy on the other," Parke C. Brinkley, president of the National Agricultural Chemicals Association had said earlier that spring. "Two of the biggest battles in this war are the battle against starvation and the battle against disease. No two things make people more ripe for Communism. The most effective tool in the the hands of the farmer and in the hands of the public health official as they fight these battles is pesticides."

It was a chord struck repeatedly during the New Orleans conference, as backward, Godless, pesticideless Russia was compared to a flourishing America. Another popular gambit used by Endrin's defenders was to try to make the Public Health Service ashamed of itself for doing its duty. "Until there is evidence to the contrary," a Shell Chemical official said, "it would be irresponsible for any reputable person to frighten people into believing that eating catfish or similar game fish is dangerous."

Velsicol's Bernard Lorant compared PHS's warnings to shouting "fire" in a crowded theater, then sounded aggrieved that the investigation had heaped extra work on the scientists. "None may allow unfounded, unthinking utterances that trigger a massive response of waste," he said. "In the present climate, should anyone recklessly conjecture as to hazard, hundreds of scientists initiate programs to prove or to disprove the remark. We do not always need more scientists; we frequently need less conjecture."

Representatives of the various states taking part in the conference apparently were more concerned with the ogre of "Big Government" than they were with the threat to their waterways. Though the conference was called because one sovereign state had been powerless to prevent pollution from pouring across its border, the representative of another state felt called upon to include among his recommendations to the conference a request that the federal government begin to know its place.

"It is not possible for the government in Washington to be all things to everybody," said E. H. Holeman, of the Tennessee Department of Agriculture, "and especially in the area of protecting wildlife, in preventing stream pollution, and in protecting the health and welfare of the consumer.

"The federal government will have to recognize this fact, and it is urged that they closely coordinate their consumer protection program with the state officials in order that we will have much better and more strict and a more harmonious consumer protection program."

This aggressive attitude toward Washington always carries with it a counteraction, much like the double standards of those foreign governments which encourage the stoning of our embassies and libraries one day, and ask for handouts the next. As in the present case, the most ardent States' Rightists are always quick to call for Washington's help when trouble crops up. A few minutes after Holeman had put forth this "recommendation," conference chairman Murray Stein pointed to another recommendation in which Holeman had asked for a federal standard on the limits of pesticides to be permitted in marketable foods.

"Aren't you worried about a federal standard usurping states' rights?" Stein asked him.

"Oh, no," Holeman said.

"Even though this might affect water pollution control and you would have a standard coming from Washington?"

"That wouldn't bother us. We have the same law in Tennessee, and so do 36 other states, as the Federal Food and Drug Act."

"It is very interesting to get the view of Tennessee on that," Stein commented.

At the conclusion of the conference, as Stein was trying to get the conferees to agree on a summary, the proceedings nearly bogged down in a spasm of local pride.

When Stein attempted to insert a phrase saying that a certain condition "may require further study," a couple of Louisiana representatives put their backs up.

"Obviously, it is true," one of them told Stein, "but I don't like to see it there. It is an invitation for you to come back, you know. We don't think we need you on this."

"I understand," Stein said.

"We have tried not to worry you for about three years, as a matter of fact," another said.

The word *must* set off another furor. When Stein suggested the inclusion of the phrase, "known sources of Endrin must be brought under control," S. Leary Jones of the Tennessee Stream Pollution Control Board spoke up.

"I object to these *musts* coming from a federal agency," Jones said. "Make it *should* or *ought to be*."

"How about *are to be?*" Stein asked.

"We are going to clean up the stuff," Jones said, "but they can't tell us what we *must* do."

"The thing is this," Louisiana's Robert LaFleur, who had made the original telephone call to Washington, interrupted. "If we are going to suffer from this next fall, I am going to be boxed into a corner, and I don't want that."

"This won't happen, I guarantee," Jones said. "But a *must* in there is just one of these words that I won't agree to."

"I sure want it to be cleaned up," LaFleur said.

"All I can tell you, Bob, is that if we say *should* it has no force and effect," chairman Stein reminded him.

"It doesn't have any force or effect either way, until you go into a hearing and into federal court," Jones said. "You know that."

"Most of these cases have been solved by conference," Stein reminded him.

"This isn't a case. This is a conference."

"When I speak of case I am using a generic term," Stein said.

"All right," Jones said. " Put *should* there."

"If that man will promise me he is going to clean it up," LaFleur nodded. "I will buy his *should*."

And so the conference sputtered to a close. Endrin, originating at Memphis, was concluded to have been a contributing factor to the previous fall's kill of Mississippi catfish, and all parties were urged to see that it did not happen again. Yet, though the government's finest scientists, equipped with the most modern machines and techniques, had come to a definite conclusion about the source and agent of the fish kill, the uproar continued. Velsicol went on maintaining its (and Endrin's) complete innocence. *Chemical Week,* a trade publication, called the conference "a kangaroo court." And, on the floor of the United States Senate, Republican leader Everett McKinley Dirksen rose to attack the United States Public Health Service, claiming it had made "wild accusations" and had "unjustly crucified" Velsicol before it had all the facts. Dirksen's tirade surprised nobody. The Illinois Senator has been for a long time the champion in Congress of the nation's drug and chemical companies, as anyone can testify who recalls his bitter opposition to the Kefauver drug bill a few years earlier.

There were expressions of dismay in the press and among public health and conservation groups when Velsicol persisted in its unregenerate stance. On the other hand Murray Stein, a man of few illusions, speaks of the case today with some satisfaction. "A lot of the criticism from the chemical people was directed at me personally," Stein says with a delighted grin. "They made a big man out of me and I got some offers for important jobs. More important though, in many aspects this was the easiest case we've ever had. It was open and shut, and our tests show that the river around there is a lot cleaner since we went after those people."

In 1965 a few fish died in the upper cane brakes after Endrin had run off the fields in the spring, but there was no slaughter on the scale of previous years, At Memphis, PHS investigators looked into a city sewer, however, and found it caked with deposits of Endrin sludge nearly three feet thick. It was estimated that 8,000 pounds of Endrin were embedded along a 3,400-foot stretch of sewer. City officials hastily closed it off and built a bypass sewer.

"The stuff is still in the sewer," Stein says. "And it will probably stay there for a while. Who would go in there after it?"

EDITOR'S COMMENTS

A number of significant points are brought out by this article. It certainly shows that both industry and government agencies will at times act in ways contrary to the welfare of the public.

Although another aspect is not emphasized, the events recorded in this article also show how significant portions of our wildlife resources can be lost in a very short time. Insecticides have been conclusively im-plicated in a number of kills of fishes, waterfowl, gamebirds, and other animals, and biocides as a group are undoubtedly responsible for the destruction of major portions of our resources of wild game and food animals, at least in certain parts of the world.

However, when contemplating the future of our fisheries and wildlife resources we must consider the effects of all factors that decrease the numbers of these animals, and we must think in terms of what these factors cause when operating in combination with one another.

Habitat destruction is perhaps the major factor causing loss of wildlife. In the United States today, destruction of habitat is proceeding at a phenomenal rate. Land alteration under the guise of "development" is replacing wildlife habitat with shopping centers, parking lots, housing developments, industrial parks and amusement parks. Usually little attempt is made to preserve wildlife habitat even if it would be possible.

Highway construction costs us millions of acres of wildlife habitat annually. Often the highways are not needed and more often their placement and design demonstrate an ignorance of ecological facts on the part of highway developers and planners. Currently several national parks and wildlife refuges are threatened by impending highways which will obliterate prime habitat or destroy unique natural features.

Even the United States government agency responsible for enhancing our wildlife resources, the Department of Interior, destroys wildlife with some of its programs.

In the West there is still a massive predator control program involving the poisoning, shooting, or trapping of coyotes, wolves, mountain lions, bobcats, bears, and other predators. This program persists in the face of the fact that many of these species exist in low populations. It is also contrary to the proven fact that predators are necessary to promote healthy prey populations. Political pressure brought to bear by powerful western cattlemen keeps this program going despite evidence that few livestock are destroyed by the predators.

Massive clearcutting, stream channelization, canal building, dredging of estuaries, land filling, oil spills, and strip mining further degrade the habitats of our important wild game and food organisms and often destroy populations outright.

All in all, within the next few decades we stand to lose the major portion of our wildlife resources. Hunters and fishermen are naturally concerned, but every human is affected as we lose potential food resources, bleach further the fading color of our land, and imbalance the ecosystems which are the basis for our future existence.

F. WAYNE KING

Adventures in the Skin Trade

Dr. F. Wayne King is curator of reptiles at the New York Zoological Park.

Writers and filmmakers have conditioned Americans to think that a trek into the jungles of Asia is a daring adventure, with tigers and leopards lurking, ready to spring from the nearest limb or rock outcrop. But today that is an event that occurs only in fiction. All the big cats are now disappearing: the tigers, leopards, cheetahs, jaguars, mountain lions, and ocelots. Many other mammals with fine furs and colorful skins are disappearing as well. They are being slaughtered, skinned, tanned, cut, and reassembled into fashion apparel. Some are now on the verge of extinction, brought there by the hunters who supply the skins for the fashion market.

It is equally difficult for many of us to envision a trip down an African river without picturing crocodiles basking on the river bank or slithering into the murky water at the approach of a boat. No jungle movie would be complete without those crocodiles; the scene featuring a river aswarm with them has become a cliché in stories about Africa. Those same Americans find it even more difficult to believe that it is a scene missing from many parts of Africa today. The crocodiles are vanishing, victims of hide-hunters' guns and harpoons and of an ignorant public's desire for expensive shoes, purses, belts, and wallets of crocodilian hide.

What has been happening to the crocodiles of Africa is not unique. Up until this year, virtually every species of crocodilian in the world was being killed faster than it could reproduce.

Most Americans think of the 1800s and early 1900s as the era of the market-hunter. During that period the passenger pigeon was exterminated by hunters who gunned the birds down by the thousands or gassed them with sulfur fires under their rookeries. Millions of the birds were sold in the meat markets of the large eastern cities. Market-hunters also wiped out the heath hen, great auk, and sea mink, while the American bison, sea otter, and fur seal were brought to the edge of extinction before the public became concerned enough to save them. But even with such a grisly track record as a basis for comparison, it is during the last thirty years that market hunting has taken its greatest toll of wildlife. Today, however, most market hunting is done outside the United States, so the effects on wild animals are not immediately visible to the American public.

As the wealthiest country in the world, the United States is the marketplace for a majority of wild animal products. Furs and skins from all parts of the world find their way to New York City's fashion industry. The money paid the professional poacher and hide-hunter comes from the sales of finished animal products and the sales, in turn, finance further slaughter of the wild animals. Eventually, the sales will finance their extinction.

In the fashion apparel field, companies have traditionally been reluctant to regulate themselves in order to save a species; they fear that competitors will make the sales that they deny themselves. The industry has also operated on the principle that rare skins bring high prices; the rarer the species, the more expensive the products made from them. It is this unrelenting pressure from commerce that accounts for much of the decline in the populations of wild animals with valuable hides. So what industry has been slow to do, government is doing through enactment of new legislation.

To counteract the role played by American commerce in the decimation of wild animal populations, Congress passed the Wildlife Preservation Act of 1969. This included the Endangered Species Conservation Act of 1969 and amendments to the Lacey Act. The Endangered Species Conservation Act permits the Secretary of the Interior to promulgate a list of animal species that are in danger of extinction and to prohibit further importation of these creatures or products made from them. If they cannot be imported, they will not be hunted. The Lacey Act, as amended, prohibits the importation of, or interstate traffic in, fish or wildlife or their products obtained illegally in their country of origin. This will aid foreign governments in their fight against poaching and the smuggling of illegal skins.

Such legislation will not prevent the extinction of animals threatened by pollution and habitat destruction. It will not save animals from the cooking pot of a protein-starved hunter and his family. It will only slow the slaughter of commercially valuable species imported for sale on the United States market. This legislation follows in the tradition of the 1913 law that stopped the trade in egret, heron, osprey, and bird-of-paradise plumes. The plumage law was one of the first major pieces of legislation enacted by one country to protect the wildlife of others. The present Endangered Species Conservation Act similarly attempts to prevent excessive commercial exploitation of all mammals, birds, reptiles, amphibians, fish, and mollusks, regardless of country of origin.

The greatest shortcomings of this legislation are in its administration and enforcement. The Department of the Interior's Endangered Species List contains names of animals in imminent danger of extinction. However, in too many instances the hides, furs, and feathers of these species resemble forms that are not endangered and are therefore not listed. Some of these look-alikes are so similar that they cannot be separated from the endangered species. Although all tigers should be considered endangered, they are not all listed and provide a good example of the problems with this legislation. While Bali, Javan, Sumatran, and Caspian tigers are on the list, the Siberian, Bengal, Chinese, Korean, and Turkestan forms are not. Yet when tiger skins are imported, no mammalogist, let alone government inspector or fur dealer, can tell the hide of one of these subspecies from another. Most tiger subspecies have been described on the bases of skull shape and minor differences in color and hair length. And it is possible to find the total range of variation in one litter of Bengal tigers.

The Nile crocodile has all but been exterminated in eastern and southern Africa and is also on the Endangered Species List. Nevertheless, its importation cannot be prohibited under the federal law, because no one can separate Nile crocodile hides from those of Morelet's crocodile (also endangered), American crocodile, or saltwater crocodile. Descriptions of crocodilian species are based on the shape and placement of skull bones and on the scales at the back of the neck and base of the tail. None of these is available to the inspector looking at commercial hides. As a matter of fact, the similarity of the belly skins of all crocodilians has permitted industry to fool the public into thinking any crocodilian item was "genuine alligator." The phrase *Genuine Alligator* on an item means only that it is made from some crocodilian, not from vinyl or grained calfskin. It is a phrase uniquely American. The American alligator lives only in the United States, nowhere else, so the American public has become accustomed to thinking in terms of alligators every time they see a crocodilian. For example, young caimans are nearly always sold in pet stores as baby alligators. In Europe and tropical Asia, the same items are sold as "genuine crocodile."

Poachers have used this identification confusion to their advantage. Skins poached illegally in one country are frequently smuggled into countries where the species is not protected and the skins can be sold openly. For years feathers of the rare gray junglefowl were exported from Nepal even though the species does not occur there. The plumes were smuggled into Nepal from neighboring India where it is legally protected. In the case of widespread species, such as leopards, tigers, and some crocodilians, no one can tell where a particular hide came from originally.

Clearly, if endangered species are going to be protected from commercial hunters, it will be necessary to prohibit not only their importation but also the importation of all species and subspecies with which they can be confused. The Department of the Interior is reluctant to take this step, however. The law does not preclude it from doing so, but the Senate Commerce Committee in-

structed it not to place a species or subspecies on the list if it is not endangered in all areas of the world. Since some of the animals involved in the identification confusion are not endangered, the Department of the Interior has been slow to add them to the list.

New York State Assemblyman Edwyn E. Mason was aware of what the Endangered Species Conservation Act was designed to do, but he also recognized its weaknesses. As chairman of the state assembly's Committee on Agriculture, he felt that the state might be able to act where the federal government's efforts had run aground. On February 3, 1970, he introduced a bill into the New York Assembly calling for an amendment to the state's agriculture and marketing laws that would prohibit the sale, or possession for sale, of leopard, snow leopard, clouded leopard, tiger, cheetah, vicuña, red wolf, polar bear, mountain lion (puma), jaguar, ocelot, margay, and all alligators, caimans, and crocodiles of the order Crocodylia. Each species was identified by its scientific name so there could be no confusion over which animals were meant. The bill, cosponsored by 44 other assemblymen, aimed at total prohibition of all species and subspecies of the big cats and crocodilians in order to protect the endangered ones with which they can be confused. Total prohibition also eliminated the problem of transshipment of skins — poached skins smuggled into another country from where they could be shipped legally.

Hearings on this bill and its companion bill were held in the New York Senate on February 20, 1970. Debate over the need for the legislation came from industry spokesmen, conservationists, state and federal wildlife officials, zoologists, and indirectly, from representatives of several concerned foreign governments.

The industry spokesmen maintained that they were true conservationists and felt that the supporters of the bill were misguided. They stated that they used only the skins of abundant species in their trade. One furrier even claimed that pelts of the rare snow leopard had not been used by the trade for ten years. To counter these industry arguments, conservationists cited newspaper advertisements for leopard, cheetah, and snow leopard coats that had appeared within the last two years.

One industry spokesman argued that while the Nile crocodile was endangered, his company used only "caimans" from Madagascar, and these were not endangered. Therefore, he pleaded, he should not be prohibited from trading in those skins. The fact is, however, that caimans are found only in the tropical Americas, and the only crocodilian in Madagascar is the Nile crocodile. Zoologists long ago developed the use of scientific names to avoid such confusion over common names.

Representatives of the fur trade worried that the law would cause the death of their industry. This belief obviously conflicts with the argument that the industry does not use endangered species. If such animals are not used, then outlawing their sale could not hurt the industry.

Some tradesmen claimed that the animals were being hurt by habitat destruction, pollution, and the human population explosion, but not by the commerce in the whole animals and their products.

The presentation of U.S. Department of Commerce statistics on importations of hides and furs clearly showed that the number of large-cat furs imported account for less than 2 percent of the total number of furs imported each year. From these cats come the prestige furs that draw customers into the stores. Once there, however, they buy mink, fox, and other furs. Mink alone accounts for about 80 percent of total fur sales. Obviously, a loss of 2 percent of sales would not kill the industry. The 2 percent is significant only to the wild populations of the animals concerned. For example, during 1968, the U.S. Department of Commerce reports that 1,283 cheetah skins were im-

ported. Yet field studies in East Africa show that there is an average of one cheetah for every 30 square miles of territory. The 1968 imports were the equivalent of taking every cheetah in an area of 38,000 square miles (*see* "This Gentle & Elegant Cat," *Natural History Magazine,* June-July, 1970). Little wonder that cheetahs are in trouble.

Conservationists pointed out that funereal forecasts had been similarly voiced by the fur industry when the uncontrolled slaughter of the Alaskan fur seal was stopped shortly after the turn of the century, but the industry did not die. A carefully controlled harvest of fur seals replaced the previous uncontrolled slaughter, and today only a small percentage of the young animals and the bachelor bulls are harvested each year. The remainder, including the breeding adults, are left untouched to produce future young. This sustained-yield harvest assures a constant supply of pelts for the market and does not threaten the continued existence of the species. Yet even with such examples to guide them, the fur industry still prefers uncontrolled exploitation for many valuable animals, even to the point of extinction. In fact, the marketing practices of the trade almost suggest that they prefer rare and endangered species — the rarer the species, the higher the price of the product.

The industry also pointed out that they did not pay the hunters, but only purchased the skins of animals already dead. The Mason bill would not resurrect those animals. While it is certainly true that a ban on sales will not restore life to dead animals, the money from retail sales pays the manufacturer and importer. He in turn pays the foreign dealer, who pays the hunters and poachers. When the whole operation is understood, it is apparent to everyone that the buying public, together with the retail dealer, is supporting the commercial slaughter of wild animals.

The industry questioned the need for protecting all tigers, all leopards, or all crocodilians, when only some species or subspecies are endangered. They asked that the Mason bill be rewritten to include only the endangered forms. Aside from not recognizing the difficulty of distinguishing the skins of endangered forms from nonendangered ones, this points up a lack of insight into the problem of commercially endangered species. Many dealers treat the absence of a particular animal on an endangered species list as license to exploit it. They reason that if it is not endangered, it must be abundant, ignoring the many intermediate states of rare, once abundant but now depleted, and declining in numbers. An animal in any of these categories should not be subject to uncontrolled exploitation.

To counter the zoologists, who supported the ban on sales of all animals that could be confused with endangered species or subspecies, the industry argued that hides could be identified from their shipping points. They claimed that African skins are shipped from Africa or, more specifically, that only Kenya skins come from Kenya and only Indian furs arrive from India. The U.S. Department of Commerce figures disprove this assumption, however. In 1968, cheetah skins were imported from India, but the Indian cheetah has been extinct since 1948. These were African skins transshipped through India. In that same year, transshipped African leopard skins were imported from Argentina, while jaguar skins from tropical America were flown in from the Netherlands, France, Germany, and South Africa. Ocelot skins arrived regularly from England. African slender-snouted crocodiles and South American caimans entered from Thailand. Transshipment is so widespread that importers cannot be sure of the country of origin. This is especially true where smuggling occurs to obscure the origin of the skins.

At the New York hearings, a letter from Mohamed Awaleh, head of the Wildlife Department of Somalia, was read. Mr. Awaleh described the difficulty of enforcing wildlife protection laws when the profit to be made from smuggling poached skins is great. He said,

I personally blame America and Europe for most of this smuggling because it is with your dollars [that] you indirectly contribute to the mass slaughter of wild game. Smuggling . . . is so great that I could not do much in spite of strong new law[s]. . . . I am now appealing to any responsible and conservation-minded American to help us by trying to discourage or forbid importation of such rare species as leopard and cheata [cheetah] from any place in Africa.

Perez Olindo, head of the Kenya National Park System, sent a similar letter pleading for passage of the Mason bill. He told how several of his wardens are killed each year by poachers and stated that African wildlife could not be adequately protected until the profit was taken out of poaching. The only way to do this is to prohibit imports into the United States and Europe. And prior to the hearing in Albany, the wife of the Indian Consul General read a statement from Indira Gandhi asking for aid from the citizens of the United States in protecting the big cats and crocodiles of India from further exploitation.

The Mason bill eventually passed the New York legislature and was due to go into effect on September 1, 1970.

In July, 1970, suit was brought in the State Supreme Court of Onondaga County by the A. E. Nettleton Company of Syracuse contesting the constitutionality of the Mason Act and the Harris Act, another piece of endangered species legislation. The Nettleton Company manufactures shoes, some of which are made from crocodilian hides. Nettleton was joined in its suit by four other fur and reptile-hide manufacturers and retailers. In their complaints, they questioned whether the state had the authority to prohibit the sale of animals not on the federal Endangered Species List. They reasoned that the Endangered Species Conservation Act of 1969 had pre-empted the field. They also questioned whether the Mason Act, in prohibiting the sale of foreign species, conflicted with the federal authority to regulate interstate and international commerce.

In defense of the law, the New York Attorney General's Office contended that the state had the authority both to ban the sales of foreign species within the state and to base the ban on an endangered species list that was at variance with the federal list. The attorney general argued that the legislature was correct in considering the consumer's right to know that the products he is purchasing are not made from endangered animals and to protect him from fraud associated with this.

In its complaint, Nettleton stated that it did not use endangered species in the manufacture of shoes. Claiming to use only "tinga" and "tinga alligator" hides, to which the company applied the scientific names *Caiman sclerops* and *C. latirostris,* Nettleton pointed out that neither of these species is on the federal Endangered Species List. According to Nettleton, these hides were imported from western Brazil, Venezuela, Colombia, Peru, Bolivia, and Paraguay. The facts dispute Nettleton's claim. Tinga and tinga alligator are trade names applied to any of the subspecies of common caiman, *Caiman crocodilus* (*C. sclerops* is an old synonym for this species). The trade names are derived from the Spanish and Portuguese common name *jacaretinga.* The species also has numerous other South American common names. In the United States it is sometimes called spectacled caiman when sold as a pet, and alligator when sold as leather goods. There are four subspecies recognized by zoologists. One is found in Central America, one in the Apaporis River of Colombia, one in northern South America, and one in central and southern South America. The last subspecies is the jacare caiman, *C. crocodilus yacare.* It is the subspecies found in western Brazil, Bolivia, Argentina, and Paraguay, and it is on the federal Endangered Species List. And there is no way to

separate this subspecies from any of the other subspecies on the basis of commercial skins alone.

Nettleton's complaint admits that the firm uses hides of *Caiman crocodilus,* and that some of these hides come from western Brazil, Bolivia, and Paraguay. Since the only representative of the species in those countries is *C. crocodilus yacare,* which is on the federal Endangered Species List, how can Nettleton sustain its claim of not using endangered species in its business?

The other species mentioned in the complaint, *Caiman latirostris,* is the broadsnouted caiman of southern South America. Its hide is sold under the common name *overo,* not tinga as claimed by the company. If Nettleton cannot distinguish between hides of the two species, this supports the conservationists' belief that it is difficult to separate species of crocodilians on the basis of commercial hides alone. If Nettleton can separate them, but called the hides tinga, it confused the facts in its complaint.

In August, the lower court ruled that the Mason Act was unconstitutional because it exceeded the state's police powers and deprived the industry of property without due process of law. The court relied heavily on the fact that

> the Act does not protect the State's domestic game and wildlife. None of the prohibited Crocodylia is indigenous to New York. In its blanket application, banning all species of crocodiles, the Mason Act is too broad and as such is prohibitive. A persuasive factor in the effect of the Mason Act is its failure to discriminate between the endangered and unendangered species, which is what the federal act does. . . . This type of legislation exceeds the bounds of necessity and is unconstitutionally oppressive.

The attorney general immediately appealed the ruling directly to the State Court of Appeals. Legal precedents were found for states protecting species that were not yet endangered, protecting them "before the danger is unmistakenly imminent," and for states protecting foreign species, as was done under New York's 1909 Bird Plumage Act. It was also pointed out that the federal government has long recognized the states' power to regulate wildlife within its borders whether indigenous or imported. A section of the Lacey Act clearly states that all dead game animals and birds, or their parts, when imported into a state become subject to the laws of the state "to the same extent and in the same manner as though such animals or birds had been produced in such state."

In October the Court of Appeals overturned the lower court by affirming the constitutionality of the Mason Act. In making the ruling the court stated that the law would be unreasonable only if the ban on all sales of the animals listed was unreasonable. Since such a ban was the only way to protect species endangered by commerce, it was not unreasonable. They did "not agree with the industry that the Mason law goes too far." They held that the state was not pre-empted by the federal Endangered Species Conservation Act, and therefore had the power to enact the Mason Act. They further held that the state had not deprived the industry of property without due process. Since the Act banned sales after September 1, the court allowed industry to dispose of animals, hides, and products that arrived before that date.

While all this had been happening in the state courts, Palladio, Inc., a Massachusetts "alligator" shoe manufacturer, had filed suit in federal court to contest the constitutionality of the Mason Act.

The Palladio suit was initiated before the Nettleton ruling had come from the State Court of Appeals, but the Palladio company had agreed to await that ruling. When the state court upheld the Mason Act, Palladio sought to bring its case to the U.S. District Court in Manhattan. Like Nettleton, Palladio argued that the federal legislation pre-empted the field of endangered species law.

The Massachusetts company and the industry also questioned whether or not the law was unreasonable, for they maintained that it is possible to distinguish between the hides of endangered and nonendangered species of crocodilians.

Federal District Judge D. J. Mansfield ruled, however, that the industry had failed to raise a substantial federal question in its complaint. Judge Mansfield, in upholding the Mason Act, stated that:

> It is now generally recognized that the destruction or disturbance of vital life cycles or of the balance of a species of wildlife, even though initiated in one part of the world, may have profound effect upon the health and welfare of people in other distant parts. We have come to appreciate the interdependence of different forms of life. We realize that by killing certain species in one area we may sound our own death knell. . . . Nowhere does the Secretary of Interior indicate that his list of endangered species is definitive. The state's list of endangered species may be broader than the federal list simply because the state legislature did not see fit to wait until only a handful of species remained before it passed a law affording protection. We cannot overrule the legislature for being cautious.

On March 22, 1971, the United States Supreme Court refused to hear the appeal of the Nettleton Company, thereby upholding Judge Mansfield's opinion on state legislative protection of wildlife. The United States District Court of Appeals similarly denied the Palladio Company's suit on March 26.

Since the year 1600, more than 120 species of animals have become extinct. Even though hundreds more are on the verge of extinction today, it would seem the American public is willing to prevent this when possible. Since the Mason Act was first signed into law, California has passed a similar bill. California did not protect the mountain lion, but they did add the sea otter and mustang to their list. Florida has banned the sales of all alligator, caiman, and crocodile products. The Massachusetts legislature is debating passage of an endangered species bill, and others are in preparation by at least four other states. The public is not willing to let animal species die unnoticed, for as noted by Judge Mansfield,

> Extinct animals, like lost time, can never be brought back. They are gone forever.

EDITOR'S COMMENTS

Of the some million and a half kinds of living things that inhabit this planet, man is only one. The others range from microscopic bacteria that only a few specialists are aware of, to the great blue whale, the largest animal that has ever existed. The fact that during the last four hundred years our fellow inhabitants have been wiped out at the rate of about one species per year seems to concern no one. The ignorant often say "Extinction is a natural process. Look at all the species that have become extinct previously. If we lose a few more, so what? It's a natural process."

It is true that extinction is natural. Species may become extinct and be replaced by others, or they may change and become others. Only in the former case is a lineage terminated. This is true extinction.

Natural extinction occurs when an organism fails to adapt to a change in the environment. Today the great majority of environmental changes are man-caused. If one wants to think of modern man as "natural" then, in a sense, all man-caused extinction is also "natural." But can we logically think of modern man as natural? It is obvious that at sometime in man's past he became dissociated from the natural checks and balances that govern the existence of all other species. Man is the only organism which has undertaken the destruction of the natural systems which support its existence. Man has purposely withdrawn from the natural world. He has sold his birthright for the sake of convenience, comfort, and to support ever-increasing numbers of his own kind. Modern man and his actions can no longer be considered natural.

Man has recently speeded up the process of extinction so that it is some thousands of times as great as that which occurred previously. The question can still be asked however, "So what, who cares about a few bugs, birds or creepy-crawlies? What good are they?" The latter question unfortunately typifies the attitude of most people. Unless something can be shown to have immediate value or use, preferably monetary, it is thought of as being worthless. Can the saving of a species be justified in the face of such motivations? The answer is often "no." But for those who think of what good a species might someday do them or other humans, a number of facts should be considered.

Before 1928, the green mold *Penicillium* was thought of as just another slimy, somewhat repulsive fungus. Who would have predicted that in 1928 Alexander Fleming would find in this mold a substance which would save more lives than any other drug?

No one believes that we can get a miracle drug or a cancer cure from every species. But the fact remains that each species is unique and may possess features which will enable man to use it in a way that he can use no other. Can we afford to throw away any of these potentially useful organisms? Is it logical to frivolously eradicate a resource which we may need in the future?

Man's survival is predicated upon the continued existence of ecosystems which he still knows little about. Reduction of species diversity in ecosystems reduces stability. Reduction of stability creates problems which often cannot be predicted. Many of these problems are greater than the problem which we thought we were solving by actions that resulted in the elimination of a species. Therefore, we cannot abandon any species as unnecessary or consider it superfluous until we know its exact role in the ecosystem; i.e., how it affects or is affected by other species. If we fail to consider these roles, we risk creating future problems which may make present ones seem small by comparison. Elimination of species is like randomly removing bricks from the building that one lives in. Sooner or later the entire structure will come tumbling down on the head of the occupants.

Many species are useful to man as indicators. An aquatic biologist can detect the presence of a disturbing factor in a lake or river by observing changes in the numbers and kinds of species living there. Many organisms respond to minute changes that man may have difficulty detecting without the presence of the organisms to serve as a warning system. Like man, these organisms are adapted to conditions on this planet. Factors which affect them detrimentally may also be damaging to man. If we discard these organisms, the results of environmental alteration may not be noticed until they affect man himself. By then, it may be too late.

It is obvious that we need to retain all existing species because of our own present and future needs. Preserving species because of self-interest is understandable, but should it be the only reason? Does not man have a responsibility to other forms of life? Man is the only animal capable of consciously eliminating any other species. This potential should bring with it a sense of responsibility. The miracle of life on earth is too precious to be randomly and carelessly discarded bit by bit.

If extinction continues at its present rate, we can look forward to a time in the future when man lives alone on the earth with his machines. The beauty of the lilies, the honking of geese, the bright eyes of the squirrel, and the majesty of the redwoods may be, by our own stupidity, denied to our descendants. It will be too late to relent when we find that this destruction of our fellow inhabitants is a major cause of our own extinction. Who will care about man when the world spins lifelessly through the void, serving only as a monument to man's destruction and ignorance?

SOURCES OF ADDITIONAL INFORMATION

BIOCIDES

Benson, R. L. 1971. On the necessity of controlling the level of insecticide resistance in insect populations. *BioScience* 21(23):1160-1165.

Blus, L., et al. 1971. Eggshell thinning in the brown pelican: Implication of DDE. *BioScience* 21(24):1213-1215.

Butler, P. A. 1969. Monitoring pesticide pollution. *BioScience* 19(10):889-891.

Carson, R. 1962. *Silent spring.* Fawcett Publications, Inc., Greenwich, Conn.

Coon, D. W., and R. R. Fleet. 1970. The ant war. *Environment* 12(10):28-37.

Edwards, C. 1969. Soil pollutants and soil animals. *Scientific American* 220(4):88-99.

Edwards, C. 1970. *Persistent pesticides in the environment.* Chemical Rubber Company Press, Cleveland, Ohio.

Enderson, J. H., and D. D. Berger. 1970. Pesticides: eggshell thinning and lowered production of young in prairie falcons. *BioScience* 20(6):355-356.

Epstin, S. S. 1970. A family likeness. *Environment* 12(6):16-25.

Galstone, A. W. 1971. Some implications of the widespread use of herbicides. *BioScience* 21(17):891-892.

Gillette, R. 1971. DDT: in field and courtroom, a persistant pesticide lives on. *Science* 174(4014):1108-1110.

Graham, F., Jr. 1970. *Since silent spring.* Houghton Mifflin, Boston, Massachusetts.

Grosch, D. S. 1970. Poisoning with DDT: second- and third-year reproductive performance of *Artemia*. *BioScience* 20(16):913.

Hinckley, A. D. 1972. The gypsy moth. *Environment* 14(2):41-47.

McCaull, J. 1971. Questions for an old friend. *Environment* 13(6):2-9.

Moats, S. A., and W. A. Moats. 1970. Toward safer use of pesticides. *BioScience* 20(8):459-464.

Peakall, D. B. 1970. Pesticides and the reproduction of birds. *Scientific American* 222(4):72-78.

Pimentel, D. 1971. Evolutionary and environmental impact of pesticides. *BioScience* 21(3):109-110.

Rudd, R. L. 1964. *Pesticides and the living landscape.* University of Wisconsin Press, Madison, Wisconsin.

Shea, K. P. 1972. Captan and folpet. *Environment* 14(1):22-32.

Westing, A. H. 1971. Ecological effects of military defoliation on the forests of South Vietnam. *BioScience* 21(17):893-898.

Whiteside, T. 1971. *The withering rain: America's herbicidal folly.* E. P. Dutton, New York.

Williams, C. M. 1967. Third-generation pesticides. *Scientific American* 217(1):13-17.

Woodwell, G. M. 1967. Toxic substances and ecological cycles. *Scientific American* 216(3):24-31.

Woodwell, G. M., et al. 1971. DDT in the biosphere: Where does it go? *Science* 174(4014):1101-1107.

PEST CONTROL WITHOUT PESTICIDES

Baumhover, A. H., et al. 1955. Screw-worm control through the release of sterilized flies. *J. Econ. Entomol.* 48:462-466.

DeBach, P., ed. 1964. *Biological control of insect pests and weeds.* Reinhold, New York.

Huffaker, C. B. 1971. *Biological control.* Plenum Publishing Corp., New York.

Maddox, D. M., et al. 1971. Insects to control alligatorweed. *BioScience* 21(19):985-991.

Ordish, G. 1967. *Biological methods in crop pest control.* Constable, London.

FOOD ADDITIVES

Kermode, G. O. 1972. Food additives. *Scientific American* 226(3):15-21.

Kohlmeier, L. M., Jr. 1969. *The regulators, watchdog agencies and the public interest.* Harper and Row, New York.

Longgood, W. F. 1960. *The poisons in your food.* Simon and Schuster, New York.

RADIATION

Curtis, R., and E. Hogan. 1969. *Perils of the peaceful atom.* Doubleday and Co., New York.

Farmer, F. 1970. Safety assessment of fast sodium-cooled reactors in the United Kingdom. *Nuclear Safety* 11:238.

Forbes, I. A., et al. 1972. Cooling water. *Environment* 14(1):40-47.

Frye, A. 1962. *The hazards of atomic wastes.* Washington Public Affairs Press, Washington, D.C.

Gillette, R. 1972. Nuclear reactor safety: at the AEC the way of the dissenter is hard. *Science* 176(4034):492-498.

Gofman, J., and A. Tamplin. 1970. Radiation: the invisible casualties. *Environment* 12(3): 12.

Gofman, J., and A. Tamplin. 1971. *Poisoned power.* Rodale Press, Emmaus, Pennsylvania.

Gough, W., and B. Eastlund. 1971. The prospects of fusion power. *Scientific American,* Feb. 1971.

Martell, E. A., et al. 1970. Fire damage! *Environment* 12(4):14-21.

Nelson, N. 1968. Some biological effects of radiation in relation to other environmental agents. *Biological implications of the nuclear age,* proceedings of a symposium at Lawrence Radiation Laboratory, Atomic Energy Commission Division of Technical Information, Oak Ridge, Tenn. pp. 223-229.

Novick, S. 1969. *The careless atom.* Houghton-Mifflin, Boston.

Novick, S. 1971. Seventeen million years. *Environment* 13(9):42-47.

Pollard, E. 1969. The biological action of ionizing radiation. *Am. Scientist* 57:206-236.

Rhoads, W. A., and R. B. Platt. 1971. Beta radiation damage to vegetation from close-in fallout from two nuclear detonations. *BioScience* 21(22):1121-1125.

Seaborg, G. T., and J. L. Bloom. 1970. Fast breeder reactors. *Scientific American* 223 (5):13-21.

Stonier, T. 1963. *Nuclear disaster.* Meridian, Cleveland.

Tamplin, A., and J. Gofman. 1970. *Population control through nuclear pollution.* Nelson Hall Co., Chicago.

Wood, L., and J. Nuckolls. 1972. Fusion power. *Environment* 14(4):29-33.

NOISE

Baron, R. A. 1970. *The tyranny of noise.* St. Martin's Press, New York.

Berland, T. 1970. *The fight for quiet.* Prentice-Hall, New York.

Berland, T. 1971. No place to hide. *Ecology Today* 1(5):8-10.

Burns, W. 1969. *Noise and man.* J. B. Lippincott, Philadelphia, Pennsylvania.

Goodfriend, L. S. 1971. *Noise pollution.* Chemical Rubber Company Press, Cleveland, Ohio.

Kryter, K. D. 1970. *The effects of noise on man.* Academic Press, New York.

Stewart-Gordon, J. 1970. We're poisoning ourselves with noise. *Readers Digest.* February, 1970:187-194.

Still, H. 1970. *In quest of quiet.* Stackpole Books, Harrisburg, Pennsylvania.

Welch, B. L., and A. S. Welch, eds. 1970. *Physiological effects of noise.* Plenum Press, New York.

WILDLIFE AND EXTINCTION

Fisher, J., N. Simon, and J. Vincent. 1969. *Wildlife in danger.* Viking Press, New York.

Laycock, G. 1966. *The alien animals.* Natural History Press, New York.

Laycock, G. 1969. *America's endangered wildlife.* W. W. Norton, New York.

MacNamara, E. E. 1971. A vanishing sport. *Ecology Today* 1(1):37-39.

McClung, R. M. 1969. *Lost wild America.* Wm. Morrow, New York.

McHugh, J. L. 1969. The United States and world whale resources. *BioScience* 19(12): 1075-1078.

Moment, G. B. 1970. Man-grizzly problems — past and present; implications for endangered species. *BioScience* 20(21):1142-1144.

Mossman, A. S. 1970. Environmental crisis and the wildlife ecologist. *BioScience* 20 (14):813-814.

Olsen, J. 1971. *Slaughter the animals, poison the earth.* Simon and Schuster, New York.

Simon, N., and P. Geroudet. 1970. *Last survivors: natural history of 48 animals in danger of extinction.* World Publishing Co., New York.

Ziswiler, V. 1967. *Extinct and vanishing animals.* Springer-Verlag New York.

Part V

The Land and Its
Resources

IRVING BENGELSDORF

Are We Running Out of Fuel?

Irving S. Bengelsdorf is Director of Science Communication at the California Institute of Technology. As former science editor of the *Los Angeles Times,* he has been writing about pollution of the global environment since 1963. Author of the booklet, "Spaceship Earth: People and Pollution," he has won numerous scientific writing awards including the Claude Bernard Science Journalism award from the National Society for Medical Research.

Love is not all it takes to make the world go round; it also takes energy. Man's pursuit of energy sources has profoundly affected the course of history, it has created severe social problems, and now it threatens our very survival.

The development of agriculture by early hunting and foraging man provided a reliable, steady energy source which allowed civilizations and populations to grow and flourish. It is estimated that without agriculture our planet could support a human population of only about 10 million. This is fewer people than live in London or the entire country of Kenya, and it is only about three-tenths of one percent of the present human population of 3.6 billion.

As man's numbers have increased, so have his energy, or fuel, demands (the words "energy" and "fuel" may be used inter-changeably). The insatiable demand for more and more energy by densely populated technological societies is now ripping the thin veneer of our global environment. Moreover, as the aspirations of the so-called underdeveloped nations mount, demands for increased amounts of energy inevitably accompany them.

Consumption of energy pollutes and warms the air above us and the seas around us; it spreads disease and destroys the aesthetic values of land. Men in general, and Americans in particular, are energy profligates and wastrels. We now are engaged in an unprecedented energy-consuming spree.

Though coal has been mined for 800 years, one-half of it has been dug in the last 33 years. Petroleum has been pumped out of the ground for about 100 years, but one-half of it has been pumped out in the last 14 years.

Stated another way, most of the world's consumption of energy from fossil fuels — from the beginning of recorded history until today — has taken place in the last 25 years!

The United States is the world's leading energy spendthrift. With less than 6 percent

of the world's population, Americans annually consume more than one-third of the world's energy expenditures. In contrast, India, with about 15 percent of the world's population, consumes only about 1.5 percent of the world's energy. What is socially and politically disturbing is that India and the other technologically underdeveloped countries cannot hope to better themselves economically unless they also greatly increase their energy consumption — which in turn causes increased pollution.

Can such an energy binge long continue? And if it can, what are the environmental prices we must pay?

Before we try to answer these questions, we must understand that all our energy comes from the sun in the form of two energy bank accounts: a *renewable* account in which energy deposits are made every day, and a *nonrenewable* account that has a fixed energy deposit which we continuously deplete by our withdrawals.

Renewable Sources

First, consider the daily renewable energy bank account. Like other stars, the sun is a huge, glowing thermonuclear furnace. Located 93 million miles from the sun, our planet is an infinitesimal speck in the cosmos that intercepts an incredibly tiny fraction of the energy that pours out from the sun. Yet, it is this exceedingly minute fraction of the total solar energy that makes life possible on earth.

PHOTOSYNTHESIS

Green plants play key roles in our renewable energy account. They alone have the incredible ability to convert the energy in sunbeams into the energy in wood, rice, corn, wheat, sugar cane, and other natural products. This is the process we call photosynthesis, and an understanding of it is the first basic lesson in ecology. Man produces nothing; he only consumes. It is the green

plants that act as intermediary energy brokers between man and the sun to keep man going as an energy consumer.

Of all the forms of energy consumed by man, none is more important — none has more consequences — than food. Historically, an increased food supply has meant an increase in population which, in turn, has increased the need for more food. It is this mutually reinforcing, positive-feedback relationship between food and people that is responsible for the ever-increasing demands on both our energy sources and the planet's environment. (It is interesting to note that there are more human "engines" in the world that burn rice as fuel, than there are engines that run on gasoline.)

Increased food production means more pesticides and fertilizers, and consequent potential pollution. It may also mean the inundation of scenic or historic landscapes by man-made lakes that extend in back of dams built to provide water for irrigation. In tropical countries, moreover, the quiet, fresh water of irrigation channels and ditches sometimes breeds disease. The construction of a dam can be a delight to the ministries of agriculture and power, but a despair to the ministry of health.

In addition to food, other sources of energy in our renewable bank account are direct solar energy, wind power, tidal power, and hydroelectric power. Though these energy sources generally have minimum impact on the environment (with hydroelectric dams the exception), none plays a significant role anymore in the world's overall energy picture, nor will in the future.

SOLAR ENERGY

The enormous amount of sun power intercepted by earth is about 100,000 times greater than the entire world's presently installed electrical power-generating capacity. But it is terribly diffuse and difficult to concentrate. The capital investment for a solar power installation is prohibitive.

Direct solar energy, of course, can be used for small-scale, special-purpose uses such as solar furnaces, solar cooking stoves, water and house heating. The sun's energy also runs our atmospheric "engine," causing winds to blow. Though wind power played a historic role in man's use of energy — windmills and Yankee clippers — it is little used today.

HYDROELECTRIC POWER

The sun's energy evaporates water from the ocean's surface, changing salty water to fresh water in the form of clouds, snow and rain. The snow melts and rain falls, and as the fresh water runs back in the form of a river to the sea, we can harness its energy to turn a turbine to produce electricity. Slightly more than 4 percent of America's total power usage is now met by hydro-electric-produced power. This may increase to about 5 percent by the year 2000.

The world has a hydroelectric power potential comparable to the *total* amount of power consumed today (with most of this potential in Africa and South America). We use only about 8 percent of this potential and any further growth in hydroelectric power must deal with these questions:

1. Does the world want to sacrifice much of its most beautiful natural scenery to dams and the resulting lakes?
2. Would the energy generated by a dam be more valuable than the energy which could be released through foods grown on the lands flooded by dams?
3. Is it worthwhile to build dams if they will last only about 50-100 years before they clog up with silt and sediment carried by the dammed streams?

TIDAL POWER

Instead of using the one-way flow of water from river to sea to generate electricity, why not use the daily two-way movement of water — the ebb and flow of the tides? A major tidal-electric power plant now operates in France, and one was once considered in Maine.

The best that can be said is that if the world's potential tidal power were fully developed, it would amount to only about 1 percent of the world's potential hydro-electric power.

This completes our inventory of our renewable energy bank account. Green plants, we have seen, are responsible for our most important renewable source of energy. But they are constantly being depleted, not only by consumption (trees cut down), but also by pollution (one can no longer grow broad-leaved vegetables in the smog of the Los Angeles basin). Furthermore, prime land to grow crops, orchards and forests is fast disappearing under such land-obliterating "advances" as highway construction, housing developments, airports and dams. Our other renewable energy sources are, for one reason or another, of limited scope.

Nonrenewable Sources

This takes us to our planetary, nonrenewable energy bank account with finite deposits of coal, oil, natural gas, shale, tar sands, uranium-235 and uranium-238, deuterium and also geothermal energy.

The so-called fossil fuel — coal, oil, natural gas, shale and tar sands — are the subterranean remains of green plants that once grew and then were buried long ago in geological time. Nonrenewable fossil fuels are thus the remnants of ancient sunbeams that slammed into earth aeons ago.

COAL

Of the fossil fuels, coal is in greatest supply. The United States has enough coal to meet industrial energy needs, at present consumption rates, for about 350-450 years. Unfortunately, coal is an "unclean" fuel, and its use leads to air pollution, especially from sulfur oxides.

While engineering research has been preoccupied with the development of novel nuclear energy, research to make cheap fuel — to remove its sulfur before or after burning — has been neglected. Some scientists feel that a "massive injection of money into coal engineering could lead to suppression of sulfur dioxide and at the same time to a lower cost of power generated from coal." Research to gasify coal — to convert it into a gaseous fuel — has also lagged badly.

NATURAL GAS

Now obtained from petroleum production, natural gas is the fossil fuel in shortest supply, and demand has tripled in the last 20 years.

Thus, in 1941, if one divided the proved reserves of natural gas by the consumption that year, there was a 33-year supply of natural gas available. But by 1965, the same ratio of proved reserves to consumption had dropped to only a 17-year supply. "Brownouts" due to short supplies of natural gas could become an ever-more frequent occurrence in the next decade.

PETROLEUM

As for petroleum, not only is there less oil than coal, but it is also being consumed at a faster rate. In 1900, America obtained 89 percent of its energy from coal and 7.8 percent from oil. But in 1965, about 68 percent of U.S. energy came from oil and 28 percent from coal.

It is estimated that American oil fields, including the new Alaska find, now have about a 30-35-year supply of petroleum remaining, at current consumption levels. The importation of ever-greater amounts of petroleum and natural gas from foreign countries is dependent upon the international political situation and is in conflict with underdeveloped nations, whose rising economic expectations are dependent upon their own increased energy consumption.

OTHER FOSSIL FUELS

There are, however, two additional fossil fuel sources. Near Fort McMurray in northeastern Alberta, there are large deposits of the *Athabasca tar sands* containing an extremely viscous, nonflowing, petroleumlike liquid fuel. Starting in 1967, a large-scale plant began extracting 45,000 barrels of tar-sand oil daily.

In Colorado, Utah and Wyoming there are deposits of *oil shale* from which a solid fuel called kerogen can be obtained. But the processing of kerogen from oil shale is in an experimental stage; no large-scale production is underway. And the disposal of tons of extracted shale rock could be a serious environmental problem since it would damage wildlife habitat (Colorado, for example, is the wintering ground for the world's largest migrating mule deer herd).

The supply of coal, oil, natural gas, oil shale and tar sands is sufficient, in terms of current consumption levels, to meet immediate future needs, but we must remember that it is finite. Or, as Dr. M. King Hubbart of the U.S. Geological Society writes,

The epoch of fossil fuel can only be a transitory and ephemeral event. . . .

With the end in sight for some of the fossil fuels in our nonrenewable energy bank

Americans make up less than 6% of the world's population, yet the mechanical "slaves" that do 98% of our work devour more than one-third of global energy expenditures

account, the world has looked to geothermal energy and nuclear energy.

GEOTHERMAL ENERGY

Using underground heat or hot water heated in the earth's interior by such naturally radioactive atoms as potassium-40, geothermal energy is now being used in Italy, New Zealand, Japan, Mexico, Iceland, the U.S.S.R. and California. But this energy is very limited in scope, suited only for a specific locale where earth's internal heat can be tapped easily.

NUCLEAR ENERGY

Uranium-235 is the only variety of atom found in nature that can fall apart (undergo fission) to release heat to be used to generate electricity, and uranium-235 is rare. Of every 140 uranium atoms in nature, only one is U-235. Moreover, our present-day, pressurized-water nuclear reactors are primitive devices, terribly inefficient, and if they were to be used to produce our future requirements of electricity, *we would use up all our U-235 in 20-30 years.*

Fortunately, there is a more sophisticated, more efficient nuclear reactor called a breeder reactor that could save the day. But breeder reactors are experimental. No large-scale breeder fission reactor is currently in operation, though a crash research program now underway may, if successful, enable us to have it by the 1980s.

Of every 140 uranium atoms in nature, 139 are uranium-238. Though U-238 does not undergo fission as does U-235, it can be changed into another variety of atom called plutonium-239. And Pu-239, like U-235, can undergo fission to produce electricity. Thus, nonfissionable U-238 can "breed" fissionable Pu-239, and U-238 is plentiful in rocks.

But the use of nuclear fission energy to generate electricity involves a radiation hazard to the environment. Proper use of nuclear fission may involve the location of power plants remote from densely populated areas, careful reactor design, establishment of suitable radiation standards, and the regulation of nuclear power plant construction and operation.

The disposal and storage of radioactive wastes from nuclear power plants will, moreover, make radioactive waste our number one garbage problem by the end of this century. Future generations may have to monitor and stand guard over some of our nuclear excreta for about 10,000 years.

THERMONUCLEAR FUSION

Instead of heavyweight nuclei releasing energy by falling apart as in the fission of U-235 or Pu-239, lightweight nuclei can combine or fuse together at extremely high temperatures to release energy by thermonuclear *fusion.* Man has mastered *uncontrolled* thermonuclear fusion, the energy of exploding H-bombs. But he has not mastered *controlled* thermonuclear fusion, the energy that powers the sun and the stars.

Who will be the modern Prometheus who kindles the celestial fires of the stars here on earth? The achievement of controlled thermonuclear fusion to generate electricity is a major engineering challenge of our time. Yet U.S. research funds for controlled thermonuclear fusion are only about $30 million per year. Many scientists feel that such research funds should be at least doubled.

Thus far, controlled thermonuclear fusion is not technically feasible. As yet, it has not even been demonstrated experimentally. But if the controlled thermonuclear fusion of deuterium atoms — a heavyweight variety of hydrogen atoms — to produce electricity becomes technically and economically feasible, it would open up "unlimited" energy vistas for all mankind.

The energy released by the controlled thermonuclear fusion of only 1 percent of the deuterium atoms present in the oceans would be about 500,000 times as much energy as our planet's total fossil fuel energy bank account originally contained. We would enjoy an energy abundance through the "burning of water" with less radiation and thermal pollution than from nuclear fission.

We may run out of certain types of fuel, but we will not run out of energy. I predict the the limitations of energy production will not depend on fuel supplies, but on the deterioration of our natural environment.

Besides air, water and land pollution, and contamination by radiation, energy production also gives rise to waste heat. Not only does the river or ocean water used for cooling an electrical power-generating plant become warmer, but so does the air. The electricity that exits from generating plants enters factories, offices and homes and dissipates heat in motors, fluorescent lamps, television sets, toasters, washing machines, dryers, refrigerators and can openers. This leads to warmer and warmer air. In turn, we install more and more air conditioners. They make our air still warmer. And so on. The amount of heat generated by man-made activities in Los Angeles now amounts to about five percent of the total sunlight the city receives daily from the sun.

Not only will it be difficult for our air and water to absorb the diverse and unwanted chemical and thermal by-products of energy production, but also our landscape will be desecrated to accommodate transmission lines, radioactive waste storage and sites for power plants. For example, if the 8.8 percent annual increase in electricity produced in California during the 16-year period 1950-1966 were to continue for the next three decades, California would have to construct 92 additional power plants, each of 4,000-megawatt capacity. That amounts to one power plant for every 10 miles of California coastline!

International agricultural authority Lester R. Brown, commenting on the world's food problems, says: "Whatever measures are taken, there is growing doubt that the agricultural ecosystem will be able to accommodate both the anticipated increase of the human population to seven billion by the end of the century and the universal desire of the world's hungry for a better diet."

"The central question is no longer, Can we produce enough food? but What are the environmental consequences of attempting to do so?"

> The big question men must face up to is: How many people can the earth support, and at what standard of living?

What goes for food production also goes for energy production. Or, to state the matter another way: How many people can the earth support, at what standard of living, and at what level of environmental deterioration? The central question is no longer, Can we generate enough energy? but, Will we wreck our environment attempting to do so?

EDITOR'S COMMENTS

As Dr. Bengelsdorf points out, our fossil fuel reserves are finite. Once chewed up and devoured, the crust of the earth cannot grow back. Fuels, however, are only one of the products of the earth's crust. We are also consuming prodigious quantities of non-fuel minerals. Among them are the metals such as iron, copper, aluminum, tin, and gold. The known reserves of some (molybdenum, mercury, copper, silver, lead, nickel, tin) have already been reduced to levels which will sustain their continued unrestricted use for only a few decades.

Nonmetallic minerals are also of critical importance although their uses are not so conspicuous. Materials such as asbestos, clays, gypsum, lime, salt, marble, sulfur, and gravels are used in large quantities. Presently we do not know how to efficiently reuse most of these.

Like the fossil fuels, the nonfuel minerals are present in limited quantities in the earth's crust. Yet today we are using many of them as if the supply was endless. This is particularly true in the United States where we often use as much of an important mineral as the entire rest of the world. New mineral discoveries cannot continue forever. Over the past 100 years only 18 percent of the aluminum, 41 percent of the silver, 28 percent of the tin, 40 percent of the iron and steel, and 42 percent of the lead have been reclaimed and recycled in the United States. Our failure to reuse critical materials cannot continue at this rate. Recycling must soon become close to 100 percent efficient. We must develop new, less wasteful technologies. We must conserve our mineral resources by eliminating wasteful uses.

Most of us alive today will never be critically affected by *our* overuse of energy and *our* overconsumption of materials. However, *our* careless use could be a major factor in pulling the rug out from under succeeding generations who may also consider these materials indispensable to their way of life.

JACK TRAWICK

Strip Mining

Jack Trawick is state news editor of the
Winston-Salem, North Carolina *Journal* and
Sentinel newspapers. He wrote and photo-
graphed a series of articles about strip mining
in Kentucky, and directed the newspapers'
coverage of a strip mining threat in Northwest
North Carolina that won for the papers the
Pulitzer Prize for Public Service in 1971.

The sign along the roadside says "Keep
Kentucky Green." But for as far as you can
see, there is very little to keep green.

It is a study in black and gray and yel-
lowish-brown, etched in scars on what were
once beautifully forested slopes.

There are broken and battered trees,
mangled by huge rocks and piles of shale
that have been pushed down the mountain-
sides to clear the path to the coal and
minerals that have been taken from the
mountains. There is garbage, and there are
the rusting hulks of junked automobiles
strewn down the slopes.

You don't have to search for the damage,
the depression, the oppressive atmosphere.
It is all around you, above and below, and
plainly visible from the main highways, such
as they are.

And even as you look, huge trucks, some
loaded with as much as 25 tons of coal,
rumble by in a steady stream, kicking up

dust and further damaging roads that, in
some places, have already been damaged
so badly that the blacktop surface has been
mashed into the dirt out of sight.

This is Letcher County, Kentucky. This
is strip mining in the Appalachian mountains. The scene is no different throughout
most of eastern Kentucky, most of West
Virginia, and huge sections of Pennsylvania, Indiana and Ohio.

Strip mining, in varying degrees, has affected all 50 states. The effects are more
apparent, and the damage more enduring, in
mountainous regions, because of the difficulty and expense in reclaiming the land
after the mining is finished.

Strip mining goes by many names. The
mining firms do not like the term "strip
mining" because it has come to carry an
unpleasant connotation. "Surface mining"
is more acceptable to them. It has been
generally defined to cover all types of mining
on the surface of the earth, as opposed to
deep mining, which is underground. Other
terms used include:

"Open cut" or "open pit" mining. This generally involves simply digging a hole in the ground and taking out the minerals being sought.

"Auger mining." Huge drills are used to bore into the earth or mountain to get to the minerals.

"Cut and fill mining." This involves extracting huge cubes from the earth, separating the minerals from the soil, and replacing the unused soil back in the hole from which it came.

The terms and methods vary, largely depending on the type of terrain being mined. But to conservationists they all carry essentially the same meaning: tearing up the earth.

In the coal fields of eastern Kentucky, the strip mining most widely used has been this:

Wide bands are stripped from the side of a mountain, moving around the circumference of the mountain, to get to the seams of coal. The coal is removed, leaving a shelf around the mountain. Work proceeds down through the hill by digging along the contour of the slope. The work may be done at several levels on the same hill.

A new method is being tested now in eastern Kentucky. It involves shearing off the top of a mountain and pushing it into the neighboring valley, exposing the mineral. The mineral is extracted, another level is sheared off and pushed into a valley, and more mineral is extracted, and so on. The end result would be to eliminate the mountains and provide level land.

Conservationists increasingly are becoming concerned about the scars left by strip mining — not only because of the effect they have on the appearance of the land, but also because of the effect on the people who must live with the scars, the damage to streams and whole watersheds, the damage to forests, the damage to wildlife, and the elimination of other potential uses of the land, such as for recreational purposes.

A survey by the U.S. Department of the Interior, completed in the summer of 1967, showed that 3.2 million acres across the United States had been surface mined. But more significantly, the survey showed that 2 million acres still needed some degree of reclamation to prevent a broad range of environmental damage. And the mining is continuing, with an estimated 20,00 mining operations across the country affecting an additional 150,000 acres a year.

As you drive from northwestern North Carolina through southwestern Virginia to the mining region of eastern Kentucky you pass through beautiful mountain countryside, as yet largely undisturbed. There are clear rivers, beautiful mountain streams, lovely hills and pastures and mountains and meadows. The contrast when you reach the mining country is startling.

The streams there are loaded with silt or have their banks lined with "spoil banks," the rubble and rock left from surface mining. Their waters run yellow or red, tainted with sulphur and acids and minerals that seep from the scars torn in the sides of the mountains.

The forests are battered and mangled. The mountains, now, have somehow lost their majesty and look beaten and scarred and ugly.

And there are the people. The men driving the trucks who eye you suspiciously, particularly when they see your camera. The children who smile wanly and wave. The women who somehow look beaten down. The men who come back from the mining operations late in the day with their faces covered with black dust. The youth who roam aimlessly through the valleys in the afternoons after school is out.

Realizing that these are the descendants of a once proud, fiercely independent people who crossed the rugged mountains from North Carolina and Virginia and elsewhere to settle eastern Kentucky in the 1700s, you can't help wondering what has happened to wear them down and make them a dependent people.

The sociologists have their theories, the politicians their promises, and the oil and steel corporations their coal and minerals. But the people have the scars and the land that is rapidly losing its usefulness. The problem is theirs.

It is increasingly becoming apparent that reclaiming mountain land that has been strip mined is virtually impossible.

In flat areas, where the topsoil and subsequent layers of soil can be stripped back one by one until the minerals being sought are reached, the minerals can be extracted and the soil replaced in its proper sequence and in a few years' time the damage is almost unnoticeable.

But in the mountains once deep cuts are made in the steep slopes, they are there to stay. It is difficult to get trees and grass to grow, and even when they do they don't fully hide the scars. And the seeping chemicals destroy the ability of the land to support vegetation.

The streams fill with silt (some studies in Kentucky have shown that the sediment yield in watersheds that have been strip mined is as much as 1,000 times as great as in undisturbed areas), and the chemicals that work their way into the streams destroy their ability to support life.

Perhaps the most startling statistic concerning strip mining is that most of what has been done in the United States has been done in the past 20 years. For 10 years it went almost unchecked. Then in the 1960s some states began to regulate strip mining. But only in the past two or three years, as an increasing national awareness of environmental problems has developed, has there been serious concern about the effects of strip mining and serious efforts to curb both the mining and the effects.

Somewhere, in some state, a new threat is almost constantly arising. Strip mining is more economical than deep mining, and

the dangers to miners are lessened. And the new federal mine safety regulations, with stringent new requirements concerning safety in deep mining operations, seems to be having the side effect of pushing more mining firms into surface mining operations.

But it has been demonstrated that concerted public reaction can halt the threat, if it comes soon enough and is persistent enough.

One case in point is what happened in a six-county area along the North Carolina-Virginia border in late 1969 and early 1970.

The Gibbsite Corporation of America, a subsidiary of Colonial Oil and Gas Corporation of Rochester, N.Y., late in 1969 began acquiring mineral rights leases in the area and in December announced plans for a mining operation to extract gibbsite, a low-grade mineral which can be used in aluminum production.

Some of the lands on which the company acquired mineral rights border the Blue Ridge Parkway, a scenic highway that stretches from Shenandoah National Park in northern Virginia to the Great Smoky Mountains National Park at Asheville, N.C. Other land involved abuts North Carolina's Stone Mountain State Park, a new park being developed around a huge solid granite formation. The entire area is largely undisturbed scenic mountain land, an area that is undergoing development as an outdoor recreational and resort area.

When a newspaper made public what the firm was doing and what its intentions were, there was an immediate public outcry. Daily and weekly newspapers took up the battle cry; and local governments, civic groups, development associations, and even state legislators joined in.

The Gibbsite Corporation let its leases lapse and abandoned its plans.

There are many cases, however, in which the outcome has been different, and the struggle more frustrating.

In some counties in eastern Kentucky, local governments have become concerned and local citizens aroused. In Pike County, Kentucky, there have been demonstrations against strip mining, with people lying down in the paths of mining equipment to try to halt the operations.

But the strip miners had a big head start in Kentucky, and the opponents have had little success.

Harry Caudill, a lawyer and author who lives in Whitesburg in Letcher County, has become a recognized spokesman for conservationists in the Appalachian region. He is a native of Letcher County and has lived all his life with the mining problems in eastern Kentucky. His book, *Night Comes to the Cumberlands,* in the early 1960s became a textbook on the problems of Appalachia.

Caudill frequently talks in terms of rape when he discusses strip mining. And rape it may well be in eastern Kentucky, for, under mineral rights leases acquired 50 to 100 years ago by major corporations outside the state, much of the land has been strip mined without the consent of the property owners.

Caudill's concern is not only for the immediate effects of strip mining. He feels strongly that the answer to the nation's growing water shortage problem may lie in the Appalachian region, where rainfall is heavy and water is stored. Damage to the watersheds could eliminate a valuable national supply of water.

He also feels that the damage being done to the forests is eliminating valuable hardwood stands (and even where reclamation is successful, most of the plantings are in pines, not hardwoods), and perhaps more significantly, is eliminating an effective means of control for the growing smog and air pollution problems in urban centers. The trees produce oxygen, helping to purify polluted air.

Caudill is a former Kentucky legislator and had a major hand in the state's strip mining laws, which he says are woefully inadequate. Caudill has suggested the following answers to the strip mining threat:

Forbidding strip mining in areas where the slopes are so steep and the rainfall so great that reclamation would be impractical or impossible, and in areas of particular scenic beauty, areas important to wildlife, and heavily populated areas where "important human values would be disrupted."

Allowing strip mining for minerals only in areas where total reclamation can be carried out "promptly and effectively."

Requiring, in areas strip mined, that the topsoil be scraped off and set aside, then the subsoil and rock strata lifted out, and all replaced in their natural order and compacted when the mining is completed; further, that the land be treated with fertilizer and limestone and planted with trees. (He says this has been done effectively, and with economic feasibility, in Germany, England, and Czechoslovakia.)

Federal purchase and reclamation of lands already stripped and not restored.

At the state level, Caudill feels that a "severance tax" — a tax on the minerals extracted — is needed. He recommends that this money — perhaps several cents a ton, or a percentage of the profits per ton — should be used partly for land reclamation and partly to provide schools, libraries, and hospitals and to repair roads in areas mined.

In the meantime, strip mining continues to spread. The Department of the Interior estimates that more than 5 million acres across the country will be affected by 1980. Conservationists are convinced that time is running out — that so much has been done in the past 20 years that irreparable damage to natural resources is a certainty unless better reclamation efforts are made now and industries stop strip mining in areas where reclamation is impossible.

EDITOR'S COMMENTS

Legislation to halt strip mining in areas where it will destroy the land, or to force restoration of the land to as near a natural state as possible is running into stiff opposition. The powerful steel and mining interests hold so much sway in Washington and the various state capitals that they can often kill any legislation that they feel will reduce their profits.

A fact to think about when contemplating the advisability of strip mining is that a large portion of the coal obtained is being shipped to countries such as Belgium, Japan, Germany, and Italy to support their steel industries. Some have questioned the wisdom in raping the American landscape to stoke the furnaces that produce steel that eventually comes to the United States in the form of foreign cars and other gadgets which compete with domestic products. The question has been bluntly phrased, "Should we desecrate our land in order to help foreign industry put American industry out of business?"

GORDON ROBINSON

Clear-Cutting and Forest Management

Gordon Robinson is a graduate of the University of California School of Forestry. For 27 years he worked for the Southern Pacific Railroad and was for a time their chief forester. For the last five years he has been a private consultant, primarily to the Sierra Club.

Excellent forestry has four characteristics: It consists of limiting the cutting of timber to that which can be removed annually in perpetuity. It consists of growing timber on long rotations, generally from one to two hundred years depending on the species and the quality of soil, but in any case allowing trees to reach full maturity before being cut. It consists of practicing a selection system of cutting wherever this is consistent with the biological requirements of the species involved and, where this is not the case, keeping the openings no larger than necessary to meet those requirements. Finally, it consists of taking extreme precaution to protect the soil, our all-important basic resource. The advantages of such forestry are overwhelming.

Low Fire Hazard

To begin with, the lowest fire hazard is in the full-canopied old growth forest. The risk of losing timber to fire is therefore least where the forest is managed on a selection system in which as full a canopy as possible is permanently maintained. Fire danger is a function of temperature and moisture. By providing shade, the closed canopy of a dense forest keeps the material on the ground cool. Also air does not circulate freely under a closed canopy and is humid from moisture given off by trees. In contrast, young plantations are highly inflammable because they tend to be hot and dry, and the combustible leaves, frequently having an oil content, are close to each other and to the ground.

While foresters frequently insist upon the felling of all dead trees during logging operations for fire suppression purposes, it is generally overlooked that these very trees are required habitat for many birds who perform great services in controlling insect enemies of our forests.

Low Windthrow Hazard

Light selective logging, or clearcutting in small openings (group selection), provides maximum assurance against windthrow. The even-aged forest canopy has a generally well-

Reprinted by permission of the author and publisher from the *Sierra Club Bulletin*.

defined, nearly horizontal upper and lower limit. The crowns are short and concentrated at the top of relatively slender stems. Such trees are not at all windfirm and may require the stand to be cut all at once unless special provisions are made to minimize severe windthrow. In uneven-aged stands the crowns are commonly larger and more dense, but since they develop in irregular canopies and are subjected to wind stresses all their life long, they develop much greater windfirmness and have stouter boles.

Minimum Risk from Insects and Diseases

Damage from insects and diseases is far more severe where clearcutting is practiced than in the selection forest. Where large areas are clearcut, as in conversion to even-age management, certain insects may breed in the slash in great numbers and later attack the young reproduction. Where clearcutting is practiced there is always a tendency to establish plantations of one species rather than mixtures without regard as to how the planted species naturally occur. A pure stand — one composed of a single species — forms an ideal situation for a disease to build up to epidemic proportions. Infection is direct and rapid from tree to tree and if one species is destroyed there is nothing left. The most hazardous pure stands are even-aged stands because fungus parasites are often virulent during only one stage of the development of the trees. Pure stands of trees outside their natural range are particularly liable to difficulty. Pure stands are partciularly susceptible to disastrous outbreak. For instance, outbreaks of the hemlock looper have been especially destructive only in stands composed of a high percentage of hemlock. Where a heavy mixture of other species occurs, infestation soon thins out and loses its destructive power. It is particularly important that the cuttings in stands that normally grow as mixed types should not favor the leaving of the single species. Since most insects and diseases of forest trees are limited rather sharply to one or a few host plants, mixed stands offer far fewer opportunities for epidemics than do pure stands. In the case of insects, every tree in a pure stand offers food and breeding ground. In the case of fungi the liberated spores find favorable hosts everywhere. In both cases destructive concentration can readily be built up in pure stands.

Yield is of Maximum Value

Forests can and should be managed to produce a continuous even flow of mature timber. Old growth is far superior to young growth, however one looks at it. Stumpage prices are much higher for old growth than for young growth timber. Furthermore, it is anticipated that young growth stumpage prices are not likely to increase substantially over the next 25 to 50 years. Prices of higher-grade commodities will increase substantially, but that can't come from young growth. There will be a great increase in the use of pulp, but the great quantities of young growth available will hold prices down. In pulp, furthermore, quality of fibre will become an important factor.

In the dense canopy of a selection forest the trees tend to grow slowly. This is not to say that the total timber grown is any less on a volume basis than in even-aged stands. Returning to quality considerations, the suitability of young growth for veneer is greatly diminished because it is not only undesirable for veneer faces but also veneer cuts are rough; the numerous knots tend to chip the knife although lathe settings are no more critical than in old growth. If lumber is produced, the yield of high grade material is lower than from old growth trees.

Wood Fibre is Highest Quality

As a tree matures and grows in girth, the cambium produces longer and thicker walled cells. The length of fibres laid down in new growth in conifers increases with the age of the tree. Length generally varies from 1 millimeter at age one to about 4 millimeters at age 70, after which length remains constant with increase in age. This means that where timber is being grown for fibre, the longest fibres occur only in that part of the tree which has grown after age 70. It would seem to be good business, therefore, to grow trees to an age of 100 to 200 years and to use for pulp chips, the slabbing from squaring or rounding the logs, and making high quality lumber and plywood from the remainder of the core. This is essentially what is done with our virgin timber today, but not with trees grown on a short rotation.

What has been said about the length of fibres is true also of the density or strength of fibres. That part of the tree which has been laid down by the cambium layer after age 70 contains the strongest fibres as well as the longest ones.

That part of the conifer grown below 40 to 50 years of age is inferior in having a high proportion of extractives. The yield of fibre will be small and the amount of dissolved material higher than in pulping slow-growth old wood. This adds to production costs as well as water pollution problems with pulp mills.

Costs No More

We hear much talk these days from both foresters and industry to the effect that they cannot afford to grow trees on a long rotation or to great size and that they must clearcut for economic reasons. These appear to be false calculations. A recent study showed that the cost of felling, limbing, and bucking trees from 45 to 48 inches in diameter cost $7.04 per thousand board feet in contrast with $18.36 per thousand board feet for trees between 12 and 16 inches in diameter. Similarly, the cost of yarding and loading was twice as much for trees 12 inches in diameter as it was for trees 30 inches in diameter.

The February, 1969 issue of the *Journal of Forestry* reports the findings of a research team studying comparative logging costs under four cutting specifications ranging from single tree selection to clearcutting. They concluded that logging costs from standing tree to truck do not differ appreciably with cutting method, and the forest manager is therefore free to choose a cutting technique on the basis of management and silvicultural consideration other than costs.

A recent study in the redwood region indicated a logging cost of $11.37 per thousand board feet in a selection forest and $11.45 per thousand board feet where clearcutting was practiced. This was a study conducted by the U.S. Forest Service in the Redwood Purchase Unit. A similar study made in the pine region showed that where clearcutting was practiced, involving 17,000 board feet per acre, 133 man minutes per thousand board feet were expended. Heavy selection cutting involving 13,000 board feet per acre required only 118 man minutes per thousand board feet. But a light, sanitation-salvage cut involving only 3,000 board feet per acre cost only 119 man minutes per thousand, considerably less than clearcutting.

These rather surprising figures are explained by the fact that where selective cutting is employed we are generally removing only the largest trees which gives us the greatest handling efficiency during each step of the logging process.

Seed Source is Reliable

Selection management provides us with many advantages in obtaining reproduction. There is no difficulty with seed source. We are assured of reforestation with trees acclimated to the particular site. Collecting seeds in one area for reforestation in another is far more hazardous than most foresters realize. In general, naturally regenerated stands are less susceptible to disease than those artificially reproduced.

Foresters would do well to heed the warning of a recent report from the Southern Forest Experiment Station. One hundred forty species were tried in southern Arkansas and northern Louisiana, mainly pine and eucalyptus. The best growth was obtained in Slash, Pond and Virginia pine, but none were as large as native Loblolly after 9 to 12 years. This experiment strongly supports the well-known principle of silviculture that one is safest with natural regeneration, or at least with perpetuation of indigenous species.

Soil is Protected

American foresters notoriously disregard the effects of logging practices upon soils. This is particularly true of the post war era in which logging has become highly mechanized and where much of the remaining timber being logged is on steep ground. The oversize and unwieldly equipment used by logging operators is totally unacceptable in the concept of excellent forestry. Logging should be conducted with light, small equipment, preferably rubber tired, in order to be maneuverable around trees left in selection forests and to function without disturbing the soil. All logging should be planned and supervised to prevent this damage, and no logging should be permitted where complete protection of the soil cannot be assured.

Clearcutting promotes erosion and compaction of the surface soil, particularly where mineral soil is exposed. Clearcutting allows organic matter to become desiccated, slowing down decay in dry climates such as characterize much of our western forests. Clearcutting exposes the forest floor to intense insolation and evaporation and, as a result, the normal soil life of fungi, bacteria, worms, microscopic plants and animals of all kinds are destroyed or at least greatly changed, with fauna and flora of open lands coming in. This is usually undesirable. Clearcutting invites invasion of vegetation that severely competes with forest tree seedlings. In the northwestern United States, clearcutting of forests and forest fires have increased floods from watersheds from both rain-snow melt floods and snow melt floods. Where stocking of the forests has recovered with time the flood peak discharges again decrease.

Landslides Minimized

It is fair to conclude from published literature that there exists a definite cause and effect relationship between clearcutting and mass-soil movement. Forest cover affects deep seated stability of a slope in two ways, by modifying the hydrologic regime in soil mantle, and by mechanical reinforcement from the root system. The former is important only the first year, before invading vegetation takes hold. The root system is far more important, and gradual deterioration of tree roots leads to progressively greater slope instability.

Soil Fertility Maintained

Something should be said for maintaining the natural mixture of species that occurs in the forest. This, too, is best done through reliance upon natural reproduction. Some species make excessively heavy demands on soil nutrients when planted in pure stands. They may do well in youth but later slow up and deteriorate. The admixture of species that makes light demand on the soil and whose leaf litter decomposes readily into a mild, rich humus is often necessary. Furthermore, pure stands may fail to utilize the site completely, either because they are composed of an intolerant species and in consequence have thin, open crowns which presumably fail to utilize the sunlight completely, or because they are shallow rooted and utilize only part of the soil.

Preserves Watershed and Fish Habitat

Selection management with careful planning of roads and logging is of great importance in sustaining the quality and productivity of the soil for these many reasons. It tends to maintain soil porosity and its water absorption qualities, thus reducing erosion and flood damage. Care of the soil and maintaining a full canopy also protect the habitat for fish in streams by keeping the water clean and cold and by preserving spawning beds. Silt and slime, the products of erosion, are unsuitable for spawning. They inhibit the flow of water through gravel where fish eggs are spawned, thus shutting off the essential supply of oxygen.

Preserves Natural Beauty

Excellent forestry largely preserves the beauty of the natural forest. For most people such well-managed forests will quite adequately serve most of their wildland recreational needs. By maintaining the natural beauty of the forests we therefore take a good deal of pressure off wilderness. In contrast, present practices on the national forests, and to a greater extent on private forest lands, is creating an ever increasing demand for more wilderness.

If national parks and wilderness areas become the only places of natural beauty we have for outdoor experiences, people who do not care for wilderness *per se* will crowd in with those who do. This would not only increase the use of such places but would add to the clamor for roads and other nonwilderness development. Furthermore, if we should reach the sad state of having no large, old-growth timber except within our national parks, we would surely face a great clamor to log that, too. Indeed, the overture to this clamor is already being heard. We had a foretaste in the ridiculous arguments advanced in opposition to the Redwood National Park which will be all too familiar to the reader.

Excellent forestry costs nothing but restraint and offers the greatest gifts a forest can provide.

EDITOR'S COMMENTS

In a recent paper, Dr. Robert R. Curry of the University of Montana indicated that if present methods of mistreating forest lands continue, certain "western forests may have something less than 200 years of productive fertility remaining before permanent eradication of productivity for saw timber production." Profit today, desolation tomorrow! Will we leave to our descendants barren hillsides, eroded gullies, and stark vistas?

Foresters who support present methods of clear-cutting and monoculture in large tracts often argue that these methods are justified in order to meet current demands for wood and wood products. What they fail to realize or admit is that what we often refer to as "demands" are not real needs.

Much of the use of paper (which is made from wood pulp) in the United States today is frivolous. We do not need our soda crackers wrapped in quadruple layers of paper. There is no good reason to carry a paper bag containing one small item away from the grocery store. The paper that this book is printed on can be recycled and thus reduce the need to cut down as many trees for pulp production. Look around in any store and see if you can estimate how many acres of forest were removed to produce the useless packaging seen on many products. It is obvious that the real need for wood is only a fraction of the amount that is called "demand."

Reducing our frivolous uses of wood and wood products and forcing the forest industry to return to realistic methods of harvesting timber are *musts*. Forests are more than just board feet of timber standing on the land. With a sensible approach to their use — their beauty, wildlife, soil, water, and wood can be forever available to future generations.

RON MOXNESS

The Long Pipe

Ron Moxness is a Foreign Service Officer
with the U.S. Information Agency at Washington, D.C., and writes on environmental matters,
narcotics problems, and urban affairs for
USIA. He has served on the editorial staffs
of two Canadian newspapers and the Portland
Oregonian prior to joining USIA in 1956.
His foreign service has included tours as press
attache to U.S. Embassies in Rabat, Morocco
and Ottawa, Canada and assignments in
Bonn and Geneva. He has taught journalism
at Lewis and Clark College and Portland
State University in Oregon. He has been the
recipient of three awards in journalism.

The years when the mountains, valleys,
rivers, and creeks of Alaska yielded fortunes
in gold have faded; now the production of
sand and gravel is valued more than the annual production of the yellow metal for
which men once struggled and died. But
Alaskans have memories and today they im-
patiently await another economic boom —
this one a river of oil which would flow
through an 800-mile-long pipeline, stretching like some huge steel serpent from Prudhoe Bay in the north to Valdez on the
Pacific, the northernmost ice-free port in
the western hemisphere.

The technical problems involved in the
oil pipeline project are as immense as the
ranges of forbidding mountains that awed
the goldseekers on the trail of '98. Alaska's
first problem, well known to those who have
looked north recently, is how to lay a steel
pipeline 48 inches in diameter whose stream
of hot oil — 176 degrees F. — will not melt
its route through the Alaskan terrain, 85
percent of which is permafrost, or permanently frozen ground.

The second problem is the demand made
by the conservationists, many of whose viewpoints are shared by the technical experts
of the U.S. government, that the pipeline
pose no threat to the ecology of what has
been described as America's last great, untouched wilderness area. The description is
particularly apt as it applies to the Brooks
Mountain Range, whose towering peaks,
some over 9,000 feet high, look north to
the Beaufort Sea and the still imprisoned
oil of Prudhoe Bay.

Today, despite the eagerness of oil companies who have already invested $900,000,-
000 in North Slope oil and gas leases and
of Alaska's resource-minded boosters who
are anxious to get on with the project at a
time of heavy unemployment, all of the
factors — technical, environmental, social,

Reprinted by permission of the author and publisher from *Environment* 12:12-23, 36. September
1970. Copyright © 1970 by the Committee for
Environmental Information.

and legal — are being carefully weighed by a Federal Task Force on Alaska Oil Development established early in 1969 by the Nixon Administration.

The task force is a government-wide body including all of the Department of the Interior's major bureaus — from the United States Geological Survey, the principal technical and engineering study unit, to the Bureau of Indian Affairs, whose responsibility it is to safeguard the rights and livelihood of Alaska's natives — an Eskimo-Aleut population of more than 28,000 and an additional 14,000 Indians. These are part of Alaska's total population of only 282,000 persons who live on 586,400 square miles of territory.

The federal task force was established by Secretary of the Interior Walter J. Hickel on April 18, 1969. The original membership of eight Interior department bureau and office heads was expanded at the request of President Nixon to include the secretaries of Commerce, Defense, Health, Education and Welfare, Transportation, and Housing and Urban Affairs. The State of Alaska and a conservation/industry ad hoc committee are also represented. The Office of Science and Technology, the National Science Foundation, and the Bureau of the Budget participate as liason members.

Dr. William D. McElroy, Director of the National Science Foundation, announced May 22 that a new coordinated research project into the potential ecological effects of the pipeline will get underway this summer.

The survey will be directed and coordinated by Dr. Jerome Brown of the U.S. Army Cold Regions Research and Engineering Laboratory and by Dr. George C. West, Professor of Zoophysiology, Institute of Arctic Biology, University of Alaska. The $300,000 project involves seven participating institutions and has two major objectives. First, the scientists want to find out how environmental disturbances by man affect the life systems of both plants and animals. Secondly, project directors plan to bring together the existing, scattered information on Arctic ecology. They also want to determine how the results of Arctic research can best be used to predict the consequences of resource development in the region. The U.S. Coast Guard is also planning a number of summer research programs dealing with the problem of oil pollution in ice, and the University of Alaska, in cooperation with industry, is studying oil pipe behavior under permafrost conditions. Studies on grass and tree plantings adaptable to the land through which the pipeline will run are also being conducted.

All of this study anticipates the exploitation of some of the largest reserves of oil ever discovered. According to Dr. Charles C. Bates, Science Advisor to the Commandant of the U.S. Coast Guard.

> In the Colville Basin of Alaska's North Slope, [running] some 50 miles parallel to the coast, the Prudhoe Bay structure has been estimated to contain five to ten *billion* barrels of oil. When one realizes that Saudi Arabia and Kuwait each took until last year to produce their ten billionth barrel and that Iran achieved this magic figure only this year, it is easy to see that the North Slope may become the land of big oil in the 1970s to the 1990s. . . .[1]

Task Force Questions TAPS

It is little wonder then that a consortium of oil companies — of which the major names are Atlantic Richfield, Humble Oil, and British Petroleum — is pressing hard to move ahead with their Trans-Alaska Pipeline System (TAPS) as early as possible to carry this oil to market. Much of the pipe has already been stockpiled at Valdez, where construction was to begin this summer.

1. Charles C. Bates, An Address to the 39th Annual Meeting of the Society of Exploration Geophysicists, Alberta, Canada: Calgary, September, 1969.

As of this writing, however, no federal authorization to go ahead with the pipeline project is forthcoming, and it is doubtful, at the present pace of negotiation, that a permit will be issued for some months in the future. In the words of John Horton, Executive Secretary of the federal task force, the consortium of nine companies making up the TAPS group has not yet presented a plan "which demonstrates that its fundamental criteria are adequate to assure integrity of the line when buried."

The current impasse in discussions between TAPS and the federal body involves both technological and environmental differences of opinion. In the view of TAPS, the pipeline would be buried for almost the entirety of its route from north to south. It would be served by a $120,000,-000 highway in the northern region of Alaska. The highway, to be paid for by the TAPS group, would serve as a secondary highway for the state. Both pipeline and highway are currently blocked by suits initiated by leading conservation and wildlife organizations and by debate over financing of the road in its construction stage. TAPS is not interested in the road unless it receives a go-ahead for the pipeline project, now projected to cost about $1,500,000,000.

The task force, on the basis of its own studies of the hazards of building in the permafrost and of questions relating to wildlife and the needs of the indigenous population, asked 79 questions for which the TAPS organization has not yet provided satisfactory answers. The questions, Mr. Horton asserted, "were about the toughest ever laid down before an industry group." The task force, in weighing the TAPS response, raised "serious questions" as to the consortium's "state of technological readiness" to proceed with the project. The task force so advised President Nixon.

The two groups are chiefly at loggerheads over placement of the line. TAPS wants to use engineering practices utilized elsewhere in the world as part of the oil industry's far-flung operations and simply bury the steel line for all but about 80 miles of its route, which would cross 23 rivers and 152 streams, and many mountains, mountain basins, and river flats.

The task force believes that at least half of the line should be built above ground on steel, timber, or concrete legs to permit free migration of caribou herds which are vital to the livelihood of native Alaskans. An elevated pipeline like that used by Soviet engineers in the U.S.S.R. would also keep the hot pipeline from any contact with the delicately balanced tundra and permafrost. The oil in the pipeline is heated to keep it fluid enough to pump easily by special heating units installed in the pumping stations along the route of the pipeline.

Federal technicians are also uneasy about the assurance of TAPS that its pipeline plans allow for a sag or differential of only three *inches* in a 50-foot section of pipe. The minimum estimate of the task force is that the potential differential to allow for soil settlement — not to mention the possibility of larger stresses — should be three *feet* in a 50-foot pipe section.

The Menlo Park working group of the U.S. Geological Survey in California, in its interim comments on engineering proposals provided by the TAPS organization earlier this year, found a number of apparent inconsistencies in the TAPS presentation and commented, "it is difficult to determine which statements represent TAPS' policies and intentions and which do not." The working group agreed that the TAPS information, set down in a number of reports, represented a forward step "in our mutual consideration of the many problems involved in the proposed pipeline project." But as of late July, Dr. Henry Coulter — one of the Geological Survey's principal technical advisors to the federal task force — points out, no reply to their interim comments had yet been received. Task force spokesmen indicated that a reply is not expected before October.[2]

One of the major areas of concern is the problem of earthquakes. The pipeline will pass through several regions of earthquake faults. Coulter indicated the task force's intention to require strict criteria for the pipeline design. "If you plan for a seven rather than a five range of [earthquake] intensity you are probably better off," he observed. "If you plan for five and are confronted with the possibility of seven it would be highly expensive to change designs."

Coulter said TAPS, in its preliminary reports, had proposed cutoff safety provisions for the pipe in fault areas to limit the amount of oil which would be lost in case of a break.

TAPS has not yet disclosed the number of cutoffs it plans to build into the line to cope with earthquakes or breaks or stoppages caused by other factors such as ground displacement in thawing or sinking permafrost. But Coulter points out that a large cutoff valve designed to really halt the flow of oil would be 32 feet high, and men would have to be stationed at various points along the route to cope with emergencies. The backup pressure, in the event of a sealed off break, would be tremendous. This is one of the points in dispute, because the TAPS people have not yet determined specific details of design. As Coulter says, "our intent is to *prevent* spills, not to provide systems for cleanup."

Coulter views bedrock construction in rocky areas as more or less conventional, but the rest of the line is where the need for "imaginative" design concepts lie. He feels that some lengthy areas of the line may need only a few cutoffs and that other stretches, in potentially dangerous fault areas, may need much more frequent installations, perhaps at half-mile intervals.

Oil spills, in the event of an earthquake, would obviously be very destructive, since one mile of pipe will contain 500,000 gallons of hot oil. But a spill caused by a break in one section of line conceivably could be strictly local in effect. The Alaskan terrain is hilly and an oil spill would run downhill and come to a stop in a reasonably short distance. "In effect, the damage could be limited to a finite distance, limited by topography," Coulter said.

Should a river basin be involved, much more extensive damage could result. In Canada recently, oil from a spill in a pipeline at Fort McMurray traveled 150 miles downstream in the Athabasca River. Great Canadian Oil Sands Ltd., at whose plant the break occurred, said the break and the loss of pressure were reflected on monitors at its Fort McMurray plant and immediate steps were taken to stop the flow.

The spill caused a shutdown of the commercial fishing season on Lake Athabasca just at a time when fish prices were rising because of mercury pollution in other areas of Canada, the Canadian Press news agency reported. The spill did not, apparently, cause much damage to wildlife breeding grounds because of the fast current flow of the Athabasca.

The Permafrost Problem

Permafrost is defined exclusively on the basis of temperature, as its name suggests. It is rock or soil material, with or without interior moisture or organic matter, that has remained below 32 degrees F. continuously for two or more years.

Permafrost may be ice-free where no water is present, the Geological Survey notes. The permafrost table consists of the upper surface of the permafrost layer and the active layer, the zone that freezes in the winter and thaws in the summer.

The Geological Survey's "Permafrost and Related Engineering Problems of Alaska"

2. Menlo Park Working Group Memorandum, "Interim Comments on TAPS Submittals of February 20, 1970," U.S. Geological Survey, Menlo Park, California, March 23, 1970.

makes it clear that American engineers who first tried to build structures — from houses to bridges and pipelines — in Alaska encountered the same problems as the Russians. The stresses and strains induced by the freezing, thawing, and heaving of permafrost soils subjected to unexpected temperature changes turned railroads into roller coasters and bridges into jigsaw puzzles.

"The permafrost region of Alaska, which includes 85 percent of the state, is characterized by a variety of permafrost-related geomorphic features including patterned ground, pingos, thaw lakes, beaded drainage, thaw or thermokarst pits, and muck deposits," states the report.

"Known permafrost thickness ranges from about 1,300 feet near Barrow in northern Alaska to less than a foot at the southern margin of the permafrost region. . . .

"The extensive permafrost region of Alaska poses special engineering problems on the design, construction and maintenance of all kinds of structures," the report notes. "Lack of knowledge about permafrost has resulted in tremendous maintenance costs and even in relocation or abandonment of highways, railroads, and other structures. Because of the unique geologic-environmental conditions that exist in permafrost areas, special engineering procedures should be used, not only to minimize disruption of the natural environment, but also to provide the most economical and sound methods for developing the natural resources of the permafrost region of Alaska."[3]

The report warns that in the Alaskan experience with construction of airfields, highways, and railroads, "improper procedures can far exceed the expense of the initial investment. In some cases structures are damaged to the extent that they become unusable after just a few months or years. The financial losses caused by such problems as impassable roads, unusable airstrips or damaged machinery in buildings which have settled [unevenly] can be extremely high."

Dr. Arthur H. Lachenbruch of the U.S. Geological Survey's Menlo Park research staff, in a report entitled "Some Estimates of the Thermal Effects of a Heated Pipeline in Permafrost," notes that the proposed Prudhoe Bay-Valdez pipeline would maintain oil temperatures in the neighborhood of 158 to 176 degrees F. when full production is achieved.

"Such an installation would thaw the surrounding permafrost," Lachenbruch asserts. "Where the ice content of permafrost is not high, and other conditions are favorable, thawing by the buried pipe might cause no special problems. Under adverse conditions, however, this thawing could have significant effects on the environment and possibly upon the security of the pipeline. It is important that any potential problem be identified prior to its occurrence so that it can be accommodated by proper pipeline design."[4]

Lachenbruch notes that the actual degree of permafrost conditions along the pipeline remains to be determined by actual measurements. Such measurements, he said, are essential to predictions of the interactions between pipeline and environment. He estimates that a pipeline 48 inches in diameter buried six feet deep in permafrost and heated to 176 degrees F. would thaw a cylindrical region around the pipeline 20 to 30 feet in diameter in a few years in typical permafrost soil.

"At the end of the second decade of operation, typical thawing depths would be 40 to 50 feet near the southern limits of permafrost and 35 to 40 feet in northern Alaska where permafrost is colder. . . . The

3. Oscor J. Ferrians, Jr., Reuben Kachadoorian, and Gordon W. Greene, "Permafrost and Related Engineering Problems of Alaska," Geological Survey Professional Paper No. 678 (Washington, D.C.: U.S. Government Printing Office, 1969).

4. Arthur H. Lachenbruch, "Some Estimates of the Thermal Effects of a Heated Pipeline in Permafrost," Geological Survey Circular 632 (Washington, D.C.: Government Printing Office).

principal effect of insulating the pipe would be to increase oil temperatures rather than to decrease thawing," he reports.

Lachenbruch asserts that if permafrost sediments have excess ice and a very low permeability when thawed, melting below the pipe could generate free water faster than it could filter to the surface. As a result, the thawed material around the pipeline could persist as a semiliquid slurry or slush. Where permeabilities are very low and excess ice contents are moderate, thawing rates would be sufficient to maintain this state for decades.

Lachenbruch explains that under certain conditions the semiliquid slurry "would tend to flow like a viscous river and seek a level. As an extreme example, if these slurries occurred over distances of several miles on almost imperceptible slopes, the uphill end of the pipe could, in a few years, be lying at the bottom of a slumping trench tens of feet deep, while at the downhill end, millions of cubic feet of mud could be extruded over the surface."

Where the pipe settled to the bottom of the trench, Lachenbruch notes, "it would accelerate thawing and flow, and the process could be self-perpetuating. The pipeline could be jeopardized by loss of support in the trench and by displacements in the mud flow, and the disruption of the landscape could be substantial."

Lachenbruch warns, too, that uneven settlement of a pipe can result from a variety of processes, the most conspicuous of which is probably the thawing of ice wedges. These massive vertical veins of ice, he notes, form polygonal networks, commonly invisible from the surface and difficult to delineate with borings. Ice wedges, he says, "are widely distributed in Northern Alaska. A statistical calculation suggests that in typical ice-wedge terrain, conditions which might exceed the design stress of the pipeline could occur on the average of once every mile. Most of these conditions could be anticipated by observations made during trenching."

Ice wedges are only one of a number of strange geological phenomena found in permafrost. Surface features include pingos (small ice-filled conical hills); stone nets (netlike concentrations of coarse rock); thaw lakes and pits, and "beaded" drainage patterns. Disturbing frozen ground, even by making small changes such as removing vegetation or putting up a building, will commonly upset the freeze-thaw balance. When certain kinds of permafrost soil thaw, what was once solid land becomes a veritable quagmire incapable of supporting any structure whatsoever.

As a result of these and other findings, to conservationists the prospect of a buried pipeline conjures pictures of an impassable "canal" of unstable land, and of slides which could bring about ruptured sections of pipe and produce ruinous oil spills which would cover vast areas of the Alaskan landscape. They reject arguments that the oil flow could be "easily turned off" in the event of a break, noting that one mile of the pipe carries three times the amount of oil that damaged the Santa Barbara coastline.

The Soviet Experience

The task force has gone to an unusual source — the U.S. petroleum industry's own survey of Soviet oil and gas pipeline construction procedures — for further evidence that burial of an oil pipeline could be a very risky business indeed, to be avoided generally in the permafrost unless new and imaginative engineering designs are developed.[5]

In commenting on the Soviet experience, D. C. Alverson, a geologist for the U.S. Geological Survey, observed:

The Soviets have engaged in research on the feasibility of laying pipelines in permafrost areas since shortly after World War II. Earliest studies were based on prob-

5. Williams Brothers, "A Survey of Soviet Pipeline Construction Techniques and Related Activities in Western Siberia" (Tulsa, Oklahoma, 1969).

lems encountered in building roads, airfields and various kinds of structures on a permafrost foundation, as well as laying water, gas distribution, heat and electric lines in cities such as Norilsk and other settlements. Experience at Ukhta in the Komi (district), in the north part of European U.S.S.R. just outside the permafrost boundary, convinced the Soviets that it was most desirable to avoid disturbing the thermal regimen of the permafrost, and where possible to construct pipelines above ground. It is less desirable, but possible, to lay pipe directly on the ground surface, with the least possible disturbance of the soil layer. Least desirable is excavation of a trench and burial; this should be confined to the active layer [of the permafrost]. Examples of the results of failure to properly accommodate to the thermal regimen of permafrost in various kinds of construction abound in the Soviet literature."[6]

Alverson notes that the Soviet experience in laying pipelines in permafrost areas has been limited to one oil line, from Krasnoyarsk to Irkutsk, where permafrost is usually less than 49 feet thick, and gas lines from Tazovskoye to Norilsk in the northern part of the West Siberian lowland; from Taas-Tumus to Yakutsk and Pokrovsk, in Yakutia, where the permafrost is commonly more than 650 feet thick.

One article referred to by Alverson notes that installation of gas pipelines involved "exceptionally complex and responsible engineering installations."[7] The underground and semi-buried installation technique may be used on a limited number of sections, where soils when thawing do not lose their weight-carrying capacity. "In the permafrost," the Soviet article states, "it is necessary to use widely the above-the-ground (on supports) installation, and in isolated sections, on-the-ground and under cover with a thermally insulated layer under the pipeline."

In a March 1969 report, I. E. Dukhin, a Soviet engineer, notes that "the construction of transmission lines in the northern part of Western Siberia in regions of permafrost is a very complex engineering task.

In spite of the complex installation of various supports and the difficult conditions of the construction itself, the possibility of excluding the heat effects of the pipeline on frozen ground and, therefore, the conservation of the best conditions guaranteeing its stability, makes it possible to consider above-the-ground laying as the most expedient laying method over almost the whole permafrost area. . . . [8]

Dukhin, in an observation echoed by ecologists pointing to similar dangers in Alaska, notes that "the main factor determining the stability of the temperature condition of grounds and their load-bearing capacity, is a sufficiently thick [eight to ten inches] moss blanket which stabilizes the inflow of heat into the ground.

"With the passage of a vehicle," he reports, "the moss blanket collapses or will be destroyed and the surface becomes uncovered; more heat flows into the ground and, therefore, the depth and intensity of the seasonal melting increases. The ground below the tracks of the vehicle melts more rapidly. As a result of the melting of the ice in ice-impregnated grounds, a significant sag arises in the area of the pipeline route which becomes a natural drain on the whole environmental surface. . . . The presence of a small amount of water in the route gives rise to the so-called hot-bed effect, which even more intensifies the melting.

"The depths of melting below the track can amount up to several yards during the season, and the sag in the track area (depending on the character of the ice) to one foot to one yard. The presence of vein ice may lead to ground collapse," he notes. "The extension of the disintegration

6. D. C. Alverson, Memorandum to the Federal Task Force on Alaska Oil Development (U.S. Geological Survey, August 5, 1969).

7. Williams Brothers.

8. *Ibid.*

to the adjacent territory and the bringing of the selected route into unfitness is extremely dangerous. The clearly expressed thixotrophy [property of becoming fluid when shaken, stirred, or otherwise disturbed] of soils which lost their load-bearing capacity under the effect of even insignificant dynamic loads, will be the source of numerous transportation delays . . . the laying of a gas pipeline in a zone of developing thermokarst formations is dangerous insofar as a guarantee of its stability is not realizable."

Dukhin, again speaking of a "cold" gasline, for which potential environmental damage is relatively minor notes that:

> A disturbance of the heat conditions of permafrost can be avoided through laying the pipeline above the ground. A gas pipeline laid above the maximum level of the snow cover has practically no heat effect on the frozen grounds of the base and guarantees maximum stability of the construction. The working of frozen ground, installing thermal insulation and other operations are not necessary for above the ground laying. However, increased heat losses during the winter period, the risk of precipitation out of the condensate, the negative effect of low temperatures on the longevity and the reliability of the insulation, and so forth, have to be considered.

Coulter points out that temperatures in Siberia and Alaska differ only by a few degrees. Geographical conditions in both regions — from mountains to river basins — offer comparable terrain, tundra and muskeg (wet, spongy ground) conditions. Both are permafrost areas. He notes that soil sagging caused by thermokarst phenomena, according to the Soviet engineer M. O. Pereltsvaig, "apparently originates dangerous stresses in an underground large diameter gas pipeline, too, as it starts floating in the soil pulp and turns up at the top of the active layer. There, soil bulging and crack formation by frost are most intensive."[9]

Coulter notes that the thrawing process, so often commented on by the Soviet en-

gineers, takes place even though the pipe is about the same temperature as the ground. The TAPS pipeline, with its oil flow at 176 degrees F., would be far more hazardous to the environment.

Other Routes

The Prudhoe Bay-Valdez route, despite all its problems, still has many sponsors. Washington State Senator Henry M. Jackson, Head of the Senate Interior Committee, as much as promised the route could be used when in April he advised a group of Alaskans "not to be in too much of a hurry" to get the line built. He said he had enough faith in American technological prowess to assure him that there would eventually be a pipeline that posed no threat of environmental disaster. Dr. William T. Pecora, Director of the U.S. Geological Survey, also believes the line will be built — although he believes about half the line should be built above ground. The TAPS consortium continues to press for the line to be buried throughout its length.

Some Canadian observers who would like to see the Alaskan oil move down through Canada to the United States doubt if the TAPS project will be built. They see too many problems for the route — the permafrost, the opposition of conservationists, and the cost of construction. They believe that the recent voyages of the S.S. *Manhattan,* exploring the possibility of moving oil by tanker through the Northwest Passage, reinforce chances for the use of Canadian harbors to ship the oil to the east coast.

A Canadian oil consortium, represented by the Bechtel Corporation, believes that the North Slope oil could be brought to the Mackenzie River Delta by a relatively short pipeline from Prudhoe Bay. From the mouth of the Mackenzie it would move, they reason, through an all-Canadian, 1,600-mile-

9. *Ibid.*

long pipeline down the valley of the Mackenzie to Edmonton, Alberta, and from there to U.S. markets. Most of this route, too, is over permafrost.

The task force in Washington, however, leans hard in the direction of the all-Alaskan pipeline, despite the problems. They note that a Prudhoe Bay-Mackenzie River connecting line would parallel the northern boundary of the huge Alaskan wildlife range, which conservationists want to see protected in perpetuity. Secondly, the oil needs of the U.S. west coast would be more efficiently met by direct oil supply via the TAPS system and tankers from Valdez. Finally, the daily estimated production of two million barrels of oil can only be handled efficiently and economically by a

pipeline. To transport the oil exclusively by sea would require dozens of supertankers (which have yet to prove they can safely and economically navigate the Northwest Passage), special equipment, and special diplomatic arrangements between Canada and the United States for the servicing of a tanker service.

In terms of ease of developing the vast oil reserves of the North Slope, the TAPS project has the edge, which may be enough. An enthusiast once suggested during Alaska's application for statehood that Alaska be maintained forever as an undeveloped wilderness area.

"We looked at him," recalled an Alaskan who had been weaned on the search for gold, "as if he were some kind of nut."

EDITOR'S COMMENTS

Presently, the need for the oil of Alaska's North Slope is not critical, except perhaps to the oil companies who invested without first investigating. To rush the construction of a pipeline without first determining the possible consequences would be foolhardy. A pipeline which breaks in a dozen places each year is inefficient in carrying oil. Since each mile of line would be carrying nearly half a million gallons of crude oil, each break could result in the loss of several million gallons. A spill could also destroy fish and wildlife and cause increased melting and further instability of the permafrost.

So many questions remain to be answered that there must be a further delay in pipeline construction. Conservationists are not anti-oil. They are not even anti-pipeline. But it seems only reasonable that any attempts to extract oil in this fragile area should be undertaken only after there is

considerable assurance that widespread damage to the environment will not result. This assurance cannot presently be given.

In April, 1970, in response to complaints filed by three environmental groups (Friends of the Earth, The Wilderness Society, and the Environmental Defense Fund) U.S. District Court Judge George L. Hart, Jr., imposed an injunction preventing construction of the pipeline. This was one of the first test cases of the National Environmental Policy Act. At issue was the adequacy of the Environmental Impact Statement required by this act. On August 15, 1972, Judge Hart dissolved the injunction and dismissed the complaints mainly to get the case off his hands. "It can be confidently anticipated that the final decision in this matter rests with the Supreme Court," he said, and indicated that he would issue no detailed legal opinion. As this goes to press, the case is in the U.S. Court of Appeals in Washington, D.C.

GEORGE W. FOLKERTS

Stream Channelization:
How a Bureaucracy Destroys a Resource

George W. Folkerts is Assistant Professor of
Zoology-Entomology at Auburn University.
His research interests center around the evolution, systematics, and ecology of aquatic
organisms. He is a member of the Board of
Directors of the Alabama Conservancy, and
has served as a consultant to the Environmental Defense Fund, National Resources Defense
Council, and other environmental groups.

Bureaucracies are not known for their al-
truism. If projects beneficial to the citizenry
also perpetuate or increase the size, power,
sphere of influence, or appropriation of the
agency responsible for administering the
project, they have the support of and are
willingly publicized by the agency. However,
if a project initiated by a bureaucracy is
found to be detrimental to the public welfare, seldom is the project cancelled, and
almost never will officials of the guilty
agency publicly admit their mistake. In
many cases agency programs are run on a
"what's good for the bureau is good for
the people!" policy. In recent years, many
United States government agencies, especially those operating under the Department
of Agriculture, seem to function mainly to
initiate huge pork barrel projects which
make work for the agency and enable
favor-trading with congressmen, but bear
little or no relationship to the public wel-

fare or need. Stream channelization is a
classic example of the results of such bureaucratic egomania.

The United States Soil Conservation Service was created over 30 years ago to handle
the growing problem of soil erosion in the
United States. Agricultural practices had
destroyed the soil in many areas. In Oklahoma, Texas, and neighboring states the
wind was removing the soil and creating
"dust bowls." Initially the Soil Conservation
Service (SCS) did its work well. Proper land
treatment was encouraged and farmers were
informed about terracing, shelter belts, cover crops, grass waterways, and other soil
conserving practices. The SCS grew and
flourished. Its representatives could be found
in almost every county in the United States.
It's activities were obviously worthwhile,
they were helpful to the farmer, and the
agency was known as the friend of the
rural landowner.

But alas! The agency functioned so well
that it became obvious that a cutback would
be necessary. In many respects it had accomplished its purposes, and there was no
longer enough to do. There were two choices.
The size and appropriation of the agency
could be reduced, or the SCS could find
some other things to do. Unfortunately, the
latter choice was the only one deemed ac-

ceptable. By influencing congressmen and calling in their political debts, the SCS and its political friends got the 83rd Congress to pass a law, now known as Public Law 566. Initially, this law gave the SCS authority to administer Small Watershed Projects for the purpose of flood prevention. Supposedly these projects are initiated by citizens who voluntarily, on their own initiative, band together to form a Soil and Water Conservation District. Funds were appropriated by Congress and the projects were designed by and in effect controlled by the SCS. From its inception, the small watershed program has been mishandled and is basically unsound. Much of this was due to the lack of expertise, and general ignorance of ecological facts in the Soil Conservation Service. Additionally, the overriding self-interest of this bureaucracy gradually surfaced and it became committed to Small Watershed Programs to an extent from which it could never withdraw.

A small watershed project is typically initiated when SCS officials contact powerful landowners and inform them that a project would reduce flooding on their land and enable increased crop production. Once the big landowners are convinced, the rest is easy. SCS officials visit other landowners in the watershed. Often a powerful landowner goes along to intimidate or cajole his neighbors. In most cases a watershed association is eventually formed. In many states this requires only the consent of 51 percent of the landowners or the owners of 51 percent of the land, whichever can be obtained more easily. The watershed association has the power of eminent domain and can force its will on landowners unwilling to cooperate. In some states this right has been given by an amendment to the state constitution.

Small watersheds under P. L. 566 must encompass less than 250,000 acres. The primary purpose of the projects is, in most cases, the alteration of the streams and small rivers included in the wastershed to prevent

them from flooding as frequently or as drastically. Obviously this appeals to many landowners because reduced flooding means more crop yield in the bottomlands. More crops mean greater profits. Who can scoff at that?

The major technique used in modifying streams is stream channelization; namely, the turning of a natural stream into a ditch which serves for little other than drainage.

A natural stream meanders through the lands it drains. Often, the stream bed contains logs, aquatic vegetation, and rocks. These serve as shelter and breeding sites for many of the animals living in the stream. The edges of the stream are stabilized by the armor formed by the roots of the bottomland hardwood trees. The upper portions of the trees overhang the stream, forming shade which keeps the water cool. Periodically the leaves are shed, fall into the water, decay, and contribute nutrients vital to the existence of the organisms in the stream. Insects inhabiting the trees frequently fall into the stream and serve as food for fishes and other animals.

The bottomland forests along a natural stream periodically flood. This is completely natural because the bottomland is the floodplain and is designed by nature to carry excess water when heavy rains swell the stream. The flooding of the bottomlands is a major factor which makes the soil rich enough to be highly prized as farmland.

The stream bed usually consists of an alternating series of shallow areas (the riffles) and deep areas (the pools). In the riffles insects and other small aquatic organisms flourish, often drifting downstream to become food for the fish in the pools.

In the rich, natural bottomland forests and the scattered swamps along the stream, wildlife is abundant. Bear, deer, and turkey feed on the berries, nuts, and rich vegetation. Near the stream otter, mink, and raccoon may be found. In the swampy areas woodducks feed and nest. A variety of songbirds, small mammals, and other nongame animals make the floodplain forest their home. In the spring the floor of the forest brings forth flowers in a variety of hues and kinds.

But the richness of the bottomlands is, in a sense, a weakness, because man desires the richness for his cultivated crops. Often where crops have been planted in the bottomlands, the natural flooding of the bottomlands destroys or reduces the yield of the crop. The goal of Public Law 566 projects is to reduce this flooding by increasing the capacity of the streams, and removing or altering any natural feature which might cause the water to remain on the fields.

The first step is usually the removal of all vegetation within 100 feet on either side of the stream. This eliminates the trees and other plants which slow the flow of flood waters and prevent rapid runoff from the land. By removal of the vegetation the terrestrial wildlife resource base of the bottomland is destroyed. Without the food and cover formerly present wildlife must evacuate the area or die.

The removal of the trees destroys the root armor along the stream bank and the bank begins to crumble and erode. The temperature of the stream water increases because of the lack of shade. Leaves and insects no longer fall into the water and the nutrient supply to the stream and, eventually, to downstream areas is reduced.

Hardwood lumber is already in short supply in the United States, and with additional destruction due to P. L. 566 projects, the situation in many states will become critical. In north Louisiana it is estimated that all hardwood forests will be gone by 1991. In Arkansas, 150,000 acres of hardwoods are being removed each year.

According to the terms of the agreement with the landowners who sponsor the watershed project, the cleared land is presumably planted with a cover crop and periodically mowed. In other words, a mature forest will never be allowed to return.

The clearing of the forest enables bulldozers and draglines to gain access to the stream and begin the actual work of channelization. This involves widening and deepening the stream bed in order to enable it to carry more water. It also entails straightening the stream because any meander or curve slows down the water flow. Often the natural channel is bypassed and a new channel is created.

The natural stream is gone and all that remains is a ditch. The pools and riffles are gone. No food or cover is left for fish. Over 90 percent of the plants and animals in the stream are killed as the bulldozer mashes them into the bottom of the channel or the dragline throws them up with heaps of mud on the bank. Others die from lack of water when the bypassed areas of the stream dry up.

The water spreads out in the wide channel and is subject to additional warming. Often, during the drier parts of the year, streams that were once permanent become intermittent after channelization.

The banks of the new channel are steep, so steep that in some instances livestock fall into the stream and become trapped. The steepness and height of the banks prevent access to the water by both livestock and any wild animals that might remain.

The soil where the forest stood, and the sides and bottom of the new channel are bare of vegetation. Erosion begins and heavy loads of silt are carried downstream when the water level is high. The speed of the water in the artificial channel increases its erosive capabilities and its silt-carrying capacity. The unstable bank is often undercut and slumps into the channel. This crumbling has caused the loss of acres of valuable farmland along some of the channels.

Pesticides and fertilizers added to farmland adjacent to the channel now flow rapidly into the stream and reach downstream areas quickly in high concentration where they cause fish kills and further disrupt natural processes. The free natural detoxifying action of the swamps and the natural stream is now gone.

The increased runoff rate hastens the flow and increases the amount of water moving down the channel. In the unchannelized downstream portions of the stream, flooding is now heavier than ever before. The benefits reaped by the upstream landowners are negated by increased flood damage downstream. It is easily seen that it is unwise to ditch streams in order to hasten the removal of water from natural floodplains (where it can be conserved and used) to downstream areas where it will cause floods that necessitate further expenditure of public funds.

The deepening of the channel interferes with the natural relationships between the water in the stream bed and the groundwater level in the adjacent soil and strata. The channel cannot recharge the water table like a natural stream. The water level in the channel is now below the water level in the ground. Water drains from the land and down the channel so rapidly that there is little recharge through percolation and seepage. Adjacent wells may drop in level or run dry. Springs and small tributary streams may become intermittent or disappear entirely. In areas where remnants of the floodplain forest occur, the drop in the groundwater level may cause the death of the trees. In coastal areas, lowered groundwater pressure may cause the intrusion of salt water into coastal plain water supplies.

In natural streams, swamps, and bottomlands, the abundant vegetation produces large amounts of oxygen and consumes large amounts of carbon dioxide. This capacity is now lost.

Local climate may be affected because the drier soil and drained swamps can no longer function to depress temperature extremes.

Repercussions caused by the lack of natural downstream nutrient flow and the rapid flowage of pollutants reduce productivity in downstream areas. Eventually the estuaries may be affected by the disturbed nutrient imbalance and estuarine fisheries may be damaged. Finally, if enough continental streams are channelized, the sea itself will begin to show the effects.

The recreational base of a natural bottomland is destroyed by channelization. After alteration the area is no longer suitable for canoeing, streamboating, hiking, swimming, hunting, fishing, bird-watching, or wildflower-hunting. The channel and scraped floodplain are an unsightly scar on the face of the landscape.

With all of the foregoing damages documented in the scientific literature, one is tempted to wonder why channelization continues. It must be understood, however, that the true worth of these projects often bears no relationship to whether or not they are initiated and constructed. The decisions are more often based on political expediency and bureaucratic self-interest.

The image of the Soil Conservation Service has been built by many years of work during which many of their endeavors were extremely laudable. A fraction of their current efforts continue to be worthwhile. Landowners have not yet realized that this agency has turned from beneficial activities to ones which are extremely destructive. This realization will take time. It is extremely difficult to disseminate the truth about an agency that can print thousands of brochures at the drop of a hat, that can push its programs with free television time, and that can distribute it's biased information through offices in every county in the country.

Further difficulty results from the fact that most of our national legislators still do not know or have not been willing to accept the truth about these projects. Many congressmen have benefitted by claiming credit for projects constructed in their districts. This benefits their image and furthers their career. It seems to matter little to some whether or not the projects are really beneficial, as long as the public can be made to believe that they are. A congressman who offends the SCS runs the risk of not being able to obtain further projects in his district and may suffer when SCS personnel impair his image with his constituents.

In the summer of 1971, Congressman Henry S. Reuss of Wisconsin introduced an amendment to the Agriculture Appropriations Bill which would have placed a one-year moratorium on stream channelization. The amendment failed because there was little time to inform members of the House of the facts which necessitated the moratorium. Additionally, the SCS and the puppet Soil and Water Conservation Districts generated publicity which implied that conservationists were trying to stop all SCS projects and were even attempting to destroy the agency itself. In the face of all this, the fact that 129 congressmen supported the amendment was encouraging.

In some cases, landowners who realized what was happening to their land have banded together and stopped a project. But few want to run the risk of alienating the SCS and the influential landowners whose friendship the SCS has cultivated. A farmer whose land has been defiled, or the owner of a cabin whose fishing has been ruined when a stream was channelized has little recourse.

All government projects, in order to be funded must be justified by data demonstrating that the benefits outweigh the costs. Honest calculations show that in most projects involving channelization, the costs outweigh the benefits appreciably, sometimes as much as ten to one. The SCS gets around this fact by contriving its benefit-cost ratios in a fashion that can only be called blatantly dishonest. Most of the damages are not even considered, the benefits are greatly inflated, and additional nonexistent benefits are claimed. Benefits are claimed to result from small lakes which are often constructed along the channel. Actually, pond and lake fishing and recreation are already in excess

supply in most of the country. Stream fishing and stream-related recreation are in short supply. Their destruction by the projects is not included in the SCS benefit-cost ratio as a loss.

Benefits are claimed due to protection of bridges against flooding when in reality, better bridge construction would be considerably cheaper.

The cost of these projects to the taxpayer is tremendous even without considering the extensive damages. In one Alabama project costing $4,417,312.00, the cost per acre to reduce flooding amounts to $405.02. The highest value of the land protected was $300.00 per acre. In other words, money used in the project could have purchased the land and a sizable chunk of funds would have been left. In this project 105 landowners were supposedly benefitted. This means that each landowner was, in effect, receiving over $42,000.00 in tax monies. If this was merely a gravy train, it would be disturbing, but when the damages of the project are considered, it becomes appalling.

Often, the actual funds spent on a project greatly exceed the projected costs. In another Alabama project the estimated cost was $226,000, but when the project was finally completed, $426,000.00 had been spent.

Another fact must be considered. The U.S.D.A., through the Soil Bank Program, has used tax funds to pay landowners to take land out of production. At the same time it uses tax funds to destroy our streams and stream-related resources so that, in some cases, the same landowners can put more bottomland areas into production. The logic behind this is completely obscure.

A memorandum issued by the Washington office of the SCS in February of 1971 directed SCS officials to reevaluate each project to make sure that "its impact on the environment as a whole is a beneficial one." As it turned out, this memo was merely lip service. In some states SCS officials have

admitted that the only result was the shuf-
fling of a few papers in the main state office.
Little attempt was made to realistically assess any of the damages. In fact, the SCS
has so little expertise in the various facets
of ecology that such an evaluation would
have been impossible. The bulk of the personnel involved in watershed projects are
engineers, draftsmen, surveyors, and other
technical people who know little (and par-
haps care little) about the natural systems
upon which man's existence depends.

Although the National Environmental
Policy Act of 1969 requires all federal agencies to prepare an environmental impact
statement concerning potential environmental damage on major projects, the SCS has,
in the past, claimed that P. L. 566 projects
are not "major," and environmental impact
statements have not been prepared for most
of these projects. The few environmental
statements available are amateurish, contrived, and incomplete. A recent North
Carolina court decision established the fact
that small watershed projects do represent
major agency actions. Hopefully this means
that in the future, environmental impact
statements will have to be furnished for all
of them.

Projects planned on nearly 9,000 small
watersheds are to be completed by the year
2000. In other words, this one agency alone
already intends to disrupt nearly half of the
small watersheds in the country. In reality,
the size of the watershed means little because the projects are often strung together,
eventually resulting in the destruction of a
large watershed.

At congressional hearings in 1971, officials from the conservation departments of
the majority of the states asked that channelization be stopped. No thinking person
can believe that channelization is beneficial.
The only real benefit is increased yield for
a few years on a few acres. Perhaps this is
all that some landowners care about. The
subsequent degeneration of the bottomland

soils in many areas eventually causes reduced
yield and increases the need for fertilizers
which, in turn, causes additional problems.

While billions of dollars worth of public
funds are being spent on programs designed
to create wildlife preserves, to increase
opportunities for recreation in natural areas,
and to promote the health of natural
streams, channelization is destroying these
resources at an alarming rate.

Stream channelization is not economy nor
is it conservation. It temporarily increases
the wealth of a few individual landowners
and strengthens a federal bureaucracy which
has obviously become irresponsible. It
demonstrates the fact that a powerful federal
agency can ram any kind of program down
the throat of the public, regardless of its
real worth.

Channelization is also often a part of projects initiated by the Corps of Engineers and
the Bureau of Reclamation. Industrial pollutants, domestic sewage, and strip-mine
runoff are ruining streams at an ever-accelerating rate.

The Soil Conservation Service whose
motto is to "hold the raindrops where they
fall" now rushes water off the land as fast
as possible. Land treatment has been essentially forgotten. Tremendous erosion
problems along secondary roads and in
strip-mined areas are left unattended. This
bureaucracy, like so many others, no longer
functions mainly in the public interest.

If the United States is to keep any
sizable portion of its extremely valuable
stream and bottomland resources, the actions of the SCS must soon be reversed. If
the natural systems upon which man depends for life are to be available to future
generations, stream channelization must be
halted. Once channelized, hundreds of years
must elapse before a stream returns to
natural conditions, assuming that no maintenance occurs and there are no further alterations. In effect, channelization destroys a
stream forever.

Once the public is informed about the results of channelization, this practice will undoubtedly be stopped. Hopefully, when that happens, there will still be a few natural, productive streams and bottomlands remaining.

ROBERT R. GRINSTEAD

The New Resource

Robert R. Grinstead is a research chemist at the Western Division Research Center of the Dow Chemical Company, Walnut Creek, California. He has devoted much of his research career to metallurgical problems including uranium and vanadium recovery from ores, and processing of brines and sea water for valuable minerals. During the past 5 years he has worked mainly in the field of water pollution problems and resource recovery from solid wastes, and has managed several federal government contracts in the area of brine treatment and water pollution problems.

"Trash Is Our Only Growing Resource," U. S. Undersecretary of the Interior Hollis Dole told participants at a conference on solid wastes in Houston last March. This point of view is becoming increasingly prevalent among public officials, scientists, and businessmen concerned with the problem of what to do with the growing mountains of solid waste accumulating in and around cities in the U.S.

Getting rid of trash has been a problem since the first caveman threw a broken bone into the nearest bush. The solutions developed by the earliest men — burning, burying, or carting the material somewhere out of the way — are still the major methods in use today, albeit with some new twists.

While these practices presented few problems for cavemen, the modern trinity of escalating population, intensifying concentration in urban centers, and skyrocketing consumption of material goods, has fashioned a triple threat to the age-old practice of dumping wastes onto the nearest unoccupied space.

Gradually, as the awareness of air pollution and public health problems has dawned, the plumes of smoke which used to identify local dumps have been disappearing; these eyesores have largely been replaced by landfills, where raw waste is quickly covered with a layer of earth. Currently, about 90 percent[1] of the trash collected in the U.S. is disposed of either by open dumping and burning or by landfilling. The latter has proven a fairly satisfactory means of solid waste disposal, since the land used has been of low economic value, and since the filled areas remain available for numerous uses, particularly recreational ones.

Reprinted by permission of the author and publisher from *Environment* 12(10):3-17. December 1970. Copyright © 1970 by the Committee for Environmental Information.
1. Office of Science and Technology, "Solid Waste Management: A Comprehensive Assessment of Solid Waste Problems, Practices, and Needs," 1969.

The landfill process, however, is a ravenous devourer of land. New York City has been consuming land for this purpose at the rate of about 200 acres a year. Some cities, including San Francisco, have already run out of space and are shipping their trash to other areas. Others have switched to incinerators, by which the volume of trash can be reduced substantially to a mineral residue, extending the life and improving the quality of the landfill site by severalfold.

The incinerator is not without its problems, however. Faced with increasingly rigid air pollution restrictions on one side, increasing corrosiveness of flue gases produced by certain plastics on another, and increasing capital and operating costs as a result of these two problems, the incinerator may well find itself becoming obsolete before it becomes fashionable.

Presented with this dilemma, authorities are thinking a good deal about longer-range solutions, and support is beginning to crystallize around the concept of reclamation — or recycling, as it is more popularly known. Rather than viewing trash as a useless waste to be stored away somewhere, the recycling concept views it as a resource to be exploited, as Undersecretary Dole suggested.

Stated in these terms, three powerful reasons support the recycling approach: first, the waste material is diminished or eliminated; second, credit may be obtained toward the cost of managing the waste material; and third, pressure on the corresponding virgin material source is reduced.

Recycling, which literally means returning to the beginning of the cycle, suggests separating the trash into its components, which may then be returned to the place of manufacture; for example, paper waste may be remade into paper products, tin cans returned to the steel mill, and bottles to the glass furnace.

However, it is not necessary to return the components of trash to their original form in order to obtain some further usefulness from them, and the aim of current recycling efforts is simply to return the wastes to the economy in a way that will provide some utility in *any* form.

With this definition, even landfilling can be termed a recycling use. Los Angeles, for example, has filled pits and gullies on which have been built golf courses and a botanical garden. Virginia Beach, Virginia is building a 60-foot hill of trash on which will be constructed an amphitheatre, a soapbox derby run, and a winter sledding course. Yet the value of fill — around one dollar per ton — is rather nominal considering the relatively expensive materials which went into the trash. The question really is: can we utilize trash in a more valuable way, and if so, how much more?

What's in Trash?

Some 200 million tons of trash (about one ton per person) are currently collected each year by towns and cities in the U.S. About 80 percent of the cost of managing this river of waste lies in the *collection* system,[2] the *disposal* currently accounting for only a minor share, due to the prevalence of relatively inexpensive landfills. Landfill costs amount to only one to three dollars per ton, compared for example to incineration, where costs run from about three to ten dollars[3] per ton, depending on the size of the installation and whether some use is made of the heat generated. Increasingly sophisticated stack gas cleaning equipment, dictated by stricter air pollution standards, can be expected to raise these costs still further. Large-scale composting, in the few places where it is done in the U.S., has a comparable price tag, about five to ten dollars per ton,[4] minus whatever credit can be

2. *Ibid.*
3. R. B. Engdahl, "Solid Waste Processing," Report SW-4C, U.S. Bureau of Solid Waste Management, 1969, p. 16.

obtained from the sale of compost and other reclaimed materials.

Against this background, let us examine the trash itself and see what is actually in it, both physically and economically. The first column in table 1 gives a very rough

TABLE 1. *Potential Values in Trash*

	Percent by Weight	Potential Value of Component	
		$/Ton of Component	$/Ton Trash
Paper, Paper-board	50	100	50
Ferrous metal	9	20	2
Aluminum	1	200	2
Glass, Ceramics	10	10	1
Garbage, Yard Waste	20	5*	1
Misc.: Plastics, Textiles, etc.	10	5**	0.50

*Value as compost
**Value as fuel

breakdown of the components of typical trash. The numbers vary, depending upon the economic level of the city, the season, and other factors, but quite clearly paper products constitute the major portion.[5] Next let us look at the potential value of this interesting ore. We shall assume, as a first step, that wastes will be recycled to those industries from which they originally came. The second column, therefore, lists the values of the bulk material (scrap iron, aluminum, scrap glass, and clean waste-paper). For the food/yard waste fraction, the value of compost is used, since although this material cannot be directly recycled to produce food and flowers, it can be *indirectly* recycled as compost to the soil.

The remainder, consisting of miscellaneous materials including plastics, rubber, fabrics, wood and leather, shall be assigned only fuel value, since the fraction contains little of any one material, and its fuel value is high. While reclamation of some of these miscellaneous materials can be envisioned,

no simple means is on the horizon.

The final column, the product of the numbers in the first two columns, gives the potential value of the components of trash if these materials could all be recycled as the forms shown.

The interesting picture that emerges from this exercise is that the potential value of paper literally dwarfs the other values in ordinary trash. The reason, of course, is twofold: the predominance of paper products in trash, and the considerably higher unit value of cellulose fiber.

It must be emphasized that a number of hurdles lie between the city dump and the industrial stockpile of recycled materials, and that the potential values listed above represent only the upper — and probably unrealizable — limits to the value of those materials. Nevertheless, the concept of potential value provides one convenient yardstick with which we may be able to compare the merits of various proposals for recycling trash.

Three other yardsticks are useful for evaluating proposals for recycling trash: one, the cost of separating the material from trash and converting it to a form which can be used by the appropriate industry (processing losses and degradation of the material are part of this cost); two, the existence of markets which are large enough to absorb the volumes of recycled materials, and which are close enough to provide acceptable shipping costs; and three, the amount and difficulty of disposal of final residue remaining after all materials which can be recycled have been removed.

4. J. R. Snell, "How Much Does Composting Cost Per Ton?" *Compost Science*, p. 17. Spring-Summer 1967. Univ. of Calif. Sanitary Engineering Lab, "Comprehensive Studies of Solid Waste Management," Second Annual Report, Report SW 3-rg, U.S. Bureau of Solid Waste Management, p. 63.

5. "Cleaning Our Environment," report by the American Chemical Society, 1969, p. 165.

Current Recycling Methods

Equipped with these yardsticks, we shall now venture into the realm of trash reclamation technology.

INCINERATION

Incineration qualifies as a recycling process on two counts: heat recovery during burning and material recovery from the residue. Incinerators with steam generation equipment for power production have been in use in Europe for many years, and new installations in the U.S. are beginning to adopt this improvement. In this instance, of course, paper serves as fuel, which is of relatively low value compared to the potential value of paper listed in table 1.

The incinerator is still an evolving species, and some newer designs involve such variations as gas turbines to generate power, or very high temperatures to melt and further shrink the volume of residue.

The major source of reclaimed values from incineration might, however, lie in the residue which, in a well-operated installation, would have a composition given in table 2.

TABLE 2. *Composition of Typical Municipal Incinerator Residue (Average of five Washington, D.C. incinerators)*

Material	Percent by Weight
Tin cans	17
Other iron and steel	11
Other metals	2
Glass	44
Ceramics, stones, bricks	2
Partially burned or unburned organic matter	9
Ash	15

Source: U.S. Bureau of Mines Report 7204, 1968.

U.S. Bureau of Mines scientists have developed a process utilizing relatively simple equipment (mainly screens and magnetic devices) which separates the major portions of this residue. In addition, a very high-intensity magnet separates the colored (iron-containing) glass from the clear glass. Costs of operating this process are estimated to be only about four dollars per ton of residue.[6] Although the value of the products has not yet been established, it will probably exceed the four-dollar-per-ton processing costs, and it seems very likely that in concert with the generation of power, incineration might be brought close to the break-even point.

The attractiveness of incineration at the present time is that it can reduce trash to somewhere between 10 and 20 percent of the original volume. For more advanced "slagging" incinerators, which operate at high enough temperatures to produce molten residue, the volume is shrunk to only 2 to 3 percent of the original.[7] Even with no reclamation of the residue, the life of an existing landfill site can thus be increased severalfold.

While the burning of trash has thus come a long way from the smoldering city dump of a generation ago, the major problem with incinerators is still air pollution. Equipped with a variety of scrubbers, filters, and precipitators, existing technology can probably cope with the increasingly strict air pollution standards in urban areas, but the question is whether it can be done economically in the face of other alternatives.

PYROLYSIS: NEW NAME, OLD PROCESS

A close cousin of incineration, pyrolysis differs only in the fact that air is excluded and heat is applied externally. Known in

6. M. H. Stanczyk, "Beneficiation of Metals and Minerals in Incinerator Residues," *Proceedings of the Second Mineral Waste Utilization Symposium,* Illinois Institute of Technology Research Institute, Chicago, Illinois, 1970, p. 255.

7. R. C. LaMantia Zinn, W. Niessen, "Total Incineration," *Industrial Water Engineering,* July 1970, p. 29.

earlier days as "destructive distillation," the process was used to convert wood and coal into charcoal and various chemical products. Recent studies using trash as a feed[8] have shown that a variety of gaseous and liquid organic materials, including methyl alcohol, acetic acid, and some heavier oils, are driven off, and charcoal and some ash are left as residues. The ash is similar to that from incinerators, but the other products are combustible and are currently viewed mainly as fuels, although some limited credit for chemical products may be obtainable. Unfortunately, none of the chemical products reported to date enjoy markets which could absorb more than a small percentage of the huge quantities of these chemicals potentially available in the U.S. trash output.

A related process developed by the U.S. Bureau of Mines involves reacting trash with carbon monoxide under high temperatures and pressures to produce an oil,[9] similar in characteristics to crude petroleum. Although this is a dramatic technical accomplishment, oil, used mainly as fuel, actually has a relatively low economic value. To be sure, the fuel value of oil is two to three times that of raw trash, but only about half of the trash weight is obtained as oil, and little, if any, increase in the overall fuel value is likely.

Construction of the first major trash pyrolysis plant[10] has been announced by the state of Delaware, where it will be located, and by the Hercules Corporation, which will operate it. The operation of the ten million dollar plant, which will handle 500 tons of wastes a day, is based on a composting step which will handle the bulk of the material, followed by removal of the metal and glass for recycling and by pyrolysis of the residual material.

One knotty problem which may prove the value of pyrolysis techniques is the recycling of old rubber vehicle tires. The problem of what to do with the 100 million tires discarded annually in the U.S. seems well on the way to a solution with the announce-

ment by the Firestone Rubber Company of a process wherein tires are pyrolyzed[11] to yield about 45 percent solid carbonized residue as in other pyrolysis operations. The remaining 55 percent is a mixture of gases and liquids similar to petroleum compounds.

The important feature of the pyrolysis process is its ability to convert most organic materials to charcoal (which may be recovered for sale or for fuel) and volatile organic compounds. Conversion of trash to more manageable fuels in this way may, some experts think, simplify the problems of extracting the heat values and meeting air pollution standards.

COMPOSTING

Although widely used in Europe, large-scale composting has never been an attractive proposition in the U.S.,[12] because it has not been economically competitive with landfilling. The compost has generally been viewed as a product to be sold, and major markets for this material have not developed here. A number of composting operations have existed in the U.S., but only three were still in operation last year,[13] and these have depended upon obtaining a disposal fee from the city.

Composting is essentially biological oxidation of the organic constituents of trash to relatively stable compounds. Trash is

8. "Refuse Can Yield Profits, Waste Technologists Say," *Chemical and Engineering News,* April 6, 1970, p. 38.

9. "Novel Process Could Aid in Waste Disposal," *Chemical and Engineering News,* Nov. 17, 1969, p. 43.

10. "Reclaiming Solid Wastes for Profit," *Environmental Science and Technology,* Sept. 1969, p. 729.

11. "Disposal Problem Solved," *Chemical and Engineering News,* June 8, 1970, p. 12.

12. S. A. Hart, "Composting: European Activity and American Potential," Report SW-2c, U.S. Bureau of Solid Waste Management, 1968.

13. "Cleaning Our Environment," p. 177.

usually ground or shredded and allowed to cure, either in windrows which are turned occasionally over a several-week period, or for three to five days in a large, slowly rotating, horizontal cylinder. Sewage sludge is often added to provide moisture and nutrients which aid in the composting process. The product is usually screened to remove plastic, metal, and larger pieces of glass. Paper and other cellulosic materials undergo composting readily, so the process has the advantage of being able to assimilate the bulk of trash components. Costs of composting are in the range of five to ten dollars per ton of trash, from which perhaps one-half or two-thirds of a ton of compost can be obtained. The finished product sells for about six dollars per ton, but is low in fertilizer nutients, and finds its main value as an additive[14] which helps to maintain good soil condition in high-value specialty crops.

In some situations compost may be in demand for reclamation of barren or dry land and strip-mined coal fields; it could also be useful for stabilization of steep slopes (as in Europe), road embankments, and mine-tailing piles.

Because of compost's relatively low value, the trend in thinking seems to be away from producing it as a salable product, and viewing it rather as simply a means of converting the unwanted organic components of trash into a material which can be returned to the environment without damage. The emphasis is accordingly shifting toward salvaging as much material as possible prior to the composting step. Typical of existing composting plants[15] is the one run by the Metropolitan Waste Conversion Corporation in Houston, Texas. Here paper and other easily identifiable materials are sorted, partly by hand and partly by mechanical methods. Iron is removed magnetically, and the residue is composted.

Viewed as simply a disposal method for the organic wastes, however, composting will have to compete with incineration or pyrolysis, which are more versatile means for accomplishing the same end. The residues from incineration and pyrolysis are smaller, and the by-product power available from both finds a ready market in the urban complex. Also, in urban areas at least, composting suffers in comparison with incineration and pyrolysis because of the distance between the urban area which produces the compost and the rural area which must absorb it.

If, as appears likely, demand for compost at any price does not materialize, it becomes simply a disposal problem instead of a resource, and the relatively large volumes and transportation requirements are distinct disadvantages. Thus, at least in more densely populated areas, composting may be heading toward the same fate as the fading landfill, which is being literally crowded into oblivion by the strangling growth of urban centers.

CELLULOSE FIBER RECOVERY

Of the roughly 55 million tons of paper and paperboard made in the U.S. each year, about 20 percent is already made from waste paper. The waste, however, comes not from trash, but mainly from commercial sources. Over 70 percent consists of either corrugated board, newsprint, or what is known as No. 1 mixed.[16] The latter is low-grade paper waste collected from office buildings and other similar commercial establishments. Much newsprint comes through collections from volunteer organizations, but the remainder is collected by

14. S. A. Hart, "Composting: European Activity and American Potential," Report SW-2c, U.S. Bureau of Solid Waste Management, 1968.

15. J. M. Prescott, "Composting Plant Converts Refuse into Organic Soil Conditioner," *Chemical Engineering*, Nov. 6, 1967, p. 232.

16. D. W. Bergstrom, "Economics of Secondary Fiber Usage," *Technical Association of the Pulp and Paper Industries Journal*, April 1968, p. 76A.

dealers, who sort, bale and ship it to paper mills. Most of this waste goes into cardboard or construction paper, where bulk, rather than high strength or whiteness, is the major consideration.

Within the past few years, two approaches to the problem of separating waste paper from trash have developed in the U.S. Some composting plants, such as Metropolitan Waste, have begun removing some paper from raw trash by various mechanical methods, and selling it.

A second approach, announced only last year by the Black Clawson Company,[17] a manufacturer of papermaking equipment, involves pulping raw trash directly in water in something resembling a giant kitchen blender. A series of mechanical separations including screens and centrifugal devices remove large nondisintegrating objects such as cans, shoes, bones, and broken glass, after which a fine screen catches the cellulose fibers. About half of the cellulose fiber can be recovered as a crude product valued, according to company officials, at about $25 a ton. Metal and glass, which are recovered separately, can be sold also.

With the aid of a grant from the U.S. Bureau of Solid Wastes Management, the city of Franklin, Ohio is constructing a 50-ton-per-day trash reclamation plant which will use this process. Company spokesmen estimate that a plant treating about 1,000 tons of trash a day (an amount equivalent to that produced by a city of about 500,000 people) would break even, while larger plants would presumably produce a profit for the operating agency.

A similar project is under way at the U.S. Forest Products Lab (FPL) at Madison, Wisconsin.[18] The project combines the "dry sort" methods of the composting plants with Black Clawson's wet-pulping method. FPL scientists envision ultimately upgrading the crude pulp to material of still higher value by appropriate chemical processing; the scientists note that this is a necessary

devolopment if recycled fiber is to compete for uses currently filled by virgin fiber. The bottleneck limiting preparation of high-grade pulp, they point out, may not be the "casual" contaminants, such as the garbage put into a paper product during use and disposal by the user, but rather the "intentional" contaminants (such as waxes, pigments, and plastics) put into the paper by manufacturers.

The second major problem in recycling paper is a marketing problem and stems from the fact that most paper products — as much as 70 to 80 percent according to one estimate — are discarded in trash. If substantial quantities of high-grade recycled fiber should become available from trash, this fiber would compete with virign material for paper products uses. To be sure, the market is large enough to absorb this recycled fiber, but only if the quality is competitive, and only at the expense of a corresponding reduction in the demand for virgin fiber. Reduction of demand on virgin raw materials is, of course, one of the aims of the recycling approach, and would be welcomed by conseravtionists as a step forward, though it might be greeted with something less than wild enthusiasm by the producers of virgin materials — in this case, the pulp manufacturers.

THE INDESTRUCTIBLE PAIR

. The above survey of current trash disposal ideas has centered on the uses to which paper wastes are put in each process. What about the metal and glass in trash?

The answer to this question is based on two factors. First of all, we saw in table 1 that the maximum credit obtainable for either fraction was only a few dollars per ton of trash. While this could be a significant

17. Ward C. Williams, "Use It — Reuse It!" *Pulp and Paper,* Sept. 1970, p. 61.
18. "FPL Recycles Municipal Trash for Fiber Products," *Forest Products Journal,* August 1970, p. 11.

credit in some cases, paper wastes are potentially more valuable and certainly more abundant; they would consequently have greater leverage in determining the economics of any given disposal scheme.

The other major factor is that, with a few exceptions, both metal and glass would be unaffected by any of the processing schemes listed. Therefore, recovery of either metal or glass could probably be accomplished either from the feed or from the residues of any of these processes, with only minor differences in equipment and economics. The exceptions to this generalization are those processes involving heating, in which alloying of the metallic constituents with each other complicates subsequent separation of the metals.

At the present time the most effective means for sorting out these materials are, for iron, various magnetic devices, and for glass, some form of air classification in which an upward air stream carries lighter materials away. No simple means has been reported for removing the aluminum, but the problem is under study.

It probably will come as a surprise to no one that the ubiquitous "tin" can is the major metal item in trash, constituting about two-thirds of the metal found there. Estimates generally place the total amount of iron and steel items in trash in the vicinity of ten to fifteen million tons per year,[19] or about 10 percent of the U.S. steel production. Another million tons or so of other metals, mainly aluminum, are also discarded in trash. Sizable quantities of cans are already salvaged in the western U.S. for use in recovering copper from low-grade-ore processing. This is a limited market, and it appears that significant expansion of steel-can reclamation will require recycling to steel furnaces, where the cans are now generally unacceptable because of their tin coating. Since the technology of detinning steel is well known, there seems to be no technological problem with recycling cans.

However, steel scrap is valued at only about twenty dollars per ton, most of which would likely be eaten up by the combination of detinning and transportation from trash collector to steel mill.

A big boost to can recycling may be on the way in the form of the trend toward what is known as TFS, or tin-free steel cans, in which the tin coating is replaced by a chromium and resin film, which would presumably be directly acceptable into the steel furnace.

All of the scrap iron, however, is not in the trash can. A large source of steel scrap is the junked automobile,[20] of which some seven or eight million appear each year in the U.S. Most of these find their way to junkyards, but probably several hundred thousand are abandoned in the countryside and in cities where they become part of the urban trash problem. New York City, for example, hauled away 50,000 such cars in 1969 alone!

The major technical problems of recycling automobiles are the same as those of recycling cans, namely, the elimination of undesirable metals and the transportation of the steel to a buyer, in this case a scrap yard. In the U.S. the principal development for separating these metals for recycling is a shearing machine which produces fist-size chunks that are sorted by magnetic equipment to yield iron and steel.

Although the glass content of trash is mainly bottles and jars, most bulk-separation methods would probably pick out stones, ceramics, and concrete, in addition to glass of nearly every shade of the visible spectrum. While scrap glass is recycled to glassmaking

19. National Academy of Engineering, National Academy of Sciences, "Policies for Solid Waste Management," Report SW-11c, U.S. Bureau of Solid Waste Management, 1970.

20. A Salpukas, "Abandoned Cars Blight the Nation," *San Francisco Chronicle*, Oct. 25, 1970. "Can Engineering Cope with the Debris of Affluence?" *Product Engineering*, Oct. 9, 1967, p. 37.

furnaces, it must be sorted by color, and extraneous materials, such as rocks and metal must be eliminated.

The nub of the problem — sorting the glass by color — is being approached from two directions. The U.S. Bureau of Mines uses a very high-intensity magnetic field to separate colored glass according to its iron content, which is related to color. Other devices divert glass fragments passing a sensor to appropriate bins, depending upon the color of light transmitted by the fragment.[21]

Since scrap glass, or cullet as it is known, is valued at about fifteen dollars per ton,[22] it is questionable whether large quantities of glass can economically be reclaimed from trash, sorted, and transported to a glass factory. In many locations the problem may be mainly a matter of how to dispose of the glass is an environmentally acceptable way. Ideas on this subject are numerous and generally involve incorporating the ground glass, which is nearly indistinguishable from sand, into building blocks, tile, or "blacktop" aggregate. The latter, dubbed "glasphalt," has been used by the Owens Illinois Company to pave a street.[23] While the value of this type of scrap glass is only that of sand or crushed rock, three to four dollars per ton, construction and paving uses represent large outlets in populated areas, eliminating the need for transportation to distant glass furnaces.

Shape of the Future

It should be clear that there has been no dearth of ideas for transmuting trash into something nobler and more valuable. Besides those described above, many others have been put forth, ranging from some interesting and potentially valuable biological processes for production of alcohol, sugar and protein,[24] to the farfetched suggestion that trash be put through a hydrogen fusion torch which would break it down

for reclamation into its constituent elements. To attempt to predict the ultimate winners in this technological contest would be as imprudent as attempting to pick the winner of a horse race before the pack rounds the first turn. Nevertheless, some conclusions are emerging, in general form if not in fine detail.

Table 3 lists the major processing schemes described above, together with some information about product yields and potential values. Estimates of final nonrecyclable residue have not been included, since most proposals envision burning or pyrolyzing any such residue to an ash. The final residues may, therefore, be roughly comparable. Based on the above discussion, an attempt has been made to provide a rough assessment of the difficulties to be expected in processing and marketing the products.

The foremost conclusion which can be drawn, and perhaps the firmest, is that the classical methods — landfilling, incinerating, and composting — are characterized mainly by the fact that the paper products are recycled into an end use of fairly low value. For the moment this may be sufficient, since the one to ten dollars-per-ton cost of the disposal process is a secondary factor alongside the twenty to fifty dollars-per-ton cost of the collection system which precedes it.

Given the range of possibilities, however, it appears that the action will inevitably shift to the reclamation of cellulose fiber, where the value of the product offers ultimately a greater chance for a net positive

21. J. H. Abrahams, Jr., "Glass Containers as a Factor in Municipal Solid Waste Disposal," *The Glass Industry,* May 1970, p. 216.

22. "Waste Recovery: Big Business in the 70s," *Chemical and Engineering News,* March 2, 1970, p. 14.

23. J. H. Abrahams, Jr., "Utilization of Waste Container Glass," *Waste Age,* July-Aug. 1970, p. 9.

24. F. H. Meller, "Conversion of Organic Solid Wastes into Yeast," Public Health Service Publ. 1909, 1969.

TABLE 3.   *Comparison of Major Trash Recycling Processes*

Process (Use)	Quantity, Tons per Ton of Wastepaper	Value, $ per Ton of Material	Value of Recycled Paper, $ per Ton of Original Paper	Processing Complexity and Cost	Marketing Fit	Probable Net Credit (+) or Cost (−) of Process, $ per Ton of Trash
Landfill	1	1	1	low	becoming poorer in urban areas	−1 to 2
Incineration* (fuel)	1	3	3	low to moderate	good	−1 to 5
Compost	0.7	6	4	moderate	poor	−5 to 10
Pyrolysis (fuel)	0.5	5-10	2-5	moderate	good	similar to incineration
Carbon Monoxide (oil)	0.3	20	6	high	good	probably (−) and large
Fiber Recovery**	0.5	25	12	moderate to high	good	about zero

*For incinerator utilizing heat
**Based on Black Clawson process

return. As exemplified by the Black Clawson and Forest Products Lab efforts, this goal has already become discernible on the technological horizon, although production of high quality, contaminant-free fiber is some years away.

This is not to predict the disappearance of other processes from the waste-processing field. Due to the spectrum of situations where domestic trash is generated, conditions may in some cases favor a process which is not applicable in others; for example, a smaller city considerably removed from markets for either pyrolysis chemicals or fiber, but surrounded by an agricultural area, might find composting an attractive process, although it might not be profitable in a major urban area.

Bypassing the Trash Collector

Up to now we have been discussing the prospects for recycling trash after it has been collected in a central location. Two other recycling routes exist, however, both of which bypass trash collection. One of these is the voluntary sorting of trash at home and delivery to collection centers, where it can be turned over directly to industries. This movement, organized by numerous ecology-oriented volunteer groups around the U.S., and assisted by the industries involved, has been the stimulus for much of the new awareness of the recycling problem in this country.

A second and similar route is utilized by the commercial scrap dealers, who collect or buy scrap metal, paper, glass, fabrics, plastics and other materials, usually from commercial and industrial sources, sort it if necessary, and sell it to manufacturing industries. This eight billion dollar secondary (waste) materials industry is responsible for most of the recycling done currently,[25] including 30 percent of all the aluminum currently produced, 45 percent of the copper and brass, 52 percent of the lead, and 20 percent of the paper.

Both the volunteers and the dealers are eager to increase the amount of recycling of materials. The question is, can an expansion of the existing channels for collection of secondary materials — home sorting, scrap dealers, and the volunteer movement — provide an alternate channel for recycling the bulk of the components of trash? At

25. J. H. Abrahams, Jr., "Packaging Industry Looks at Waste Utilization," *Compost Science,* Vol. 10, no. 1-2, 1969.

this writing the answer seems to be no, for a number of reasons.

The secondary materials industries now work mainly with commercial scrap and obtain very little of their material from trash sources. If they tried to expand by sorting material from trash, it would be a very costly operation since, at the current state of technological development, it would probably require expensive hand labor, plus some additional processing to clean up the material for sale.

With some form of subsidy, either in the form of volunteer effort, or from the public treasury, no doubt an extra increment of value could be skimmed from trash. However, neither the volunteer movement nor the commercial scrap dealers seem likely to be able to manage the entire trash problem, including disposal of those final residues remaining after sorting out the materials of value.

Finally, to the extent that recycled materials are diverted from trash through either of these channels, additional collection systems, be it trucks or individual autos, are required. Since in conventional trash management practice the collection process usurps some 80 percent of the cost, further fragmentation of the collection system seems likely to be a step in the wrong direction. Rather, as the technology of recycling develops, it seems probable that there will be an increasing reliance on a single trash collection system, combined with large-scale sorting and processing methods at a central location.

This is not to deny the value of the volunteer recycling drives or the commercial scrap industry. Central sorting plants and sophisticated recycling processes are not yet in sight, and for the time being there is no alternative to everyone saving his own aluminum, washing labels off his own bottles, and tying up his own newspapers. Perhaps even more important, however, is the educational impact resulting from involvement in recycling drives. Through the efforts of recycling centers, and through the publicity given their activities by the press, millions of Americans are aware that newspapers can be recycled and that aluminum is a relatively valuable material, and they are developing some long overdue appreciation for the unbridled extravagance of the U.S. materials economy.

New Attitudes and Technologies Needed

In very general terms, the roadblock to recycling our trash has been the attitude that materials are to be used once and discarded, and that the management of the waste piles thus created can somehow be taken care of.

Thanks to the new awareness of and concern about the environment, this attitude is changing. But we are finding that more than attitudes may need changing if many of our environmental problems are to be solved.

Looking at the trash problem, one of the major deficiencies seems to be that our materials technology needs to be extended to include the production of materials not only from virgin sources, but also from wastes. A tree contains about 50 percent cellulose fiber, just about the same as a truckload of urban trash. Yet we got most of our paper from trees, because, at our present state of knowledge, it is simply less expensive to do so. A large part of the reason for this is that the technology of papermaking arose at a time when wastes were almost nonexistent and virgin sources unchallenged. The technologies of papermaking, steelmaking, glassmaking, and numerous other industries, have all been laboriously constructed over many decades to their present highly refined state on a foundation of virgin material. Yet to a hypothetical scientist from outer space, unfamiliar with our history, there would seem to be no *a priori* reason why we could not, with adequate research effort, utilize the 50 percent of cellulose fiber, or, for that matter, the glass, iron, aluminum, and other materials in the trash.

Thus we need, among other things, new attitudes about producing materials which will be reused, rather than discarded after a single pass through the economy. But we need just as badly some new technology for salvaging these materials from wastes. This will cost money, and it will take time. It is at this point that the need for federal government activity becomes visible.

The Solid Waste Act of 1965 placed the primary responsibility for dealing with the solid waste problem in the Bureau of Solid Wastes Management (BSWM) in the Department of Health, Education and Welfare, some additional duties for mineral and fuel wastes being given to the Bureau of Mines in the Department of the Interior. The interest at that time was nominal by current standards of funding, and the total budgets of these two agencies have since then amounted to only about fifteen million dollars per year. Much of the effort of the BSWM during this initial period was devoted simply to assessing the problem and the existing means for dealing with it.

The mood is now shifting. A bill introduced in Congress in 1969 by Senator Muskie to extend the Solid Waste Act of 1965 was buffeted about for over a year and emerged as the Resource Recovery Act of 1969. Development of technology for recycling of materials is a major emphasis in this bill, for which $461 million was authorized,[26] several times the 1968 budget for for solid wastes. While expenditures are thus *authorized,* funds have yet to be *appropriated,* and the sincerity of Congress will be more adequately measured by the extent to which their appropriations match their rhetoric.

Two changes in our official attitudes seem called for, if we are serious about increasing our utilization of waste materials. First, we need to treat waste material industries on at least an equal basis with virgin material industries. In fact, until the technology of recycling matures, we may have to go a step further and favor it for a time, using such devices as subsidies for waste material industries, and a reduction or elimination of existing depletion allowances, favored tax positions, and lower freight rates for virgin materials.

The second change would be the establishment of some sort of feedback between the disposal process and the material manufacturing process. Thus, while it may be perfectly possible to come up with ways to recycle currently available materials, in the absence of restraints, the rapid appearance of new items in our trash cans may outstrip the ability of the waste processor to separate and reclaim them.

If the material producer can somehow be given at least part of the responsibility for the disposal problem, a powerful brake on extravagance would exist. At this time, however, no consensus has been reached on how to do this.

The role of the federal government in this field so far has thus been neither carrot nor stick — neither taxes nor incentives — for the management of trash and solid wastes. It is, to pursue the analogy, rather more like the shovel, which through the support of research and development, is smoothing the path along which the proverbial animal must tread. Plenty of carrot-and-stick legislation has been discussed and even introduced in Congress and state legislatures to accomplish a variety of ends. Few bills have actually been passed into law, because in this rapidly developing field it is not clear how the government should play its regulatory and incentive cards.

26. "Solid Waste Bill Signed," *Air & Water News,* Nov. 2, 1970, p. 1.

EDITOR'S COMMENTS

Trash is a problem because: (1) materials that should be reused are being thrown away, and (2) many current methods of trash disposal despoil the land or cause air and water pollution. Realistically we can only afford to throw away trash that cannot be reused and which will break down quickly under conditions in nature. A very small amount of our current solid waste is of this type.

Anything that is discarded will remain in the environment forever unless it is biodegradable or can rust or be oxidized away. Biodegradable items are those which bacteria and fungi can break down to their component molecules. By natural processes these molecules can then be returned to the ecosystem. Paper and organic garbage are biodegradable. Plastic, glass and metals are not, although some metals may be oxidized and eventually disappear. Paper, glass, and metals can be recycled. Plastics are not recyclable and thus present a major problem. To truly solve solid waste problems, we must either devise ways to recycle plastics or at least invent usable plastics that are biodegradable.

Much of our solid waste problem stems from frivolous use of materials. It is possible, for instance, to build an automobile that would last for several decades. The same is true for many of our other devices and appliances. However, planned obsolescence and the shoddy workmanship that go with it, cause many products to be useless after a few years, either because they are no longer functional or because they are out of style.

Manufacturing products that last, reducing needless use of materials, and recycling will greatly reduce the drain on our resources and, at the same time, cut down significantly our solid waste volume. Only in this way do we stand a chance of leaving to future generations an earth that will supply their needs and be free of the mountains of litter that will result if present trends continue.

SOURCES OF ADDITIONAL INFORMATION

POWER AND ENERGY

Barnea, J. 1972. Geothermal power. *Scientific American* 226(1):70-77.

Bernshtein, L. B. 1965. *Tidal energy for electric power plants.* English translation of the Russian edition. Israel Program for Scientific Translations, Jerusalem.

Catz, M. 1971. Decision-making in the production of power. *Scientific American* 225 (3):191-200.

Chough, C. W., and B. J. Eastlund. 1971. The prospects of fusion power. *Scientific American* 224(2):50-64.

Daniels, F. 1964. *Direct use of the sun's energy.* Yale University Press, New Haven, Connecticut.

Duncan, D. C., and V. E. Swanson. 1965. *Organic-rich shales of the United States and world land areas.* U.S. Geol. Survey Circ. 523, Washington, D.C.

Grimmer, D. P., and K. Luszczynski. 1972. Lost power. *Environment* 14(3):14-23.

Hubbert, M. K. 1971. The energy resources of the earth. *Scientific American* 225 (3): 60-70.

Leff, D. N. 1970. Familiar story. *Environment* 12(4):11-13.

Luten, D. B. 1971. The economic geography of energy. *Scientific American* 225(3):164-175.

Nowinson, D. 1971. Full steam ahead. *Ecology Today* 1(9):2-5.

Odum, H. T. 1971. *Environment, power, and society.* John Wiley and Sons, Inc., New York.

Starr, C. 1971. Energy and power. *Scientific American* 225(3):36-49.

White, D. E. 1965. *Geothermal energy.* U.S. Geol. Survey Circ. 519, Washington, D.C.

STRIP MINING

Caudill, H. M. 1963. *Night comes to the cumberlands: a biography of a depressed* area. Little, Brown and Co., Boston, Massachusetts.

Hill, R. 1971. Restoration of a terrestrial environment — the surface mine. *ASB Bulletin* 18(3):107-116.

Katz, M. 1969. *The biological and ecological effects of acid mine drainage with particular emphasis to the waters of the appalachian region.* Appalachian Regional Commission, Washington, D.C.

Kinney, E. C. 1964. *Extent of acid mine pollution in the United States affecting fish and wildlife.* U.S. Busport Fish, and Wildlife Circ. 191.

Nephew, E. A. 1972. Healing wounds. *Environment* 14(1):12-21.

U.S. Department of Interior. 1967. *Surface mining and our environment.* Washington, D.C.

FOREST PRACTICES

Bormann, F., et al. 1968. Nutrient loss accelerated by forest clear-cutting of a forest ecosystem. *Science* 159:882-884.

Curry, R. 1971. Soil destruction associated with forest management and prospects for recovery in geologic time. *ASB Bulletin* 18(3):117-129.

Frome, M. 1971. *The forest service.* Praeger, New York.

Klein, R. 1969. The Florence floods. *Natural History* Aug.-Sept., 1969:46-55.

U.S. Senate, Ninety-second Congress. 1st session, April 1971. Clear-cutting on the national forests. *Hearings before the subcommittee on public lands of the committee on interior and insular affairs.* U.S. Govt. Printing Office, Washington, D.C.

Vogl, R. J. 1971. The future of our forests. *Ecology Today* 1(1):6-8.

ECOSYSTEM DESTRUCTION

Briggs, J. C. 1969. The sea-level Panama Canal: potential biological catastrophe. *BioScience* 19(1):44-47.

Carr, A. 1964. *Ulendo — travels of a naturalist in and out of Africa.* Alfred A. Knopf, New York.

Caudill, H. M. 1968. A wild river that knew Boone awaits its fate. *Audubon* September-October, 1968.

Dorst, J. 1970. *Before nature dies.* Wm. Collin Sons, London.

Ehrenfeld, D. W. 1970 *Biological conservation*. Holt, Rinehart and Winston, Inc., New York.

Gifford, J. 1972. *On preserving tropical Florida*. University of Miami Press, Coral Gables, Florida.

Gillette, R. 1972. Stream channelization: conflict between ditchers, conservationists. *Science* 176(4037):890-894.

Idyll, B. 1969. The everglades: a threatened ecology. *Science Journal* 5A(2):66-71.

Laycock, G. 1970. *The diligent destroyers*. Ballantine Books, New York.

Low-McConnel, R. H., ed. 1966. *Man made lakes: proceedings*. Academic Press, New York.

Maass, A. 1951. *Muddy waters — the army engineers and the nation's rivers*. Harvard University Press, Cambridge, Massachusetts.

Marine, G. 1969. *America the raped — the engineering mentality and the devastation of a continent*. Simon and Schuster, New York.

Mobray, A. 1969. *Road to ruin*. Lippincott, Philadelphia, Pennsylvania.

Morgan, A. 1971. *Dams and other disasters. a century of the army corps of engineers in civil works*. Sargent, Lawrence, Massachusetts.

Smith, F. E. 1969. Today the environment, tomorrow the world. *BioScience* 19(4):317-320.

U.S. House of Representatives, Ninety-second Congress. 1st session, May-June, 1971. Stream channelization. *Hearings before a subcommittee of the committee on government operations*. U.S. Govt. Printing Office, Washington, D.C.

U.S. Senate, Ninety-second Congress. 1st session, July 27, 1971. The effect of channelization on the environment. *Hearing before the subcommittee on flood control — rivers and harbors of the committee on public works*. U.S. Govt. Printing Office, Washington, D.C.

SOLID WASTES

Dean, K. C., C. H. Chindgren, and L. Peterson. 1971. Preliminary separation of metals and nonmetals from urban refuge. *U.S. Bureau Mines Reports*. TPR 34.

Dornby, N. L., H. E. Hull, and F. Pestin. 1971. *Recovery and utilization of municipal solid waste*. U.S. Public Health Service Publication No. 1908.

Engdahl, R. B. 1969. *Solid waste processing*. U.S. Public Health Serv. Publ. No. 1856. U.S. Govt. Printing Office, Washington, D.C.

Grinstead, R. R. 1972. Bottlenecks. *Environment* 14(3):2-13.

Grinstead, R. R. 1972. Machinery for trash mining. *Environment* 14(4):34-42.

Hannon, B. M. 1972. Bottles, cans, energy. *Environment* 14(2):11-21.

Herbert, W., and J. Backster, Jr. 1971. Reclaiming municipal garbage. *Environmental Science and Technology* 5:998.

Myer, J. G. 1971. Back in circulation. *Environment* 13(7):30-33.

Packard, V. 1960. *The waste makers*. McKay, New York.

Piburn, M. 1972. New beaches from old bottles. *Natural History* 81(4):48-51.

Part VI

Law, Economics, and Religion:
Important New Factors
in Environmental Management

INTRODUCTION

The sixties represented a period of environmental awakening. Hopefully, the seventies will be a period of positive environmental action and all of us will quickly come to realize that most of the needed action will be started and carried out by persons other than ecologists.

We have already mentioned some of the environmental problems which must of necessity be solved by engineers. Cleaning the air and water, and recycling wastes are primarily engineering problems. The development of new fuel and power sources are engineering tasks. The development of new biological control techniques is dependent upon biological research. Agronomists, plant and animal breeders, and foresters all have important future environmental roles to play. Doctors, politicians, and individual citizens must begin to understand and be willing to take action against continued uncontrolled population growth. It is increasingly clear that bringing human life into balance with nature depends so much on the understanding and cooperation of many people.

In the coming years the fields of law, economics, and religion will undoubtedly come to play major roles in changing some of man's basic attitudes about himself, his world, and his relationships with his fellow man and the environment. We think the following few brief articles demonstrate an awakening of environmental interests and abilities in these fields.

JOSEPH L. SAX

Environment and the Courts of Law

Joseph L. Sax is Professor of Law at the
University of Michigan and a specialist in en-
vironmental law. He is a member of the
Environmental Studies Board of the National
Academy of Sciences.

What have the courts to offer in the resolution of environmental disputes that other
institutions, either public or private, lack?
Certainly judges are no wiser in such matters
than those who hold administrative posts.
They are no less amenable to corruption.
Nor, certainly, are they better equipped to
design highways or pipelines.

The judiciary has several virtues which
have thus far been largely lacking in those
who attempt to deal with environmental
quality. First, judges are outsiders. The
amenability to political pressures of the
kind that can loom so large in major environmental controversies, and which can
be critical in many cases, except in the rarest
situations has no place in judicial process.
Judges do not ordinarily receive telephone
calls, for example, from Senators or the
brothers of Governors, and they do not
have a federal or state agency's program
or budget to balance against the merits of
a particular case. All things which make
an administrative agency so much a political
institution, are essentially lacking in the

courts. In this respect, a change of institutions can be more than a change of form —
it gets to the heart of the matter, the problem of insider perspective.

The court is an outsider in another sense
as well, which distinguishes it from even new
organizations like the Environmental Quality Council. Judges will spend only a tiny
fraction of their time and energy dealing
with environmental disputes. For this reason
the process of judicial selection is not significantly affected by anyone's estimate of a
given judge's attitude about those issues.
This is a most important fact, one which
can hardly be applied to any institution that
deals regularly with environmental matters.
A President or a Governor who is choosing
an environmental council cannot avoid consideration of the attitude that important interest groups — whether the oil industry or
conservation organizations — will adopt toward that choice. But the very diversity of
the judicial role and the large numbers of
judges among whom such cases will be divided tend to reduce this consideration virtually to the zero point. And this, of course,
is a tremendously liberating factor when one

considers the political dimension that plays so important a role in the administrative process. While judical selection is itself tempered by consideration of matters which dominate the attention of the courts, such as the criminal law, a judge's attitudes about law and order (for example) in no way necessarily affect his judgments about potential environmental cases. This is a valuable advantage, and it should be exploited.

By the same token, the breadth of judicial work and diffusion of environmental issues among many courts and judges, free any given judge very substantially from the concerns which inevitably affect a specialized administrator or advisor, particularly the need to maintain some sort of politically balanced position among the constituencies with which he regularly deals. Any official who deals routinely with particular interest groups inevitably feels the need to do some "trading" in order to maintain a credible position in the eyes of those constituencies. This pressure towards sub-optimizing too is virtually absent in the judicial process.

It may seem a paradox that the greatest strength of an institution is its lack of expertise, that quality much vaunted among administrators, but to understand and appreciate this paradox is to understand the heart of the administrative dilemma — the problem of the insider viewpoint. The issue of expertise, and whether judges are to be asked to design bridges and power plants, is complex. For the moment, suffice it to note that those who actually make the decisions in controversial environmental cases turn out ordinarily not to be technical experts, making technical decisions, but (most frequently) lawyers in high position making policy judgments.

Yet another virtue of the judicial process, and perhaps the most important, is the opportunity which the lawsuit provides for private-citizen initiatives. We should remember that one must distinguish between the ability of agencies or officials to cope with problems they have undertaken to resolve (such as the Everglades jetport dispute) and their inability to cope with *all* the issues which deserve attention. Plainly, one of the greatest difficulties is in getting a dispute upon the action agenda of an environmental committee. Not only are time and energy limited, but the very pressures which lead in the first instance to questionable decisions often serve to make it imprudent for agencies or officials to take needed initiatives.

It is in this respect that courts are perhaps outstandingly unique. In a lawsuit no public official need take any initiative. A case is instituted by private citizens who feel they have a legitimate grievance. The court is spared the responsibliity for opening sensitive questions — indeed, in a number of environmental lawsuits, judges have made it a point to comment from the bench that they do not seek out controversies and would be just as happy to be left alone, but that if a citizen comes to them with a complaint, they have a duty to respond. Moreover, the traditional legal process is particularly responsive to this problem of citizen initiative. Not only is there no "political screening" of cases, but once a complaint is filed, the judicial process moves inexorably forward. Pleadings are filed, testimony taken, requests for particular relief are put forward and must be acted upon. It is not in the nature of the judicial process — as it so often is with complaints made elsewhere in the governmental system — for a matter to be shelved, put off for interminable study, or met with a form letter noting that some official is glad to hear of the matter and will certainly give it his consideration (someday, maybe).

These elements of the judicial process strongly support the need, averred to earlier, for citizens to feel that they are not merely passive bystanders in making their government work. The opportunity for anyone to obtain at least a hearing and honest consideration of matters that he feels important must not be underestimated. The availability of a judicial forum means that access to a government is a reality for the ordinary citizen — that he can be heard and that, in a setting of equality, he can *require* bureaucrats and even the biggest industries to respond to his questions and to justify themselves before a disinterested auditor who has the responsibility and the professional tradition of having to decide controversies upon the merits. The citizen asserts rights which are entitled to enforcement; he is not a mere supplicant.

The judicial process also demands that controversies be reduced to rather concrete and specific issues rather than allowed to float around in the generality that so often accompanies public dispute. It is easy for agencies to put off decisions by throwing into the controversy some vague comments about "loss of jobs" or "world oil supplies," or "building a tax base." Judges, on the other hand, must make specific decisions, and those who appear before them are necessarily required to shape their controversies to precise, manageable issues that can be the subject of specific orders. This is not to say that large issues, such as population control, ought to have no forum. Quite the contrary, it is to suggest the usefulness of a forum which permits us to *begin* examining those large and underlying issues in discrete and manageable contexts. It is to move toward the general through the specific. We have far too little of this sort of public debate, and the opportunity to enhance such particularized resolution of disputes is nowhere better presented than by the courts.

Finally, it should again be made clear that to enlarge the ambit of judicial activity in environmental matter is not to restrict or supplant other modes for public debate or the resolution of controversy. Administrative regulations will go on, legislative standards will be set, hearings and investigations will continue. Task forces and advisory panels will continue to engage in both long-range planning and some degree of specific dispute management. Courts serve only to supplement these activities and to encourage them to be carried forward more adequately in the knowledge that there remains another source of redress and review when they can be shown to be inadequate.

In this regard, it is essential to understand that litigation is not antithetical to planning. Indeed, one of its principal functions is to promote intelligent planning and the consideration of large, long-range issues. The principal function of courts in environmental matters is to restrain projects that have not been adequately planned and to insist that they not go forward unless and until those who wish to promote them can demonstrate that they have considered, and adequately resolved, reasonable doubts about their consequences. Similarly, courts frequently require fuller and more open debate (as by a remand to the legislature) in cases in which action is about to be undertaken before important policy matters have been satisfactorily resolved. In this sense, courts exercise an overview designed to assure that democratic processes are made to work and reflect the full range of public attitudes.

In the largest and most important sense, judicial intervention forces officials to take into account the wide implications and consequences of their proposals by challenging them at the operative level. For example, no one would expect a court to enjoin the federal highway program in general and order that the funds be reallocated to a more effective program of mass transit. But by restraining particular elements of that program, where inadequate provision has been made for accommodating public dissatisfactions or for taking into account the potential losses to important public resources such as parks and open space, congestion, noise, and air pollution, the courts thrust back on the highway builders some of the difficulties that the "true cost" of their proposal implies.

To the extent that this sort of judicial activity requires officials to consider alternatives, such as mass transportation schemes, which may seem relatively less costly, the courts have helped to promote precisely the sort of broad planning that we all approve but find so difficult to implement through traditional institutions.

The same sort of analysis may be made of private enterprises. Companies engaged in the production of electric power lament the constraints that judicial intervention has imposed upon their planning. On the other side, many wonder how we can ever bring home to the public the true costs of ever-increasing demands for electric power. The courts help to focus the issue. By imposing restraints on the construction of new facilities that inadequately compensate for losses in public amenities and natural habitats, they discourage to an extent the traditional search for ever more power. In so doing, they encourage the search for less costly — that is, less harmful — solutions, and they have the power to transform the sense of urgency about the need for such solutions from rhetoric to reality.

Litigation, then, provides an additional source of leverage in making environmental decision-making operate rationally, thoughtfully, and with a sense of responsiveness to the entire range of citizen concerns. Courts alone cannot and will not do the job that is needed. But courts can help to open the doors to a far more limber governmental process. The more leverage citizens have, the more responsive and responsible their officials and fellow citizens will be.

RUSSELL D. BUTCHER

Conservationists Go to Court

Russell D. Butcher of Seal Harbor, Maine is a free-lance conservation writer and photographer. He has served on the staffs of the National Audubon Society, the Save-the-Redwoods League, the Museum of New Mexico, and Sierra Club Books. For the past nine years he has written for the editorial department of *The New York Times*.

In addition to the land-related cases previously discussed, [in a previous article] there are many more suits concerned with such problems as endangered wildlife, the use of pesticides, and air, water, and noise pollution.

In New York State, the legality of the Mason Act, prohibiting the importation and sale of the skins of certain endangered species of wildlife, including rare spotted cats, alligators, and crocodile, was challenged by a shoe manufacturer, A. E. Nettleton Company. With a lower court striking down the law, the State appealed (with national Audubon Society and Environmental Defense Fund (EDF) filing *amicus curiae* briefs). An appellate court upheld the law.

Pesticide cases, many of them filed by the EDF, include suits to force the Department of Agriculture to ban the use of DDT, halt broadcast spraying of DDT in Michigan and Wisconsin, end the pollution of the waters of a national wildlife refuge in Alabama by a DDT manufacturer and the pollution of California's Santa Monica Bay by the nation's largest DDT producer, block the Agriculture Department's fire ant eradication program with the pesticide called mirex, prevent deregistration of 17 mercury fungicides by the federal government, and a $3 billion damages suit against all DDT manufacturers.

In a recent encouraging case against DDT, brought by EDF, Sierra Club, National Audubon Society, and others, the U.S. Court of Appeals for the District of Columbia Circuit, on January 7, 1971, ordered William D. Ruckelshaus, chief of the new Environmental Protection Agency, to cancel registration of DDT, and further ordered him to investigate the possibility of suspending DDT use — a step that, if taken, would prohibit even the use of existing supplies of the persistent hydrocarbon. The court ruled that, under the Federal Insecticide, Fungicide, and Rodenticide Act, Congress intended *immediate* notice of cancellation when there are substantial questions of safety of a pesticide.

Reprinted by permission of the author and publisher from *American Forests* 77(6):33-35, 55. June 1971. Copyright © 1971 by the American Forestry Association.

319

In concluding its opinion, the court made this significant observation:

> For many years, courts have treated administrative policy decisions with great deference, confining judicial attention primarily to matters of procedure. On matters of substance, the courts regularly upheld agency action. . . . Courts occasionally asserted, but less often exercised the power to set aside agency action on the ground that an impermissible factor had entered into the decision, or a crucial factor had not been considered. Gradually, however, that power has come into more frequent use, and with it, the requirement that administrators articulate the factors on which they base their decisions.

There are many water pollution cases. For instance, in December, 1970, the State of Vermont filed a lawsuit with the U.S. Supreme Court against the International Paper Company and the State of New York, claiming that serious sludge pollution of Lake Champlain by the pulp and paper mill at Ticonderoga has been "willful, intentional, reckless, and wanton," and that a fish and recreation area has been destroyed. The multimillion dollar suit asks that the company be compelled to remove the 40-year accumulation of sludge; and Vermont further seeks punitive as well as compensatory damages. There is also a multi-million dollar class-action suit on behalf of owners of lakeshore property in Vermont opposite the mill. These cases are pending.

In Florida, a property owner filed suit in January, 1971, to stop hot acid sulfate waste pollution of the Amelia River by an ITT-Rayonier cellulose mill. The same company is the target of a suit in Washington State for polluting Port Angeles Harbor, filed in July, 1970, by the federal government and two citizens, under the Refuse Act of 1899.

Other suits have been brought to stop the discharge of phosphates into Florida waters — a successful case; to prevent industrial solid waste pollution of Lake Muskegon, Michigan; to curtail the flow of taconite mine tailings into Lake Superior; and suits brought by the federal government against seven companies in the New York City area and eleven firms in the Chicago area for various kinds of water pollution, in violation of the Refuse Act.

Mercury pollution has recently been the cause of particular alarm, with the federal government filing suits against ten major industrial firms for dumping highly poisonous mercury wastes into the rivers, lakes, and harbors of the country. The U.S. Supreme Court has recently agreed to hear a suit brought by the State of Ohio which seeks to prevent Wyandotte and Dow chemical companies from discharging mercury into Lake Erie.

In Alabama, a private suit was brought last July by the Bass Anglers Sportsmen Society to block pollution of that state's waterways by 214 companies. When the Army Engineers announced they would enforce the Refuse Act against the offenders, the group dropped its charges against all but 14 of the firms which include pulp and paper, textile, steel, and chemical plants.

Only recently have the Army Engineers insisted on refuse discharge permits under the 72-year-old law. Violations of this provision have resulted in many of the suits in this area of environmental defense in recent months.

Oil pollution is another active area of court action. As a result of the massive oil spill off the Santa Barbara, California coast in early 1969, some $2 billion in lawsuits have been filed for damages against Union Oil, other companies, and the federal government. Suits to block further oil drilling and the erection of new rigs, under federal lease, have so far met with no help from the courts, however, even though there are no guarantees against increasing numbers of accidents in the future.

In another large oil spill, off the Louisiana coast, Chevron Oil was indicted by a federal grand jury, and on August 26, 1970, was fined $1 million by a federal district court. (This was the first such case to be filed under the Outer Continental Shelf Lands Act of 1953.) On December 3, the same court fined Humble, Union, and Continental oil companies $500,000 for their failure to install the kind of safety devices that would have prevented the Chevron accident and a more recent disaster at a Shell well.

In October, 1970, New York State's Attorney General went to court to ask that the Mobil Oil refinery at Buffalo be closed down. Prior to this step, the State Supreme Court had fined Mobil $10,000 and, to no avail, had given several extensions in time to initiate pollution abatement measures. The appeal is still pending.

As in the case of an oil slick in Florida's Tampa Bay in February, 1970, tanker oil spills are also the subject of litigation.

Air pollution is in court, too. In January, 1970, residents of El Paso, Texas, and Juarez, Mexico. filed a suit for $1 million against American Smelting and Refining Company, seeking also to close the plant.

In Arizona, two university professors filed suit in January, 1970, on behalf of the citizens of the State, for $2 billion in damages against American Smelting, and three other companies, and seeking an injunction against pollution.

In Washington State, conservationists are seeking an injunction against American Smelting to halt pollution from its Tacoma smelter. But on the reverse side, the company is suing the Puget Sound Air Pollution Control Agency, alleging that the sulfur dioxide emission standards, set by the agency, are unconstitutional.

In Richmond, Virginia, the Fourth Circuit Court of Appeals ruled in March, 1970, that Bishop Processing Company, a rendering and animal reduction plant in Maryland, must be shut down on the grounds that manufacturing plants have no right to pollute the air of nearby residents. This conclusion is surprisingly broad, but one wonders how far this reasoning will be followed in suits against major industries, in contrast to this relatively small operation.

In Montana, the EDF sued in 1968 to end severe air pollution of the Missoula Valley by a pulp and paper mill of Hoerner-Waldorf Corporation. While the case was in court, the company undertook a $13.5 million abatement program which, according to EDF "is well on its way to solving the problem." The court, therefore, ultimately dismissed the case, but the judge had "no difficulty in finding that the rights to life and liberty and property are constitutionally protected . . . and surely a person's health is what . . . sustains life. So it seems to me that each of us is constitutionally protected in our natural and personal state of life and health."

One serious weakness of pollution controls laws is that industry may find it easier and cheaper to pay fines while continuing to pollute, rather than go to the expense of pollution abatement. In March, 1970, a New York Court of Appeals decision held that a cement plant would not be required to close down until pollution control measures were taken. Instead, the firm was told it could continue operations, as long as it paid for damages to nearby homes. As a dissenting justice pointed out, decisions of this kind amount to "licensing a continuing wrong."

To help curtail such temptations, Illinois has provided that a polluter may be imprisoned for six months if he fails to take necessary steps with a specified time schedule. Fines, too, have been increased.

The most universal form of air pollution is from the automobile, from the internal combustion engine, and lawsuits have been brought to force manufacturers into quicker and more complete solution to this growing crisis. For instance, the U.S. Supreme Court may agree to hear a case brought by 15 states versus the automobile industry. The airlines and jet engine manufacturers have also been sued to speed up pollution control of aircraft.

Atomic pollution is another topic of litigation, with suits to block nuclear projects until higher safety standards are met. In January, 1970, the American Civil Liberties Union and the Colorado Open Spaces Council claimed that safety standards of the Atomic Energy Commission "grossly underestimate possible damage from radiation." The suit was specifically directed against the planned release of natural gas resulting from Project Rulison in which a 40-kiloton nuclear fission explosion was designed to stimulate underground production of natural gas in western Colorado. A federal district court agreed to take jurisdiction of the project, which may include several hundred more underground explosions. Hopefully, the courts will demand stricter safety standards than those of the AEC, although it should be questioned just how a court can actually oversee such a complex program.

When the State of Minnesota attempted to set far higher radiation pollution standards for nuclear power plants than those of the AEC, it was sued by Northern States Power Company on the grounds that federal regulation preempts this special field. A federal district court agreed with the company and ruled on December 22, 1970, that the State lacks authority to set stricter standards.

Among private suits against nuclear power plants is a case filed in October, 1970, by the Sierra Club and Citizens for Clean Air and Water to block construction of the Davis-Besse Nuclear Power Station near Port Clinton, Ohio. The case is pending.

Noise pollution is still another environmental cause of litigation. A suit brought by EDF, in the spring of 1970, seeks a court order requiring the Federal Aviation Administration to set noise standards for the projected supersonic transport, and requests that current airplane noise levels not be relaxed for the SST.

What right does a citizen have to bring lawsuits to protect the environment? In most instances, he must show some kind of injury or grievance. Michigan, however, is the first state to enact a law specifically permitting a citizen to sue to protect the air, water, or natural beauty, *even though he claims no personal injury or loss.*

When the Michigan law took effect on October 1, 1970, among the first cases filed were a property owners' suit to end pollution of a lake, a state legislator's suit to prevent the issuance of oil and gas drilling permits in a state forest area, and a suit by Wayne County against several industrial firms for air pollution — one of which, Chrysler Corporation, has challenged the law's constitutionality.

At the federal level, several members of Congress, notably Senators Philip Hart (D-Mich.) and George McGovern (D-S.D.) and Rep. Morris K. Udall (D-Ariz.), have sponsored measures similar to the Michigan law that would apply to the federal courts.

As an August 3, 1970, editorial in the *New York Times* explains, there is need for such laws:

> . . . because governmental agencies, federal or state, are so frequently derelict in the enforcement of the very standards they were created to enforce that a way must be found for the citizen to seek judicial relief. . . . A plaintiff in environmental cases should have to present a serious cause of action. When he does, he is surely entitled to more than the quick brushoff or the endless delay which are the twin traits of administrative bureaucracy.

Professor Joseph L. Sax of the University of Michigan Law School, author of the book, *Defending the Environment,* drafted the landmark Michigan law and the proposed federal legislation. He is one of the country's leaders in the effort to knock down the legal barriers to citizen suits on behalf of the environment.

Among the many attorneys now devoting themselves (sometimes with little or no pay) to conservation lawsuits are:

Victor John Yannacone, Jr., of Long Island, N.Y., who in 1966 brought the first case against DDT and who was a founder and the first attorney of the Environmental Defense Fund. An imaginative, tough, outspoken defender of conservation causes, Mr. Yannacone has courageously helped mold new court attitudes toward a wide range of ecological questions, one of the most unusual of which was his "buying of time" in a lawsuit against a land developer until Florissant Fossil Beds National Monument could be authorized by Congress.

David Sive, a New York City lawyer, who has been effective in such suits for the Sierra Club as the Hudson River Expressway case.

James W. Moorman, of the Center for Law and Social Policy, 1600 20th Street, N.W., Washington, D.C., who is an attorney on the suits against the Alaskan pipeline and Three Sisters Bridge, the West Virginia Highlands Conservancy case, and a key pesticides case.

H. Anthony Ruckel of Denver, who was counsel in the East Meadow Creek case.

Among the organizations working to promote environmental law are:

The Environmental Defense Fund, 162 Old Time Road, East Setauket, New York 11733, which is a nonprofit membership organization composed of an advisory panel of eminent scientists and a staff of attorneys, including Edward Lee Rogers and Edward Berlin, who represent EDF in legal actions to protect the environment from threats identified by EDF's scientists.

The Environmental Law Institute, 1346 Connecticut Ave., N.W., Washington, D.C. 20036, which is performing an invaluable service by publishing the *Environmental Law Reporter* and other case and statute compilations.

The National Environmental Law Society, Stanford, Calif. 94305, which encourages and helps coordinate environmental law research and action projects at many of the nation's law schools.

What are the reactions to the newly opening avenue of conservation action through the judicial system?

Last October, the Nixon Administration, through the Internal Revenue Service (doubtless responding to pressures from big business), started suddenly to deny tax exemption to organizations suing in ecological matters. Rebuffed by widespread strong public opposition, the IRS reversed its position a month later. As Sen. Sam J. Ervin, Jr., wrote in a letter appearing in the *New York Times:*

By withdrawing tax exemption from otherwise exempt organizations because they seek redress in the courts, the Service is striking at the heart of one of the most effective, traditional, and basic of American freedoms. . . . To say that citizens who join together to pursue litigation for nonbusiness, nonpersonal reasons may not deduct their litigation expenses . . . is a denial of the equal protection of the laws.

Even though environmental lawsuits are not always successful it is certainly a fact that within the past five years, in a remarkably rapid evolution of American legal attitudes, conservationists have been discovering how to use what Senator Ervin calls an "effective, traditional, and basic" right. Gradually, a body of case law is being created which is not only beginning to be effective in itself, but which hopefully will encourage far more vigorous and careful administration of environmental laws and regulations, and, where necessary, will bring about enactment of new laws. This is the broader goal behind the current vast array of environmental lawsuits.

The American judiciary has indeed come a long way since the historic *Berman v. Parker* case in which, for the first time, a court held that the protection or restoration of the environment is included within the scope of the welfare clause of the federal constitution. Said Supreme Court Justice William O. Douglas:

> The concept of the public welfare is broad and inclusive. . . . The values it represents are spiritual as well as physical, esthetic as well as monetary.

LAURENCE I. MOSS

Taxing U.S. Polluters

▶ Environmentalists previously opposed the idea, but
experience has changed their minds.

Lawrence I. Moss, a director of the Sierra
Club, is Executive Secretary of the Committee
on Public Engineering Policy of the National
Academy of Engineering. He is also a member
of the Council of the Federation of American
Scientists. The views expressed in the article
are his own.

Sulfur oxides are emitted in enormous
quantities (now about 33 million tons per
year, and increasing every year) from coal-
and oil-burning power plants, smelters, oil
refineries, sulfuric acid plants, furnaces
burning fuel oil, and a few other miscellaneous sources. The cost of significant reduction in emissions of sulfur oxides is likely
to be large (perhaps on the order of a few
billion dollars per year). The proven technology to achieve these reductions, according to a recent report of the National Academy of Engineering, is not yet available for
power plants, which emit 60 percent of all
sulfur oxides.

One could argue that it serves the economic self-interest of industry that solutions
not be found. If solutions are found, then
industry will be obliged to implement them,
thereby substantially increasing costs of production and perhaps even drastically changing the way in which business is done. If
solutions are not found (or if government

regulators cannot prove they exist), industry will be able to present government with
a choice of postponing implementation of
the standards or shutting down an activity
vital to the economic welfare of the United
States.

Does anyone seriously believe that the
Environmental Protection Agency (EPA)
in 1975 will shut down all electrical generating capacity within areas having concentrations of sulfur oxides in excess of the
national ambient air quality standard if a
substantial fraction of U.S. electrical generating capacity lies within such areas?

There is a need to supplement the conventional regulatory process in these difficult
cases, to establish a condition whereby government and industry are similarly motivated rather than motivated to act at cross-
purposes. I believe that pollution taxes will
fill that need by generally making it more
costly for industry to continue to pollute
than to stop polluting. Under such taxation,
industry could be expected to generally increase its investment in research and development and to quickly apply any promis-

Reprinted by permission of the author and publisher from Saturday Review, August 7, 1971.
Copyright © 1971 by Saturday Review, Inc.

ing technologies if for no other reason than that the return on such an investment would be higher than the return available from competing investments.

By encouraging marginal cost decision-making, the tax has the potential of achieving the desired level of environmental quality at lowest cost. This is why almost every economist who has studied the problem has become an advocate of the pollution tax approach to environmental quality. Robert H. Haveman, a Wisconsin University professor formerly on the staff of the Joint Economic Committee of the Congress, has calculated that the net budgetary cost of five years of water quality control under an effluent tax system would be $4.3-billion, as compared to the $12-billion the Nixon administration proposes to spend to clean up the streams, and the $14-billion appropriation advocated by Senator Edmund Muskie.

With specific reference to emissions of sulfur oxides, I applaud the President's repeated endorsement of a tax on them. I believe that the measure should include the following features:

1. A tax of 20 cents per pound of sulfur, achieved in full by 1975. This is somewhat greater than the estimated cost of abatement of sulfur oxide emissions, which ranges from about 5 to 15 cents per pound. The 20-cent charge is, incidentally, somewhat less than the measurable health and property costs to society of pollution from sulfur oxides. EPA estimates these at 25 cents per pound.

2. Uniform application of the tax throughout the nation, for reasons of administrative simplicity and to avoid creating havens for polluters.

3. Revenue from the tax should go into the general fund rather than to a trust fund. The purpose of the tax would be to abate pollution, not to raise revenue.

Candidates for pollution taxes, other than sulfur oxides, might include nitrogen oxides (from automobile exhaust), carbon monoxide, hydrocarbons, and particulate matter in the air and BOD (the biological oxygen demand made by effluent) in water.

PHILLIP S. BERRY

Corporate Responsibility and the Environment

Phillip S. Berry is a practicing attorney in San Francisco, California. He is a member of the Board of Directors of the Sierra Club.

Nations of the world must confront the problem of corporate irresponsibility towards the environment. Incorporation allows the organization and concentration of wealth and power far exceeding the capacity of single individuals or partnerships. Some of the most important decisions affecting our planet's environment are not made by governments or by peoples, but rather by the men who wield corporate power. And, too often, corporate decisions involve only minimal concessions to the public interest while every effort is bent to maximize profits.

There is nothing wrong with the profit motive in itself. It is wrong, however, to make it the *controlling* influence in corporate decision making. The environment must come first.

The problem goes back to the basic nature of a business corporation. Viewed in one sense, the private corporation is the part of government which 'got away.' The first corporate charters were grants of the English kings' sovereign power, and the notion that corporations receive special privilege from some governments remains in the

law today. In granting the first corporate charters, sovereigns placed conditions upon corporate powers but failed, for obvious reasons, to specify protection of the environment as one of the corporate purposes. This can and should be done, by enactment of National Corporation Codes to protect the environment, in every major country in the world.

Envisioned is a legal requirement that, in exchange for the privilege of doing business as a corporate entity, every corporation would be obliged to provide reasonable protection for the environment in every phase of its operations. This would answer the worries of corporate officers who are genuinely concerned about the environment but at the same time are unsure of legal parameters for resolution of conflict between the legitimate desire to make a profit and the more important interest of keeping the world livable. Meanwhile, as is already happening in some quarters, for example in the United States of America, commercial and allied enterprises would budget for the cost of the necessary arrangements to satisfy regulations to safeguard the local (and hence general) environment. Indeed, some forward-looking companies budget the cost of environmental safeguards ahead of time and consider this to be merely part of good business.

Amending all corporate charters in a single stroke, as these laws might do, would have a heavy impact upon how corporate decisions are made. It would force inquiry into environmental effects at every stage and level of decision-making. From beginning to end in every project, in every major country, and from bottom to top in the corporate hierarchy, every employee would be bound to consider not just the costs and possible return from each new project or product, but whether or not the broad public interest, and the environment of the planet, would be served thereby. If, according to some standard of reasonableness, the manu-

facturing process would degrade the environment or the end-product itself would pose such a hazard, the plan to produce it simply would not go forward. If it did, lawsuits could remedy the situation.

This is one method which would cause private industry to assume forcefully a new and positive attitude towards the environment. If such a new attitude is not widely inculcated within a reasonable time, it could well be that proposals now heard from some militant conservationists from different parts of the globe for public takeover of chronically offending businesses, would be implemented. Another possibility lies in enlightened trade (labor) union action, which is already proving effective in some countries in precluding activities that are considered potentially harmful to the environment and hence detrimental to the general well-being.

A. A. BERLE, Jr.

What GNP Doesn't Tell Us

▶ The Gross National Product—our standard index of economic
growth—measures everything from the price of hospital care to
the wages of belly dancers. What we need, argues an economist,
is an index of social—as well as dollar—benefits.

The late A. A. Berle, Jr., was formerly an
Assistant Secretary of State. He is the author
of a number of books, the most recent of
which is *The Three Faces of Power*.

It is nice to know that at current estimate
the Gross National Product of the United
States in 1968 will be above 850 billions of
dollars. It would be still nicer to know if
the United States will be better or worse
off as a result. If better, in what respects?
If worse, could not some of this production
and effort be steered into providing more
useful "goods and services"?

Unfortunately, whether the work was
sham or useful, the goods noxious, evan-
escent or of permanent value will have no
place in the record. Individuals, corporations, or government want, buy and pay for
stuff and work — so it is "product." The
labor of the Boston Symphony Orchestra
is "product" along with that of the band in
a honky-tonk. The compensated services
of a quack fortune teller are "product" just
as much as the work of developing Salk
vaccine. Restyling automobiles or ice chests
by adding tail fins or pink handles adds
to "product" just as much as money paid
for slum clearance or medical care. They
are all "goods" or "services" — the only

test is whether someone wanted them badly enough to pay the shot.

This blanket tabulation raises specific
complaints against economists and their
uncritical aggregated figures and their acceptance of production as "progress." The
economists bridle. "We," they reply, "are
economists, not priests. Economics deals
with satisfaction of human wants by things
or services. The want is sufficiently evidenced by the fact that human beings, individually or collectively, paid for them. It is
not for us to pass on what people ought to
have wanted — that question is for St. Peter.
A famous statistic in *America's Needs and
Resources* — published by the Twentieth
Century Fund in 1955 — was that Americans in 1950 paid $8.1 billion for liquor
and $10.5 billion for education. Maybe they
ought to have cut out liquor and paid for
more education instead — but they didn't,
and value judgments are not our job. Get
yourself a philosopher for that. We will go
on recording what did happen."

What they are saying — and as far as
it goes, they are quite right — is that nobody
has given economists a mandate to set up

a social-value system for the country. Fair enough — but one wonders. Closer thinking suggests that even on their own plane economists could perhaps contribute a little to the subject, although, as will presently appear, we must get ourselves some philosophy, too. One branch of social indicating may not be as far removed from cold economics as it would appear. Another branch is more difficult, though even it may yield to analysis.

Any audit of social result, any system of social indicators, requires solving two sets of problems. First, with all this Gross National Product reflecting payment to satisfy wants, did America get what it paid for? In getting it, did it not also bring into being a flock of unrecorded but offsetting frustrations it did not want? Essentially, this is economic critique. Second — and far more difficult — can a set of values be put forward, roughly expressing the essentials most Americans would agree their society ought to be, and be doing, against which the actual record of what it was and did can be checked? This second critique, as economists rightly contend, is basically philosophical.

As for the economic critique, let us take the existing economic record at face. Work was done, things were created, and both were paid for. The total price paid this year will be around $850 billion. But, unrecorded, not included and rarely mentioned are some companion results. Undisposed-of junk piles, garbage, waste, air and water pollution come into being. God help us, we can see that all over the country. Unremedied decay of parts of the vast property we call "the United States" is evident in and around most American cities. No one paid for this rot and waste — they are not "product." Factually, these and other undesirable results are clear deductions from or offset items to the alleged "Gross National Product" we like so well.

The total of these may be called "disproduct." It will be a hard figure to calculate in dollar figures. Recorded as "product" is the amount Americans spent for television sets, stations, and broadcasts. Unrecorded is their companion disproductive effect in the form of violence, vandalism, and crime. Proudly reported as "product" are sums spent for medical care, public health, and disease prevention; unheralded is the counter-item, the "disproduct" of loss and misery as remediable malnutrition and preventable disease ravage poverty areas. Besides our annual calculation of "gross" national product, it is time we had some ideas of Gross National Disproduct. Deducting it, we could know what the true, instead of the illusory, annual "net national product" might be. (Economists use "Net National Product" to mean Gross National Product less consumption of capital — but it is not a true picture.)

There is a difference, it will be noted, between "disproduct" and "cost." Everything made or manufactured, every service rendered by human beings, involves using up materials, if only the food and living necessities of labor. These are "costs." They need not enter into this calculation. Conventional statistics already set up a figure for "capital consumption," and we deduct this from "Gross National Product." That is not what we have in mind here. We are trying to discover whether creation of "Gross National Product" does not also involve frustration of wants as well as their satisfaction. Pollution of air and water are obvious illustrations but there are "disproducts" more difficult to discern, let alone measure.

Scientists are increasing our knowledge of these right along. For example, cigarettes (to which I am addicted) satisfy a widespread want. They also, we are learning, engender a great deal of cancer. Now it is true that at some later time the service rendered in attempting to care for cancer (generated by cigarettes manufactured five years ago) will show up as "product"; so the work of attempted cure or caretaking will later appear as a positive product item. But that item will not be known until later. What we do know without benefit of figures is that against this year's output of tobacco products whose cash value is recorded we have also brought more cancer into being — an unrecorded "disproduct." We know at the end of any year how many more automobiles have been manufactured. We also know that each new car on the road means added injury and accident overall. Carry this process through our whole product list, and the aggregate of "disproduct" items set against the aggregate of production will tell us an immense amount about our progress toward (or retrogression from) social welfare.

Once we learn to calculate disproduct along with product and discover a true "net" as well as a "gross," we shall have our first great "social" indicator. We shall know what the country accomplished.

It could be surprising and disillusioning. It might disclose that while satisfying human wants as indicated by the "gross" figure, in the process we had also violated, blocked, or frustrated many of these same wants and, worse, had done a great deal we did not want to do. Carrying the calculation further, we would probably find (among other things) that while satisfying immediate wants from today's productivity, we had been generating future wants (not to say needs) to repair the damage, waste, and degeneration set up by current production.

Some of today's "gross" product carries with it a mortgage — it sets up brutal defensive requirements that must be met by tomorrow's work and things. Some forms of productivity may prove to generate more decay, damage, or waste annually than their total amount, while neglect of some production may annually place a usurious claim on future years. Failure to maintain cities at acceptable standards is a case in point: it sets up huge but unrecorded claims on the manpower and product of coming decades. It is entirely possible to score annual increases of Gross National Product as we presently figure it — and yet, after reckoning "disproduct," be little better off at the end of any year than at its beginning.

Calculation of "disproduct" is admittedly difficult. If seriously tackled, I think it at least partially possible. At first it would be far indeed from exact. All the same, "disproduct" is a plain fact of life — look out of your window and you can see some. Crude calculation of the probable amounts needed to offset many items of "disproduct" is not insoluble; technicians in some lines have fairly concrete ideas along these lines already. Actuaries compute the "disproduct" resulting from automobile accidents, and your car insurance bill is calculated accordingly. Carry the process through and a crude though probably incomplete item could be developed. Using it, one could judge whether, materially at least, the country had moved forward or backward.

In this first bracket of critique, economists are not required to make value judgments of what is "good" or "bad." They, with the advice of the technical men in the various sectors, could merely be asked to tackle calculation of "disproduct" as well as of "product."

The second branch of the problem is harder. It raises the question of whether a good deal of Gross National Product should not be steered by social or political action toward creating a more satisfactory civilization. That, of course, requires some elementary assumptions as to what a satisfactory civilization ought to be and do. Can any such assumptions be made?

The question has not gone unnoticed. A philosopher, Sidney Hook (it would be Sidney Hook!), two years ago organized a combined conference of philosophical and economic pundits on the subject. Their proceedings were published in a book called *Human Values and Economic Policy*. They had themselves a fancy time. The opening gun was fired by Professor Kenneth J. Arrow of Stanford University, a mathematical economist. Consider, said Professor Arrow, a country that is not a dictatorship. In it, individuals have wide opportunity to find their own way to personal development and satisfaction. Then, he said, no picture can be drawn. Staffing it through equations, he evolved an "impossibility theorem," and thereupon tossed the ball to his fellow pundits. A colleague economist, Kenneth Boulding, rebutted, but it fell to a philosopher, Professor Paul Weiss of Yale, to counterattack. Professor Weiss forthrightly said that economists had been operating with an "unnecessary scarcity of ideas." The world, after all, is there — so they ought to add some conceptions of a "common-sense world and actual society, and a lived-through time."

Constructing enough of a value system to use as critique of a Gross National Product indeed does seem not beyond commonsense possibility. The job does without question, require setting out some values on which there is sufficient agreement to engage social opinion and one hopes, social action. Production steered toward realizing these values can be described as "good." Production frustrating or tearing them down can be stigmatized as "bad." Let us try drawing up a list, tentative in the extreme. I think there would probably be considerable agreement that it is "good"; but if not, make a dinner table game of drawing a better one:

1. People are better alive than dead.
2. People are better healthy than sick.
3. People are better off literate than illiterate.
4. People are better off adequately than inadequately housed.
5. People are better off in beautiful than in ugly cities and towns.
6. People are better off if they have opportunity for enjoyment — music, literature, drama, and the arts.
7. Education above the elementary level should be as nearly universal as possible through secondary schools, and higher education as widely diffused as practicable.
8. Development of science and the arts should continue or possibly be expanded.
9. Minimum resources for living should be available to all.
10. Leisure and access to green country should be a human experience available to everyone.

Anyone can add to or change this list if he likes; my point is that at least a minimum set of values can be agreed on. We have done more here than draw up a list of pleasant objectives. We have set up criteria. By applying our list to the actual and recorded output of our Gross National Product, we begin to discern that some of these values are perhaps adequately pursued, some inadequately, some not served at all. Even now, the Gross National Product figure is broken down into many lines. It would have to be split up further or differently for purposes of criticism. The elementary value-system we have projected (or some better edition of it) could provide the basis for critique. It could permit discovery of whether the recorded outturn of our vast hubbub of activity, after subtracting "disproduct" from "product," tended toward producing social results more or less in accord with the objectives implied by our values. If Governor Nelson Rockefeller is right in believing that in a decade the Gross National Product of the United States will be a trillion and a half dollars, it should be possible to steer increasing amounts of it toward realization of this or any similar list of values, and the objectives it suggests.

I am aware that no American value-system can be real except as it expresses a common divisor of the thinking of 200 million Americans. Beyond that point, Professor Arrow's "impossibility theorem" probably was right enough. Only totalitarian police state dictatorships, denying their citizens choice of life and action, can lay down complete and all-inclusive value-systems, force their populations and their production into that mold, and audit the results in terms of their success in doing so. Free societies cannot. They must content themselves with common denomination of basic value judgments on which most of their people have substantial consensus — leaving them free to do as they please in other respects. When a free society attempts to impose value judgments going beyond consensus — as they did when the Prohibition Amendment was adopted in 1919 — it fails. Yet because there is a wide measure of consensus on values, America does move along, does generate its enormous Gross National Product (and let us hope solid Net National Product) precisely because there is substantial agreement on what its people really want.

Also there is probably a high factor of agreement on priorities — that is, on what they want most. There are doubtful areas, of course. I will not risk a guess whether priority would be given to military preparedness over education were a Gallup Poll taken — more expenditures for defense and less for aid to education. But I am clear that both in values and in priorities a large enough measure of agreement does exist so that if we put our minds to it a critique of our outturn performance expressed in Gross National Product can be had.

And we ought not to be stopped or baffled or bogged down because philosophers cannot agree on the nature of the "good," or because scientists cannot predict with certainty the social effects of value judgments carried into action. Wrong guesses about values show up in experience, as happened in the Prohibition experiment. In light of experience, they can be corrected. With even rudimentary social indicators, the current cascade of emotional and sterile invective might be converted into rational dialogue. Constructive use of social-economic forces and even of currents of philosophical thinking might become possible.

I realize, of course, that up to now it has been assumed that social indicators, based on an expressed value-system, could not be achieved. Well, only a generation ago scholars assumed nothing could be done to alleviate the impact of assumedly blind economic forces, let alone guide them. We know better today; rudimentary capacity to control and steer these forces already exists; the so-called New Economics increasingly guides their use. Similar thinking and similar tools can provide material on which social policy can be based. Combined with the economic tools currently being forged, social objectives might be brought out of dreamland into range of practical achievement.

Discussion and debate would inevitably result from comparison of actual operations with desired results. More intense and perhaps more fruitful controversy would be engendered in areas where there were items not appearing in our tentative list of values for lack of sufficient consensus. Protagonists would insist they be included; opponents would object. This could be healthy. It would be ballasted by realization that, were consensus achieved, constructive action could be possible. Any caterwaul that American society is "sick" could be qualified by emerging factual knowledge showing that either the accusation was untrue or, if true, that measures for cure could be taken. The debate might disadvantage some people; for one thing it might reduce the torrent of boring despair-literature presently drowning the reading public. Possibly even contrasting currents of new Puritanism might emerge perhaps providing a not unpleasant contrast, if not relief.

Knowing where American civilization is going is the first essential to saving it (if it is to be saved) or changing it (if it is to be altered.)

ROBERT C. ANDERSON

The Church and the Environment

Robert C. Anderson is Minister of the Parkside Community Church (United Church of Christ) in Sacramento, California. He has long been active with conservation groups and environmental concerns, giving special effort to bring these matters to the attention of the religious community.

Speaking of the role of the church, and particularly the Judeo-Christian tradition, in the environmental crisis, perhaps the first proper response is a confession of the church's own sins of commission and omission. With a few lonely prophets in the wilderness, the church is late in coming to the scene of the current environmental action. To use the familiar imagery of the earth as spaceship, the church has long been concerned with the character and fate of its passengers, but has only started to turn its attention to the health of the craft as it begins to grasp the ecological fact that passengers and craft alike share a common destiny.

Apart from the need for activism on currently crucial issues (which may not be the strong suit of the church), an even more fundamental task faces the religious community and the general public, and the task is germane to the role of the church. It is a question of values. What do we want life to *be*? Dr. Paul Sears has put it this way:

Behind the fact of life is the problem of its meaning. The creative genius of mankind is challenged in all its range to design a future not only for survival, but for a kind of survival that has meaning.

When the discussion of environment issues enters the realm of values, it clearly becomes a religious matter. Others have said this, not always to the favor of the Christian faith. In an article in *Science* (March 10, 1967) called "The Historical Roots of Our Ecological Crisis," Professor Lynn White of UCLA points to the man-centered character of Christianity, stating that

Christianity . . . not only established a dualism of man and nature but also insisted that it is God's will that man exploit nature for his proper ends.

With all things under his domination, man too often chose to interpret this as a license to consume, rather than as a trust to keep. Content that it was "right" to exploit nature, man produced a devastating impact of exploitative practices with the possibilities offered by an increasingly efficient technology.

Thus, where there was once a time when the need was for man to save himself from nature, now a time has come when the need is to save nature from man, and man from himself.

But if the historical development of western religious attitudes permitted and even encouraged the exploitation of the earth, Professor White suggests that it will also require religious attitudes to redeem the situation.

> Since the roots of our trouble are so largely religious, the remedy must also be essentially religious, whether we call it that or not. We must rethink and refeel our nature and destiny.

What can the religious community do? It is imperative that some churches take corrective action on specific doctrines that violate the demands of the times and the true cause of humanity. The restriction on birth control is the obvious example. Every church can encourage its people to take their places with those agencies and groups that work for a better environment, and to learn from the persons who are doing the hardest thinking about these problems. The church (both as individuals and as an institution) can support legislation designed to heal the current afflictions. It can interpret the need to sacrifice some of the things we think of as "rights," and encourage a willingness to pay the costs of a clean environment.

However, before any of these things can be done with conviction or sincerity, the church must reassess its own values and beliefs — beginning by taking seriously the Christian teaching that this is a finite world that demands living out the Christian concept of stewardship with new sophistication and wisdom. The earth *is* a trust to keep for the sake of all men, and not a thing to destroy for personal gain or pleasure. Thus the church must help people to ponder what it means for man to be a part of the natural order, and not a creature who thinks of himself as independent of it. It can help in generating a new commitment to the earth and to the other things and creatures of creation — helping us sense, with St. Francis, what it means to say "brother wind," "sister water," "mother earth." It can foster in parishioners and citizens the development of an ecological conscience that is sensitive to the rights of other creatures, and evaluates the things of the earth in terms of ethics and esthetics, as well as economics. It can open our eyes to the fact that we are related in a profound way to the vast and complicated web of life that exists within the thin biosphere of earth, and that our own fate is tied up with the fate of other life on the planet. And in keeping with its prophetic heritage, it can proclaim the inevitable judgment of a self-wrought wrath that will befall the race if it persists in the exploitation and destruction of the Creation.

The duration of man's moment in time will depend, in part, on how well we learn the ecological lessons as to what earth is and who we are; and the meaning of each person's life can be enhanced by the same lesson. For in our growing concern for the environment and all its parts we learn something new about ourselves. In the durability of life we see strength, in its complexity there is wonder, in its fragility there is beauty. And in both the deepening mystery and the increased understanding of our place in the scheme of creation we may discover something new about humility, fraternity, and oneness.

People of the Judeo-Christian faith should be in the first ranks of those who draw wisdom from the environmental crisis, and and bring creative resolution to it. For whatever the historical distortions may have been, this is a faith that is, at its heart, not exploitative, but rather the agent of healing, redemptive love — to be extended now to earth and nature, as well as to man.

SOURCES OF ADDITIONAL INFORMATION

LAW, POLITICS, AND THE ENVIRONMENT

Allan, J. D., and A. J. Hanson. 1971. The politics of ecology. *Ecology Today* 1(3):38-40.

Anderson, W., ed. 1970. *Politics and environment: a reader in ecological crisis.* Goodyear Publishing Co., Inc., Pacific Palisades, California.

Billings, L. G. 1971. Prospects for environmental legislation. *Ecology Today* 1(3):37.

Clark, J. S. 1964. *Congress: the sapless branch.* Harper and Row, New York.

DeBell, G., ed. 1970. *The voter's guide to environmental politics.* Ballantine Books, New York.

Graham, F., Jr. 1966. *Disaster by default: politics and water pollution.* M. Evans and Co., Inc., New York.

Landau, N. J., and P. G. Rheingold. 1971. *The environmental law handbook.* Ballentine Books, New York.

Lowe, D. 1966. *Abortion and the law.* Pocket Books, New York.

McCaull, J. 1972. The politics of technology. *Environment* 14(2):2-10.

McIntire, M. V. 1971. Bringing polluters to justice. *Ecology Today* 1(1):48-51.

Sax, J. 1971. *Defending the environment: a strategy for citizen action.* Alfred A. Knopf, New York.

Sprout, H., and M. Sprout. 1971. *Toward a politics of the planet earth.* Van Nostrand-Reinhold Co., New York.

Udall, S. W. 1968. *1976, agenda for tomorrow.* Harcourt, Brace and World, Inc., New York.

Wheeler, H. 1970. The politics of ecology. *Saturday Review* 53(10):51-52, 62-64.

Wurster, C. F. (1969). DDT goes to trial in Madison. *BioScience* 19(9):809-813.

ECONOMICS VS. ENVIRONMENT

Boulding, Kenneth, E., et al. 1971. *Economics of pollution.* New York University Press, New York.

Carter, A. P. 1966. The economics of technological change. *Scientific American* 214(4):25-35.

Cipolla, C. M. 1965. *The economic history of world population.* Penguin Books, Baltimore.

Dales, J. H. 1968. *Pollution, property, and prices.* Univ. of Toronto Press, Toronto.

Enke, S. 1966. The economic aspects of slowing population growth. *The Economic Journal* 76(301):44-56.

Heller, W., ed. 1968. *Perspectives on economic growth.* Random House, New York.

Herfindahl, O. C., and A. V. Kneese. 1965. *Quality of the environment: an economic approach to some problems in using land, water, and air.* Resources for the Future, Washington, D.C.

Jarrett, H., ed. 1966. *Environmental quality in a growing economy.* Johns Hopkins Press, Baltimore.

Leontief, W. W. 1965. The structure of the U.S. economy. *Scientific American* 212(4):25-35.

Meadows, D., et al. 1972. *The limits to growth.* Universe Books, New York.

Mintz, M., and J. S. Cohen. 1971. *America Inc.: who owns and operates the United States.* Dial Press, New York.

Mishan, E. 1967. *The costs of economic growth.* Frederick A. Praeger, New York.

Pincus, J. A., ed. 1968. *Reshaping the world economy.* Prentice-Hall, Englewood Cliffs, N. J.

ENVIRONMENT AND RELIGION

Fagley, R. M. 1960. *The population explosion and Christian responsibility.* Oxford Univ. Press, New York.

Fiske, E. 1970. The link between faith and ecology. *New York Times.* 4 Jan., 1970, sec. 4, p. 5.

Harris, M. 1965. *The myth of the sacred cow.* Man, Culture, and Animals. Edited by A. Leeds and P. Vayda. American Association for the Advancement of Science Publ. No. 78, pp. 217-228. Washington, D.C.

Weber, M. 1958. *The protestant ethic and the spirit of capitalism.* Scribner's, New York.

White, L., Jr. 1967. The historical roots of our ecological crisis. *Science* 155:1203-1207.

Wright, R. T. 1970. Responsibility for the ecological crisis. *BioScience* 20(15):851-853.

Part VII

The Anti-Environment
Movement:
Plot, Backlash, or Apathy?

INTRODUCTION

Every cause has its detractors. For every blatantly obvious fact that exists, searching will reveal some who would prefer to believe the opposite. The environmental movement is not a cause to which all have flocked with religious-like fervor. Increasingly, in past months, loud voices have been heart "pooh-poohing" environmental concern; scoffing at the idea that changes must be made in our way of life; and railing at environmentalists, calling them "emotionalists," "prophets of doom," and "eco-freaks." What are the motives behind this criticism? Are there individuals and groups who genuinely feel that there are no reasons to be concerned about the future of the life-support systems of the earth? What could cause disagreement with the precepts of a movement when its main goal is to make the earth a hospitable planet which man can happily inhabit forever? In most cases it doesn't take a social psychologist to answer the foregoing questions.

A major problem is apathy. The average American is not willing to take action to solve problems unless they affect him directly. If we were all coughing up chunks of lung tissue, the air pollution problem would probably be solved in a matter of weeks. However, the damage done by most types of destructive environmental tampering is insidious. The effects come slowly, although ultimately they are just as fatal. It's easy to say, "I haven't noticed anything, so I'm not going to worry about it." "I can't be bothered," is another common reaction.

Change, even if it is for the better, always involves effort and often brings trauma. Change is therefore often resisted. It is easy to cling to the old ways. The familiar rut is comfortable to slide along in. Rather than change, it is easier to convince oneself that change really isn't necessary. The old ways die hard, and many will fight to keep them.

Prominent among anti-environmentalists are representatives of polluting industries. Reducing effluent output or eliminating a destructive practice costs money, mainly because of the technological modifications involved. Most large corporations have emphasized profits for so long that anything that interferes with profits is automatically attacked. To counter concern about pollution, industries often hint that if they are forced to clean up, the job market and total economy in the area will suffer. Another device used is to point with pride to token efforts to clean up, in the hopes of distracting the public from the fact that major problems still remain. It is a well-known fact that last year in the United States, big industry spent more money telling the public how much it was doing to conquer pollution than was spent on solving the problems big industry was causing. Those who most frequently call the environmentalists "emotionalists" base their actions on the lowest human emotion, greed.

There is little doubt that the public is beginning to tire of hearing about the environment. This is mainly due to overstimulation. "Ecology" and "environment" are catch words. Advertizing agencies stick them in any commercial whether they fit or not. Politicians sprinkle them into speeches indiscriminately. Everyone has hopped on the bandwagon. Unfortunately, little of the talk is backed up by action, support, or real concern. Environmental problems are beginning to resemble the weather. Everyone is talking about them, but few are doing anything about them. The public, being the public, rebels at overstimulation, and at times the very attempt to solve environmental problems may thus suffer from guilt by association.

The forces behind the anti-environmental movement are tremendously powerful. The results reaped when these forces go into action are the weakening of anti-pollution legislation, the intimidation of government agencies charged with cleaning up pollution, the silencing of individuals who have spoken out for wise use of resources, and the lulling of the public into feeling that "it's not all that bad."

The following selections are examples of anti-environmental literature, the motives behind some of them will be obvious—others are more subtle.

GLENN T. SEABORG

Those Good New Days

▶ They are sure to come, a scientist says, and a new science will bring them.

Glenn T. Seaborg, Nobel Laureate, is University Professor of Chemistry at the University of California, Berkeley, of which he is a former Chancellor. For the past ten years, he served as Chairman of the U.S. Atomic Energy Commission. He is presently (1972) President of the American Association for the Advancement of Science.

There seem to be many people today who deplore the fact that we did not, long before now, predict our population growth and our growing productivity with its accompanying waste, and somehow forecast our current environmental dilemma. Unfortunately, most great minds of the past foresaw only small segments of the evolving problem. And the values of the past were centered upon unlimited growth because this seemed to be to the advantage of the individual and his society. In a world of seemingly endless physical frontiers, where the exploration and exploitation of these frontiers by new human creativity generated and fulfilled new human needs and values, few if any could think in terms of limits, balance, and stability.

It does little good to make scapegoats of our ancestors or of one or another segment of our society for the crisis we face today. Our environmental crisis in particular could not have been theorized or accepted in the abstract before. It was an experiment that had to be lived in conjunction with the other problems of human growth that have evolved and that we must now resolve. It was inevitable that man had to grow to this point. He is now entering what must be a period of tremendous maturity.

Science and technology are said to be the cause of most of our ills today. By conquering disease and extending life they have been responsible for an explosion of population. By increasing productivity and raising living standards they have been responsible for depleting resources and polluting nature. By expanding knowledge and emphasizing efficiency, they have been responsible for deflating myths and diminishing man. And by placing enormous power in the hands of man, they have brought him to the brink of his own destruction. The list of accusations is endless, and it is not fashionable today to attempt to answer the charges or put the matter in perspective. It is more fashionable to dwell on man's relationship to the natural world, to lament that he is not more like the animal life from which he ascended, and to wish for his return to a simpler, perhaps more primitive, existence.

This approach may be more fashionable; it may even contain a certain amount of wisdom we should heed, but it is not the whole message we should be hearing. The major part of that message should tell us not to deny our dependence on nature but neither to deny our differences from what we left behind in our evolution. It is this recognition of what we are — with all its potential as well as its shortcomings — and the emphasis on what we must and can become that are important. In this transitional period from tribal man to a truly organic mankind, and to a world in which we can live in harmony with each other and in balance with our global environment, we need a new level of excellence in our science and technology and a new degree of integration between them.

There is, no doubt, a great deal of pain and shock involved in this transitional period, for we are breaking one set of long-established natural bonds and forming new ones. The whole process of change produces shock, reaction, and readjustment. There is always a tendency to turn back, to flee from the new and challenging, before new understanding and confidence allow us to move ahead. We are living through such times. We are experiencing what Alvin Toffler refers to as "future shock," and it is often difficult to sort out our movement and its direction. For example, take note of the action and reaction of our youth as it resists some change with an anti-rational thrust — and often a flight from reality — while it at the same time demands realization of a new level of idealism that can only be achieved through change employing the highest form of rationality.

A similar dichotomy and flux exist in our confrontation with environmental problems. Many feel the need for simplicity, limits, and balance. Yet, we know that to accomplish the goals we express in these terms involves the mastery of a greater complexity, new growth, and a dynamic rather than static type of balance. We really do not want to freeze the world as it is now or go back to "the good old days." What we want is a world far different from what we have ever known. We struggle fiercely but fruitfully to clarify our conception of that world and work toward its realization. We must not weaken or lose heart in this struggle.

What will be the outcome when we begin to succeed? What will the evolution of this new mankind mean? And what will be some of the manifestations that it is taking place?

Perhaps most important, we shall see the elimination of war as an attempt to resolve human differences. It will not be only that war becomes untenable as a form of such resolution. Neither will it be only that through the wisest and fullest application of science and technology we shall eliminate most of the physical insecurity and want at the root of war. What may be most significant as both a cause and an effect in establishing world peace will be a sublimation of man's territorial instinct, and the aggressiveness that is tied to it, to a new feeling of the communality of man in possession of the entire Earth.

Men are already sharing the Earth through international travel, communication, and exchange of resources. As this sharing is enhanced by a parallel releasing of the age-old bond of fear of scarcity — and adjustments in the economic system we have built to institutionalize that bond — we will begin to see the true meaning of the brotherhood of man materialize. And as this happens the tribal loyalty that Arthur Koestler has seen as the root of much of man's conflict will be broken and shift to a new global loyalty: a loyalty of man to all his fellow men.

Concurrently with this establishment of world peace (and again as both a cause and effect of it) will be the closing of the chasms between the peoples of the world. Aurelio Peccei, Barbara Ward, and many others have warned us that we cannot live in a world growing apart in the rate of development of its peoples. What we will see is a new concerted effort to raise the standard of living and productivity of the underdeveloped areas of the world while readjusting the growth of what many feel are becoming overdeveloped areas, harming themselves and others by unwise management of their power and affluence.

Another manifestation of our evolving mankind will be the reduction and eventual elimination of environmental pollution. Organic mankind could exist but momentarily on this Earth if it were to act as a parasite or cancer. It must learn to exist as an integral and contributing part of the Earth that up to now has supported it unquestioningly. Such balance can be achieved only by the formulation and application of a whole new scientific outlook and new ecological-technological relationship. This relationship must be based on a non-exploitive, closed-cycle way of life that is difficult to conceive of in terms of the way we live today. We will have to achieve what René Dubos has referred to as a "steady-state world." We will have to think and operate in terms of tremendous efficiencies. We will have to work with natural resources, energy, and the dynamics of the biosphere as a single system, nurturing and replenishing nature as she supports and sustains us. Such a system can be operated at various levels. A steady-state world does not have to be one in which mankind merely subsists and waits for natural evolution to take place. In fact, a steady-state world would be a challenge and stimulus to man's creative evolution, which I believe we should not deny is a natural process, and which may be the

highest form of natural evolution. Perhaps the organic global mankind I have portrayed will be the acme of physical evolution on this planet.

Undoubtedly, many people envision the concept of such a complex, efficient, and organic mankind as a nightmare, an ant-hill civilization in which individuals are mere automatons or mindless cells in an emotionless body. I do not agree. I see quite the opposite: a world in which the sphere of freedom of action and choice, individual creativity, and sensitivity are enlarged by the growth and application of knowledge and by greater efficiency and organization. These elements buy time and provide freedom. It is ignorance, confusion, and waste that enslave and eventually destroy.

Of course, new values and greater education must accompany the transition to this type of civilization. That is why the age of enlightenment we enter must be one that combines scientific understanding with a new humanistic philosophy. We need both now to survive and grow.

What will be the role and direction of science in achieving this new age?

First, science must return to the broad and general philosophy from which it originated. It had departed from this generality into a growing number of more precise disciplines — each becoming more productive the narrower its focus became. In so doing, science traded off wisdom for knowledge and, to some extent, knowledge for information.

We are now seeing the growth of inter-disciplinary sciences and a striving for an all-encompassing grasp of the physical world and even broader relationships. This type of growth is essential if science is to be the guiding force behind our evolving mankind. Science must grow stronger by continuing to nourish and improve its individual disciplines. We need the specific knowledge they offer. At the same time, it must grow wiser through its correlation of knowledge. And it must be able to transmit its wisdom in the most effective way to society.

We have a tremendous task before us in humanizing the focus and feeling of science, while at the same time organizing and rationalizing the forces of humanity. In recent years, we have not been too successful in either of these directions. That is the reason why we are faced today with a decline in the prestige of science, an antirational reaction on the part of many of our disillusioned youth, talk of the "eroding integrity of science," and even a feeling of guilt and despair in much of the scientific community. We must move away from all this. We must work toward a unification of the scientific spirit and a restoration of our self-confidence, as well as a new degree of respect for science on the part of those who have lost faith and hope in it.

Let me offer some specific proposals.

We should establish more international interdisciplinary conferences and more organizations that integrate our various disciplines, within and outside of the sciences. These conferences and organizations should bring together visionaries and realists, environmentalists and technologists, ecologists and economists, theorists and activists for positive, constructive exploration, discussion, and action — participation of varied interests, opinions, and talents. But the purpose of these meetings should not be confrontation. We should seek not the degraded power of polarization but the more beneficial strength of unity achieved through recognizing and working toward common goals.

In this regard, I would like to see those scientists who in recent years have done a great service to man by calling attention to his environmental problems now contribute an even greater service by joining their colleagues in a concerted effort to solve those problems. We must give our

activists something constructive to act upon and encourage the idea that many small positive measures can add up to a significant force.

We have been very unsuccessful in communication with the public. Now not only must we communicate, we must involve. We should particularly encourage the participation of youth in scientific and technical activities. Merely to decry their alienation, to speak of their immaturity or their unrealistic, "non-negotiable" approach to achieving their ideals, is pointless. More than that, it is disastrous. We must at all levels engage them in the realities of life, not to blunt their ideals or enthusiasm, but for the purpose of capturing what is good and constructive in them, of harnessing their energy and creativity, of growing with them.

If some sparks must fly between the gap of our generations, let us not use them to ignite conflagrations but rather to fire an engine of human progress. We in the scientific community in particular need our young people working with us, and it is one of the tragedies of our time that so many of them have become cynical about the accomplishments and prospects of science. I believe we can win many of them back, especially by showing them how effective we can be in working toward the solution of our environmental ills. We must prove to them that science and technology are among man's most creative and constructive forces — when they are used by creative and constructive men.

Finally, in bringing together the many forces I have referred to, and in emphasizing the importance of their working together, we must establish the leadership and goals to direct and sustain their efforts. Never before has the world had such a desperate need for greatness, for inspiration, for vision. The cynics today will tell us that any vision we would have now would be a delusion. But I cannot agree. I feel as is said in Proverbs: "Where there is no dream the people perish."

EDITOR'S COMMENTS

Dr. Seaborg's remarks undoubtedly stem in part from his long association with American technology. Perhaps some of his attitude can also be attributed to the fact that the Atomic Energy Commission, of which he was previously the chairman, has been under attack for its irresponsibility in the handling of radioactive materials and for encouraging the proliferation of nuclear power plants without adequate safeguards. He may think he has reason to resent environmentalists.

In one sense, most of the author's comments are positive in that they point to a bright and encouraging future. We all like to look ahead to happiness. However, it may be a disservice to point to a glowing future utopia when the facts indicate otherwise.

Very little is actually said in this article although it is full of highsounding phrases and exhortations to goodness. What, for instance, does he mean by his reference to "our differences from what we left behind in our evolution"? This phrase can be applied to any organism that has ever existed.

Perhaps the author is using evolution in the social sense. Hopefully he is not hypothesizing that a "technological man" is evolving that is very different from "natural man."

The major damaging effect of articles such as this one is that they create the impression that we can all sit around and wait for a natural progression of events to lead us to tomorrow's nirvana. Perhaps Dr. Seaborg did not intend to give this impression, because he certainly makes some suggestions as to what we will have to do.

There are two basic flaws in the argument presented in this paper. First, the author assumes that creative and constructive men will somehow be given control of technology by the profit-motivated forces which currently control it. Second, he assumes that presently-existing technology, which is exploitative, can solve the problems that it has created. A little "hair of the dog that bit you" may work on the morning after a party. There is some doubt that it will work in restoring a planet to ecological balance.

MAURICE H. STANS

Common Sense and Ecology

Maurice H. Stans was formerly U. S. Secretary of Commerce. Early in 1972 he resigned to direct President Nixon's re-election campaign.

For too many years, all of us treated the environment — air, water and land — as though it could absorb unlimited amounts of anything and everything.

But no more. In the 1970s the profligate era is being brought to a shuddering halt.

We have launched the first comprehensive cleanup of the nation's air, water and land in our country's history, and we will succeed in this task. This is just the kind of problem that American technology is equipped to solve.

Orderly Approach

But in approaching solutions to our environmental problems, we have also come close to creating new ones.

Frequently we attack environmental matters individually, and sometimes on a local basis, which more often than not just increases the cost and lowers the efficiency of the effort.

As a result, and with more emotion than knowledge, we are rapidly developing a patchwork of laws and regulations, often at variance with each other, with a dearth of scientific and technological facts, usually enforced by new agencies at various levels of government which operate according to a wide variety of standards.

What we need is something else.

We must consider technological limitations and economic factors as well as ecological goals in approaching environmental decisions affecting the national interest.

We need to clean up the environment in an orderly way, at reasonable cost, over a fixed period of time, comparing cost with benefits at each point along the way.

We must achieve orderly progress by local governments, by agriculture, by the public and others equal to the progress demanded of industry.

This task is tremendously large and complex. It will not yield to the quick, easy, simplistic solutions that some people might seem to think are readily available. Nor will those solutions become available just by setting unrealistic timetables.

Reprinted by permission of the author and publisher from *Commerce Today*. September 20, 1971.

Hasty Solutions

Some of our most eminent scientists warn us against hasty, ill-conceived solutions in the environmental area.

Dr. Philip Handler, President of the National Academy of Sciences, has warned that a combination of "emotional zeal and technological ignorance" could lead us to "substitute environmental tragedy for existing environmental deterioration."

"Let us not," he says, "replace known devils by insufficiently understood, unknown devils."

The fact is that our knowledge in this area is extremely limited. The science of ecology is in its infancy. Much of the technology required to clean up the environment is nonexistent.

Common Sense Decisions

If ever there was a time and place to look before we leap, that time is here and now.

We must not make decisions on an emotional basis, in a state of ecological hysteria, which we will live to regret later.

We must not add the environment to the list of problems to which we apply more dollars than sense — common sense.

All of this does not mean we should not spend what is necessary to clean up the environment. It does mean we must plan our spending wisely, with regard for priorities, taking all of the factors into account before we plunge into these efforts — doing first the things we can do, but seeking the breakthroughs as we go, in an orderly way.

EDITOR'S COMMENTS

The "it's great, but" approach is a favorite ploy in debate. First one agrees with an idea, then proceeds to pick it apart. In conclusion, one claims that what was obviously meant wasn't really intended.

Mr. Stans was Secretary of Commerce of the United States when he wrote this article. Secretaries of Commerce can benefit their administration by catering to the powers that be in commerce. An anticipated result is that big business will reciprocate. The administration speaks through many mouths, some pro-environment, some anti-environment. A problem exists in determining which is the real one.

The author uses many anti-environmental cliches and demonstrates a number of the facets of anti-environmental bigotry. His implication that environmental factors are being considered before economic factors is ludicrous. Quoting a prominent anti-environmentalist lends little credence to his arguments. Totally, the author's remarks seem to mean only one thing — that corporate profits should not suffer because of concern for public welfare. This is a novel brand of common sense. It differs little from the philosophy that is at the root of our present problems.

The most jolting fact realized after reading this article is that environmental backlash is present at the cabinet level in the current administration. With this type of attitude in such lofty places, it is evident that the battle for a livable planet is far from won.

THOMAS R. SHEPARD, Jr.

Speech Given Before the 44th Annual Meeting of the Soap and Detergent Association

Thomas R. Shepard, Jr., was formerly the Publisher of *Look* magazine.

One morning last fall I left my office here in New York and hailed a cab for Kennedy Airport. The driver had the radio tuned to one of those daytime talk shows where the participants take turns complaining about how terrible everything is. Air pollution. Water pollution. Noise pollution. Racial unrest. Campus unrest. Overpopulation. Under employment. You name it, they agonized over it. This went on all the way to Kennedy and as we pulled up at the terminal the driver turned to me and said — and I quote — "if things are all that bad, how come I feel so good?"

Ladies and gentlemen, I wonder how many Americans, pelted day after day by the voices of doom, ever ask themselves that question: "If things are all that bad, how come I feel so good?"

Well, I think I have the answer. We feel good because things *aren't* that bad. Today I would like to tell you how wrong the pessimists are, and to focus an overdue spotlight on the pessimists themselves. These are the people who, in the name of ecology or consumerism or some other "ology" or "ism," are laying siege to our state and federal governments, demanding laws to regulate industry on the premise that the United States is on the brink of catastrophe and only a brand-new socio-economic system can save us. I call these people The Disaster Lobby, and I regard them as the most dangerous men and women in America today. Dangerous not only to the institutions they seek to destroy but to the consumers they are supposed to protect.

Let's begin with a close-in look at that drumbeat of despair I heard in the taxicab and that all of us hear almost every day. Just how much truth is there to the Disaster Lobby's complaints?

Take the one about the oxygen we breathe. The Disaster folks tell us that the burning of fuels by industry is using up the earth's oxygen and that, eventually, there won't be any left and we'll suffocate. False. The National Science Foundation recently collected air samples at 78 sites around the world and compared them with samples taken 61 years ago. Result? There is today precisely the same amount of oxygen in the air as there was in 1910 — 20.95 percent.

But what about air pollution? You can't deny that our air is getting more fouled up all the time, says the Disaster Lobby.

Reprinted by permission of the author. Speech given January 28, 1971 before the 44th Annual Meeting of the Soap and Detergent Association.

346

Wrong. I *can* deny it. Our air is getting less fouled up all the time, in city after city. In New York City, for example. New York's Department of Air Resources reports a year-by-year *decrease* in air pollutants since 1965. What's more, the New York City air is immeasurably cleaner today than it was a hundred years ago, when people burned soft coal and you could cut the smog with a knife.

Which brings us to water pollution. The Disaster Lobby recalls that, back in the days before America was industrialized, our rivers and lakes were crystal clear. True. And those crystal-clear rivers and lakes were the source of the worst cholera, yellow fever and typhoid epidemics the world has ever known. Just one of these epidemics — in 1793 — killed one of every five residents of Philadelphia. Our waterways may not be as pretty as they used to be, but they aren't as deadly, either. In fact, the water we drink is the safest in the world. What's more, we're making progress cosmetically. Many of our streams will soon *look* as wholesome as they *are*.

Perhaps it's the fear of overpopulation that's getting you down. Well, cheer up. The birth rate in the United States has been dropping continuously since 1955 and is now at the lowest point in history. If the trend continues, it is remotely possible that by the year 4000 there won't be anyone left in the country. But I wouldn't fret about *under*population, either. Populations have a way of adjusting to conditions, and I have no doubt that our birth rate will pick up in due course.

I now come to the case of the mercury in tuna fish. How did it get there? The Disaster Lobby says it came from American factories. The truth, as scientists will tell you, is that the mercury came from deposits in nature. To attribute pollution of entire oceans to the 900 tons of mercury released into the environment each year by industry — that's less than 40 carloads — is like blaming a boy

with a water pistol for the Johnstown Flood. Further proof? Fish caught 44 years ago and just analyzed contain twice as much mercury as any fish processed this year.

Speaking of fish, what about the charge that our greed and carelessness are killing off species of animals? Well, it's true that about 50 species of wildlife will become extinct this century. But it's also true that 50 species became extinct *last* century. And the century before that. And the century before *that*. In fact, says Dr. T. H. Jukes of the University of California, some 100 million species of animal life have become extinct since the world began. Animals come and animals go, as Mr. Darwin noted, and to blame ourselves for evolution would be the height of foolishness.

Then there is the drug situation. Isn't it a fact that we are becoming a nation of addicts? No, it is not. Historically, we are becoming a nation of *non*addicts. Seventy years ago, one of every 400 Americans was hooked on hard drugs. Today, it's one in 3,000. So, despite recent experimentation with drugs by teenagers, the long-range trend is downward, not upward.

Another crisis constructed of pure poppycock is the so-called youth rebellion, to which the Disaster Lobby points with mingled alarm and glee. But once you examine the scene in depth — once you probe behind a very small gaggle of young troublemakers who are sorely in need of an education, a spanking and a bath, not necessarily in that order — you can't find any rebellion worth talking about. A while back *Look* commissioned Gallup to do a study on the mood of America. Gallup found that, on virtually every issue, the views of teenagers coincided with those of adults. And on those issues where the kids did *not* see eye-to-eye with their elders, the youngsters often tended to be more conservative.

The same assessment can be made of the putative black rebellion. There isn't any. Oh, there are the rantings of a lunatic fringe — a few paranoid militants who in any other country would be behind bars and whose continued freedom here is testimony to the fact that we are the most liberated and least racist nation on earth. But the vast majority of black Americans, as that same Gallup study revealed, are staunch believers in this nation.

How about unemployment? The Disaster people regard it as a grave problem. Well, I suppose even one unemployed person is a grave problem, but the record book tells us that the current out-of-work level of six percent is about par. We've had less, but we've also had more — much more. During the Kennedy Administration unemployment topped seven percent. And back in the recovery period of Franklin Roosevelt's second term, unemployment reached 25 percent. So let's not panic over this one.

That word "panic" brings me to the H-bomb. Some people have let the gloommongers scare them beyond rational response with talk about atomic annihilation. I can't guarantee immunity from the bomb, but I offer the following as food for thought. Since World War II, over one billion human beings who worried about A-bombs and H-bombs died of other causes. They worried for nothing. It's something to think about.

One final comment on the subject. Members of the Disaster Lobby look back with fond nostalgia to the "good old days" when there weren't any nasty factories to pollute the air and kill the animals and drive people to distraction with misleading advertisements. But what was life *really* like in America 150 years ago? For one thing, it was very brief. Life expectancy was 38 years for males. And it was a gruelling 38 years. The work week was 72 hours. The average pay was $300. Per *year,* that is. The women had it worse. Housewives worked 98 hours a week, and there wasn't a dishwasher or vacuum cleaner to be had. The food was monotonous and scarce. The clothes were rags. In the winter you froze

and in summer you sweltered and when an epidemic came — and they came almost every year — it would probably carry off someone in your family. Chances are that in your entire lifetime you would never hear the sound of an orchestra or own a book or travel more than 20 miles from the place you were born.

Ladies and gentlemen, whatever American businessmen have done to bring us out of that paradise of 150 years ago, I say let's give them a grateful pat on the back — not a knife *in* it.

Now I'm not a Pollyanna. I am aware of the problems we face and of the need to find solutions and put them into effect. And I have nothing but praise for the many dedicated Americans who are devoting their lives to making this a better nation in a better world. The point I am trying to make is that we are solving most of our problems, that conditions are getting better, not worse, that American industry is spending over $3 billion a year to clean up the environment and additional billions to develop products that will keep it clean, and that the real danger today is not from the free enterprise establishment that has made ours the most prosperous, most powerful and most charitable nation on earth. No, the danger today resides in the Disaster Lobby — those crapehangers who, for personal gain or out of sheer ignorance, are undermining the American system and threatening the lives and fortunes of the American people.

When I speak of a threat to lives, I mean it literally. A classic example of the dire things that can happen when the Disaster Lobby gets busy is the DDT story.

It begins during World War II when a safe, cheap and potent new insecticide made its debut. Known as DDT, it proved its value almost overnight. Grain fields once ravaged by insects began producing bumper crops. Marshland became habitable. And the death rate in many countries fell sharply. According to the World Health Organization, malaria fatalities dropped from four million a year in the 1930s to less than a million by 1968. Other insect-borne diseases also loosened their grip. Encephalitis. Yellow fever. Typhus. Wherever DDT was used, the ailment abated. It has been estimated that a hundred million human beings who would have died of one of these afflictions are alive today because of DDT.

But that's not the whole story. In many countries famine was once a periodic visitor. Then, largely because of food supplies made possible by DDT, famines became relatively rare. So you can credit this insecticide with saving additional hundreds of millions of lives. Then in 1962 a lady named Rachel Carson wrote a book called *Silent Spring* in which she charged that DDT had killed some fish and some birds. That's all the Disaster Lobby needed. It pounced on the book, embraced its claims — many of them still unsubstantiated — and ran off to Washington to demand a ban on DDT. And Washington meekly gave them their ban in the form of a gradual DDT phase-out. Other countries followed the U.S. lead.

The effects were not long in coming. Malaria, virtually conquered throughout the world, is having a resurgence. Food production is down in many areas. And such pests as the gypsy moth, in hiding since the 1940s, are now munching away at American forests. In some countries — among them Ceylon, Venezuela and Sweden — the renaissance of insects has been so devastating that laws against DDT have been repealed or amended. But in our country the use of DDT, down to 10 percent of its former level, may soon be prohibited entirely.

The tragedy is that DDT, while it probably did kill a few birds and fish, never harmed a single human being except by accidental misuse. When the ultimate report is written, it may show that the opponents of DDT — despite the best of intentions — contributed to the deaths of more human beings than did all of the natural disasters in history.

In addition to endangering human life, the Disaster Lobbyists are making things as difficult as possible for us survivors. By preventing electric companies from building new power plants, they have caused most of those blackouts we've been experiencing. By winning the fight for compulsory seat belts in automobiles, they have forced the 67 percent of all Americans who do not use seat belts to waste $250 million a year buying them anyway. By demanding fewer sizes in package goods on the ground that this will make shopping easier for the handful of dumbbells in our society, they are preventing the intelligent majority of housewives from buying merchandise in the quantities most convenient and most efficient for their needs.

And I don't have to tell anyone in this room what the Disaster crowd has done and is doing to make washday a nightmare in millions of American homes. By having the sale of detergents banned in some areas and by stirring up needless fears throughout the country, they have missed the point entirely. As Vice President Charles Bueltman of the Soap and Detergent Association recently pointed out, detergents with phosphates are perfectly safe, eminently effective and admirably cheap. And if they foam up the water supply in some communities, the obvious remedy is an improved sewer system. To ban detergents is the kind of overkill that might be compared with burning down your house to get rid of termites.

But of all activities of the Disaster Lobbyists, the most insidious are their attempts to destroy our free enterprise system. And they are succeeding only too well. According to Professor Yale Brozen of the University of Chicago, free enterprise in the United States is only half alive. He cited as evidence our government's control of the mail, water supplies, schools, airlines, railroads, highways, banks, farms, utilities and insurance companies, along with its regulatory involvement in other industries. And his statement was made prior to introduction in Congress last year of 150 bills designed to broaden government influence over private business. Fortunately, most of the bills were defeated or died in committee. But they will be back in the hopper this year, along with some new bills. And they will have support from the darlings of the Disaster Lobby — senators like Moss, Proxmire and Hart and representatives like Rosenthal of New York.

If so many important people are against free enterprise, is it worth saving? I think it is. With all its faults, it is by far the best system yet devised for the production, distribution and widespread enjoyment of goods and services. It is more than coincidence that virtually all of mankind's scientific progress came in the two centuries when free enterprise was operative in the western world, and most of the progress was achieved in the nation regarded as the leading exponent of free enterprise: the United States of America.

For in the past 200 years — an eyeblink in history — an America geared to private industry has conquered communicable diseases, abolished starvation, brought literacy to the masses, transported men to another planet and expanded the horizons of its citizens to an almost incredible degree by giving them wheels and wings and electronic extensions of their eyes, their ears, their hands, even their brains. It has made available to the average American luxuries that a short time ago were beyond the reach of the wealthiest plutocrat. And by developing quick-cook meals and labor-saving appliances, it has cut kitchen chores in most homes from five hours a day to an hour and a half — and as a result has done more to liberate women than all of the bra-burning Betty Friedans, Gloria Steinems and Kate Milletts combined.

But the practical benefits of free enterprise are *not* my principal reason for wanting to preserve the system. To me, the chief advantage of free enterprise is in the word "free." "Free" as opposed to controlled. "Free" as opposed to repressed. "Free" as in "freedom."

I am always amazed that members of the Disaster Lobby — libertarians who champion the cause of freedom from every podium, who insist on everyone's right to dissent, to demonstrate, to curse policemen and smoke pot and burn draft cards and fly the flags of our enemies while trampling our own — these jealous guardians of every citizen's prerogative to act and speak without government restraint are also the most outspoken advocates of eliminating freedom in one area. When it comes to commerce, to the making and marketing of goods, our liberty-loving Disaster Lobby is in favor of replacing freedom with rigid controls.

And let us not minimize the value of this freedom of commerce to every man, woman and child in our country. This is the freedom that makes it possible for the consumer to buy one quart of milk at a time — even though a government economist may think gallon containers are more efficient and quarts should be abolished. This is the freedom that enables the consumer to buy rye bread if he prefers the taste — although someone in Washington may feel that whole-wheat is more nutritious and rye should be outlawed. This is the freedom that allows the consumer to buy a refrigerator in avocado green despite some bureaucrat's desire to have all refrigerators made in white because it would be more economical that way.

For in a free economy, the consumer — through his pocketbook — determines what is made and what is sold. The consumer dictates the sizes, the shapes, the quality, the color, even the price. And anyone who doubts the importance of this element of freedom ought to visit one of those grim, drab countries where the government decided what should not be marketed.

But this is the direction in which the Disaster Lobby is pushing *our* country.

What surprises me is how few of us seem to recognize the enormity of the threat. Instead of fighting back, we keep giving in to each insane demand of the consumerists — in the hope, I suppose, that if we are accommodating enough the danger will go away. Well, ladies and gentlemen, it *won't* go away. If I accomplish nothing else today, I hope I can make that fact transparently plain.

Take the Nader group, for example. I have heard many businessmen dismiss Ralph Nader and his associates as well-meaning fellows who sincerely want to help the consumer by improving business methods. Forget it. Mr. Nader isn't interested in seeing American industry clean house. What he wants is the *house* — from cellar to attic. His goal is a top-to-bottom takeover of industry by the government, with Mr. Nader, himself, I would guess, in charge of the appropriate commission. Find it hard to believe? Then listen to this Associated Press report of a speech he made last September: "Consumer advocate Ralph Nader has proposed that corporations that abuse the public interest should be transferred to public trusteeship and their officers sent to jail."

Well, we all know which corporations abuse public interest in the eyes of Mr. Nader, don't we. *All* of them. The automobile companies. The tire companies. The appliance companies. The drug companies. The food companies. And yes, indeed, the soap and detergent companies. What Mr. Nader really desires, ladies and gentlemen, is for the government to take over *your* companies and to toss all of you into the calaboose, presumably without a trial. At least he never said anything about a trial. Does anyone still think Mr. Nader and the rest of the Disaster Lobby are just some harmless do-gooders? Those who know them best don't think so. Federal Trade Commissioner Paul Rand Dixon, for example. Not long ago, he said of Mr. Nader — and I quote — "He's preaching revolution, and I'm scared."

So let's start fighting back! It's not an impossible task because the Disaster Lobby is, by and large, not too bright and far too preposterous. All we have to do to win over the American people is acquaint them with the facts. We must show them that the consumerists are for the most part devout snobs who believe that the average man is too stupid to make his own selections in a free marketplace.

Our Disaster group opponents also have the most cockeyed set of priorities I have ever encountered. To save a few trees, they would prevent construction of a power plant that could provide essential electricity to scores of hospitals and schools. To protect some birds, they would deprive mankind of food. To keep fish healthy, they would allow human beings to become sick.

One curious feature of the Disaster Lobby is an almost total lack of ethics. I say "curious" because these are the people who demand the maximum in ethics from private industry. Not long ago, an organization favoring clean air ran an ad soliciting funds from New Yorkers. It was full of half-truths and non-truths, including this sentence: "The longer you live with New York's polluted air and the worse it gets, the better your chances of dying from it." But we know that New York's air is *not* getting worse. Just let some private company run that ad and see how fast the consumerism boys would have a complaint on file with the FTC.

Immaturity is also a characteristic of the Disaster man. His favorite question is, Why can't we have everything? Why can't we have simon-pure air *and* plentiful electricity *and* low utility rates, all at the same time? Why can't we have ample food *and* a ban on pesticides? I recommend the same answer you would give a not-too-intelligent five-year-old who asks, "Why can't I eat that cookie and still have it?" You explain that you just *can't* under our present technology.

Just recently the Coca-Cola Company felt it necessary to reply to environmentalists who demand immediate replacement of glass and metal soft drink containers with something that will self-destruct. "A degradable soft drink container sounds like a fine idea," said Coca-Cola, "but it doesn't exist. And the chances are that one can't be made." And Edward Cole, president of General Motors, responding to a government mandate for drastic reductions in exhaust emissions within the next four years, stated: "The technology does not exist at this time — inside or outside the automobile industry — to meet these stringent emission levels in the specified time."

This inability of the Disaster people to accept reality is reflected in their frequent complaint that mankind interferes with nature. Such a thing is patently impossible. Man is *part* of nature. We didn't come here from some other planet. Anything we do we do as card-carrying instruments of nature. You don't accuse a beaver of interfering with nature when it chops down a tree to build a dam. Then why condemn human beings for chopping down a lot of trees to build a lot of dams — or to do anything else that will make their lives safer or longer or more enjoyable? When it comes to a choice between saving human lives and saving some fish, I will sacrifice the fish without a whimper. It's not that I'm anti-fish; it's just that I am pro-people.

The Disaster Lobbyist's immaturity shows up again and again in his unwillingness to compromise, to understand that man must settle for less than perfection, for less than zero risk, if he is to flourish. Failing to understand, they demand what they call "adequate testing" before any new product is released to the public. But what they mean by adequate testing would, if carried out, destroy all progress. If penicillin had been tested the way the Disaster Lobby wants all products tested — not only on the current generation but on future generations, to determine hereditary effects — this wonder drug would not be in use today. And mil-

lions of people whose lives have been saved by penicillin would be dead. We simply cannot test every aspect of human endeavor, generation after generation, to make *absolutely* certain that *everything* we do is *totally* guaranteed not to harm *anybody* to *any* degree whatsoever. We must take an occasional risk to do the greater good for the greater number. But that is a rational, mature evaluation — something of which the Disaster Lobby seems utterly incapable.

So this is the face of the enemy. Not a very impressive face. Not even a pleasant face. We have nothing to lose, therefore, by exposing it to the American people for what it is. The time for surrender and accommodation is past. We must let the American public know that, once free enterprise succumbs to the attacks of the consumerists and the ecologists and the rest of the Disaster Lobby, the freedom of the consumer goes with it. His freedom to live the way he wants and to buy the things he wants without some Big Brother in Washington telling him he can't.

Truth and justice and common sense are on our side. And Americans have a history of responding to these arguments. All we have to do is get the story out — as often as possible, in as many forms as possible. And let's not vitiate our efforts by talking to each other — one businessman to a fellow businessman. The people we must reach are the *consumers* of America, and they're out there right now listening to propaganda from the other side and, as often as not, agreeing with it. But why shouldn't they? They have yet to hear the truth.

It's a bit late to make a New Year's resolution, but I suggest this one for anyone willing to chip in with a tardy entry. Let us resolve that 1971 will be the year we help convince the people of America that our nation is a great one, that our future is a bright one and that the Disaster Lobby is precisely what the name implies. A disaster.

EDITOR'S COMMENTS

As you might assume, this speech was well-received by those attending the meeting of the Soap and Detergent Association. Mr. Shepard's remarks illustrate many of the methods of distortion and smoke-screening often used to make points that are contrary to the facts. He points to bad conditions in the past and implies that if conditions are better today, there is no need for further improvement. He attempts to equate natural extinction of life forms with man-caused extermination. He is cheered over the fact that the birth rate is dropping, but either fails to realize or fails to admit that any birth rate above zero still adds to the population. He ignores the fact that bans on DDT have not caused an increase in malaria. The increases, where they occurred, were due to the failure of local health authorities to treat infected persons who entered the community after they thought the disease was eradicated.

The *Chicago Tribune* had its environment editor, Casey Bukro, analyze Mr. Shepard's speech. The results of Mr. Burko's research are reprinted here with permission of the Chicago Tribune.

BY CASEY BUKRO

Shepard: "But what about air pollution? You can't deny that our air is getting more fouled up all the time, says the Disaster Lobby. Wrong. I *can* deny it. Our air is getting less fouled up all the time, in city after city. In New York City, for example. New York's Department of Air Resources reports a year-by-year *decrease* in air pollutants since 1965."

Dr. Edward Ferrand, assistant commissioner for science and technology, New York City Department of Air Resources, said sulfur dioxide gas is the only air pollutant in New York City that has shown any decrease since 1966. And that was the result of an environmental control ordi-

nance in 1966 which required reductions in the sulfur content of fuel burned in New York City.

Nineteen air contaminants are monitored in New York air, said Dr. Ferrand. With the exception of sulfur dioxide gas, none of the others has shown any improvement, although there were no major increases, either.

"In terms of dirt and particles in the air, there has been no decrease because we have made no change in emissions into the air," said Dr. Ferrand, adding that environmental improvements have been directly the result of public demands.

The Council on Environmental Quality, in its second annual report on the state of the nation's environment last August, said, "more of every major pollutant was emitted in 1969," compared with 1968. Figures for 1970 were not available.

Shepard: "Which brings us to water pollution. The Disaster Lobby recalls that, back in the days before America was industrialized, our rivers and lakes were crystal-clear. True. And those crystal-clear rivers and lakes were the source of the worst cholera, yellow fever and typhoid epidemics the world has ever known. . . . Our waterways may not be as pretty as they used to be, but they aren't as deadly, either. In fact, the water we drink is the safest in the world."

Shepard is talking about public drinking water supplies, which must be purified and account for less than one per cent of the total daily water usage in America. Shepard named Harold Gotaas, dean of the Technological Institute at Northwestern University, as the source of his information and the basis for saying that today's concern over water pollution stems from aesthetic rather than health considerations.

"That's not true," said Dean Gotaas. No one would say all waters are better today than they have ever been." Dean Gotaas did say in a speech several years ago that water quality in the United States has never been better in terms of human health, speaking only about water-borne diseases. But Gotaas pointed out that Shepard neglected to mention that the same speech expressed concern for other forms of water pollution and its effect on fish and wildlife, ecology, aesthetics and recreation.

Still, the federal Environmental Protection Agency has designated five major municipal water supplies in the nation as potential health hazards.

The Council on Environmental Quality reported that almost one-third of United States stream miles are polluted, while 10 per cent of the watersheds are unpolluted or moderately polluted. Industrial wastes were given as the largest source of organic water pollution nationwide. It also reported that 41 million fish were killed in 1969 by water pollution, up from 15 million in 1968.

Dr. Bertram Carnow, head of the environmental health department at the University of Illinois Medical School, said that the cholera and typhoid mentioned by Shepard are water-borne diseases caused by poor sanitation practices which allowed human wastes to contaminate drinking water—essentially an early environmental problem. Yellow fever is transmitted by mosquitoes.

As a result of the man-made epidemics, said Carnow, stringent laws creating public health departments and regulating the disposal of wastes resulted in improved drinking water. In effect, he said, these are controls of the kind sought by ecologists today.

Shepard: "Perhaps it's the fear of overpopulation that's getting you down. Well, cheer up. The birth rate in the United States has been dropping continuously since 1955 and is now at the lowest point in history."

"That is about as kooky a remark as anybody can make," said Dr. Philip Hauser,

director of the Population Research Center at the University of Chicago. Dr. George Hay Brown, United States census director, also said, "That is not an absolutely true statement."

Both men said that the United States birth rate did decline between 1957 to an historical low in 1968 of 17.6 births per 1,000 population, but rose again in 1969 and 1970.

"We haven't gotten down to the numbers required for zero population growth," said Dr. Hauser.

Shepard: "I now come to the case of the mercury in tuna fish. How did it get there? The Disaster Lobby says it came from American factories. The truth, as scientists will tell you, is that the mercury came from deposits in nature."

Victor Lambou, an authority on mercury in the United States Environmental Protection Agency water program, said there is no agreement among scientists that the major source of mercury in the ocean is natural deposits.

"I don't think our present state of knowledge is detailed enough to say one way or another," said Lambou, although he emphasized that surveys have shown that most mercury contamination of inland and estuarine waters definitely is manmade.

Shepard: "Fish caught 44 years ago and just analyzed contain twice as much mercury as any fish processed this year."

Shepard said his statement was based on a New York newspaper article last year which reported that the New York State Department of Environmental Conservation "found levels of mercury in preserved fish caught up to 43 years ago that are more than twice as high as levels that now bar fish from the market." In his source material, Shepard said the fish under question are small mouth bass taken from Long

Pond and Boyd Pond in the Adirondacks in 1930 (which is 41 years ago).

Carl Parker, fisheries biologist for the New York State Department of Environmental Conservation, said it would be impossible to draw Shepard's conclusion from the information available. Parker explained that the fish from Boyd Pond contained .53 parts per million (ppm) of mercury and the fish from Long Pond contained .32 ppm of mercury. The Food and Drug Administration has said that fish containing more that half a part per million (.50 ppm) of mercury should not be sold for consumption.

Clearly, the mercury contents of the fish caught in 1930 are not twice the levels that bar fish from the market. Parker also said that fish have not been taken from Boyd or Long Ponds since 1930 to compare their mercury content.

Fish caught recently in New York inland waters, said Parker, have shown mercury contents ranging generally from .05 ppm to 2 ppm. One exception is Onondaga Lake near Syracuse, where fishing is prohibited, where mercury levels in fish have ranged from 1 to 8 ppm because of an industrial discharge.

Shepard: While speaking on the disappearance of animal species, Shepard said, "In fact, says Dr. T. H. Jukes of the University of California, some 100 million species of animal life have become extinct since the world began." Shepard went on to say, "Animals come and animals go, as Mr. Darwin noted, and to blame ourselves for evolution would be the height of foolishness."

Dr. Jukes, a professor of medical physics, said it is foolish to confuse evolution with extermination, and complains that Shepard has misquoted him. Dr. Jukes said he estimates that 100 million species of all forms of life—animals, birds, fish, reptiles, plants and insects—probably have become extinct in the 3 billion years since life has existed on Earth.

But Dr. Jukes, who is president of Trustees for Conservation in San Francisco, said he would be the first to admit that thoughtless acts by man have pushed lifeforms to extinction and should be stopped.

Shepard: "Members of the Disaster Lobby look back with fond nostalgia to the 'good old days' when there weren't any nasty factories to pollute the air and kill the animals. . . . But what was life *really* like in America 150 years ago? For one thing, it was very brief. Life expectancy was 38 years for males. . . . Whatever American businessmen have done to bring us out of that paradise of 150 years ago, I say let's give them a grateful pat on the back—not a knife in it."

Dr. Carnow of the University of Illinois Medical School points out that not a single year had been added to human longevity in the last 30 years for American males, a period of unprecedented technological advancement. Meanwhile, more than a million people are dying each year of cardiovascular diseases and 60,000 from lung cancer.

"If he suggests that progress is trading an epidemic of typhoid for an epidemic of heart attacks or lung cancer, he is out of his skin," said Dr. Carnow.

Shepard: The use of DDT was defended by Shepard who contended that 100 million lives have been saved through the use of DDT. He named the World Health Organization as the source of information showing reduction in malaria by using DDT. Then, he said, the Disaster Lobby acted to ban the use of DDT. "The effects were not long in coming. Malaria, virtually conquered throughout the world, is having a resurgence. . . . In some countries—among them Ceylon, Venezuela and Sweden—the renaissance of insects has been so devastating that laws against DDT have been repealed or amended."

Dr. Jose A. Najera, research officer of the department of malaria eradication for the W.H.O. in the Americas, flatly denies that bans on the use of DDT have resulted in the rise in malaria cases. The reason for increasing cases of malaria in Ceylon, for example, is the failure of local health authorities to treat new cases of infection introduced by newcomers to the community after malaria had been thought to be eradicated in 1961.

"This is what Ceylon failed to do after 1961," Dr. Najera said. "They failed to control secondary cases produced from imported infections." Dr. Najera said he knows of no laws against the use of DDT in Ceylon or Venezuela, where reintroduction of malaria once it has been eliminated in a specific area also is the problem.

> Shepard: "The tragedy is that DDT, while it probably did kill a few birds and fish, never harmed a single human being except by accidental misuse."

Dr. Charles F. Wurster, associate professor of environmental sciences, State University of New York at Stony Brook, N.Y., said that DDT has killed millions of birds, but that is not the central issue.

Of major importance, said Dr. Wurster, is that DDT affects bird reproduction so that the number of some species has declined sharply while entire populations of some birds have disappeared. This is especially true among predatory birds, which tend to get the highest DDT doses. DDT also has been known to cause cancer in test animals, he said.

To speak of toxic substances only in terms of whether they kill things outright avoids the larger question of chronic long-term effects, said Dr. Wurster.

> Shepard: "In addition to endangering human life, the Disaster Lobbyists are making things as difficult as possible for us survivors. By preventing electric companies from building new power plants, they have caused most of those blackouts we've been experiencing."

The Federal Power Commission News has reported 42 cases of power failures and voltage reductions for a period covering Oct. 1, 1970 to June 30, 1971, and their causes. In a vast majority of the cases, mechanical failures, accidents or heavy power demands coming at a time when key generating equipment had been shut down were given as causes.

> Shepard: "But of all activities of the Disaster Lobbyists, the most insidious are their attempts to destroy our free enterprise system. And they are succeeding only too well. According to Professor Yale Brozen of the University of Chicago, free enterprise in the United States is only half alive."

Professor Brozen, professor of business economics in the graduate school of business at the University of Chicago, said Shepard was referring to a magazine article he wrote about a year ago in which he said governmental economic controls are hampering free enterprise.

"I was not thinking of environmentalists when I wrote that thing," said Professor Brozen, who said he is in favor of conserving natural resources that are being used and polluted without restraint.

"We've got to establish some way of getting economic use of the air and water, but at the same time conserve them," said the professor. "That is what economic use means—conserving it."

> Shepard: "When it comes to a choice between saving human lives and saving some fish, I will sacrifice the fish without a whimper. It's not that I'm anti-fish; its just that I am pro-people."

"I don't know anybody who prefers fish over people or birds over people," said Dr. Wurster. "That is not at stake. Ultimately, it is likely to be both or neither. They both live in the environment. If the environment is destroyed, they will both be destroyed. It is a matter of doing things intelligently."

JOHN CAREW

In Balance with Nature

John Carew is chairman of the Department of Horticulture at Michigan State University. He is past president of the American Society for Horticultural Science. Dr. Carew is well-known for his writings dealing with the production of fruits and vegetables and the uses of ornamental plants.

In the Beginning
There was Earth; beautiful and wild;
And then man came to dwell.
At first, he lived like other animals
Feeding himself on creatures and plants around him.
And this was called *in balance with nature*.

Soon man multiplied.
He grew tired of ceaseless hunting for food;
He built homes and villages.
Wild plants and animals were domesticated.
Some men became Farmers so that others might become Industrialists, Artists, or Doctors.
And this was called Society.

Man and Society progressed.
With his God-given ingenuity, man learned to feed, clothe, protect, and transport himself more efficiently so he might enjoy Life.

He built cars, houses on top of each other, and nylon.
And Life *was* more enjoyable.

The men called Farmers became efficient.
A single Farmer grew food for 28 Industrialists, Artists, and Doctors.
And Writers, Engineers, and Teachers as well.
To protect his crops and animals, the Farmer produced substances to repel or destroy Insects, Diseases, and Weeds.
These were called Pesticides.
Similar substances were made by Doctors to protect humans.
These were called Medicine.
The Age of Science had arrived and with it came better diet and longer, happier lives for more members of Society.

Soon it came to pass
That certain well-fed members of Society
Disapproved of the Farmer using Science.
They spoke harshly of his techniques for feeding, protecting, and preserving plants and animals.
They deplored his upsetting the Balance of Nature;

Reprinted by permission of the author and publisher from the *American Vegetable Grower,* January 1968. Copyright © 1968 by Meister Publishing Company.

They longed for the Good Old Days.
And this had emotional appeal to the rest
of Society.
By this time Farmers had become so effi-
cient, Society gave them a new title:
Unimportant Minority.

Because Society could never imagine a
shortage of food
Laws were passed abolishing Pesticides,
Fertilizers, and Food Preservatives.
Insects, Diseases, and Weeds flourished.
Crops and animals died.

Food became scarce.
To survive, Industrialists, Artists, and Doctors were forced to grow their own food.

They were not very efficient.
People and governments fought wars to
gain more agricultural land.
Millions of people were exterminated.
The remaining few lived like animals
Feeding themselves on creatures and plants
around them.
And this was called *in balance with nature*,

EDITOR'S COMMENTS

This poem typifies the attitude of many individuals and groups associated with American agriculture. In one breath they scream, "You'll all starve!" if controls are placed on the use of agricultural chemicals. In the next breath they label environmentalists as "emotionalists."

Note the attempt to liken pesticides to medicines. No mention is made, however, of the fact that pesticides are made to kill, whereas medicines are designed to cure. Note the veiled effort to imply that all of our modern "conveniences" come from God and are therefore good. No mention is made of the fact that misuse of these very "conveniences" has, in large measure, destroyed the earth as God made it.

This poem depicts the farmer as the victim of the environmental movement, seeking thereby to bring to the surface the respect and love that most Americans have for farmers, and to use it to counteract environmental concern. In reality, this poem insults the American farmer and the agricultural profession as a whole by implying that there is not enough innovative ability or inventive genius present in agriculture to raise the needed food without also despoiling the life-support systems upon which man depends.

This poem is based on the false and naive assumption that foreign materials in the environment will do us nothing but good. This poem and the philosophy behind it are detrimental to man.

Preparing for a New Competitor

Frank W. Considine is President of The
National Can Corporation.

Mr. Chairman, honored guests and members
of the packaging fraternity:

I used the term packaging fraternity since
in a personal way it fits so well — few
members ever leave our industry although
some do move within its various segments
— and most important, our continued success is dependent one upon the other. A
problem in one segment of our industry
affects all of us in the achievement of our
personal as well as corporate goals.

Gentlemen, your industry profits are under pressure. You have a new competitor
and all the packaging progress and our
continued important contributions to the
people of the world are challenged as never
before.

Why? Because we are being hit throughout the country by the new competitor in
the form of precipitious, ill-advised, emotional actions by municipalities, state legislatures, and Congress to ban nonreturnable
packaging for beverages and it won't stop
with beverages. And why are the legislators
yielding to public pressures? Because we
have not made them aware of the facts concerning litter and solid waste disposal. Nor
have we made them aware of the size and
importance of the packaging industry in our
economy. To illustrate the threat, it is
reliably estimated that there will be three
hundred (300) pieces of legislation introduced by legislators in the year beginning
1971 to ban, tax, require deposits or in some
way restrict nonreturnable containers.

Let's get down to brass tacks and identify
ourselves as an industry so we can measure
the impact we have and how we should use
it.

Packaging is a major industry — the
third largest in our nation — with sales over
20.5 billion dollars. In terms of total employees (over one million) we are number

Packaging
$\begin{cases}
\text{is the third largest user of steel.} \\
\text{consumes 50 percent of all paper and paperboard.} \\
\text{consumes 90 percent of aluminum foil.} \\
\text{consumes 96 percent of all non-flat glass.} \\
\text{consumes 20 percent of all plastics products.}
\end{cases}$

Reprinted by permission of Frank W. Considine,
President, National Can Corporation. Adapted
from a speech delivered to the U.S.A. Packaging
Institute's 32nd Annual National Packaging
Forum. October 5, 1970.

1. In terms of plants we are number 2 with over 5,000. The automobile industry, steel and chemical producers, all giants in the eyes of the public are considerably smaller than packaging.

Now, if we take this thought one step further and consider the suppliers to and customers of the packaging industry, you're looking at the bulk of our nation's economy today. All industries will be affected along with us. Measure the potential impact and you'll wonder how we were caught off base last spring when the emotional public began demanding ill-conceived laws from our public officials. But we were. . . .

Further, each of you present today has a position of responsibility within your company. From the registration lists I noted, in fact, that many of you are top executives of large and prosperous packaging corporations and companies in industries related to or strongly dependent upon the growth of the packaging industry.

But, for far too long we have been talking to ourselves, complaining about mutual problems, participating in charitable drives, supporting government leaders when they call for action, and at times taking sporadic action individually or in small groups to counteract certain individual threats when in the big picture our virtual existence has been challenged by some of the consumers we serve — and by some of the very people who seek our help in so many ways. Up to now, we have been able to get by with weak and ineffective responses, but with the current threat, time is running out.

Let me ask you: *Have we examined our spheres of influence and taken action to capitalize on our many assets?* Have we taken a look at our dimensions extending a direct payroll into over a million homes . . . our indirect influence through suppliers and customers and total services supporting the distribution system we have made possible and now serve so well?

We have not or we wouldn't be so much on the defensive. We are so busy growing, competing, researching and developing new products for the consumer, that we ignored reality and as a consequence find ourselves battered on all sides — standing naked, unprepared and disorganized — unable to counter the offensive. For the future, it will not be enough to sporadically challenge opposition and figure it will go away. Ecology consideration and consumerism are here to stay and it's our big challenge to profit in the 70s.

Why such a challenge? Because present profit levels depend on volume, and productivity improvement is possible only with sustained volume. Restrictive legislation could curtail the volume for which today's production capacity has been built. Prices must increase or lesser volume will produce less profit when excess capacity exists and high cost investment lays idle.

Production curtailment means fewer jobs from the nation's largest employer . . . and so the industry spiral starts and where is your future and the future of those men now dedicating their careers to our industry . . . and where are our hourly employees who have developed skills in our field that may not be easily transferred to other jobs . . . and what happens to the strength of our unions and their objectives on behalf of their people? What incentives exist to make the creative moves, that will bring about greater production efficiencies and the incorporation of higher levels of consumer appeal into our products?

Now, I don't have to tell you about the many contributions made by our industry to the progress of mankind and to the progress of our economy and our country. You know of the importance of modern packaging and packaging methods to the success of many products on the shelf today. You also know about the industries born of your creativity and those who have grown largely because of the convenience factor you have now integrated with their product. You are aware of the huge distribution system from farm to processor to supermarket chains — all a result of packaging industry innovations. And you also know the vast sums of money your firms generate and distribute to the government, to employees and to social institutions.

Your industry is asked to support many worthwhile projects to help make the world, your country, state, and community a better place in which to live.

And, you assume your responsibilities willingly. And that's good.

But whom do you tell of your importance and our problems? No one who can benefit from that knowledge and help us — not your elected government officials; not your large and assorted publics, including educational institutions; not even the governing body and citizens of your own community; not even the Consumer . . . — *and that's bad!* And THAT, gentlemen, explains why our problems are increasing, and why you have a new competitor.

Look about you and see what emotional and hysterical propositions are being offered to an uninformed public. Ridiculous questions frequently being posed include:

Why should man fear pollution more than the atom bomb?
How many mass suicides result from pollution?
Why may the earth become another moon?

Ridiculous, emotional, sensational, senseless catch statements that originate and disseminate hysteria.

History shows that progress has never been associated with this level of fear, but, progress has been the goal of all economic systems from the very first civilizations.

As our GNP approaches the trillion mark, the economy of this country demonstrates in a very large way our ability to alter the environment to satisfy human wants. Logically, as these "wants" become increasingly environment oriented, a system must be developed utilizing the same technology that helped solve previous problems and move us into our advanced stage of packaging technology. Every problem has been a challenge for those of us in packaging and our investment in research, engineering and marketing have all developed answers to some very special problems.

Put another way, our industry has concentrated on the creation of products — on the *distribution* of products while for the most part *neglecting* the other end of the cycle by not providing for final disposition of our creations. It was a happenstance neglect and we can chastise ourselves only a little for not looking far enough into the future to see the problem our degree of technology was creating. We can meet this challenge by utilizing the same problem-solving technical might on the other end of the cycle that we used on the front end.

The problems I am referring to specifically are litter, pollution, solid waste disposal, and the recycling of our resources. Although each is quite different, they are erroneously lumped together in the eyes of the public. Litter and pollution are separate and distinct. Litter has a high irritancy factor because it is so visible. Litter is a critical problem. But oft times, it is *caused* by some of the same people who protest against it the loudest. It will be solved by education, equipment and enforcement of litter laws. As for solid waste — the solution to this pressing problem lies in developing a totally integrated system's approach to solid waste disposal and recycling of our products.

Many of our packaging products are now already being recycled. Paper currently utilizes 20 percent of their waste product and their objective is to use 35 percent by 1980. Glass now can utilize up to 30 percent of their batch from returned glass made into cullet. Aluminum cans are easily melted and rerolled into aluminum sheets. The basic oxygen furnace of the steel companies makes steel cans of all types recyclable. Tin, tin-free, and tin cans with aluminum tops are now no problem for recycling by steel mills.

It is important for you to know that machinery now exists to handle solid waste as it is brought to the depot. It can sort various products like cans, glass, plastic and ready them for recycling. There is *urgent* need to combine this existing hardware into *one total, unified system at a pilot solid waste disposal center*. I repeat — recycling equipment *is* on hand, but we need a complete systems setup in a pilot plant to demonstrate its ability. Industry has already done far more than it is being credited for. Specifically, I have seen a proposal set forth after over a year of research engineering by one of the country's leading firms — which details the operation of a proposed Solid Waste Disposal Center costing $15 million. This would serve a city with a population of 250,000 and completely handle the total solid waste. This depot will process and sell recoverable solid waste components to offset its operating cost. Figures show this project to be a paying proposition.

Much work has been done, but there is much left to do. But will we put the energy and dollars behind such a project to make it go? I predict we will.

Will we get the message of the long-range unemotional solution across to our leaders in government? It is urgent that we do, and I am sure we will.

There are 8 bills to ban N/R bottles and cans already introduced in the U.S. Congress — plus 12 bills for financing research on solid waste.

Yes — the problems of which I speak are very real and very imminent. This positions you with a new and effective competitor, gentlemen, and you had better be felt against this competition. I urge you to deal with this competition using the same zeal with which you market your products — or this new form of competition is going to take your market from you. Call it Consumerism — Environmentalism — it's basically the same for your industry — it's potentially explosive and it seems to stem from an unanalyzed dissatisfaction of a segment of American people — and much of it directed against the business community — it's a conflict business must win for the good of our country and the people who out of ignorance or possibly action on their own social conscience seek to destroy or emasculate the fundamental underpinnings of our society — our country and thus negate all our successes since this Nation began.

Our industry has evidenced a total unpreparedness in coping with this new threat — and I mean all of us. We are not organized and have been groping for the answers. To date we have not found them.

Up to now I have pointed out some very important dimensions of our industry — the roots of some of our problems that now present challenges and opportunities, and hopefully I have alerted you to a very serious threat to the health and profit of our industry.

In 1970, 64 bills in 25 states have been presented with the same objective. In Bowie, Maryland, a ban was recently enacted preventing the sale of one-way containers and will possibly serve as a springboard for other municipalities across the country. Richmond County in Wisconsin now plans to ban one-way containers effective 7/1/71. The people of the state of Washington have proposed a minimum deposit of 5¢ per container for N/Rs. There will be 49 states in session in 1971 and as I mentioned earlier, it is estimated that some 300 bills will be initiated in the various legislation.

The years ahead, therefore, are filled with challenges to the survival of our industry. Gentlemen, isn't it logical to organize

THE ANTI-ENVIRONMENT MOVEMENT

and participate together in local, state and federal activity to counter this new competition. Realistically, we must. You must each get the message across to your associates at all levels of your company that we need action now.

We must organize for *impact* by first examining our spheres of influence, your importance to others — your employees — your suppliers — customers — farmers who grow products for our packages — transportation and all the other service industries who depend on the vitality of your industry — and very important too, our labor unions who are taking an All American approach to dealing with some current issues . . . . *Together labor and industry are vital spheres of influence*. Examine these and then get all to participate. Let's all speak out to our Congressmen, state legislators, and local officials. Let them know who you are and what impact you have and what you think they should be doing when it involves our industry and people they represent. How else are they going to know what it is you stand for?

The next step is to have effective task force groups in each state — and these task groups now exist in many states based around the USBA field services organization — and everyone knows the brewers are packaging oriented. These task groups must be augmented and reinforced so all segments of the packaging industry are involved. As an industry, we must have the facts concerning our importance by State, Country, Municipality so we can be ready to go on the offensive with a positive program dedicated to achieving a solution to litter and solid waste.

Speak out to the National Association of Manufacturers. Urge them to utilize their offices and take leadership to oppose detrimental bills proposed in Congress. Your impact is not being felt in these business associations since they haven't taken the

leadership I think they could have to help our segment of their membership.

Join with merchandisers of your products — the supermarkets and large chains. The average supermarket offers for sale some 10,000 different items, virtually all of these are packaged. An unnecessary upset of one-way packaging would be a disastrous change to their distribution system — a change for which they are not now geared. There should be substantial support for your industry among these giants.

Let's go on the offensive. Fortify current efforts by assigning the responsibility for action and results to one person in your company or association. Demand results and you'll get them — it's your responsibility to your employees, shareholders, and it's a responsibility you have but may not realize . . . but, after your business erodes you'll know how essential a responsibility it was.

So far, I've described the industry's problems and opportunities. I also attempted to inspire each of you to take immediate and decisive individual and group action, as we can no longer depend upon reason to prevail in the general public.

There is an urgent need for a positive plan for effective action; and one has come to the fore and I'm going to tell you about it. It's absolutely necessary we identify and establish a sound leadership vehicle with the objective of negating unfavorable legislation. Also, it is essential to have a vehicle for research, planning, communicating, and for implementation of hardware requirements to solve both the near-term and long-range problems of litter and solid waste disposal. In short a vehicle dedicated to results.

I am proud to tell you that for the past 8 months, men of ability and vision at Anheuser Busch developed and presented a program to the board of directors of the USBA that was enthusiastically endorsed by the brewers and packaging industry members on the board. And, as a result, the National Center for Solid Waste Disposal has been brought into being.

I happen to be one of the incorporators of the National Center for Solid Waste Disposal. The first steps of incorporation were taken on August 6 and the entire project has enthused all of us who are privy to the plans . . . and things are moving fast. The day after tomorrow in Washington we'll have a Board of Directors meeting and soon after will announce the new chairman for the Center . . . a national figure you will all quickly recognize.

The Center will have a Board of Directors made up of top executives from the food, beverage, and packaging industries. Also included will be representatives from government, labor, the academic world, and the public. (Total membership est. 25.)

The Center's Research policy panel will include highly qualified experts from a variety of academic disciplines, including physical and biological scientists (ecologists), engineers, psychologists, city planners, economists, and operations analysts. (Est. 12 members.)

The mission of the Center will be to test concepts, conduct exploratory research and develop prototype systems to help industry and government find solutions to vital national problems posed by litter and solid waste. The Center is designed to operate as a sponsor of research projects and participate in design and operation of prototype disposal systems. A special report about the National Center will be made to President Nixon within the next week.

Is my telling you of this organization a little premature — YES, just a little — you'll see considerable press on it in the coming weeks, but I prevailed on the other organizers of NCSWD to let me unfold it to you today because of the importance of this audience — it demonstrates action and results, vision and fulfills an absolute need. The Center will need your support and the support of your company — it will be well funded by 8-11 key packaging associations and individual companies. Talk it up, it's alive and working for you. It is the brainchild of the leaders of our industry, and the National Center will serve you well. But this is only a first step, a beginning.

In closing, I urge the packaging industry as a group to strive for more interaction with other segments of our society. We need to make a substantial effort to get involved in community, state and national projects. We ought to also take a more participative posture in the world of education to balance the flow of anti-business propaganda which all too often makes its mark on impressionable young minds. If the future leaders of our economy and society refuse to buy the notion of free enterprise, it will be because the most imaginative marketing people in the world have not sold it.

We can expect to see strife in this free, active, and diverse society of ours; but, we must continue to reaffirm our belief in those things that formed and developed this great country if we are to preserve these very freedoms. When we protect our way of doing business, we assure the continued health and vitality of the economy and insure the future of our industry and those in it who have accomplished so much.

This is a noble undertaking ladies and gentlemen . . . *and I suggest we get on with it*.

Thank you!

EDITOR'S COMMENTS

Mr. Considine's basic philosophy is revealed in the first sentence of the second paragraph when he says, "Gentlemen, your industry profits are under pressure." He lays it on the line when he refers to consumer interests and environmentalists as "the opposition."

However, Mr. Considine does encourage recycling, and this is to his credit. Unfortunately, the only objective he sees in encouraging this process is to continue making profits in the face of opposition from "ridiculous, emotional, sensational" sources. He doesn't even admit that environmental problems really have anything to do with the goals of the packaging industry.

When the people in industry finally realize that industrial processes must soon come into a balance with nature, we may as a species begin to learn to live in harmony with nature. Conservationists are not against the packaging industry, but rather against the needless waste of natural resources and the creation of unsightly litter and difficult disposal problems. Wasting natural resources and properly disposing of (recycling where possible) packaging materials should be charged against the production of these materials as a social cost. When this very real expense is added to the manufacturing cost of packaging materials, we will quickly see a drastic decline in much of their unnecessary use.

When the social costs associated with all industrial activities are considered and compensated for, we will just begin to understand that much of our way of life today is very similar to that of one who lives off his capital (indiscriminate use of natural resources) rather than his interest — that which can be used without upsetting the balance of nature or without depleting nonrenewable resources — let us hope that this happens while enough capital remains to promote a decent life style.

JERRY PROCTOR

Ecology Jitters—
It's Doomsday! Well, Uh, Almost

Jerry Proctor is the City Editor of the *Birmingham News,* Birmingham, Alabama.

That Amchitka nuclear test was eerily almost like living through the last days of Pompeii.

Vesuvius-like, our dedicated and panicky environmentalists boomed and rumbled warnings: (a) The Pacific Basin would be pulverized by earthquakes; (b) Hawaii would be swallowed up by a tidal wave; (c) the Eskimos and polar bears of Alaska would be slain by lethal radiation.

When, in fact, nothing happened but a successful nuclear shot — one which enhanced our nation's security immeasurably — everyone was vastly relieved. Even the tense jowls of frightened TV commentators momentarily relaxed.

But our dedicated and panicky environmentalists lost not one bit of face. That's the strangest asset of today's wide-eyed environmental set. They never seem to lose public credence, no matter how fantastic or idiotic their charges.

When one charge is discredited, they manufacture three to take its place. Countering these charges thus becomes an impossible task, something like using a fly swatter to rid the world of gnats.

Nuclear power has become a special target of panicky environmentalists — despite the fact that presently it seems to be the most practical alternative to all the dirty coal and oil that panicky environmentalists hate so much.

Scarcely had mankind learned to generate electric power from nuclear energy than thousands of bright-eyed and dedicated environmentalists began seeking to block construction of atomic power plants over the nation. At Columbia University they even halted construction of a nuclear reactor for basic research.

The first and the biggest lie they've compounded is that reactors are simply big atomic bombs, weakly chained under tenuous human control and likely to explode at any moment, wiping out whole cities and regions. The fact that this charge was fashioned from pure fear and ignorance hasn't impaired its popularity.

Panicky environmentalists seem to be paralyzed by the awful power of all that uranium burbling away inside nuclear reactors. ("It was uranium that blew up Hiro-

Reprinted by permission of author, editor, and publisher from *The Birmingham News,* Birmingham, Alabama, Wednesday, December 1, 1971, p. 48.

shima and Nagasaki, wasn't it?") Yes, it was. And it was coal tar which reduced German, British and Russian cities to ashes during World War II — or, more specifically, TNT made from coal tar.

However, compared with the scientific miracles needed to make uranium detonate, it is childishly simple to turn coal tar into high explosives.

First off, ordinary uranium is not an explosive. It requires extremely expensive and time-consuming processes to turn it into the dangerous U-235 isotope which is the stuff of atomic bombs. Even then it must be machined to exact geometrical forms and driven into critical mass in microseconds before it will release its energy into that familiar and hellish fireball.

Unless all these steps are carried out with the greatest precision, the uranium charge simply melts. And that's what would happen inside a nuclear electric generating plant in the very unlikely event all its safety devices should fail and the charge "ran wild." All the uranium would melt or "slag down" and cease reacting.

The latest attack launched by our frightened environmentalists upon the atomic age is the highly dubious charge of "thermal pollution."

The more astute among them have noticed that nuclear plants manufacture a lot of excess heat, which must be gotten rid of somehow. Currently, most N-plants are using river or lake water to carry off heat, a fact which has sent some environmentalists into spasms of indignation over the danger to aquatic life. (Let's just skip the fact that nobody's yet proved that this heat actually is a danger to fish.)

Their howls have taken on such ferocity that most nuclear plants under construction are being equipped with cooling towers to remove heat from the water before it is returned to the rivers. This is a cute technological trick, but all it means in practical

terms is that the heat is jettisoned into surrounding air.

And since heat is the main generating force behind the world's weather, our environmentalists may get some unpleasant climatic changes they haven't bargained for.

The strange capability of some environmentalists to retain credence through a series of silly fiascos is nowhere more apparent than in the Great Mercury Scare. (Remember, it wasn't too long ago that people were afraid to eat fish because it was "full of mercury.")

Our environmentalists came up with such a beauty of a theory that it came close to closing down commercial fishing throughout Alabama. Industrial plants, they assured us with absolute certainty, were dumping poisonous mercury into our rivers. Fish were absorbing this mercury. We reabsorbed it when we ate the fish. It gradually accumulated in our frail bodies until it killed us.

The only trouble with this beautifully logical theory is that a research team at Saratoga General Hospital in Detroit got around to doing some actual scientific research on it. The findings seem to indicate the story was spun out of whole cloth.

The team did an analysis of tissue taken from human organs in autopsies between 1913 and 1970. They found that mercury levels in humans actually have declined since 1913.

Moreover, they found no scientific basis for the federal government's standard of .5 parts per million as the maximum permissible in fish.

Then comes the clincher: Mercury, reported the team, does not "accumulate" in humans. Mercury levels appear to rise and fall with age. It reaches peaks of perhaps 34 parts per million in childhood and middle age.

Summing it up, the team reported the Great Mercury Scare "had profound social reverberations in the form of mass anxiety leading to . . . action — often with little or no scientific basis — resulting in chaos, fear, and the economic pain of damaged or killed sectors of industry and commerce."

It would seem a rebuke this pointed would slightly abash our dedicated but panicky environmentalists. But it won't.

Tomorrow, you'll find them out on the soapbox again, yelling the latest Doomsday.

EDITORS' COMMENTS

The most disturbing feature about this article is that its type is becoming commonplace in the public press. This author, like many newspapermen who fail to understand environmental problems, jumps to the conclusion that they do not exist. Not only does this article evidence the author's lack of knowledge about environmental problems but its tone is inflammatory, if not abusive. He calls environmentalists "panicky," "wide-eyed," "idiotic," and characterizes their actions with words such as "pure fear and ignorance," "first and biggest lie," and "their howls."

The errors of logic and misinformation contained in this article are too numerous to analyze in detail, but perhaps a glance at a few of them might make their presence evident. First, the author failed to mention the real dangers of nuclear power plants such as, problems of radioactive waste disposal, magnification of radioactivity in biological food chains, and the genetic effects of long term exposure to increased radiation levels. His allegation that no one has proven that thermal pollution is dangerous to fish is untrue and shows that he has ignored or is unaware of a tremendous amount of scientific research.

Second, his comments on mercury show that he has failed to correctly interpret the research results of the Detroit team, and has ignored the bulk of the data relating to the mercury problem.

All in all, the article comes over as a defense of the nuclear power industry and other industries responsible for mercury pollution. The article must be considered in light of the fact that public newspapers depend, in large part, on advertising paid for by industry. If they offend industry, advertising may be withdrawn. These facts may be behind an evident trend toward anti-environmentalism in many of our newspapers. Perhaps it is a matter of survival. But where are the crusading editors and public-spirited reporters of song and story? Are they cowed by pressure from powerful polluting industries and reduced to producing pro-industry nonsense such as this?

Epilogue

If the reader of the previous selections is left with the feeling that the future of this planet is bleak, this is precisely as it should be. A natural response is to pass this feeling off as pessimism, but it is realism. Those who think of a human population explosion as an event of some vague point in the future, are themselves part of the explosion. The idea that pollution and environmental degradation are not yet a significant problem can only be held by one blind to obvious fact.

However, for some reason, most authors and editors seem to feel that a book must be ended with optimism. Perhaps we should be saying things like "Man's spirit will rise to the occasion," or "human ingenuity will solve environmental problems like it has solved similar problems in the past." Perhaps we can expect individuals and mankind as a whole to shed sluggishness and inaction and don a cloak of responsibility. Maybe the malnourished and underfed hordes, the bulk of mankind, will forget about the exigencies of everyday life and look to the future. Possibly the economic and political forces which run the world are even now readying themselves to take positive action to halt the destruction of the earth's life support systems. Bluntly, these things are not likely to occur.

Is the situation hopeless? Are the problems insoluble? Certainly not! But they will not be solved by depending on the actions of visionaries, searching for messiahs, or sitting back on our haunches. Time is growing short. Effort on the part of every individual is vital. Action must be taken before we reach that not-too-distant point beyond which continuing degradation of the environment will be irreversible.

Survival alone is not enough. With it must also come a world in which man's humanity can survive. Such a world is still within man's attainment, if we discard many of the false values that we have inherited from the time when man's main goal was to subdue to earth. The change must be made within the lifetime of most humans now alive.

Enumerated below is a list of actions that individuals can initiate to help alleviate certain environmental problems. It must be remembered that these are, in most cases, stop-gap measures that are not in themselves solutions. Additionally, many of them are compensatory in that they function as substitutes for the absence of responsibility in industry, in government, or on the part of our fellow citizens.

The Five Most Effective Individual Actions in Helping to Solve Environmental Problems

1. Be informed. Become familiar with the facts about environmental problems. Do not allow false or distorted publicity to confuse you. Become aware of the motives behind anti-environment publicity.
2. Join and become an active member in a conservation or environmentally oriented group of one kind or another.

3. Speak out, pass the word along, and inform others about environmental problems whenever you can. In other words, be a missionary.

4. Write or contact your national, state, county, and local elected and appointed officials giving them details about environmental problems. Ask them to take immediate action to solve the problems. When they fail to take action in the public interest, tell them so. Timing is very important here.

5. Decide now to limit your family to two children. If you want more, adopt them.

In the Home . . .

1. Repair and keep repaired all leaky faucets. A leaky faucet can waste 25 gallons of water a day.

2. Take brief showers or shallow (2 inches of water) baths.

3. Don't wash dishes, brush your teeth, comb your hair, or wash out clothes with the water running.

4. Put a brick in the toilet tank to keep down the volume of water used. Bend the float arm down to create a lower full water level.

5. Run your dishwasher, clothes washer and other water-using appliances once a day or less. Do not run them with partial loads.

6. Do not use toilets as sewage disposals for household items that can be disposed of without water.

7. Do not hose down walks, driveways, patios or other areas to clean them. Sweep them with a broom.

8. Find out if your city water system gives discounts to users who consume large quantities of water. If they do, gripe the next time you pay your bill. Making water cheaper in large quantities encourages waste of water.

9. Save extra coat hangers and return them to the cleaner for re-use.

10. Use soap with washing soda in your washer. If you use a detergent use a low- or non-phosphate one. Measure carefully.

11. Save newspapers and magazines for recycling. Do the same for cans and bottles if there are recycling centers in your area.

12. Power pollutes! Conserve it by turning off lights, not using unnecessary appliances, and using your air conditioning and heating systems only when needed.

13. Use cloth napkins, and non-disposable cups.

14. Be aware of environmental values and natural surroundings when you buy or build a house. Inform the builder or developer.

15. Avoid using noisy appliances, especially during evening hours.

16. Don't waste anything.

Concerning Your Car . . .

1. Drive less. Walk, ride a bicycle, jog, get a horse. If you must have a mechanical conveyance get a purring motor scooter. Motorcycles are major causes of noise pollution.

2. Form car pools.

3. Use mass transit when possible.

4. Support the development of mass transit systems in your community.

5. Buy only as much car as you need. Neither high speed nor monstrous power is necessary.

6. Be sure your car has emission-control features and keep them in working order.

7. Buy lead-free gasoline.

8. Do not let your car's gas tank be topped off, since this results in spillage. When the pump stops automatically, the proper level has been reached.

9. Urge auto makers to manufacture long-lasting cars. Planned obsolescence is a major cause of metal wastage.
10. Drive sanely. Jack-rabbit starts and screeching stops result in excessive fuel consumption and increased tire wear.
11. Dispose of worn out or wrecked cars carefully so that the metal will be reused. Don't burn old tires.
12. Don't let your motor idle unnecessarily.
13. Keep a litter container in your car. Never throw anything out of the windows.
14. Use a bucket and sponge to wash your car, not a running hose.
15. Replace faulty, noisy mufflers.
16. Use your horn only when absolutely necessary.
17. Actively support the development of alternatives to the internal combustion-powered automobile.

In the Yard and Garden . . .

1. Compost organic wastes such as clippings, weeds, coffee grounds, vegetable wastes, etc. They make good topsoil.
2. Collect branches for trash or make brush piles for birds and other animals. Do not burn trash.
3. Limit pesticide use. Learn how to garden organically. If you must use pesticides try to stay away from the organic phosphates and chlorinated hydrocarbons. Use the kinds derived from plants such as rotenone, pyrethrums, and nicotine sulfate.
4. Mulch your garden to limit watering. If you must water, one good soaking is often better than sprinkling. Water in the evenings to reduce evaporation.
5. Do not overfertilize. Have your soil analyzed to see if it needs fertilizer or to determine the correct amounts to use.

6. Use live Christmas trees and replant them or give them to schools and parks to be replanted.

When Shopping . . .

1. Take a shopping bag. Re-use it.
2. Do not buy small items packaged individually, especially if the packaging includes non-biodegradable plastic. If you must buy them, let the cashier, manager, or owner know you object. In some cases you may want to remove the packaging and leave it at the store.
3. Do not accept bags for items you can carry. If a store forces you (security reasons?) to take a bag whether you want it or not, object to the manager.
4. Avoid using merchandise packaged in non-biodegradable and/or non-returnable cans, bottles or containers.
5. Do not buy disposable diapers. The plastic portions do not break down, and if flushed, cloggage of plumbing may result.
6. Do not buy materials in aerosol cans. They are costly, dangerous, and difficult to dispose of or to recycle.
7. Buy things in bulk if possible, without wastage. It's cheaper, more efficient, and wastes less container material.
8. Make your own baby food. Baby food jars and lids represent 36 percent of the cost of the merchandise.
9. Ask for fresh meat wrapped in paper rather than in styrofoam and plastic.
10. Support advertisers that use small concise ads. Big ads in newspapers are a major cause of paper waste.
11. Read the labels carefully on everything you may buy. This enables you to save money and allows you to stay away from foods containing potentially harmful or useless additives.

12. Do not buy novelties, clothing, or accessories made from the skins or other parts of rare or endangered animals.

In Your Community . . .

1. Learn about zoning and planning action and encourage environmental awareness in these activities.
2. Don't litter. Object when you see litter or see someone littering.
3. Protest unnecessary roads, highways, airports, and other land clearing activities.
4. Actively resist the building of unnecessary dams, stream channels, and canals.
5. Support the local development of effective sewage processing facilities, even if it means higher taxes.
6. Encourage the development of green belts and natural areas.
7. Encourage the municipal government to begin trash separation and recycling of solid wastes.
8. Do not allow your community government or chamber of commerce to encourage the locating of polluting industries in or near your city.
9. Be knowledgeable when you vote. Vote for and work for candidates with an ecological conscience.

You must close these pages and begin now. These actions may seem insignificant when done by one person alone, but when millions begin to cooperate they become enormously important. Set an example. Begin now! GOOD LUCK!

Glossary

Many of the terms defined below have a variety of meanings. The definitions given here only apply in the sense and context that the words or terms are used when discussing ecological principles or environmental problems. This list is by no means exhaustive. Most of the terms not appearing here can be found in an ecology textbook or in one of the several biological, zoological, or ecological dictionaries or encyclopedias currently on the market.

abortion — removal or expulsion of a fetus or embryo from the body of the mother at a time before it is capable of independent life.

adaptation — a structural, physiological, or behavioral trait of an organism which functions in fitting the organism to its particular mode of life; the evolutionary process by which an organism becomes more suited to its environment.

aerobic — occurring in the presence of molecular oxygen. *See* anaerobic.

aerosol — a dispersion of solid or liquid particles of microscopic size in a gaseous medium.

aesthetic pollution — environmental disturbances which result in situations unpleasant to the eye or which impair an individual's ability to take pleasure from his surroundings or the world as a whole.

age distribution — the classification of members of a population according to age classes, or life periods such as immature, reproductive, and postreproductive.

air pollution — the presence of the atmosphere of man-made contaminants at levels injurious to plant life, animal life, or property or in quantities which interfere with the enjoyment of life.

algae — a group of relatively simple, green, mainly aquatic plants which lack true roots, stems, and leaves. Some are referred to as seaweeds.

alluvial — referring to the sedimentary matter transported and deposited by streams and rivers.

alpha radiation — radiation consisting of a stream of alpha particles (helium nuclei). Alpha radiation has a very low penetrating power.

anabolism –- all metabolic processes by which substances in an organism are synthesized; the building of protoplasm. *See* catabolism, metabolism.

anaerobic — occurring in the absence of molecular oxygen. *See* aerobic.

antibiotic — a substance produced by an organism that inhibits or prevents the growth of certain other species in the area, (e.g., penicillin, aureomycin, chloromycetin).

anti-environmentalism — a philosophy or point of view in which individuals or groups deny the existence of environmental problems, make light of the problems, or take actions which impede solutions to the problems.

aquaculture — the use of artificial methods to increase the production of aquatic food organisms. *See* mariculture.

aquatic — pertaining to or inhabiting water, either fresh or marine. *See* marine, terrestrial.

aquifer — the underground layer of water-bearing rock, sand, gravel, or other material through which water moves. The source of water for springs and wells. *See* groundwater, water table.

arid — dry or lacking sufficient moisture for crop production; receiving low amounts of precipitation.

assimilation — the absorption and construction of the complex organic constituents of protoplasm from simpler food materials.

atmosphere — the envelope of air surrounding the earth. *See* biosphere, hydrosphere, lithosphere.

autecology — the ecology of a single individual or a single species; the study of the multiplicity of factors affecting a single kind of organism. *See* synecology.

autotrophic — capable of using simple inorganic substances for the synthesis of complex organic compounds. This process is generally accomplished by photosynthesis. *See* heterotrophic.

background radiation — the total of all natural ionizing radiation coming from cosmic radiation, radioactive elements in the body, and radioactive elements in the earth's crust.

bacteria — a group of microscopic, unicellular, usually parasitic or saprophytic plants. They are considered fungi and compromise the phylum Shizomycophyta.

balance of nature — a general term referring to the dynamic equilibrium which under natural conditions, is maintained by the totality of the actions of all living things.

beta radiation — radiation consisting of a stream of beta particles (electrons) which have greater penetrating power than alpha particles, but less penetrating power than gamma rays.

biochemical oxygen demand (B.O.D.) — the amount of oxygen necessary for the biological oxidation of organic matter under a set of standardized conditions. Used as an index of water pollution. In general, the higher the BOD the more organic pollution present.

biocide — a substance designed to kill living things.

biodegradable — capable of being chemically broken down or decomposed by the action of organisms in the environment.

biogeochemical cycle — a process which circulates elements, such as nitrogen, carbon, etc. from the living portions of the environment to the nonliving portions, and back again.

biological control — the use and enhancement of natural diseases or parasites to control organisms which man considers pests.

biology — the study of living things. *See* botany, zoology.

biomass — the total quantity (weight) of all members of a species or of all of the organisms in a specific habitat or area.

biome — a major biotic community including all of the living things in a large, possibly discontinuous area characterized by the prevailing climatic and soil conditions, (e.g., the grassland biome, composed of grasslands everywhere).

biometer — an organism that can be used to indicate conditions, such as soil type, pollutant concentration, or climate.

biosphere — the portion of the earth which is inhabited by living things, (i.e., the upper crust and the lower atmosphere).

biota — collectively the kinds of plants and animals which inhabit a given area. *See* fauna, flora.

biotic potential — the inherent ability of an organism to reproduce and survive. In a sense, it is this ability which is pitted against the limiting factors in the environment.

biotic resistance — environmental factors which work against the survival and reproduction of an organism.

birth control — any process which prevents reproduction, including mainly contraception and abortion.

bloom — an obvious and visible concentration of algae or other plants in a body of water above the level at which they would normally occur. Blooms often result from nutrient enrichment.

botany — the study of plants. *See* biology, zoology.

calorie — the amount of heat energy necessary to raise one kilogram of water from 15° to 16° Centigrade. Used in measuring the metabolism or energy output of animals.

capillary water — the portion of the water in the soil that is held by capillary forces around and between the soil particles.

carbon dioxide — a colorless, odorless, incombustible gas formed by the respiration of organisms, combustion, and decomposition.

carbon monoxide — a colorless, odorless, highly poisonous gas formed by the incomplete combustion of carbon or any carbon-containing material.

carcinogen — a substance capable of producing a cancerous growth. *See* mutagen, teratogen.

carnivore — a flesh eater; an animal or plant which preys or feeds on animals. *See* herbivore, omnivore.

carrying capacity — the maximum number or weight of individuals of a species which can be maintained in a habitat without depleting the needed resources.

catabolism — all metabolic processes such as respiration and digestion by which organic compounds in an organism's body are broken down to form simpler substances. *See* anabolism, metabolism.

catalyst — a substance which increases the rate at which a chemical reaction occurs but is not itself permanently altered. *See* enzyme.

celluose — a polysaccharide (carbohydrate) which is the major constituent of the cell walls of most plants. Cellulose is indigestable to humans.

cereal — a plant of the grass family, the grains of which may be used for food, (e.g., wheat, maize (corn), oats).

chlorinated hydrocarbon — a group of synthetic insecticides which have a relatively low immediate toxicity but persist for long periods in the environment, (e.g., DDT, endrin, dieldrin, heptachlor, aldrin, lindane, toxaphene). *See* organic phosphate.

chlorophyll — a green magnesium porphyrin pigment found in algae, most higher plants, and certain bacteria. Plants use chlorophyll to capture light energy which is used to manufacture carbohydrates from carbon dioxide and water.

clear-cutting — a method of harvesting timber in which all trees in a stand are removed at the same time regardless of their size. *See* selective cutting, monoculture.

climate — the general aggregate of all weather conditions such as moisture, temperature, wind, pressure, etc., which in combination are characteristic of an area. *See* weather.

climax — the final stable type of community that develops as the end-product of ecological succession. The climax perpetuates itself unless disturbed. *See* disclimax.

closed community — a community in which all available niches are occupied by organisms well suited to them. Closed communities can only be invaded by new organisms with great difficulty.

coaction — an interaction between organisms; the effect of one organism on another.

coliform count — an index of water pollution by human waste in which bacteria which are normally inhabitants of the human intestine are counted. The presence of these forms indicates the possibility of the presence of disease-causing bacteria.

commensalism — a physical relationship between two kinds of organisms in which one benefits and the other is neither harmed nor benefitted.

community — all of the organisms inhabiting a given area.

competition — an indirect rivalry of two or more species for the same resources such as food, or shelter.

composting — a technique for processing solid organic wastes into compost which can be used as a soil conditioner. Usually involves allowing the organic material to decompose and adding nitrogen, lime, and phosphorus.

condom — contraceptive device consisting of a flexible cap, usually made of latex, which fits over the male organ. Condoms prevent the liberation of sperm into the vagina during intercourse.

coniferous — cone-bearing; referring to the gymnosperms such as pine, spruce, fir, and hemlock. Coniferous trees are often evergreen.

conservation — the wise use of resources on a permanent, continuing basis. Effective conservation involves detailed knowledge and precise planning.

consumer — collectively, those organisms in an ecosystem which feed on other organisms. *See* producer, decomposer.

contraceptive — a device or chemical which prevents conception or impregnation; a birth control device. *See* IUD, condom, contraceptive pill.

contraceptive pill — a chemical means of contraception which involves the female taking oral doses of female sex hormones which function to prevent the production of an ovum. *See* contraception, sperm, ovum.

contrail — streak-line, narrow, shallow clouds created by condensation caused during the passage of high-flying airplanes.

controlled burning — the use of controlled fires in forests for the purpose of removing underbrush and preventing the reproduction of unwanted tree species.

corrosion — slow destruction of materials or tissue by chemical action. A problem involved in certain types of air and water pollution.

cosmic radiation — various types of radiations of high energy and short wavelength which come to the earth from space.

crowding — a condition in which organisms have less than the minimum space necessary to carry on life activities without disruption by other members of the species.

curie — a unit used in measuring the radioactivity of materials. Technically, that amount of radioactive substance undergoing decay at the rate of 3.7×10^{10} disintegrations per second. Roughly, a curie equals the radioactivity of one gram of radium plus it's decay products. *See* roentgen, rem, rad.

cycle — a series of events or changes which returns to it's starting point or in which the condition returns to the original; the circulation of substances through a system.

decibel — a unit which measures the relative loudness of sounds audible to the human ear.

deciduous — having leaves which are all shed at a certain time of year, usually fall. *See* evergreen.

decomposers — collectively, those organisms in an ecosystem which convert dead organic materials into inorganic materials. In general these are the agents of decay and are mainly fungi and bacteria. *See* producer, consumer.

defoliant — a substance which causes plants, especially trees, to lose their leaves, (e.g., picloram).

demography — the study of populations with reference to their age distribution, birth rate, death rate, geographical distribution, and environment.

density — the number of individuals per unit of area occupied.

density dependent factors — mortality factors in the environment whose effectiveness (intensity and severity) increases as the population density increases, (e.g., composition, food supply, predation, disease). *See* density independent factors.

density independent factors — mortality factors in the environment whose effectiveness is not directly related to population density, (e.g., extreme temperatures, floods, storms). *See* density dependent factors.

desalination — the conversion of sea (salt) water to fresh or drinking water.

desiccation — a drying out process. A process by which water in an organism or area becomes less abundant.

detergent — a cleansing agent which chemically includes a surface active agent (surfactant), and which functions by a process not involving mere dissolving of the dirt or material to be removed.

detritus — in the ecological sense any fine particulate material of organic origin. Debris resulting from decomposing plants and animals.

disclimax — an enduring community or apparent climax which results from direct or indirect disturbance by man, (e.g., the prickly pear cactus disclimax in Australia which resulted from man's introduction of this plant).

dispersal — the transfer or movement of organisms from place to place, (e.g., in flowering plants, seeds and fruits are a means of dispersal.)

dispersion — the pattern of spatial distribution or placement of individuals in a population.

diversity index — the ratio between the number of species and the number of individuals in an area. The more complex the community, the higher the diversity index.

dominant — a characteristic of a species which because of its size, numbers, area covered, or other factors, exerts a major influence on the other species associated with it.

dry-farming — cultivation of land in dry or desert regions without the use of irrigation, often involves mulching and allowing tilled land to lie fallow to accumulate water and nutrients.

dystrophic lake — a type of lake or pond with brown water having a high humus content. The number of organisms present is usually low.

earth week — currently, the fourth week in April. A week during which activities involving environmental concern are emphasized throughout the nation.

ecofreak — an individual who energetically and uncomprisingly works for sane use of the environment, especially one who courageously voices his views; originally used in a derogatory fashion by anti-environmentalists.

ecological equivalent — an organism which, because of similar characteristics, occupies a niche in one area similar to the niche occupied by a different organism in another area.

ecological indicator — *See* Indicator.

ecological succession — the series of progressive changes in vegetation and animal life which eventually result in the climax. *See* primary succession, secondary succession.

ecology — the study of the relationships of organisms or groups of organisms to their environment. *See* autecology, synecology.

ecosystem — the living things plus the non-living things in a particular habitat, i.e., the community plus all of the associated environmental factors.

ecotone — a transitional or borderline area between two communities or two different habitat types, (e.g., a zone where a forest and grassland merge). *See* edge effect.

edaphic — referring to the soil or to factors related to the soil.

edge effect — the increased capacity to support populations of larger, especially game animals, by creating ecotones, i.e., by creating a mixture of different habitat types.

effluent — pollutant-containing wastes released into the environment. Specifically the liquid coming from a sewage treatment plant.

electrostatic precipitation — the process of removing liquid droplets or small particles from a gas in which they are suspended by charging the particles by passing them through an electrically charged screen and then attracting the charged particles to a charged plate.

emigration — the movement of an organism out of a locality, usually permanently.

emotionalism — a charge leveled by anti-environmentalists at citizens concerned about the environment. The accusation seeks to imply that a person angered or sorrowed at the destruction of his world cannot have anything worthwhile to say.

endangered species — a kind of plant or animal that exists in low numbers, in a restricted habitat, or in an area which man is likely to disturb, and is therefore likely to become extinct unless measures are initiated to save it.

endemic — restricted to a specified area.

endocrine gland — ductless gland which secretes hormones directly into the blood. Endocrine glands are important because their secretions often regulate behavior, and they often respond to environmental stresses.

energy — the ability to do work. Energy is one of the two fundamental physical components of the universe, the other being mass.

energy flow — the intake, conversion, and passage of energy through organisms and from one trophic level to the next.

environment — the sum total of all conditions under which an organism lives. Everything affecting an organism in any way.

Environmental Impact Statement (102 statement) — a statement which under the National Environmental Policy Act, all government agencies must make as to the possible environmental effects of any action they might take See NEPA.

environmental resistance — all factors which would tend to limit the numerical increase of a species.

environmentalist — an individual who is concerned about and supports sane use of the environment.

enzyme — an organic substance which greatly speeds up the rate at which chemical reactions take place in the bodies of organisms; an organic catalyst. See catalyst.

equilibrium — a state of balance; a condition in which interacting factors cause no major ultimate change.

erosion — slow destruction of a substance by chemical or physical effects. More specifically, the removal of soil from the land by the action of wind, water, ice, or earth movements.

estuary — the area where a river flows into the sea and there is a mixing of marine and fresh waters.

euphotic zone — the upper level of a body of water in which there is enough light penetration for green plants to live.

eutrophic — referring to bodies of water which are rich in mineral nutrients and organic materials and therefore very productive. Waters that are highly eutrophic may suffer periodically from oxygen difficiencies.

eutrophication — the process of nutrient enrichment of a body of water. Man-caused eutrophication, due to adding sediments, fertilizers, detergents, etc., often causes ultimate oxygen deficiencies and the subsequent death of aquatic organisms.

evaporation — the process by which a liquid or solid becomes a vapor without boiling.

The change of liquid water into water vapor.

evergreen — possessing leaves throughout the year. Evergreen plants do lose leaves, but they are lost and replaced gradually.

excretion — the process of concentrating and eliminating metabolic waste materials.

exotic — not native to an area. Generally used in referring to plants and animals that have been introduced in a country or continent where they are not native.

extinction — the termination of a lineage; the failure of a type of organism to leave descendants.

fallout — radioactive substances (dust and debris) which result from and are dispersed after a thermonuclear explosion.

fault zone — an area in which major geological earth movements (earthquakes) have occurred or are likely to occur. Geologically, an area where a crack has developed between major rock masses in the earth's crust.

fauna — a collective term referring to all of the kinds of animals inhabiting a specific area. *See* flora, biota.

fecundity — the number of offspring, or gametes produced by an animal; the capability of an organism to reproduce.

feral — referring to a domestic animal that has become wild.

fertilization — the union of gametes; the fusion of sperm and egg or more specifically the fusion of two unlike nuclei.

flora — a collective term referring to all of the kinds of plants inhabiting a specific area. *See* fauna, biota.

food chain — the series of organisms involved in the transfer of food energy from its source in green plants through the other organisms which eat the plants and are in turn eaten. A component, or oversimplified version of a food web. *See* food web.

food habits — the kinds and amounts of food items that are eaten by an organism.

food web — all of the interconnecting food chains in a community. The complex food-energy interrelationships in a community. *See* food chain.

forest — a stand of trees growing close together.

fossil fuel — fuels formed by alteration of the remains of ancient plant and animal life, (e.g., coal, petroleum, natural gas, peat).

gamete — a neutral term referring to either of the sex cells, sperm, or ovum (egg). *See* sperm, ovum.

gamma radiation — radiation with exceptionally strong powers of penetration. Much of the damage to organisms done by radioactivity is due to gamma radiation. *See* alpha radiation, beta radiation.

gene — a unit of hereditary material governing one characteristic of the organism.

genetics — the study of heredity and variation.

geology — the study of the earth from the point of view of its physical and chemical composition and the changes which have occurred and are occurring.

geothermal power — power obtained by tapping natural hot areas deep in the earth's crust.

grassland — an area in which most of the plants are densely aggregated grasses, and trees are absent or sparsely distributed.

green belt — a zone in which development is prohibited and vegetation is maintained or planted to provide beauty, recreation, wildlife habitat, and a refugium for plants and animals. Natural green belts are to be encouraged. Highly artificial ones provide little benefit.

green revolution — man's success in increasing crop yields by planting, breeding, fertilization, and other artificial methods; not a solution to the population problem, merely a means of staving off the end.

greenhouse effect — a phenomenon that results in the trapping of heat when light passes through a substance or permeable layer and produces heat internally which is trapped in the confined space. The carbon dioxide in the upper atmosphere creates a greenhouse effect on the earth.

groundwater — water standing in or moving through the soil or underlying strata. *See* water table, aquifer.

habitat — the type of area in which an organism lives as characterized by the physical, biological, and climatic conditions present. *See* niche.

half-life — the time necessary for half the amount of a pollutant originally present to lose its power to damage. This term may be applied to radioactive materials, persistent pesticides, or other pollutants.

herb — a plant with little or no woody tissue, and hence relatively small and flexible.

herbicide — a substance designed to kill plants, (e.g., 2,4-D, 2,4,5-T).

herbivore — an animal that feeds exclusively on plants.

heterotrophic — a type of nutrition in which the organism depends on complex organic food molecules which have originated in the bodies of other organisms. Most animals and the parasitic plants fall into this category.

homeostasis — a state of stability which fluctuates within tolerable limits; stability in metabolic or ecological conditions.

home range — the general area traveled or covered during the normal daily or seasonal activities of an animal. *See* territory.

homing — the process of returning to a given site. The ability 'to home' is not well understood, (e.g., return to the home stream by migrating salmon).

hormone — a chemical messenger secreted by an endocrine gland and reaching its site of action in the body by flowing in the blood.

host — the organism on which a parasite or other physically associated organism lives.

human ecology — the study of the effects of the environment on man, especially of how man-made changes are affecting man himself.

humidity — the amount of moisture in the air.

humus — organic matter which has reached a more or less stable, advanced state of decomposition.

hydroelectric power — power manufactured by energy of falling water. Most hydroelectric plants are located in dams which back up rivers to form artificial lakes.

hydrologic cycle — the cycle which involves the movement of water from the atmosphere to the earth by rain, and the return to the atmosphere by processes including run-off, infiltration, percolation, storage, evaporation, and transpiration.

hydrosphere — the total of all water surrounding the earth, i.e., oceans, lakes, rivers, streams, ground water, etc. *See* biosphere, atmosphere, lithosphere.

immigration — the movement of an organism into an area, usually permanently.

immunity — the general ability of an organism to resist infections or infestations of disease-causing organisms or parasites.

incineration — the burning of waste material. More specifically, the burning of refuse to remove much of the water and reduce the remainder to a safe, non-burning, sometimes usable, ash.

indicator — organism which can be used to detect or interpret environmental changes, (e.g., tubifex worms indicate low oxygen concentrations).

insecticide — a substance designed to kill insects, (e.g., DDT, parathion, endrin). *See* organic phosphate, chlorinated hydrocarbon.

instinct — an innate, simple or complex, largely invariable, behavior pattern. Instinctive actions are not based on learning or experience, (e.g., fear of loud noises in humans is instinctive).

intelligence — the ability to associate facts and meanings; the ability to reason abstractly; the capacity for understanding and initiating subsequent action.

IUD — intra-uterine device; a device for prevention of pregnancy which consists of a stainless steel or non-reactive plastic unit of varying shape which is inserted semi-permanently into the uterus.

inversion — the condition in which a layer of cool air is trapped by a layer of warm air above it. This situation aggravates air pollution problems since neither the cool air nor the pollutants in it can rise and be dispersed.

ionizing radiation — radiation types including alpha, beta, and gamma radiation which cause the ionization of molecules; hard radiation. *See* alpha radiation, beta radiation, gamma radiation.

irrigation — the artificial addition of water, in excess of rain, to crops for the purpose of increasing yield or in order to grow crops in areas otherwise too dry.

isotope — forms of the same element which have different atomic weights.

LD 50 — the dose rate of a biocide or radioactivity that will kill fifty percent of the individuals to which it is applied. The LD 50 is used in evaluating toxicity.

landfill — the open dumping of solid wastes followed by covering them with soil.

land use planning — the making of long range decisions as to the use of the land that will ultimately be to the benefit to the populace. Land use planning involves the zoning of floodplains, the protection of natural areas, the limiting of industrial expansion, proper highway planning, etc.

lentic — referring to standing water habitats such as lakes, ponds, and swamps, *See* lotic.

lichen — a "plant" formed by a mutually beneficial physical combination of an alga and a fungus. Lichens are able to grow in harsher situations than most plants.

life table — a table including information about life expectancy, age specific mortality and reproduction, and the numbers of individuals in an age group. A life table describes the probable history of the individuals composing a population.

limiting factor — the environmental influence which first stops the growth or spread of an organism. The limiting factor outweighs all others in restricting the organism.

limnology — the study of fresh waters and the organisms inhabiting them.

lithosphere — the land mass portions of the earth's crust. Parts of the lithosphere, hydrosphere, and atmosphere comprise the biosphere. *See* atmosphere, hydrosphere, biosphere.

littoral — pertaining to the coastal or edge regions of a body of water; strictly speaking, the area along the sea coast between the high and low tide marks.

lotic — referring to running water habitats such as rivers, streams, and springs. *See* lentic.

lunar cycle — a cycle correlated with the phases or periodicity of the moon; a twenty-eight day cycle.

macronutrient — an element or compound necessary in relatively large amounts for the proper functioning of an organism. *See* micronutrient.

malnutrition — improper nutrition in which the right types of foods are not being eaten, even though the food energy taken in each day may be sufficient. *See* undernutrition.

mariculture — the practice of farming the oceans; controlling the oceans to increase food production. *See* aquaculture.

marine — referring to organisms which inhabit the oceans; anything associated with oceans. *See* aquatic.

marine biology — the study of organisms which inhabit the oceans. *See* oceanography.

metabolism — all of the chemical and physical life processes in an organism.

meteorology — the study of weather and climate.

microclimate — the climate of the immediate surroundings of an organism; the climate on which the life of the organism depends. The microclimate may or may not be similar to the overall climate of an area.

microenvironment — the immediate environment of an individual.

microhabitat — the actual place occupied by an organism; a small uniform area within a larger more heterogeneous habitat.

micronutrient — an element or compound necessary in very small amounts for the proper functioning of an organism. *See* macronutrient.

migration — the periodic movement of an organism or population from one area to another.

monoculture — the practice of growing crops or timber in large acreage consisting of only one species.

monophagous — feeding only on one type of food. Monophagous animals are prone to extinction, (e.g., the barnacle goose feeds only on eelgrass).

mortality — the death of an individual; the removal of individuals from a population by death.

multiple use — the practice of using an area or resource simultaneously for a number of purposes. In forestry, the currently neglected practice of using forests for timber, recreation, wildlife, aesthetics, species preservation, and water conservation without extreme emphasis on any one use.

mutagen — a substance or influence capable of causing mutations. *See* mutation, carcinogen, teratogen.

mutation — a minute change in the amount, kind, or position of the genetic material, which causes a corresponding change in the cell or organism. Most mutations are harmful.

mutualism — a physical relationship between two kinds of organisms in which both benefit.

natality — the production of offspring; the addition of individuals to a population by reproduction.

National Environmental Policy Act (NEPA) — a 1969 law which has been an effective legal tool in preventing environmental degradation, especially of the type resulting from the activities of federal agencies.

natural area — an area left in its natural state, or left undisturbed so that it may return to as natural a state as possible.

natural history — a loosely defined discipline dealing with the life history, behavior, and ecology of any organism.

natural resource — a material or value that can be obtained from nature and is useful to man.

natural selection — the controlling force in evolution; the process by which species change: Natural selection occurs as individuals with certain genetic make-ups are more successful in reproducing than others. It is these individuals that are the "fittest."

niche — all factors acting upon an organism and everything which the organism acts upon; the mode of life of an organism. *See* habitat.

nocturnal — active during the night.

noise pollution — an excess of sound to the extent that it interferes with pleasure or relaxation, damages property, or causes damage to hearing and mental stability.

non-renewable resource — a resource which once used cannot be used again in its original form and does not by natural processes regenerate itself, (e.g., coal, ores).

noosphere — the world dominated by the mind of man.

nuclear fission — the splitting of the nucleus of an atom into two parts with a large amount of energy and neutrons being given off in the process. The neutrons may split more nuclei causing a chain reaction. *See* nuclear fusion.

nuclear fusion — the uniting of the nuclei of two atoms of small mass, with an amount of energy being given off in the process. *See* nuclear fission.

nuclear power plant — an electric power plant in which the steam which drives the turbine to create the electricity is created by heating water by nuclear fission.

nutrient — a substance needed by an organism for proper functioning.

nutrition — the use of food material in the life processes of an organism; the study of the processes involved in the proper use of food by an organism.

oceanography — the study of the geography, history, movements, and physical and chemical characteristics of the ocean. *See* marine biology.

oil spill — pollution of a body of water when oil escapes from tankers, offshore oil wells, or other sources.

oligotrophic lake — lakes lacking large amounts of the nutrients necessary for plant growth and with oxygen distributed rather uniformly throughout. Oligotrophic lakes are low in productivity. *See* dystrophic lake, eutrophic lake.

omnivorous — feeding on both animals and plants, (e.g., man).

open range — an area for grazing livestock in which the movements of the animals are unrestricted by fences or other artificial barriers.

organic — having to do with living things; derived from living things. Specifically, in chemistry, all compounds containing carbon and hydrogen are called organic.

organic farming — the production of crops without the use of synthetic chemicals such as fertilizers and pesticides.

organic phosphate — a group of synthetic insecticides with high immediate toxicity but not persistent in the environment, (e.g., parathion, malathion). *See* chlorinated hydrocarbon.

overgrazing — the consumption of vegetation by livestock or herbivorous animals at a rate faster than it can be replaced by growth. Overgrazing reduces the capacity of the area to support livestock or game, damages habitat for other animals, and often bares the soil to erosion.

overpopulation — the presence of a species in numbers so large that the functioning of the individuals is impaired or ultimately all cannot survive.

ovum — the egg or female reproductive cell. *See* gamete, sperm.

oxidation — the breaking down of organic materials or chemicals by combining oxygen with them; the chemical combination of oxygen with any substance.

ozone — a colorless, gaseous, pungent form of oxygen (O_3) produced in smog, electrical discharge, and in the upper atmosphere. Toxic to plants and animals in low concentrations.

paleontology — the study of fossil organisms and their distribution in times past.

parasite — an organism which while physically associated with another organism, benefits itself, and harms the other organism without immediately killing it. *See* host, predator.

pathogen — any organism or virus that produces disease.

peck order — a system of social dominance in flocks of birds or groups of other organisms. The individuals at the top of the peck order have priority in feeding, reproducing, etc., and therefore benefit from their position.

pelagic — referring to the open water of the ocean or to organisms which inhabit open water.

permafrost — permanently frozen ground in arctic and subarctic regions.

pesticide — a substance designed to kill organisms which interfere with man's activities. *See* biocide, insecticide, herbicide.

pheromones. — a substance secreted by an animal that influences the behavior of other members of the same species. The pheromones used by female insects to attract the male have been useful in controlling insects.

phosphate — a phosphorus-containing compound. Phosphates from detergents and fertilizers have been implicated as causes of eutrophication. *See* eutrophication.

photochemical smog — *See* smog.

photosynthesis — the process by which plants use chlorophyll and light energy to combine carbon dioxide and water to form carbohydrates.

physiography — the study of landforms.

phytoplankton — the small floating plants inhabiting a body of water. *See* zooplankton.

"pill" — *See* contraceptive pill.

plankton — the small floating or weakly swimming plants and animals inhabiting a body of water. *See* phytoplankton, zooplankton.

plankton bloom — *See* bloom.

pollution — the presence of an interfering substance or activity in the environment which makes it less usable for a purpose which will benefit man.

population — a group of interacting individuals of the same species inhabiting a defined area.

population ecology — the ecology of a given population with special emphasis on factors related to the growth, maintenance, or decline of the population.

precipitation — the condensation and falling of atmospheric water in the form of rain, snow, sleet, etc.

predator — animals which attack and kill other animals for the purpose of feeding on them. *See* parasite.

primary sewage treatment — the first process in sewage treatment involving the removal of materials that will settle. It is accomplished by using screens and settling tanks.

primary succession — ecological succession that begins on an area that is bare of soil where no life has existed before or where the previous life has been completely destroyed.

producer — an organism in an ecosystem which uses sunlight energy to produce food. All producers are chlorophyll-bearing plants.

productivity — the amount of material or number or mass of organisms produced in excess of the original stock.

prophet of doom — a term used by anti-environmentalists to attempt to discredit the views of those who warn that man must change the way he is treating the world or suffer the consequences.

pyramid of numbers — the phenomenon involved in food chains or successive trophic levels in which the number of organisms at a certain level is always less than the number on which they feed.

race — a characteristic, recognizable population of a species which inhabits a certain geographic area.

RAD — the unit of ionizing radiation absorbed by the tissues of an organism;

equal to 100 ergs of energy per gram. *See* curie, rem, roentgen.

radiation — the transmission of energy from a source by waves. *See* ionizing radiation.

radioisotope — a radioactive isotope of an element. *See* isotope.

rain shadow — an area in which rainfall is low because it lies to the leeward side of mountains which cause the rain to be dropped on the opposite side.

rare species — a species in which the individuals or populations are in low abundance and scattered.

reclamation — the process by which areas are modified to make them more suitable for man's purposes. Unfortunately, much reclamation is destructive because it involves swamp drainage, the dredgeing of estuaries, or the agriculturization of deserts. Reclamation is a process often promoted by developers.

recruitment — the addition of individuals to a population by the production of young.

recycling — the practice of using a resource or material repeatedly by treating or processing it so it can again serve the original or a related purpose.

red tide — population explosions of small reddish algae (dinoflagellates) in the ocean. The wastes produced by these algae kill fishes and other marine organisms.

relative humidity — the ratio of the amount of water present in the air to the amount that the air could hold when saturated at that temperature.

REM — a unit of absorbed dose which takes into account the biological effects of a type of radiation. *See* curie, rad, roentgen.

renewable resource — a resource which, if properly cared for, can regenerate itself by natural processes and be used again, (e.g., food organisms, timber).

reproductive potential — the maximum ability of an organism to reproduce under optimum conditions. Actual reproduction is much lower than the reproductive potential.

respiration — the metabolic processes by which organisms obtain energy from nutrient materials.

riparian — referring to the areas bordering rivers, streams or tidewaters.

roentgen — a measure of the number of ionizations caused by radiation in air. A roentgen equals 1.6×10^{12} ionizations per cubic centimeter of air. *See* curie, rad, rem.

saprophyte — an organism which lives by taking in simple organic compounds and dissolved salts. Saprophytes live in areas where decay is occurring and are often the agents of decay.

scavenger — an animal that eats dead organic material or the bodies of animals killed by agents other than itself.

science — a body of exact, tested, and verified knowledge; the development and understanding of such a body of knowledge.

secondary sewage treatment — the second step in sewage treatment in which bacterial action breaks down the organic parts of the wastes. Secondary treatment is accomplished by trickling filters or by the activated sludge process.

secondary succession — ecological succession which takes place on an area following the complete or partial destruction of the vegetation by man or natural processes. *See* primary succession.

sediment — materials carried in and deposited by water.

selective cutting — the system of harvesting timber in which only certain trees, usually the largest are removed. *See* clear-cutting.

sewage — organic wastes composed of animal waste products and other materials of plant or animal origin; the used water supply of a community.

siltation — the deposit of water-borne sediments in and around bodies of water.

soil conservation — the prevention of soil degradation and the control of erosion, runoff, and siltation by proper land treatment practices.

sonic boom — the loud noise often made when an airborne vehicle exceeds the speed of sound. Caused by the build-up and release of shock waves. An important noise pollutant.

species — a kind of organism; a group of organisms which over time exchange significant amounts of genetic material.

sperm — the motile male reproductive cell. *See* gamete, ovum.

standing crop — the amount of an organism or organisms existing in a given area at a given time. Standing crop is a measure or productivity or yield and may be expressed as numbers, biomass, or energy content.

stimulus — an influence that causes a response or reaction of some type in an organism or part of an organism.

stream channelization — the process of changing a natural stream into a straight, steep-sided ditch for purposes of increased drainage.

strip mining — a process by which relatively shallow veins of coal or minerals are removed by digging in from the surface, heaping the covering soil and strata to the side, and extracting the desired material. Strip mining is generally very destructive to soil, water, vegetation, and wildlife resources.

substrate — the surface, foundation, or material upon which an organism lives.

succession — *See* ecological succession.

supersonic transport (SST) — a proposed, exceptionally large, supersonic (1800 mph), high-flying jet transport. The SST may cause considerable problems due to sonic booms and the formation of persistent blending contrails.

synecology — the ecology of communities; the study of the environmental relationships of a group of individuals of a number of different species. *See* autecology.

taxonomy — the study dealing with the kinds of organisms and their naming and classification.

technology — the use of science; the practical application of science to problem solving; the processes of industry.

teratogen — a substance which causes an abnormality or malformation in the structure of an organism; a substance which causes abnormalities in the offspring of exposed parents.

terrestrial — referring to the land or to organisms which live on land. *See* aquatic, marine.

territorial — referring to organisms which defend or protect an area against intruders.

territory — an area occupied by an individual or group; an area which an animal protects against intruders.

tertiary sewage treatment — the third step in sewage treatment in which the remaining suspended and collodial nutrient materials are removed. Territary treatment may involve many processes such as filtration, chlorination, and the use of activated carbon.

thermal inversion — *See* inversion.

thermal pollution — the discharge of waste heat, usually in the form of heated water, into natural waters; the discharge of heat into the environment.

topography — the characteristics of the ground surface, especially of relief, steepness, and elevation.

transpiration — the loss of water vapor from the bodies of plants.

trophic level — one of the levels in a food chain, food web, or series of energy transfers. *See* producer, consumer, decomposer.

tundra — the region between the northern limit of tree growth and the area permanently covered by ice. Tundra is characterized by dwarf or small types of vegetation.

turbidity — the degree of opaqueness produced by suspended matter in water.

undernutrition — improper nutrition in which not enough food is taken in each day to meet energy requirements. *See* malnutrition.

upwelling — an area where nutrient-rich deep water comes to the surface of the ocean causing a marked increase in productivity.

urbanization — the process of transforming rural areas into cities, especially the encroachment of housing developments, shopping centers, etc., into agricultural or natural land.

vagility — the ability of an animal to disperse or to move from one area to another.

vector — an organism that transmits a disease-causing agent form one host organism to another, (e.g., *Anopheles* mosquitoes are the vector for malaria).

virus — a submicroscopic, disease-causing parasite composed of a nucleic acid and a protein. Viruses are capable of reproducing only when inside of or attached to the cell of a host.

vitamin — organic substances needed in very small amounts for the proper health and functioning of an organism. The absence of a vitamin results in a deficiency disease.

water pollution — the alteration of water in a way that makes it less usable for man and other organisms than it is in its pure state.

watershed — the area of land drained by a river or stream.

water table — the upper level of the ground water in the soil or rock beneath an area. *See* aquifer, groundwater.

weather — the condition of all atmospheric factors at a given time. *See* climate.

wilderness — an area in which man's disturbances are so slight that they are insignificant or not easily noticed; a natural area.

wildlife — in the broad sense, all animals except man; in a narrower sense the terrestrial game birds, terrestrial game mammals, waterfowl, and furbearers.

X-rays — a type of electromagnetic radiation similar to but longer in wavelength and not as harmful as gamma radiation.

zoology — the study of animals. *See* biology, botany.

zooplankton — the small floating or weakly swimming animals inhabiting a body of water. *See* phytoplankton.

Index

abortion, 45

adaptation, 21-23

additives. *See* food additives; fuels

AEC. *See* Atomic Energy Commission

Agency for International Development. *See* AID

agriculture, and food production, 77-87

Agriculture, U.S. Department of. *See* USDA

AID, 77, 82

air. *See* air pollution

air pollution, 93-117
  amounts from various sources, 103
  components of, 95-99
  court suits relating to, 321-22
  fallout and ocean pollution, 131
  fate of, 100-101
  present state in U.S., 347-48, 353
  by radioactive materials, 99, 215-27
  sources of, 95-99
  transport of, 99-102

airplanes, and noise pollution, 226, 228, 230-31

Alaska, oil pipeline and, 281-89

aldehydes, as air pollutants, 97

aldrin, 203, 237

algae
  effects of thermal pollution on, 166-67
  and eutrophication, 155-63

aluminum
  recycling of, 269, 306, 361
  strip mining for, 272

use in packaging, 359

Atlantic Ocean, plankton production in, 66

atomic bomb, 216

Atomic Energy Commission, 215-27

automobiles
  and air pollution, 104-11
  exhaust and eutrophication, 158
  and noise pollution, 229

autotrophic, defined, 6

bacteria
  and eutrophication, 156
  and formation of hydrogen sulfide, 96
  and oil degradation, 143
  and oxygen depletion in waters, 119
  and sewage treatment, 121-25

behavior
  effect of noise on, 225, 228, 230
  and population regulation, 20, 68-73

benzopyrene, in diesel exhaust, 109

beryllium, poisoning by, 117

biochemical oxygen demand (BOD), 120, 326

biocides, 175-83
  as air pollutants, 98-99
  See also herbicides; insecticides; pesticides

biodegradation, or solid wastes, 309

biological control, 198-201

biological magnification
  after oil spills, 139-43
  of pesticides, 133, 177-79